Taking Issue Charts

Taking Issue charts present arguments on both sides of controversial topics in the education field.

In This Case

NEW *In This Case* feature provides case scenarios that help students apply and think critically about concepts discussed in each chapter.

Foundations of Education

Foundations of Education

> ## NINTH EDITION

Allan C. Ornstein
St. John's University

Daniel U. Levine
Emeritus, University of Missouri at Kansas City and
University of Nebraska at Omaha

Houghton Mifflin Company   Boston   New York

This edition is dedicated in memory of First Lieutenant Michael Lawlor, a very special young man who died serving his country in 2004. He is dearly missed by family and friends.

Publisher & Editor-in-Chief: Patricia Coryell
Senior Sponsoring Editor: Sue Pulvermacher-Alt
Senior Development Editor: Lisa A. Mafrici
Project Editor: Lindsay Frost
Senior Project Editor: Aileen Mason
Editorial Assistant: Neil Reynolds
Senior Manufacturing Coordinator: Marie Barnes
Marketing Manager: Jane Potter
Marketing Assistant: Erin Lane

Cover: Conestoga Valley Middle School, The Foreman Group/Gary Yon Photography

Part opener credits: Part One, Jim Cummins/CORBIS; Part Two, The Hulton Archive/Getty Images; Part Three, Chuck Savage/CORBIS; Part Four, © Ed Bock/CORBIS; Part Five, Stone/Getty Images; Part Six, Jose Luis Pelaez, Inc./CORBIS.

Printed in the U.S.A.

Library of Congress Catalog Card Number: 2004113506
ISBN: 0-618-47406-4

23456789-DOW-09 08 07 06 05

► Brief Contents

Gratis

► Contents

Preface

The Ninth Edition of *Foundations of Education* provides a comprehensive overview and analysis of topics and material typically taught in foundations courses in the United States. We have written this text for students who are preparing for a teaching career as well as for those who simply wish to learn more about the key educational issues and policies affecting American education.

Audience and Purpose

This text is designed for use in both introductory courses in the foundations of education and in a variety of upper-level foundations courses. For beginning students in education, it provides a clear understanding of the teaching profession and the issues and controversies confronting American education today. The book is also appropriate for upper-level courses because of its solid research base and documentation drawn extensively from primary sources and its systematic attention to providing up-to-date references.

Our purposes in writing this book remain the same as in the previous eight editions: to provide a comprehensive body of knowledge and information on the various foundations of education and significant contemporary issues, while incorporating relevant interdisciplinary perspectives. We have sought to summarize and synthesize fundamental concepts and research findings in a practical way and to provide balanced treatment of controversial issues without making the text either too simplistic or too complicated.

Goals and Features of the Revision

Three goals directed the work on this new edition: (1) to make sure it is contemporary and substantive in identifying and analyzing appropriate subject matter; (2) to increase the effectiveness of the text for student learning; and (3) to provide material that instructors are likely to want emphasized in preparing their students for teaching careers.

To meet our first goal of including an appropriate mix of contemporary and substantive classic subject matter, we have worked to refine the themes that recur throughout the book:

- **Diversity** We continue to place emphasis, throughout this revision, on student diversity and multiculturalism. For example, we discuss the importance of diverse populations in the teaching profession, the current status of desegregation and other important equal opportunity trends, and educational responses to the increasing diversity of students in the United States. In light of current world and U.S. events, we have made a special effort in this edition to expand the information we provide about Muslim populations.

- **Technology** We have systematically placed emphasis on the growing role of technology in education. Our emphasis on technology includes sections on the history of technology in education, the place of technology in school reform, and the effects of digital technologies on children.

■ **Standards and Accountability** We have added new information to several chapters that addresses the growing emphasis on holding students, teachers, and schools accountable for performing at levels specified by local, state, and national standards. We also provide basic information in several chapters on the No Child Left Behind Act and its provisions dealing with accountability and educational reform.

■ **Developing One's Own Philosophy of Education** In this edition, we continue to stress, in several sections throughout the book, the development of a personal philosophy of education and the relevance of a personal philosophy to the realities of day-to-day teaching.

Other current and important topics that receive particular emphasis in the Ninth Edition include professional development, school-based management, character education, the history of education in China and India, legal protections regarding assaults on teachers and students, school choice and charter schools, curriculum and testing standards, promising instructional innovations and interventions, approaches for helping disadvantaged students and for equalizing educational opportunity, collaboration between schools and other institutions, research on class size, and international achievement patterns.

New sections or subsections include those on the No Child Left Behind Act in Chapters 1, 2, 7, 8, 12, and 13; "Islam, Arabic Learning, and Education" in Chapter 3; "Postmodernism" in Chapter 4; "Paulo Freire" in Chapter 5; "Arab Americans" in Chapter 6; "Government Guidelines Regarding Prayer and Religion in Schools" and "Zero Tolerance and Its Effects on Schools" in Chapter 9; "Latchkey Children and Community Learning Centers" and "Research on Bullying and Its Prevention" in Chapter 10; "Social Class, College Participation, and National Problems" in Chapter 11, "Technology Education" in Chapter 14; and "After-School and Summer Programs" in Chapter 16.

We have also worked diligently to obtain the latest available data on contemporary topics such as teacher employment trends, student and school demographics, school finance trends, changes in the family, school governance changes, and student performance.

Our updating has drawn, to a considerable extent, on resources available on the Internet. For this reason, many of the citations do not have page references. Students can explore areas of personal interest by scrutinizing the printed versions of many sources we cite—including news sources such as the *New York Times* and *Education Week* and journal sources such as the *American School Board Journal* and *Scientific American*—at college, community, and university libraries. But in general, instructors should recognize that a substantial proportion of our citations are available to their students on the Internet. (For *Education Week*, most articles can be accessed easily by searching the Archives at **www.edweek.org.**) To facilitate access, we frequently provide URLs that students can access from any computer linked to the World Wide Web. (The Web sites were active at the time we prepared this text.) For many scholarly papers and for articles in periodicals, we provide initial URLs; the reader then can click on "Archives" or "Back Issues" (or similar terms) on the first screen to find the designated issue, or can use a search function provided in the initial screen. All Web sites mentioned in the text are links on the companion Web site.

To meet our second goal, the enhancement of student understanding, we have retained and thoroughly updated key pedagogical features that helped students in previous editions, including focusing questions, marginal notes, the **Taking Issue** feature, chapter summaries, key terms lists, Suggested Projects for Professional Development, and an extensive glossary, discussion questions, and lists of selected Internet and reading resources. In addition, we have paid considerable attention to making our textual descriptions of both new and continuing topics as clear and informative as possible, revising many of the discussions retained from previous editions to further enhance readability and understanding. We have provided more summaries of key textual discussions in our popular topical Overview charts, which now appear in every chapter of the text.

Finally, to highlight our third goal of helping students prepare for teaching careers, we have added in each chapter a new **In This Case** feature. In each of these boxed inserts students read a brief fictional case scenario related to the content of the chapter and answer questions designed to encourage them to apply and think critically about concepts discussed in the chapter. Each chapter also has a **Technology @ School** feature to help keep students up-to-date on relevant developments regarding educational technology and provide information about potential use during their teaching careers.

Content and Organization

The text consists of sixteen chapters divided into six parts. Part One ("Understanding the Teaching Profession") considers the climate in which teachers work today and its impact on teaching. Changes in the job market and in the status of the profession and issues such as teacher empowerment, school-based management, and alternative certification are treated in detail.

The four chapters in Part Two ("Historical and Philosophical Foundations") provide historical and philosophical contexts for understanding current educational practices and trends by examining the events and ideas that have influenced the development of education in the United States. These chapters allow students to develop a philosophical understanding early in the course, providing a knowledge base that will help them comprehend and think critically about the material on more modern foundations that appear later in the text.

Part Three ("Political, Economic, and Legal Foundations") presents an overview of the organization, governance, and administration of elementary and secondary education; the financing of public education; and the legal aspects of education.

Part Four ("Social Foundations") examines the relationships between society and the schools that society has established to serve its needs. The three chapters in this part discuss culture and socialization; the complex relationship between social class, race, and educational achievement; and the various programs aimed at providing equal educational opportunity for all students.

Part Five ("Curricular Foundations") examines the ways in which changes in societies have led to changes in educational goals, curriculum, and instructional methods. Throughout these chapters we explicitly point out how the particular philosophical ideas discussed in Chapter 4 are linked to goals, curriculum, and other facets of contemporary education. This section concludes with a look at emerging curriculum trends.

Part Six ("Effective Education: International and American Perspectives") provides a comparative look at schools and their development throughout the world and an in-depth analysis of current efforts to improve school effectiveness in the United States.

Special Pedagogic Features

The Ninth Edition of *Foundations of Education* includes many special features designed to help students easily understand and master the material in the text. Several pedagogical features are particularly noteworthy:

- **New—In This Case** features in every chapter help students apply and think critically about concepts discussed in the chapter. In each of these boxed inserts, students read vignettes that describe situations in which new teachers might find themselves and answer questions that encourage critical and applied thinking about how they might best respond in each situation. Further In This Case features are found on the Web site that accompanies the text.

- **Expanded topical overview charts,** now found in every chapter of the text, summarize and compare key developments and topics.

- **Technology @ School** features in every chapter help keep students up-to-date on relevant developments regarding educational technology and provide information that they may find valuable to apply during their teaching careers. Some examples of this feature include "Connecting with Schools Around the World" (Chapter 3), "Helping Students Develop Media Literacy" (Chapter 10), and "Protecting Students from Undesirable Material on the Web" (Chapter 13).

- **Focus and Refocus Questions.** Focus Questions appear at the beginning of each chapter to provide students with an advance organizer of chapter material. Related to the Focus questions, Refocus Questions, which appear after major sections of each chapter, are designed to help students reinforce their comprehension by applying the concepts discussed in the book to their own personal situations.

- **Taking Issue charts** present controversial issues in the field of education, offering arguments on both sides of a question so that students can understand why the topic is important and how it affects contemporary schools. One of these charts appears in each chapter, covering issues such as alternative certification, merit pay, magnet schools, character education, and establishing a national curriculum. Instructors may wish to use these charts as the basis for class discussion or essay assignments.

- **Internet and video resources** at the end of each chapter connect both the reader and instructor to technology resources.

- **Getting to the Source** features for each chapter of the text are now available on the companion Web site for *Foundations of Education*. Corresponding to every chapter, Getting to the Source consists of brief excerpts from a variety of high-interest, significant, and relevant primary source materials, along with author commentary and questions. They offer students the opportunity to become familiar with a wide variety of primary source materials through topics that include "A Confucianist View of Good Teaching," "Rousseau on Natural Education," and "Every Child Reading."

To help you easily locate the features just listed, special indexes for each of them appear on the inside cover at the front of this book.

In addition, other key pedagogic features of the preceding edition have been retained, including the following:

- *Focusing questions* at the beginning of each chapter highlight the major topics to be discussed.

- *Marginal notations* reinforce central points throughout the text.

- *Annotated lists of selected readings and resources for further learning* that may be of special interest to readers appear at the end of each chapter.

- *A list of key terms,* with cross-references to text pages, appears near the end of each chapter as a convenient recapitulation and guide for the student.

- *End-of-chapter features* also include *summary lists* that facilitate understanding and analysis of content and *discussion questions* to stimulate class participation in examining text material.

- *An extensive glossary* at the end of the book defines important terms and concepts.

As in the previous edition, the text is in **full color.** This design enhances the format and presentation of material, giving a thoroughly modern look and feel to the text.

Ancillaries

Accompanying the text are the following ancillaries:

- An ***Instructor's Resource Manual with Test Items,*** prepared by David E. Vocke of Towson University. It contains hundreds of test items, developed according to sound principles and standards of test construction. The multiple-choice items have been extensively revised and include many items that test for higher-order thinking skills. In addition, the instructional resource material of the manual has been thoroughly updated and revised to reflect new text content; it offers for each chapter of the text a chapter outline, a chapter overview, student objectives, lecture and discussion topics, student projects, selected references and resources, a transition guide, and model syllabi.

- An ***Instructor's Class Prep CD*** offers the test items from the *Instructor's Resource Manual* in an electronic format, plus a PowerPoint slide program for class presentation.

- An expanded *companion Web site* (**http://college.hmco.com** and go to "Education") contains many valuable resources for both students and instructors using the text, including Getting to the Source primary source material readings related to the content of each chapter of the textbook, additional In This Case studies, PowerPoint slides, ACE self-quizzes, glossary flashcards, video clips, and more.

- ***Houghton Mifflin Video Cases*** let preservice teachers experience the complex multiple dimensions of true classroom dilemmas that teachers face every day. Each case includes a 3- to 5-minute video and audio module presenting actual classroom scenarios, as well as key "artifacts" that provide background information and allow preservice teachers to realistically and thoroughly analyze the problems and opportunities in the case.

- For instructors who teach the course online, Houghton Mifflin's new ***Eduspace course*** offers a convenient format. Eduspace is Houghton Mifflin's proprietary version of Blackboard. In addition to its handy gradebook and other course management tools, Eduspace includes special interactive components such as videos, a discussion board, reflective journal questions, test items, and additional materials to aid students in studying and reflecting on what they have learned.

Acknowledgments

The Ninth Edition would not have been possible without the contributions and feedback from many individuals. In particular, James Lawlor, Professor of Education at Towson University, planned and carried out many quite substantial revisions in Chapters 2, 7, 8, 13, and 14. His outstanding contributions to this volume are in themselves a testimonial to the breadth of his knowledge and the acuity of his insight as an educator dedicated to improving professional preparation. Gerald Gutek, Professor Emeritus of Education and History at Loyola University of Chicago, has also made an outstanding contribution to the book as the author of Chapters 3, 4, 5, and 6, which he thoroughly revised and updated for this edition.

A number of reviewers made useful suggestions and provided thoughtful reactions that guided us in every edition. We thank the following individuals for their conscientiousness and for their contributions to the content of this edition:

Barbara R. Bridges, Bemidji State University

Theresa J. Canada, Western Connecticut State University

Eric J. Heinrich, Limestone College

William R. Martin, George Mason University

Susan L. Peterson, Slippery Rock University

William C. Rietschel, Concordia University

In addition, we thank the numerous reviewers who have contributed to prior editions. They include

H. Rose Adesiyan, Purdue University, Calumet

Louis Alfonso, Rhode Island College

Terryl J. Anderson, The University of Texas of the Permian Basin

Mario L. M. Baca, California State University, Fresno

Harold B. Bickel, University of South Alabama

Nancy A. Blair, Ball State University

Les Bolt, James Madison University

John A. Bucci, Rhode Island College

Paul R. Burden, Kansas State University

John Caruso, Jr., West Connecticut State University

Charles R. Colvin, SUNY, Fredonia

Jack Conklin, North Adams State, Massachusetts

James F. Cummings, Newberry College, South Carolina

Arnold Danzig, Northern Arizona University

Donald C. Edinger, Grand Valley State College

Virden Evans, Florida A&M University

Jerry R. Franklin, Morehead State University

Kate Friesner, The College of Santa Fe

F. H. George, Southeastern Oklahoma State University

Judith A. Green, Kansas State University

Thomas W. Gwaltney, Jr., Eastern Michigan University

Dwight Hare, Northeast Louisiana University

JoAnn Hatchman, California State University, Hayward

Ralph R. Karst, Northeast Louisiana University

James Lawlor, Towson University

Edith Lombardo, West Virginia State College

Derwyn McElroy, Auburn University, Montgomery

Colleen A. Moore, Central Michigan University

William Phillips, Fairmont State College

Richard R. Renner, University of Florida

Maureen A. Reynolds, Indiana University, Kokomo

Patrick Socoski, West Chester University

Jack Stirton, San Joaquin Delta Community College

John P. Strouse, Ball State University

T. Lavon Talley, Oglethorpe University, Georgia

Margaret Tannenbaum, Rowan University

Sevan G. Terzian, University of Florida

Roderick M. Thronson, Carroll College

Cheryl Valdez, Chapman University, California

J. W. Weatherford, University of Central Oklahoma

Lowell E. Whiteside, Central Missouri State University

Jody Messinger Wolfe, West Virginia University

We also want to acknowledge and express appreciation for the work of Sheralee Connors who, as Development Editor, made crucial contributions in every aspect involved in revising this text. In particular, she played a large part in preparing the *Technology @ School* features, in suggesting organizational improvements across and within chapters, in preparing overview charts, in gracefully helping the authors avoid missteps and unproductive byways, in calling attention to generalizations that needed firmer support, and in helping to find and incorporate quality material within a tight revision schedule. Marion Czaja provided excellent ideas and help in creating the new *In This Case* features. At Houghton Mifflin, Senior Development Editor Lisa Mafrici and Senior Sponsoring Editor Sue Pulvermacher-Alt provided overall leadership and supervision to make sure that this edition would be worthwhile and timely. Other persons who made creative contributions included Lindsay Frost and Aileen Mason, Project Editors; Neil Reynolds, Editorial Assistant; Jean Hammond, Designer and Art Editor; and Marie Barnes, Manufacturing Coordinator. We'd also like to thank Karen Keady, who copyedited the manuscript, Norma Frankel, who proofread the pages, and Edwin Durbin, who created the indexes.

PART ONE

Understanding the
Teaching Profession

CHAPTER 1

Motivation, Preparation, and Conditions for the Entering Teacher

Some of your relatives or friends may have questioned you about your interest in becoming a teacher. "Are you sure you want to deal with kids?" Or "Why don't you pick a business specialty with a big salary and forget about children unless you have some of your own?"

Perhaps you tried to explain the importance of helping children and young people become capable and responsible adults. You may have pointed out that teachers in today's schools are gaining more power and more responsibilities, not to mention higher salaries. Of course, you may still be pondering your own motives for teaching, as well as the potential opportunities, rewards, and difficulties of a teaching career. This chapter will examine such topics, including motivations for becoming a teacher, teacher supply and demand, pay scales, career preparation, and efforts to improve the teaching work force and to give teachers more decision-making power. To help focus your thoughts, keep the following questions in mind:

FOCUS QUESTIONS

- What are the usual reasons for becoming a teacher, and how do your reasons compare with them?
- What are the current employment trends for teachers?
- What salaries and benefits do teachers earn? How do these compare with other occupations?
- How are teachers prepared? How are they certified?
- What are the current trends in teacher education?
- What do teachers find satisfying and dissatisfying about their work?
- What are some current developments in teacher work-force quality and teaching conditions?

▶ **Choosing a Career in Teaching**

The path to becoming a teacher starts when you first choose teaching as a career. In this section, we'll review some motives for choosing a teaching career. We'll also examine the growing concern that too few minority college students are becoming teachers.

Motivations for Choosing Teaching

▪ Reasons for teaching

We have many motives, both idealistic and practical, for choosing a career in teaching. Often, a person's reasons for wanting to teach stem from his or her *personal philosophy of education,* a topic we will revisit throughout the book. If you are thinking of entering the teaching profession, ask yourself why. Your motives may include (1) love of children, (2) desire to impart knowledge, (3) interest in and excitement about teaching, and (4) desire to perform a valuable service to society. Perhaps you hope for job security, pension benefits, and relative ease in preparing for teaching compared with the training required by some other professions.

▪ Reasons for entering the profession

One study asked future teachers from a representative sample of seventy-six schools and colleges of teacher education to state their reasons for selecting the teaching profession. Ninety percent of the respondents cited "helping children grow and learn" as a reason. Next highest was "seems to be a challenging field" (63 percent), followed closely by "like work conditions" (54 percent), "inspired by favorite teachers" (53 percent), and "sense of vocation and honor of teaching" (52 percent). These reasons resembled those cited in several other studies conducted during the past fifteen years. Some of these studies also concluded that admiration for one's elementary and secondary teachers is often important in shaping decisions to become a teacher.[1] This chapter's In This Case box also looks at the reasons people decide to become teachers.

REFOCUS | How do your reasons for becoming a teacher compare with those of the teachers surveyed? Does your list rank in the same order? What other reasons might you add to this list?

Teaching Force Diversity: A Growing Concern

Although the U.S. school population is becoming increasingly diverse, the teaching force has not kept pace. For example, African American, Asian American, and Hispanic American students make up almost 40 percent of the public school student population, but the proportion of elementary and secondary teachers from these minority groups is generally estimated at 16 percent or less. The disparity is particularly acute in the largest urban districts, where minority students comprise nearly 90 percent of enrollment.

▪ Need for teacher diversity

This underrepresentation of minority groups in the teaching force is expected to grow even more severe in the future. Currently, only about 10 percent of teacher-

---

[1]Donald B. Cruickshank, *Research That Informs Teachers and Teacher Educators* (Bloomington, Ind.: Phi Delta Kappa, 1990); *The Metropolitan Life Survey of the American Teacher* (New York: Metropolitan Life, 1995); Steve Farkas, Jean Johnson, and Tony Foleno, *A Sense of Calling* (New York: Public Agenda, 2000), available at **www.publicagenda.org/specials/teachers/teachers.htm**; AARP Knowledge Management, NRTA, and HarrisInteractive, "Exodus," 2003 report prepared for the AARP, available at **http://research.aarp.org/general/exodus.html**; and Sonia M. Nieto, *What Keeps Teachers Going?* (New York: Teachers College Press, 2003).

IN THIS CASE

Considerations

"Are each of you certain that you want to enter the teaching profession?" asked Professor Johnson. "Remember the challenges of the profession often become stressors. About half of the teachers who enter the profession leave within a few years. So, tell me why you want to become a teacher. Josephine?"

"My grandmother was a teacher, and my mother is a teacher. Both of them have told me how rewarding the career can be. I like children. I've loved my experiences with children in summer camps, so now I'm choosing elementary school teaching."

"I want to coach and teach," said Mark. "Some of the best times in my life have been when I played basketball or tennis. The coaches made it their business to see that I followed their discipline and that I paid attention to academics, too. These experiences taught me new values and new disciplines and gave me a vision for what I want to do with my life. I want to work at the high school level."

"I don't have any great yearning to teach," said Patricia. "I have to support myself after I graduate—my parents made it plain that I'm on my own financially after next year. I want to be an artist, and I think I can do that if at first I support myself by teaching. There are several galleries in the area, and if I could get a job teaching junior or senior

high, maybe I could get some work shown locally, earn a few commissions, and be on my way."

"I know I won't get rich," said Peter, "but there is something compelling about watching the 'aha' experience in a student's face. I've taught swimming and diving during the summers. When a skill finally clicks in, the triumph of that young boy or girl makes it all worthwhile. I want to teach physical education in an elementary school."

"Each of you seems to have considered this choice for some time. I will share a few other reasons mentioned by other students. Teaching is one profession you can use to travel the world. International schools and foreign private schools search regularly for people such as you. Teaching English as a second language has given many a free ticket to China, Japan, and Korea. Or you can teach as a missionary in church schools.

"Another primary consideration is that state retirement systems usually provide fairly secure long-term benefits. That kind of security can be hard to find in the business world today.

"As a follow-up to this discussion, write a reflection paper about the discussion and your reasons for choosing education. Bring it to class next week."

Questions

1. Why is it important that preservice teachers reflect on their motivations for selecting the teaching profession?

2. Why are you choosing the teaching profession?

3. Geographically, where do you think you might want to teach? Why? What are the projected job opportunities in that area at the time you finish your education?

---

education majors are African American or Latino; yet members of these minority groups are predicted to constitute a still higher percentage of elementary and secondary students in the near future. In recent years the shortage of Asian American teachers has also become an important problem. Asian Americans now constitute nearly 4 percent of the population of K–12 students, but they account for only 2 percent of the teaching force.[2]

---

[2]John Gehring, "Minority-Serving Colleges Call for Teacher-Training Help," *Education Week*, October 4, 2000; Jennifer McNulty, "Breaking Down the Barriers that Keep Asian Americans Out of Teaching," *UC Santa Cruz Currents*, February 14, 2000, available at **www.ucsc.edu/ currents/99-00/02-14**; and Rona F. Flippo and Julie G. Caniff, "Who Is Not Teaching Our Children?" *Multicultural Perspectives* (Issue 2, 2003).

The teaching force is much less diverse than the U.S. student population, and the shortage of minority teachers is expected to grow more severe. Some groups are working to enact new programs to increase the number of minority teachers. *(Stone/Getty Images)*

■ Reasons for increasing teacher diversity

Increasing teaching force diversity to better reflect the student population is widely viewed as an important goal. For one thing, teachers from a cultural or ethnic minority group generally are in a better position than are nonminority teachers to serve as positive role models for minority students. In many cases, minority teachers also may have a better understanding of minority students' expectations and learning styles (see the chapter on Social Class, Race, and School Achievement and the chapter on Providing Equal Educational Opportunity), particularly if minority teachers working with low-income students grew up in working-class homes themselves. For example, Lisa Delpit and other analysts have pointed out that many African American teachers may be less prone than nonminority teachers to mistakenly assume that black students will respond well to a teacher who is overly friendly. In addition, teachers from Asian American, Latino, and other minority groups are in demand for working with students who have limited English skills.[3]

■ Proposals for promoting diversity

Officials of the American Association of Colleges of Teacher Education (AACTE) have stated that data on the low proportion of minority teachers constitute a "devastating" crisis. Along with other organizations, the AACTE has proposed and helped initiate legislation for various new programs to increase the number of minority teachers: increasing financial aid for prospective minority teachers, enhancing recruitment of minority candidates, and initiating precollegiate programs to attract minority students.[4]

[3]Lisa D. Delpit, "The Silenced Dialogue: Power and Pedagogy in Educating Other People's Children," *Harvard Educational Review* (August 1988), pp. 280–298; Gilbert Brown, "The Role of the African-American Teacher," *Black Collegian* (October 2000), pp. 88–91; Terry Burant, Alice Quiocho, and Francisco Rios, "Changing the Face of Teaching," *Multicultural Perspectives* (Issue 2, 2002); and Thomas S. Dee, "The Race Connection," *Education Next* (Spring 2004), available at **www.educationnext.org.**
[4]*Minority Teacher Supply and Demand* (Washington, D.C.: American Association of Colleges of Teacher Education, 1990), p. 3. See also Susan Melnick and Kenneth Zeichner, "Teacher Education Responsibilities to Address Diversity Issues," *Theory into Practice* (Spring 1998); Kenneth Zeichner, "The New Scholarship in Teacher Education," *Educational Researcher* (December 1999), pp. 4–14; and "Recruitment and Retention of Minority Teachers," undated posting at the National Education Association Web site, **www.nea.org/recruit/minority.**

REFOCUS What do you think might make teaching a more attractive career option for today's college students, minority and nonminority? If you are a member of a minority group, what attracts you to teaching? How will you prepare to work with students who may have a different ethnic or socioeconomic background from your own?

▶ Supply and Demand

Will you find work as a teacher? How much money will you earn? These two questions are related, following the economic principle of **supply and demand**. When the supply of teachers exceeds demand, salaries tend to decline. Conversely, high demand and low supply tend to increase salaries. As discussed in the chapter on The Teaching Profession, supply and demand also affect the social status and prestige accorded to a particular occupation.

Job Opportunities

■ Changing pattern

In the 1960s and 1970s, a falling birthrate resulted in a surplus of teachers. As college students and teacher educators recognized the substantial oversupply, enrollment in teacher-education programs decreased, and the percentage of college freshmen interested in becoming teachers declined from 23 percent in 1968 to 5 percent in 1982. Since then, the trend has reversed. The percentage of college students interested in teaching rose by nearly 100 percent during the late 1980s and 1990s.[5]

Analysts predict many candidates in upcoming years, but also many teaching jobs. More than two million new teachers will be needed in the next decade, for several reasons:[6]

■ Reasons to expect a teacher shortage

1. When the post–World War II baby boom generation began to produce its own children, a "mini" baby boom developed. Those children are now in K–12 schools. In addition, many immigrant families have entered the United States in recent years. As a result, school enrollment has been increasing (see Table 1.1).

2. A significant proportion of the current teaching force will reach retirement age in the coming decade.

3. Educational reformers in many locations are attempting to reduce class size, expand preschool education, place greater emphasis on science and mathematics, and introduce other changes that require more teachers.

Standards & Assessment ✔ 4. Higher standards for becoming a teacher are limiting the supply.

Standards & Assessment ✔ 5. Many states are requiring more teachers to be certified for the courses they teach.

6. Job dissatisfactions or desires to pursue other careers lead many teachers to resign their positions each year.

---

[5]Somini Sepgupta, "A Traditional Career Gains New Class," *New York Times,* August 3, 1997; and F. Howard Nelson and Rachel Drown, *Survey and Analysis of Teacher Salary Trends 2002* (Washington, D.C.: American Federation of Teachers, AFL-CIO, 2003), available at **www.aft.org.**
[6]Richard W. Riley, "High Quality Teachers for Every Classroom," *Teaching K–8* (January 1999), p. 6; and Richard Ingersoll, "Is There Really a Teacher Shortage?" 2003 report prepared for the Center for the Study of Teaching and Policy, available at **http://depts.washington.edu/ctpmail/Descriptions.htmlShortage.**

Table 1.1	Public- and Private-School Kindergarten Through Grade 12 Enrollments, 1990 to 2012 (in millions)			
	Total	Public	Private	Private as Percentage of Total
1990	46.4	41.2	5.2	11.2
2000	53.1	47.7	5.9	11.1
2012 (projected)	53.7	47.7	6.0	11.1

Note: Data include most kindergarten and some pre-kindergarten students.
Source: Debra E. Gerald and William J. Hussar, *Projections of Education Statistics to 2012.* (Washington, D.C.: U.S. Government Printing Office, 2002), Table 1.

■ Reasons to expect no shortage

Other educators, however, argue against a widespread shortage of teachers in the next ten years. For one thing, recent shortages have mainly involved large urban districts and specialized fields such as math and science; many districts have reported no shortage of potential teachers. In addition, it seems that fewer teachers are leaving the profession than in earlier years, and increased enrollment of students may be leveling off. Improved salaries may also bring ex-teachers back to the schools and attract people who trained as teachers but did not enter the profession. Moreover, many states are simplifying becoming a teacher through alternative certification (discussed later in this chapter).[7]

■ Shortages in "special-needs" fields

Given the arguments on each side of the issue, it is difficult to determine whether major teacher shortages will be widespread in the next decade. However, shortages should continue to exist in "special-needs" fields such as education of students with disabilities, remedial education, bilingual education, science and mathematics, and foreign languages. In addition, teachers will remain in short supply in many rural areas and in some city and suburban communities that register significant population growth, particularly in the South and Southwest.[8]

■ Upgraded programs

Opportunities in Nonpublic Schools. Prospective teachers may find numerous job opportunities in nonpublic schools during the next decade. As Table 1.1 shows, private schools enroll more than 10 percent of the nation's elementary and secondary students. Like the public schools, many private schools are upgrading their instructional programs, often by hiring more teachers who specialize in such areas as science, math, computers, education of children with disabilities, and bilingual education.

■ Changing enrollment patterns

Years ago, a large majority of students attending nonpublic schools were in Catholic schools, but this situation has now changed. In the past three decades, Catholic enrollment has declined and many other nonpublic schools have been established. Enrollment has increased most in the independent (nonreligious) sector and in schools sponsored by evangelical and fundamentalist church groups. More-

[7]Patrick Murphy and Michael DeArmond, "A National Crisis or Localized Problems? *Education Policy Analysis Archives,* July 31, 2003, available at **http://epaa.asu.edu**.
[8]Elizabeth F. Fideler, Elizabeth D. Foster, and Shirley Schwartz, *The Urban Teacher Challenge* (Washington, D.C.: Council of Great City Schools, 2000); and Andrew J. Rotherham, "The Wrong Teacher Shortage," *Blueprint* (March/April 2003), available at **www.ndol.org/blueprint**.

OVERVIEW 1.1 *Ways to Improve Your Employment Prospects*

Advance Preparation	Scouting and Planning	Assembling Materials	Applying for a Job	Preparing for an Interview
Check your state's certification requirements and follow them correctly. Acquire adjunct skills that make you multidimensional, ready to assist in activities such as coaching or supervising the student newspaper. Maintain an up-to-date file listing all your professional activities, accomplishments, and awards. Keep well-organized notes on what you learn from classroom observations. Begin a journal specifically related to teaching concerns. Use it to reflect on what you see and hear and to develop your own ideas.	Collect information on school districts that have vacant positions. Possible sources of information include your career planning or placement office and the state education department's office of teacher employment. Look into computerized job banks operated by professional organizations or available elsewhere on the Internet. Visit, call, or write to school districts in which you are particularly interested. Plan your application strategy in advance.	Prepare a neat, accurate, clear résumé. Prepare a professional portfolio including lesson plans, peer critiques, descriptions of relevant experience, supervisors' evaluations, and, if possible, a videotape of you teaching. Ask your career planning or placement office for advice on other materials to include with the credentials you will submit.	Begin applying for teaching jobs as soon as possible. Apply for several vacancies at once.	Take time to clarify your philosophy of education and learning. Know what you believe, and be able to explain it. Be prepared for other interview questions as well. In particular, anticipate questions that deal with classroom management, lesson design, and your employment history. Learn as much as you can about the school district *before* the interview: for instance, its organization, its levels of teaching positions, its types of schools, and its use of technology.

over, many Catholic schools have been increasing the percentage of lay teachers on their faculties, and this trend is likely to continue.[9]

Regardless of whether a large teacher shortage does or does not develop in the next ten years, astute prospective teachers will take certain steps to enhance their opportunities for rewarding employment. Some of these are outlined in Overview 1.1.

 Are you preparing to enter a high-demand teaching specialty? If not, what can you do to improve your employment prospects?

---

[9]David Baker and Cornelius Riordan, "The 'Eliting' of the Common American Catholic School and the National Education Crisis," *Phi Delta Kappa* (September 1998), pp. 16–23; and G. Jeffrey MacDonald, "Prep Schools Open Their Doors Wider," *Christian Science Monitor,* October 28, 2003.

Pay Scales and Trends

■ Increase in salaries

Traditionally, teachers had relatively low salaries. In 1960, for example, the average teacher salary in current dollars was slightly less than $26,000. By 2003 this figure had risen to more than $45,000. Today experienced teachers in wealthy school districts frequently earn $80,000 to $100,000. Moreover, teachers have opportunities to supplement their income by supervising after-school programs, athletics, drama, and other extracurricular activities, and some advance to administrative positions with annual salaries well over $100,000. In addition, keep in mind that public-school teachers usually have excellent benefits (such as pensions and health insurance) compared to other workers.[10]

■ Differences among states

Teaching pay varies considerably among and within states. Figure 1.1 shows the range of variation among states. Average overall salaries in the three highest-paying states (California, Michigan, and Connecticut) were much higher than those in the three lowest-paying states (North Dakota, Oklahoma, and South Dakota). Of course, we must take into account comparative living costs. It is much more expensive to live in New York, for example, than to live in the northern plains states. Salaries differ widely within states, too, where average state pay scales are high. Salary sched-

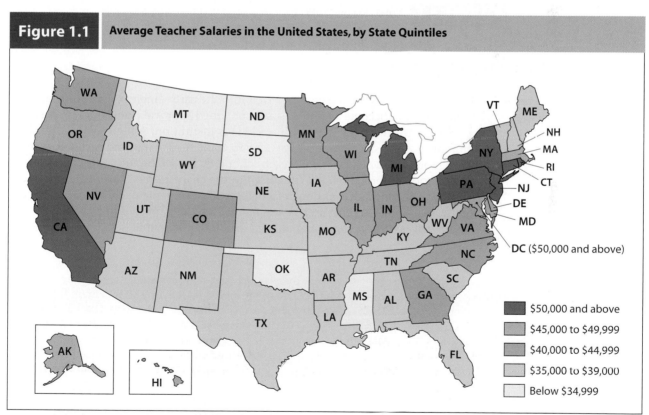

Figure 1.1   **Average Teacher Salaries in the United States, by State Quintiles**

DC ($50,000 and above)

- $50,000 and above
- $45,000 to $49,999
- $40,000 to $44,999
- $35,000 to $39,000
- Below $34,999

Source: Adapted from F. Howard Nelson and Rachel Drown, Survey and Analysis of Teacher Salary Trends 2002 (Washington, D.C.: American Federation of Teachers, AFL-CIO, 2003) Table I–1, available at **www.aft.org**.

---

[10]Jay Chambers and Sharon Bobbitt, *The Patterns of Teacher Compensation* (Washington, D.C.: U.S. Department of Education, 1996); and "Rankings and Estimates Updates," 2003 paper published by the National Education Association.

ules in wealthy suburban districts generally are substantially higher than those in most other school districts.

■ Salaries vary with experience and education

The greatest variation in salaries relates to years of experience and education. Teachers with more experience and more education earn more than those with less of either. Table 1.2 shows the range based on years of experience and additional education in a typical salary schedule—that of the St. Mary's County, Maryland, public schools. The salary schedule negotiated for 2004 provided $35,272 for the first-year teacher with a standard certificate and $68,119 for a teacher at the highest level of experience and education. Although numbers change from district to district and state to state, the wide difference between upper and lower pay levels is fairly common.

■ Starting salaries

Although a teacher at the top of the salary schedule can earn an attractive salary (especially considering that the academic year is less than ten months long), starting salaries still tend to be lower than in some other professions. Recognizing this problem, many political and educational leaders have been working to increase salaries for both first-year and experienced teachers in order to attract and retain high-quality staff. Figure 1.2 shows the results of such efforts. During the inflationary 1970s, teachers' salaries declined relative to inflation and to the average salary of all workers, but gains in both these measures have been registered since 1980.

REFOCUS   **What do you expect to earn in your first teaching position?**

▶ Preparing Teachers

■ Evolution of teacher training

During the U.S. colonial period and well into the early nineteenth century, anyone who wanted to become a teacher usually obtained approval from a local minister or a board of trustees associated with a religious institution. A high-school or college diploma was considered unnecessary. If you could read, write, and spell and were of good moral character, you could teach school. By the 1820s, future teachers had begun attending normal schools (discussed in the chapter on Historical Development of American Education), although formal certification remained unnecessary. Eventually, the normal schools became teacher colleges, and most of the teacher colleges are now diversified colleges and universities. Today, all public school teachers must

Table 1.2	Selected Steps in the Salary Schedule for the St. Mary's County, Maryland, Public Schools, 2004			
	Bachelor's Degree and Standard Certificate	Master's Degree or Advanced Certificate	Master's Degree and Advanced Certificate +15 Approved Hours	Master's Degree and Advanced Certificate +51 Approved Hours
First year	$35,272	$37,224	$38,206	$40,163
Fifth year	37,058	40,090	41,605	46,251
Tenth year	44,730	46,749	49,326	53,920
Thirtieth year	49,731	60,909	63,556	68,119

Note: All teachers must earn an advanced certificate within ten years of initial state certification.
Source: Internet site of the St. Mary's County, Maryland, Public Schools at **www.smcps.k12.md.us**.

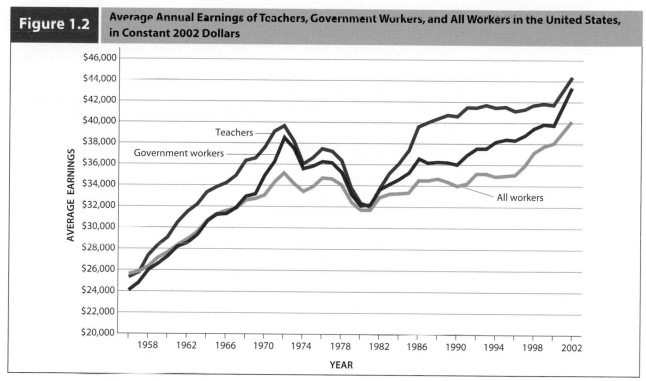

Figure 1.2 Average Annual Earnings of Teachers, Government Workers, and All Workers in the United States, in Constant 2002 Dollars

Source: Adapted from F. Howard Nelson and Rachel Drown, *Survey and Analysis of Teacher Salary Trends 2002* (Washington, D.C.: American Federation of Teachers, AFL-CIO, 2003), Table II–2, available at **www.aft.org.**

be certified. Except for alternative certification or temporary certification, all states require a bachelor's degree or five years of college work for entrance into teaching.

Standards & Assessment

Certification

■ Requirements for certification

Prospective teachers who wish to teach in a U.S. public school must be certified by the state in their chosen subject areas or grade levels. At one time, most states granted **certification** based on documentation that the candidate possessed appropriate professional preparation and good moral character. However, increasing public dissatisfaction with the quality of education led to changes in certification practices.[11]

■ Renewable certificates

In past decades teaching certificates usually were issued for life. Now some states issue certificates valid for only three to five years. Although teachers currently holding life certificates are unaffected, those with renewable certificates usually must furnish proof of positive evaluations or university coursework to have their certificates renewed.

■ Wide differences among states

Variation in Certification Requirements. Certification requirements vary widely from state to state. The resulting variance in teacher-preparation programs leads to

[11]Elizabeth A. Kaye, ed., *Requirments for Certification of Teachers, Counselors, Librarians, and Administrators of Elementary and Secondary Schools, 2003–2004,* 7th ed. (Chicago: University of Chicago Press, 2003).

problems in determining how well prepared entering teachers are. The required semester hours in general education (that is, arts and sciences) for a secondary certificate varies nationwide from about thirty hours to about seventy-five hours. The minimum hours required in professional teacher-education courses and the number of semester or quarter hours needed to teach an academic subject also vary in accordance with state requirements. Add to this the fact that courses with the same title may have drastically different content from one institution to another, and you'll see why state and institutional requirements, even when taken together, do not guarantee that teachers have studied a uniform set of skills and concepts.

■ Interstate movement of teachers

Reciprocity of Teacher Certificates. Differences in certification requirements between states also traditionally inhibited the movement of teachers throughout the country. If you were certified to teach in New York, for example, you might not meet the requirements for teaching in Illinois. Organizations concerned with the quality of education generally criticized this lack of reciprocity among states. Many educators argued that easing interstate movement of teachers would help (1) balance teacher supply and demand, (2) improve opportunities for teachers, (3) reduce inbreeding and provincialism in local school systems, and (4) increase morale among teachers.

■ Regional certificates

Reciprocity compacts of varying success were established between some states as early as 1900. In recent years, regional agreements have developed that recognize preparation requirements across states. Most states have signed interstate contracts in which they agree to issue comparable certificates or licenses to teachers who have completed a state-approved program at an institution accredited by the region covered in the contract. In addition, various organizations are developing nationwide approaches to improve teachers' geographic mobility.[12]

REFOCUS Does your state participate in regional teacher-education agreements with other states? If yes, are graduates of your institution automatically qualified to apply for teaching positions in cooperating states? If not, in which nearby states could you most easily obtain a teaching certificate?

■ Nontraditional preparation

Alternative Certification. Most states have introduced **alternative certification** programs, partly to attract more talented candidates to teaching and partly in reaction to current or anticipated shortages in teaching fields such as science and math. These programs help prospective teachers pursue certification without following the traditional preparation path at schools and colleges of education. A New Jersey program, for example, seeks to attract "talented persons who did not study education in college." Nationwide, more than 200,000 teachers have been certified through alternative certification programs. Many new teachers within this group pursue teaching careers after leaving the armed forces.[13]

■ Critiques of alternative certification

Alternative certification programs promote intense supervision and compressed formal coursework during the first few years of teaching assignment. Such programs almost always require professional development activities and courses while learning to teach. Several systematic examinations of alternative certification programs have provided some encouraging indications that they are attracting well-educated

---

[12]The organizations include the National Association of State Directors of Teacher Education Certification (NASDTEC), the Council of Chief State School Officers, and the Educational Testing Service. See the *NASDTEC Communicator* and other documents available at **www. nasdtec.org.**
[13]C. Emily Feistritzer, "Alternative Teacher Certification: A State-by-State Analysis," 2003 summary available at **www.ncei.com.**

individuals and are frequently meeting their goal of intense supervision. However, some recent assessments have raised questions. For example, data on several alternative certification programs indicate that many participants received little or none of the training or supervision that school districts were supposed to provide. Some participants acquired large debts and were unable to find teaching jobs afterward.[14]

■ Teach for America

Probably the best-known alternative certification program is a national effort called Teach for America. Designed to attract recent graduates from colleges at which students have high achievement scores, Teach for America has spent tens of millions of dollars to recruit potential teachers, train them intensively for eight weeks, and place them in school districts with severe urban problems. Some initial reports were promising. For example, in some years more than one-quarter of the participants were minority individuals, and many of the secondary-school participants had much-needed skills in math or science. More than 10,000 teachers have been trained, and about 6,000 participants are still teaching or have other jobs in school districts. Several studies have reported promising results regarding the contributions of TFA participants. But other studies indicated that many of these potential new teachers were frustrated by conditions in difficult schools and/or withdrew before completing their teaching assignments.[15]

Despite the growing popularity of alternative certification programs, most teachers attend more traditional teacher-education programs. The Taking Issue box presents some arguments for and against alternative certification programs.

REFOCUS What are the certification requirements in the state where you wish to teach? How can you find out? How might you prepare yourself for geographic mobility during your teaching career?

Trends in Preservice Education

Over the past two decades, many teacher-education programs have placed significant emphasis on earlier field experience. In recent years major developments also have included movements toward fifth-year and five-year programs; increased emphasis on producing "reflective" teachers; growing use of computers and other technology; requirements that future teachers learn about methods for teaching students with disabilities and other "special" populations; and programs to prepare

---

[14]John M. Miller and Michael C. McKenna, "A Comparison of Alternatively and Traditionally Prepared Teachers," *Journal of Teacher Education* (May–June 1998), pp. 167–176; Barnett Berry, "Quality Alternatives in Teacher Preparation," *The State Education Standard* (Winter 2000), available at **www.nasbc.org/Standard**; Anne T. Lockwood, "Who Prepares Your Teachers? The Debate Over Alternative Certification," 2002 paper prepared for the American Association of School Administrators, available at **www.aasa.org/issues_and_insights/issues_dept**; Albert Cortez, "Prepared Teachers Needed," *IDRA Newsletter* (April 2003), available at **www.idra.org**; R. Clarke Fowler, "The Massachusetts Signing Bonus Program for New Teachers," *Education Policy Analysis Archives*, April 22, 2003, available at **http://epaa.asu.edu**; and Barnett Berry, Mandy Hoke, and Eric Hirsch, "The Search for Highly Qualified Teachers," *Phi Delta Kappan* (May 2004), pp. 684–689.

[15]Wendy Kopp, "A Case for Professional Corps," *National Civic Review* (Fall 1997), pp. 211–217; Raymond Macke, Stephen H. Fletcher, and Javier Luque, "Teach For America: An Evaluation of Teacher Differences and Student Outcomes (Houston, Texas)," 2001 paper prepared for the Houston Independent School District, available at **www.teachforamerica.org/pdfs/TFA_final.pdf**; Ildiko Laczko-Kerr and David C. Berliner, "The Effectiveness of 'Teach for America' and Other Under-certified Teachers on Student Academic Achievement," *Education Policy Analysis Archives*, September 6, 2003, available at **http://epaa.asu.edu**; and Molly Ness, *Lessons to Learn* (New York: Routledge/Falmer, 2004).

taking issue

Question Should we encourage alternative certification programs that bypass traditional teacher-education requirements?

Alternative Certification

Many states have introduced alternative certification programs that bypass traditional teacher-education requirements. In general, these programs help orient college graduates to the teaching experience and then place them in full-time teaching positions, where they receive training that leads to certification while they learn about teaching and education.

Arguments PRO

1 Learning to teach on the job can provide better opportunities to determine what does and doesn't work in the real world and to talk with, observe, and emulate successful teachers.

2 Professional studies integrated with full-time teaching are likely to be more meaningful and practical than studies presented in largely theoretical college courses.

3 Alternative programs, which avoid years of study for certification, can attract teacher candidates to shortage areas such as mathematics, science, and bilingual education.

4 Alternative programs help attract minority teachers, retired persons with special skills in technical subjects, and other candidates who can make important contributions in improving the education system.

5 Competing alternative programs will stimulate colleges and universities to improve their teacher-training programs.

Arguments CON

1 Learning to teach on the job frequently proves unsuccessful because many participants find the immediate demands overwhelming and fail to develop and hone their skills adequately.

2 Initial data on several alternative certification programs show that, in practice, school districts either lack sufficient resources to provide professional studies for participants or have other priorities.

3 These programs offer short-term relief only. Many participants realize they are unsuited for or not interested in the work and withdraw during or soon after the first year.

4 Alternative certification reinforces inequity in education because it often places inexperienced persons at inner-city schools, which have high turnover and the most need for well-trained and experienced faculty.

5 Competing alternative programs may distract colleges and universities from offering training that develops the understanding and skills of reflective teachers over several years of study.

teaching candidates for the diverse cultural and ethnic settings of contemporary American schools.

■ Early assignments in schools

Early Field Experience. Many teacher-education programs have become more practical by requiring future teachers to spend a significant amount of time in elementary or secondary schools early in their preparation. If you are a student in one of these programs, you will likely find that your professional courses, which address subjects such as educational psychology or pedagogical methods, coordinate closely with classroom observation, assignments as a teacher aide, or other field experiences in local schools. Institutions that require early and continual field experience have constructed a sequence by which students move from observation to service as

Preparing Teachers ■ 15

a teacher's aide and into relatively full-scale teaching responsibility, much as in the traditional "practice teaching" semester.[16]

■ Scheduling professional-study components

Fifth-Year and Five-Year Programs. During the 1980s several states and numerous schools and colleges of education either introduced fifth-year programs or expanded teacher education across five years of preparation. *Fifth-year programs* include few or no professional-study components during the four years in which the future teacher earns a bachelor's degree; professional preparation is concentrated in the fifth year. In contrast, *five-year programs* spread professional preparation across the undergraduate years and focus increasingly on clinical experience and training.[17]

■ "Thoughtful" practitioners

Reflective Teaching. In accordance with recent emphasis on improving students' thinking and comprehension skills, many institutions emphasize **reflective teaching** as a central theme in teacher education. Reflective teachers frequently observe and think about the results of their teaching and adjust their methods accordingly. Closely related terms such as *inquiry-oriented teacher education, expert decision making,* and *higher-order self-reflection* also describe this concept. Hundreds of schools of education have reorganized their programs to prepare reflective teachers, but the programs are diverse and show little agreement on what reflective teaching should mean.[18]

■ Technology training for teachers

Computer and Technology Use. Most likely, your teacher-education program offers you some training and access to a computer lab. National surveys of teacher-education programs indicate that more than 90 percent have established computer or technology laboratories. These laboratories encompass a wide variety of activities and objectives, such as orienting future teachers in computer use, introducing hardware and software developed for elementary and secondary schools, and strengthening interest and capability in technology for lesson design or delivery. Many students also encounter technology in their teaching methods courses. Some programs, however, apparently lack sufficient funds for high-quality efforts to prepare their future teachers to use contemporary technologies.[19]

Standards & Assessment ✓
■ Preparation for mainstreaming and inclusion

Requirements for Teaching Disabled Students. Many states and teacher-training institutions now require that all future teachers receive some preparation in working with students who have significant disabilities. As a teacher, you will likely have

---

[16]Judy Swanson, "Systemic Reform in the Profesionalism of Educators," *Phi Delta Kappan* (September 1995), pp. 36–39; David C. Berliner, "A Personal Response to Those Who Bash Teacher Education," *Journal of Teacher Education* (November–December 2000), pp. 358–371; and Anders Hove and Brian Gill, *The Benedum Collaborative Model of Teacher Education* (Washington, D.C.: ERIC Document Reproduction Service, 2003), available at **www.edrs.com**, search for ED469940.

[17]Linda Darling-Hammond, "Teachers and Teaching," *Educational Researcher* (January–February 1998), pp. 5–15; and "Teacher Preparation and Induction," *The Progress of Education Reform 1999–2001* (October–November 2000), available at **www.ecs.org**.

[18]Dorothy K. Stewart, "Reflective Teaching in Preservice Teacher Education," *Journal of Teacher Education* (September 1994), pp. 298–302; Deborah S. Yost, Sally M. Sentner, and Anna Forlenza-Bailey, "An Examination of the Construct of Critical Reflection," *Journal of Teacher Education* (January–February 2000), pp. 39–49; and Victoria J. Risko, Carol Vukelich, and Kathleen Roskos, "Preparing Teachers for Reflective Practice," *Language Arts* (November 2002), pp. 134–145.

[19]Donald R. Coker and Mary Wilson, "Reconceptualizing the Process of Teacher Preparation," *Education* (Summer 1997), pp. 500–506; American Association of Colleges for Teacher Education, *Log On or Lose Out: Technology in 21st Century Teacher Education* (Washington, D.C.: AACTE, 2000); and Kristen Loschert, "Are You Ready?" *NEA Today* (April 2003), available at **www.nea.org/neatoday**.

special-needs students in your classes. The law demands that disabled students be *mainstreamed* in regular classes as much as is possible and feasible, and the growing trend is toward full *inclusion* of disabled students no matter how extensive their special needs. (See the chapter on Providing Equal Educational Opportunity for information about mainstreaming, inclusion, and related topics.) As a consequence, most teachers can expect certain responsibilities for working with special-needs students. Typical teacher-training requirements involve the following:[20]

■ Typical requirements

- Cooperative, interdisciplinary efforts in which both higher-education faculty and knowledgeable field educators help future teachers learn approaches for working with students with disabilities

- Arrangements to bring together programs that prepare "regular" teachers and those that prepare "special-education" teachers

- Requirements in many states that all future teachers complete one or more courses in education for special-needs students, and/or that existing courses incorporate substantial amounts of material on the subject

■ Preparing for multicultural classrooms

Preparation for Teaching in Diverse Settings. Increasing enrollment of racial and ethnic minority students in U.S. schools is prompting programs to prepare future teachers by adding components to help candidates function successfully in diverse settings. Similar efforts are under way in teacher licensing. For example, the Praxis III teacher performance assessment approach, developed by the Educational Testing Service (ETS), specifies that a candidate for a teaching license should be able to demonstrate a "comprehensive understanding" of why it is important to become familiar with students' background knowledge and experiences.[21]

 R E F O C U S   What trends listed here especially describe your teacher-education program? Do any of the trends describe directions in which you *wish* your program would head?

▶ Prospective Teachers: Abilities and Testing

Standards & Assessment ✔

In recent years, much discussion has centered on improving the quality of the teaching work force, particularly on improving the abilities of prospective teachers and on testing their competence for teaching.

Teacher Abilities

■ Standardized test scores

Discussions of the "quality" of the teaching work force frequently focus on "ability" scores derived from standardized tests such as the Scholastic Assessment Test (SAT) and the American College Test (ACT). Among potential teachers, such test scores declined in the 1970s, as they did for students majoring in business and numerous

---

[20]Carol Strawderman and Pamela Lindsey, "Keeping Up with the Times," *Journal of Teacher Education* (March–April 1995), pp. 95–100; and Denise Littleton, "Preparing Teachers for Hard-to-Staff Schools," *State Education Leader* (Spring–Summer 2000).

[21]G. Pritchy Smith, *Common Sense About Uncommon Knowledge* (Washington, D.C.: American Association of Colleges of Teacher Education, 1998); Carla Claycomb, "High-Quality Urban School Teachers," *The State Education Standard* (Winter 2000), available at **www.nasbc.org/ Standard**; and Lisa Holm and Carol Horn, "Priming Schools of Education for Today's Teachers," *Education Digest* (March 2003), pp. 25–31.

other subjects. For example, between 1973 and 1981, the average SAT verbal score of college students intending to teach fell from 418 to 397. Since 1982, however, test scores of college students who say they intend to become teachers have appreciably increased and generally resemble those of students majoring in business, psychology, and the health professions. In addition, recent studies have found that teachers' average test scores are about the same as those of other college-educated adults.[22]

Testing Teachers

■ Testing basic skills

Some efforts to improve the teaching force focus on **basic skills testing** of preservice teachers, new teachers, and sometimes experienced teachers. Drawing on the argument that teachers low in reading, mathematics, communications, and/or professional knowledge probably are ineffective in their teaching, many states have introduced requirements that prospective teachers pass some form of minimum skills test in reading and language, math, subject-area specialty, and/or professional knowledge. More than forty states now use the Praxis test developed by the Educational Testing Service for this purpose, and to become a certified teacher, you likely will need to pass a series of Praxis exams.[23]

■ Praxis examination

■ Criticisms of testing

Testing of prospective and current teachers remains a controversial topic. Many political leaders see testing as one of the few feasible steps they can take to improve public confidence in the teaching force. Opponents argue that the process unjustifiably excludes people who do poorly on paper-and-pencil tests. Many opponents believe that existing tests are biased against minorities and other candidates not from the cultural mainstream. Critics also cite data indicating that scores on standardized tests taken by future teachers correlate poorly with subsequent on-the-job measures of teaching effectiveness.[24]

■ In support of testing

Proponents of testing generally counter that all or nearly all teachers must be able to demonstrate that they can function at least at the seventh- or eighth-grade level in reading, writing, and math—the minimum level currently specified on some tests—to perform effectively in their jobs. Many proponents also argue that research has provided enough information to justify minimum standards and to allow for the creation of more valid exams.[25] In any case, testing remains highly popular, and you should make sure that your teacher preparation program and general studies help you prepare to pass any exams that you must take.

---

[22]Catherine E. Cardina and John K. Roden, "Academic Proficiency of Students Who Reported Intentions of Majoring in Education," *Journal of Teacher Education* (January–February 1998), pp. 38–46; Barbara A. Brusch and Richard J. Coley, *How Teachers Compare* (Princeton, N.J.: Educational Testing Service, 2000), available at **www.ets.org**; and Andrew S. Latham, Drew Gitomer, and Robert Ziomek, "What the Tests Tell Us About New Teachers," undated paper prepared for the Educational Testing Service, available at **www.ets.org/textonly/ teachingandlearning/edstnew.html.**

[23]Linda Darling-Hammond, *The Evolution of Teacher Policy* (Santa Monica, Calif.: Rand, 1998); and David Imig, "National Test Is a Good Plan," *USA Today,* February 25, 2003.

[24]Ayres G. D'Costa, "The Impact of Courts on Teacher Competence Testing," *Theory into Practice* (Spring 1993), pp. 104–112; and Ann Bradley, "National Research Panel Tepid over Tests for Licensing Teachers," *Education Week,* March 15, 2000.

[25]Richard J. Murname, "The Case for Performance-Based Licensing," *Phi Delta Kappan* (October 1991), pp. 137–142; Allen Glenn, "Passing the Test," *AACTE Briefs,* August 10, 1998; Kate Zernike, "Teachers Union Proposes a National Test for Recruits," *New York Times,* April 14, 2000; and Peter Youngs, Allan Odden, and Andrew C. Porter, "State Policy Related to Teacher Licensure," *Educational Policy* (May 2003), pp. 217–236.

 Are teachers in your state required to pass a test? If yes, what are the requirements? What are the passing and failing rates in your state and at your institution?

■ Controversy in Massachusetts

Controversy regarding testing of prospective teachers became nationally prominent in 1998 after Massachusetts administered its first statewide test for this purpose. Thirty percent of the candidates failed the reading and writing test, and 63 percent of candidates for mathematics certification failed the subject-matter test in their field. After the chairman of the state board of education stated that "the real story . . . is that so many prospective public school teachers failed a test that a bright 10th grader could pass without difficulty" and that "no responsible person would subject anyone's children, much less his own, to teachers who had failed these topics," legislators and educators in Massachusetts and elsewhere initiated ongoing debates and arguments concerning appropriate test performance levels for entering and exiting teacher-preparation programs and for obtaining and retaining teaching certificates.[26]

▶ Job Conditions for Teachers

Are people who become teachers generally satisfied with their work? Job conditions strongly affect satisfaction, and, as we'll see in this section, job conditions are changing in response to many calls for educational reform. Several of these changes seem likely to improve teachers' job satisfaction.

Teacher Satisfaction

■ National surveys

In a poll conducted for the Metropolitan Life Insurance Company, teachers were asked, "All in all, how satisfied would you say you are with teaching as a career?" Most of the respondents answered either "very satisfied" or "somewhat satisfied." Nearly half reported that they were more enthusiastic about teaching than when they began their careers. Similar results have been documented in several other recent polls.[27]

■ Reasons for satisfaction

One important reason for teachers' job satisfaction is that they often feel successful in advancing their students' learning and growth. Recent increases in teacher salaries, widespread recognition of teachers' expertise, and the quality of their interpersonal relationships with students and parents also promote satisfaction. Because teachers appear mostly positive about these and other aspects of their jobs, it is not surprising that they generally indicate they have high satisfaction in their work.

■ Reasons for dissatisfaction

Many teachers do, however, report dissatisfaction with their work. Nationwide surveys show that significant percentages believe they have insufficient time for

[26]John Silber, "Those Who Can't Teach," *New York Times,* July 7, 1998. See also David J. Hoff, "Massachusetts to Put Math Teachers to the Test," *Education Week,* May 31, 2000; and Larry H. Ludlow, "Teacher Test Accountability," *Education Policy Analysis Archives,* February 22, 2001, available at **http://epaa.asu.edu.**

[27]National Center for Education Statistics, *America's Teachers Ten Years After "A Nation at Risk"* (Washington, D.C.: U.S. Department of Education, 1995); Andrew S. Latham, "Teacher Satisfaction," *Educational Leadership* (February 1998) pp. 82–83; Steve Farkas, Jean Johnson, and Ann Duffett, "Stand By Me," 2003 paper prepared for Public Agenda, available at **www.publicagenda.org/PDFStore/pdfs/stand_by_me.pdf;** and Jack Buckley, Mark Schneider, and Yi Shang, "The Effects of School Facility Quality on Teacher Retention in Urban Districts," 2004 paper posted by the National Clearinghouse for Educational Facilities, available at **www.edfacilities.org.**

counseling students, planning lessons, and other instructional functions. Other complaints include ambiguity in supervisors' expectations; unresponsive administrators, decrepit facilities, and obligations to participate in staff development perceived as irrelevant or ineffective; lack of supplies and equipment; extensive paperwork and record keeping; and insufficient input on organizational decisions. Improvements in teacher salaries and teaching conditions may reduce these aspects of dissatisfaction in the future.[28]

Standards & Assessment ☑

■ "High-stakes" tests

State and District Standards and Teacher Stress

Teaching is a difficult profession that usually involves significant stress. In recent years the introduction of state and district standards for student performance has substantially increased this stress. Standards are often accompanied by accountability mechanisms involving standardized testing and publication of achievement scores for schools and, sometimes, individual classrooms. All states now require some degree of uniform testing in all school districts. Many of these tests carry "high stakes," such as whether students pass from one grade to another, become eligible to graduate, or must attend summer school, and whether or not schools may be closed or intensely scrutinized because of low test scores.

■ Teaching to the tests

With such consequences, many teachers feel severe pressure to improve their students' test scores. This reaction is particularly prevalent at low-performing schools, but it also occurs even at some high-performing schools in locations where states or districts set high requirements for improved performance every year. Faculty in many schools wind up devoting much of the school year to preparing for tests and to emphasizing test-preparation materials in obtaining and using teaching resources, practices known collectively as "teaching to the test." As we point out elsewhere in this book, this situation has raised controversial questions as to whether the standards movement facilitates or impedes improvements in student performance, as teachers narrow their instructional focus to the tested skills. Although some teachers report finding ways to provide engaging, quality instruction within frameworks that require continuous attention to the many learning objectives specified on state and district tests, even these teachers typically experience high-level stress as they learn to function effectively within such frameworks.[29]

Coping with Stress

■ Teaching can be stressful

As we've seen, teaching has its difficult and stressful moments. Research also indicates that elementary and secondary teaching has become more stressful in recent years. In response, many professional organizations and school districts offer courses or workshops emphasizing coping techniques and other stress-reduction approaches.

[28]Connie Anderson, "Time Well Spent," *Teaching K–8* (January 1999), pp. 80–81; Wade A. Carpenter, "Ten Years of Silver Bullets," *Phi Delta Kappan* (January 2000), pp. 383–389; Peter D. Hart and Robert M. Teeter, "A National Priority," 2002 paper prepared for the Educational Testing Service, available at **www.ets.org/download.html**; and Richard M. Ingersoll, "The Teacher Shortage: Myth or Reality," *Educational Horizons* (Spring 2003), available at **www. pilambda.org.**

[29]Linda McNeil, "Creating New Inequalities," *Phi Delta Kappan* (June 2000), pp. 729–734; Robert Rothman, ed., "Giving All Students a Fair Shot," *Achieve Policy Brief* (Fall 2000), available at **www.Achieve.org,** search for "policy brief"; and Sandra Mathison and Melissa Freeman, "Constraining Elementary Teachers' Work," *Educational Policy Analysis Archives,* September 24, 2003, available at **http://epaa.asu.edu.**

In national surveys, most teachers express satisfaction with their careers. Common frustrations of teachers, however, include insufficient time, ambiguous expectations, and new demands for teacher accountability. The first year of teaching can be especially stressful, and new teachers should make stress-reducing activities a priority.
(© *Elizabeth Crews*)

■ Coping techniques

Counselors point out that exercise, rest, hobbies, good nutrition, meditation or other relaxation techniques, efficient scheduling of personal affairs, and vacations can help individuals cope with high-stress jobs. You may also reduce stress if you participate in professional renewal activities or support groups, separate your job from your home life, and keep an open mind attitude toward change. Because first-year teachers experience special stress as they enter new jobs, professional organizations, school districts, and even the U.S. Department of Education offer supportive programs. The Technology @ School box in this chapter describes one such effort.

As you see, most teachers are motivated by a desire to work with young people and to enter a challenging and honorable field and most are satisfied with most aspects of their jobs. Some dissatisfaction arises, however, with various "nonteaching" considerations and with demands of the contemporary movement to raise standards of performance. As we shall see next, nationwide efforts are under way to address some of the teaching conditions that teachers find difficult.

Educational Reform and Teaching Conditions

Among many calls for educational reform over the past two decades, the most widely known come from a series of **national reports** on the state of education in the United States. One of the most prominent reform efforts is the federal No Child Left Behind Act. This and other reform efforts that we describe here have changed, and will continue to change, job conditions for teachers in fundamental ways.

■ Problems identified in *A Nation at Risk*

National Reports. Since the mid-1980s numerous reports have focused on problems of education in the United States. *A Nation at Risk* (1983), the best known and most influential of the national reports, was prepared by the National Commission on Excellence in Education sponsored by the U.S. Department of Education. Arguing that the United States is "at risk" in the sense that its "once unchallenged preeminence in commerce, industry, service, and technological innovation is being overtaken by competitors throughout the world," the commission concluded that one major aspect of decline has been a "rising tide of mediocrity" in

An Internet Location for Prospective Teachers

Go to **www.ed.gov/inits/teachers/archive-wantobe.html** and open a screen headed "So You Want to Be a Teacher?" Clickable hypertext headings on this page include:

■ "Teacher Recruitment Clearinghouse" is an "online resource for prospective teachers seeking jobs and for schools, districts, and states seeking qualified teachers."

■ "What to Expect Your First Year of Teaching" offers a "compilation of frank discussions by award-winning first-year teachers."

■ "Survival Guide for New Teachers," now available at **www.ed.gov/teachers/become/about/survivalguide/index.html,** offers a "collection of reflections by award-winning first-year teachers." Sections in this document advise you on how to work with veteran teachers, parents, and principals. Here is an excerpt from the introductory message.

What Does "Sink or Swim" Mean?

To start with, first-year teachers are still liable to be assigned the most challenging courses—the ones with a heavy developmental emphasis and students who need additional expertise to teach. Moreover, many new teachers receive little more than a quick orientation on school policies and procedures before they start their jobs. And there is often no time in the day—or week, for that matter—allotted for sitting down with colleagues to discuss pedagogical methods, daily dilemmas like time and classroom management, and coping strategies. . . .

Fortunately, some promising new initiatives are already under way. For example, 100 percent of the graduates of a program for first-year teachers from Texas A&M University–Corpus Christi, Texas, have stayed on the job after five years of teaching. Meanwhile, a statewide retention rate is about 50 percent after five years, according to the university.

Texas's Induction Year Program is designed to provide support and instruction to first-year teachers while getting them started toward master's level professional development. The program focuses on practical issues such as classroom management, communication skills, and discipline. Also, faculty members regularly visit the classes of participants to evaluate the teacher's performance. . . .

In addition to university teacher-preparation programs, school districts are doing more to make first-year teaching a success. Districts from Delaware to Columbus, Ohio, to Omaha, Nebraska, have instituted induction programs for new teachers that include mentoring, peer assistance, and other forms of guidance and support.

You will also find headings for links to state departments of education and an Educational Resources Information Center (ERIC) document, "So You Want to Be a Teacher." In addition to digesting the information and suggestions provided in these documents, you can discuss their meaning and implication with other prospective teachers or familiarize yourself with information on certification and assistance possibilities in your own or other states.

the schools. Here, we should note the report's suggestions for making teaching a more rewarding and respected profession:[30]

---

[30]National Commission on Excellence in Education, *A Nation at Risk: The Imperitive for Education Reform* (Washington, D.C.: U.S. Department of Education, 1983), p. 5; and Paul D. Houston, "Do We Suffer from Educational Glaucoma?" *School Administrator* (January 1999). See also *The Full Circle: Building a Coherent Teacher Preparation System* (Washington, D.C.: National Association of State Boards of Education, 2000).

■ Proposals for the teaching profession

- Set higher standards for entry into the profession
- Improve teacher salaries so they are "professionally competitive, market-sensitive, and performance-based," thus making them part of a system that rewards superior teachers (in other words, institute merit pay, a practice discussed in the chapter on The Teaching Profession)
- Add an additional month of teacher employment with pay
- Institute a *career ladder* so that qualified people progress from beginning teacher to experienced teacher and finally to the level of *master* teacher
- Use incentives such as grants and loans to attract outstanding candidates into teaching, particularly into shortage areas such as science and mathematics
- Involve master teachers in preparing and supervising probationary teachers

Standards & Assessment ☑

■ No Child Left Behind Act

The No Child Left Behind Act. In 2001 teacher-quality-improvement activities became an integral part of the national school reform movement with passage of the **No Child Left Behind Act** (NCLBA). We will discuss major components of NCLB dealing with student achievement elsewhere, particularly in the chapter on Providing Equal Educational Opportunity. Here we review the key sections dealing with requirements that by 2005–2006 teachers in school districts receiving federal funding must be "highly qualified."

■ Highly qualified teachers

Requirements in these sections were explained in a 2003 U.S. Department of Education document (see "A Toolkit for Teachers," available at **www.ed.gov/teachers/nclbguide/nclb-teachers-toolkit.pdf**). The toolkit notes that the NCLBA "represents a sweeping overhaul of federal efforts to support elementary and secondary education" and "sets the goal of having every child making the grade on state-defined education standards by the end of the 2013–2014 school year." As part of the overhaul, NCLB "outlines the minimum qualifications needed by teachers and paraprofessionals who work on any facet of classroom instruction. It requires that states develop plans to achieve the goal that all teachers of core academic subjects be highly qualified by the end of the 2005–06 school year."[31]

■ Three requirements

Under NCLB, a "**highly qualified teacher**" must have (1) a bachelor's degree, (2) full state certification and licensure as defined by the state, and (3) "demonstrated competency as defined by the state in each core academic subject he or she teaches."

■ Defining competency

New elementary teachers can demonstrate competency by "passing a rigorous state test on subject knowledge and teaching skills in reading or language arts, writing, mathematics and other areas of the basic elementary school curriculum." New middle and high school teachers can demonstrate competency "either by passing a rigorous state test in each subject they teach, or by holding an academic major or course work equivalent to an academic major, an advanced degree or advanced certification or credentials." Those already employed as teachers at any level can demonstrate competency by meeting the requirements for new teachers or by meeting a state-defined "high, objective, uniform state standard of evaluation (HOUSSE)." States are now defining and establishing their HOUSSE standards for competency among current teachers. Many are using point systems that allow teachers to count a combination of years of successful classroom experience, participation in high-quality professional development that evaluates what the teacher has learned, service on curriculum development teams, and other activities related to developing knowledge in an academic area.

---

[31]U.S. Department of Education, *No Child Left Behind: A Toolkit for Teachers* (Washington, D.C.: U.S. Department of Education, 2003).

Developments with respect to implementation of NCLB teacher quality goals have included the following:[32]

■ Early developments

■ Following passage of the NCLBA, the federal government has begun to distribute millions of dollars for activities such as devising and implementing alternative certification programs for teachers and administrators, establishing teacher merit pay, providing bonus pay for teaching in high-need subjects and high-poverty schools, testing teachers in their subjects, and forming a Teacher Assistance Corps to help states carry out their quality-improvement initiatives. In addition, the Educational Testing Service is working with twenty-three states to set a common cut-off score for licensing on its Praxis II test, which covers subject-matter knowledge.

■ Progress report

■ In 2003 Secretary of Education Rod Paige issued a *Second Annual Report on Teacher Quality,* in which he provided data on state efforts to comply with the NCBLA. For example, in the first two years following the act, thirty-five states had developed and linked teacher certification requirements to student achievement content standards, thirty-two states required teaching candidates to pass a test in at least one academic content area, and all but eight states required statewide assessments for beginning teachers.

■ Controversy over data

■ Unfortunately, controversy has also arisen regarding state progress toward ensuring highly qualified teachers in all classrooms. For example, a U.S. General Accounting Office investigation reported in 2003 that many states were not collecting the kind of data Congress needed to assess progress toward the NCLBA's requirement for qualified teachers. Data submitted (or not submitted) in 2003 to the Department of Education indicated that many states had not defined their criteria for demonstrating competency.

Among states that had moved more speedily, twenty-two reported that at least 90 percent of courses were taught by highly qualified teachers. Some disagreeing observers cited various data indicating that numerous staff teaching science, math, and other specialty subjects were working "out-of-field," or teaching in areas where they had not demonstrated competency, particularly in high-poverty schools. They concluded that either the data were incorrect or criteria for defining "highly qualified" had been set low, or both.

■ Impatience and skepticism

■ Several organizations expressed impatience and/or skepticism regarding NLCB implementation. For example, The Education Trust criticized the federal government for doing little to ensure that teachers in urban schools are becoming truly qualified to raise the achievement of minority students. The Association of Community Organizations for Reform Now concluded that NCLB commitments to notify parents about the presence of unqualified teachers locally were not being met. Although the NCLBA promises reforms that will increase the professionalism of teachers and in some ways may improve their working conditions, it remains to be seen whether those ambitious promises can be met.

---

[32]Bess Keller, "States Claim Teachers Are 'Qualified'," *Education Week,* October 29, 2003; "Leaving Teachers Behind," 2003 paper prepared for ACORN, available at **www.acorn.org**; "Meeting the Highly Qualified Teacher Challenge," 2003 Second Annual Report on Teacher Quality by the U.S. Secretary of Education; "More Information Would Help States Determine Which Teachers Are Highly Qualified," 2003 paper published by the U.S. General Accounting Office, available at **www.gao.gov**, search for GAO–03–631; and Michael A. Rebell and Molly A. Hunter, "'Highly Qualified' Teachers," *Phi Delta Kappan* (May 2004), pp. 690–696.

Standards & Assessment ☑

■ NBPTS certification

The NBPTS and the INTASC.   In 1987, in accordance with a recommendation of its Task Force on Teaching as a Profession, the Carnegie Corporation helped establish the **National Board for Professional Teaching Standards** (NBPTS), a nonprofit organization that issues certificates to teachers who meet its standards for professional ability and knowledge. The standards, which focus on both content knowledge and effective teaching methods, are considerably more rigorous than those for state certification tests. Assessment methods include interviews, portfolios, computer and video simulations, and other innovative elements. To qualify for national board certification, teachers must have a bachelor's degree, a state teaching license, and at least three years of successful teaching. Most states provide a salary supplement or bonus to teachers who receive the certification. More than thirty thousand candidates have earned NBPTS certificates.[33]

■ INTASC standards

Standards for teacher performance—in this case for beginning teachers—are also being developed by the Interstate New Teacher Assessment and Support Consortium (INTASC) with funding from the U.S. Department of Education. Look for current information concerning INTASC at **www.cesso.org/acadfact.html.** More than thirty states are participating in INTASC.

■ Holmes Group recommendations

Holmes and Other Groups.   Since 1986 teaching profession reform has been a primary concern of the Holmes Group, a consortium of deans of education at major research universities. Renamed the Holmes Partnership in 1996, Holmes commissioned a series of reports, including *Tomorrow's Teachers* (1986), *Tomorrow's Schools* (1990), and *Tomorrow's Schools of Education* (1995). In addition to the reforms emphasized in other reports, the Holmes Partnership has emphasized the need for teacher-education students to have early experience in schools. Consequently, the group has focused on the creation of **professional development schools** (PDSs). Like a traditional "laboratory" school, the PDS is designed to link a local school district with a college or school of education, but in a more comprehensive and systematic fashion. College faculty members function as classroom teachers and serve as mentors for new teachers. According to advocates, PDSs allow experienced teachers, beginning teachers, teacher educators, and administrators to work together to create a community of learners and to improve educational opportunities for low-achieving students. There are now more than one thousand professional development schools.[34]

■ In Support of PDSs

Other groups, including the American Federation of Teachers, the American Association of Colleges of Teacher Education (AACTE), and the National Education Association, have been working to establish plans for schools similar to PDSs. Although these are in the early stages, AACTE surveys indicate that many schools and colleges of education are cooperating with professional development schools or

---

[33]Iris C. Rotberg, Mary H. Futrell, and Joyce M. Lieberman, "National Board Certification," *Phi Delta Kappan* (February 1998), pp. 462–466; Kristen Loschert, "Pursuing Teaching Excellence," *NEA Today Online* (April 2003), available at **www.nea.org/neatoday/0304**; Dan Goldhaber and Emily Anthony, "Can Teacher Quality Be Effectively Assessed?," 2004 report prepared for the Urban Institute, available at **www.urban.org**; and general information available at **www.nbpts.org.**
[34]Holmes Group, *Tomorrow's Teachers* (East Lansing, Mich.: Holmes Group, 1986); Holmes Group, *Tomorrow's Schools* (East Lansing, Mich.: Holmes Group, 1990); and Holmes Group, *Tomorrow's Schools of Education* (East Lansing, Mich.: Holmes Group, 1995). See also Wendy Schwartz, "The Impact of Professional Development Schools on the Education of Urban Students," *Clearinghouse on Urban Education Digest* (September 2000); Marsha Levine, "Why Invest in Professional Development Schools?," *Educational Leadership* (March 2003), pp. 65–68; and "Professional Development Schools (PDS) Network," 2003 posting at the Web site of the Nystrand Center, available at **www.louisville.edu/edu/collaboration.**

■ Renaissance Group proposals

similar institutions. On the other hand, progress has been hampered by lack of funds and other obstacles to collaboration among both school districts and higher-education institutions.[35]

Additional support for teaching profession reform has come from the Renaissance Group, a consortium of higher-education institutions composed primarily of former teacher-training colleges. The Renaissance Group contends that teacher training should be integrated throughout a student's university experience rather than reserved for the student's final year and should incorporate extensive, sequenced field and clinical experience. In 1999, ten members of the group obtained an $8.55 million grant to enhance their teacher-education programs.[36]

■ Critiques of national reports and recommendations

Reactions to the National Reforms. Reactions have been mixed toward the plethora of national reports and subsequent developments described above. We already have noted the emergence of some controversy and dissatisfaction with respect to implementation of teacher-quality provisions in the NBCLA. No doubt these developments have helped focus attention on the problems of education; the specific proposals have generated a great deal of support. However, many educators believe that the reports and legislation have been too simplistic in their diagnoses and solutions, and some of the proposals have met with substantial resistance and criticism.[37]

For example, many teachers and administrators as well as researchers have criticized the emphasis on "lead teacher" and "career ladder" approaches that give some teachers greater authority and remuneration than their colleagues. In addition, critics of professional development schools have focused on the high costs of PDSs and the lack of available funds, as well as the divergent interests that hamper collaboration between school districts and higher-education institutions. There is concern, as well, that teachers participating in reform activities will be overburdened by numerous and conflicting demands for change.[38]

■ State reforms

Despite the lack of consensus, nearly all state governments have taken actions consistent with one or another of the national reports and all have initiated activities to comply with NCLB. Most states have raised teacher salaries, stiffened entrance and exit requirements for teacher education, and/or expanded testing of new teachers.

■ School-based management

Educational Reform and Teacher Empowerment. Some reform efforts deal specifically with **teacher empowerment**, which frequently includes *school-based* management to increase the role of teachers in decision making. For example, contractual agreements reached between teacher associations and school boards in many districts have given teachers a larger role in determining school policies and

---

[35]Anne Lieberman and Lynne Miller, "Teacher Development in Professional Practice Schools," *Teachers College Record* (Fall 1990), pp. 105–122; Marsha Levine, ed., *Professional Practice Schools* (New York: Teachers College Press, 2002); and information available at **www.aacte.org/eric/pds_glance.htm.**

[36]Informaion about the Renaissance Group is available at **www.emporia.edu/rengroup.**

[37]For examples, see Joseph Murphy, ed., *The Educational Reform Movement of the 1980s* (Berkeley, Calif.: McCutchan, 1990); Michael Fullan et al., *The Rise and Stall of Teacher Education Reform* (Washington, D.C.: American Association of Colleges of Teacher Education, 1998); Susan L. Melnick and Diana Pullin, "Can You Take Dictation?" *Journal of Teacher Education* (September–October 2000), pp. 262–275; and Monty Neill, "Leaving Children Behind," *Phi Delta Kappan* (November 2003), pp. 225–228.

[38]William R. Johnson, "Empowering Practitioners: Holmes, Carnegie, and the Lessons of History," *History of Education Quarterly* (Summer 1987), pp. 221–240; Susan M. Johnson, "Can Professional Certification for Teachers Reshape Teaching as a Career?" *Phi Delta Kappan* (January 2001), pp. 393–399; and "Is It a Real PDS or a Wannabe?" undated posting at the Trilemma Solutions Web site, **www.trilemmasolutions.com/lectures.html.**

practices. Such provisions typically give faculties greater opportunities to select instructional methods and materials and to determine how funds will be spent in their schools. (School-based management is discussed in detail in the next chapter on The Teaching Profession.)

■ Self-governance in Dade County

Several recent experiments to improve education through teacher empowerment are even more ambitious and comprehensive. For example, many Dade County, Florida, schools have adopted a self-governance approach in which teachers and administrators work together to redesign the educational programs in their schools. To a significant extent, faculties can determine staff numbers and functions. As part of this project, the board of education suspended requirements in such areas as maximum class size, length of the school day, and number of minutes per subject.[39]

■ Comprehensive reforms in Rochester

From some points of view, the approach in Rochester, New York, has been even more comprehensive. Since 1987 contracts between the board of education and the Rochester Teachers Association have included the following key provisions:[40]

1. Based on the Carnegie model for "lead" teachers, a teaching career program was established. In this program, teachers move through four stages: (a) *intern,* (new) teachers work under the supervision of experienced colleagues; (b) *resident,* teachers have completed internship and have provisional certification; (c) *professional,* teachers have a permanent certificate; and (d) *lead,* teachers with at least ten years of experience work 10 percent longer hours and devote as much as half their time to serving as mentors, to planning instructional improvements, or to other leadership roles. Lead teachers, selected by panels consisting of four teachers and three administrators, earn more than $75,000 per year.

2. Instead of following traditional seniority practices in determining teachers' assignments, a faculty committee in each school interviews teachers who wish to transfer and makes decisions based on the needs of that school. At the same time, professional teachers and lead teachers are assigned according to need rather than seniority and thus more frequently teach the lowest-achieving students and classes. As Rochester Teachers Association President Adam Urbanski put it, "Success with these students shouldn't be expected of first-year teachers, who have enough to do just to learn the job. Rookie teachers taking on the toughest assignments would be tantamount in the medical profession to interns performing open-heart surgery while master surgeons treat skin abrasions."

It is still premature to reach conclusions about the success or failure of such experiments. These reform efforts will encounter many obstacles, and educators involved in them will have to learn how to translate teacher empowerment into improved school functioning.

[39]Susan H. Fuhrman and Richard F. Elmore, *Ruling Out Rules* (New Brunswick, N.J.: CPRE, 1995); and "Preliminary Report, Highlights," 2003 posting at the Florida School Report Internet site, **www.floridabestpractices.com/casestudies/fascell.html.**
[40]Joanna Richardson, "Rochester, N.Y., Contract Links Accountability, Resources," *Education Week,* December 15, 1993, p. 3; Christine E. Murray, Gerald Grant, and Raji Swami-Nathan, "Rochester's Reforms," *Phi Delta Kappan* (October 1997), pp. 148–155; *Eliminating Barriers to Quality Teaching* (Washington, D.C.: U.S. Department of Education, 2000); and Julia Koppich, Carla Asher, and Charles Kerchner, *Developing Careers, Building a Profession* (Washington, D.C.: National Commission on Teaching and America's Future, 2002).

REFOCUS Which of the reform efforts described here would you most like to see in a school district in which you wanted to teach? Which of the reforms do you think might cause teachers dissatisfaction or stress? Why?

▶ Outlook for Teaching

▪ Bright prospects for teachers

Until the school reform movement of the 1980s, college students majoring in education confronted a buyer's market for teachers, and many questioned the wisdom of entering a field apparently declining in salary, status, and general attraction. Now national attention has focused on education, and there is good news regarding teachers' prospects. The pattern of teacher oversupply has been alleviated, and governments at all levels are acting to improve teacher recruitment and preparation. Individuals dedicated to helping young people learn and grow in school should have considerable professional opportunities to realize their ambitions. In the years to come, the teaching profession should continue to experience a renewed excitement and an even greater sense that the work is of vital importance to American society.

▶ Summing Up

1. Although we see many reasons for entering the teaching profession, research indicates that most teachers do so to help young children and to provide a service to society.

2. Many educators are focusing on ways to increase diversity in the teaching work force to better reflect the student population.

3. Demand for new teachers will likely continue.

4. Teacher salaries have improved rapidly in recent years.

5. Requirements for teacher certification vary from state to state and among institutions of higher learning.

6. In general, teacher education is becoming more practical and reality oriented. Trends in this direction include provision of early field experience in elementary and secondary classrooms. Other important trends include the introduction of five-year and fifth-year programs and the interest in developing reflective teachers. Teachers also are increasingly prepared to use up-to-date technology, to work with students who have special needs, and to teach in widely diverse settings.

7. Most teachers are satisfied with most aspects of their jobs, despite some dissatisfaction with starting salaries and certain other aspects of the profession.

8. National concern remains widespread over teaching work force quality. The major national reports on education and the No Child Left Behind Act have led to higher standards for licensing and to establishment of the highly paid position of "lead" or "master" teacher.

9. Many school districts are working out approaches for empowering teachers in order to make schools more effective.

10. Increasing public concern for education, changes occurring in the schools, and improvements in the outlook for teachers are bringing new excitement and importance to the role of the teacher.

▶ Key Terms

The numbers in parentheses indicate the pages where explanations of the key terms can be found.

supply and demand (6)
certification (11)
alternative certification (12)
reflective teaching (15)
basic skills testing (17)
national reports (20)

A Nation at Risk (20)
No Child Left Behind Act (22)
highly qualified teacher (22)
National Board for Professional Teaching Standards (24)
professional development school (PDS) (24)
teacher empowerment (25)

▶ Discussion Questions

1 Have your reasons for becoming a teacher changed over time? If so, what caused the change or changes? What might be most likely to change your motivation in the future?

2 Do you believe that the trends in teacher education identified in this chapter are desirable? Do you think they will improve education in the schools? What conditions are necessary to make them effective?

3 What steps might improve teacher salaries? Which are most likely to succeed? What will determine whether they are successful?

4 What jobs other than teaching in elementary or secondary schools may be open to persons with a teaching certificate? What additional preparation might be necessary or helpful in obtaining such jobs?

▶ Suggested Projects for Professional Development

1 Collect and analyze information on teacher salary schedules in several nearby school districts. Compare your data with information other members of your class acquire from additional districts. What patterns do you see? What might be the advantages and disadvantages involved in teaching in these districts?

2 Investigate funding for teacher education at your campus. Does your school or college of education serve as a "cash cow" that provides substantial funding for other campus units?

3 Interview an elementary-school teacher and a high-school teacher about their satisfaction with their work and their reasons for being satisfied or dissatisfied. Compare your findings with those of other students in your class.

4 Individually or as a team member, prepare a report on projects and organizations that work to ensure that teachers possess a high level of preparation for their jobs. You might, for example, research the the Interstate New Teacher Assessment and Support Consortium (**www.ccsso.org/Projects**) and the National Board for Professional Teaching Standards (**www.nbpts.org**).

5 Find out what your state has done with respect to reviewing and modifying certification requirements, and to defining competency of new and employed teachers in response to the No Child Left Behind Act of 2001. Have these actions created changes in your preparation program? Are they raising issues for beginning teachers, or controversies regarding the status of current teachers in your state? (Information may be available at your state department of education's Web site, which you can find on the first screen at **www.ccsso.org**.)

► Suggested Resources

Internet Resources

The federal government maintains various sites on the World Wide Web. Many topics in this chapter (and in this book) can be explored at **www.ed.gov.** Various professional organizations, such as the Association for Supervision and Curriculum Development (**www.ascd.org**) and Phi Delta Kappa (**www.pdkintl.org**), also sponsor relevant sites.

"A New Teacher Guide Book" is a useful resource available at **http:hannahmeans. bizland.com.**

Teacher Quality Bulletin is a weekly publication available by e-mail or online from the Teacher Quality Clearinghouse at **www.nctq.org**.

Comparisons of characteristics of private and public schools are available at **http:// nces.ed.gov/programs/coe/2002/analyses/private.**

Information about teachers and teaching as well as jobs and how to obtain them is available at **www.rnt.org.**

Materials at **www.new-teacher.com** are relevant for future as well as new teachers.

Publications

Draper, Sharon M. 2000. *Teaching from the Heart.* Westport, Conn.: Heinemann. *A winner of the Teacher of the Year award recounts her career and what she has learned from it.*

Herndon, Joseph. *The Way It Spozed to Be.* New York: Bantam, 1968. *A classic when it was published, this book, which describes the satisfactions and difficulties of teaching in the inner city, remains relevant in the new millennium.*

Johnson, Susan M. "Can Professional Certification for Teachers Reshape Teaching as a Career?" *Phi Delta Kappan* (January 2001). *This article discusses numerous issues involving teaching as a career.*

Journal of Teacher Education. Regularly provides information and analysis regarding important issues in preservice and in-service education.

McNeil, Linda M. *Contradictions of Control.* New York: Routledge and Kegan Paul, 1986. *Analyzes teachers' reactions to legislative and administrative mandates that sometimes distort instruction toward low-level concentration on facts.*

National Conference on Teacher Quality Exemplary Practices. Exemplary practices and programs are described at **www.ed.gov/inits/teachers/exemplarypractices/index.html**.

Nettles, D. H., and Pamela B. Petrick. *Portfolio Development for Preservice Teachers.* Bloomington, Ind.: Phi Delta Kappa, 1995. *Describes major steps involved in preparing a professional portfolio.*

CHAPTER 2

The Teaching Profession

Until the twentieth century, teachers received relatively little preparation and had little say in the terms of their employment. Teacher training consisted of one or two years and sometimes less at a normal school or teacher college, and teachers had to follow strict rules and regulations concerning their behavior outside the school. Unorganized and isolated from one another in small schools and school districts, teachers could be summarily dismissed by a board of education. Many were told they could not teach material that a community member might find objectionable.

Times have changed. Today, teachers aspire to be professionals with expert knowledge concerning instruction, content, and methods in their particular fields. In addition, they are well organized as a group and have gained greater rights to be judged on their work performance rather than on their behavior outside school. Often, too, they participate in decision making about work conditions. In many cases, they are forging stronger links with school administrators, university researchers, government officials, and the communities they serve. The first part of this chapter describes ways in which teachers are striving for full professional status, and the second discusses how teacher organizations have grown in power and prominence. As you read this chapter, think about the following questions:

FOCUS QUESTIONS

- What trends show that teaching is becoming a full-fledged profession?
- In what ways is teaching *not* fully a profession?
- How does merit pay help or hinder the teaching profession?
- What are the goals and activities of the two main professional organizations, the NEA and the AFT?
- What are other important professional organizations for teachers?
- What professional organizations might education students and beginning teachers join?

▶ Is Teaching a Profession?

The question of whether or not teaching is a profession in the fullest sense has greatly concerned educators for many decades. Some have tried to identify the ideal characteristics of professions and, by rating teachers on these items, determine whether teaching is a profession. The following are characteristics of a full **profession**, based on the works of noted authorities over a twenty-five-year period.[1]

■ Characteristics of a profession

1. A sense of public service; a lifetime commitment to career
2. A defined body of knowledge and skills beyond that grasped by laypersons
3. A lengthy period of specialized training
4. Control over licensing standards and/or entry requirements
5. Autonomy in making decisions about selected spheres of work
6. An acceptance of responsibility for judgments made and acts performed related to services rendered; a set of performance standards
7. A self-governing organization composed of members of the profession
8. Professional associations and/or elite groups to provide recognition for individual achievements
9. A code of ethics to help clarify ambiguous matters or doubtful points related to services rendered
10. High prestige and economic standing

■ Teaching as a "semiprofession"

The general consensus is that teaching is not a profession in the fullest sense because it lacks some of the above characteristics, but it may be viewed as a "semiprofession" or an "emerging profession" in the process of achieving these characteristics.[2] Several sociologists contend that nursing and social work are also semiprofessions.

In particular, teaching seems to lag behind professions such as law and medicine in four important areas: (1) a defined body of knowledge and skills beyond that grasped by laypersons, (2) control over licensing standards and/or entry requirements, (3) autonomy in making decisions about selected spheres of work, and (4) high prestige and economic standing. In the following sections we explore these four aspects of teaching.

A Defined Body of Knowledge

■ No agreed-upon knowledge

All professions have a monopoly on certain knowledge that separates their members from the general public and allows them to exercise control over the vocation. Members of the profession establish their expertise by mastering this defined body of knowledge, and they protect the public from quacks and untrained amateurs by denying membership to those who have not mastered it. In the past "education" or "teaching" has had no agreed-upon specialized body of knowledge.[3] Nor has

---

[1]Ronald G. Corwin, *Sociology of Education* (New York: Appleton-Century-Crofts, 1965); Robert B. Howsam et al., *Educating a Profession* (Washington, D.C.: American Association of Colleges for Teacher Education, 1976); and Susan J. Rosenholtz, *Teachers' Workplace: The Social Organization of Schools* (New York: Longman, 1989).
[2]Amitai Etzioni, *The Semiprofessions and Their Organizations: Teachers, Nurses, and Social Workers* (New York: Free Press, 1969), p. v.
[3]Robert J. Yinger and Amanda L. Nolen, "Surviving the Legitimacy Challenge," *Phi Delta Kappan* (January 2003), pp. 386–390; Susan Moore Johnson, "Can Professional Certification of Teachers Reshape Teaching as a Career," *Phi Delta Kappan* (January 2001), pp. 393–399.

An occupation's level of professionalism and prestige relates to the complexity of the work and to having a defined body of knowledge that practitioners must master. How do you think teaching ranks on these indicators? *(© David Young-Wolff/ PhotoEdit)*

▪ Lack of agreement on teacher education

▪ Major components of preservice preparation

teaching been guided by the extensive rules of procedure and established methodologies found in professions such as the physical sciences and health care. As a result, too many people, especially the lay public, talk about education as if they were experts—the cause of much conflicting and sometimes negative conversation.[4]

The ill-defined body of knowledge also allows teacher-education course content to vary from state to state and even among teacher-training institutions within a given state. Teacher preparation usually consists of three major components: (1) liberal (or general) education, (2) specialized subject-field education—the student's "major" or "minor," and (3) professional education. Almost all educators agree that preparing good teachers rests on these three components. Strong arguments arise, however, over the relative emphasis that each component should receive. How much time, for example, should the education student devote to liberal-education courses versus courses in a specialized subject field and professional education? Viewpoints also differ concerning the extent to which clinical experience, which emphasizes practice in actual school settings, should be incorporated in professional education courses. Thus, your teacher-education program may differ from one at a different college of university.

James Koerner described the problem further in his highly critical book *The Miseducation of American Teachers*. Koerner argued that by requiring too many education courses—as many as sixty hours at some state teacher colleges—and by making these courses too "soft," colleges of education were producing teachers versed in pedagogy at the expense of academic content.[5] Although critics have helped reduce

---

[4]Hendrik D. Gideonse, *Relating Knowledge to Teacher Education* (Washington, D.C.: American Association of Colleges for Teacher Education, 1989); Brian Rowan, "Comparing Teachers' Work with Work in Other Occupations: Notes on the Professional Status of Teaching," *Educational Researcher* (August–September 1994), pp. 4–17, 21; and Jonathan Saphier, *Bonfires and Magic Bullets: Making Teaching a True Profession* (Carlisle, Mass.: Research for Better Teaching, 1995).
[5]James D. Koerner, *The Miseducation of American Teachers* (Boston: Houghton Mifflin, 1963).

Standards & Assessment
■ NCATE standards

the number of required education courses, the controversy continues,[6] making it especially difficult to establish clear national standards for teacher preparation.

The situation is gradually changing, however. The **National Council for Accreditation of Teacher Education (NCATE)** has set standards that specify courses to be taken and faculty qualifications for teaching those courses. At this point, many teacher-education institutions still fail to meet NCATE's standards; as recently as 2003, 45 percent of the twelve hundred colleges involved in training teachers were not accredited by NCATE. However, most NCATE members have worked diligently to meet NCATE standards, and 85 percent of member programs had obtained NCATE approval by 2003. Also by 2003, thirty-six states had adopted NCATE unit standards for state evaluation of teacher-education programs. NCATE standards are increasingly the norm in teacher preparation.[7] Moreover, the American Association of Colleges for Teacher Education (AACTE) decided in 1995 to promote the pursuit of NCATE accreditation. To further this end, AACTE is expanding technical assistance, such as consultants to nonaccredited institutions, during the accreditation process.[8]

REFOCUS   **Is your institution accredited by NCATE? Find out and learn more about the NCATE standards at their Web site, www.ncate.org.**

Controlling Requirements for Entry and Licensing

■ Variations in certification

Whereas most professions have uniform requirements for entry and licensing, teaching historically has lacked this. As indicated in Motivation, Preparation, and Conditions for the Entering Teacher, recent reforms have required prospective teachers in most states to pass minimum competency tests, and bodies such as the National Board for Professional Teaching Standards are establishing methods for measuring a person's ability to teach. However, certification requirements still vary greatly from state to state, and the trend toward teacher testing has generated widespread controversy. You may wish to research the qualifications and testing required in your state to compare with others nearby.

Moreover, many teachers working in the secondary schools appear to be teaching out of license—in other words, outside their recognized areas of expertise. This problem is especially acute in science and mathematics.

■ Debate about alternative certification

The outlook is further clouded by the trend toward alternative certification, discussed in the chapter on Motivation, Preparation, and Conditions for the Entering Teacher. This process, by which teachers are recruited from the ranks of college-educated retirees, industrial personnel, and experienced people seeking second careers, is intended to eliminate teacher shortages in certain subject areas such as mathematics, science, and computer instruction or to upgrade the quality of new teachers. Alternative certification is often praised as practical and innovative by laypeople and school board members. Most teacher organizations, on the other hand,

---

[6]See, for example, Pamela C. Boyd, "Professional School Reform and Public School Renewal: Portrait of a Partnership," *Journal of Teacher Education* (March–April 1994), pp. 132–139; and Arthur E. Wise, Creating a High Quality Teaching Force," *Educational Leadership* (December 2000–January 2001), pp. 18–21.

[7]See "Quick Facts" at **www.ncate.org/ncate/fact_sheet.htm** (2003); National Council for the Accreditation of Teacher Education, *A Decade of Growth: 1991–2001* (Washington, D.C.: National Council for Accreditation of Teacher Education, 2001), p. 4.

[8]"AACTE Strategic Plan Includes Focus on Accreditation," *NCATE Reporter* (Washington, D.C.: National Council for Accreditation of Teacher Education, 1998), p. 5; and AACTE, "NCATE Creates Task Force to Improve Program Reviews," *AACTE Briefs*, August 25, 2003, pp. 1, 3.

see alternative certification as a threat to the profession. One critic wrote, "The assumption that those who know something can automatically teach . . . [will] not solve the problem of teacher quality."[9] The AACTE has taken a middle position, supporting alternative licensing procedures only at the master's-degree level and in conjunction with supervised field training.[10]

Standards & Assessment ☑
■ Involvement of teacher organizations

Whatever they may think about differing requirements for certification, teachers traditionally have had little to say in these matters. However, teacher organizations are beginning to cooperate with state legislatures and departments of education to modify certification standards and establish professional practice boards (discussed later in this chapter). The more input teachers have—the more control they exercise over their own licensing procedures—the more teaching will be recognized as a full profession.

Autonomy in Deciding About Spheres of Work

■ Professional control versus lay control

In a profession, every member of the group, but no outsider, is assumed to be qualified to make professional judgments on the nature of the work involved. Indeed, control by laypersons is considered the natural enemy of professions; it limits the professional's power and opens the door to outside interference. Professionals usually establish rules and customs that give them exclusive jurisdiction over their area of competence and their relationships with clients.

■ Traditional lack of teacher input

Teachers, in contrast, have traditionally had little input in curriculum decisions, and they are vulnerable when they seek to introduce textbooks or discuss topics that pressure groups consider controversial. In fact, school officials often hire outside "experts" with little teaching experience to help them select books, write grant proposals, or resolve local school–community issues.[11] Even school reform initiative often comes from government officials, business leaders, and civic groups rather than from teachers.

Standards & Assessment ☑
■ Standardizing teaching methods

Educational Reform and Teacher Empowerment.   Reform efforts in many states and local school districts have included particular methods of planning and delivering instruction. Teachers are evaluated, in large part, by their ability to follow these standard methods. In Arkansas, Missouri, and Texas, to take three examples, guidelines for teacher assessment have specified the general instructional sequence that teachers should follow in executing a "model" lesson—introduce the topic, present material, check for understanding, provide guided and independent practice, and discuss homework.

■ Adverse effects of standardized methods

One researcher concluded that legislative requirements for extensive testing of students, combined with administrative prescriptions of appropriate teaching methods, have contributed to "deprofessionalization" and "deskilling" of the teaching force. **Deprofessionalization** occurs when policies encourage or require teachers to

---

[9]Lee S. Shulman, "Knowledge and Teaching: Foundations and the New Reform," *Harvard Educational Review* (February 1987), p. 324; Vicky Dill and Delia Stafford-Johnson, "No Shortcuts to Preparing Good Teachers," *Educational Leadership* (May 2001), pp. 32–36.

[10]*Alternative Paths to Teaching* (Washington, D.C.: American Association of Colleges for Teacher Education, 1995); Glen Buck et al., "Alternative Certification Programs," *Teacher Education and Special Education* (Winter 1995), pp. 39–48.

[11]Michael W. Apple, "Is There a Curriculum Voice to Reclaim?" *Phi Delta Kappan* (March 1990); Alfred G. Hess, "The Changing Role of Teachers: Moving from Interested Spectators to Engaged Planners," *Education and Urban Society* (May 1994), pp. 248–263; John J. DiNatale, "School Improvement and Restructuring: A Threefold Approach," *NASSP Bulletin* (October 1994), pp. 79–83; and Susan Moore Johnson, "Can Professional Certification for Teachers Reshape Teaching as a Career," *Phi Delta Kappan* (January 2001), pp. 393–399.

simplify curriculum and instruction to ensure that students demonstrate mastery on easy-to-grade tests. Linda McNeil, Robert Rothman, and other observers have reported that many teachers respond with "defensive teaching," in which they fragment the curriculum to fit tests, "mystify" topics by emphasizing factual regurgitation over understanding, and simplify material to gain the compliance of students.[12] Perhaps you recall experiencing defensive teaching as a student or in classroom observations or field experiences.

■ Rewarding passivity

Specifying instructional methods seems to have produced similarly negative consequences in teacher evaluation. As described by one observer in the Southwest, evaluative approaches frequently reward teachers who "lecture and question a relatively passive class but not teachers who help students struggle through difficult tasks—such as science experiments, English composition, or computer programming—on their own." Researchers elsewhere have described cases in which prescribing specific teaching methods has led teachers to emphasize passive learning and memorization of low-level material.[13] Only recently, with the advent of school-based management (discussed later in this chapter) and other forms of teacher participation, has this situation begun to change, as teachers, supervisors, and school administrators show increasing commitment to constructivist teaching methods. You, we hope, have had the opportunity to struggle through difficult but active learning tasks in your student career.

■ Public accountability

Although collective bargaining has produced new arrangements between teachers and administrators, most people still see teachers as public servants and therefore accountable to the people and to the school officials hired, elected, or appointed by the people. Taxpayers and their representatives are said to "reasonably" claim a large share in decision making because they foot the bill and provide the clients. Thus, in many situations, teachers must defer to parents, principals, superintendents, and school board members, even when directives go against teachers' professional judgments.

High Prestige and Economic Standing

■ High-prestige occupations

Occupational prestige refers to the esteem a particular society bestows on an occupation. Do you consider teaching a high-prestige occupation? Occupations rate high in prestige if they are generally perceived as making an especially valuable contribution to society. Occupations that require a high level of education or skill and little manual or physical labor also tend to be prestigious. On these aspects of social status, the job of elementary or secondary teacher historically has ranked relatively high.

---

[12]Linda M. McNeil, *Contradictions of Control* (New York: Routledge and Kegan Paul, 1986); Patricia Rochard-Amato, "Sharing Power in the Classroom," *ESL Magazine* (January–February 2002), pp. 16–18; Patricia A. Watson et al., "Stories from the Shadows: High Stakes Testing and Teacher Preparation," *Language Arts* (January 2002), pp. 216–225; Robert Rothman, *Measuring Up* (San Francisco: Jossey-Bass, 1995); William L. Sanders and Sandra P. Horn, "Educational Assessment Reassessed," *Educational Policy Analysis Archives,* March 3, 1995, available at **olam.ed.asu.edu;** and Chris Richards, "Popular Culture, Politics, and the Curriculum," *Educational Researcher* (June–July 1998), pp. 32–34.
[13]Harriett Tyson-Bernstein, "The Texas Teacher Appraisal System," *American Educator* (Spring 1987), pp. 26–31; Arthur E. Wise, "Legislative Learning Revisited," *Phi Delta Kappan* (January 1988), pp. 328–333; Daniel U. Levine and Rayna F. Levine, *Society and Education,* 9th ed. (Needham Heights, Mass.: Allyn and Bacon, 1996); and John Smyth, Geoff Shacklock, and Rob Hattam, "Teacher Development in Difficult Times," *Teacher Development,* November 1, 1997, available at **www.triangle.co.uk;** Geoffrey Caine, "Guiding the Innate Constructivist," *Educational Leadership* (October 2002) p. 70.

■ Teacher prestige

Perhaps the best-known studies of occupational prestige are those conducted by the National Opinion Research Center (NORC). In these studies of more than five hundred occupations, the highest average score for a major occupation was eighty-two for physicians and surgeons, and the lowest was nine for shoe shiners. Elementary school teachers were rated at sixty and secondary school teachers at sixty-three—both above the ninetieth percentile. In addition, the percentage of teachers who say they "feel respected in today's society" has increased substantially in recent decades. In one cross-national study, 70 percent of U.S. respondents believed that high-school teachers are either "very respected" or "fairly respected."[14]

■ Prestige derived from complex work

One reason why teachers have maintained or even increased their occupational prestige is that their average level of education has risen greatly over the past century. Another reason may be the complex nature of teaching. Brian Rowan, comparing teachers' work with other occupations, found that work complexity related directly to occupational prestige. Teaching, more complex than 75 percent of all other occupations, ranked quite high in prestige. The complexity of teachers' work is manifested in their need to apply principles of logical or scientific thinking to define problems, collect data, establish facts, and draw conclusions. To be a teacher, you must be highly proficient in language (reading, writing, and speaking), and, most of all, you must work effectively with many kinds of people—children, adolescents, parents, colleagues, and superiors. This work with people sets teaching apart from most other occupations. However, society accords higher prestige (and, of course, higher pay) to professionals such as physicians, academics, lawyers, and engineers, mainly because they must deal with information generally regarded as more abstract (complex) and because these fields require more rigorous academic preparation and licensure.[15]

■ Salary trends

■ Status-consistency hypothesis

Although teachers' salaries since 1930 have increased more than those of the average industry worker, teacher pay remains lower than that of the average college graduate, such as an engineer, nurse, accountant, or business major.[16] In addition, teachers still earn far less than lawyers, business executives, and some other professionals with similar levels of formal education. For example, your classmates who become business executives with a level of formal education similar to yours as a teacher might earn $150,000 per year, and some might earn $500,000 or more. Nevertheless, the *status-consistency hypothesis* holds that a group tends to compare its achievements (both prestige and salary) with those of other groups, striving to match the rewards of people with similar jobs and similar years of education.[17] If this is true, we can expect teachers to compare their lot with other groups' and feel somewhat dissatisfied. In the past this dissatisfaction has been a major reason for teacher militancy, and it has motivated some teachers to leave the profession.[18]

---

[14]C. C. North and Paul K. Hatt, "Jobs and Occupation: A Popular Evaluation," *Opinion News*, September 1, 1947, pp. 3–13; Robert W. Hodge, Paul M. Siegel, and Peter H. Rossi, "Occupational Prestige in the United States, 1925–63," *American Journal of Sociology* (November 1964), pp. 286–302; Donald J. Treiman, *Occupational Prestige in Comparative Perspective* (New York: Academic Press, 1977); and Rowan, "Comparing Teachers' Work," pp. 4–17.
[15]Eric Hoyle, "Teaching: Prestige, Status and Esteem," *Educational Management and Administration* (April 2001), pp. 139–152.
[16]Victor R. Lindquist and Frank S. Endicott, *The Northwestern Lindquist–Endicott Report: Employment Trends for College Graduates*, Forty-sixth Annual Survey (Evanston, Ill.: Northwestern University, 1992); "Teaching Low on the Pay Scale," *NEA Today* (March 1995), p. 5; see also "Just the Stats," at **www.nea.org/publiced/edstats/;** Steven L. Denlinger, "A Look at the Problem of Teacher Deficits," *Clearing House* (January–February 2002), pp. 116–117.
[17]Ronald G. Corwin, *Militant Professionalism: A Study of Militant Conflict in High Schools* (New York: Appleton-Century-Crofts, 1970).
[18]Jo Anna Natale, "Why Teachers Leave," *Executive Educator* (November 1993), pp. 8–15; and Patricia Gonzales, "Strategies for Teacher Retention," *NSTEP Information Brief* (Alexandria, Va.: National Association of State Directors of Special Education, 1995).

▇ Teacher status on the rise

To its credit, educational reform has put teachers in the limelight and has brought pressure on school districts to increase salaries. Though optimistic projections have not always been fulfilled,[19] the earnings gap between teachers and other highly educated groups may now begin to close. With help from their own professional organizations, coupled with pressure to upgrade educational standards, teachers should continue to experience increased status.

REFOCUS **Which of the preceding areas of professionalism—a defined body of knowledge, control of licensing and entry, autonomy in decision making, or high prestige and economic standing—is most important to your personal definition of a profession? Is it important to you that teaching seems to lag behind other professions in these areas? Why or why not?**

▶ Trends Toward Professionalism

Although teaching, as we have seen, probably should not be considered a fully professionalized occupation, certain trends have helped it move in that direction. **Collective bargaining** , for example, can enhance teachers' capacity to make decisions about their classroom work. Let's look at several other major aspects of a long-range trend toward professionalizing teaching.

The Scope of Collective Bargaining

By 1980 teachers had won the right to have their representatives formally bargain with their employers in most of the United States. If you went to public schools, your teachers' contracts were probably negotiated through collective bargaining. The extent and nature of collective bargaining varied from negotiations conducted in the absence of a law allowing or forbidding it to full-scale contract bargaining backed by the right to strike. In contrast, the private school sector has no collective bargaining.

▇ Is collective bargaining professional?

In some ways, collective bargaining may be considered a nonprofessional or even antiprofessional activity. In law, medicine, or the ministry, for example, few professionals work in organizations in which collective bargaining determines terms of employment. Collective bargaining, however, can significantly enhance teaching's professionalism by giving teachers greater authority to determine their work conditions and their effectiveness as teachers.

▇ Changing focus of collective bargaining

Collective bargaining has increasingly affected concerns other than the fundamental salary issue. Today, the focus is often on peer review, career ladders, merit pay, standards setting, and school-based management,[20] subjects discussed in later sections of this chapter. Teachers' bargaining units often feel the "push/pull" of addressing bread-and-butter issues as opposed to professional concerns.[21] In upcoming

---

[19]Allan C. Ornstein, "Teacher Salaries in Social Context," *High School Journal* (December–January 1990), pp. 129–132; see also "Just the Stats," at **www.nea.org/publiced/edstats;** and Southern Regional Education Board, *SREB Teacher Salaries: Update for 1995–96 and Estimated Increases for 1997* (Atlanta, Ga.: SREB, 1996).
[20]Louis Fischer, David Schimmel, and Leslie Stellman, *Teachers and the Law* (New York: Longman, 2003), pp. 45–58; Lynn M. Cornett, "Lessons from 10 Years of Teacher Improvement Reforms," *Educational Leadership* (February 1995), pp. 26–30; and William A. Firestone, "Redesigning Teacher Salary Systems for Educational Reform," *American Educational Research Journal* (Fall 1994), pp. 549–574.
[21]Denny G. Bolton, "Better Bargaining: Common Mistakes in Contract Negotiations and How to Avoid Them," *American School Board Journal* (March 2001), pp. 16–20.

years, movements toward school reform, school restructuring, and teacher empowerment will give teachers more professional autonomy, union strength, and higher salaries, in exchange for greater accountability and reduced adversarial bargaining. Continuing in this vein, collective bargaining can go beyond resolving conflicts between school boards and teachers and raise the overall status of the profession.[22]

Standards & Assessment ✓

Professional Practice Boards

■ Setting professional standards

Educators are unlikely to achieve complete autonomy in setting professional practice standards, but their role has increased. Today all states except two (Maine and South Dakota) have established state **professional practice boards**, or similar bodies, which set standards for teacher certification. These boards upgrade the profession by defining standards for minimum competency, by reprimanding teachers for unprofessional or unproductive behavior, and in extreme cases by suspending teachers' certificates. However, few of these state boards are composed of a majority of teachers, and some states do not even require teacher participation on the board.[23]

■ NEA's position

The National Education Association (NEA) has endorsed the idea of professional practice boards but believes they should be controlled by teachers—with other groups, such as school administrators and universities, given minority representation. The NEA argues that teachers are as capable of governing their own profession as are attorneys, doctors, and accountants.[24]

■ A national board

Other educators favor a single national board rather than independent state boards. This has always been the position of the American Federation of Teachers (AFT), and the idea has been welcomed by many national task force groups. As mentioned in Chapter 1, Motivation, Preparation, and Conditions of the Entering Teacher, the Carnegie Corporation has helped to found the **National Board for Professional Teaching Standards** (NBPTS). The NEA now supports this organization because two-thirds of the NBPTS directors are "teaching professionals"—that is, representatives of teacher unions, subject-area associations, and teachers noted for classroom excellence.[25] Currently, the NBPTS has granted national certification to more than sixteen thousand teachers in twenty-four certificate fields.[26] Eventually the program is expected to cover more than forty certification areas. Although NBPTS certification is voluntary and cannot be required as a condition of hiring, many educators hope that local school boards and superintendents will develop in-

[22]Perry A. Zirkel, "Striking Results," *Phi Delta Kappan* (February 2003), pp. 478–479; and William Keene, *"Win/Win or Else": Collective Bargaining in an Age of Public Discontent* (Thousand Oaks, Calif.: Corwin Press, 1996).

[23]*Teacher Education Policy in the States: A 50-State Survey of Legislative and Administrative Actions* (Washington, D.C.: American Association of Colleges for Teacher Education, 1990); Ann L. Wood, "What Does Research Say About Teacher Induction and IHE/LEA Collaborative Programs," *Issues in Teacher Education* (Fall 2001), pp. 68–81.

[24]Ann E. Harman, "A Wider Role for the Professional Boards," *Educational Leadership* (May 2001), p. 54–55; and National Education Association, "Professional Standards Boards," *NEA Handbook,* 1994–95 (Washington, D.C.: NEA, 1994), p. 311.

[25]John W. Porter, "A Call for National Certification of Teachers," *NASSP Bulletin* (October 1990), pp. 64–70; Arthur E. Wise, "Teaching the Teachers," *American School Board Journal* (June 1994), pp. 22–25; Donna H. Leuker, "Certification: Teachers at the Top of Their Profession," *American School Board Journal* (June 1994), p. 24; and Albert Shanker, "Quality Assurance: What Must Be Done to Strengthen the Teaching Profession," *Phi Delta Kappan* (November 1996), pp. 220–224.

[26]Available at **www.nea.org/national,** board/background-facts; Holly Thornton, "The Meaning of National Board Certification for Middle Grades Teaching," *Middle School Journal* (March 2001), pp. 46–54.

centives to encourage teachers to apply for national certification.[27] Forty-nine states have already initiated support in the form of certification fee reimbursement or salary supplements.[28] For more information on national board standards and the forty certification areas, see **new.nbpts.org**.

Mediated Entry

Mediated entry refers to the practice of inducting persons into a profession through carefully supervised stages that help them learn how to apply professional knowledge successfully in working environments. For example, aspiring physicians serve one or more years as interns and then as residents before being considered full-fledged professionals.

■ Lack of assistance for new teachers

Dan Lortie has studied the teacher's job from a sociological perspective and has concluded that teaching ranks between occupations characterized by "casual" entry and those that place difficult demands on would-be members. For example, secretarial knowledge and skills are significantly less demanding than those of a medical doctor or even a nurse.[29] The lack of more carefully mediated entry means that new teachers have relatively little opportunity to benefit from the principles and practices developed by earlier educators. Too often teachers report learning to teach through trial and error in the classroom. They also report that the beginning years of teaching can be a period of anxiety, loneliness, and fear, even of trauma.[30] Although

Teacher-preparation institutions and school districts are working to make entry into the field less stressful for new teachers through early experience in professional development schools, mentoring, and transition guidance. *(Bob Rowan/CORBIS)*

---

[27]The National Board for Professional Teaching Standards 2003, at **www.nbpts.org**.
[28]American Association of Colleges of Teacher Education, "NBPTS Study: Teachers Who Attained Board Certification Outperform Those Who Didn't Succeed," *Teacher Education Reports*, November 27, 2000, p. 2.
[29]Dan C. Lortie, *Schoolteacher: A Sociological Study* (Chicago: University of Chicago Press, 1975).
[30]Barry A. Farber, *Crisis in Education: Stress and Burnout in the American Teacher* (San Francisco: Jossey-Bass, 1991); Pamela L. Grossman, *The Making of a Teacher* (New York: Teachers College Press, 1990); Susan Moore Johnson, *Teachers at Work* (New York: Harper and Row, 1990); and Anne Cockburn, *Teaching Under Pressure* (Bristol, Pa.: Falmer, 1996).

almost any occupation or profession produces problems and anxieties at first, a more systematic mediated entry would probably alleviate some stress.

■ Professional development schools as clinical settings

More colleges and universities are using professional development schools (described in the chapter on Motivation, Preparation, and Conditions for the Entering Teacher) as clinical settings where aspiring teachers gain a year of classroom experience before student teaching (residency). This multisemester approach—in actual classrooms under the guidance of experienced teachers and their university professors—provides a more systematic induction into the teaching profession.[31]

■ Establishing a transition period

The teaching profession now recognizes the need to develop a period of induction and transition into teaching. During your first few years of teaching, you may be considered a probationary teacher. Since the early 1980s, more than thirty states have mandated statewide initiatives or have provided funds for this purpose. Some school districts, such as Toledo, Ohio, provide probationary or intern teachers with feedback and assistance from experienced teachers. Performance-assessment approaches can help determine whether new teachers have mastered some of the most important teaching skills. Other districts assign especially trained mentor teachers or support teams to work closely with new teachers, particularly those assigned to teach "high-risk" students.[32] Mentor teachers may receive released time or stipends for helping new teachers. In many other school districts, all teachers are evaluated, but expectations and training sessions differ for probationary teachers and experienced teachers.[33] Some colleges and universities provide transitional guidance for graduates who will teach, either through direct supervision or through staff development or both. Overall, the trend toward more carefully mediated entry should continue; major teacher unions and several education reform groups support it, as does federal legislation such as No Child Left Behind, which mandates "highly qualified teachers." (We define and discuss *highly qualified* in the chapter on Motivation, Preparation and Conditions for the Entering Teacher.)

Staff Development

■ Keeping up to date

Your teacher training does not end when you begin teaching full time. Teaching demands rigorous and continuous training, which we often refer to as **staff development**, or further education and training for a school district's teaching staff. To stay up to date in their preparation and to acquire new classroom skills, teachers have traditionally participated in various kinds of in-service training.

■ Rising importance of staff development

Both the NEA and the AFT support the concept of staff development as integral to a teacher's professional growth. U.S. teachers are an aging group (the average teacher is about fifty years old and has twenty years of experience), and many states now require teachers to participate in staff development programs in order to retain

[31]Ismat Abdul-Haqq, *Professional Development Schools: Weighing the Evidence* (Thousand Oaks, Calif.: Corwin Press, 1997); Thomas Guskey, "What Makes Professional Development Effective," *Phi Delta Kappan* (June 2003), pp. 748–750; Ann Reynolds, Steven Ross, and Janine Rakow, "Teacher Retention, Teaching Effectiveness, and Professional Preparation: A Comparison of Professional Development School and Non-Professional Development School Graduates," *Teaching and Teacher Education* (April 2002), pp. 289–303.
[32]Susan Moore Johnson and Susan Kardos, "Keeping New Teachers in Mind," *Educational Leadership* (March 2002), pp. 12–16.
[33]Arthur E. Wise, Linda Darling-Hammond, and Barnett Berry, *Effective Teacher Selection: From Recruitment to Retention* (Santa Monica, Calif.: Rand Corporation, 1987). See also David Holdzkom, "Teacher Performance Appraisal in North Carolina: Preferences and Practices," *Phi Delta Kappan* (June 1991), pp. 782–784; and Joseph Kretovics, Kathleen Farber, and William Armaline, "Reform from the Bottom Up," *Phi Delta Kappan* (December 1991), pp. 295–299.

their teaching certificates. Younger teachers, those with less than ten years' experience, tend to use staff development programs to pursue new degrees (mostly master's degrees), whereas veteran teachers with ten or more years' experience are more likely to participate in specialized workshops or in-service training.[34] Staff development topics in high demand include improving students' reading and writing skills, work with special-needs and inclusion students, active learning strategies, curriculum revision, site-based management, and legal issues and concerns.

■ Training in educational technology and research

Another important focus for staff development is improving teachers' knowledge and skills in using educational technology. This effort ranges from teaching basic computer literacy, such as word processing and making grade spreadsheets, to teaching more sophisticated use of Internet resources, interactive video, CD-ROM videodisks, and distance learning.[35]

The AFT has also developed its Educational Research and Dissemination (ER&D) program to expose teachers to the growing body of important education research findings. A series of collegial workshops explore the latest research and practical classroom applications. Universities have trained more than fifteen hundred teachers to act as workshop leaders, and the program continues to grow.[36] As the Technology @ School box describes, teachers can also use the Internet for professional development.

New varieties of staff development programs are giving teachers a major voice in decisions that affect their professional careers. These programs also help to establish the concept that teaching, like other full-fledged professions, requires lengthy and ongoing training,

Merit Pay

■ Critiques of merit pay

Real changes in teacher remuneration are under way. A growing number of school boards have taken the position that **merit pay** (a supplement to a teacher's base salary to reward superior performance) is a cost-effective method of motivating teachers and encouraging excellence in teaching. However, teacher unions and other critics have expressed reservations about merit pay plans. Some argue that teachers' work is complicated and difficult to measure, and assessments of merit are too often subjective, especially when left in the hands of a single person—the school principal.[37] Teachers and their professional organizations feel more comfortable with peer evaluations. Where merit plans have been implemented, according to some reports, teachers have often believed that the wrong people were selected for preferential pay. Some observers fear that such rewards go to relatively few teachers at the expense of many others and threaten unity and collegiality among

---

[34]*The Condition of Education* (Washington, D.C.: U.S. Government Printing Office, 2002), p. 139.

[35]Judith Duffield, "Trials, Tribulations and Minor Successes: Integrating Technology into a Preservice Teacher Preparation Program," *Tech Trends* (September 1997), pp. 22–26; and John Norton, "Grounded in Research," *Journal of Staff Development* (Summer 2001), pp. 30–32; Van E. Cooley, "Implementing Technology Using Teachers as Trainers," *Journal of Technology and Teacher Training* 9, no. 2 (2001), pp. 269–284; Paula Galland, "Techie Teachers—Web-Based Staff Development at Your Leisure," *Tech Trends* (May–June 2002), pp. 7–10.

[36]*AFT Educational Research and Dissemination Program* (Washington, D.C.: AFT, 1990); and telephone conversation with Deanna Woods, assistant director of the Educational Research and Dissemination Program, American Federation of Teachers, November 14, 1995; Hayes Mizell, "How to Get There from Here," *Journal of Staff Development* (Summer 2001), pp. 18–20.

[37]Ron Brandt, "On Research on Teaching," *Educational Leadership* (April 1992), pp. 14–19; and Stephen Jacobsen, "Money Incentives and the Reform of Teacher Compensation: A Persistent Dilemma," *International Journal of Educational Reform* (January 1995), pp. 29–35.

TECHNOLOGY @School

Professional Development Opportunities on the World Wide Web

Whether you are preparing to teach, experiencing your first year in the classroom, or a veteran professional, professional growth and development are critical to your success in teaching. The Internet provides a rich array of technology resources for teachers, students, and even parents.

Novice teachers especially need job search information, such as résumé writing and interviewing tips, as well as information on substitute teaching, certification, and professional expectations and behavior. New-Teacher.com (at **www.geocities.com/Athens/Delphi/7862**) covers all of these topics and more. New teachers can also consult New-Teacher.com for tips on organizing classrooms, bulletin board ideas, teaching strategies, resources for educators, and even workshops on assessment rubrics, block schedules, and motivating students.

Beginning and veteran teachers eager to expand their Internet skills and their students' Internet skills can look at Kathy Schrock's "Guide for Educators—Internet Information" (**school.discovery.com/schrockguide/yp/iypabout.html**). Click on "About the Net" for tutorials on finding information and resources on the Internet. Click on "Graphics" and access clip art for kids and teachers, Web graphics, photographs for educational purposes, and links to school-related graphics sites. These are only a few of the many resources available at this site. Also beginning teachers can visit Jennifer Cox's "Annotated List of Useful Websites," available at **www.daisy7693@aol.com.**

Kathy Schrock's "Guide for Educators—Educational Resources Lists" (at **school .discovery.com/schrockguide/edres.html**) has a wealth of general education resources for elementary and secondary teachers as well as a special section on early childhood resources. Each resource area has links to additional resource sites, which makes exploring Schrock's site an easy lesson in navigating the Internet for teacher resources. Additionally, this site has information on professional development, lesson plans, thinking skills, learning centers, special education, Internet projects, and online publications.

Veteran teachers interested in helping new teachers will find an excellent professional development experience by clicking on "Mentoring New Teachers" at New-Teacher.com, where research summaries, ideas for developing mentor programs and new teacher induction, as well as Web sites and listservs assist mentor teachers.

---

educators. Moreover, merit pay funding has often been inadequate. The need, critics say, is to increase all teachers' salaries, not just a few, and not to pit teachers against one another.[38] The Taking Issue box presents some arguments for and against merit pay.

■ Career ladders

Even as the arguments continue, the concept of merit pay has spread to many school districts and to entire states. Today, merit pay plans are sometimes linked with *career ladders,* which establish clear-cut stages through which a teacher may advance. North Carolina in 1991 implemented a statewide merit plan called "differential pay," whereby local school districts receive up to 3 percent above their normal salary totals to allocate to teachers on the basis of merit or additional re-

---

[38]Carolyn McCreight, "Teacher Attrition, Shortage, and Strategies for Teacher Retention" (2000), ERIC Document: ED 444986; and Allen Odden and Carolyn Kelley, *Paying Teachers for What They Know and Do* (Thousand Oaks, Calif.: Corwin Press, 1997); Dale Ballou, "Pay for Performance in Public and Private Schools," *Economics of Education Review* (February 2001), pp. 51–61; and Larry Lashway, "Incentives for Accountability," 2002, ERIC No: ED 457598.

taking issue

Question Should individual teachers receive special pay increases based on merit?

Merit Pay

Traditionally, teachers have earned salaries based on their years in teaching and their highest degree obtained. Recent plans, however, offer extra pay to teachers considered above average in teaching skills, work habits, leadership, or student achievement.

Arguments PRO

1 Teachers whose students consistently score high on achievement tests or have healthy social attitudes must be outstanding teachers or models for citizenship. Such teachers merit extra compensation for their work.

2 Teachers who provide their students with creative and interesting educational experiences, work hard in preparation, and give many hours of their own time to their students also deserve special compensation.

3 Merit pay reduces teaching conformity by encouraging teachers to develop different teaching approaches, become more independent in thought, and exceed text or teaching guide presentations.

4 Some merit pay plans allow teachers to earn $75,000 or more. Without such opportunities to earn above the base salary, capable and ambitious people will choose incentive-producing careers such as business.

5 Merit pay promotes excellence in teaching by acting as an incentive for teachers to improve their performance. Each teacher is encouraged to develop better teaching behaviors and a deeper concern for student welfare. Business and most other professions offer such motivators, why not in teaching?

Arguments CON

1 Factors related to achievement and social attitudes are so diverse that it is impossible to differentiate the teacher's contribution from home, social class, and peer group influences.

2 Hard work can perhaps be measured, but many "creative" activities do not necessarily correlate with good teaching. If creativity is a criterion, merit pay may be awarded more for the teacher's apparent inventiveness than for students' learning.

3 Those who evaluate teachers' merit may unconsciously favor people who do not challenge district policy or seem not to threaten school stability with innovative approaches. Thus, merit pay may encourage conformity.

4 Businesses can offset extensive merit pay rewards by raising prices, but schools must raise taxes. Taxpayers often will not or cannot support such rewards.

5 Incentive pay, by definition, goes to only a few. Such a plan penalizes equally qualified teachers who miss out for lack of enough positions. Moreover, competition for merit pay pits one teacher against another, encourages political games, and destroys the collegial cooperation essential to good education.

sponsibilities.[39] Overall, the trend toward raising the ceiling on teachers' salaries and making distinctions based on merit should attract brighter students into the profession and keep good teachers from leaving classrooms for more competitive salaries in other fields.

---

[39]Jeffrey T. Sultanik, "Bonus Pay for Teachers," *American School Board Journal* (February 2000), pp. 34–36; Marge Scherer, "Improving the Quality of the Teaching Force: A Conversation with David C. Berliner," *Educational Leadership* (May, 2001), pp. 6–10.

School-Based Management

▪ Decision making at the school level

Many educational reforms, as we have seen, involve a movement toward teacher empowerment—increasing teachers' participation in decisions that affect their own work and careers. One such reform is **school-based management** (also known as *site-based management, site-based decision making,* or *collaborative decision making*), a system in which individual schools rather than superintendents or boards of education make many decisions about curriculum, instruction, staff development, allocation of funds, and staffing assignments. School teachers, administrators, and often parents together develop their own plan for the school's future.

▪ Teachers as experts

The assumption underlying school-based management is that people who share in responsibilities and decisions will believe in what they are doing and will work more effectively toward common goals. This concept of reform also recognizes that teachers are experts whose talents should be put to use in planning. The reform plans in Dade County, Florida, and Rochester, New York (described in the chapter on Motivation, Preparation, and Conditions for the Entering Teacher), include a generous dose of school-based management. Other districts with similar plans include Louisville, Chicago, Denver, Los Angeles, Philadelphia, and Baltimore.

▪ Willingness to get involved

The fate of school-based management rests especially on the relationship between principals and their teachers, on the willingness of teachers to take responsibility for directing their own behavior, and on the amount of extra time teachers are willing to devote to working out problems and reaching consensus.[40] Advocates of school-based management claim that most teachers welcome the increased involvement and that teacher morale and the overall climate of the school dramatically improve.[41]

▪ Critiques of school-based management

Critics contend that the result of collaboration is often not useful. Considerable time, they say, is devoted to discussing daily teaching problems such as classroom management, equipment needs, clerical routines, and working conditions; thus little time remains for the larger issue of school effectiveness. In addition, some administrators argue that many teachers untrained in shared leadership, instead of cooperating, may revert to a hostile collective-bargaining stance.[42] In addition, some districts have found it difficult to develop meaningful parental involvement in school-based decision making.[43]

Expanding school-based management will require patience and a willingness to work out differences in expectations. Once in practice, however, shared decision making helps empower teachers and further enhances their professional status.

---

[40]Gordon Cawelti, "Key Elements of Site-Based Management," *Educational Leadership* (May 1989), pp. 46–54; and Frank Brown, "Site-Based Management: Is It Still Central to the School Reform Movement?" *School Business Affairs* (April 2001), pp. 5–6, 8–9.

[41]Mary Apodaca-Tucker, "School-Based Management: Views from Public and Private Elementary School Principals," *Education Policy Analysis Archives* (April 2002), p. 23; Hess, "The Changing Role," pp. 248–263; and Neil Dempster, "The Impact and Effects of Site-Based Management on Schools," *Journal of Educational Administration* (January 2000), pp. 47–63.

[42]Mary L. Radnofsky, "Empowerment and the Power Not to Change: Teachers' Perceptions of Restructuring," *International Journal of Educational Reform* (April 1994), pp. 154–164; Alan B. Henkin, Peter J. Cistone, and Jay Dee, "Conflict Management Strategies of Principals in Site-Based Managed Schools," *Journal of Educational Administration* (February 2000), pp. 42–58; and Bruce R. Brown and G. Robb Cooper, "School-Based Management: How Effective Is It?" *NASSP Bulletin* (May 2000), pp. 77–85.

[43]Eddy Van Meter, "Implementing School-Based Decision Making in Kentucky," *NASSP Bulletin* (September 1994), pp. 61–70; Alan Riley, "Parent Empowerment: An Idea for the Nineties," *Education Canada* (Fall 1994), pp. 14–20; and Lynn Beck and Joseph Murphy, "Parental Involvement in Site-Based Management: Lessons from One Site," *International Journal of Leadership in Education* (April–June 1999), pp. 81–102.

REFOCUS How do you believe movements toward increasing professionalism in teaching will affect you? Will you look for a position in a school that makes a strong effort to help new teachers? Would you prefer a mediated-entry program similar to that in the medical profession, with intern and resident teacher levels, before you become a full-fledged professional teacher? How can you prepare yourself to effectively carry out the shared leadership responsibilities of school-based management?

IN THIS CASE

The SBDM Team

During a break in the teachers' lounge, Anna Solemini, a first-year teacher, listened to her colleagues talk about the recent staff development day. Several complaints focused on the lack of helpful professional development provided by the school administration. Julia Smith, an experienced teacher, questioned, "Why did they make all of us sit there and listen to another presentation on learning styles? Most of us have heard that at least three times!"

Robert Garza, another long-time staff member, said, "I wish they would pay attention to what we want for professional development. I cannot remember one topic that our group requested. The site-based decision-making team seems to consistently ignore the survey that we complete in the spring. I know I requested help to improve teachers' use of technology. A couple of my friends requested help with classroom management. Learning styles may touch on that, but it doesn't hit the bull's-eye."

Another teacher added an important point that helped Anna better understand some of the differing views. She explained that the site-based decision-making team (SBDMT) decided topics for professional development, and that perhaps ideas from the teachers were not well presented to that team. The teachers wanted to know if an actual tabulation of the surveys had been created and presented to the team. After all, each of them had completed a survey last spring to select a couple of topics for this fall's professional development. Her new colleagues also expressed the opinion that if asking for their views on professional development was a way of empowering teachers as professionals, ignoring the survey results was equally a way to deprofessionalize the teachers.

After hearing about some of the SBDMT's other roles, Anna began to think that serving on the SBDMT could be a service to the school. The experience could help her develop professionally, too. She asked Julia how she might become involved. Julia said, "Don't worry. Until you have several years of experience and can influence other teachers, the administration won't even consider you for that position."

"But I thought that the teachers were elected to the positions on the SBDMT," said Anna. "What factors do the teachers consider important?"

"The same items I have already noted—experience and influence."

"But I think that it could be a great learning experience for a beginning teacher like myself," said Anna.

"Well, I think you will probably find this first year challenging enough without taking on the site-based decision-making team. If you believe you can find time for all those meetings and really want to do this, though, make that known to our principal and to our fellow teachers. Just try not to be too idealistic. I am sure you have a lot of new ideas from your recent training, but decisions in the real world can get a little stickier."

Questions

1. What further information should Anna seek before trying to join the site-based decision-making team?

2. What do you think about Julia's view that only experienced teachers will be selected or elected to serve on the SBDMT?

3. Why might some teachers object to serving on an SBDMT?

4. In your opinion, is Anna's plan likely to be more or less effective than complaints in the teachers' lounge?

▶ Teacher Organizations

■ NEA and AFT

Although today's working conditions need improvement, they sharply contrast with the restrictions teachers once endured. For example, a Wisconsin teacher's contract for 1922 prohibited a woman teacher from dating, marrying, staying out past 8 P.M., smoking, drinking, loitering in ice cream parlors, dyeing her hair, and using mascara or lipstick.[44] A critical factor in the development of teaching as a profession has been the growth of professional organizations for teachers. The **National Education Association (NEA)** and the **American Federation of Teachers (AFT)**, the two most important, usually are considered rivals, competing for members, recognition, and power. Overview 2.1 sums up major differences between the two organizations. Although some educators believe that this division produces healthy professional competition, others consider it detrimental to the teaching profession—a splitting of power and a waste of resources. Still others argue that teachers will not attain full professional status until one unified voice speaks for them.

■ Benefits of organizational membership

Regardless of which teacher organization you prefer or are inclined to join, the important step is to make a commitment and be an active member. Organizational membership will increase your own professionalism and gain you collegial relationships. Your support also helps to improve salary, working conditions, and benefits for many teachers. In addition, reading the journals, magazines, or newsletters that most professional organizations publish will keep you abreast of the latest developments in the field.

National Education Association (NEA)

■ NEA membership

The National Education Association is a complex, multifaceted organization involved in education on many local, state, and national levels. Unlike the AFT, the NEA includes both teachers and administrators at the national level. As shown in Table 2.1, membership totaled 2.7 million in 2003.[45] Among NEA members in 2002 more than two million were classroom teachers.[46] This figure comprises three-

Table 2.1	Membership in the NEA and AFT	
Year	**NEA Membership**	**AFT Membership**
1960	714,000	59,000
1970	1,100,000	205,000
1980	1,650,000	550,000
1990	2,050,000	750,000
1995	2,200,000	875,000
1998	2,300,000	950,000
2003	2,700,000	1,000,000

Source: "The AFT Soars," *The 1988–90 Report of the Officers of the American Federation of Teachers* (Washington, D.C.: AFT, 1990), p. 15; *NEA Handbook, 1986–87* (Washington, D.C.: NEA, 1986), Table 4, p. 142; *NEA Handbook, 1994–95* (Washington, D.C.: NEA, 1995), Table 1, p. 164; and *NEA Handbook, 1997–98,* Table 1, p. 166; see **http:www.nea.org/aboutnea/faq.html** (2003).

---

[44]*Chicago Tribune,* September 28, 1975, sect. 1, p. 3.
[45]See **http:www.nea.org/aboutnea/faq.html** (2003).
[46]See **http:www.nea.org/publications** (2003).

OVERVIEW 2.1 *Comparison of the National Education Association (NEA) and the American Federation of Teachers (AFT)*

	NEA	AFT
Total membership (2003)	2,700,000	1,000,000
Members who are classroom teachers	2,200,000	500,000
President	Reg Weaver	Sandra Feldman
President's term	2 years (maximum 6 years per person)	2 years (no maximum)
Organizational view	Professional association	Union affiliation with AFL-CIO
Organizational atmosphere	Relatively formal (white collar)	Relatively informal (blue collar)
Geographic strength	Suburban and rural areas	Large and medium-size cities

fourths of the nation's 2.7 million public-school teachers. Primarily suburban and rural in its membership, the NEA represents the fifth-largest lobbying force in the country. State affiliates are usually among the most influential state-level education lobbies.[47]

■ NEA services

The NEA offers a wide range of professional services. The research division conducts annual studies on the status of the profession; it also publishes research memos and opinion surveys on an annual basis. The NEA's major publication is a monthly newspaper, *NEA Today*. Most of the fifty state affiliates publish a monthly magazine as well.

American Federation of Teachers (AFT)

■ AFT membership

Formed in 1916, the AFT is affiliated with the AFL-CIO labor organization. Originally open only to classroom teachers, in 1976, to increase membership, the AFT targeted professional employees such as nurses and nonprofessional school personnel such as cafeteria, custodial, maintenance, and transportation workers. Membership in 2003 stood at just over one million (Table 2.1), of whom 500,000 were teachers.

■ AFT services

In the past, the AFT has supported less research and publication than the NEA, but the union does publish a professional magazine, *American Educator,* and a monthly newspaper, *American Teacher.* In addition, local affiliates each produce a monthly newsletter. Unlike the NEA, the AFT has always required its members to join the local, state (twenty-two in all), and national organizations simultaneously.[48]

■ The AFT and teacher militancy

The AFT expanded rapidly in the 1960s and 1970s when its affiliates spearheaded a dramatic increase in teacher strikes and other militant actions. The AFT became the dominant teacher organization in many large urban centers where unions have traditionally flourished, where militant tactics have been common, and where teachers in general have wanted a powerful organization to represent them. In rural and suburban areas, where union tactics have received less support, the NEA remains dominant.

---

[47]See **www.nea.org/publications** (2003).
[48]See "About AFT" at **http:www.aft.org/about** (2003).

In addition to the NEA and AFT, more than 325 other national teacher organizations exist.[49] In the following sections we describe some of the basic types.

 Which goals and activities seem more appealing to you, those of the NEA or those of the AFT? Why?

Specialized Professional Organizations

■ Subject-related associations

At the working level, the classroom, the professional organization that best serves teachers (and education students) is usually one that focuses on their major field. Each such subject-centered professional association provides a meeting ground for teachers of similar interests. These professional organizations customarily provide regional and national meetings and professional journals that offer current teaching tips, enumerate current issues in the discipline, and summarize current research and its relationship to practice. The first column of Overview 2.2 lists fifteen major organizations that focus on specific subject matter.

■ Student-related organizations

Other organizations, also national in scope, focus on the needs and rights of particular kinds of students, ensuring that these children and youth are served by well-prepared school personnel. Fifteen such organizations are listed in the second column of Overview 2.2. These associations hold regional and national meetings and publish monthly or quarterly journals.

■ Other professional associations

Still another type of organization is the professional organization whose members cut across various subjects and student types, such as the Association for Supervision and Curriculum Development and Phi Delta Kappa. These organizations tend to highlight general innovative teaching practices, describe new trends and policies affecting the entire field of education, have a wide range of membership, and work to advance the teaching profession in general.

Religious Education Organizations

■ Religious education organizations

In grades K–12 there are approximately 375,000 nonpublic-school teachers, of whom 135,000 belong to religious education associations. One of the largest religious teacher organizations is the National Association of Catholic School Teachers (NACST), founded in 1978 and now comprising more than five thousand teachers, mainly from large cities.[50] Few Catholic K–12 schoolteachers belong to either the NEA or the AFT.

The largest and oldest Catholic education organization is the National Catholic Education Association, comprising 8,146 institutions and 200,000 Catholic educators. Most members are administrators who serve as principals, supervisors, or superintendents of their respective schools. Few teachers are members.[51]

Parent-Teacher Groups

Parent-teacher groups provide a forum for parents and teachers to work together in resolving educational problems on the local, state, and national levels. As a

---

[49]See *Directory of Education Associations, 2001–2002* (Washington, D.C.: U.S. Department of Education, 2001).
[50]Letter from and telephone conversation with Heidi Wunder, public relations assistant, National Catholic Education Association, August 27, 2003; telephone conversation with Virginia Crowther, office manager–membership, National Association of Catholic School Teachers, March 16, 2001.
[51]Wunder, NCEA, March 16, 2001; see **www.pta.org/aboutus** (2003).

OVERVIEW 2.2 *Major Specialized Professional Organizations for Teachers*

Organizations that Focus on Specific Subject Matter	**Organizations That Focus on Student Type or Age Level**
1. American Alliance for Health, Physical Education, Recreation and Dance	1. American Association for Gifted Children
2. American Council on the Teaching of Foreign Languages	2. American Association of Workers for the Blind
3. American Industrial Arts Association	3. American Association for Asian Studies
4. American School Health Association	4. American Montessori Society
5. American Vocational Association	5. American Speech-Language-Hearing Association
6. Association for Education in Journalism	6. Association for Childhood Education International
7. International Reading Association	7. Association for Children with Learning Disabilities
8. Modern Language Association	8. Council for Exceptional Children
9. Music Teachers National Association	9. Music Teachers National Association
10. National Art Education Association	10. National Art Education Association
11. National Business Education Association	11. National Business Education Association
12. National Council for the Social Studies	12. National Council for the Social Studies
13. National Council of Teachers of English	13. National Council of Teachers of English
14. National Council of Teachers of Mathematics	14. National Council of Teachers of Mathematics
15. National Science Teachers Association	15. National Science Teachers Association

teacher, you can take an active part in these associations and work with parents on curriculum and instructional programs, student policy, and school-community relations.

■ PTA membership

Founded in 1897, the **Parent-Teacher Association (PTA)**—the most prominent of the groups—is a loose confederation of fifty-four branches and 23,000 local units in all fifty states, with more than 6,554,000 members (mostly mothers) in 2003. Every PTA unit devises its own pattern of organization and service to fit its school and neighborhood. (Some units now use the acronym PTSA, emphasizing their inclusion of students.) PTA membership is open to anyone interested in promoting the welfare of children and youth, working with teachers and schools, and supporting PTA goals.[52] *Our Children: PTA Today* and *What's Happening in Washington* are the official monthly magazines of the association.[53] The "Where We Stand" section of the PTA Web site **(www.pta.org)** offers their online press room and legislative information.

■ National PTA activities

As the nation's largest child-advocacy organization, the National PTA is constantly assessing children's welfare to respond to changes in society and in children's needs. For years, the National PTA has lobbied to reduce violence on television

---

[52]*Partners in Education: Teachers in the PTA* (Chicago: National PTA, 1987); and telephone conversation with Patricia Yoxall, director of public relations, National PTA, March 16, 2001; Ginny Markel, "Rural Communities Matter: How PTAs Can Increase Parent Involvement in Our Nation's Small Towns," *Our Children* (November 2000), p. 3.
[53]See **www.pta.org/pta/washington.**

and to improve the quality of children's television programming. It also has active programs related to reading, urban education, sex education and AIDS education, child nutrition and safety education, and drug abuse prevention, as well as improving school discipline and combating censorship of school and library materials.

Organizations for Prospective Teachers

■ Help in understanding the profession

Students considering teaching careers may join professional organizations. These organizations can help you answer questions; investigate the profession; form ideals of professional ethics, standards, and training; meet other students and educators at local and national meetings; and keep up with current trends in the profession.

Overview 2.3 lists professional organizations that students can join. Ask your professors for appropriate information if you are interested in joining any of these organizations. Some offer student membership rates. Your college library most likely carries the respective journals for each organization. The first or second page of each issue lists membership information and costs and the Internet address.

REFOCUS
- Which of the professional organizations listed in this chapter hold the most interest for you? Which might be useful to join later in your career?
- How can you find out more information about professional organizations in which you are interested?

OVERVIEW 2.3 *Professional Organizations Students Can Join*

Name and Location	Membership Profile	Focus	Major Journals
Student National Education Association, Washington, D.C. **www.nea.org**	Undergraduate students (46,000)	Future teachers, understanding the profession, liability coverage	*Tomorrow's Teachers* (annual), *NEA Today* (monthly)
Pi Lambda Theta, Bloomington, Ind.	Undergraduate and graduate students, teachers, and administrators (11,500)	Honorary association, teaching	*Educational Horizons* (quarterly)
Phi Delta Kappa, Bloomington, Ind. **www.pdkintl.org**	Undergraduate and graduate students, teachers, administrators, and professors (130,000)	Honorary association; research; service, leadership, and teaching; issues, trends, and policies	*Phi Delta Kappan* (monthly), *Fastbacks* at reduced rates
Kappa Delta Pi, Lafayette, Ind. **www.kdp.org**	Graduate students, teachers, administrators, and professors (29,700); undergraduate students (25,300)	Honorary association, teaching	*Educational Forum* (quarterly), *Kappa Delta Pi Record* (quarterly)
American Educational Research Association, Washington, D.C. **http:aera.net**	Graduate students and professors (22,500), undergraduate students (4,500)	Research and its application to education	*Educational Researcher* (bimonthly), *American Educational Research Journal* (quarterly), *Review of Educational Research* (quarterly), *Educational Evaluation and Policy Analysis* (quarterly)

▶ Summing Up

1 It is generally agreed that teaching, although not yet a full profession, is moving toward becoming one.

2 Collective bargaining is an integral part of the teaching profession, giving teachers greater authority to determine working conditions and their effectiveness as teachers.

3 Many education trends are raising the level of teacher professionalism. State professional practice boards and the National Board for Professional Teaching Standards, for example, enable teachers to participate in setting criteria for entering the profession. Mediated-entry and staff development programs help establish the idea that teaching is a full-fledged profession requiring lengthy and continued training. Merit pay and school-based management provide opportunities for increased salaries and more professional responsibilities.

4 The NEA and AFT now represent a large majority of classroom teachers; these organizations have improved teachers' salaries and working conditions and have gained them a greater voice in decisions that affect teaching and learning in schools.

5 Many professional organizations are open to undergraduate students or to graduate students and teachers. All provide valuable information and services to educators at different career levels.

▶ Key Terms

profession (31)
National Council for
   Accreditation of Teacher Education
   (33)
deprofessionalization (34)
occupational prestige (35)
collective bargaining (37)
professional practice board (38)
National Board for Professional
   Teaching Standards (38)

mediated entry (39)
staff development (40)
merit pay (41)
school-based management (44)
National Education Association (NEA)
   (46)
American Federation of Teachers (AFT)
   (46)
parent-teacher groups (48)
Parent-Teacher Association (PTA) (49)

▶ Discussion Questions

1 In your opinion, is teaching a profession or not? What changes might make teaching a true profession? What does teacher professionalism mean to you?

2 What special relationships does your college of education have with area school districts and/or schools? How do these relationships enhance your preparation as well as the work of the teachers and administrators? How could these be improved?

3 Are staff development programs essential for maintaining high-quality teaching? If so, what should their main focus be? Who should design these programs and how?

4 Do you agree with proponents of school-based management that teachers should have a greater role in managing schools? As a teacher, what kinds of decisions would you like to be involved in? In what, if any, areas of school management would you rather *not* be involved, and why?

▶ Projects for Professional Development

1 Using local newspapers, professional journal articles, and conversations with teachers and administrators, identify an educational issue or trend of importance in a local school district. Why is the issue or trend important? What are the differing views on the issue (for/against; pro/con)? What implications do you see for teachers and administrators as professional people? Talk with your instructor about selecting several classmates to present their issues and analyses as a panel before the class.

2 Survey local public-school teachers and your education faculty regarding their views on merit pay. Compare and contrast your results with the views expressed in the Taking Issue feature. What is your opinion? What are you uncertain about? How can you find more information to clear up these uncertainties?

3 Either by telephone or over the Internet, contact your local NEA and AFT affiliates and ask for information on membership costs, benefits, and services and for position statements on key educational issues. Talk with teachers in the schools you visit, asking them which of the organizations tend to represent teachers in your area and why. Make a chart to display your information and share it with the class.

4 Talk with teachers in the schools you visit and your education professors to find out which professional organizations they belong to—and why. Review the list of specialized professional organizations in Overview 2.2 and select two or three that most interest you. Using the Internet addresses below, contact these organizations about student membership costs, special benefits, publications, and special programs.

▶ Suggested Resources

Internet Resources

Information about many of the organizations discussed in this chapter can be found on the World Wide Web. For example, the NEA maintains a home page at **www.nea.org**; the AFT is at **www.aft.org**; and the National PTA is at **www.pta.org**. In addition, the Usenet offers access to many news and discussion groups related to education; some of them, such as **k12.chat. teacher**, focus on topics of particular concern to elementary and secondary school teachers. In exploring specific topics such as staff development and educational technology; the biggest problem often is deciding which of the many good sites to visit first. A general Internet search will provide a good start. For staff development, try the National Staff Development Council at **www.nsdc.org**. For educational technology, search the federal government site at **www.ed. gov**. For information on national board certification standards, consult the NBPTS site at **www.nbpts.org**.

Publications

Abdul-Haqq, Ismat, *Professional Development Schools: Weighing the Evidence.* Thousand Oaks, Calif.: Corwin Press, 1997. *An excellent book on professional development school partnerships in teacher education.*

Bascia, Nina. *Unions in Teachers' Professional Lives.* New York: Teachers College Press, 1994. *A case study book on teachers' unions.*

Brimelow, Peter. *The Worm in the Apple: How Teacher's Unions Are Destroying Public Education.* New York: HarperCollins, 2003. *A one-sided, but thoughtful, view of teachers' unions, their philosophies and tactics.*

Conant, James B. *The Education of American Teachers.* New York: McGraw-Hill, 1964. *A classic text on improving teacher education and teacher professionalism.*

Elliot, Emmerson J. *Assessing Education Candidate Performance: A Look at Changing Practices.* Washington, D.C.: National Council for the Accreditation of Teacher Education, 2003. *Describes a shift from what institutions offer their candidates to what candidates receive—that is, evidence that candidates have the knowledge, skills, and dispositions necessary to teach and put these attributes into action so that all students will learn.*

Johnson, Susan Moore. *Teachers at Work.* New York: Harper and Row, 1990. *The rules and responsibilities teachers adopt in classrooms and schools.*

Lieberman, Myron, and Gene Geisert. *Teacher Union Bargaining: Practice and Policy.* Chicago: Precept Press, 1994. *A book on collective bargaining issues and teachers' unions.*

Maeroff, Gene I. *Education and Change: A Personal Critique.* Fastback #466. Bloomington, Ind.: Phi Delta Kappa Educational Foundation, 2000. *A thoughtful reflection on and analysis of changes in public education and suggestions for schools in the twenty-first century.*

McCarty, Hannoch, and Frank Siccone. *Motivating Your Students: Before You Can Teach Them You Have to Reach Them.* Boston: Allyn and Bacon, 2001. *A stimulating book written for both new and veteran teachers with scores of suggestions for motivating both students and teacher.*

Murray, Frank. *The Teacher Educator's Handbook: Building a Knowledge Base for the Preparation of Teachers.* San Francisco: Jossey-Bass, 1996. *This is a thorough examination of the need for a knowledge base in teaching, based on research and school reform issues.*

National PTA. *National Standards for Parent/Family Involvement.* Chicago: National PTA, 1997. *A comprehensive set of standards to help schools, families, and parent groups work cooperatively to help children and effect educational change.*

Ornstein, Allan C. *Teaching: Theory into Practice.* Boston: Allyn and Bacon, 1995. *Designed to help students reflect on teaching in both the theoretical and the practical sense.*

Perlmutter, Jane, and Louise Burrell. *The First Weeks of School: Laying a Quality Foundation.* Portsmouth: Heinemann, 2001. *An excellent book for beginning teachers that addresses the weeks before the school year begins, the first day of school, those early weeks, survival, and roadblocks to success. Must reading for first-year teachers!*

Reynolds, Larry J. *Successful Site-Based Management: A Practical Guide.* Thousand Oaks, Calif.: Corwin Press, 1997. *An excellent guidebook for introducing a system-wide approach to site-based management as a strategy for school improvement.*

Walling, Donovan R., ed. *Teachers as Leaders: Perspectives on the Professional Development of Teachers.* Bloomington, Ind.: Phi Delta Kappa Educational Foundation, 1994. *A handbook for recruiting teachers, especially minorities, with general information on the teaching profession and professional development.*

Warner, Jack, and Clyde Bryan. *The Unauthorized Teacher's Survival Guide.* Indianapolis: Park Avenue, 1995. *Must reading for all new teachers—a how-to-survive guide that covers everything a young professional needs to know from "soup to nuts."*

PART TWO

Historical and Philosophical Foundations

CHAPTER 3

World Roots of American Education

For a healthy perspective on issues you'll confront as a teacher, let's start now to build your understanding of how education and schooling originated, developed, and reached their present condition. Even the most urgent contemporary educational issues lack perspective until we examine their historical roots. As the Bradley Commission put it, students "need to confront the diverse cultural heritages of the world's many peoples, and they need to know the origins and evolution of the political, religious, and social ideas that have shaped our institutions and those of others."[1] This chapter's In This Case feature explores how understanding the origins of some Western educational practices can contribute to the day-to-day practice of today's teachers.

This chapter examines how diverse cultures have contributed to contemporary education. Taking a global perspective, we discuss educational developments in Chinese, Indian, Egyptian, and Western cultures. Tracing how educational institutions and practices arose in the past, we use history to illuminate the present and as a tool to build toward the future.

Throughout history, teachers have faced many reoccurring and unresolved questions about the nature of knowledge, education, schooling, and teaching and learning. How have personal and group rights to participate in schooling changed, for example, and how have educational opportunities been limited by gender, race, and socioeconomic class biases? As you read this chapter, consider the following questions:

This chapter was revised by Dr. Gerald Gutek.
[1]The Bradley Commission on History in Schools, *Building a History Curriculum: Guidelines for Teaching History in Schools* (Washington, D.C.: Educational Excellence Network, 1988), pp. 3–4.

- How were knowledge, education, schooling, teaching, and learning defined in the major historical periods?
- What concepts of the educated person were dominant during each period of history discussed in this chapter?
- How did racial, gender, and socioeconomic factors affect educational opportunities in the past?
- When and how has schooling been used for cultural transmission or change?
- What curricula (the content of education) and what teaching methods were used in the various historical periods?
- How did the ideas of leading educators contribute to modern education?

IN THIS CASE

The Old and the New

Eddie Albrecht strolled up and down the aisles in the classroom, talking all the time. He dictated the causes of the important battles, the names of the generals involved, and the result of each. As he walked, he made sure that the students were dutifully taking notes. He wanted them to learn all this and be ready for the exam he was going to give them next week.

After observing Eddie's teaching, Dr. Allredd, supervising professor, said, "I want you to think about strategies to improve your teaching, Eddie. You used a Homeric teaching style, *telling* your students most of the information. Perhaps you remember your own history teacher teaching that way, but how stimulating was it?"

Dr Allredd continued, "Next time, try the Socratic method. *Ask* questions in class and draw out what knowledge the students have before you proceed. Or you might give them a chance to research the information in teams and report their findings together."

"I thought you wanted us to use some of the traditional approaches to education," said Eddie.

"I want you to be familiar with how ancient, medieval, and Renaissance educators approached teaching and learning," replied Dr. Allredd. "I also want you to understand why they taught as they did. Understand this, and you'll see how current educational methods may include some of those techniques. For instance, we still need a certain amount of memorization in today's schools. You may consider some facts essential for your students to know, and certainly the state tests require students to know some basics, but facts alone are not the answer. We also need to help students develop higher-level thinking skills. Erasmus, you'll recall, did much the same in his teaching."

"Dr. Allredd, I think I understand. You know, I did suffer a little in my history classes, but I really enjoyed most of them. They got me involved in research, reading, and writing. I liked reading the journals of some of my favorite historical figures. And I really enjoyed field trips to see the historical sites where these American heroes lived and worked. I guess you'd say those experiences incorporated both the humanistic and scientific approaches. I want my lessons to reflect those approaches, too. Heck, if I emphasize my kids' abilities to think and work to develop their reasoning abilities, I'll be using concepts straight out of the Enlightenment."

Dr. Allredd laughed. "Good thinking, teacher! And I want you to keep thinking about the purposes of schooling today and what education could mean for each of your students. Remember, not everything done in the past is appropriate for today."

Questions

1. How would a review of past educational approaches help you in preparing to teach?
2. What do you believe are the purposes for schooling in the United States today?
3. What cultural heritages do you think had the most influence on your education? Explain.

▶ Education in Preliterate Societies

■ Cultural transmission

Our narrative begins in preliterate times, before the invention of reading and writing, when our ancestors transmitted their culture orally from one generation to the next. We can find the origins of informal learning in families and appreciate why it remains so powerful even today. Although we live in a time when information is electronically stored and retrieved by computers, an examination of preliterate education can help us understand why schools often tend to resist change as they train the young in essential "survival" skills.

■ Trial-and-error learning

Preliterate people faced the almost overwhelming problems of surviving in an environment that pitted them against drought and floods, wild animals, and attacks from hostile groups. By trial and error, they developed survival skills that over time became cultural patterns.

For culture to continue, it must be transmitted from adults to children. By **enculturation**, children learn the group's language and skills and assimilate its moral and religious values.

■ Moral codes

Over time, groups developed survival skills and passed these on to their young. They marked the passage from childhood to adulthood with ritual dancing, music, and dramatic acting to create a powerful supernatural meaning and evoke a moral response. Thus children learned the group's prescriptions (acceptable behaviors) as well as its proscriptions or taboos (forbidden behaviors).

■ Oral tradition

Lacking writing to record their past, preliterate societies relied on oral tradition—storytelling—to transmit their cultural heritage. Elders or priests, often gifted storytellers, sang or recited narratives of the group's past. Combining myths and legends, the oral tradition told young people about the group's heroes, victories, and defeats. The songs and stories helped the young learn the group's spoken language and develop more abstract thinking about time and space.

■ Storytelling

Stories and storytelling remain an important and engaging educational strategy today, especially in preschools and the primary grades. Through stories, children meet their culture and its heroes, legends, and past.

■ Literacy

As toolmakers, humans made and used spears, axes, and other tools, the earliest examples of technology. Similarly, as language users, we created and manipulated symbols. Beginning to express these symbols in signs, pictographs, and letters, and creating a written language constituted our great cultural leap to literacy and then to schooling.

A global frame of reference will help you understand the worldwide movement to develop schools in literate societies. For that reason, our historical survey begins with the ancient empires of China, India, and Egypt.

▶ Education in Ancient Chinese Civilization

Chinese civilization's long history and vast influence offer significant insights into education's evolution. With the world's largest population, modern China is an important global power. Historically, it was a great empire whose civilization reached high pinnacles of political, social, and educational development. The empire was ruled by a series of dynasties spanning more than forty centuries, from 2200 B.C. to A.D. 1912.[2] Many educational traditions—especially Confucianism—that originated in imperial China still have influence today. (See Overview 3.1 for key periods in China and other countries.)

---

[2]Edward Shaughnessy, *China: Empire and Civilization* (New York: Oxford University Press, 2000).

The Chinese educational heritage reveals persistent efforts to maintain unbroken cultural continuity. Like many people, the early Chinese were ethnocentric and believed their language and culture to be superior to all others.[3] Scorning foreigners as barbarians, the Chinese were inward looking, seeing little of value in other cultures. Eventually, imperial China's reluctance to adapt technology from other cultures isolated and weakened it and, by the nineteenth century, made it vulnerable to foreign exploitation. The challenge of how to adapt to new ideas, especially in science and technology, and maintain one's own culture remains an important educational issue in China today and in other countries as well. Their efforts help us understand questions that you as a teacher must ask yourself: How can you provide students with an appreciation for the cultural and scientific achievements of the past as well as an openness to social and technological change? What is the relationship between cultural continuity and change, and how does education promote one or the other?

Confucian Education

■ Group loyalty

Many people, especially in China, Japan, South Korea, and Singapore, highly esteem **Confucius** (551–479 B.C.) as the world's greatest philosopher and teacher. For more than two thousand years Confucius' ethical system, with its emphasis on personal discipline, loyalty to the family and group, and the need for social and political harmony, has shaped Chinese civilization and education.[4]

■ Need for harmony

Confucius lived during "the warring states period" of Chinese history, a time of chaotic turmoil, treachery, and conflict. Rival warlords—using cunning, duplicity, and brute force—struggled for power. Treaties were made and then ignored; bribery helped secure favors; assassinations were commonplace. In response to this time of troubles, Confucius formulated an ethical and educational philosophy to restore peace and harmony in China. Convinced that knowledge could replace force, he established a school where he would educate future government officials to rule China with justice, fairness, and order.

■ Rituals and manners

For Confucius, education's paramount goal is to develop persons of noble character who by diligent and continuous study acquire the necessary knowledge to follow the "way," the path that leads to benevolence rather than violence. Seeking to reduce the anxiety caused by rapid change, Confucius organized his ethical and educational system around learning how to observe the rituals and manners that governed human relationships in a hierarchical society. His ideal of hierarchical relationships can be depicted as an ethical ladder on which the person standing on each rung is connected to the people standing above and below. Everyone in the hierarchy should clearly know her or his status, duties, and responsibilities, and the proper way of behaving toward others.

■ Hierarchy

As a teacher, how will you help your students to develop positive human relationships and values? Will these values reflect traditional standards or will they be open-ended? The concept of hierarchical ethical relationships has important implications for education, especially character formation. Confucius' concept of hierarchical relationships in which some individuals are superior and others subordinate differs significantly from our common idea in the United States today of human relationships based on equality.

---

[3]Roxann Prazniak, *Dialogues Across Civilizations: Sketches in World History from the Chinese and European Experiences* (Boulder, Colo.: Westview of HarperCollins, 1996).
[4]See Peimin Ni, *On Confucius* (Belmont, Calif.: Wadsworth, 2002) and Jennifer Oldstone-Moore, *Confucianism* (Oxford and New York: Oxford University Press, 2002).

OVERVIEW 3.1 *Key Periods in Educational History*

Historical Group or Period	Educational Goals	Students
Preliterate societies 7000 B.C.–5000 B.C.	To teach group survival skills and group cohesiveness	Children in the group
China 3000 B.C.–A.D. 1900	To prepare elite officials to govern the empire according to Confucian principles	Males of gentry class
India 3000 B.C.–present	To learn behaviors and rituals based on the Vedas	Males of upper castes
Egypt 3000 B.C.–300 B.C.	To prepare priest-scribes to administer the empire	Males of upper classes
Greek 1600 B.C.–300 B.C.	Athens: To cultivate civic responsibility and identification with city-state and to develop well-rounded persons Sparta: to train soldiers and military leaders	Male children of citizens; ages 7–20
Roman 750 B.C.–A.D. 450	To develop civic responsibility for republic and then empire; to develop administrative and military skills	Male children of citizens; ages 7–20
Arabic A.D. 700–A.D. 1350	To cultivate religious commitment to Islamic beliefs; to develop expertise in mathematics, medicine, and science	Male children of upper classes; ages 7–20
Medieval A.D. 500–A.D. 1400	To develop religious commitment, knowledge, and ritual; to prepare persons for appropriate roles in a hierarchical society	Male children of upper classes or those entering religious life; girls and young women entering religious communities; ages 7–20
Renaissance A.D. 1350–A.D. 1500	To cultivate humanist experts in the classics (Greek and Latin); to prepare courtiers for service to dynastic leaders	Male children of aristocracy and upper classes; ages 7–20
Reformation A.D. 1500–A.D. 1600	To instill commitment to a particular religious denomination; to cultivate general literacy	Boys and girls ages 7–12 in vernacular schools; young men ages 7–12 of upper-class backgrounds in humanist schools

Instructional Methods	Curriculum	Agents	Influences on Modern Education
Informal instruction; children imitating adult skills and values	Survival skills of hunting, fishing, food gathering; stories, myths, songs, poems, dances	Parents, tribal elders, and priests	Emphasis on informal education to transmit skills and values
Memorization and recitation of classic texts	Confucian classics	Government officials	Written examinations for civil service and other professions
Memorizing and interpreting sacred texts	Vedas and religious texts	Brahmin priest-scholars	Cultural transmission and assimilation; spiritual detachment
Memorizing and copying dictated texts	Religious or technical texts	Priests and scribes	Restriction of educational controls and services to a priestly elite; use of education to prepare bureaucracies
Drill, memorization, recitation in primary schools; lecture, discussion, and dialogue in higher schools	Athens: reading, writing, arithmetic, drama, music, physical education, literature, poetry Sparta: drill, military songs, and tactics	Athens: private teachers and schools, Sophists, philosophers Sparta: military officers	Athens: the concept of the well-rounded, liberally educated person Sparta: the concept of serving the military state
Drill, memorization, and recitation in primary schools; declamation in rhetorical schools	Reading, writing, arithmetic, Laws of Twelve Tables, law, philosophy	Private schools and teachers; schools of rhetoric	Emphasis on education for practical administrative skills; relating education to civic responsibility
Drill, memorization, and recitation in lower schools; imitation and discussion in higher schools	Reading, writing, mathematics, religious literature, scientific studies	Mosques; court schools	Arabic numerals and computation; reentry of classical materials on science and medicine
Drill, memorization, recitation, chanting in lower schools; textual analysis and disputation in universities and in higher schools	Reading, writing, arithmetic, liberal arts; philosophy, theology; crafts; military tactics and chivalry	Parish, chantry, and cathedral schools; universities; apprenticeship; knighthood	Established structure, content, and organization of universities as major institutions of higher education; the institutionalization and preservation of knowledge
Memorization, translation, and analysis of Greek and Roman classics	Latin, Greek, classical literature, poetry, art	Classical humanist educators and schools such as the lycée, *gymnasium,* and Latin school	An emphasis on literary knowledge, excellence, and style as expressed in classical literature; a two-track system of schools
Memorization, drill, indoctrination, catechetical instruction in vernacular schools; translation and analysis of classical literature in humanist schools	Reading, writing, arithmetic, catechism, religious concepts and ritual; Latin and Greek; theology	Vernacular elementary schools for the masses; classical schools for the upper classes	A commitment to universal education to provide literacy to the masses; the origins of school systems with supervision to ensure doctrinal conformity; the dual-track school system based on socioeconomic class and career goals

In conditions of equality, individuals engaged in a relationship continually redefine the relationship and create new openings to each other, and often establish or reestablish boundaries. Character education in situations of equality carries the ethical prescriptions that we should treat each person as an equal and that we should respect and even value their differences from us.

In contrast, Confucianist ethics set up definite patterns of behavior rather than flexible or fluid ones. People are accorded various levels of respect based on their position, status, and achievements. Character education means to learn one's roles in the network of relationships that form the community and to fulfill the prescribed role behaviors that will ensure social harmony.

Because change, novelty, and innovations can bring about the unexpected—and unexpected change was a social problem during his time—Confucius based his ethical system on tradition. A certain practice or behavior that contributed to maintaining peace, security, and tranquility in the past was worthy of being encased in a ritualized way of behaving and transmitted to and practiced by people in the present. According to Confucius, "A man worthy of being a teacher gets to know what is new by keeping fresh in his mind what he is already familiar with."[5]

■ Respect for teachers

In China, teacher–student relationships, like other relationships, were well known and followed with precision. Students were to hold their teachers in high regard and respect. Confucius' own students referred to him as "the master." This respect for education, learning, and teachers became an important characteristic of education in China and in East Asia where Confucianism became a major intellectual and educational force.[6]

China's Contribution to World and Western Education

■ Importance of examinations

An important educational legacy from ancient China was its system of national examinations. Chinese educators developed comprehensive written examinations to assess students' academic competence. Students prepared for the examinations by studying ancient Chinese literature and Confucian texts with master teachers at imperial or temple schools. The examinations emphasized recalling memorized information rather than solving actual problems. The examination process, like the society, operated hierarchically and selectively. Students had to pass a series of rigorous examinations in ascending order; if they failed, they were dismissed from the process.[7] In imperial days, only a few finalists were eligible for the empire's highest civil service positions. The educational and examination systems were reserved exclusively for upper-class males. Women, ineligible for government positions, were excluded from schools as well.

Currently, national examinations, especially for university entrance, dominate education in modern China and Japan. Other countries such as the United Kingdom have also developed national tests.

Standards & Assessment ✔

In the United States, the Education Act of 2001, "No Child Left Behind," mandates annual testing of students in grades 3–8 to measure academic achievement in reading and mathematics.[8] You may have taken standardized tests as a student. As a

---

[5]Confucius, *The Analects*, Book II, in D. C. Lau, "Introduction," *The Analects*, trans. D. C. Lau (New York: Penguin Books, 1979), p. 64.

[6]T. R. Reid, *Confucius Lives Next Door: What Living in the East Teaches Us About Living in the West* (New York: Vintage Press, 2000).

[7]Conrad Schirokauer, *A Brief History of Chinese Civilization* (New York: Harcourt Brace Jovanovich, 1991), pp. 57, 124, 128.

[8]U.S. Department of Education, Office of the Secretary, *No Child Left Behind*, 2001 (Washington D.C.: U.S. Department of Education, 2001), pp. 3, 8.

teacher, you will most likely administer them, and thus must determine the extent to which external examinations will affect your teaching. The act's premise is that this kind of testing will hold schools accountable for their students' academic achievement. Critics, however, contend that using standardized tests to measure student achievement may lead to standardized instruction that teaches for the test.

REFOCUS Think back to the Focus Questions listed at the beginning of this chapter. How would you answer those questions if you were asked to summarize education in ancient China? In what ways would national examinations in U.S. schools affect your teaching?

▶ Education in Ancient Indian Civilization

■ Cultural equilibrium

Like China, India is an ancient civilization. River valley civilizations flourished on the banks of India's Indus River at Mohenjo-daro and Harrapa from 3000 B.C. to 1500 B.C. India's educational history reveals a general pattern of intrusion by invaders, followed by a cultural clash with the indigenous people, and then the restoration of sociocultural equilibrium. In this cultural equilibrium, the invaders were absorbed into India's culture while at the same time the indigenous people borrowed some of the invaders' ideas.[9]

■ Brief history

Among India's early invaders were the Aryans, ancestors of India's Hindi-speaking majority, who conquered India in 1500 B.C. and imposed their rule over the indigenous Dravidian inhabitants. They were followed by the Muslims, who established the Mughul dynasty in the thirteenth century. Then, in the eighteenth century, the British gained control over India.

Cultural changes introduced by the Aryans exerted powerful social and educational influences that continue even today. The Aryans introduced their religion, Hinduism, and their highly stratified social order, the **caste system**.

■ Hinduism

Hinduism, a powerful cultural force in India, incorporates a wide range of religious beliefs and elaborate rituals. Hinduism emphasizes transmigration of souls—a person's soul experiences a series of reincarnations, and that person's position in the cosmic scale depends on how well he or she performs duties and rituals. Reincarnation ends only when a soul reaches the highest spiritual level and is reabsorbed in Brahma, the divine power.[10]

■ Caste system

The four original castes were **Brahmins**, priest-educators; Kshatriyas, rulers, judges, and warriors; Vaishyas, merchants; and Shudras, the farmers. At the bottom of the caste system were the untouchables, who performed the most menial work. Social mobility did not exist. People stayed in the caste into which they were born, and learned their duties and roles by imitating parents and other adults. Schooling was reserved for the upper castes, primarily the Brahmins. By outlawing caste-based discrimination, modern India has imposed an "affirmative action" for lower caste members. However, like racism in the United States, discrimination still exists.

[9]See Stanley A. Wolport, Herman Kulke and Dietmar Rothermund, *A History of India* (New York: Routledge, 1998).
[10]Arvind Sharma, ed. *The Study of Hinduism* (Columbia: University of South Carolina Press, 2003; also see Mehdi Nakosteen, *The History and Philosophy of Education* (New York: Ronald Press, 1965), pp. 23–40.

Evolution of Indian Education

Education in India reflects the general historical pattern of assimilating different cultures. Earlier schools reflected cultural changes brought by the Aryans. Ancient India had the following types of schools:

■ Vedas

- Brahminic schools, for the priestly caste, stressed religion, philosophy, and the **Vedas**. The Vedas, the Bhagavad Gita, and the Upanishads, Hinduism's sacred religious books, portray the goal of life as a search for universal spiritual truths. The quest for truth, Indian educators believe, requires disciplined meditation. Contemporary transcendental meditation and yoga follow these ancient Indian principles for finding inner spiritual truth and serenity.
- *Tols* were one-room schools where a single teacher taught religion and law.
- Court schools, sponsored by princes, taught literature, law, and administration.

■ Schools and teaching

Hindu educational philosophy, emphasizing religious purposes, prescribed appropriate teacher–student relationships. The teacher, an *ayoha,* was to encourage students to respect all life and to search for truth. Students were to respect teachers as a source of wisdom, and teachers were to refrain from humiliating students.[11]

■ Mughuls

The Mughul dynasty, established after the Muslim invasions, introduced the Islamic religion and Persian and Arabic philosophy, science, literature, astronomy, mathematics, medicine, art, music, and architecture.

■ English entry

By the time the English entered India in the late eighteenth century, India's schools were conducted either by Hindus or Muslims or by smaller sects such as Buddhists, Jains, and Parsis. Only about 10 percent of India's children, mostly boys, attended. Hindu higher schools, conducted by Brahmins, emphasized religious literature, mathematics, astronomy, and Sanskrit grammar. Muslim schools, called *madrassahs,* were attached to mosques and emphasized grammar and the Koran.[12]

When the British established their colonial rule in India, they encountered an ancient civilization with many languages and religions. The British, valuing English more than India's tongues, made English the official language for government and commerce and established English-language schools to train Indians for positions in the British-controlled civil service.

India's Contribution to World and Western Education

Ancient India's legacy to the world is its example of how education can help a civilization endure over the centuries. Through cultural assimilation and readaptation, Indian civilization has survived to the present. In today's climate of rising ethnic and religious tensions, India continues to face profound challenges in assimilating and respecting diverse cultures. The United States and other culturally pluralistic nations face similar challenges. India's situation reveals how caste, like racism in the United States, was once perpetuated by society and indoctrination but is now being corrected through educational processes. You, as a teacher, will probably be challenged by your students' diversity. How will you use multiculturalism as a means of promoting cultural diversity in your classroom?

---

[11]Nandish Patel, "A Comparative Exposition of Western and Vedic Theories of the Institution of Education," *International Journal of Educational Management* 8 (1994), pp. 9–14.
[12]Lawrence James, *Raj: The Making and Unmaking of British India* (New York: St. Martin's Press, 1998).

REFOCUS **Think back to the Focus Questions listed at the beginning of this chapter. How would you answer the first five questions if you were asked to summarize education in ancient India? What similarities and differences exist in the Indian and American approaches to cultural pluralism?**

▶ Education in Ancient Egypt

Ancient Egypt—one of the world's earliest civilizations—developed, like other early populations—as a river-valley culture. Because of the Nile River's life-sustaining water, agricultural groups established small village settlements, organized into tribal kingdoms, on the riverbanks. About 3000 B.C. these kingdoms consolidated into a large empire, which eventually became a highly organized and centralized political colossus.

■ An unchanging cosmos

An important Egyptian religious and political principle affirmed that the pharaoh, the emperor, was of divine origin. The concept of divine emperorship gave social, cultural, political, and educational stability to the Egyptian empire by endowing it with supernaturally sanctioned foundations. Knowledge and values were seen as reflecting an orderly, unchanging, and eternal cosmos. The concept of a king-priest also gave the priestly elite high status and considerable power in Egyptian society. The educational system reinforced this status and power by making the priestly elite guardians of the state culture.

Religious and Secular Concerns

Educationally, the Egyptians were both worldly and otherworldly. Although preoccupied with the supernatural, they also developed technologies to irrigate the Nile Valley and to design and build the massive pyramids and temples. To administer and defend their vast empire, they studied statecraft, and their concern with mummification led them to study medicine, anatomy, and embalming. The Egyptians also developed a system of writing, a hieroglyphic script that enabled them to create and transmit a written culture.

■ Temple and court schools

The Egyptian empire required an educated bureaucracy to collect and record taxes. By 2700 B.C. the Egyptians had in place an extensive system of temple and court schools. A basic school function was to train scribes, many of whom were priests, in reading and writing. Schools often were part of the temple complex, which furthered the close relationship between formal education and religion.[13] After receiving preliminary education, boys studied the literature appropriate to their future professions. Special advanced schools existed for certain kinds of priests, government officials, and physicians.

■ Educating scribes

In the scribal schools, students learned to write the hieroglyphic script by copying documents on papyrus, sheets made from reeds growing along the Nile. Teachers dictated to students, who copied what they heard. The goal was to reproduce a correct, exact copy of a text. Often students would chant a short passage until they had memorized it thoroughly. Those who advanced studied mathematics, astronomy, religion, poetry, literature, medicine, and architecture.

---

[13]James Mulhern, *A History of Education, A Social Interpretation* (New York: Ronald Press, 1959), pp. 55–79.

Egypt's Historical Controversies

■ Traditional interpretation

Ancient Egypt's role in shaping Western civilization has become controversial. In 332 B.C. Egypt was conquered by Alexander the Great and incorporated into Hellenistic civilization, which in turn had been shaped by ancient Greek culture. The conventional historical interpretation was that ancient Egyptian civilization was a highly static despotism and that its major cultural legacy was its great architectural monuments. This interpretation saw Greek culture, especially Athenian democracy, as the cradle of Western civilization.

■ Bernal's theory

A highly controversial interpretation by Martin Bernal argues that the Greeks borrowed many of their concepts about government, philosophy, the arts, and sciences from ancient Egypt. Furthermore, the Egyptians, geographically located in North Africa, were an African people, and the origins of Western culture are therefore African.[14] Though they recognize the interactions between Egyptians and Greeks, Bernal's critics contend that he greatly overemphasizes Egypt's influence on ancient Greece. While historians continue to debate the matter, tentative findings indicate that Egyptian–Greek contacts, particularly at Crete, introduced the Greeks to Egyptian knowledge such as mathematics, and to Egyptian art forms.

■ The past as a source of power

This intriguing historical controversy has important ideological significance. Whoever interprets the past gains the power of illuminating and shaping the present. In particular, the controversy relates to a current debate about Afrocentrism and an Afrocentric curriculum in schools. In the next section we turn to the ancient Greeks. Whether influenced directly or indirectly by the Egyptians, the Greeks continue to hold an important place in the history of education. Keep in mind, however, that most historical cultures have borrowed from one another in many ways, and the roots of Greek thought may indeed be traceable to Egypt or elsewhere.

► Education in Ancient Greek and Roman Civilizations

The educational history of ancient Greece and Rome illuminates the origin of many persistent issues that today's teachers face. Among the educational questions the Greeks and Romans debated were What is the true, the good, and the beautiful? Who are worthy models for children to imitate? How does education shape good citizens? How should education respond to social, economic, and political change?

■ Homeric education

Generations have thrilled to the dramatic suspense of Homer's epic poems, the *Iliad* and the *Odyssey*. Appearing about 1200 B.C., Homer's epics helped Greeks define themselves and their culture. Like ritual ceremonies in preliterate societies, Homer's dramatic portrayal of the Greek warriors' battles against the Trojans served important educational purposes: (1) it preserved the culture by transmitting it from adults to the young; (2) it cultivated Greek cultural identity based on mythic and historical origins; and (3) it shaped the character of the young.[15] Agamemnon, Ulysses, Achilles, and other warriors dramatically personified life's heroic dimensions. Using these heroes as role models, young Greeks learned about the values that made life worth living, the behaviors expected of warrior-knights, and the character defects that led to one's downfall.[16]

---

[14]Martin Bernal, *Black Athena: The Afroasiatic Roots of Classical Civilization: The Fabrication of Ancient Greece 1785–1985* (New Brunswick, N.J.: Rutgers University Press, 1987), pp. 2–3.
[15]Louis Goldman, "Homer, Literacy, and Education," *Educational Theory* (Fall 1989), pp. 391–400.
[16]Robert Holmes Beck, "The *Iliad*: Principles and Lessons," *Educational Theory* (Spring 1986), pp. 179–195.

An illustration of a student learning the alphabet at a school in ancient Greece. From a vase by Duris, fifth century B.C., Ashmolean Museum, Oxford.
(© Corbis-Bettmann)

■ Citizenship education

Ancient Greece also illuminates education's role in forming good citizens. Just as Americans are likely to disagree on the precise formula for educating good citizens, so the Greeks debated the issue. Unlike the great empires of China and Egypt, ancient Greece was divided into small and often competing city-states that, like Athens and Sparta, defined civic responsibilities and rights differently. After experimenting with different forms of government, Athens became a democracy that emphasized the shared public responsibility of its citizens. Sparta, Athens' chief rival, was an authoritarian military dictatorship.[17] To match its distinctive government, each city-state, or polis, had its own type of citizenship education.

■ Enculturation and formal education

The Greeks recognized the importance of interrelating enculturation—immersion and participation in the city-state's total culture—with formal education. Through enculturation Greek youths were prepared to become citizens of their society. Formal education, in turn, provided the knowledge needed to fulfill more completely the society's expectations of the good life. For example, the Athenians believed that a free man needed a liberal education to perform his civic duties as well as to develop personally.[18] In contrast, Sparta used formal education for military training.

■ The role of slaves

Greek society rested at least partially on slave labor. The majority of slaves, including women and children, were prisoners of war or those judicially condemned to servitude. Although a few educated slaves tutored wealthy children in Athens, most slaves were trained to perform specific farming or commercial skills. The Athenians

[17]Nigel M. Kennell, *The Gymnasium of Virtue: Education and Culture in Ancient Sparta* (Chapel Hill: University of North Carolina Press, 1995).
[18]Kevin Robb, *Literacy and Paideia in Ancient Greece* (New York: Oxford University Press, 1994).

believed that the liberal education appropriate for free men was useless for slaves. Contemporary debates between proponents of vocational and liberal education go back to the Athenian distinction between vocational training for slaves and a liberal education for free citizens.

■ Education of women

In male-dominated Greek society, only a minority of exceptional women received any formal education. In Athens women had severely limited legal and economic rights, and few attended schools. More fortunate young women received instruction at home from tutors. Others, such as priestesses of religious cults, learned religious rituals at temple schools. In contrast, Sparta's young women received athletic and military training to prepare them to be healthy mothers of future Spartan soldiers.

The Sophists

In the fifth century B.C., a changing economy brought new social and educational patterns to Greece, especially Athens. The older landed aristocracy was displaced by new commercial classes that had profited from Athenian expansion and colonization. This socioeconomic change created the conditions for the **Sophists**.

■ Wandering teachers

■ Grammar, logic, and rhetoric

The Sophists, a group of traveling educators, developed new teaching methods to instruct this emergent commercial class in the skills of public speaking. Proficiency in oratory was highly important in a democracy such as Athens, where it could be used to persuade the assembly and the courts in one's favor.[19]

The Sophists sought to develop their students' communication skills so they could become successful advocates and legislators. The Sophists' most important subjects were logic, grammar, and rhetoric—subjects that later developed into the liberal arts. Logic, the rules of correct argument, trained students to organize their presentations clearly, and grammar developed their powers of using language effectively. **Rhetoric**, the study of persuasive speech, was especially important for future orators.

■ Knowledge as an instrument

The Sophists claimed that they could educate their students to win public debates by teaching them (1) how to use crowd psychology to know what would appeal to an audience; (2) how to organize a persuasive and convincing argument; and (3) skill in public speaking—knowing what words, examples, and lines of reasoning to use to win the debate or the case.

If they were alive today, the Sophists would probably argue that their approach to education gives people what they want—the ability to organize ideas and to present them so forcefully that people would be persuaded to accept their claims. Critics of the Sophists, however, accused them of emphasizing argument-winning techniques over seeking the truth of the matter at hand.

The Sophists were like modern image-makers who use the media to "package" political candidates and celebrities. Although today political discussion and candidates' debates take place on television rather than live in the Athenian town center, the Sophists would argue their techniques remain valid. It is still important to know one's audience, to appeal to their needs, and to use skilled persuasion to convince them. They would consider focus groups, public opinion polls, and negative advertising useful persuasive tools.

■ Protagoras's method

In many ways, the Sophists developed a strikingly modern approach to education. Protagoras (485–414 B.C.), one of the most prominent Sophists, developed a

---

[19]"The Philosophy of the Sophists," **http:www.radicalacademy.com/philsophists.htm**.

highly effective five-step teaching strategy.[20] He (1) delivered an outstanding speech so that students knew their teacher could do what he was attempting to teach them; this speech also gave them a model to imitate. Then Protagoras had the students (2) examine the great speeches of famous orators to amplify the available models; (3) study the key subjects of logic, grammar, and rhetoric; and (4) deliver practice orations, which he assessed to provide feedback to students. Finally, (5) the student orators delivered public speeches. Protagoras's method resembles present-day teacher-education programs, in which prospective teachers study the liberal arts and professional subjects, learn various teaching strategies, and do practice teaching under the guidance of an experienced cooperating teacher.

■ Enduring truth or relativism?

The Sophists' appearance on the scene in ancient Greece raised serious educational questions whose answers led to controversies still with us today. The Sophists were moral relativists, arguing that what we need to know depends on the circumstances in which we live. Socrates, Plato, and Aristotle all challenged their relativism and insisted on the existence of enduring truths that we must know. Isocrates, a teacher of oratory, tried to resolve the controversy by saying that we need to know what is true but also to apply it to the situations in which we live. We'll discuss the views of all four of these educational philosophers.

Socrates: Education by Self-Examination

■ Universal principles

Unlike the Sophists, who claimed that knowledge depended on the situations in which people used it, Socrates (469–399 B.C.) believed that knowledge was based on what was true universally—at all places and times. Socrates is important in educational history because he firmly defended the academic freedom to think, question, and teach. He was also significant as the teacher of Plato, who later systematized many of Socrates' ideas.[21]

■ Moral excellence

Socrates' philosophy stressed the ethical principle that a person should strive for moral excellence, live wisely, and act rationally. Moral excellence, Socrates believed, was far superior to the Sophists' technical training.

■ Role of the Socratic teacher

Socrates' concept of the teacher differed from that of the Sophists. He did not believe that knowledge or wisdom could be transmitted from a teacher to a student because he believed the concepts of true knowledge were present, but buried, within the person's mind. The teacher must ask the right questions so that students think critically about important issues. A truly liberal education would stimulate learners to discover ideas by bringing to consciousness the truth that was present but latent in their minds.

■ Self-examination, dialogue, and the Socratic method

Socrates' educational aim was to help individuals define themselves through self-examination. In this way each person could seek the truth that is universally present in all people. As a teacher, Socrates asked leading questions that stimulated students to investigate perennial human concerns about the meaning of life, truth, and justice. The students then became involved in lively but rigorous discussion, or dialogue, in which they clarified, criticized, and reconstructed their basic concepts. For Socrates, dialogue did not mean merely sharing opinions; it meant reflecting on and criticizing them to find the underlying truth. This approach is still known as

---

[20]Edward Schiappa, *Protagoras and Logos: A Study in Greek Philosophy and Rhetoric* (Columbia: University of South Carolina Press, 2003; also see L. Glenn Smith, *Lives in Education: People and Ideas in the Development of Teaching* (Ames, Iowa: Educational Studies Press, 1984), pp. 7–9.
[21]Gary Alan Scott, *Plato's Socrates as Educator* (Albany: State University of New York Press, 2000), pp. 1–12. Also see Alven Neiman, "Ironic Schooling: Socrates, Pragmatism and the Higher Learning," *Educational Theory* (Fall 1991), pp. 371–384.

the **Socratic method**. As a teacher, you might use the Socratic method by asking students questions designed to elicit their critical thinking on a current or historical issue, or about a work of literature that they have been assigned to read.

Frequenting Athens' marketplace, Socrates attracted a group of young men who joined him in critically examining all kinds of issues—religious, political, moral, and aesthetic. But as a social critic, Socrates made powerful enemies. Then, as now, some people, including those in high places, feared that critical thinking would challenge the status quo and lead to unrest. In 399 B.C., after being tried on the charge of impiety to the gods and corrupting Athenian youth, Socrates was condemned to death, a sentence he refused to avoid.

Plato: Eternal Truths and Values

■ Reality as universal, eternal ideas

Socrates' pupil Plato (427–346 B.C.) followed his mentor's educational path. Plato founded the Academy, a philosophical school, in 387 B.C. He wrote *Protagoras*, a discourse on virtue, and the *Republic* and the *Laws*, treatises on politics, law, and education.[22] Rejecting the Sophists' relativism, Plato argued that reality consisted of an unchanging world of perfect ideas—universal concepts such as truth, goodness, justice, and beauty. Individual instances of these concepts, as they appear to our senses, are but imperfect representations of the universal and eternal concepts that reside in an absolute idea, the Form of the Good.

■ Reminiscence

Plato's theory of knowledge is based on **reminiscence**, a process by which individuals recall the ideas present but latent in their minds. Reminiscence implies that the human soul, before birth, has lived in a spiritual world of ideas, the source of all truth and knowledge. At birth, these *innate* ideas are repressed within one's subconscious mind. For Plato, learning means that one rediscovers or recollects these perfect ideas.[23]

■ Universalism versus relativism

Unlike relativism's fluidity, universalism asserts that because sense impressions distort reality, genuine knowledge is intellectual, changeless, and eternal, not sensory. There is but one idea of perfection for all human beings regardless of when or where they live. Because what is true is always true, education should also be universal and unchanging. The debate over this idea is presented in the Taking Issue box.

■ Innate ideas

The belief that innate ideas are latently present in the mind has had a powerful influence on early Western education. Education in India also reflected belief in innate knowledge, as described earlier in the chapter. Vedic education encouraged meditation to discover innate knowledge. In the West, the theory of innate ideas was challenged by later educational reformers such as Locke, Pestalozzi, Dewey, and others, whose ideas are described in the chapter on Pioneers in Education. Many later educational controversies, even the current interest in constructivism, can be seen as counterarguments to Plato's theory of ideas.

■ *The Republic*

Plato's Ideal Society. In Plato's *Republic*, Plato projected a plan for a perfect society ruled by philosopher-kings, an intellectual elite. Although Plato's utopian state was never implemented, his ideas are useful in portraying an idealized version of a certain kind of education.[24] *The Republic* divided inhabitants into three classes:

[22]Devin Stauffer, *Plato's Introduction to the Question of Justice* (Albany: State University of New York Press, 2001).
[23]Gerald L. Gutek, *Historical and Philosophical Foundations of Education: A Biographical Introduction* (Columbus, Ohio: Merrill/Prentice Hall, 2005), pp. 37–40.
[24]Plato, *Republic* (London: Folio Society, 2003; also see *Selected Dialogues of Plato: The Benjamin Jowett Translation* (New York: Modern Library, 2001).

taking issue

Universal Truth or Cultural Relativism?

In classical Greece, the question of whether education should reflect universal truth or the beliefs relative to different peoples living at a particular place and time was debated. Plato, who argued that truth was unchanging, debated this issue with the Sophists, who considered everything relative to time and circumstances. The issue is debated today by those who want schools to instill basic morality and by others who want students to clarify their values.

Universalists contend that what is true today has always been true. Relativists argue that changing values make life satisfying at a particular place and time.

Arguments PRO

1 Truth is universal and eternal. As human beings search for truth, their quest will bring them to the same general ideas and values. What is true is true in all places and at all times. Changing public opinion polls do not change truth.

2 Although different races and ethnic and language groups inhabit the earth, they are all members of the same human family and thus share common hopes and dreams.

3 Education, as Socrates and Plato argued, should engage students in seeking answers to the great questions, such as What is true, good, and beautiful? Especially in the new computer-driven information age, we need educational programs based on enduring truth and value.

4 Schools should emphasize the universal truths and values found in religion, philosophy, mathematics, science, and other subjects that transcend particular cultural and political barriers.

Arguments CON

1 What is called "truth" is really a tentative knowledge claim that is relative to different groups living in different places at different times. What is true at a given time is that which solves a problem in living.

2 Society is relative and changing. Human behavior needs to be flexible to adapt to social, economic, political, and technological change.

3 Education is a pragmatic tool, a means of personal and social adaptation. As such, it emphasizes new ways of learning to prepare people to be efficient users of new technologies. It is more important for students to be computer competent than to ponder unanswerable questions about the true, the good, and the beautiful.

4 Schooling, based on people's needs, will differ from culture to culture and from time to time. That is why the constructivist approach, by which students create their own conceptions of reality, is so useful in today's schools.

(1) the philosopher-kings, the intellectual rulers; (2) the auxiliaries, the military defenders; and (3) the workers, who produced goods and provided services. A person's intellectual capacity would determine his or her class assignment.

A similarity exists between the ideas of Confucius, the ancient Indians, and Plato. In all three instances, society would be structured into a hierarchy, with the most intellectual persons located at the highest level in positions of authority. In contrast to these hierarchical societies, the Sophists argued that anyone could rise to the top if they acquired the techniques that empowered them.

■ Education corresponding to social role

Once assigned to a class, individuals in the Republic would receive the education appropriate to their social role. The philosopher-kings, educated for leadership, also were responsible for identifying the intellectually able in the next generation and preparing them for their destined roles. The second class, the warriors, courageous rather than intellectual, would be trained to defend the Republic and to take orders from the philosopher-kings. The third and largest class, the workers, would be trained as farmers and artisans. With an educational track for each group, the Republic prepared its members for their appropriate functions, which in turn contributed to the community's harmony and efficient functioning. Modern-day critics of tracking students in schools argue that screening devices, such as Plato's, actually tend to reproduce the existing class situation rather than encourage movement among social classes.

■ Women's education

Unlike Athenians, Plato believed that women should have the same privileges and responsibilities accorded men.[25] Women, too, fell within the three classes to which Plato assigned human beings. Women who possessed high-level cognitive powers could become members of the ruling philosophical elite; others of lesser intellect would be assigned to lower ranks. Like men, women would receive the education or training appropriate to their abilities and their destined occupations.

■ State-run nurseries

Plato's Curriculum. Plato's curriculum fits the educational objectives of a hierarchical rather than an egalitarian society. Fearing that parents would pass on their ignorance and prejudices to their children, Plato wanted children reared by experts in child care. Children, separated from their parents, would live in state nurseries and so acquire good habits and purge harmful ones.

■ Plato's basic curriculum

From ages six to eighteen, children would be in schools, where they studied music and gymnastics. "Music," in Plato's definition, was a broad subject that included reading, writing, literature, arithmetic, choral singing, and dancing. After mastering reading and writing, students would read the approved classics. Plato regarded literature as a powerful force in character formation and believed that children should read only poems and stories that epitomized truthfulness, obedience to authorities, courage, and control of emotions. After mastering basic arithmetic, students would apply themselves to geometry and astronomy. Gymnastics, which consisted of functional exercises useful for military training, such as fencing, archery, javelin throwing, and horseback riding, were considered essential for character building and for physical development. Plato also included rules of diet and hygiene in his curriculum.

■ Higher education

From ages eighteen to twenty, students would pursue intensive physical and military training. At twenty, the future philosopher-kings would be selected for ten years of additional higher education in mathematics, geometry, astronomy, music, and science. At age thirty, the less intellectually capable among this group would become civil servants; the most intellectually capable would continue the higher philosophical study of metaphysics, the search for the principles that explained ultimate reality. When their studies were completed, the philosopher-kings would begin to direct the Republic's military and political affairs. At age fifty, the philosopher-kings would become the Republic's elder statesmen.

Aristotle: Cultivation of Rationality

Plato's student Aristotle (384–322 B.C.) was the tutor of Alexander the Great. Aristotle founded the Lyceum, an Athenian philosophical school, and wrote exten-

---

[25]Robert S. Brumbaugh, "Plato's Ideal Curriculum and Contemporary Philosophy of Education," *Educational Theory* (Spring 1987), pp. 169–177.

sively on physics, astronomy, zoology, botany, logic, ethics, and metaphysics. His *Nicomachean Ethics* and *Politics* examine education in relation to society and government.[26]

■ An objective reality

Unlike his mentor Plato, who believed that reality exists in the realm of pure ideas, Aristotle held that reality exists objectively. Whereas Plato founded philosophical idealism, Aristotle established realism. (Both idealism and realism are discussed in the chapter on Philosophical Roots of Education.)

Aristotle noted that objects exist outside of our minds but believed that, by sensation and abstraction, we can acquire knowledge about them. Aristotle insisted that humans possess intellect—the power to think and to reason. As rational beings, they have the potential to know and to live according to the natural laws governing the universe.

■ Sensation as the root of knowledge

For Aristotle, knowing begins with one's sensation of objects in the environment. From this sensory experience, one forms concepts about objects. The Aristotelian emphasis on sensory experience as the beginning of knowing and of instruction was later stressed by eighteenth- and nineteenth-century educators such as Locke and Pestalozzi.

■ Education as cultivation of rationality

Aristotle on Education.   In his *Politics,* Aristotle argues that the good community rests on its members' rationality. If education, the cultivation of rationality, is neglected, then the community suffers. Like Plato, Aristotle distinguished between liberal education and technical training. Aristotle saw the liberal arts as enlarging a person's horizons, consciousness, and choices, and he saw vocational training as having only limited value. Contemporary debates between liberal and career educators often reflect the same issues Aristotle and other Greek theorists examined, and as a teacher you may encounter a version of the same debate when students ask you why they should learn something they are convinced they will never use. What is your rationale for teaching certain skills and subjects but not others?

■ Aristotle's curriculum

Aristotle recommended compulsory schooling. Infant schooling was to consist of play, physical activity, and appropriate stories. Children from ages seven to fourteen learned basic numeracy and literacy and proper moral habits to prepare them for future study in liberal arts. Their curriculum also included physical education and music to cultivate proper emotional dispositions. From age fifteen through twenty-one, youths would study mathematics, geometry, astronomy, grammar, literature, poetry, rhetoric, ethics, and politics. At age twenty-one, students would proceed to more theoretical subjects, such as physics, cosmology, biology, psychology, logic, and metaphysics.

■ Limited roles for women

Believing women were intellectually inferior to men, Aristotle was concerned only with male education. Girls were to be trained to perform the household and child-rearing duties necessary for their future roles as wives and mothers.

■ Knowledge as concepts based on objects

Aristotle's Theory of Knowledge.   Aristotle, a Realist, differs from Plato, an Idealist, in that his concepts of knowledge arise in objects rather than from preexisting ideas in the mind. Knowledge, according to Aristotle, is always about objects; education focuses on the classification of objects into subject matters. For example, if you were teaching botany using the Aristotelian method, you could teach about trees as a class, a general category in botanical reality, and also about the particular trees that are individual members of the class.

---

[26]Christopher Rowe and Sarah Brodie, *Aristotle: Nicomachean Ethics* (Oxford U.K.: Oxford University Press, 2002); also see Mary M. Spangler, *Aristotle on Teaching* (Lanham, Md.: University Press of America, 1998).

■ Aristotle's lasting influence

An Aristotelian school's primary goal is to cultivate each student's rationality. As academic institutions, schools should offer a prescribed subject-matter curriculum based on scholarly and scientific disciplines. Teachers must possess expert knowledge of their subjects and be skilled in motivating and transmitting knowledge to students. Aristotle's philosophy has had great significance in Western education. Along with Christian doctrine, it became a foundation of medieval Scholastic education, discussed later in this chapter, and of Realism, discussed in the chapter on Philosophical Roots of Education.

Isocrates: Oratory and Rhetoric

The Greek rhetorician Isocrates (436–388 B.C.) is significant for his exceptionally well-constructed educational theory, which emphasized both knowledge and rhetorical skills.[27] His theory took a middle course between the conflicts of the Sophists and Plato. Isocrates' treatise *Against the Sophists* explained the method used at his school.

■ Emphasis on rhetoric

Isocrates considered education's primary goal was to prepare clear-thinking, rational, and truthful statesmen. Civic reform, he believed, required educating virtuous leaders who could be effective administrators. Of the liberal studies, Isocrates held that rhetoric, defined as the rational expression of thought, was most important in cultivating morality and political leadership. Rhetorical education should combine arts and sciences and effective communication. The worthy orator should argue for honorable causes that advance the public good. Above reproach, the orator would persuade people to follow good policies. Isocrates opposed Sophist teaching of rhetoric as merely persuasive routines or public relations techniques.

Isocrates' students, who attended his school for four years, studied rhetoric, politics, history, and ethics. They analyzed and imitated model orations and practiced public speaking. As a model teacher, Isocrates believed that he was responsible for influencing students by his own demonstration of knowledge, skill, and ethical conduct.

■ Balancing Plato and the Sophists

Although Isocrates opposed the Sophists' crass opportunism, he also rejected Plato's contention that education was purely theoretical and abstract. For Isocrates, education contributed to public service guided by knowledge. Isocrates influenced the rhetorical tradition in education, in particular the Roman educational theorist Quintilian. By recognizing the humanistic dimension of rhetoric, Isocrates also contributed to the ideal of the liberally educated person.

Education in Ancient Rome

While Greek culture and education were developing in the eastern Mediterranean, the Romans were consolidating their political position on the Italian peninsula and throughout the western Mediterranean. In their movement from small republic to great empire, the Romans initially were preoccupied with war and politics. Once they became an imperial power, they concentrated on the administration, law, and diplomacy needed to maintain the empire. Whereas the Greeks were noted for philosophy, the Romans concentrated on educating practical politicians, able administrators, and skilled generals.

---

[27]Ekaterina V. Haskins. *Logos and Power in Isocrates and Aristotle* (Columbia: University of South Carolina Press, 2004); also see Gerald L. Gutek, *A History of the Western Educational Experience* (Prospect Heights, Ill.: Waveland Press, 1995), pp. 52–54.

■ Access to education

As in ancient Greece, only a minority of Romans was formally educated. Schooling was reserved for those who had both the money to pay the tuition and the time to attend school.

■ Primary and secondary schools

Whereas upper-class girls often learned to read and write at home or were taught by tutors, boys from these families attended a *ludus,* a primary school, and then secondary schools taught by Latin and Greek grammar teachers. Boys were escorted to these schools by educated Greek slaves, called *pedagogues,* from which the word *pedagogy,* meaning the art of instruction, is derived.

■ Ideal of the orator

Rome's educational ideal was exemplified in the orator. The ideal Roman orator was the broadly and liberally educated man of public life—the senator, lawyer, teacher, civil servant, and politician. To examine the Roman ideal of oratory, we turn to Quintilian.

Quintilian: Master of Oratory. Marcus Fabius Quintilianus (A.D. 35–95), or Quintilian, was one of imperial Rome's most highly recognized rhetoricians. The emperor appointed him to the first chair of Latin rhetoric.

■ Instruction based on stages of growth

Quintilian's *Institutio Oratoria,* a systematic educational treatise, included (1) the education preparatory to studying rhetoric, (2) rhetorical and educational theory, and (3) the practice of public speaking or declamation. Quintilian made the important educational point that instruction should be based on stages of human growth and development. Anticipating the modern teacher's concern for learners' individual differences, he advised that instruction be appropriate to students' readiness and abilities. He stressed the importance of early childhood in forming behavior, and he recommended that teachers motivate students by making learning interesting and attractive.

For the first stage, from birth until age seven, when the child was impulsive and concerned with immediate needs and desires, he advised parents to select well-trained and well-spoken nurses, pedagogues, and companions for their children.

■ Reading and writing

In Quintilian's second stage of education, from seven to fourteen, the child should learn from sense experiences, form clear ideas, and train his memory. He now learned to write the languages that he already spoke. The primary teacher, the *litterator,* who taught reading and writing in the ludus, must have a worthy character and teaching competence. Instruction in reading and writing should be slow and thorough, and children would learn the alphabet using a set of ivory letters. Like Montessori many centuries later, Quintilian advised that children learn to write by tracing the letters' outlines. Anticipating modern education, he urged that the school day include breaks for games and recreation so that students could refresh themselves and renew their energy.

■ Study of liberal arts

For the third stage of education, from fourteen to seventeen, Quintilian emphasized the liberal arts. Students studied Greek and Latin grammar, literature, history, and mythology bilingually and biculturally. Students also studied music, geometry, astronomy, and gymnastics.

■ Rhetorical studies

Prospective orators undertook rhetorical studies, the fourth stage, from ages seventeen to twenty-one. In rhetorical studies Quintilian included drama, poetry, law, philosophy, public speaking, declamation, and debate.[28] Declamations—systematic speaking exercises—were of great importance. After being properly prepared, the novice orator spoke to a public audience in the forum and then returned to the master rhetorician for expert criticism. The teacher corrected the student's mistakes with a sense of authority but also with patience, tact, and consideration.

---

[28]James J. Murphy, ed., *Quintilian on the Teaching of Speaking and Writing* (Carbondale: Southern Illinois University Press, 1987).

The Greek and Roman Contributions to Western Education

■ Liberal arts

Western culture and education inherited a rich legacy from ancient Greece and Rome. Many of the cultural and educational structures that shaped Western civilization developed in classical Greece and Rome. Believing it possible to cultivate human excellence, the Greeks and Romans gave education an important function in society's political well-being. Some Greco-Roman educational practices, however, including the distinction between liberal education and vocational training, have led to curricular controversies lasting throughout Western educational history.

Many ideas of the Greeks and Romans influenced Arab scholars, who preserved and interpreted them. As Europeans encountered Arabic scholarship, these ideas were transmitted to European and later American culture.

REFOCUS Think back to the Focus Questions listed at the beginning of this chapter. How would you answer those questions if you were asked to summarize educational contributions from ancient Greece and Rome? Which contributions from these periods are you glad to inherit as a teacher? Which ones will you work to modify?

▶ Islam, Arabic Learning, and Education

Islamic civilization, originating with the Arabs, became a global cultural and educational force through its ability to absorb, reinterpret, and transmit knowledge from one world region to another.[29] The origins of Islamic culture began with Mohammed (569–632), an Arab religious reformer and proselytizer. Mohammed began his religious mission in Arabia, in Mecca, in 610, where he preached the need for repentance and living an upright, moral life. Gradually, he organized his ideas into **Islam**, a new religion. Today, Islam is the religious faith of an eighth of the world's

Islamic religion and culture are widespread and in the twenty-first century interactions are increasing between Muslims and others throughout the world. This photograph is of students at an Islamic school in Asia. *(Stone/Getty Images)*

[29]Malise Ruthven, *Islam in the World* (New York: Oxford University Press, 2000).

population. It is the dominant religion in the Arab countries of the Middle East and North Africa, and its influence extends to Indonesia, Malaysia, and Pakistan, as well as other countries in Asia. In addition, Muslims, followers of Islam, live in countries throughout the world, although often as minorities.

Revered as a prophet, Mohammed's followers believed he spoke the revealed word of Allah, or God, which is recorded in the **Koran**. Written in Arabic, the Koran became not only Islam's most sacred religious book, but also the authoritative ethical and legal source in Arab and other Islamic countries. Much of the Koran also contributed to a sense of Arabic and Islamic cultural unity. Once feuding Arab clans united under the banner of extending Islam throughout the world.

By 661 Arabian forces had occupied and established Islam as the official religion in Palestine, Syria, Persia, and Egypt. The cities of Baghdad, Cairo, Damascus, and Cordoba became renowned centers of Islamic culture and education. Baghdad, in particular, was a prominent educational center, where Arab, Greek, Persian, and Jewish scholars exchanged ideas.

Followers of Mohammed then proceeded to extend Islamic influence through conquest and conversion. After conquering most of North Africa, Arab power flowed into Spain. Here, Islamic Arabs and western Christians struggled for power and territory, but also borrowed ideas from each other.[30] The Islamic, or Moorish, kingdoms of Spain persisted until 1492, when they were conquered by the armies of Christian Spain.[31] During the Moorish period, Cordoba, with a population of 500,000 people, 700 mosques, and 70 libraries, became a leading Arab cultural and educational center.[32]

Islamic scholars translated many ancient Greek authors such as Aristotle, Euclid, Archimedes, and Hippocrates into Arabic. The translated works became important in Islamic education and, through contacts between Arabs and Europeans, were reintroduced into Western education. In particular, Ibn-Rushd, or Averroës (1126–1198) wrote important commentaries on Aristotle that influenced medieval European scholastic educators.

Islamic scholarship led to advances in astronomy, mathematics, and medicine. In mathematics, Arab scholars adopted the number system from the Indians but made the crucial addition of zero. This innovation made it possible to replace the cumbersome Latin system.

In the twenty-first century, interaction has continued between the Arabic and Islamic cultures and the Western world. Despite a great deal of recent conflict between the West, especially the United States, and Arab and Islamic groups, more positive encounters have occurred between Arabs and Americans. In particular, many Americans are giving more attention to and learning more about the contributions of Arabic civilization and the Islamic religion to world culture.

In the aftermath of the attack on the World Trade Center on September 11, 2001, and the United States' response with a "war on terrorism," attention has increased toward studying Arabic culture and the Islamic religion. Although some of the terrorists were identified as nationals of Arabic countries, the actions of the few do not represent the thinking of all Arab people nor do they reflect Islamic beliefs. To understand changing world dynamics, American schools and colleges are making greater efforts to include units and courses on Arabic peoples and cultures and the Islamic religion.

---

[30]**Http://www.islamicity.com/mosque/ihame/Sec5.htm** (09/25/2003), pp. 1–2.
[31]Mortimer Chambers, Raymond Grew, David Herlihy, Theodore Rabb, and Isser Woloch, *The Western Experience* (New York: Knopf, 1983), pp. 228–235.
[32]**Http://www.islamicity.com/mosque/ihame/Sec5.htm** (09/25/2003), pp. 1–2.

REFOCUS Think back to the Focus Questions listed at the beginning of this chapter. How would you answer those questions if you were asked to summarize educational contributions from the Arabic tradition? How can you combine contributions from diverse sources in your teaching?

▶ Medieval Culture and Education

■ Decline, then revival in learning

Historians designate the millennium between the fall of Rome and the Renaissance (c. 500–1400) as the Middle Ages, or medieval period. This era of Western culture and education spanned the time between the end of the Greco-Roman classical era and the beginning of what we call the modern period. The medieval period was characterized first by a decline in learning and then by its revival by Scholastic educators.

■ Institutions of learning

After the Roman Empire in the west collapsed, the Catholic Church, headed by the pope in Rome, partially filled the resulting political, cultural, and educational vacuum. During the medieval period, European formal primary education fell to the church in parish, chantry, and monastic schools. At the secondary level, both monastic and cathedral schools offered a general studies curriculum. Higher education occurred in the universities of Paris, Bologna, Salerno, Oxford, and Cambridge.[33] Merchant and craft guilds also established some schools that offered basic education as well as training for a trade. Knights learned military tactics and the chivalric code in the castles.

■ Access to schooling

As in the earlier Greek and Roman eras, few people attended medieval schools, primarily men who planned to enter religious vocations as priests, monks, or members of other clerical orders. The vast majority of people were serfs—agricultural workers on the estates of feudal lords—and generally illiterate.

■ Education of medieval women

The condition of women in medieval society varied according to their socio-economic class. Although medieval Christianity stressed the spiritual equality of women and the sacramental nature of marriage, women continued to be consigned to traditional gender-prescribed roles. Girls of the serf and peasant classes learned household and child-rearing chores by imitating their mothers. Women of the noble classes also followed the prescriptions of their class and learned the roles appropriate to the code of chivalry, which often meant managing the domestic life of castle or manor.[34] The medieval church provided an educational opportunity for women through religious communities. Convents, like monasteries, had libraries and schools to prepare nuns to follow the religious rules of their communities.

Aquinas: Scholastic Education

■ Faith and reason combined

By the eleventh century, medieval educators had developed **Scholasticism**—a method of inquiry, scholarship, and teaching. The Scholastics, as the teaching clerics were called, relied on faith and reason as complementary sources of truth. They accepted the sacred scriptures and the writings of the church fathers as sources of God's revealed word, but they also trusted in human reason. The Scholastics believed that

---

[33]C. Stephen Jaeger, *The Envy of Angels: Cathedral Schools and Social Ideals in Medieval Europe, 950–1200* (Philadelphia: University of Pennsylvania Press, 1994), p. 153.
[34]Judith M. Bennett, *Medieval Women in Modern Perspective* (Washington, D.C.: American Historical Association, 2000).

the human mind could deduce first principles that, when illuminated by scriptural authority, were a source of truth.

■ Reconciling scriptures with Greek reasoning

Scholastic philosophy and education reached its zenith in the *Summa Theologiae* of Saint Thomas Aquinas (1225–1274), a Dominican theologian at the University of Paris. Aquinas was primarily concerned with reconciling authorities—that is, linking scriptural faith with Aristotle's Greek philosophy. Aquinas used both faith and reason to answer basic questions about the Christian concept of God, the nature of humankind and the universe, and the relationship between God and humans.[35] For Aquinas, humans possess a physical body and a spiritual soul. Although they live temporarily on Earth, their ultimate purpose is to experience eternity with God. Like Aristotle, Aquinas asserted that human knowledge begins in sensation and is completed by conceptualization. (See Overview 3.2 for the ideas of Aquinas and other educators discussed in this chapter.)

In *de Magistro* (*Concerning the Teacher*), Aquinas portrayed the teacher's vocation as combining faith, love, and learning. Teachers need to be contemplative scholars, active agents of learning, experts in their subjects, skillful instructors, and lovers of humanity.

■ Subject-matter disciplines

Scholastic teachers were clerics, and schools were governed and protected by the church. The curriculum was organized into formal subjects, following the liberal arts tradition; for example, in higher education the subject disciplines were logic, mathematics, natural and moral philosophy, metaphysics, and theology. In their teaching, Scholastics used the syllogism—deductive reasoning—to create organized bodies of knowledge. They emphasized basic principles and their implications. In addition to formal schooling, Aquinas recognized the importance of informal education through family, friends, and environment.[36]

Long after the medieval period and up to the present day, Aquinas's philosophy, called Thomism, has influenced education in Catholic schools, where it is used as the basis of a school-faith community. In the United States, Catholic schools are the largest nonpublic school system, enrolling 2,511,040 students in 8,102 schools.[37] Thomism also influenced nonreligious humanists such as Mortimer Adler, who developed the Paideia proposal, discussed further in the chapter on the Philosophical Roots of Education.

The Medieval Contribution to Western Education

■ Preserving and institutionalizing knowledge

The medieval educators contributed to Western education primarily by preserving and institutionalizing knowledge—that is, by presenting it within an organized framework. Parish, monastic, and cathedral schools all transmitted knowledge in this manner. The epitome of this trend was the medieval university, the foundation for the modern university. Within its walls, medieval educators not only taught but also preserved knowledge by recording and codifying it.

REFOCUS Think back to the Focus Questions listed at the beginning of this chapter. How would you answer if you were asked to summarize educational contributions from medieval Europe?

---

[35]Francis J. Selman, *Saint Thomas Aquinas: Teacher of Truth* (Edinburgh, Scotland: T&T Clark, 1994); and Etienne Gilson, *The Christian Philosophy of St. Thomas Aquinas* (Notre Dame, Ind.: University of Notre Dame Press, 1994).

[36]John W. Donohue, *St. Thomas Aquinas and Education* (New York: Random House, 1968), pp. 76–89.

[37]"Private School Universe Survey, 1999–2000," **http:nces.ed.gov/pubsearch** (01/12/2003).

OVERVIEW 3.2 *Major Educational Theorists, to A.D. 1600*

Theorist	Philosophical Orientation	View of Human Nature
Confucius 551–478 B.C. (Chinese)	Developed ethical system based on hierarchical ordering of human relationships and roles; emphasized order and stability through subordination.	Human beings need the order of a highly stable society in which people accept the duties that come with their station in life.
Socrates 469–399 B.C. (Greek)	Social and educational iconoclast; tended toward philosophical idealism and political conservatism.	Human beings can define themselves by rational self-examination.
Plato 427–346 B.C. (Greek)	Philosophical idealist; sociopolitical conservative.	Human beings can be classified on the basis of their intellectual capabilities.
Aristotle 384–322 B.C. (Greek)	Philosophical realist; view of society, politics, and education based on classical realism.	Human beings have the power of rationality, which should guide their conduct.
Isocrates 436–388 B.C. (Greek)	Rhetorician; oratorical education in service of self and society.	Humans have the power to use speech (discourse) for social and political improvement.
Quintilian A.D. 35–95 (Roman)	Rhetorician; oratory for personal gain and public service.	Certain individuals have the capacity for leadership, based on their disposition, liberal knowledge, and oratorical skill.
Aquinas A.D. 1225–1274 (Italian medieval theologian)	Christian theology and Aristotelian (realist) philosophy.	Human beings possess both a spiritual nature (soul) and a physical nature (body).
Erasmus A.D. 1465–1536 (Dutch Renaissance humanist)	Christian orientation; the educator as social and intellectual critic.	Human beings are capable of profound achievements but also of great stupidity.
Luther A.D. 1483–1546 (German Protestant)	Protestant theological orientation; salvation by faith and individual conscience.	Human beings are saved by faith; individual conscience shaped by scripture and Reformed theology.

▶ Renaissance Classical Humanism

◼ Reviving humanistic aspects of the classics

The Renaissance, which began in the fourteenth century and reached its zenith in the fifteenth century, marked a revival in the humanistic aspects of the Greek and Latin classics. It is considered a period of transition between the medieval and modern ages. Renaissance scholars of **classical humanism**, like medieval Scholastics, found their authorities in the past and stressed classical literature. Unlike the Scholastics, however, classical humanists were interested more in literature than in theology.[38]

◼ Classical humanism in Italy

The Renaissance was particularly notable in Italy, where commercial revival funded a proliferation of art and literature. Italian classical humanists, considering themselves a literary elite, were self-proclaimed "custodians of knowledge." In Italy, the works of Dante, Petrarch, and Boccaccio reflected the humanist literary revival. Italian nobles established humanist schools to prepare their children in the revived classical learning.

---

[38]J. R. Hale, *Renaissance Europe* (New York: Basil Blackwell, 2000).

Views on Education and Curriculum	Contribution and Influence
Education prepares people for their sociopolitical roles by cultivating reverence for ancestors and traditions; curriculum of ancient Chinese classics and Confucius's *Analects;* highly selective examinations.	Confucianist ethics shaped Chinese culture for centuries, creating a value system of enduring importance.
Use of probing intellectual dialogue to answer basic human concerns; education should cultivate moral excellence.	Socratic dialogue as a teaching method; teacher as a role model.
Reminiscence of latent ideas; music, gymnastics, geometry, astronomy, basic literary skills; philosophy for ruling elite of philosopher-kings.	Use of schools for sorting students according to intellectual abilities; education tied to civic (political) purposes.
Objective and scientific emphasis; basic literary skills, mathematics, natural and physical sciences, philosophy.	Emphasis on liberally educated, well-rounded person; importance of reason.
Rhetorical studies; basic literary skills; politics, history, rhetoric, declamation, public speaking.	Use of knowledge in public affairs and in political leadership; teacher education has both content and practice dimensions.
Basic literary skills; grammar, history, literature, drama, philosophy, public speaking, law.	Role of motivation in learning; recognition of individual differences.
Education should be based on human nature, with appropriate studies for both spiritual and physical dimensions.	Teacher as moral agent; education related to universal theological goals; synthesis of the theological and philosophical; basis of philosophy used in Roman Catholic schools.
Education for a literary elite that stressed criticism and analysis.	Role of secondary and higher education in literary and social criticism; emphasis on critical thinking.
Elementary schools to teach reading, writing, arithmetic, religion; secondary schools to prepare leaders by offering classics, Latin, Greek, and religion; vocational training.	Emphasis on universal literacy; schools to stress religious values, vocational skills, knowledge; close relationship of religion, schooling, and the state.

▪ The courtier as a model

Rejecting Scholasticism, classical humanist educators turned again to Isocrates and Quintilian. In the Greek and Latin classics, they found models of literary excellence and style, the ideal of the educated person, and a view that cherished antiquity's wisdom. For humanist educators, the courtier became the model of the educated person. A person of style and elegance, liberally educated in classical literature, the courtier was a tactful diplomat who could serve his ruler well in affairs of state. Baldesar Castiglione (1478–1529) described the courtier and his education, which featured classical Greek and Latin literature as well as courtly civility, in his work, *The Book of the Courtier*.[39]

▪ Educating the courtier

▪ Critical thinking

The Renaissance humanist educators were literary figures—writers, poets, translators, and critics. Artist-teachers, critics of society and taste, they brought wit, charm, and satire as well as erudition to their work. Anticipating today's emphasis on critical thinking, they sought to educate critically minded people who could challenge existing customs and expose and correct mediocrity in literature and life. In northern Europe, classical humanist scholars critically examined medieval theological works.

---

[39]Baldesar Castiglione, *The Book of the Courtier,* trans. C. S. Singleton (New York: Doubleday, 1959). A commentary is Peter Burke, *The Fortunes of the Courtier: The European Reception of Castiglione's Cortegiano* (University Park: Pennsylvania State University Press, 1996).

But Renaissance humanists often kept a distance between themselves and the mass of people, distilling their conception of human nature from a carefully aged literature. As a vintage wine is used to grace an elegant dinner, humanist education was for the connoisseur. It was not provided to everyone but reserved for an elite.

■ Limited access to schools

The Renaissance did not dramatically expand school attendance. Humanist preparatory and secondary schools educated children of the nobility and upper classes. Elementary schools served the commercial middle classes. Lower-socioeconomic-class children received little, if any, formal schooling.

Erasmus: Critic and Humanist

■ Erasmus on education

Desiderius Erasmus (1465–1536), the leading classical humanist scholar of the Renaissance, described the model teacher as a cosmopolitan humanist.[40] A cosmopolitan teacher's attitude would be global and not restricted by parochialism. A humanist teacher would be well grounded in the liberal arts, especially in subjects such as literature, languages, history, and religion, which were useful in interpreting the classical works. Like Quintilian, Erasmus took a broad view of education, advising parents that early education was crucial in forming a child's attitudes and behavior for later education. Children were entitled to parents and teachers who were models of civility and culture.

■ Promoting books and literature

As a humanist, Erasmus was most concerned with the teaching of literature. He suggested motivating students to read good books by having them explore an au-

During the Renaissance, the curriculum for young upper-class women reflected the notion that certain studies—such as art, music, needlework, dancing, and poetry—were appropriate for their gender. *(© Giraudon/Art Resource, NY)*

[40]For biographies of Erasmus, see Leon E. Halkin, *Erasmus: A Critical Biography* (Oxford, U.K., and Cambridge, Mass.: Basil Blackwell, 1993); and James McConics, *Erasmus* (New York: Oxford University Press, 1991).

thor's meaning in their own lives. He encouraged teachers to use conversations, games, and activities to illustrate the meaning of a book. Erasmus developed the following method for teaching literature: (1) present the author's biography; (2) identify the type, or genre, of the work; (3) discuss the plot; (4) reflect on the book's moral and philosophical implications; (5) analyze the author's writing style.[41]

■ Opposition to violence

Erasmus's opposition to war and violence is conveyed in his book, *The Education of the Christian Prince* (1516).[42] He advised those who would tutor a prince to make sure that he learned as much as he could about the people of his kingdom—about their traditions, customs, work, and problems. Unlike Machiavelli, who urged that the king should rule by fear and manipulation, Erasmus advised the prince to gain the love of his subjects and to study the arts of peace, especially diplomacy, and avoid war.

The Renaissance Contribution to Western Education

■ Emphasis on classical languages and literature

Renaissance humanists emphasized Latin and Greek knowledge as hallmarks of the educated person. For centuries, this classical humanist preference shaped Western secondary and higher education. In Europe and the United States, many colleges and universities required knowledge of Latin for admission until the late nineteenth century.

■ Humanistic (not scientific) knowledge

It is also important to note that Erasmus and other Renaissance educators were moving to a humanistic, or human-centered, conception of knowledge. Rather than approaching their human subject through scientific inquiry, however, humanist educators explored their concerns through literature. This approach was later resisted in the educational reforms of Rousseau, Comenius, Pestalozzi, and Dewey (discussed in the chapter on Pioneers in Education), who all argued against instruction that emphasized literature while neglecting experience.

■ The printing press

The invention of the printing press in 1423 in Europe advanced literacy and schooling dramatically. Before the printing press, students painstakingly copied dictation from teachers. The university lecture was essentially an experience in which students recorded their professor's words.

By mid-fifteenth century, Europeans were experimenting with movable metal type in printing. Johannes Gutenberg, a German jeweler, invented a durable metal alloy to form letters for the printing press. His Bible, in 1455, was the first major book printed thus. Printing spread throughout Europe, multiplying the output and cutting the costs of books. It made information accessible to a larger reading population.[43] The printing press inaugurated the "information revolution." It was a momentous technological innovation whose consequences recollect that of the advent of computer information dissemination. (See Overview 3.3 for the invention of the printing press and other significant events in the history of education.)

REFOCUS Think back to the Focus Questions listed at the beginning of this chapter. How would you answer them if you were asked to summarize educational contributions from the Renaissance? What elements of the humanist position do you see in schools today?

---

[41]William H. Woodward, *Desiderius Erasmus: Concerning the Aim and Method of Education* (New York: Teachers College Press, 1964).
[42]Robert D. Sider and John B. Payne, eds. *Collected Works of Erasmus* (Toronto: University of Toronto Press, 1994).
[43]Lucien Febvre and Henri-Jean Martin, *The Coming of the Book: The Impact of Printing, 1450–1800* (London: Verso, 1990).

OVERVIEW 3.3 *Significant Events in the History of Western Education, to A.D. 1650*

Period	Political and Social Events	Significant Educational Events
Greek	1200 B.C. Trojan War 594 B.C. Athenian constitutional reforms 479–338 B.C. Golden Age of Greek (Athenian) culture 445–431 B.C. Age of Pericles 431–404 B.C. Peloponnesian War between Athens and Sparta	c. 1200 B.C. Homer's *Iliad* and *Odyssey* 399 B.C. Trial of Socrates 395 B.C. Plato's *Republic* 392 B.C. School established by Isocrates in Athens 387 B.C. Academy founded by Plato 330 B.C. Aristotle's *Politics*
Roman	753 B.C. Traditional date of Rome's founding 510 B.C. Roman republic established 336–323 B.C. Alexander the Great 272 B.C. Rome dominates Italian peninsula 146 B.C. Greece becomes Roman province 49–44 B.C. Dictatorship of Julius Caesar 31 B.C. Roman empire begins A.D. 476 Fall of Rome in the West	449 B.C. References appear to the existence of Latin primary schools, or *ludi* 167 B.C. Greek grammar school opened in Rome A.D. 96 Quintilian's *Institutio Oratoria*
Medieval	713 Arab conquest of Spain 800 Charlemagne crowned Holy Roman Emperor 1096–1291 Crusades to the Holy Land 1182–1226 St. Francis of Assisi	1079–1142 Abelard, author of *Sic et Non* 1180 University of Paris granted papal charter and recognition 1209 University of Cambridge founded 1225–1274 Thomas Aquinas, author of *Summa Theologiae*
Renaissance	1295 Explorations of Marco Polo 1304–1374 Petrarch, author of odes and sonnets 1313–1375 Boccaccio, founder of Italian vernacular literature 1384 Founding of Brethren of the Common Life 1393–1464 Cosimo de' Medici encourages revival of art and learning in Florence 1423 Invention of printing press	1428 Da Feltre, classical humanist educator, established court school at Mantua 1507–1589 Sturm, creator of gymnasiums in Germany 1509 Erasmus's *Praise of Folly*
Reformation	1455 Bible printed 1492 Columbus arrives in America 1517 Luther posts *Ninety-five Theses* calling for church reform 1509–1564 John Calvin, Protestant reformer, founder of Calvinism 1509–1547 King Henry VIII of England, founder of the Church of England 1540 Jesuit order founded by Loyola 1545 Council of Trent launches Roman Catholic Counter Reformation	1524 Luther's "Letter . . . in Behalf of Christian Schools" 1524 Melanchthon, an associate of Luther, organizes Lutheran schools in German states 1630–1650 Calvinist schools organized in Scotland by John Knox

▶ The Religious Reformation and Education

■ Freedom from papal authority

The religious reformation of the sixteenth and seventeenth centuries was stimulated by northern European humanist criticism of medieval institutions and authorities. As humanism replaced medieval Scholasticism, the Catholic Church's central authority to enforce religious conformity eroded. This paved the way for diverse religious opinions, which ultimately led to disputes about education.

The rise of the commercial middle classes and strong national states contributed to the reformation movements. Primarily, however, Protestant religious reformers—including John Calvin, Martin Luther, Philipp Melanchthon, and Ulrich Zwingli—sought to free themselves and their followers from papal authority and to interpret their own religious doctrines and practices.[44] While doing so, the Protestant reformers formulated their own educational theories, established their own schools, structured their own curricula, and reared their children in the reformed creeds.

■ Extension of popular literacy

Luther, Melanchthon, Calvin, and other Reformation leaders concerned themselves with questions of knowledge, education, and schooling because they wanted these powerful weapons to advance the Protestant cause. On questions of knowledge, their supreme authority was the Bible. Regarding Bible reading as essential to salvation, the Protestant reformers promoted universal primary schooling to advance literacy.

Protestants established **vernacular schools** to instruct children in their common language—for example, German, Swedish, or English rather than Latin. These primary schools offered a basic curriculum of reading, writing, and arithmetic as well as religion. Catholic Masses and liturgies remained in Latin rather than vernacular languages, although, to compete with Protestants, Catholic schools also began to teach vernacular languages along with Latin.

■ The catechism

Both Protestants and Catholics used schools to indoctrinate children with "correct" religious beliefs and practices. Only members of the officially sanctioned church were hired as teachers, and teachers were carefully supervised to make certain they taught approved doctrines. To ensure doctrinal conformity, religious educators developed the catechistic method of instruction. In question-and-answer form, catechisms summarized the particular denomination's doctrines and practices. Although memorization had always been a feature of schooling, the catechistic method emphasized it. The objective was to have children memorize the catechism and thereby internalize the doctrines of their church. The question-and-answer format gained such a powerful hold on schools that it was also used in teaching secular subjects such as history and geography.

For example, Calvin's *Catechism of the Church of Geneva* used the question and answer method:

> Master: What is the chief end of human life?
> Scholar: To know God by whom men were created.

In the nineteenth century, the same method appeared in Davenport's *History of the United States*:

> Q. When did the battle of Lexington take place?
> A. On the 19th of April, 1775; here was shed the first blood in the American Revolution.[45]

---

[44]W. Robert Godfrey, *Reformation Sketches: Insights into Luther, Calvin, and the Confessions* (Phillipsburg, N.J: P&R Publishers, 2003).

[45]John Calvin, *Tracts and Treatises on the Doctrine and Worship of the Church, II,* Translated by Henry Beveride (Grand Rapids, MI: Wm. B. Erdmans Publishing Co., 1958), p. 37; and Bishop Davenport, *History of the United States* (Philadelphia: William Marchall and Co. 1833), p. 31.

■ Rising literacy

By emphasizing popular literacy and increasing school attendance, the Protestant Reformation inaugurated a major change in education and in literacy rates. For example, only 10 percent of men and 2 percent of women in England were literate in 1500. By 1600 the numbers had risen to 28 percent for men and 9 percent for women, and by 1700 nearly 40 percent of English men and about 32 percent of English women were literate. Literacy rates were higher in northern Europe than in southern Europe, in urban as opposed to rural areas, and higher among upper than lower classes.[46]

■ Increasing school attendance

As these figures suggest, reformers wanted both girls and boys to attend the primary vernacular schools, and their efforts increased school attendance for both sexes. Nevertheless, Protestant reformers continued to reserve the prestigious classical humanist preparatory and secondary schools for upper-class boys. Preparatory and secondary schools such as the German *gymnasium*, the English Latin grammar school, and the French *lycée* prepared upper-class boys in Latin and Greek, the classical languages needed for university entry. This elite was destined for leadership roles in the church and state.

Many strong characters—Calvin, Zwingli, Ignatius Loyola, and Henry VIII among them—made an impact on the Protestant Reformation and the Roman Catholic Counter Reformation. German Martin Luther was a leading reformer.

Luther: Protestant Reformer

■ Luther challenges the Catholic Church

Martin Luther (1483–1546) stands out as one of the most important religious reformers in shaping Western history and education.[47] An Augustinian monk in Germany, Luther had grown increasingly critical of Catholic practices. In 1517 at Wittenberg, he posted his famous *Ninety-five Theses* on the door of the castle church, challenging the Roman Catholic Church and the pope. Luther's challenges were a catalyst for the Protestant Reformation, which spread throughout Western Europe.

■ Education as part of religious reform

Luther recognized education as a potent ally of religious reformation. He saw church, state, family, and school as crucial reform agencies. Believing that the family had a key role in forming children's character and behavior, Luther encouraged family Bible reading and prayer. He also wanted parents to make sure that children had vocational training so they could support themselves as adults and become productive citizens.

■ Luther on schooling

Luther's "Letter to the Mayors and Aldermen of All Cities of Germany in Behalf of Christian Schools" advised public officials to take educational responsibility and emphasized schooling's political, economic, and spiritual benefits. Schools, Luther insisted, should be organized and inspected by state officials to train literate, orderly, and productive citizens and members of the church. Advanced education in the *gymnasium* and in universities would prepare well-educated ministers for the Lutheran Church.

■ Luther on women's education

Luther's views on women's education reflected traditional restrictions but also contained liberating ideas. Influenced by Saint Paul, he believed that the husband, as the head of the household, had authority over his wife. Domestic duties and child-rearing remained women's appropriate roles. On the other hand, Luther's em-

---

[46]Mary Jo Maynes, *Schooling in Western Europe: A Social History* (Albany: State University of New York Press, 1985).

[47]Biographies of Luther are James A. Nestigen, *Martin Luther: A Life* (Minneapolis, Minn.: Augsburg, 2003); Fredrick Nohl, *Luther: Biography of a Reformer* (St. Louis, Mo.: Concordia Publishing House, 2003); James M. Kittelson, *Luther: The Reformer* (Philadelphia: Penn.: Fortress, 2003).

■ School codes

phasis on reading the Bible in one's own language meant that girls as well as boys were to attend primary schools. Schooling thus gave women a shared, if subordinate, role in educating their own children.

To design and implement educational reforms, Luther relied heavily on Philipp Melanchthon (1497–1560). Seeking to end the Roman Catholic Church's control over schools, Luther and Melanchthon wanted the state to supervise schools and license teachers. In 1559, Melanchthon drafted the *School Code of Würtemberg,* which became a model for other German states. The code specified primary vernacular schools in every village to teach religion, reading, writing, arithmetic, and music. Classical secondary schools, *gymnasien,* were to provide Latin and Greek instruction for those select young men expected to attend universities.

The Reformation's Contribution to Western Education

The Protestant Reformation reconfirmed many institutional developments from the Renaissance, especially the **dual-track system of schools**. While vernacular schools provided primary instruction to the lower socioeconomic classes, the various classical humanist grammar schools prepared the upper classes for higher education. European colonists in turn brought this two-track school structure to the New World.

Through their stress on Bible reading, Protestant reformers also bequeathed to later educators the all-important emphasis on literacy. This attitude helped accelerate the movement toward universal schooling.

Religion has had a tremendous impact on education and schooling from ancient times through the twenty-first century. Many schools were tied to churches, temples, and mosques. In the United States, too, early schools and colleges were closely tied to religions. Currently, about 4,354,420 U.S. elementary and secondary students attend religiously affiliated schools.[48]

In the eighteenth century, however, religious influence over education met with challenge. The naturalism and rationalism of the Enlightenment, the Age of Reason, spread throughout Western Europe.

REFOCUS Think back to the Focus Questions listed at the beginning of this chapter. How would you answer them if you were asked to summarize educational contributions from Europe during the Reformation? How might you use that popular Reformation technique, memorization, in your classroom?

▶ The Enlightenment's Influence on Education

As we examine the eighteenth-century Age of Enlightenment (also called the Age of Reason), recall that the United States' political institutions are products of that era. Enlightenment ideas influenced such major educational reformers as Rousseau, Pestalozzi, and Froebel, discussed in the chapter on Pioneers in Education. The ideas of these European reformers traveled to America.

■ Reason and the scientific method

Foremost among the Enlightenment's ideas was the power of reason. The Enlightenment philosophers, scientists, and scholars firmly believed that humans could improve their lives and institutions by using reason to solve problems.[49] Emphasizing scientific inquiry, these thinkers attempted to discover "natural laws," the orderly

---

[48]"Private School Universe Survey, 1999-2000"; **http:nces.ed.gov/pubsearch/** (01/12/2003).
[49]Ulrich Im Hoff, *The Enlightenment* (Cambridge, Mass.: Basil Blackwell, 1994).

processes by which the universe functioned. They also devised theories for social reform. For example, the ideologies underlying the American and French revolutions sought to reconstruct the political order according to reason. Enlightenment ideologies implied that schools should cultivate students' ability to reason and thereby free themselves from superstition.

■ Belief in progress

Notable Enlightenment figures such as Diderot, Rousseau, Franklin, and Jefferson saw humanity as marching progressively forward to a new and better world. They no longer needed to look backward to the "golden age" of Greece or Rome. Using reason and the scientific method, humans could achieve progress on Earth. Schools must be progressive institutions that encouraged students to develop an open-minded, questioning attitude and an eagerness to use science's empirical method.

Enlightenment ideas took root in the United States, where they developed into an optimistic faith in political democracy and universal education. They were behind Benjamin Franklin's emphasis on utilitarian and scientific education and Thomas Jefferson's arguments for state-supported schools. Convinced of their ability to direct their own future, Americans saw education as the key to progress.[50]

The chapter entitled Philosophical Roots of Education examines the philosophies of education in our history. Several of those philosophies developed in the historical periods discussed in this chapter. The Technology @ School box suggests ways to learn about education around the world.

R E F O C U S **Think back to the Focus Questions at the beginning of this chapter. How would you answer them if you were asked to summarize educational contributions during the Enlightenment? In particular, identify the trends that had the greatest impact on American education.**

TECHNOLOGY @ School

Connecting with Schools Around the World

Many different cultures and traditions have contributed to the evolution of U.S. education. Educational systems in other parts of the world have also been shaped by global traditions. (The chapter on International Education explores this topic in more depth.) When you explore with your students differences and similarities in schools around the world, start by visiting Intercultural E-mail Classroom Connections (**www.teaching.com/IECC**), which provides information and an electronic mailing list to help teachers connect with colleagues and schools in other countries.

If it fits your objectives, you may wish to encourage your students to correspond with students in other countries. Students can directly share information about school and everyday life in their country. Valuable tips about setting up e-mail exchanges appear on several sites, including Intercultural E-Mail Classroom Connections at **www.teaching .com/IECC**; Global Schoolhouse at **www.gsh.org**; International Friendship Programs at **www.globalschoolnet.org/programs/friendship.html**; ePals Classroom Exchange at **www .epals.com**; KidLink at **www.kidlink.org**; or the Key Pals Club at **www.teaching. com/ keypals/**. These sites also suggest ideas for collaborative projects you can arrange between your students and those in another country.

Be sure to explore all arrangements and correspondents thoroughly before involving students, and encourage your students to adhere to your school's acceptable-use policy and to use good "netiquette" when corresponding with other students.

---

[50]Daniel Feller, *The Jacksonian Promise: America, 1815–1840* (Baltimore: Johns Hopkins University Press, 1995), pp. xiii–xiv.

▶ Summing Up

1 We have examined in historical context questions about the nature of teaching and learning raised at the beginning of this chapter: What is knowledge? What is education? What is schooling? Who should attend school? How should teaching and learning be carried on? Contemporary educators continue to examine these powerful questions. Some emphasize traditional knowledge and values, as did Confucius in ancient China, or the preservation of the culture, as in Egypt. Some seek to answer in universal terms, as did Plato; others shape their responses according to changing perceptions of knowledge and the role of education.

2 As in preliterate societies, schooling continues to transmit cultural heritage from one generation to the next.

3 Growing international interdependence increases the importance of the global context of education. By examining education in such culturally diverse societies as ancient China, India, Egypt, and Greece, we explored themes about knowledge, the purpose of education, and who should attend school.

4 Many American educational institutions and processes originated in Europe. In ancient Greece, the concepts of the educated person, rational inquiry, and freedom of thought were enunciated by Socrates, Plato, and Aristotle. The concept and methods of rhetorical education were devised by the Sophists, refined by Isocrates, and further developed by the Roman rhetorician Quintilian.

5 During the medieval period, the foundations of the university were established. Medieval education reflected mathematical and scientific contributions that entered the Western world by way of the Arabs. Renaissance classical humanist educators developed the concept of the well-rounded, liberally educated person. The Protestant Reformation's emphasis on literacy and vernacular education directly influenced colonial American schools. The Enlightenment was especially influential in America.

6 From the classical period of ancient Greece and Rome to the Protestant Reformation in the fifteenth century, only a minority of children attended schools. School attendance began to increase during the Protestant Reformation.

7 Schools in Western European societies developed into a two-track set of institutions based on socioeconomic class differences. Common people attended primary schools, and upper-class males attended preparatory schools that prepared them for university entrance. Girls attended primary schools but were generally excluded from secondary and higher education.

▶ Key Terms

enculturation (58)
Confucius (59)
caste system (63)
Brahmins (63)
Vedas (64)
Sophists (68)
rhetoric (68)
Socratic method (70)

reminiscence (70)
Plato's *Republic* (70)
Islam (76)
Koran (77)
Scholasticism (78)
classical humanism (80)
vernacular schools (85)
dual-track system of schools (87)

▶ Discussion Questions

1 Observe classes in kindergartens and the primary grades and note how holiday observances, stories, and art are used to introduce children to their culture. How are these examples similar or unlike education in preliterate societies?

2 Examine the Confucian ethical principle of appropriate behavior. Compare and contrast the concept of Confucianist ethical behavior with that of modern American society.

3 Compare and contrast the effects on education of caste in India with race in the United States.

4 Whereas the Arabic scholars tended to absorb knowledge from other cultures, the ancient Chinese tended to resist cultural borrowing. In your judgment, is the adaptation of "foreign" concepts in American education positive or negative? How has this phenomenon manifested itself in U.S. education in recent years?

5 Compare and contrast the Sophists' educational objectives with those found in modern political and advertising campaigns.

6 Consider who in contemporary America has the greatest opportunities to attend preschools, elementary schools, secondary schools, and colleges and universities. How do patterns of opportunity vary at each level? How do these educational opportunities compare with the historical patterns discussed in this chapter?

7 Historically, how have changes in women's education reflected changing roles of women in society?

▶ Suggested Projects for Professional Development

1 Visit the Web site of the Asia Society, **http:askasia.org**, for information on Asian culture and education. Use this site to explore articles on Confucius and other Asian philosophers and educators.

2 Visit the education center of IslamiCity (**www.islamicity.com**) for information and resources on Islam and Islamic history in Arabia and the Middle East. Determine how Islam's history has influenced contemporary interest in Arabic and Islamic education.

3 Visit the "Classic Philosophers" series on the Radical Academy Web site (**www .radicalacademy.com**) for information on the Sophists, Plato, Aristotle, and other ancient Greek philosophers. Determine the Sophists' historical and contemporary relevance.

4 The "Gallery of Educational Theorists," created by Edward G. Rozycki, is a useful Web site for students of education history and philosophy. The site is **www.newfoundations.com/GALLERY/Gallery.html**. The site analyzes theorists such as Aquinas, Aristotle, Locke, Luther, and Plato, all treated in this chapter, as well as other world educational figures, in terms of such questions as What is knowledge? What is learning? and How is knowledge to be transmitted? Use this site to help you develop your own philosophy of education.

5 Information, sources, and links related to educators treated in this chapter can be found at **www.infed.org/thinkers**. This site examines educators in terms of their theories of informal education. Use the information provided to answer such questions as What is informal education? How does informal education differ from formal education? What were the ideas of leading educators in informal education?

6 A biography and other information related to Erasmus, the Renaissance humanist, are provided at **www.ciger.be/erasmus**. Access the site and determine why an entire site is devoted to Erasmus.

7 To gain a global perspective on professional development, interview international students on education in their country, especially on the status of the teacher.

8 To gain a historical perspective on professional development, interview experienced teachers on how the teaching profession has changed since they began teaching.

9 Professional development includes a sense of ethics. To compare and contrast ethics, conduct a survey among students in your course or colleagues to identify the three people in the world who are most worthy of imitation by young people. How do these role models compare with the models of the educated person in ancient China, India, Egypt, Greece, and in the medieval, Renaissance, and Reformation periods?

▶ **Suggested Resources**

 Internet Resources

For the biography, philosophy, and works of Erasmus, consult **www.ciger.be/erasmus**.

For biographies of educators and an analysis of their theories from the perspective of informal education, consult **www.infed.org/thinkers**.

The "Gallery of Educational Theorists," created by Edward G. Rozycki, is a very useful Web site for students of education history and philosophy at **www.newfoundations.com/ GALLERY/Gallery.html**.

For a discussion of Confucius and Confucianism, visit **www.askasia.org**.

For information and illustrations of the ancient Greek Spartans, visit **http:www.legion-fourteen.com/greeks.htm**.

For the history, mythology, art, and culture of ancient Greece, visit **http:www.ancientgreece .com**.

For a discussion of the ancient Greek Athenians, visit **http:arwhead.com/Greeks**.

For a discussion and comparison of the ancient Greek Spartans and Athenians, visit **http:www.essene.com/History/greek1.html**.

For a discussion of the Sophists and other Greek philosophers, visit **www.radicalacademy .com**.

For a discussion of Islam and Islamic history, visit **www.islamicity.com**.

For a discussion and sources of Aquinas and Thomist philosophy, visit: **www.aquinasonline .com**.

Publications

Barzun, Jacques. *From Dawn to Decadence: 500 Years of Western Cultural Life, 1500 to the Present.* New York: HarperCollins, 2001. *A highly recognized historian and educator presents a large-scale reexamination of Western cultural life, institutions, trends, and revolutions that have shaped Western civilization.*

Black, Robert. *Humanism and Education in Medieval and Renaissance Italy: Tradition and Innovation in Latin Schools from the Twelfth to the Fifteenth Century.* New York: Cambridge University Press, 2001. *Examines how Latin schools in the medieval and Renaissance periods were agencies of educational transmission and change.*

Gutek, Gerald. *Historical and Philosophical Foundations of Education: A Biographical Introduction.* Columbus, Ohio: Merrill/Prentice Hall, 2005. *Contains essays that provide biographies and discussions of the educational ideas of Confucius, Plato, Aristotle, Aquinas, Erasmus, Calvin, and others in their historical contexts.*

Gutek, Gerald. *Historical and Philosophical Foundations of Education: Selected Readings.* Columbus, Ohio: Merrill/Prentice Hall, 2001. *Primary source documents highlight the educational philosophies of Plato, Aristotle, Aquinas, Erasmus, Calvin and other educational thinkers.*

Hanson, Victor D., and Heath, John. *Who Killed Homer? The Demise of Classical Education and the Recovery of Greek Wisdom.* New York: Encounter Books, 2001. *Analyzes the declining study of Western culture and argues for its inclusion in general education.*

Lascarides, V. Celia, and Hinitz, Blythe F. *History of Early Childhood Education.* New York: Falmer Press, 2000. *A large-scale and comprehensive treatment of the origins and historical development of early childhood education.*

Palmer, Joy A, Cooper, David E., and Bresler, Liora, eds. *Fifty Major Thinkers on Education: From Confucius to Dewey.* New York: Routledge, 2001. *Provides biographical sketches and discusses the principal educational ideas and contributions of leading educators, including Confucius, Plato, St. Augustine, and Erasmus.*

Ruthven, Malise. *Islam in the World.* New York: Oxford University Press, 2000. *A global treatment of the rise and influence of Islam.*

Shigeki, Kaizulka. *Confucius: His Life and Thought.* Mineola, N.Y.: Dover Publications, 2002. *Provides a biography of Confucius and discusses his philosophy.*

CHAPTER 4

Philosophical Roots of Education

Teachers face important daily challenges: preparing lessons, assessing student performance, and creating and maintaining a fair and equitable classroom environment.[1] How well you meet these challenges determines your success as a teacher. From informal conversations in the teachers' lounge to professional workshops and conferences, you'll hear many opinions on how to meet these challenges. The urgent problems teachers face each day may diminish opportunities to do so, but in considering and sharing opinions about these apparently everyday issues, they take on deeper and more philosophical dimensions.

This chapter provides you with a philosophical and theoretical map, a locating grid upon which you can examine your opinions about education and formulate them into your own philosophy of education. The following basic questions can guide you in reading the chapter and aid you as you build your own philosophy of education:

FOCUS QUESTIONS

- What are the subdivisions of philosophy, how are they defined, and how do they reflect your beliefs and your teaching about truth and values?

- What are the leading philosophies and theories of education? Are certain philosophies and theories present in your educational experiences? Do these philosophies help you examine your beliefs about knowledge and your practice of ethical values in the school and classroom?

- How do philosophies and theories of education influence curriculum and teaching and learning in schools, including what the curriculum claims is true, methods of instruction, teachers' ethical relationships with students and with each other, and attitudes toward cultural diversity?

This chapter was revised by Dr. Gerald Gutek.

[1]Useful books on the philosophy of education are Robert D. Heslep, *Philosophical Thinking in Educational Practice* (Westport, Conn.: Praeger Publishers, 1997); and Nel Noddings, *Philosophy of Education* (Boulder, Colo.: Westview Press, 1995).

■ How do contemporary trends in education such as the standards movement and the growing importance of educational technology affect your overall philosophy of education?

As a teacher, you will reflect on what you are teaching and how you teach it. You will consider how your presence in a classroom makes a difference in the lives of your students.[2] These serious reflections mark the beginnings of a teacher's self-examination. You can begin to to create your own philosophy of education by asking the following questions:

■ What is truth, and how do we know and teach it?

■ What are right and wrong, and how can we teach ethical moral values?

■ How can schools and curricula exemplify what is true and valuable?

■ How do teaching and learning reflect one's beliefs about truth and value?

■ Basic questions and philosophical issues

Throughout the chapter we refer to these as "the basic questions." They are not easy to answer, nor can they be answered in true-false, multiple-choice format. Most likely, your answers to these questions will change over time, become more complex, and upon reflection help you formulate your philosophy of education. Just as we use portfolios for ongoing student assessment, teachers often keep journals with daily entries about classroom events, successes, and problems. Both portfolios and journals provide a personal framework of educational events upon which you can reflect. Constructing a personal philosophy of education is neither easy nor quick, but you will find it both personally and professionally rewarding.

■ Philosophies and theories

This chapter examines five educational philosophies and four educational theories. Systematic **philosophies**, such as idealism and realism, refer to complete bodies of thought that present a worldview of which education is a part. In contrast, educational **theories** focus on education itself and on schools. (See Figure 4.1.) The general philosophies examined in this chapter link closely to the more specific theories of education, which form their school-based components. For example, the theory of essentialism is closely related to the philosophy of realism. Similarly, progressivism derives from pragmatism.

To understand current disputes about educational goals and curricula, we must explore these often conflicting philosophical roots. Before doing so, we must define certain terms and areas of philosophy.

▶ Special Terminology

Every field of inquiry has a special terminology. Philosophy of education uses the basic terms *metaphysics, epistemology, axiology,* and *logic.* The relationship between philosophical terms and education is summarized in Figure 4.2.

■ Reality and existence

Metaphysics examines the nature of ultimate reality. What is real and what is not real? Is there a spiritual realm of existence separate from the material world? Idealists, for example, see reality primarily in nonmaterial, abstract, or spiritual terms. Realists see it as an objective order that exists independently of humankind. Much instruction in schools represents the efforts of curriculum makers, teachers, and textbook writers to describe "reality" to students. As a teacher you will find that

---

[2]For the relevance of educational philosophy to classroom practices, see Tony W. Johnson, *Discipleship or Pilgrimage? The Study of Educational Philosophy* (Albany: State University of New York Press, 1995).

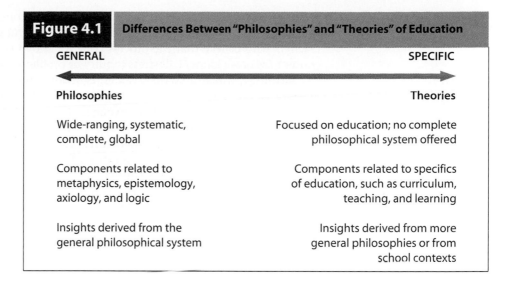

Figure 4.1 Differences Between "Philosophies" and "Theories" of Education

GENERAL ⟷ SPECIFIC

Philosophies	Theories
Wide-ranging, systematic, complete, global	Focused on education; no complete philosophical system offered
Components related to metaphysics, epistemology, axiology, and logic	Components related to specifics of education, such as curriculum, teaching, and learning
Insights derived from the general philosophical system	Insights derived from more general philosophies or from school contexts

different textbooks have competing interpretations of reality, or at least different emphases.

■ Knowledge and knowing

Epistemology, which deals with knowledge and knowing, influences methods of teaching and learning. It raises such questions as On what do we base our knowledge of the world and our understanding of truth? Does our knowledge derive from divine revelation, from ideas latent in our own minds, from empirical evidence, or from something else? Again, different philosophies hold different epistemological conceptions.

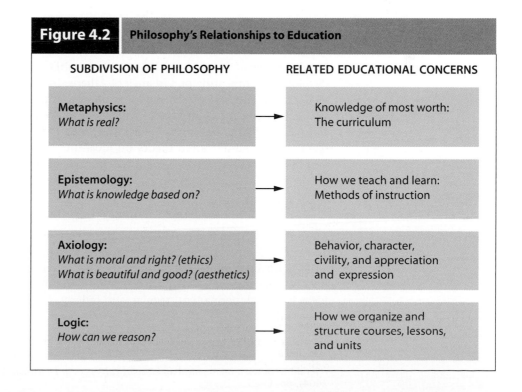

Figure 4.2 Philosophy's Relationships to Education

SUBDIVISION OF PHILOSOPHY	RELATED EDUCATIONAL CONCERNS
Metaphysics: *What is real?*	Knowledge of most worth: The curriculum
Epistemology: *What is knowledge based on?*	How we teach and learn: Methods of instruction
Axiology: *What is moral and right? (ethics)* *What is beautiful and good? (aesthetics)*	Behavior, character, civility, and appreciation and expression
Logic: *How can we reason?*	How we organize and structure courses, lessons, and units

Teachers who believe that human ideas should conform to the ordered structure of reality will stress orderly and sequential teaching of subjects. In contrast, teachers who believe that the process (*how* we know) is more important than the content (*what* we know) will stress inquiry or problem solving.

■ What is of value?

Axiology, which prescribes values, is divided into *ethics* and *aesthetics*. **Ethics** examines moral values and the rules of right conduct; **aesthetics** addresses values in beauty and art. Whether a school explicitly teaches such values or not, teachers—like parents and society in general—convey values implicitly by rewarding or punishing behavior depending on whether it conforms to their conceptions of what is right, good, and beautiful. Moreover, the school climate as a whole represents the values of the educational community.

■ Deductive and inductive thinking

Logic, which is concerned with correct and valid thinking, examines the rules of inference that help us correctly frame our propositions and arguments. **Deductive logic** moves from general statements to particular instances and applications. **Inductive logic** moves from the particular instance to tentative generalizations subject to further verification. Curriculum and instruction are organized on conceptions of logic. Does something in the subject itself logically dictate how lessons should be organized and presented to students (the deductive approach)? Or should teachers take their cue from students' interest, readiness, and experience in deciding how to present instruction (an inductive approach)?

With this background in terminology, we can examine different philosophies and theories. After discussing the key concepts of each one, we will see how it answers the basic questions raised at the beginning of the chapter and helps a teacher construct his or her own philosophy of education. (See Overview 4.1 for the philosophies discussed in this chapter.)

REFOCUS Which area of philosophy most influences you as a teacher: metaphysics, epistemology, axiology, or logic? Why?

▶ Idealism

■ Notable idealist thinkers

Idealism, one of the oldest of the traditional philosophies, goes back to Plato, who developed idealist principles in ancient Athens. In Germany, Georg W. F. Hegel created a comprehensive worldview based on idealism, and in the United States, Ralph Waldo Emerson and Henry David Thoreau developed a variety of idealism known as transcendentalism. Friedrich Froebel (described in the Pioneers in Education chapter) based his kindergarten theory on idealism.[3] Asian religions such as Hinduism and Buddhism also rest on the spiritual outlook associated with idealism.

Key Concepts

■ Universal, eternal truth

Metaphysics. Idealists believe that only the mental or spiritual is ultimately real. They see the universe as an expression of a highly generalized intelligence and will—a universal mind. The person's spiritual essence, or soul, is the permanent aspect of human nature that provides vitality and dynamism. This mental world of ideas is eternal, permanent, regular, and orderly. Truth and values are absolute and universal.

---

[3]Gerald L. Gutek, *Philosophical and Ideological Voices in Education* (Boston: Allyn and Bacon, 2004), pp. 15–27.

OVERVIEW 4.1 *Philosophies of Education*

Philosophy	Metaphysics	Epistemology	Axiology	Educational Implications	Proponents
Idealism	Reality is spiritual or mental and unchanging.	Knowing is the rethinking of latent ideas.	Values are absolute and eternal.	A subject-matter curriculum emphasizes the culture's great and enduring ideas.	Emerson Froebel Hegel Plato
Realism	Reality is objective and is composed of matter and form; it is fixed, based on natural law.	Knowing consists of sensation and abstraction.	Values are absolute and eternal, based on nature's laws.	A subject-matter curriculum emphasizes humanistic and scientific disciplines.	Aquinas Aristotle Broudy Maritain Pestalozzi
Pragmatism (experimentalism)	Reality is the interaction of an individual with environment or experience; it is always changing.	Knowing results from experiencing, use of scientific method.	Values are situational or relative.	Instruction is organized around problem solving according to the scientific method.	Childs Dewey James Peirce
Existentialism	Reality is subjective, with existence preceding essence.	Knowing is to make personal choices.	Values should be freely chosen.	Classroom dialogues stimulate awareness that each person creates a self-concept through significant choices.	Sartre Marcel Morris Soderquist
Postmodernism	Rejects metaphysics as historical constructions used for socioeconomic domination.	Deconstructs texts (canons) to find their origin and use by dominant groups and classes.	Emphasizes the values of marginalized persons and groups.	Schools are sites of democratic criticism and social change to empower dominated groups.	Derrida, Foucault

■ Macrocosm and microcosm

Idealists such as the transcendentalists use the concepts of macrocosm and microcosm to explain their version of reality. **Macrocosm** refers to the universal mind, the first cause, creator, or God. Regardless of the particular name used, the macrocosmic mind is the whole of existence. It is the one, all-inclusive, and complete self of which all lesser selves are parts. The universal, macrocosmic mind is continually thinking and valuing. The **microcosm** is a limited part of the whole—an individual and lesser self. But the microcosm is of the same spiritual substance as the macrocosm.

■ Latent knowledge

Epistemology. Idealism emphasizes the recognition or reminiscence of latent ideas—those already present but not conscious in the mind. These **a priori ideas** concern knowledge that exists prior to and independent of human experience about them. Through introspection the individual examines his or her own mind and finds a copy of the macrocosmic mind. The teacher's challenge is to bring this latent knowledge to consciousness. Education thus helps students arrive at a broad, general, and unifying perspective of the universe.[4]

■ Hierarchy of subjects

Idealist teachers prefer a hierarchical curriculum based on traditional disciplines or subject matter. At the top of the hierarchy are the most general disciplines, philosophy and theology. These general and abstract subjects transcend the limitations of time, place, and circumstance, and they transfer to a wide range of situations. Mathematics is valuable, too, because it cultivates the power to deal with abstractions. History and literature rank high as sources of moral and cultural models. Somewhat lower in the curriculum, the natural and physical sciences address particular cause-and-effect relationships. Language is important because it is an essential tool at all levels of learning. For the idealist, the highest level of knowledge recognizes the relationships among all these subject matters and integrates them.

■ Enduring values

Axiology. Because idealists see the universe in universal and eternal terms, they prescribe values that are unchanging and applicable to all people. Thus ethical behavior reflects the enduring knowledge and values of human culture. Philosophy, theology, history, literature, and art are rich sources for transmitting this heritage of values. Such an education requires that students encounter worthy models, especially the classics—the great works that have endured over time.

■ Logical consistency

Logic. For idealists, logic, too, is based on the whole-to-part relationship. The part, a particular idea or principle, is derived from and agrees with the whole, which is more general. Idealist teachers would organize lessons following a deductive logical arrangement that emphasizes general principles or rules and then draws more specific illustrations from them. For example, an idealist teacher would introduce the general concept of nonviolence before discussing the harmful consequences of bullying one's classmates.

The Basic Questions

■ Knowledge of universal ideas

If you were to ask an idealist teacher, "What is knowledge?" he or she would reply that knowledge concerns the spiritual principles that form the base of reality. This knowledge of reality takes the form of ideas. If knowledge is about universal ideas, then education is the intellectual process of bringing ideas to the learner's consciousness.

■ Schooling: an intellectual pursuit of truth

If you further ask the idealist teacher, "What is schooling?" he or she would say that the school is an institution where students seek to discover and pursue truth. It is an intellectual institution where teachers and students explore the questions Socrates and Plato first asked: What is truth? What is beauty? What is the good life? These answers are present but hidden in our minds, and we must reflect deeply to bring them to our consciousness. We should allow nothing to distract us from the intellectual pursuit of truth.

Who should attend school? The idealist would say everyone. Not all students have the same intellectual aptitude, but all must cultivate their minds to the limits of their capacities. Gifted students need the greatest intellectual challenges that the teacher can provide.

---

[4]Gerald L. Gutek, *Philosophical and Ideological Perspectives on Education,* 2nd ed. (Boston: Allyn and Bacon, 1997), pp. 13–25.

■ Socratic method

How should we teach? The idealist would say that thinking and learning are names for the process of bringing ideas to consciousness. An effective means of doing this is the **Socratic method**, in which the teacher stimulates the learner's awareness of ideas by asking leading questions. Another important aspect of idealist methodology is modeling. Teachers should be models worthy of student imitation—they should have wide knowledge of the cultural heritage and lead exemplary lives.

Standards & Assessment ☑
■ High standards

Idealists want to safeguard the quality of education by maintaining high intellectual standards and resisting any tendency toward mediocrity. In Plato's *Republic,* for example, intellectual standards were so high that only a gifted minority entered the ruling elite of philosopher-kings. Today's idealists would not go that far, but their educational goals encompass developing intellectual capacity, and they generally accept the fact that not all students will go on to the highest stages of education.

Standards & Assessment ☑

Although idealists might not view standardized test results as the only measures of assessing academic achievement, they would generally support the standards movement in education. For them, high standards set high expectations for both teachers and students.

Implications for Today's Classroom Teacher

■ Intellectual development, not vocational training

Idealism seeks to create an intellectual environment for teaching and learning. It rejects the consumerism and vocationalism that often shape attitudes in contemporary society. It sees teachers as vital agents in helping students realize their fullest potential, and it encourages teachers to acquaint themselves and their students with the finest elements of the cultural heritage. Teachers expose students to the classics—great and enduring works of art, literature, and music—so that they can experience and share in the time-tested values these cultural works convey.

Although technology can convey the great works of literature and art to students, idealists would insist on technology use as a means, as an instrument, of education rather than an end. The content matters most, not the technical apparatus that conveys it.

■ An idealist lesson

How might a teacher use idealism in developing a lesson? A fifth-grade social studies teacher might illustrate the power of ideas and the higher ethical law by a unit on the life and moral impact of Mohandas Gandhi, the father of India's independence. Students would study Gandhi's biography and reflect on his principles of nonviolent protest against injustice that guided his movement against racism in South Africa and British colonialism in India.

REFOCUS What elements of idealism have you noticed as a student? What elements of this philosophy most immediately appeal to you as a teacher? Which appeal least? Why?

▷ Realism

■ A real world of objects

The ancient Greek philosopher Aristotle developed **realism**, which stresses objective knowledge and values. As described in the chapter on World Roots of American Education, Thomas Aquinas during the Middle Ages articulated a variety of religious realism known as Thomism, a synthesis of Aristotelianism and Christian doctrine. Alfred North Whitehead continued the realist tradition in the early twentieth century. Realism holds that (1) there is a world of real existence not made by human be-

Realist philosophy emphasizes sensory learning and organizing objects into categories such as mineralogy, as these students are doing in a science class. (© Bob Daemmrich/Stock Boston)

ings; (2) the human mind can know about the real world; and (3) such knowledge is the most reliable guide to individual and social behavior. These doctrines provide a starting point for considering realism's educational implications.

Key Concepts

■ Knowing: sensation, then abstraction

Metaphysics and Epistemology.   Realists believe in a material world independent of and external to the mind of the knower.[5] All objects are composed of matter. Matter, in turn, must assume the structure of particular objects.

Human beings can know these objects through their senses and their reason. Knowing is a process that involves two stages: sensation and abstraction. First, the knower perceives an object and records sensory data about it in the mind, such as color, size, weight, smell, or sound. The mind sorts these data into qualities always present in the object and those sometimes present. By identifying the necessary qualities (those always present), the learner forms a concept of the object and recognizes it as belonging to a certain class. This classification lets the learner understand that the object shares certain qualities with other members of the same class but not with objects of a different class.

■ Curriculum of organized subjects

Like idealists, realists believe that following a curriculum of organized, separate subjects is the most effective way of learning about reality. Organizing subject mat-

---

[5]William P. Alston, *A Realist Conception of Truth* (Ithaca, NY: Cornell University Press, 1996).

ter, as scientists and scholars do, is a sophisticated method of classifying objects. For example, past human experiences can be organized into history. Botany studies plants systematically according to their classifications. Political organizations such as nations, governments, legislatures, and judicial systems can be grouped into political science. The realist acquires knowledge about reality through systematic inquiry into these subjects.

■ Rational behavior, based on reality

Axiology. In the realist's conception of knowledge, certain rules govern intelligent behavior. For example, human beings ought to behave in a rational way, and behavior is rational when it conforms to the way in which objects function in reality. From their study of reality, people can develop theories based on natural, physical, and social laws. Natural laws are universal and eternal, as are the values based on them.

■ Deductive and inductive logic

Logic. Realist teachers often use logic both deductively and inductively. For example, students in a botany class might examine roses that differ in color, scent, and size but conclude, through induction, that all are members of the same genus. However, when the class plants a rose garden on the school grounds as a project, the students can consult plant-care literature and deduce the correct locations and amounts of fertilizer and water for each rose they plant.

The Basic Questions

■ Knowledge concerns objects

To begin our philosophical cross-examination, we again ask, What is knowledge? Realists would reply that knowledge concerns the physical world in which we live. When we know something, our knowledge is always about an object. Our concepts are valid when they correspond to those objects as they really exist in the world.[6]

■ Education via subject-matter disciplines

Formal education, the realists would say, is the study of knowledge organized and classified into subject-matter disciplines. History, languages, science, and mathematics are a few of these organized bodies of knowledge. If we know them, we will know more about the world in which we live. This knowledge is our best guide in conducting our daily affairs.

Realists view schools as primarily academic institutions that societies establish to provide students with knowledge about the objective world. Because all persons have a rational potentiality, schooling should be available to all, with students pursuing the same academic curriculum that will prepare them to make rational decisions.

Implications for Today's Classroom Teacher

■ Classrooms for learning, not therapy

In realist classrooms, the teacher's primary responsibility is to teach skills such as reading, writing, or computation, or some body of disciplined knowledge, such as history, mathematics, or science. Although they appreciate that their students are emotional as well as rational persons, realist teachers do not turn classrooms into therapeutic centers for emotional or behavioral adjustment. Realist teachers would oppose those nonacademic activities that interfere with the school's primary purpose as a center of academic learning.

■ Teachers as subject-matter experts

In order to perform their primary educational responsibility, realist teachers must know their subject well. For example, the history teacher should be a historian

---

[6]Andrew Newman,. *The Correspondence Theory of Truth: An Essay on the Metaphysics of Prediction* (New York: Cambridge University Press, 2002).

with a thorough background in that discipline. In addition, realist teachers should have a general education in the liberal arts and sciences that allows them to demonstrate relationships between their areas of expertise and other subject-matter areas. Realist teachers may employ a wide repertoire of methods, such as the lecture, discussion, demonstration, or experiment. Content mastery is most important, and methodology is a necessary but subordinate means to reach that goal.

■ Example of a realist approach

How might a high-school physics teacher with a realist philosophical orientation plan a unit on Isaac Newton's laws of motion? First, the teacher would help students place Newton in historical context and would comment on his scientific contributions. Second, the teacher might illustrate the laws of motion in a laboratory demonstration. Third, the students might discuss the demonstration and frame the scientific generalization that it illustrated. Finally, students would take a test to demonstrate their understanding of Newton's laws of motion.[7]

Standards & Assessment ✔

Realists would applaud the movement to set standards that specify student academic achievement goals, especially in skill areas such as reading and in subject content areas such as mathematics, science, and history. Standardized tests provide hard and comparable data about how well students are mastering curriculum subjects and how well teachers are instructing students. Standards help keep schools and teachers accountable.

Realists would endorse technology use that complements other methods of developing skill and subject-matter competency. They would want programs as "realistic" and effective as possible.

> **REFOCUS** Do you recall any instances of realism in your own education? Do you find any similarities to realist philosophy in your personal educational beliefs?

▶ Pragmatism

■ Founders of pragmatism

Pragmatism emphasizes the need to test ideas by acting on them. Among its founders were Charles S. Peirce (1839–1914), William James (1842–1910), George Herbert Mead (1863–1931), and John Dewey (1859–1952). Peirce emphasized using the scientific method to validate ideas empirically, and James applied pragmatic philosophy to psychology, religion, and education. Mead emphasized children's development as learning and experiencing human organisms. Dewey, in particular, applied pragmatism to education.[8]

The chapter on Pioneers in Education examines Dewey as an educational pioneer. Here we focus on his pragmatic or experimentalist philosophy, which featured change, process, relativity, and the reconstruction of experience.

■ Organism and environment

Influenced by Charles Darwin's evolutionary theory, Dewey applied the terms *organism* and *environment* to education. Dewey saw human beings as biological and sociological organisms who possess drives or impulses that sustain life and promote growth and development. Every organism lives in a habitat or environment. Education is a process of creating a learning environment that will promote experiences for optimum human growth.

[7]Philip H. Phenix, *Philosophies of Education* (New York: Wiley, 1961), pp. 22–24.
[8]John Dewey, *The Child and the Curriculum* (Chicago: University of Chicago Press, 1902); John Dewey, *Democracy and Education* (New York: Macmillan, 1916); John Dewey, *The School and Society* (Chicago: University of Chicago Press, 1923); and John Dewey, *Experience and Education: The 60th Anniversary Edition* (West Lafayette, Ind.: Kappa Delta Pi, 1998).

■ Problem solving

Whereas idealism and realism emphasized bodies of substantive knowledge or subject-matter disciplines, Dewey stressed the *process* of problem solving. For Dewey, learning occurs as the person engages in problem solving. In this experimental epistemology, the learner, as an individual or as a member of a group, uses the scientific method to solve both personal and social problems. For Dewey, the problem-solving method can be developed into a habit that transfers to a wide variety of situations.[9]

Key Concepts

■ Experience

Metaphysics and Epistemology.   Unlike idealism and realism, which both rest on a metaphysical foundation of a universal and unchanging reality, pragmatism or experimentalism dismisses metaphysics as unverifiable speculation. Rather than metaphysics, pragmatists are most concerned with epistemology, how we know what we know.

In Dewey's philosophy of experimentalism, the epistemological, or knowing, situation involves a person, or organism, and an environment. **Experience**, defined as the interaction of the person with the environment, is a key concept. The person interacts with the environment to live, grow, and develop. This interaction may alter or change both the person and the environment. Knowing is thus a *transaction,* a process, between the learner and the environment.[10]

■ Test of experience

Rejecting the a priori idealist and realist perspectives, Dewey applied a test of experience. Human purposes and plans could be validated only by acting on and judging them by their consequences. Although each interaction has generalizable aspects that carry over to the next problem, each episode will differ somewhat. Effective people use the scientific method to solve problems and add the features of a particular problem-solving episode to their ongoing experiences.

Dewey also applied judgment by consequences to educational programs. Did a particular educational program, curricular design, or methodological strategy achieve its anticipated goals and objectives? The only valid test, Dewey believed, was to try out the proposal and judge the results.[11]

■ No permanent realities

A reality that continually changes renders a curriculum based on supposedly permanent realities or universal truth untenable. Human beings must interact with the environment guided only by tentative assertions subject to further research and verification. Therefore, according to pragmatists, we need a method for dealing with change in an intelligent manner. The Deweyites stress problem solving as the most effective method for directing change toward desired outcomes. Even though reality involves constant transformation or *reconstruction* of both the person and the environment, humankind can benefit from the process. Every human experience reconstructed to solve a problem adds to humanity's fund of experience.

■ "Reconstruction" of person and environment

■ Relativity of values

Axiology and Logic.   Pragmatic axiology is highly situational. A constantly changing universe means that values, too, must change and are relative to time, place, and circumstance. What contributes to personal and social growth we consider valuable; what restricts or limits experience is unworthy. Further, we can clarify our

---

[9]Lawrence J. Dennis and George W. Stickel, "Mead and Dewey: Thematic Connections on Educational Topics," *Educational Theory* (Summer–Fall 1981), pp. 320–321.
[10]For an analysis of Dewey's pragmatic perspective, see Christine L. McCarthy and Evelyn Sears, "Deweyan Pragmatism and the Quest for True Self," *Educational Theory* (Spring 2000), pp. 213–227.
[11]Stephen M. Fishman and Lucille McCarthy, *John Dewey and the Challenge of Classroom Practice* (New York: Teachers College Press, 1998).

values by testing and reconstructing them in the same way we verify scientific claims.[12]

■ Inductive logic

Following the scientific method, experimentalist logic is inductive rather than deduced from first principles as in idealism and realism. Tentative assertions rely on empirical evidence and must be tested.

The Basic Questions

■ Knowledge is tentative

The pragmatist's answers to questions about knowledge, education, schooling, and instruction differ significantly from those of idealism and realism. Because knowledge claims are tentative and subject to revision, pragmatists are more concerned with the process of constructing and using knowledge than with truth as a body of permanent knowledge.

■ An experimental process

The pragmatist considers education an experimental process—a method of solving problems that challenge people as they interact with their world. Dewey argued that human beings experience the greatest personal and social growth as they interact with the environment in an intelligent and reflective manner. The most intelligent way of solving problems is to use the scientific method.

■ Interdisciplinary approach

Pragmatists favor interdisciplinary education. When you face a problem, pragmatists say, you draw the information you need to solve it from many sources, not from a single discipline or academic subject. For example, to define the problem of environmental pollution and suggest ways of solving it, we must consider sources that are historical, political, sociological, scientific, technological, and international. An educated person, in the pragmatic sense, knows how to apply information from all of these sources to the problem. In contrast to this pragmatist view, idealists and realists are suspicious of interdisciplinary education because they believe students must first acquire a knowledge base by studying organized subjects.

■ School as microcosm of society
■ Transmitting cultural heritage

Pragmatists such as Dewey see the school as a small, local community of learners and teachers intimately connected to the larger society. The school exercises three major functions: to simplify, purify, and balance the cultural heritage. To simplify, the school selects elements of the heritage and reduces their complexity to units appropriate to learners' readiness and interest. To purify, it selects worthy cultural elements and eliminates those that limit human interaction and growth. To balance, the school integrates the selected and purified experiences into a harmony.

■ Cultural diversity, but shared learning processes

In a society of diverse cultural groups, the pragmatic school helps children of one culture understand and appreciate members of other cultures. Although cultural diversity enriches the entire society, pragmatists want all cultural groups to use the scientific method. They also believe that schools should build social consensus by stressing common processes of learning. As genuinely integrated and democratic learning communities, schools should be open to all and encourage the widest possible sharing of resources among people of all cultures.

Implications for Today's Classroom Teacher

■ Subject matter as instrumental

Idealist and realist teachers see teaching subject matter as their primary responsibility, but pragmatist teachers are more concerned with the process of solving problems intelligently. Rather than ignore subject matter, they make it an instrument in

---

[12]William R. Caspary, "Judgments of Value in John Dewey's Theory of Ethics," *Educational Theory* (Spring 1990), pp. 155–169. See also Robert B. Westbrook, *John Dewey and American Democracy* (Ithaca, N.Y.: Cornell University Press, 1991), pp. 151–156.

problem-solving activities. They do not dominate the classroom but guide learning as facilitators of student research and activities. Pragmatist teachers also help students find other resources useful in problem solving, such as those accessible through classroom technology.[13]

■ Applying the scientific method

Students in a pragmatist classroom share the experience of applying the scientific method to a full range of personal, social, and intellectual problems. Teachers expect that students using the problem-solving method will learn to apply the process to situations both in and out of school and thus connect the school to society. Communication technologies such as e-mail and the Internet also create a larger community with more opportunities to share ideas, insights, and experiences.

■ Classroom as community

Pragmatist teachers work to transform classrooms into collaborative learning communities by encouraging students to share their interests and problems. Pragmatist educators also encourage both cultural diversity and commonalities. Although they recognize that each culture has something of value to share with other cultures, they stress shared communication between members of different cultures so that all students together can help create the larger democratic community. Instead of simply preserving the status quo, pragmatist teachers must take risks. They must see knowledge as indeterminate and open-ended, and their educational goals must constitute an ongoing inquiry that leads to action.

■ Teachers as risk takers

Standards & Assessment ☑

■ Questions the standards movement

Pragmatists would raise serious questions about the standards movement, especially its heavy reliance on standardized testing. Such tests burden students with goals and expectations set by other people and agencies rather than those that arise from the students' own experiences, issues, and problems. Further, "pencil-and-paper" tests measure only how well students assimilate prescribed and derived content, rather than genuinely test problem-solving skills. Teachers whose competency is judged by how well students perform on standardized tests focus instruction on passing tests rather than solving problems.

■ A pragmatist lesson

How might we apply pragmatism to classroom teaching? Let us say a college teacher-education class is examining using standardized tests as a means of setting national educational standards, as in the "No Child Left Behind" Act. (See the Technology @ School box for more on standardized testing.) The class members do the following:

1. Establish the issue's context: Why is this an issue? Who supports and who opposes using standardized tests to set national standards?

2. Define the problem by defining its key terms.

3. Conduct interdisciplinary research and locate information about the issue from various sources such as professional educators, educational psychologists, and politicians.

4. Conjecture about possible solutions, ranging from acceptance to rejection of the proposition.

5. Resolve the issue by reaching consensus and acting—for example, carry out an agreement to write a position paper and send it to decision makers.

REFOCUS Pragmatism has had significant influence on education in America. What influences of this philosophy can you identify in your own educational experiences? Will you carry these influences into your own teaching?

---

[13]For an examination of the philosophical implications of technology, see Larry A. Hickman, *Philosophical Tools for Technological Culture* (Bloomington: Indiana University Press, 2001).

The Debate over Standardized Testing

The United States is experiencing a major movement toward standardized testing at local school district, state, and national levels. Indeed, the federal No Child Left Behind Act mandates state standardized testing. In many states, standardized tests help determine student promotion and teacher effectiveness.

Standardized testing's proponents see it as an important way to reform American education. Its opponents see it as a reactionary rather than reformist movement. As a classroom teacher, you will be involved in this far-reaching and rapidly changing debate. You can follow the debate on the Internet as you form your opinion on this important issue.

Begin your research by visiting the U.S. Department of Education Web site—**www.ed.gov**—to determine the status and recent initiatives for state and national standardized testing, including No Child Left Behind.

Then, consult two opposing philosophical perspectives on standardized testing by visiting the John Dewey Project on Progressive Education at the University of Vermont Web site (**www.uvm.edu/~dewey**) and the Council for Basic Education Web site (**www.c-b-e.org**).

Based on your research, begin to develop your own philosophical position on the issue of standardized testing. Consider the arguments for and against standardized testing. What philosophies and theories of education tend to support it, and which tend to oppose it? What is your position, based on your personal philosophy of education?

▶ Existentialism

Existentialism, representing both a feeling of desperation and a spirit of hope, examines life in a personal way. An existentialist education encourages deep personal reflection on one's identity, commitments, and choices.

Key Concepts

■ Personal reflection

■ Creating one's essence through choices

The existentialist author Jean-Paul Sartre (1905–1980) stated that "Existence precedes Essence." In other words, human beings are born and enter the world without being consulted. We simply are here in a world we did not make or shape. However, we possess volition, or will, and thus are to make choices and to create our own purposes for existence. In our lives, we are thrust into choice-making situations. Some choices are trivial, but those that deal with the purpose and meaning of life lead to personal self-definition. We create our own definition and make our own essence. We are what we choose to be. Human freedom is total, say the existentialists, as is our responsibility for choice.[14]

■ Existential *Angst*

This conception of a human being as the creator of his or her own essence differs substantially from that of the idealists and realists, who see the person as a universal category. Moreover, whereas the idealist or realist sees the individual as an inhabitant of a meaningful and explainable world, the existentialist believes that the universe is indifferent to human wishes, desires, and plans. Existentialism focuses on the concept of *Angst,* or dread. We each know that our destiny is death and

---

[14]Gutek, *Philosophical and Ideological Voices in Education,* pp. 86–96.

that our presence in the world is temporary. From this sense of philosophical dread each person must make choices about freedom and slavery, love and hate, peace and war. As we make these choices, we carry before us this question: What difference does it make that I am here and that I have chosen to be what I am?

■ Choosing self-determination

According to the existentialists, we must also cope with the constant threat others—persons, institutions, and agencies—are to our choice-making freedom. Each person's response to life reflects an answer to the question, Do I choose to be a self-determined person or do I choose to be defined by others? But existentialism does see hope behind the desperation. Each person has the potential for loving, creating, and being. Each can choose to be an inner-directed, authentic person. An authentic person, free and aware of this freedom, knows that every choice is in fact an act of personal value creation.[15]

The Basic Questions

■ Creating personal values

Because existentialists have deliberately avoided systemization of their philosophy, it is difficult to categorize its metaphysical, epistemological, axiological, and logical positions. As already stated, existentialists believe that we create our own self-definition, or essence, by the personal choices we make. Epistemologically, the individual chooses the knowledge that he or she wishes to possess. Existentialists consider axiology most important because human beings create their own values through their choices.

■ Awakening consciousness of the human condition

Existentialists realize that we live in a world of physical realities and that we have developed a useful and scientific knowledge about these realities. However, the most significant aspects of our lives are personal and nonscientific. Thus, existentialists believe that knowledge about the human condition and the personal choices we make is most important and education's most significant goals are to awaken human consciousness to the freedom to choose and to create a sense of self-awareness that contributes to our authenticity.

■ Same opportunities for all

At school, existentialists say, individuals should pursue discussion about their own lives and choices. Because we are all in the same predicament and have the same possibilities, we all should have opportunities for schooling. In the school, both teachers and students should have the chance to ask questions, suggest answers, and engage in dialogue.

■ Questioning and dialogue

■ An existential curriculum

An existentialist teacher would encourage students to philosophize, question, and participate in dialogues about the meaning of life, love, and death. The answers to these questions would be personal and subjective, not measurable by standardized tests. An existentialist curriculum would consist of whatever might lead to philosophical dialogue. Particularly valuable are subjects that vividly portray individual men and women in the act of making choices, including emotional, aesthetic, and poetic subjects.[16] Literature and biography are important for revealing choice-making conditions. Students should see and discuss drama and films that vividly portray the human condition and human decision-making.

■ Self-expression needed

In addition to literary, dramatic, and biographical subjects, students must create their own modes of self-expression.[17] They should be free to experiment with

---

[15]Maxine Greene, *Landscapes of Learning* (New York: Teachers College Press, 1978); and Van Cleve Morris, *Existentialism in Education* (New York: Harper and Row, 1966).

[16]Maxine Greene, *The Dialectic of Freedom* (New York: Teachers College Press, 1988).

[17]For an approach that uses narrative and dialogue to examine philosophical issues in education, see Carol Witherell and Nel Noddings, eds., *Stories Lives Tell: Narrative and Dialogue in Education* (New York: Teachers College Press, 1991).

artistic media and to dramatize their emotions, feelings, and insights. Educational technology that enhances personal choice and freedom might be useful in existentialist education. For example, students might benefit from expressing themselves by creating multimedia productions. Technological applications that create conformity in thinking and in accessing information, on the other hand, would be viewed with suspicion.

Implications for Today's Classroom Teacher

■ Teacher encourages awareness

Teaching from an existentialist perspective is not easy because teachers cannot specify goals and objectives in advance—these are determined by each student as an individual person. Rather than imposing goals on students, the existentialist teacher seeks to create an awareness in each student of ultimate responsibility for her or his own education and self-definition. In creating this awareness, the teacher encourages students to examine the institutions, forces, and situations that limit freedom of choice. Further, existentialist teachers seek to create open classrooms to maximize freedom of choice. Within these open learning environments, instruction is self-directed.

Standards & Assessment ✔

■ External standards depersonalize education

Existentialists would oppose the standards movement, especially its emphasis on standardized testing to measure academic success. The whole standards movement is a trend away from individuality and personal choice and freedom. Making instruction in every classroom follow the same standards eliminates the unique character of each educational setting.

An Existentialist School: Summerhill

■ Summerhill: an example of freedom

Although A. S. Neill's Summerhill School in the United Kingdom defies neat classification in terms of philosophies of education, it exemplifies existentialist themes in its mission, curriculum, and approach to teaching and learning. Neill created his school as an educational experiment in students' freedom to choose what and when they wanted to learn. When they were free from externally prescribed restrictions and prohibitions, Neill found that students actually wanted to learn and eagerly pursued their own learning agendas.[18]

■ An existentialist lesson

Literature, drama, and film are especially powerful in existentialist teaching. An example of existentialist teaching might be a senior high school history class that is studying the Holocaust, the genocide of six million Jews in Europe during World War II. The class views Steven Spielberg's movie, *Schindler's List,* in which an industrialist, Oscar Schindler, who initially profits from the forced labor of Jewish concentration camp inmates, makes a conscious decision to save his workers from death in the Nazi gas chambers. The class then probes the moral situation of one man, Schindler, and the choice that he made in a senseless and cruel world.

 **REFOCUS** Can you recall any influences of existentialism in your own education? What place does this philosophy hold in your plans for teaching?

---

[18]Neill described his approach to education in A. S. Neill, *Summerhill: A Radical Approach to Child Rearing* (New York: Hart Publishing, 1960; also see his autobiography, *"Neill! Neill! Orange Peel!"* (New York: Hart Publishing, 1972). The Web site for Neill's Summerhill School is **http:www. summerhillschool.co.uk/pages/index.html**.

▶ Postmodernism

Postmodernism, a leading contemporary philosophy, contends that the modern period of history has ended and that we now live in a postmodern era. Postmodernism's origins can be found in the ideas of German philosophers Friedrich Nietzsche (1844–1900) and Martin Heidegger (1899–1976). Nietzsche dismissed metaphysical claims about absolute truth, suggesting that they were contrived to replace worn-out myths and supernatural beliefs with newer but equally false assertions.[19] Formulating a philosophy called phenomenology, Heidegger asserted that human beings construct their own subjective truths about reality from their intuitions, perceptions, and reflections as they interact with phenomena.

■ Relationship to constructivism

Postmodernism has several implications for **constructivism**, a psychology and method of education. Postmodernists and constructivists agree that we make, or construct, our beliefs about knowledge from our experiences. Learners therefore create their view of knowledge by interacting with their environment. Knowledge, a human construction, is tentative and conjectural and subject to ongoing revision as learners acquire more experience. Knowledge is never complete; we add to it and revise it based on our experience. *Collaborative learning,* the sharing of experiences and ideas through language, makes knowledge both a personal and a social construction.[20]

Key Concepts

■ Derrida and Foucault

Postmodernism is associated with the work of the French philosophers, Michel Foucault and Jacques Derrida. Foucault discounts claims to universal and unchanging truths. He contends that what some people, especially experts, claim as objective truth, analysis reveals as a rationale those in power use over others at a given time in history.[21] Postmodernists also use the concepts of subordination and marginalization. In any society, especially a modern capitalist one like the United States, certain economically, socially, and educationally favored classes and groups dominate those pushed to the margins of society.

Derrida developed **deconstruction** as a method to trace the origin, the genealogy, and the meaning of texts or canons. (A canon is a work, often a book, prized as having authoritative knowledge in a given culture.) A text is often a book, but it might also be a dialogue, a movie or a play, or another type of cultural representation. In education, a text is often a curriculum guide, a video, or a book, including a textbook, such as the one you are reading. The purpose of deconstruction is to show that texts, rather than reflecting metaphysical truths, are historical and cultural constructions that involve political power relationships.

For example, proponents of the "great books" curriculum discussed later in this chapter use the books as canons, but many postmodernist thinkers suggest that these texts emphasize Western culture while marginalizing Asian and African cultures. Postmodernists would say that texts such as Plato's *Republic* and Aristotle's

[19]Friedrich Nietzsche, *The Will to Power,* trans. Walter Kaufmann (New York: Vintage, 1967); also see David E. Cooper, *World Philosophies: An Historical Introduction* (Oxford, U.K., and Cambridge, Mass.: Blackwell, 1996), p. 467.

[20]John A. Zahorik, *Constructivist Teaching* (Bloomington, Ind.: Phi Delta Kappa Educational Foundation, 1995), pp. 10–13.

[21]For Foucault as a philosopher of dialogue, see Christopher Falzon, *Foucault and Social Dialogue: Beyond Fragmentation* (New York and London: Routledge, 1999). Also see Gavin Kendall and Gary Wickham, *Using Foucault's Methods* (New York: Sage, 1999); and Mark Olsen, *Michel Foucault: Materialism and Education* (New York: Bergin and Garvey, 1999).

Nicomachean Ethics lack enduring, universal authority; they are mere historical pieces that can be deconstructed.

■ Deconstructing a text

In deconstructing a canon or text, postmodernists ask (1) What events and situations at a particular time gave prominence to the canon? (2) Who gives a canon a privileged status in a culture or society, and who benefits from its acceptance as an authority? (3) Why do canons exclude the voices of underrepresented and marginalized individuals and groups? The answers to these questions point to those who hold actual social, economic, political, and educational power in a particular culture and society.

Questions regarding formal education focus on how curriculum is constructed. What texts represent official knowledge in the curriculum? What texts and experiences do we exclude? How do we interpret texts to establish and maintain power relationships among different groups?

The Basic Questions

The postmodernist educator seeks to raise consciousness and bring about change by deconstructing traditional assumptions about knowledge, education, schooling, and instruction. Postmodernists consider the school's curriculum not a repository of objective truths and scientific discourses but an area of conflicting viewpoints—some dominate and others are marginalized.

■ Schools reproduce status quo

Postmodernists contend that American public schools are key agencies in the social, political, and economic system justified by official rationales. These rationales, made by those seeking to legitimize their own privileged societal status and to disempower other, less fortunate people, include claims that schools (1) fairly and equitably educate the children of all the people; (2) facilitate upward social and economic mobility; and (3) are necessary for the continuation of a democratic society. Disputing these official claims, postmodernists argue that public schools, like other official institutions, help reproduce a society that is (1) patriarchal—it favors men over women—(2) Eurocentric—its so-called knowledge is largely a construction of white people of European ancestry—and (3) particularly in the United States, capitalist—private property and the corporate mentality are glorified in the free-market ideology. The experiences of other groups such as people of color, for example, are excluded from the curriculum's official narratives.[22]

■ Struggle over curriculum

Postmodernists see the curriculum as a locus of struggle, a cultural war among groups contending to assert power. If we think of the curriculum as a contested area, we can see how deconstruction operates. Many arguments have been advanced for a standard cultural "core" curriculum in secondary and higher education. Suggestions for core requirements often reflect the traditional canons of Western culture. Postmodernists challenge these canons as representing male-dominated, European-centered, Western and capitalist culture. They argue that the works of underrepresented groups—African, Asian, Latino, and Native Americans; feminists, the economically disadvantaged, and gays and lesbians—should be included in the curriculum, even at its core, if there is still a core. The diverse curriculum favored by postmodernists would allow all children to feel represented and to gain from schooling.

■ Teaching as representation

Postmodernists believe that instruction involves "representation," meaning any kind of cultural expression or discussion, including language, stories, images, music,

---

[22]Angeline Martel and Linda Peterat, "Margins of Exclusion, Margins of Transformation: The Place of Women in Education," in Rebecca A. Martusewicz and William M. Reynolds, *Inside/Out: Contemporary Critical Perspectives in Education* (New York: St. Martin's Press, 1994), p. 152.

and other cultural constructions.[23] Postmodernists urge teachers to become conscious of their powerful role and their need to critically examine the representations they make to students. Rather than transmit only officially approved knowledge, teachers must critically and reflectively present a wider range of human experience.[24] Students in postmodern-era schools should hear many voices and many stories, including the autobiographies and biographies—the personal and social history—of the students who attend the school. It is crucial that marginalized groups are heard and seen and become participants in consciousness-raising dialogues.[25]

Implications for Today's Classroom Teacher

■ Teacher empowerment

Postmodernists urge teachers to empower themselves through critical review of their school's purpose, its curriculum content and organization, and the role and mission of the teaching profession. Empowerment means that teachers take responsibility for shaping their own futures and for helping students to shape their own lives.[26]

■ Site-based philosophy

The process of empowering teachers and students begins in the schools and communities where they work and live. Unlike idealists and realists, who derive a philosophy of education from abstract metaphysical speculation, postmodernists urge teachers to create their own site-based educational philosophy. Teachers, students, and community members must begin a local, site-based examination of key control issues by examining such questions as (1) who actually controls their school, establishes the curriculum, and sets the academic standards; (2) what motivates those who control the school; and (3) what rationale justifies the existing curriculum? Curriculum in a postmodern school should analyze issues of personal and group identity, and control and power relationships, and encourage the cultural politics and social criticism that lead to collective action. This kind of critical analysis will empower people and transform society by challenging special economic and political interests and privileges.

Standards & Assessment ✅

■ Postmodernists deconstruct standards

The postmodernist emphasis on hearing from diverse groups resonates well with arguments for cultural diversity and multiculturalism in the schools. In addition, postmodernist educators ask critical questions about standards, especially when schools use standardized tests to measure student achievement, as in the No Child Left Behind Act. In particular, they would search for power relationships by asking who mandates the testing; who develops the test; who interprets the test results; how results will be used; and what roles politicians, parents, teachers, and students play in setting standards and using tests to verify if standards are met.

Similar questions would apply to analyzing technology use in the classroom. The World Wide Web and Internet can empower people by creating quick communication means to share ideas and common concerns with each other. Likewise, technology, if controlled by dominant groups, can help indoctrinate people to accept the status quo that disempowers them. A postmodernist teacher would be sure

---

[23]Elizabeth Ellsworth, "Representation, Self-Representation, and the Meanings of Difference: Questions for Educators," in Rebecca A. Martusewicz and William M. Reynolds, *Inside/Out: Contemporary Critical Perspectives in Education* (New York: St. Martin's Press, 1994), p. 100.
[24] Ibid., pp. 100–101.
[25] William E. Doll, Jr., *A Post-Modern Perspective on Curriculum* (New York: Teachers College Press, 1993).
[26]Joe L. Kincheloe, *Toward A Critical Politics of Teacher Thinking: Mapping the Postmodern* (Westport, Conn.: Bergin & Garvey, 1993), p. 35.

A student shares part of his personal life in a poem about his brother. Postmodernists urge teachers to include the personal stories of all students in the curriculum and to avoid representations that transmit only knowledge approved by the dominant groups of society. (© *Nancy Sheehan/ PhotoEdit*)

to examine the representations in software for student use, as well as to consider issues of power involved in arranging for students to have access to technology.

■ Postmodern lesson

What would a postmodernist lesson be like? Students in a high school American history class might examine how Mexicans living in the territories that Mexico was forced to cede to the United States after the Mexican War were marginalized. Then, they might discuss how Latinos and other marginalized groups have made their voices heard throughout U.S. history. The lesson might include a journal assignment in which students examine areas of their own lives where they feel powerful or marginalized and suggest some actions they believe would help make their voices heard in constructive ways.

REFOCUS Can you recall any influences of postmodernism in your own education? What place does this philosophy hold in your plans for teaching?

▶ Educational Theories

In the following sections we examine four educational theories: progressivism, critical theory, perennialism, and essentialism (see Overview 4.2). Whereas philosophies encompass metaphysics, epistemology, axiology, and logic, theories seek to explain more particular phenomena and processes. Educational theories attempt to

OVERVIEW 4.2 *Theories of Education*

Theory	Aim	Curriculum	Educational Implications	Proponents
Progressivism (rooted in pragmatism)	To educate the individual according to his or her interests and needs	Activities and projects	Instruction that features problem solving and group activities; teacher acts as a facilitator	Dewey Kilpatrick Parker Washburne
Critical Theory (rooted in neo-Marxism and postmodernism)	To raise consciousness about critical issues	Autobiographies about oppressed peoples	Focus on social conflicts	McLaren Giroux
Perennialism (rooted in realism)	To educate the rational person	Subject matter hierarchically arranged to cultivate the intellect (great books, etc.)	Focus on enduring human concerns as revealed in great works of the Western cultural heritage	Adler Bloom Hutchins Maritain
Essentialism (rooted in idealism and realism)	To educate the useful and competent person	Basic education: reading, writing, arithmetic, history, English, science, foreign languages	Emphasis on skills and subjects that transmit the cultural heritage and contribute to socioeconomic efficiency	Bagley Bestor Conant Morrison

explain the role and functions of schools, curriculum, teaching, and learning. Some theories are derived from philosophies and others arise from practice.

▶ Progressivism

■ A widespread reform movement

Progressive education was part of the general reform movement in American life in the late nineteenth and early twentieth centuries. Although it is often associated with John Dewey's experimentalism, the progressive education movement wove together diverse strands. Whereas some progressives sought to use education for social reform, other progressives, especially administrators, concentrated on making schools more efficient and cost effective. Administrative progressives sought to build larger schools that could house more class sections and create more curriculum diversity.[27]

■ Progressives in education

Progressive education arose from a rebellion against traditional schooling. Educators such as G. Stanley Hall, Francis Parker, and William H. Kilpatrick argued against mindless routine, rote memorization, and authoritarian classroom management. Progressive teachers developed teaching styles and methods that emphasized students' own interests and needs. Their classrooms were flexible, permissive, and open-ended.

[27]Arthur Zilversmit, *Changing Schools: Progressive Education Theory and Practice, 1930–1960* (Chicago: University of Chicago Press, 1993).

Key Concepts

■ Practices opposed by progressives

The Progressive Education Association, an organization that incorporated a variety of views, did not fashion a comprehensive educational philosophy because progressive educators often disagreed among themselves. Nevertheless, they generally condemned the following traditional school practices: (1) authoritarian teachers, (2) book-based instruction, (3) passive memorization of factual information, (4) the isolation of schools from society, and (5) using physical or psychological coercion to manage classrooms. Although they had more difficulty in agreeing about what they favored, members of the Progressive Education Association generally believed that (1) the child should be free to develop naturally; (2) interest, stimulated by direct experience, is the best stimulus for learning; (3) the teacher should facilitate learning; (4) close cooperation is essential between the school and the home; and (5) the progressive school should be a laboratory for experimentation.

■ Practices favored by progressives

■ Progressive reforms in schools

Opposing the conventional subject-matter curriculum, progressives experimented with alternative curricula, using activities, experiences, problem solving, and projects. Child-centered progressive teachers also emphasized collaborative learning rather than competition. More socially oriented progressives, called **social reconstructionists**, sought to make schools centers of larger social reforms.[28] Moreover, progressive schools, especially private ones, sought to free children from conventional restraints and repression.

The Basic Questions

■ Antitraditional

Progressives dislike dogma and would not answer questions about knowledge, education, the school, teaching, and learning with a single voice. In general, however, progressives view knowledge as relative, arising from human experience, rather than in universal terms. Education is a means of liberating human creativity in thinking and feeling. Progressives believe that all children have the right to attend schools.

■ Child-centered and social reformist

Although united against traditionalism and authoritarianism, some progressives emphasize children's freedom and others emphasize social reform. Child-centered progressives want schools in which children are free to experiment, play, and express themselves. Social reform progressives want schools to be agencies of social change.

■ Readiness, interests, and needs

For progressives, children's readiness and interests and not predetermined subjects shape curriculum and instruction. Instructionally flexible, progressive teachers use a repertoire of learning activities such as problem solving, field trips, creative artistic expression, and projects. They see teaching and learning as active, exciting, and ever-changing processes.

■ Constructing reality

As educational community builders, progressive teachers want students to work collaboratively on projects based on their shared experience. This approach has similarities to popular constructivist approaches. Constructivism, like progressivism, emphasizes socially interactive and process-oriented "hands-on" learning in which students work collaboratively to expand and revise their knowledge base.[29]

---

[28]The definitive history of progressive education remains Lawrence A. Cremin, *The Transformation of the School* (New York: Random House, 1961).
[29]For a discussion of the challenges of translating constructivist epistemology into classroom practice, see Peter W. Airasian and Mary E. Walsh, "Constructivist Cautions," *Phi Delta Kappan* (February 1997), pp. 444–449.

Implications for Today's Classroom Teacher

■ Example of a progressive strategy

How might a progressive strategy work in today's schools? A junior high or middle school social studies class might examine Latinos' contributions to American life. After defining the term *Latino* and identifying the various ethnic groups included in that designation, the class might be divided into research and reporting teams. Each team would focus on a particular Latino group and prepare a report to be shared collaboratively with the class. The team activities might include the following: Team A would trace the origins, migration, major areas of residence, and problems of Mexican Americans; Team B would conduct similar research on Puerto Rican Americans; and Team C would do the same on Cuban Americans. The teams would be encouraged to create multidimensional reports that use printed material, films, illustrations, and invited speakers representative of the particular group. Then, the entire class, as a collaborative learning experience, would use the research teams' reports to identify cultural similarities and differences between the three ethnic groups and their contributions to American society.

The teacher would act as a resource facilitator during the project. Consulting with each team, he would suggest library, Web, and community resources and help students discover ways of researching the project and solving the problems it presented. The teacher would also guide the students in sharing their information and reaching a collaborative conclusion.

REFOCUS Progressive influences are strong in many American schools. Would you like to teach in such a school? Why?

▶ Critical Theory

Critical theory, a highly influential contemporary theory of education, urges a rigorous analytical critique of schools and society to uncover exploitative power relationships and bring about equity, fairness, and justice. Many of its theoretical assumptions stem from the postmodernist and existentialist philosophies, neo-Marxism, feminist and multicultural theories, and from Paulo Freire's liberation pedagogy. (Freire is discussed in the Pioneers in Education chapter.) Among the highly visible leaders of critical theory are Henry Giroux and Peter McLaren.

Key Concepts

■ Neo-Marxist influence

Critical theory has been influenced by the ideology of Karl Marx, an important nineteenth-century philosopher who argued that all institutions rest on an economic base and that human history is a struggle of socioeconomic classes for social and economic control.[30] Critical theorists often use such Marxist concepts as class conflict and alienation. Alienation refers to the social and psychological state of people who have been marginalized and pushed to society's edges.

■ Powerful groups dominate

According to critical theorists, critical consciousness requires recognition that an individual's social status, including educational and economic expectations and opportunities, is largely conditioned by race, ethnicity, gender, and class. The dominant, higher socioeconomic class that controls social, political, economic, and

---

[30]For an assessment of Marxist educational theory, see Frank Margonis, "Marxism, Liberalism, and Educational Theory, *Educational Theory* (Fall 1993), pp. 449–465.

educational institutions uses its power to maintain, or reproduce, its favored position and to subordinate socially and economically disadvantaged classes.[31] In the United States the historically subordinate groups are the urban and rural poor, African and Native Americans, Latinos, women, and gays and lesbians.[32] Through a critical education, however, subordinated classes and groups can become conscious of their exploitation, resist domination, overturn the patterns of oppression, and empower themselves.

The Basic Questions

■ A new public philosophy

Drawing a great deal of their influence from the postmodern philosophy described earlier in this chapter, critical theorists want to raise consciousness about questions dealing with knowledge, education, the school, and teaching and learning. They believe that knowledge is about issues of social, political, economic, and educational power and control. In particular, critical theorists want to raise the consciousness of those who are forced into lesser, marginal, and subordinate positions in society because of race, ethnicity, language, class, or gender.[33]

■ Social control

Critical theorists contend that economically, politically, and socially dominant classes control and use schools for social maintenance and control. To maintain the status quo that affords them a commanding position, children of the dominant classes attend prestigious educational institutions and receive educations that prepare for high-level careers in business, industry, and government. Children of subordinate groups and classes are indoctrinated to accept the conditions that disempower them as the "best of all possible worlds." Schools in economically disadvantaged urban and declining rural areas, for example, serve mainly the poor, African Americans, and Latinos. Typically underfinanced, these schools often are housed in deteriorating buildings and lack needed resources.

■ Teacher empowerment

The typical inner-city school and many other schools as well are enmeshed in a large, hierarchical educational bureaucracy. With orders coming down from the top, teachers have little or no power in setting goals or making decisions about how schools will run. Within the school, teachers tend to be isolated from each other in self-contained classrooms. Further, parents and others in the local community are kept at a distance, with little involvement or interaction with the school. The curriculum, too, is determined by higher-level administrators, with little room for local initiatives that relate to the life experiences of students or community people.

■ Official curriculum

Critical theorists see the curriculum as existing in two spheres: the formal official curriculum and the **"hidden" curriculum**. The officially mandated curriculum contains skills and subjects purposely taught and transmitted to students. The "hidden" curriculum conveys behaviors and attitudes imposed on students through the school environment. Critical theorists suggest that both of these curricula preserve the status of dominant social classes.

---

[31]Martin Carnoy, "Education, State, and Culture in American Society," in Henry A. Giroux and Peter L. McLaren, eds., *Critical Pedagogy, the State, and Cultural Struggle* (Albany: State University of New York Press, 1998), pp. 6–7.

[32]Angeline Martel and Linda Peterat, "Margins of Exclusion, Margins of Transformation: The Place of Women in Education," in Rebecca A. Martusewicz and William Reynolds, eds., *Inside/Out: Contemporary Critical Perspectives in Education* (New York: St. Martin's Press, 1994), pp. 151–154.

[33]Henry A. Giroux and Peter L. McLaren, "Schooling, Cultural Politics, and the Struggle for Democracy," in Henry A. Giroux and Peter McLaren, eds., *Critical Pedagogy, the State, and Cultural Struggle* (New York: State University of New York Press, 1989), pp. xi–xii.

The dominant classes use the official curriculum to transmit their particular beliefs and values as the legitimate version of knowledge for all students. For example, the official version of history portrays the American experience as a largely European American series of triumphs in settling and industrializing the nation. African and Native Americans and Latinos are relegated to the margins or as "add-ons" to the official narrative. Critical theorists point out that many schools' preferred method of instruction is to use officially sanctioned textbooks to transmit approved information to students. This process of transmission, instead of critical thinking and analysis, reproduces in students the officially constructed version of knowledge.

■ Hidden curriculum

A key element in school-based social control is lodged in the hidden curriculum. "Hidden" because it is not stated in published state mandates or local school policies, it permeates the public-school milieu. For example, sexist attitudes that males are better than females in mathematics and science courses preserve gender-specific patterns of entry into ongoing education and careers in those fields.

Although the privileged classes have historically dominated schools, critical theorists do not see their domination as inevitable. They challenge current patterns of control and work to break the cycle of domination. They believe that teachers and schools can help raise the consciousness of the exploited and empower the dispossessed. They want schools to become democratic public spheres in which young people learn to live the ethics of equality.

■ Students' life stories

Critical theorists argue that the truly legitimate knowledge and the values in schools and curriculum arise in students' local context, the immediate situation and the community in which they live and in the school they attend. Teachers should begin consciousness raising with the students in their classes, by examining the conditions in their neighborhood communities. Students can share their life stories to create a collaborative group autobiography that recounts experiences at home, in school, and in the community. They can further connect this group autobiography to the larger histories of their respective economic classes and racial, ethnic, and language groups.

The United States' truly multicultural society provides many more versions of the American experience story than an officially approved one. Members of each race, ethnic, and language group can tell their own story rather than having it told for them. After exploring their own identities, students can develop ways to recognize stereotyping and misrepresentation and to resist indoctrination both in and out of school. They can learn how to take control of their own lives and shape their own futures.[34]

Implications for Today's Classroom Teacher

■ Teachers must empower themselves

Critical theorists urge teachers to (1) find out who their real friends are in the struggle for control of schools; (2) learn who their students are by helping them to work toward their own self-identities; (3) collaborate with local people for school and community improvement; (4) join with like-minded teachers in teacher-controlled professional organizations that work for genuine educational reform; (5) take part in a critical dialogue about political, social, economic, and educational issues that confront American society.

Standards & Assessment ✔

■ External limits on teachers' power

In critiquing teachers' working conditions, critical theorists find teachers' power in determining their own professional lives severely limited. State boards, not teachers'

---

[34]Christine E. Sleeter and Peter L. McLaren, eds. *Multicultural Education, Critical Pedagogy, and the Politics of Difference* (Albany: State University of New York Press, 1995).

professional organizations, largely determine entry requirements into the profession. Where student performance on standardized academic achievement tests determine schools' effectiveness and teachers' competency, teachers are judged by criteria mandated by state legislators and prepared by "experts" external to the particular school and classroom.

■ Question uses of technology

Michael Apple, an educator who analyzes curriculum from a neo-Marxist orientation, warns that much discussion about educational technology in the classroom is rhetorical rather than motivated by a desire for genuine change. Apple believes the real questions regard the purposes of educational technology. Unless educational technology helps uncover the root issues of discrimination and poverty critical theorists raise, it is likely to bring an externally derived, "impersonal,

IN THIS CASE

Students' Perceptions and Feelings and the Official Curriculum

The following case study is excerpted from Peter McLaren, *Life in Schools: An Introduction to Critical Pedagogy in the Foundations of Education.* The case study is based on the experiences of McLaren, a critical theorist philosopher, while teaching in a school in the Toronto suburb of North York, Canada. The school's neighborhood includes many low-income residents, giving the school characteristics of an inner-city school. The case study discussion appears as a diary entry in which Fred, the school principal, and McLaren discuss students' feelings or perceptions of their own reality.

Tuesday, April 25 For the first time since I came to this school, most of the parents showed up for interviews. Although I had scheduled parents for only fifteen minutes each, sometimes the interviews lasted over an hour.

When they had all left, I saw Fred in the hallway and we walked down to his office for a quiet talk. I told him how depressed I was to find that over half my class came from single-parent families who lived below the poverty line.

Fred cleared his throat, leaning forward. "What we have to do in this school is to accept the child for who he or she is. We can't cloud our minds with the fact that the child comes from a single-parent family, or that the father is an alcoholic, or that the mother is rarely home.

"As teachers, we can't ignore that, but we can't let it get in our way, either. We have to try to make these kids feel like people who feel like they're worth something.". . .

"You have to ask yourself if there is any way you can get children to feel good about themselves. . . .

"Listen. Teachers have to understand about the prejudices they bring to their job. Somehow, they have to respect the kids' own values, and where the kid is at. We can impose our values on them, but that implies their values aren't any good. That would be destructive. We've got to develop relationships with these kids, and relationships involve feelings, not simply content or information. With poor kids, it's even harder, because you almost have to say to them that they are worthwhile human beings, that you don't care how they dress or where they come from." Fred was getting very emotional. His jaw tensed, his arms waved as he spoke, his eyes burning right through me.

"The way you reach a poor kid who's doing badly at school is not by concentrating on arithmetic, but by getting something going with him or her that tells them that you care about them as people. Forget about the curriculum, at least for the time being. Reach your kids through feelings." *(Peter McLaren, Life in Schools)*

Questions:

1. What is Fred's opinion about the role of the official curriculum in the students' education?

2. What importance does Fred give to students' experiences, their autobiographies, as a basis for teaching and learning?

3. How would Fred resolve the tension between thinking (the cognitive dimension) and feeling (the affective dimension) in education?

4. What meaning would a critical theorist find in the discussion between Fred and McLaren?

prepackaged style" in education rather than one derived from the schools' internal conditions.[35]

■ A lesson with a critical-theory approach

Teachers using a critical-theory approach might design a lesson in which in middle-school social studies students explore their racial and ethnic heritages. Students begin by sharing their impressions of their heritage by telling stories about their families, their customs, and celebrations. Then, parents and grandparents are invited in as guest speakers to share experiences about their cultures with the students. Students then create a multicultural display that includes family photographs, artifacts, and other items that illustrate the lives and cultures of the people who live in the local community.

REFOCUS How might critical theory influence your approach, as a teacher, to issues of cultural diversity in your classroom? What is the critical-theorist strategy for teacher empowerment?

▶ Perennialism

■ Truth in the classics

Perennialism, a culturally conservative educational theory, centers on the authority of tradition and the classics. It believes that (1) truth is universal and does not depend on circumstances of place, time, or person; (2) a good education involves a search for and an understanding of the truth; (3) truth can be found in the great works of civilization; and (4) education is a liberal exercise that develops the intellect.

Perennialism draws heavily on realist principles. The educational similarities between idealism and realism lead some educational theorists to relate perennialism to idealism. However, leading perennialists such as Robert Hutchins and Mortimer Adler based their theory of education on Aristotle's realism

■ Schools cultivate rationality

Agreeing with Aristotle that human beings are rational, perennialists see the school's primary role as intellectual development. They oppose theories that would turn schools into multipurpose agencies, especially economic ones that would use them for vocational training. Although perennialists understand the need for vocational skills and competencies, they believe that other agencies such as business and industry can provide on-the-job training more efficiently than schools. Placing nonacademic demands such as social adjustment or vocational training on schools diverts time and resources from their primary purpose, which is students' intellectual development.

■ Perennial curriculum

Perennialists' most important educational goals are searching for and disseminating truth. They believe that as truth is universal and unchanging, a genuine education also is universal and constant. Thus the school's curriculum should consist of permanent, or perennial, studies that emphasize the recurrent themes of human life. It should contain cognitive subjects that cultivate rationality and the study of moral, aesthetic, and religious principles to develop ethical behavior and civility. Like idealists and realists, perennialists prefer a subject-matter curriculum that includes history, language, mathematics, logic, literature, the humanities, and science. The classical works of literature and art should provide content for these subjects. Perennialists regard mastering these subjects as essential for training the intellect.

■ Hutchins: Education develops the mind

Robert Hutchins, a former president of the University of Chicago, was a highly articulate perennialist theorist. Hutchins described the ideal education as "one that develops intellectual power. . . . The ideal education is not an *ad hoc* education, not

---

[35]Michael W. Apple, *Official Knowledge: Democratic Education in a Conservative Age* (New York and London: Routledge, 2000), pp. 132–133.

an education directed to immediate needs; it is not a specialized education, or a pre-professional education; it is not a utilitarian education. It is an education calculated to develop the mind."[36]

■ Great books of Western civilization

Hutchins particularly recommended intensive study and discussion of the great books of Western civilization. The great books, he reasoned, place the members of each generation in dialogue with the great minds of the past. These classic works, containing persistent or perennial themes, help a person become a genuine cultural participant. They cultivate the intellect and prepare students to think critically. In addition to the classics, he urged the study of grammar, rhetoric, logic, mathematics, and philosophy.

■ Critique of great books curriculum

As we noted earlier in this chapter, postmodernist critics saw Hutchins's great books curriculum as an attempt to give western European cultures predominance over other cultures, such as those of Asia and Africa. In this view, Hutchins's prized great books merely asserted dominant-class interests at a given time in history. For example, postmodernists seek to deconstruct the texts of the great books to find their historically based meaning.

The Paideia Proposal

■ Paideia curriculum

Mortimer J. Adler's **The Paideia Proposal**: *An Educational Manifesto* is a revival of perennialism.[37] *Paideia,* a Greek word, means the total educational formation of a person. Affirming the right of all people to a general education, Adler wants all students in America's democratic society to have the same high quality of schooling. The *Paideia* curriculum includes language, literature, fine arts, mathematics, natural sciences, history, geography, and social studies. These studies help develop a repertoire of intellectual skills such as reading, writing, speaking, listening, calculating, observing, measuring, estimating, and problem solving, which lead to higher-order thinking and reflection.[38]

The Basic Questions

■ A general education

Progressives criticize perennialism for fostering educational elitism. Denying this allegation, perennialists defend their program as genuinely democratic, arguing that all persons have the right to the same high-quality education. Students, they contend, should not be grouped or streamed into "tracks" that prevent some from acquiring the general education to which they are entitled by their common humanity. To track some students into an academic curriculum and others into vocational curricula denies genuine equality of educational opportunity.

■ Against cultural relativism

Perennialists strongly oppose **cultural relativism**, which is associated with pragmatism, progressivism, and critical theory. According to cultural relativism, our "truths" are temporary statements based on our coping with changing circumstances. The change in environments over time and differences from place to place, make truth, rather than permanently and universally valid, temporarily and situa-

---

[36]Robert M. Hutchins, *A Conversation on Education* (Santa Barbara, Calif.: The Fund for the Republic, 1963), p. 1. See also Robert M. Hutchins, *The Learning Society* (New York: Praeger, 1968); and Hutchins, *The Higher Learning in America* (New Haven, Conn.: Yale University Press, 1962).

[37]Mortimer J. Adler, *The Paideia Proposal: An Educational Manifesto* (New York: Macmillan, 1982); see also Mortimer J. Adler, *Paideia Problems and Possibilities* (New York: Macmillan, 1983).

[38]Adler, *Paideia Proposal,* pp. 22–23.

tionally valid. Perennialists, like Allan Bloom in *The Closing of the American Mind*, condemn cultural relativism for weakening ethical character. They claim it denies universal standards by which certain actions are consistently either morally right or wrong.[39]

Implications for Today's Classroom Teacher

Perennialists, like idealists and realists, see the classroom as an environment for students' intellectual growth. To stimulate students' intellects, teachers must be liberally educated people who love truth and desire to lead a life based on it. Indeed, a liberal education is more important for perennialist teachers than courses in educational methods.

■ Enduring human concerns

In primary grades, the perennialist teacher would emphasize learning fundamental skills such as reading, writing, and computation to build literacy and readiness to begin the lifelong quest for truth. Perennialist secondary teachers would structure lessons around enduring human concerns explored in the great works of history, literature, and philosophy. Like idealists, perennialists emphasize the classics that have engaged the interest of people across generations. In perennialist schools, administrators, teachers, and students maintain high standards for academic work.

Standards & Assessment ✔
■ Emphasis on academic content

Perennialists endorse high academic standards, but they would question the content tested to assess students' competency. If the tests reflect knowledge of the enduring subjects and great books, they would favor them. Standards not based on this kind of content would raise questions regarding the assessment process. The same criteria would apply to educational technology. They would favor technology used to transmit the great works of art and literature, but technology used as a substitute for the great books would be considered another way to trivialize the educational process.

■ A perennialist lesson

An illustration of the perennialist emphasis on recurring human concerns and values can be seen in a middle-school literature class that is reading and discussing Louisa May Alcott's *Little Women*. The students have discussed the main characters—Marmee, Jo, Beth, Meg, and Amy—and the issues the March family faced. The class discussion reveals that the March family's sad times and happy times exist in family life today. That evening at dinner her grandmother asks Alice, a student in the class, "What are you studying in school?" Alice replies, "We just finished reading *Little Women*." Alice's mother and grandmother say that they, too, read and enjoyed the book when they were girls. In the ensuing conversation, Alice, her mother, and her grandmother share their impressions of the book. In such ways perennial themes can become memories that transcend time and generations.

The Taking Issue box explores the question of child-centered or subject-matter–centered curricula, an issue on which perennialists take a definite stand.

REFOCUS Did your own educational experiences include strong influences from perennialism? How do you think this theory will influence your teaching?

---

[39]Allan Bloom, *The Closing of the American Mind* (New York: Simon and Schuster, 1987).

taking issue

Question Should education be child centered, focusing on children's interests and needs?

Education: Child Centered or Subject Matter?

A persistent issue in American education is whether curriculum and instruction should focus on the child's interests and needs or on cultural transmission. Pragmatists and progressives contend that education should arise from children's interests. These interests, they say, lead to projects that connect children with the larger world. Idealists, realists, perennialists, and essentialists disagree, arguing that schools should prescribe subjects that transmit cultural heritage from adults, society's mature members, to children, its immature members.

Arguments PRO

1 Experience in their immediate environment leads children to realize needs and interests in learning skills and knowledge. Children learn most effectively when guided by interests arising from their direct experience.

2 Learning is a process that engages children with their environment; projects give children a hands-on learning process by which to construct their own concepts about reality.

3 When allowed to follow their interests, children will exert the necessary effort to solve problems and work on projects.

4 Child-oriented process learning results in collaborative learning that develops a genuine community of learners.

Arguments CON

1 Over time, civilized people have developed culture, often through trial and error. Thus, relying primarily on children's interests and needs to repeat this trial and error is a needlessly inefficient waste of time. It is crucial to transmit this cultural heritage from adults to children deliberately and efficiently.

2 Certain skills, especially literacy and numeracy, and certain subjects, such as mathematics, science, language, and history, have been developed by the culture's great thinkers. This organized knowledge must be taught deliberately and sequentially to children.

3 Even if children are not initially interested in learning the culture's skills and subjects, these must be transmitted to them so they can participate in society.

4 To rely on children's interests as the foundation of the curriculum is to jeopardize the transmission of the culture from one generation to the next.

▶ Essentialism

Essentialism, also known as basic education, asserts that certain fundamental skills and subjects are crucial to perpetuating and continuing human civilization. These fundamentals or essentials are the skills of literacy (reading and writing) and computation (arithmetic) and the subjects of history, mathematics, science, languages, and literature. Deliberate instruction that transmits the basic skills and knowledge areas from one generation to the next guarantees civilization's perpetuation and survival. Failure to transmit these necessary skills and subjects puts civilization in peril. The great amount to learn and limited time to learn it mean that curriculum and instruction must be carefully planned and organized and efficiently transmitted by teachers to students.

Neo-Essentialism

The 1980s and 1990s witnessed a strong revival of basic education and a new, or neo-essentialist, movement developed. The neo-essentialists, often allied with political and cultural conservatives, developed a critique of existing schools and proposed a program to remedy perceived deficiencies in the educational system, especially in the public schools.

■ New approaches neglected basics

Neo-essentialists contended that new and sometimes experimental approaches to teaching had resulted in a neglect of systematic direct instruction in basic skills of reading, writing, and computation. This, in turn, had caused a decline in literacy standards. Social promotion policies, which promoted children in public schools to higher grades to keep them with their age cohort, even if they had not mastered grade-appropriate skills and subjects, had eroded academic standards. These policies, neo-essentialists charged, had lowered academic standards and produced a notable decline in scores on standardized tests such as the SAT and ACT. In addition, some neo-essentialists were concerned that a morally permissive environment in the schools had weakened fundamental civic values of industriousness, responsibility, and patriotism.

■ "New basics"

To correct these deficiencies, *A Nation at Risk,* a national report sponsored by the U.S. Department of Education, recommended that all high-school students complete a rigorous curriculum of "new basics" consisting of English, mathematics, science, social studies, and computer science.[40] (See the chapter on The Purposes of Education for more details on *A Nation at Risk.*)

Standards & Assessment ✓
■ Start of standards movement

Stimulated by *A Nation at Risk* and other critical reports that asserted basic educational themes, a standards movement developed. The essential theme of the standards movement is that American education will be improved by creating high academic standards, or benchmarks, for students' academic achievement and by measuring progress toward achievement of those benchmarks via standardized tests. By 2000, the standards movement was affecting schools throughout the United States as states enacted legislation requiring standardized testing in basic subjects.

Standards & Assessment ✓
■ No Child Left Behind

A pronounced endorsement of standards came with the enactment of the federal Elementary and Secondary Education Act of 2001, the No Child Left Behind Act (NCLB). Although NCLB is comprehensive legislation, its key features reinforce an essentialist basic education approach. It identifies the key basics as reading and mathematics. The act is also based on the neo-essentialist premise running through the standards movement—students' academic achievement can be measured objectively by standardized tests.

Standards & Assessment ✓
■ Terms of NCLB

To qualify for federal aid under the terms of NCLB, states must establish annual assessments in reading and mathematics for every student in grades 3 through 8. Proponents of this approach contend that these tests will help identify schools in which large numbers of students fail to achieve to the standard and provide remediation to improve the average academic performance of their students.[41] The law holds school districts accountable for improving the performance of disadvantaged students as well as the overall student population. Schools and districts failing to make adequate yearly progress are to be identified and helped. If the schools fail to meet standards for three years, their students may then transfer to a higher performing public or private school.[42]

---

[40]National Commission on Excellence in Education, *A Nation at Risk: The Imperative for Educational Reform* (Washington, D.C.: U.S. Department of Education, 1983), pp. 5, 24.
[41]*No Child Left Behind* (Washington, D.C.: U.S. Printing Office, 2001), p. 1.
[42]Ibid., pp. 8–9.

The Basic Questions

■ Role of school to teach basics

Essentialists argue that schools and teachers must stay with their primary task and not be diverted into nonacademic areas. They oppose using schools in attempts to solve social and economic problems. Although these problems may be examined in relevant subjects, schools should not be politicized and used to advance political, social, and economic agendas. The appropriate role of the school is to teach students the basic skills and subjects that will prepare them to function effectively and efficiently in society.

■ Favor defined subject-matter boundaries

Essentialists favor a subject-matter curriculum that differentiates and organizes subjects according to their internal logical or chronological principles. Curriculum that ignores the past, rejects subject-matter boundaries, and prides itself on being interdisciplinary or transdisciplinary often, in reality, causes educational confusion. Essentialists consider progress through the curriculum a cumulative process. Basic skills—such as reading, writing, and computing—have generative power in that they transfer to other subjects and functions. From the basics, students advance to more complex subjects that require higher-order thinking. The curriculum's skills and subjects should be well defined as to scope and have a sequence that is cumulative and designed to prepare students for the future.

■ Suspicious of innovations

Essentialists are highly suspicious of so-called innovative or process learning approaches, such as constructivism, in which students construct or create their own knowledge in a collaborative fashion. Essentialists argue that civilized people learn effectively and efficiently by using knowledge developed and organized by scientists, scholars, and other experts. We need not continually reinvent the wheel, wasting time and resources by "discovering" what is already known.

Implications for Today's Classroom Teacher

■ Transmitting essential skills

The essentialist goal of education is to transmit and preserve the necessary elements of human culture. Schools have the specific and well-defined task of transmitting essential human skills and subjects to the young so that civilization can be maintained and passed on to future generations.[43] To accomplish this goal, teachers should (1) develop a well-defined curriculum of basic skills and subjects; (2) inculcate traditional values of patriotism, hard work, effort, punctuality, respect for authority, and civility; (3) emphasize a core based on Western civilization and traditional American values; (4) operate classrooms efficiently and effectively as spheres of discipline and order; (5) promote students on the basis of academic achievement and not social promotion.

■ An essentialist lesson

Essentialist logic proceeds deductively, with emphasis on first mastering facts and then basing generalizations on those facts. Consider a high-school American history class studying the differences between the two African American leaders, Booker T. Washington and W. E. B. Du Bois. First, the teacher assigns reading on both men. Then she leads a discussion in which the students carefully identify Washington's and Du Bois's differences in background, education, and policy. After such teacher-led research, the students must reach a judgment about why Washington and Du Bois acted as they did and assess their influence in African American and United States history.

---

[43]Diane Ravitch, *Left Back: A Century of Failed School Reforms* (New York: Simon and Schuster, 2000), pp. 465–467.

 In what ways do you believe the essentialist-influenced trend toward increased standardized testing will affect your teaching?

▶ Constructing Your Personal Philosophy of Education

Now that we have examined the major philosophies and theories of education, we can return to the questions about knowledge, education, schooling, and teaching and learning raised at the beginning of the chapter. You can now begin to construct your own philosophy of education by reflecting on and recording your answers to such questions as

- Do you believe that knowledge is based on universal and eternal truths or is it relative to different times and places?
- What is the purpose of education? Is it to transmit cultural heritage, to provide economic and social skills, to develop critical-thinking skills, or to criticize and reform society?
- What are schools for? Are they to teach skills and subjects, encourage personal self-definition, develop human intelligence, or create patriotic and economically productive citizens?
- What should curriculum contain? Should it include basic skills and subjects, experiences and projects, the great books and classics, inquiry processes, critical dialogues?
- What should the relationship be between teachers and students? Should it include transmitting heritage, teaching and learning skills and subjects, examining great ideas, encouraging self-expression and self-definition, constructing knowledge, or solving problems?

▶ Summing Up

1 To provide an orientation for developing your philosophy of education, the text defined the terms *metaphysics, epistemology, axiology (ethics* and *aesthetics),* and *logic,* and how these subdivisions of philosophy relate to questions of education, schooling, knowledge, and teaching and learning.

2 To provide a frame of reference for developing your philosophy of education, we examined the philosophies of education of idealism, realism, pragmatism, existentialism, and postmodernism and the educational theories of progressivism, critical theory, perennialism, and essentialism.

3 By studying these philosophies and theories of education, you can work toward formulating your personal philosophy of education and come to understand the underlying philosophical bases of curriculum and teaching and learning.

▶ Key Terms

philosophies (94)
theories (94)
metaphysics (94)
epistemology (95)

axiology (96)
ethics (96)
aesthetics (96)
deductive logic (96)

inductive logic (96)
idealism (96)
macrocosm (97)
microcosm (97)
a priori ideas (97)
Socratic method (99)
realism (99)
pragmatism (102)
experience (103)
existentialism (106)
postmodernism (109)

constructivism (109)
deconstruction (109)
progressivism (113)
social reconstructionism (114)
critical theory (critical pedagogy) (115)
"hidden" curriculum (116)
perennialism (119)
The Paideia Proposal (120)
cultural relativism (120)
essentialism (122)

▶ Discussion Questions

1 Reflect on your ideas about knowledge, education and schooling, and teaching and learning. What would you say is your philosophy of education? If you have the opportunity, share your thoughts with your classmates and listen to their philosophies. Discuss the agreements and disagreements that emerge.

2 Reflect on how your philosophy of education has been influenced by significant teachers in your life or by books and motion pictures about teachers and teaching. Share and discuss such influences with your classmates.

3 What underlying philosophical orientations can you identify in courses you are taking or in your teacher-education program as a whole?

4 Of the philosophies and theories examined in this chapter, which is most relevant and which is least relevant to contemporary American education? Why?

▶ Suggested Projects for Professional Development

1 Contemporary papers on the philosophy of education presented at the Twentieth World Congress of Philosophy are available at **www.bu.edu/wcp/MainEduc.htm**. Identify and review the papers most useful in helping you create your own philosophy of education.

2 Consult the Council for Basic Education Web site at **www.c-b-e.org** and examine the council's educational philosophy. Is this philosophy similar to perennialism and essentialism? How does it differ from pragmatism, progressivism, and critical theory?

3 In your field-based or clinical experience, keep a journal that identifies the philosophy or theory underlying the school, curriculum, and teaching-learning methods you have observed. Share and reflect on these observations with the members of your class.

4 Create and maintain a clippings file of articles about education that appear in the popular press—newspapers and magazines—either critiquing schools or proposing educational reforms. Analyze the philosophical and theoretical positions underlying these critiques and proposed reforms. Share and reflect on your observations with other class members.

5 Create and maintain a clippings file of articles about education that appear in local newspapers near the school where you are doing clinical experience, student teaching, or teaching. Analyze the philosophical and theoretical positions underlying these articles. Share and reflect on your observations with other class members.

6 Research and prepare a statement on the school district philosophy of education approved by the board of education where you are doing clinical experience, student teaching, or teaching. Compare and contrast the board's philosophy of education with the philosophies and theories discussed in this chapter. Share and reflect on your observations with other class members.

7 Prepare a set of questions to use as a guide for interviewing key educators—deans, department chairs, professors—at your college or university about their educational philosophies. Share and reflect on your observations with other class members.

8 Prepare a set of questions to use as a guide for interviewing administrators and teachers in the school district in which you are engaged in clinical experience, student teaching, or teaching. The questions should relate to their educational philosophies. Share and reflect on your observations with other class members.

9 Prepare a set of questions to use as a guide for interviewing key community leaders—editors, politicians, media persons, officers of service organizations and unions—about their educational philosophies. Assign class members to report their interview findings.

10 Prepare a set of questions to use as a guide for interviewing key campus leaders who represent a wide cultural diversity—officers of African American, Latino, and Asian American organizations; gay or lesbian alliances; Young Republicans; Young Democrats; socialist youth groups; leftist organizations; right-wing organizations; religious fundamentalists; right to life groups; freedom of choice groups—about their educational philosophies. Assign class members to report their interview findings.

▶ Suggested Resources

 Internet Resources

For an introduction to an extensive collection of materials about pragmatism, consult the Pragmatism Archive at Oklahoma State University, John R. Shook, director: **www.pragmatism.org/archive**.

For recent research, projects, and programs on John Dewey and progressive education, consult the John Dewey Project on Progressive Education at the University of Vermont: **www.uvm.edu/~dewey**.

For commentaries on philosophers and philosophies, consult the Internet Encyclopedia of Philosophy: **www.utm.edu/research/iep**.

For materials on Dewey's life and philosophy, consult the Center for Dewey Studies, Southern Illinois University: **www.siu.edu/~deweyctr**.

For commentaries and analysis of the educational philosophies and theories of selected educators, consult the Gallery of Educational Theorists organized and maintained by Edward G. Rozycki: **www.newfoundations.com/GALLERY/Gallery.html**.

For discussions of informal education in the philosophies and theories of selected educators, consult **www.infed.org/thinkers**.

For information and materials about basic education, consult the Council for Basic Education at **www.c-b-e.org**.

The Foundation for Critical Thinking provides information and resources at **www.criticalthinking.org**.

For papers presented at the Twentieth World Congress of Philosophy on the philosophy of education, consult: **www.bu.edu/wcp/MainEduc.htm**.

For sources, materials, organizations, and links related to the philosophy of education, consult the Open Directory Project at **www.dmoz.org**. Link to the Society/Philosophy listings, then to Philosophy of Education.

Publications

Achterhuis, Hans, ed. *American Philosophy of Technology: The Empirical Turn.* Bloomington: Indiana University Press, 2001. *Examines the rise of technology in philosophical perspective.*

Apple, Michael W. *Democratic Education in a Conservative Age.* New York and London: Routledge, 2000. *Apple identifies educational trends and movements threatening and undermining critical and democratic educational processes in schools.*

Cahoone, Lawrence E. *From Modernism to Postmodernism: An Anthology.* Oxford, U.K.: Blackwell Publishers, 1996. *Provides an anthology of source readings in contemporary philosophy that highlights the movement from modernism to postmodernism.*

Dewey, John. *Experience and Education: The 60th Anniversary Edition.* West Lafayette, Ind.: Kappa Delta Pi, 1998. *This anniversary of Dewey's highly influential book includes commentaries by Maxine Greene, Philip W. Jackson, Linda Darling-Hammond, and O. L. Davis, Jr.*

Falzon, Christopher. *Foucault and Social Dialogue: Beyond Fragmentation.* New York and London: Routledge, 1999. *Falzon examines Foucault as a philosopher of dialogue, especially in relationship to ethical critique and analysis.*

Fishman, Stephen M., and McCarthy, Lucille. *John Dewey and the Challenge of Classroom Practice.* New York: Teachers College Press, 1998. *The authors examine key Deweyan concepts such as student-curriculum integration, interest and effort, and continuity and interaction in terms of schools and classrooms.*

Gutek, Gerald L. *Philosophical and Ideological Perspectives on Education.* Boston: Allyn and Bacon, 1997. *Gutek examines the major philosophies, ideologies, and theories of education.*

Gutek, Gerald L. *Philosophical and Ideological Voices in Education.* Boston: Allyn and Bacon, 2004. *Provides discussions of the major philosophies, ideologies, and theories of education with representative primary source selections.*

Heslep, Robert D. *Philosophical Thinking in Educational Practice.* Westport, Conn.: Praeger Publishers, 1997. *Heslep, a well-respected educational theorist, relates the philosophy of education to classroom practices.*

Hickman, Larry A. *Philosophical Tools for Technological Culture: Putting Pragmatism to Work.* Bloomington: Indiana University Press, 2001. *Provides an examination of the philosophical implications of technology in the modern world.*

Hinchey, Patricia H. *Finding Freedom in the Classroom: A Practical Introduction to Critical Theory.* New York: Peter Lang, 1998. *Hinchey's book examines critical theory in ways applicable to schools and classrooms.*

Johnson, Tony W. *Discipleship or Pilgrimage? The Study of Educational Philosophy.* Albany: State University of New York Press, 1995. *In his critique of educational philosophy and the assumptions of educational philosophers, Johnson argues for the need to rethink the field in terms of school practices.*

Kanpol, Barry. *Critical Pedagogy: An Introduction.* Westport, Conn.: Bergin and Garvey, 1994. *Kanpol's book provides a useful and readable treatment of critical theory, a highly significant contemporary educational theory.*

Martusewicz, Rebecca A., and Reynolds, William M., eds. *Inside/Out: Contemporary Critical Perspectives in Education.* New York: St. Martin's Press, 1994. *Provides a range of essays that analyze critical theory from a variety of perspectives.*

Noddings, Nel. *Educating Moral People: A Caring Alternative to Character Education.* New York: Teachers College Press, 2002. *Noddings, a distinguished philosopher of education, examines the relationships between character education, ethics, and caring in schools and curriculum.*

Noddings, Nel. *Philosophy of Education*. Boulder, Colo.: Westview Press, 1995. *In her well-reviewed book, Noddings relates general issues in the philosophy of education to important questions of educational policy making and classroom practices.*

Ravitch, Diane. *Left Behind: A Century of Failed School Reforms*. New York: Simon and Schuster, 2000. *Ravitch appraises the failure of selected educational reforms based on progressive and social reconstructionist theories of education.*

Thayer-Bacon, Barbara, with Bacon, Charles S. *Philosophy Applied to the Education: Nurturing a Democratic Community in the Classroom*. Columbus, Ohio: Merrill, 1998. *The authors relate philosophy of education to transforming classrooms into democratic spheres of teaching and learning.*

CHAPTER 5

Pioneers in Education

This chapter examines how the great educational pioneers constructed their philosophies and theories of education. Despite their differences, these pioneers all emphasized the importance of childhood and the educational role of the environment. Early pioneers such as Johann Amos Comenius, Jean-Jacques Rousseau, and Johann Heinrich Pestalozzi challenged the inherited concepts of child depravity and passive learning that had long dominated schooling. The child depravity theory insisted that children are born with a tendency to evil and that this inclination to misbehavior could be exorcised by authoritarian teachers who dominated the classroom. In contrast, the early educational pioneers asserted that children are naturally good and that nature provided the cues for their education.

Later educators such as Friedrich Froebel, Maria Montessori, Herbert Spencer, John Dewey, Jean Piaget, and Paulo Freire extended the naturalistic theory of the early pioneer educators. They argued that (1) education should follow the natural stages of human growth and development and (2) children learned by interacting with the objects and situations in their everyday environments. Froebel's kindergarten and Montessori's prepared environment were deliberate efforts to construct learning environments based on children's development. Both Dewey and Piaget emphasized the importance of children's interactions with their environments as the foundation of education. Herbert Spencer made the case for a utilitarian education to enable individuals to adapt to their environments. Freire called for a liberating education in which individuals could transform the conditions in their social and political environments to improve their lives.

As you read this chapter, consider the following questions:

This chapter was revised by Dr. Gerald Gutek.

- Who qualifies as an educational pioneer?
- How did the pioneers develop their philosophies of education?
- How did they redefine knowledge, education, schooling, teaching, and learning?
- How did they challenge and change traditional concepts of the child and the environment?
- Which ideas or practices among the pioneers' contributions are present in today's teaching and learning?
- What contributions from the pioneers are useful to you in developing your philosophy of education?

▶ Comenius: The Search for a New Method

■ Pansophism

Jan Komensky (1592–1670), known as Comenius, was born in the Moravian town of Nivnitz.[1] He lived during Europe's post–Reformation religious wars between Catholics and Protestants—a time of hatred and violence. His family belonged to the Moravian Brethren, a small Protestant church that suffered persecution. Comenius, a bishop and educator of the Brethren, was forced to flee his homeland and lived in exile in other European countries. Hoping to end religious intolerance, he constructed a new educational philosophy, *pansophism,* to cultivate universal understanding. A pioneering peace educator, he believed that universally shared knowledge would generate a love of wisdom that would overcome ethnic and religious hatreds and create a peaceful world order.[2]

■ Learning language by natural means

Comenius was a transitional figure between the Renaissance humanist educators discussed in the chapter on World Roots of American Education, and later naturalistic reformers. His educational philosophy, pansophism, resembled realism in its emphasis on sensory learning. This emphasis would later be developed further by Locke, Rousseau, and Pestalozzi.

Although Comenius stressed the importance of the Latin language in the curriculum, his teaching method used the senses instead of passive memorization. His book, *Gate of Tongues Unlocked,* related Latin instruction to the students' vernacular language. Lessons began with short, simple phrases and gradually proceeded to longer, more complex sentences. A highly inventive educator, Comenius wrote one of the earliest picture books, *The Visible World in Pictures,* as a teaching aid.[3]

■ Respecting children's needs and development

Principles of Teaching and Learning. Comenius respected children's natural needs and interests and strongly opposed the conventional wisdom that children were inherently bad and that teachers needed corporal punishment to discipline them. Instead, Comenius wanted teachers to be gentle and loving persons who would create joyful and pleasant classrooms. He urged teachers to make their lessons and materials appropriate to children's natural stages of growth and development.

---

[1]For a biography of Comenius, see Daniel Murphy, *Comenius: A Critical Reassessment of His Life and Work* (Dublin, Ireland: Irish Academic Press, 1995).
[2]Johann Comenius, *The Labyrinth of the World and the Paradise of the Heart,* translated and introduced by Howard Louthan and Andrea Sterk (New York: Paulist Press, 1998), pp. 17–26.
[3]Edward A. Power, *A Legacy of Learning: A History of Western Education* (Albany: State University of New York Press, 1991), pp. 195–197.

An illustration for Johann Amos Comenius's *Orbis Pictus,* one of the earliest illustrated school texts. The picture illustrates the word, which then appears in Latin and German. *(© Hulton Archive)*

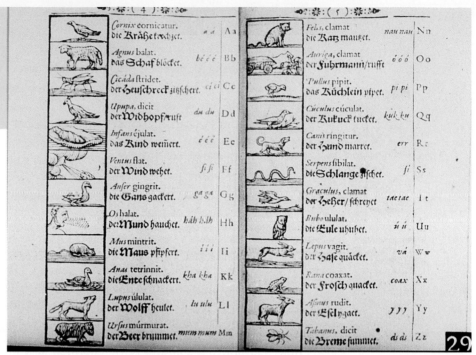

■ Principles of teaching

Warning against hurrying or pressuring children to learn, Comenius advised that children learn most efficiently when they are ready to learn a particular skill or subject. He advised teachers to organize lessons into easily assimilated small steps that made learning gradual, cumulative, and pleasant.

In constructing his philosophy of education, Comenius emphasized the following principles for teachers: (1) use objects or pictures to illustrate concepts; (2) apply lessons to students' practical lives; (3) present lessons directly and simply; (4) emphasize general principles before details; (5) emphasize that all creatures and objects are part of a whole universe; (6) present lessons in sequence, stressing one thing at a time; (7) do not leave a specific subject until students understand it completely.[4] Comenius's principles about basing instruction on the learners' readiness, using concrete objects and examples and illustrations, and moving systematically through a lesson remain useful for teachers.

■ Universal knowledge, a force for peace

Education and Schooling.   Comenius honored multicultural principles that respected religious and cultural diversity. He believed that schooling, by cultivating universal knowledge and values, could promote international understanding and peace. He was also an innovator who incorporated the technological changes of his time, such as the invention of the printing press, by writing widely used textbooks that promoted his new educational methods. Comenius's use of education to promote ethnic and religious tolerance remains important to us today, especially to a world torn by violence and terror.

■ Anticipating progressivism and naturalism

Influence on Educational Practices Today.   Though he lived in the seventeenth century, Comenius's ideas fit well with modern education. He developed plans for

---

[4]Gerald L. Gutek, *Historical and Philosophical Foundations of Education: Selected Readings* (Columbus, Ohio: Merrill, 2001), pp. 50–57.

efficient and effective schools, and his encouragement of children's active and engaged learning anticipated child-centered progressive education. With patience and kindness, teachers should lead children to understand the larger world in which they lived. Later theorists such as Rousseau and Pestalozzi, as well as the progressives mentioned in the chapter on Philosophical Roots of Education, were inspired by Comenius's pioneering work in naturalistic education.

REFOCUS After reading about Comenius, think back to the questions at the beginning of the chapter. How would you relate each of those questions to Comenius? How would Comenius educate children to understand and relate to contemporary threats of violence and terrorism?

▶ Locke: Empiricist Educator

■ Inalienable rights

John Locke (1632–1704), an English physician and philosopher, supported the important political changes that gave England a more representative government. He attacked Plato's idealist epistemology of innate ideas, emphasizing instead that ideas arose from sensation.

Locke opposed King James II, who wanted to be England's absolute ruler. James was overthrown in the Glorious Revolution of 1688. In his *The Second Treatise of Government,* in 1689, Locke argued that the political state was founded on a contract between the people and the government, which ruled by the consent of those who had established it. He asserted that all persons possessed inalienable rights of life, liberty, and property.[5] Locke's philosophy contributed to the concepts of representative government and checks and balances among a government's legislative, executive, and judicial branches. Thomas Jefferson and other founders of the American republic borrowed many of Locke's ideas.

■ Education for self-governance

Locke's theory implied that citizens should establish their own government and elect their own leaders. To do this intelligently and responsibly, they had to be educated. This idea of civic education became a significant principle of the nineteenth-century American common-school movement and remains a major responsibility of public schools. (For Locke's ideas on education as well as those of other pioneers discussed in this chapter, see Overview 5.1.)

■ The mind as a blank slate

Principles of Teaching and Learning.   Locke's *An Essay Concerning Human Understanding*, published in 1690, examined how we acquire ideas.[6] He held that at birth the human mind is a blank slate, a *tabula rasa*, empty of ideas. We gradually acquire knowledge about the world from information our senses bring to us. Simple ideas become compound ideas as we combine them, and these in turn become more complex through comparison, reflection, and generalization.

■ Empiricism and the scientific method

Although Locke's emphasis on the senses resembled realism, his philosophy of **empiricism**, which asserted that all human ideas were based on sensation, went beyond Aristotle, Comenius, and other realists. Its emphasis on sensation links empiricism to induction, the logic of arriving at explanations or hypotheses by observing phenomena. Further developers of Locke's emphasis on learning from the environment were Rousseau and Pestalozzi, and also Dewey, who declared the scientific method—testing hypotheses by experimentation—the best approach for teaching

---

[5]John Locke, *The Second Treatise of Government and A Letter Concerning Toleration* (New York: Dover 2002).
[6]John Locke, *An Essay Concerning Human Understanding* (New York: Prometheus Books, 1994).

OVERVIEW 5.1 *Educational Pioneers*

Pioneer	Historical Context	Purpose of Education	Curriculum
Comenius 1592–1670 (Czech)	Seventeenth-century religious war following Protestant Reformation	Relate education to children's natural growth and development; contribute to peace and understanding	Vernacular language, reading, writing, mathematics, religion, history, Latin; universal knowledge
Locke 1632–1704 (English)	England's Glorious Revolution of 1688	Develop ideas in the mind based on sense perception; educate individuals capable of self-government	Reading, writing, arithmetic, foreign language, mathematics, history, civil government, physical education
Rousseau 1712–1778 (Swiss-French)	Eighteenth-century French Enlightenment	Create a learning environment that allows the child's innate, natural goodness to flourish	Nature; the environment
Pestalozzi 1746–1827 (Swiss)	Early nineteenth century, post-Napoleonic period and beginnings of industrialism	Develop the human being's moral, mental, and physical powers harmoniously; use sense perception in forming clear ideas	Object lessons; form, number, sound
Froebel 1782–1852 (German)	Nineteenth-century resurgence of philosophical idealism and rise of nationalism	Develop the latent spiritual essence of the child in a prepared environment	Songs, stories, games, gifts, occupations
Spencer 1820–1903 (English)	Darwin's theory of evolution in 1859 and rise of nineteenth-century industrial corporations	Enable human beings to live effectively, economically, and scientifically	Practical, utilitarian, and scientific subjects
Dewey 1859–1952 (American)	Early-twentieth-century American progressive movement, growth of science, and rise of pragmatic philosophy	Contribute to the individual's personal, social, and intellectual growth	Making and doing; history and geography; science; problems
Addams 1860–1935 (American)	First half of twentieth century, period of massive immigration and urban change	Assimilate immigrants into American society while preserving their ethnic cultural heritages	Wide range of practical skills for life in urban centers, along with arts and sciences and problem solving
Montessori 1870–1952 (Italian)	Late nineteenth and early twentieth century assertion of feminism; greater attention to early childhood education	Assist children's sensory, muscular, and intellectual development in a prepared environment	Motor and sensory skills; preplanned materials
Piaget 1896–1980 (Swiss)	Twentieth-century developments in psychology by Freud, Hall, Jung, and others	Organize education in terms of children's patterns of growth and development	Concrete and formal operations
Freire 1921–1997 (Brazilian)	Late twentieth-century critique of neo-colonialism and globalism	Raise consciousness about exploitative conditions	Literary circles and critical dialogues

Methods of Instruction	Role of the Teacher	Significance	Influence on Today s Schools
Based on readiness and stages of human growth; gradual, cumulative, orderly; use of objects	A permissive facilitator of learning; bases instruction on child's stages of development	Developed a more humane view of the child; devised an educational method incorporating sensation	Schools organized according to children's stages of development
Reliance on sensation; slow, gradual, cumulative learning	Encourages sense experience; bases instruction on empirical method	Developed a theory of knowledge based on sensation	Schooling that emphasizes sensory observation
Reliance on sensation; experience with nature	Assists nature, rather than imposing social conventions on the child	Led a Romantic revolt against the doctrine of child depravity; a forerunner of child-centered progressivism	Permissive schooling based on child freedom
Reliance on sensation; object lessons; simple to complex; near to far; concrete to abstract	Acts as a loving facilitator of learning by creating a homelike school environment; skilled in using the special method	Devised an educational method that changed elementary education	Schooling based on emotional security and object learning
Self-activity; play; imitation	Facilitates children's growth	Created the kindergarten, a special early childhood learning environment	Preschools designed to liberate the child's creativity
Reliance on sensation and the scientific method; activities	Organizes instruction in basic activities	A leading curriculum theorist who stressed scientific knowledge	Schooling that stresses scientific knowledge and competitive values
Problem solving according to the scientific method	Creates a learning environment based on learners' shared experiences	Developed the pragmatic experimentalist philosophy of education	Schooling that emphasizes problem solving and activities in a context of community
Begin with learner's neighborhood, culture, and needs; lead to broader social realities and connections	Engages in a reciprocal or mutual learning experience with students	Developed a progressive theory of urban and multicultural education	Respect for cultural diversity and pluralism in a shared American cultural context
Spontaneous learning; activities; practical, sensory, and formal skills; exercises for practical life.	Acts as a facilitator or director of learning by using didactic materials in a prepared environment	Developed a widely used method and philosophy of early childhood education	Early childhood schooling that is intellectually and developmentally stimulating
Individualized programs; exploration and experimentation with concrete materials	Organizes instruction according to stages of cognitive development	Formulated a theory of cognitive development	Schooling organized around cognitive developmental stages
Use of personal and group autobiographies	Stimulates awareness of real conditions of life	Formulated a theory and praxis of critical consciousness	Influenced critical theory and liberation pedagogy

and learning. In fact, Locke's empiricism was a forerunner of pragmatism, a philosophy discussed in the chapter on Philosophical Roots of Education.

■ Necessity of a good environment

Education and Schooling.　In his 1697 *Some Thoughts Concerning Education*, Locke wrote that a proper education began in early childhood. Emphasizing a sound mind in a strong and healthy body, he called attention to the importance of a child's physical and social environments, diet, and activities. Children should breathe fresh air, have plenty of sleep, eat nourishing and plain food, bathe frequently, exercise regularly, and have time for recreation and play.

■ Slow and cumulative learning

Learning, Locke said, should be a gradual process; instruction in reading, writing, and arithmetic should be slow and cumulative. In addition to these basics, Locke's curriculum included conversational foreign-language learning, especially French; higher mathematics; and history. Physical education, games, and athletics were encouraged. He believed that this foundation would achieve the educational goal of cultivating ethical individuals and competent managers of social, business, and political affairs.[7]

■ Impact on modern pragmatic approaches
■ Citizenship education

Influence on Educational Practices Today.　Locke's advocacy of representative political institutions helped shape American democracy and public schools' role in citizenship education. His empiricist epistemology, which emphasized sensation as the process by which we construct our ideas, encouraged experiential process learning and use of the scientific method in instruction. Pragmatic experimentalist philosophy and constructivist psychology owe much to Locke's pioneering work.[8]

REFOCUS　After reading about John Locke, think back to the questions at the beginning of the chapter. How would you relate each of those questions to Locke? How did Locke's ideas influence modern education, especially experimentalism and constructivism?

▶ Rousseau: Educating the Natural Person

■ Noble savages in the state of nature

Jean-Jacques Rousseau (1712–1778), a Swiss-born French theorist, lived during an era of intellectual ferment that anticipated the American and French Revolutions.[9] He belonged to a group of Paris intellectuals who questioned the status quo of the established church and absolute monarchy. His works *On the Origin of the Inequality of Mankind* and *The Social Contract* condemn distinctions of wealth, property, and prestige that cause social inequalities.[10] In the original state of nature, according to Rousseau, people were "noble savages," innocent, free, and uncorrupted by socioeconomic artificialities. Rousseau is often criticized for his personal inconsistency regarding children. In his writing, he emphasized respecting children's freedom but

[7]Ruth W. Grant and Nathan Tarcov, eds. *John Locke: Some Thoughts Concerning Education and the Conduct of the Understanding* (Indianapolis: Hackett, 1996), p. 187.
[8]John Locke, *Essays on the Law of Nature* (New York: Oxford University Press, 2002).
[9]For Rousseau's autobiography, see Jean-Jacques Rousseau, *Confessions*, Patrick Coleman, ed. and Angela Scholar, trans. (New York: Oxford University Press, 2000). For biographies, see Maurice W. Cranston, *Jean-Jacques: The Early Life and Work of Jean-Jacques Rousseau, 1712–1754* (Chicago: University of Chicago Press, 1991); and Maurice W. Cranston, *The Noble Savage: Jean-Jacques Rousseau, 1754–1762* (Chicago: University of Chicago Press, 1991).
[10]Jean-Jacques Rousseau, *Discourse on the Origin of Inequality* (Indianapolis: Hackett, 1991); see also Daniel Cullen, *Freedom in Rousseau's Political Philosophy* (DeKalb: Northern Illinois University Press, 1993).

he placed his own children in orphanages instead of rearing and educating them himself.

■ Emile: A novel of education

Rousseau conveyed his educational philosophy through his famous 1762 novel, *Emile*, which tells the story of a boy's education from infancy to adulthood.[11] The novel attacks the child depravity theory and an exclusively verbal and literary education, which Rousseau believed ignored the child's natural interests and inclinations. He also believed that the child must be freed from society's imprisoning institutions, of which the school was one of the most coercive.

Rousseau's theory of education blended several philosophies and theories that were discussed in Philosophical Roots of Education. Like Locke, he rejected idealism's epistemology of innate ideas and turned instead to realism. Rousseau's pioneering ideas that children needed freedom to explore their environment and his emphasis on learning from direct experience with the environment would find reaffirmation among progressive educators.

■ Stages of development

Principles of Teaching and Learning. Like Comenius, Rousseau recognized the crucial importance of stages of human development. In *Emile*, Rousseau identified five developmental stages: infancy, childhood, boyhood, adolescence, and youth. Each stage requires an appropriate education to lead to the next stage.[12] To preserve the child's natural goodness, Rousseau insisted that the early formative stages be free from society's corruption. Thus Emile was to be educated by a tutor on a country estate away from the temptations of a ruinous society.[13] Rousseau's setting for Emile's education anticipated today's home schooling movement, in that Emile was taught at home by a tutor. Rousseau believed that schools often stressed the wrong lessons and miseducated children.

■ Infancy: first contacts with environment

In Rousseau's first stage, infancy (birth to age five), the child makes his first contacts with objects in the environment and learns directly from his senses.

■ Childhood: exploring the world through senses

During childhood (ages five to twelve), the child constructs his personality as he becomes aware that his actions cause either painful or pleasurable consequences. Motivated by curiosity, he actively explores his environment, learning more about the world through his senses. Rousseau called the eyes, ears, hands, and feet the first teachers and considered the senses better and more efficient than the schoolmaster, who teaches words the learner does not understand, and better than the schoolroom's silence and the master's rod. Emile's tutor deliberately refrained from introducing books at this stage to avoid substituting reading for the child's direct interaction with nature.

■ Boyhood: natural science

During boyhood (ages twelve to fifteen), Emile learned natural science by observing the cycles of growth of plants and animals. By exploring his surroundings, he learned geography far more realistically than from studying maps. In addition, Emile also learned a manual trade, carpentry, to make the connection between mental and physical work.

■ Adolescence: entering society

Next in Rousseau's developmental schema is adolescence (ages fifteen to eighteen). Emile was now ready to cope with the outside world and to learn about society, government, economics, and business. His aesthetic tastes were to be cultivated by visits to museums, art galleries, libraries, and theaters. During the last stage of

---

[11]William Boyd, *The Emile of Jean-Jacques Rousseau* (New York: Teachers College Press, 1962); and Allan Bloom, *Emile, or On Education* (New York: Basic Books, 1979).

[12]Christopher Winch, "Rousseau on Learning: A Re-Evaluation," *Educational Theory* (Fall 1996), pp. 424–425.

[13]David B. Owen, "History and the Curriculum in Rousseau's *Emile*," *Educational Theory*, 32 (1982), pp. 117–130.

education (ages eighteen to twenty), Emile traveled to Paris and to foreign countries to visit different peoples and societies. After meeting his future wife, Sophie, the book ends with Emile telling his tutor that he will give his children the same natural education that he had received.

■ Education versus schooling

Education and Schooling. Rousseau preferred the natural to the social and emphasized human instincts as the initial means to knowledge.[14] He believed that the school often interferes with learning. As a social institution, the school conditions children to accept confining traditional customs and institutions. Schooling teaches children to play the roles that adults prefer, rather than being their natural selves. Emile, a child of nature, followed rather than repressed his natural instincts and impulses. If pleasure was the result, Emile earned his reward. If his actions caused pain, Emile brought these consequences upon himself. Either way, he learned from the experience. Rousseau used the following key ideas in formulating his personal philosophy of education: (1) childhood is an important foundation of human development; (2) children's natural interests and instincts are valuable beginnings of a more thorough exploration of the environment; (3) human beings, in their life cycles, go through necessary stages of development; (4) adult coercion has a negative impact on children's development. These ideas have had a continuing influence on education and schooling.

■ Impact on progressive educators

Influence on Educational Practices Today. One of Rousseau's significant ideas was that curriculum should reflect children's interests and needs; it should not force them to conform to adult prescriptions. This idea was deeply influential on child-centered progressive education. In the United States, child-centered progressives discussed in the chapter on Philosophical Roots of Education devised a pedagogy based on children's interests and needs. Rousseau's ideas also anticipated the constructivist view of child development in which children interpret their own reality rather than learn information from indirect sources.

R E F O C U S   After reading about Jean-Jacques Rousseau, think back to the questions at the beginning of the chapter. How would you relate each of those questions to Rousseau? How did Rousseau's ideas anticipate contemporary child-centered and constructivist education?

▶ Pestalozzi: Educator of the Senses and Emotions

The life of the Swiss educator, Johann Heinrich Pestalozzi (1746–1827), coincided with important changes in both Europe and America. He lived during the early industrial revolution when factory-made products were replacing home handicrafts. Early industrialization changed family life as women and children entered the workforce. Concerned about the impact of this economic change on families and children, Pestalozzi sought to develop schools that, like loving families, would nurture children's development. His ideas about the relationship of families and schools are useful in today's rapidly changing society. Pestalozzi was an attentive reader of Rousseau's *Emile*. He agreed with Rousseau that humans were naturally good but spoiled by a corrupt society, that traditional schooling was a dull mess of deaden-

---

[14]J. J. Chambliss, *Educational Theory as Theory of Conduct: From Aristotle to Dewey* (Albany: State University of New York Press, 1987), pp. 101–115.

ing memorization and recitation, and that pedagogical reform could generate social reform.[15]

■ Group instruction by the object lesson

Pestalozzi established schools at Burgdorf and Yverdon to educate children and prepare teachers. Here he devised an efficient method of group instruction by which children learned in a loving and unhurried manner.[16]

Philosophically, Pestalozzi, a realist, asserted that the mind formed concepts by abstracting data gathered by the senses. His method of using objects in instruction influenced Froebel and Montessori, discussed later in this chapter, as well as the progressive educators described in the Philosophical Roots of Education chapter.

■ Warm, secure school

Principles of Teaching and Learning. Pestalozzi's approach to teaching can be organized into "general" and "special" methods. The general method created a permissive and emotionally healthy homelike learning environment that had to be in place before more specific instruction occurred. This required teachers who, emotionally secure themselves, could gain students' trust and affection.

■ Sensory learning

Once the general method was in place, Pestalozzi implemented his special method. Believing like Locke that thinking began with the senses, Pestalozzi developed his **object lesson**, which stressed sensory learning. In this approach, children studied the common objects in their environment—plants, rocks, artifacts, and other objects encountered in daily experience. To determine the form of an object, they drew and traced it. They also counted and then named objects. Thus they learned the form, number, and name or sound related to objects. From these lessons grew exercises in drawing, writing, counting, adding, subtracting, multiplying, dividing, and reading. The first writing exercises consisted of drawing lessons in which the children made a series of rising and falling strokes and open and closed curves. These exercises developed the hand muscles and prepared children for writing. Here Pestalozzi was following Rousseau's rule that mere verbal learning or abstract lessons are futile. Like Rousseau, he wanted lessons based on sense experiences that originated in the learner's home and family life. This basic innovation later became an important part of progressive school reform.

■ Instructional strategies

To ensure that instruction followed nature, Pestalozzi developed the following strategies. Instruction should (1) begin with the concrete object before introducing abstract concepts; (2) begin with the learner's immediate environment before dealing with what is distant and remote; (3) begin with easy exercises before introducing complex ones; and (4) always proceed gradually, cumulatively, and slowly.

■ Naturalistic schooling

Education and Schooling. Like Rousseau, Pestalozzi based learning on natural principles and stressed the importance of human emotions. Unlike Rousseau, however, Pestalozzi relied not on individual tutoring but on group instruction. Both Rousseau and Pestalozzi defined "knowing" as understanding nature, its patterns, and its laws. Like Locke, Pestalozzi stressed empirical learning, through which people learn about their environment by carefully observing natural phenomena.

■ Slow, precise learning in a loving environment

Like Comenius, Pestalozzi believed children should learn slowly and understand thoroughly what they were studying. He was especially dedicated to children who were poor, hungry, and socially or psychologically handicapped. If children were hungry, Pestalozzi fed them before he attempted to teach them. If they were frightened, he comforted them. For him, a teacher was not only skilled in instructional

---

[15]Gerald L. Gutek, *Pestalozzi and Education* (Prospect Heights, Ill.: Waveland Press, 1999), pp. 21–51.
[16]Johann Heinrich Pestalozzi, *How Gertrude Teaches Her Children,* trans. L. E. Holland and F. C. Turner (Syracuse, N.Y.: Bardeen, 1900).

method but also capable of loving all children. In fact, Pestalozzi believed that love of humankind was necessary for successful teaching.

■ Pestalozzianism brought to United States

Influence on Educational Practices Today.   Pestalozzi's object lessons were incorporated into the American elementary school curriculum in the nineteenth century. His emphasis on having students manipulate the objects in their environment was a forerunner of process-based learning. His belief that education should be directed to both the mind and the emotions stimulated educators to develop instruction to encourage both cognitive and affective learning. As American educators continue to focus on the needs of at-risk children, Pestalozzi's ideas, especially his general method, take on a renewed relevance.[17] His assertion that emotional security is a necessary precondition for skill and subject learning strongly parallels the contemporary emphasis on supportive home–school partnerships.

R E F O C U S   After reading about Johann Pestalozzi, think back to the questions at the beginning of the chapter. How would you relate each of those questions to Pestalozzi?

▶ Froebel: The Kindergarten Movement

■ Idealism and nationalism

German educator Friedrich Froebel (1782–1852) is renowned for his pioneering work in developing a school for early childhood education—the *kindergarten*, or children's garden.[18] Froebel was influenced by two trends in the first half of the nineteenth century: (1) a resurgence of philosophical idealism and (2) the rising nationalism of the post-Napoleonic eras. As discussed in the chapter on Philosophical Roots of Education, idealism emphasizes a spiritually based reality. Idealists saw nations as embodying the world spirit on Earth. Froebel believed that an education emphasizing German traditions and folk tales would advance efforts to unite the various small German kingdoms into one large nation. His idealism was a reaction against the empiricism of Locke, but his educational philosophy emphasized the dignity of child nature recommended by Rousseau and Pestalozzi. Thus Froebel attempted to weave several threads into his philosophy of education: idealism, nationalism, and child freedom.

■ Student of Pestalozzi

Froebel's attraction to teaching led him to Pestalozzi's institute at Yverdon, where he interned from 1808 to 1810. Although he accepted certain aspects of Pestalozzi's method—the emphasis on nature, the permissive school atmosphere, and the object lesson—he believed that Pestalozzi's theory lacked an adequate philosophical foundation. Froebel gave Pestalozzi's object lesson a more symbolic meaning by asserting that the concrete object would stimulate recall of a corresponding idea in the child's mind. He readily accepted Pestalozzi's vision of schools as emotionally secure places for children but elevated the concept to a highly spiritual level. Like Pestalozzi, he wanted teachers who were sensitive to children's readiness and needs rather than taskmasters who heard preset recitations and forced children to memorize words they did not understand.

■ Kindergarten: a prepared, permissive environment

Principles of Teaching and Learning.   A philosophical idealist, Froebel believed that every child's inner self contained a spiritual essence that stimulated self-active

---

[17]Rebecca Wild, *Raising Curious, Creative, Confident Kids: The Pestalozzi Experiment in Child-based Education* (Boston: Shambhala, 2000).

[18]Norman Brosterman, *Inventing Kindergarten* (New York: Harry N. Abrams, 1997), pp. 14–18, 22–29.

learning. He therefore designed a kindergarten that would be a "prepared environment" designed to externalize children's interior spirituality through self-activity.

■ Gifts and occupations

Froebel's kindergarten, founded in 1837 in Blankenburg, was a permissive environment featuring games, play, songs, stories, and crafts. The kindergarten's songs, stories, and games, now a standard part of early childhood education, stimulated children's imaginations and introduced them to the culture's folk heroes and heroines and values. The games socialized children and developed their physical and motor skills. As the boys and girls played with other children, they became part of the group and were prepared for further socialized learning activities.[19] The curriculum also included "gifts," objects with fixed form, such as spheres, cubes, and cylinders, which were intended to bring to full consciousness the underlying concept represented by the object. In addition, Froebel's kindergarten featured "occupations," which consisted of materials children could shape and use in design and construction activities. For example, clay, sand, cardboard, and sticks could be manipulated and shaped into castles, cities, and mountains.[20]

■ Importance of teacher's personality

Education and Schooling.   Many of us form our first impressions of schools and teachers in kindergarten. Froebel considered the kindergarten teacher's personality of paramount importance. The kindergarten teacher should respect the dignity of human personality and personify the highest cultural values so that children could imitate those values. Above all, the kindergarten teacher should be sensitive, approachable, and open.

■ Spread of the kindergarten movement

Influence on Educational Practices Today.   Froebelianism soon grew into an international education movement. Immigrants who fled Germany after the Revolution of 1848 brought the kindergarten to the United States, where it became part of the American school system. A key person in incorporating the Froebelian kindergarten into American education was Elizabeth Peabody, who founded an English-language kindergarten and worked to make the kindergarten part of the American school system.[21]

 REFOCUS   After reading about Friedrich Froebel, think back to the questions at the beginning of the chapter. How would you relate each of those questions to Froebel?

▶ Spencer: Social Darwinist and Utilitarian Educator

■ Theory of evolution

Herbert Spencer (1820–1903) was an English social theorist whose ideas enjoyed great popularity and influence in late nineteenth and early twentieth-century America. He lived when Charles Darwin was changing the ways people thought about nature and change. According to Darwin, species evolved naturally and gradually over

---

[19]*The Origins of Nursery Education,* a series edited by Kevin Brehony (New York and London: Routledge, 2001), provides reprints of the following works by Friedrich Froebel: *The Education of Man,* vol. 1 (1885); *Letters on the Kindergarten,* vol. 2 (1887); *Pedagogics of the Kindergarten,* vol. 3 (1900); *Friedrich Froebel's Education by Development,* vol. 4 (1896); *Mother's Songs and Women's Work,* vol. 5 (1900).
[20]Scott Bultman, *The Froebel Gifts: The Building Gifts 2–6, Ages 3 & Up* (Grand Rapids, Mich.: Kindergarten Messenger, 2000). Also see Joachim Liebschner, *A Child's Work: Freedom and Practice in Froebel's Educational Theory and Practice* (Cambridge, U.K: Lutterworth, 2001).
[21]Peabody's contributions to kindergarten education are described in Ruth M. Taylor, *Elizabeth Palmer Peabody: Kindergarten Pioneer* (Philadelphia: University of Pennsylvania Press, 1965); and Caroline Winterer, "Avoiding a 'Hothouse System of Education': Nineteenth-Century Early Childhood Education from the Infant Schools to the Kindergartens," *History of Education Quarterly* (Fall 1992), pp. 310–311.

long periods of time. Members of certain species survived and reproduced themselves by adapting to changes in the environment. As their offspring inherited adaptive characteristics, they too survived and continued the life of the species. Those unable to adapt—the unfit—perished.[22]

■ A social theory based on Darwin

Spencer, a key proponent of **Social Darwinism**, believed that the "fittest" individuals of each generation would survive because of their skill, intelligence, and adaptability. Competition, a natural ethical force, induced the best in the human species to climb to the top of the socioeconomic ladder. As winners of the competitive race over slower and duller individuals, the fittest would inherit the earth and populate it with their intelligent and productive children. Individuals who were proved lazy, stupid, or weak would slowly disappear. According to Social Darwinism, competition would bring about gradual but inevitable progress.[23]

■ Opposition to public schools

Spencer argued against public schooling, which he claimed would create a monopoly for mediocrity by catering to the lowest common denominator. Private schools, he thought, should compete with each other for students. Like some contemporary proponents of a voucher system, Spencer believed the best schools would attract the brightest students and the most capable teachers.[24]

■ Education for utilitarian purposes

Principles of Teaching and Learning.   In addition to being a staunch Social Darwinist, Spencer followed the naturalist tradition in education.[25] Rather than a humanist classical education, he believed that industrialized society requires a **utilitarian education** based on useful scientific objectives. As a founder of modern curriculum theory, Spencer argued that education should be based on the necessary activities that sustain survival.

■ Vocational studies

Spencer advocated sensory learning that involved the learner with the environment. He opposed rote memorization and recitation and wanted instruction to be gradual, cumulative, and unhurried. Spencer also favored education directed to the marketplace and strongly advocated technical and professional preparation based on science and engineering.[26]

Spencer's educational theory blended naturalism with a view of essentialism that emphasized science and technology. He argued that the curriculum should keep pace with scientific and technological innovations and criticized the schools of his day for failing to educate students in using technology.

Education and Schooling.   Spencer opposed the traditional schools' highly verbal literary and classical curriculum. The most valuable subjects, in his opinion, were the physical, biological, and social sciences as well as applied technology in fields such as engineering.

■ Science emphasis

Using a rationale that anticipated modern curriculum making, Spencer classified human activities according to their capacities for advancing human survival and progress. Science was especially important because it could be applied to the ef-

---

[22]For Darwin, see Charles Darwin, *The Autobiography of Charles Darwin, 1809–1883*, Nora Barlow, ed. (New York: Norton, 1993); Darwin, *The Descent of Man* (New York: Prometheus Books, 1997); Darwin, *Origin of the Species* (New York: Gramercy Press, 1995).
[23]Recent reprintings of Spencer's works are Herbert Spencer, *Essays: Scientific, Political, and Speculative* (London: Routledge/Thoemmes Press, 1996); Spencer, *Collected Writings* (London: Routledge/Thoemmes Press, 1996); Spencer, *The Principles of Psychology* (London: Routledge/ Thoemmes Press, 1996).
[24]Andreas Kazamias, *Herbert Spencer on Education.* (New York: Teachers College Press, 1966).
[25]For a critique of Spencer, see Kieran Egan, *Getting It Wrong from the Beginning: Our Progressivist Inheritance from Herbert Spencer, John Dewey, and Jean Piaget* (New York: Yale University Press, 2002).
[26]R. S. Dreyer, "Take a Tip from Herbert Spencer," *Supervision* (May 1993), pp. 22–23.

fective performance of life activities.[27] Spencer identified five types of activities to include in the curriculum: (1) self-preservation activities, which are basic to all other activities; (2) occupational or professional activities, which make a person economically self-supporting; (3) child-rearing activities; (4) social and political participation activities; and (5) leisure and recreation activities.

■ Impact on curriculum design

Influence on Educational Practices Today.   American educators were receptive to Spencer's ideas. In 1918, a National Education Association committee, in its landmark *Cardinal Principles of Secondary Education,* reiterated Spencer's list of basic life activities. Modern curriculum designers continue to reflect Spencer's influence when they base curriculum on human needs and activities.

After dominating American social science in the late nineteenth century, Social Darwinism was pushed aside by John Dewey's Experimentalism and progressive reform. Key Social Darwinist ideas reemerged in the contemporary neoconservative agenda, however, which included offering vouchers to attend private schools, reducing government's regulatory powers, and increasing economic productivity through basic skills that have market value.

REFOCUS   After reading about Herbert Spencer, think back to the questions at the beginning of the chapter. How would you relate each of those questions to Spencer? Do you find aspects of Spencer's ideas in current educational initiatives?

▶ Dewey: Learning Through Experience

■ School and society
■ Laboratory school

John Dewey (1859–1952) is one of the most important American philosophers.[28] He developed his pioneering Experimentalist philosophy of education against the backdrop of the social, political, scientific, and technological changes taking place in the United States in the first half of the twentieth century.[29] The progressive reform movement in politics stimulated his thinking, and he sought to incorporate the concept of relativism current in science into his philosophy. Keenly aware of technology's power to transform society, Dewey wanted it used for democratic purposes. He saw education as an instrument of social progress and envisioned schools closely connected to society. While director of the University of Chicago Laboratory School from 1896 to 1904, he tested his pragmatic educational philosophy by using it as the foundation for children's learning activities and projects.[30] (For a discussion of pragmatism, see the chapter on Philosophical Roots of Education.)

■ Confronting problems

Principles of Teaching and Learning.   Dewey's *The Child and the Curriculum* provides a guide to principles and practices used at the University of Chicago Laboratory School. Children were seen as socially active human beings eager to explore and gain control over their environment. By interacting with their world, learners confront both personal and social problems. Such problematic encounters stimulate

---

[27] Valerie A. Haines, "Spencer's Philosophy of Science," *British Journal of Sociology* (June 1992), pp. 155–172.

[28] For a biography of Dewey, see Jay Martin, *The Education of John Dewey: A Biography* (New York: Columbia University Press, 2002); for a commentary on Dewey, see Walter Feinberg, "Dewey and Democracy: At the Dawn of the Twenty-first Century," *Educational Theory* (Spring 1993), pp. 195–216.

[29] For Dewey's relationship to the development of pragmatism, see Louis Menard, *The Metaphysical Club: The Story of Ideas in America* (New York: Farrar, Straus and Giroux 2001).

[30] John Dewey, *The Child and the Curriculum* (Chicago: University of Chicago Press, 1902). A commentary is Laurel N. Tanner, *Dewey's Laboratory School: Lessons for Today* (New York: Teachers College Press, 1997).

children to use their intelligence to solve the difficulty, and their knowledge in an active, instrumental manner.[31] Arguments for and against Dewey's approach are presented in the Taking Issue box.

Standards & Assessment

taking issue

Question   Should Dewey's Experimentalist method of inquiry be the basis of teaching and learning in American schools?

Dewey's Learning by Experience

Since John Dewey developed his Experimentalist or pragmatic philosophy and applied it to education, his approach has been vigorously debated. Proponents of Dewey's method, many of whom are professors of education, emphasize learning by experience through the scientific method. Opponents of Dewey's method claim that it lowers academic standards and achievement by weakening systematic subject-matter learning and encouraging relativistic values.

Arguments PRO

1 Dewey's method provides continuity between children's direct experience and a school curriculum that arises from and develops that experience. Because of this continuity, students readily become interested and motivated, eager to pursue their interests into areas of broader educational importance.

2 Free from absolutes based on a priori concepts of reality, Dewey's method encourages students to question inherited traditions and values. It fosters an experimental attitude that leads to invention, discovery, and innovation and equips people to use knowledge as an instrument to solve the problems of a changing world.

3 Dewey's method of inquiry requires the freedom to think and to question and thus encourages democratic participation in society. Dewey's method is therefore well suited to American cultural emphasis on representative institutions and open discussion of issues.

4 Dewey's educational goal—human growth for the sake of further growth—promotes an instructional flexibility in which teachers and students are free to respond to personal and social issues. This type of education encourages flexible responses to the environment, sorely needed in today's technological and interdependent world.

Arguments CON

1 By stressing the interests and needs of children and adolescents, Dewey's method fails to emphasize the important role of adults in transmitting the cultural heritage. It also minimizes the fact that learning often requires the child to apply effort before developing interests.

2 Dewey's method falsely assumes that the scientific method can be applied to any problem without a deep knowledge of the problem's context. On the contrary, it is important that students learn subjects systematically, not experimentally. Failure to master subject matter develops deficiencies in American students, especially in mathematics and science.

3 Dewey's method is highly relativistic and situational, denying the existence of universal truths and values. In order to survive and prosper, American democracy must reaffirm certain basic and traditional values, not call all values into question.

4 Dewey's argument that the only goal of education is growth for further growth neglects the need for standards that encourage intellectual achievement and economic productivity. Schools, teachers, and learners need substantive goals to guide the educational process; vague notions about human growth are not sufficient.

---

[31]For an analysis of Dewey's democratic approach to education, see Sandra Rosenthal, "Democracy and Education: A Deweyan Approach," *Educational Theory* (Fall 1993), pp. 377–389.

For Dewey, the **scientific method** is the most effective process we have to solve problems. When they use the scientific method to solve problems, children learn how to think reflectively and to direct their experiences in ways that lead to personal and social growth. The following steps are extremely important in Dewey's application of the scientific method to teaching and learning:

■ Steps in learning by the scientific method

1. The learner is involved in a "genuine experience" that truly interests him or her.

2. Within this experience, the learner has a "genuine problem" that stimulates thinking.

3. The learner acquires the information needed to solve the problem.

4. The learner frames possible, tentative solutions that may solve the problem.

5. The learner tests the solutions by applying them to the problem. In this way, the learner constructs and validates his or her own knowledge.[32]

■ Reconstructing knowledge to solve problems

Dewey saw knowledge not as inert information but as an instrument to solve problems. We use our fund of human knowledge—past ideas, discoveries, and inventions—to frame hypothetical solutions to current problems and then test and reconstruct this knowledge in light of present needs. Because people and their environments constantly change, knowledge, too, is continually reconfigured or reconstructed. Once a problem has been solved, its solution enters into the knowledge fund.

■ Education for personal and social growth

Education and Schooling.   Dewey considered education a social process by which the group's immature members, especially children, learn to participate in group life. Through education, children are introduced to their cultural heritage and learn to use it in problem solving. Education's sole purpose is to contribute to a person's personal and social growth. As Dewey put it, education "is that reconstruction or reorganization of experience which adds to the meaning of experience, and which increases ability to direct the course of subsequent experience."[33]

■ Three levels of curriculum

Dewey's curriculum consisted of three levels of learning activities and processes. The first level, "making and doing," engaged children in projects in which they explored their environment and put their ideas into concrete form. These first activities developed sensory and motor skills and encouraged socialization through collaborative group projects. The second level enlarged students' concepts of space and time through projects that involved them in history and geography. The third level, "science," brought students into contact with various subjects such as biology, chemistry, and social studies that they could use as sources of information to solve problems.

These three curricular levels moved learning from simple impulses to careful observation of the environment, to planning actions, and finally to reflecting on and testing the consequences of action.

■ Schools are liberating and democratic

As an advocate of democratic education and schooling, Dewey wanted schools to be liberating environments in which students were free to test all ideas, beliefs, and values. As democratic institutions, schools should be open to and used by all. Opposing the separation of people from each other because of ethnic origin, race, gender, or economic class, Dewey believed that communities were enriched when people shared their experiences to solve their common problems.

■ Impact on progressivism

Influence on Educational Practices Today.   John Dewey exercised an enormous influence on American education. By applying pragmatism to education, he helped

---

[32]John Dewey, *Democracy and Education* (New York: Macmillan, 1916), p. 192.
[33]Ibid., pp. 89–90.

to open schooling to change and innovation. Dewey's ideas about socially expanding children's experience stimulated progressive education, which emphasized children's interests and needs. Today, educators who relate schooling to social purposes are often following Dewey's pioneering educational concepts.[34]

Dewey's influence can also be seen in teaching that takes a "hands-on" or process-oriented approach. For example, the "whole language" approach, with its emphasis on teaching language arts through the entire educational environment, is a recent development stemming from Dewey's pioneering experimentalist philosophy.

REFOCUS After reading about John Dewey, think back to the questions at the beginning of the chapter. How would you relate each of those questions to Dewey? Do you find any evidence of Dewey's philosophy in current educational reforms?

▶ Addams: Socialized Education

Jane Addams (1860–1935), founder of Hull-House and a pioneering figure in social work and women's rights, developed an educational theory called **socialized education**. Her educational philosophy emphasized immigrant, urban, and women's education, and was a forerunner of modern multicultural and feminist education.

■ Hull-House

Jane Addams established Hull-House on Chicago's near west side in 1889 in a culturally diverse neighborhood of recent immigrants. Addams and her coworkers, a cadre of young middle-class women, educated the immigrants and, in turn, were educated by them. Hull-House provided a place where immigrants learned how to find jobs, pay rent, find health care, and educate their children.[35]

■ Proponent of multiculturalism

Principles of Teaching and Learning. Addams believed that urbanization, industrialization, and technology had challenged and enlarged the meaning and purposes of education. Modern professions and occupations needed deliberate connection to a sense of social purpose and the social relationships necessary to re-create a true democratic community.[36]

An early proponent of multiculturalism, Addams sought to create connections between new immigrants and the larger American society. She believed that cultural diversity could coexist within a larger American common culture. Addams wanted the public schools to include the history, customs, songs, crafts, and stories of various ethnic and racial groups in the curriculum.[37]

Addams, an advocate of women's rights, rebelled against the restrictions of Victorian society. She rejected the traditional curriculum that limited women's educational choices and opportunities. She wanted women to have educations that encouraged them to define their own lives and choose their own careers. She wanted women to

[34]For analyses of Dewey's work in educational philosophy, see Matt Parmental, "The Structure of Dewey's Scientific Ethics"; and Eric Bredo, "Understanding Dewey's Ethics," in *Philosophy of Education* (Urbana: Philosophy of Education Society/University of Illinois at Urbana-Champaign, 2000), pp. 143–154.

[35]Biographies of Addams are Allen F. Davis, *American Heroine: The Life and Legend of Jane Addams* (Chicago: Ivan R. Dee, 2000); Gioia Dilberto, *A Useful Lady: The Early Life of Jane Addams* (New York: Scribner/ Lisa Drew, 1999); Barbara G. Polikoff, *With One Bold Act: The Story of Jane Addams* (Chicago: Boswell Books, 1999); and James W. Linn, *Jane Addams: A Biography* (Urbana and Chicago: University of Illinois Press, 2000).

[36]Jane Addams, *Democracy and Social Ethics* (New York: Macmillan, 1905), pp. 178–181.

[37]Jane Addams, *The Spirit of Youth and the City Streets* (New York: Macmillan, 1909), pp. 98–103.

participate fully in politics and society and to work for reforms such as ending child labor and bringing about world peace.[38]

■ Multifunctional education

Education and Schooling. Addams's "socialized education," influenced by progressivism and pragmatism, sought to restore a sense of community as America experienced a profound transition from a rural to an urban industrialized society. She believed that education was multifunctional. The school, as a community agency, was connected to another community agency dedicated to social work, the settlement house. Likewise, the teacher was connected to the social worker. Addams believed that schools could be multifunctional only after progressive reform reduced their isolation from society. The curriculum should provide broadened experiences that explored children's immediate environment in a way that highlighted connections with a technological society.

Influence on Educational Practices Today. Addams's philosophy is significant for today's education. Her belief that education must be free from gender biases corresponds with the goals of contemporary women's education, especially equal rights for women and their freedom to define their lives and choose their careers. Her belief that industrialism should be infused with broad social purposes can be applied to the argument that technology should advance greater communication and sharing rather than generate consumer-oriented materialism. Her crusade in the women's peace movement for a world without war provides a needed message for a world wracked by violence and terrorism.

REFOCUS After reading about Jane Addams, think back to the questions at the beginning of the chapter. How would you relate each of those questions to Addams? How well do Addams's ideas apply to contemporary social and educational issues?

▶ **Montessori: The Prepared Environment**

■ Early childhood and feminism

Italian educator Maria Montessori (1870–1952) devised an internationally popular method of early childhood education.[39] Two important trends highlight Montessori's life and times: emphasis on early childhood and the rise of feminism. Like Pestalozzi and Froebel, Montessori recognized that children's early experiences have an important influence on their later lives. As a pioneering women's educator, she vigorously challenged those who, because of sexist stereotyping, argued that women should not be admitted to higher and professional programs of study. Defying the barriers on women's education, Montessori was admitted to the University of Rome and was the first woman in Italy to be awarded the degree of doctor of medicine.

As a physician, Montessori worked with children regarded as mentally handicapped and psychologically impaired. Her methods with these children were so effective that she concluded they were useful for all children.

■ Emphasis on structured work

Principles of Teaching and Learning. In 1908 Maria Montessori established a children's school, the Casa dei Bambini, for impoverished children from the slums

---

[38]Jane Addams, Emily G. Balch, and Alice Hamilton, *Women at the Hague: The International Congress of Women and Its Results* (Urbana and Chicago: The University of Illinois Press, 2002).
[39]Biographies of Montessori are Rita Kramer, *Maria Montessori: A Biography* (Reading, Mass.: Perseus Books, 1988); and E. M. Standing, *Maria Montessori: Her Life and Work,* introduction by Lee Havis (New York: Plume/Penguin Books, 1998).

of Rome. In this school, Montessori fashioned a "specially prepared environment" that featured methods, materials, and activities based on her observations of children.[40] She also refined her theory by doing extensive research on the theories of Itard and Sequin, two early pioneers in special education. Montessori argued that children, contrary to the assumptions of conventional schooling, have an inner need to work at what interests them without the prodding of teachers and without being motivated by external rewards and punishments. Children, she found, are capable of sustained concentration and work. Enjoying structure and preferring work to play, they like to repeat actions until they master a given activity. In fact, children's capacity for spontaneous learning leads them to begin reading and writing.

■ Types of activity

Education and Schooling.   Montessori's curriculum included three major types of activity and experience: practical, sensory, and formal skills and studies. It was designed to introduce children to such practical activities as setting the table, serving a meal, washing dishes, tying and buttoning clothing, and practicing basic manners and social etiquette. Repetitive exercises developed sensory and muscular coordination. Formal skills and subjects included reading, writing, and arithmetic. Children were introduced to the alphabet by tracing movable sandpaper letters. Reading was taught after writing. Colored rods of various sizes were used to teach measuring and counting.

■ Didactic materials

The Montessori school had preplanned teaching (didactic) materials designed to develop the practical, sensory, and formal skills. Examples included lacing and buttoning frames, weights, and packets to be identified by their sound or smell. Because they direct learning in the prepared environment, Montessori educators are called directresses rather than teachers. Under the guidance of the directress, children use materials in a prescribed way to acquire the desired skill mastery, sensory experience, or intellectual outcome.

■ Key contributions

Influence on Educational Practices Today.   Montessori's pioneering contribution to education was her emphasis on the formative significance the early childhood years have for later development. Her other important educational contributions were her (1) concept of sensitive periods, phases of development, when certain activities and materials are especially useful in sensory, motor, and cognitive learning; (2) recognition that learning is complex and involves a variety of experiences; (3) emphasis on the school as part of the community and the need for parent participation and support. She anticipated the current movement to provide earlier enrichment opportunities for children.[41]

■ Montessori movement in United States

Among the thousands of **Montessori schools** worldwide, six thousand are operating in the United States. Most of these are private schools, enrolling children between the ages of two and six. A recent but still limited effort has emerged to establish Montessori divisions in the public-school system, especially as magnet or charter schools.[42]

REFOCUS   **After reading about Maria Montessori, think back to the questions at the beginning of the chapter. How would you relate each of those questions to Montessori?**

[40]Maria Montessori, *The Montessori Method,* introduction by J. McV. Hunt (New York: Schocken Books, 1964), pp. 48–70.
[41]Gerald L. Gutek, "Maria Montessori: Contributions to Educational Psychology," in Barry J. Zimmerman and Dale H. Schunk, *Educational Psychology: A Century of Contributions* (Mahwah, N.J.: Lawrence Erlbaum, 2003), pp. 171–186.
[42]Timothy D. Seldin, "Montessori" in James W. Guthrie, ed., *Encyclopedia of Education,* 2nd ed., vol. 5 (New York: Macmillan Reference USA/Thomson Gale, 2003), p. 1697.

Children in today's Montessori schools use specially designed didactic materials in an environment prepared to encourage learning. *(Ellen Senisi/ The Image Works)*

▶ Piaget: Developmental Growth

Swiss psychologist Jean Piaget (1896–1980) made pioneering contributions to educational psychology that provided new insights into children's cognitive, moral, and language development. Rather than relying on philosophical speculation, Piaget closely observed children to determine how they develop and act on their ideas.[43]

■ Cognitive development

Principles of Teaching and Learning. Piaget based his principles of education on his investigations of how children think and learn. He believed that children explore their environment as active agents of their cognitive development. According to Piaget, intelligence develops through a series of stages, characterized by the child's set of mental structures and operations at a particular age. With each new stage, children's attainment of new mental abilities enables them to reconstruct the concepts formed at an earlier stage and to develop a more complex cognitive map of the world.[44] Based on his stage-learning theory of development, Piaget identified four qualitatively distinct but interrelated periods of cognitive growth:

■ Sensorimotor stage

1. The **sensorimotor stage**, from birth to two years when children learn from experience and activity in exploring their immediate environment. Children begin their earliest environmental explorations using their senses—their mouths, eyes, and hands. Displaying a largely nonverbal intelligence, they learn to coordinate their senses and to construct simple concepts of space, time, and causality at the visual, auditory, tactile, and motor levels. These rudimentary concepts, however, are limited to children's immediate situations.[45]

---

[43]David Elkind, "Piaget, Jean (1896–1980)," in James W. Guthrie, ed., *Encyclopedia of Education,* 2nd ed., vol. 5 (New York: Macmillan Reference USA/Thomson Gale, 2003), p. 1895.
[44]Ibid., p. 1897.
[45]Ibid.

■ Preoperational stage

2. The **preoperational stage**, from two to seven years, when intuition combines with speech to lead to operational thought involving concepts of space, time, and cause-and-effect relationships that extend beyond the immediate situation. Children now organize their concepts by grouping and naming objects. They use signs and symbols to represent their ideas and experiences as they reconstruct the mental structures and networks constructed in the first stage into a more complex, higher-order, view of reality.[46]

■ Concrete-operational period

3. The **concrete-operational period**, from seven to eleven years, when children begin thinking in a mathematical and logical way. They become adept at recognizing such general characteristics as size, length, and weight and use them in more complex mental operations. As at every stage, they reconstruct the concepts arrived at in the earlier two stages into more abstract and complex levels. Coinciding with the years of elementary school, children in the concrete-operational stage exercise their reasoning skills and deal with clock and calendar time, map and geographical space, and experimental cause and effect.[47]

■ Formal-operational period

4. At the **formal-operational period**, from age eleven through early adulthood, individuals deal with logical propositions and form abstract hypotheses. At this stage, they can understand and interpret space, historical time, and multiple cause-and effect relationships. They use such multivariate thinking to construct possible plans of action.[48] Now that adolescents understand cause-and-effect relationships, they can use the scientific method to explain reality and can learn complex mathematical, linguistic, and mechanical processes.[49]

Piaget's stage-learning theory of development has many important applications to education. Piaget emphasizes that children view the world differently from adults. Further, they constantly reconstruct, reshape, and repattern their view of reality as they pass through the stages of development. Thus, children's conception of reality differs from the kinds of curriculum and instruction adults often impose on them.

Early childhood and elementary education should reflect how children develop and act on their thinking and learning processes. It is important to recognize that as they move through the stages of development, children have their own readiness for new learning. Children's ability to learn depends on and varies with the cognitive level they have reached. This, in turn, determines their readiness for new and higher-order learning experiences.[50] Although a rich environment can stimulate readiness, we cannot force learning on children.

Education and Schooling. Piaget accentuated their environment as children's setting for learning. Outside of school, children learn directly and informally from their environment. The most effective teaching strategies replicate the informal learning children use in their everyday out-of-school lives.[51]

---

[46]Ibid.
[47]Ibid.
[48]C. J. Brainerd, "Jean Piaget, Learning Research, and American Education," in Barry J. Zimmerman and Dale H. Schunk, ed., *Educational Psychology: A Century of Contributions* (Mahwah, N.J.: Lawrence Erlbaum, 2003), p. 257; and Elkind, p. 1897.
[49]Jean Piaget, *The Origins of Intelligence in Children*, trans. Margaret Cook (New York: Norton, 1952), pp. 24–40; also see William O. Penrose, *A Primer on Piaget* (Bloomington, Ind.: Phi Delta Kappa Educational Foundations, 1979).
[50]Brainerd, p. 260.
[51]Ibid., p. 284.

■ Constructivism

As they interact with their environment, children construct their knowledge of their world through a process of creative invention known as **constructivism**. As they move through the stages of development, children discover inadequacies between their existing knowledge and the new situations they encounter as they explore their environment. They then reconstruct or reconceptualize their existing knowledge with their new information to construct more complete and higher-order concepts.[52] To stimulate children's explorations, teachers must make sure their classrooms are arranged with learning centers and are rich in materials that stimulate and engage children's curiosity.[53] The following guidelines can help teachers apply Piaget's principles in the classroom:

1. Teachers should encourage children to explore and experiment.

2. Instruction should be individualized so that children can learn at their own level of readiness.

3. The classroom should be stocked with concrete materials that children can touch, manipulate, and use.

As you read the In This Case feature, examine the lesson described to determine to what extent the teacher is using a constructivist approach.

■ Informal learning and constructivism

Influences on Educational Practices Today   Piaget's research about developmental processes connected how children learn to think and reason with teaching and learning in schools. His developmental psychology stimulated revolutionary changes in early childhood and elementary education, not only in the United States, but throughout the world. His ideas stimulated a movement to make classroom settings less formal and more related to how children learn. Today, Piaget's psychology of children's development is a widely accepted contribution to psychology and education. Contemporary constructivist education originated with Piaget's pioneering assertion that children do not copy but rather construct reality.[54]

REFOCUS   After reading about Jean Piaget, think back to the questions at the beginning of the chapter. How would you relate each of those questions to Piaget? Do you find evidence of Piaget's developmental psychology in current educational practices?

▶ Freire: Liberation Pedagogy

Brazilian educator Paulo Freire (1921–1997) developed his philosophy of **liberation pedagogy** while working in a literacy campaign among the impoverished illiterate peasants and urban poor of his native country. For Freire, literacy meant more than learning to read and write; it raised people's consciousness about conditions of their lives, especially those that exploited and marginalized them.[55] Freire's *Pedagogy of the Oppressed,* his most important book, established the foundations of his theory of liberation pedagogy, an educational theory designed to empower people to resist and overcome the forces that oppressed them.[56]

---

[52]Ibid., p. 271.
[53]Piaget, *Origins of Intelligence,* pp. 23–42.
[54]Elkind, p. 1894.
[55]Richard Shaull, preface to Paulo Freire, *Pedagogy of the Oppressed* (New York: Continuum, 1984), pp. 9–11.
[56]Among several editions, a recent one is Paulo Freire, *Pedagogy of the Oppressed* (New York: Continuum, 1996).

IN THIS CASE

A New Lesson

Nancy sat and watched her mentor teacher, Ms. Walker, engaging the students in a lesson. This was one of several lessons about the importance of DNA duplication during cell division through a process called mitosis. The students had some background reading in their text, but no other preparation.

Ms. Walker had asked Nancy how she would approach the subject if this were her class. Nancy wasn't certain—one lesson would include a laboratory experience—but introducing the topic and deciding points of emphasis would be difficult. Teaching was a lot harder than Ms. Walker made it look.

Ms. Walker introduced the lesson with a series of questions. She started with broad questions. "What makes each of you unique? What characteristics do you have that seem to link you to your mom and dad, your brother or sister? How do you explain similarities and differences?"

The students wrote out their initial understanding in their notebooks. Then Ms. Walker showed a video that explained the basics of mitosis in simple plant and animal cells. It illustrated genes, composed of particular DNA strands, and showed the normal sequence and pairing of substances in the DNA in detail.

Class discussion followed. Nancy watched as the discussion became somewhat random. A few students seemed confused. One asked about evolution and Darwin's theory. Another asked about cancer, and another about mutations. One student inquired about the balance of genes and the environment. Still others wanted to focus on what they had to learn to pass.

Ms. Walker was not in the least disturbed by all of this. She recorded the questions on the board. Then she divided the class up into small groups to research some answers. Each group had to explain how the duplication of DNA strands related to their question. The groups would bring their work to class the next day, to summarize and clarify findings. After a review by Ms. Walker, each group would present their information to the class.

During the conference hour that followed class, Ms. Walker explained to Nancy that she thought both content and process were important. She wanted to be sure that the content was correct, but she also wanted students to learn to find the information they needed and to apply it to a problem at hand. She wanted the students to learn to think. Ms. Walker also wanted students to know how such knowledge might apply to them and their families.

Nancy thought, "If only I can learn to be as challenging as she is and yet be as comfortable as she is in the classroom. I've got a lot to learn—not only content, but also how to conduct a class so that students learn as I want them to learn."

Questions:

1. What philosophical approach(es) did Ms. Walker utilize? How can you tell?

2. What approach might you use if you were to teach a similar lesson?

3. Have you ever had a teacher like Ms. Walker? How was it?

4. Which pioneer's approach to education does Ms. Walker tend to favor?

Principles of Teaching and Learning. An important goal of Freire's philosophy is *conscientizaçao*, a Portuguese word meaning to be conscious and critically aware of the social, political, and economic conditions and contradictions that affect a person's life. To raise their consciousness, students, in dialogue with their teachers, must study their own life stories and the collective histories of their racial, ethnic, language, economic, and social groups. They must consciously examine the objective conditions in which they live, identifying those conditions and persons who limit their freedom for self-definition.[57]

---

[57]Paulo Freire, *Pedagogy of Freedom: Ethics, Democracy, and Civic Courage* (Lanham, Md.: Rowman and Littlefield, 1998), p. 51.

Education and Schooling.   Freire asserted that the school's curriculum and instruction can either indoctrinate students to conform to an official version of knowledge or it can challenge them to develop a critical consciousness that empowers them to engage in self-liberation. For example, an official version of history that celebrates the achievements of white Euro-American males and minimizes the contributions of women, African Americans, Latinos, and other minority groups creates a false consciousness. An education that defines a person's worth in terms of wealth and power and sees schooling as a ticket to a success in an exploitative economic system cannot be truly humanizing.[58]

- Reality of school situations
- Teachers need commitment

Freire's teachers should be neither impartial nor uncommitted on social, political, and economic issues.[59] Rather, he wants teachers to develop a critical consciousness of the real power relationships in the schools and of the conditions that affect their students. For example, teachers in schools in economically depressed areas need to know that their students' lives are being blighted by poverty, poor access to health care and recreational services, drug abuse, and gang violence. When they understand the true reality of their school situations, teachers can resist these oppressive conditions and work to empower their students.

Standards & Assessment ✓
- Opposes teacher talk

For Freire, real learning takes place as teachers and students engage in an open and ongoing dialogue. He attacks instruction that leads to false, rather than critical, consciousness in students' perceptions of reality. An example is "teacher talk." Teacher talk implies that teachers can transmit knowledge to students by telling them what is true: students memorize what the teacher says and passively deposit it in their minds for later recall. Freire calls the teacher-talking–student-listening method educational "banking" in which each bit of information is deposited to be cashed in the future, usually for an examination.[60] The standardized tests favored in the contemporary standards movement provide an example of the banking model. The tests, constructed from officially transmitted knowledge, sort students into groups, often isolating marginalized students and thereby reproducing the inequalities of the existing system.

Influence on Educational Practices Today.   Freire is esteemed as a genuine educational reformer and pioneer by contemporary critical theorists. (See the Philosophical Roots of Education chapter for more on critical theory.) His ideas have stimulated efforts to reconceptualize teaching and learning. Freire worked to transform teaching and learning from the limited concept of transmitting information to engaging in the project of completing one's identity and meaning in a world that needs to be made more equitable, humane, and just.

REFOCUS   **After reading about Paulo Freire, think back to the questions at the beginning of the chapter. How would you relate each of these questions to Freire? How well do Freire's ideas apply to contemporary social and educational issues?**

▶ Thinking About Pioneers in Education

This chapter on pioneers examined the significant contributions of major educators in the past. Often our choice of who is a pioneer depends on the situations in which we find ourselves. The pioneers examined in this chapter developed innovative ideas on education through research and teaching and many constructed unique

---

[58]Stanley Aronowitz, introduction to Freire, *Pedagogy of Freedom*, p. 4.
[59]Freire, *Pedagogy of Freedom*, p. 22.
[60]Freire, *Pedagogy of the Oppressed*, trans. Myra Bergman Ramos (New York: Continuum, 1984), pp. 57–59.

philosophies of education. We can look to these pioneers for insights that may aid us in understanding and solving current problems in education.

You can play a role in determining who qualifies as a pioneer in education. As a student of education and a teacher, you will continue to encounter potential pioneers—scholars, authors, professors, practitioners, and others—who have developed new theories and methods of education. As you appraise these present-day educators, try to identify those you think will become a pioneer in education, those whose ideas will help generations of educators understand and solve their problems.

Building Your Philosophy of Technology in Education

Technology is a highly important force in contemporary education. Schools throughout the country now have computers and other instruments of electronic data retrieval and instruction. Some theorists believe that technology will dramatically change the culture and revolutionize the processes of education. Others see it as a cultural and educational add-on that will speed up information transmission but will not exert a profound transformation. Considering the pioneers, philosophers, and theorists of education can clarify your thinking about the broad philosophical meaning of technology in relationship to culture and education.

Throughout the chapter on Philosophical Roots of Education and the chapter on Pioneers in Education, we have briefly mentioned the relative importance of technology to the thinking of different educational pioneers and in different philosophies of education. Comenius, for example, enthusiastically embraced the new technology of his day, the printing press, and worked to create appropriate educational applications for that technology by writing textbooks. Other educational pioneers and their followers may not have been quite so enthusiastic. Rousseau's distrust of modern technology is suggested by his insistence, in *Emile*, that the student should not even be allowed to read books until approximately age twelve. For a modern-day perspective, consider the Montessori position on television and computers in the learning environment, posted at the International Montessori Index Web site: **http://www.montessori.edu/prod.html**.

For the broad impact of technology on society and culture, you might consider how John Dewey, a leading pragmatist and progressive, would have reacted to technological change. Visit the Web site of the John Dewey Project on Progressive Education at **http://www.uvm.edu/~dewey/**. Compare and contrast the position of Dewey and other progressives on technology's application to education with that of the Council for Basic Education at **http://www.e-b-e.org/**. Given this information, will you encourage students to experiment with computers, digital cameras, and other technologies to solve their own problems, or will you use those tools for more efficient drill learning of basic skills?

Give careful consideration to the legacy of the educational pioneers as you start constructing your educational philosophy. Your general philosophy of education will certainly influence your ideas about educational technology, but it is also worthwhile to spend time considering your philosophy toward educational technology in particular.

Visit some of the Web sites recommended at the end of the chapter and look for evidence about the pioneers' attitudes toward educational technology. Then, reflect on the same questions you used to help guide your general philosophical inquiry. Consider, too, how you would answer such questions as the following: Is technology a transforming force or an add-on to culture and education? What kinds of technological programs and information best agree with your ideas about knowledge, values, and logic? Which of the pioneers' ideas do you see as most valuable? Which would you wish to incorporate into your philosophy? Which ideas do you wish to confront and possibly discard?

The pioneers can help you as well. As you construct your philosophy of education, think back to the work of the pioneers in education examined in this chapter. Which of their ideas do you assess as valuable contributions that you may wish to incorporate into your philosophy? Which of their ideas do you wish to challenge and possibly reject as you build your philosophy as an educator?

The Technology @ School box considers the educational pioneers' attitudes about technology and invites you to form your own perspective.

▶ Summing Up

1. The pioneers discussed in this chapter made distinctive contributions to the development of education in their countries and throughout the world.

2. In challenging the dogma of child depravity, Comenius, Locke, and Rousseau developed a method of education based on children's natural growth and goodness.

3. Pestalozzi developed teaching methods that used objects in children's immediate environments. Froebel's theory was the basis of the kindergarten. Both Pestalozzi and Froebel liberated early childhood education by encouraging teachers to be sensitive to children's interests and needs.

4. Spencer's sociology of education was a pioneering effort to relate the school to society. His identification of social activities contributed to curriculum development.

5. Dewey's pioneering work at the University of Chicago Laboratory School stimulated progressive educational reform. Montessori's prepared environment is currently popular in early childhood education.

6. Addams's theory of socialized education contributed to multicultural education, to an examination of technology's impact on society, and to the movement for women's rights and education.

7. Piaget's developmental psychology illuminated thinking on children's cognitive operations.

8. Freire's liberation theory calls for a radical transformation of education and schooling to make them into instruments of human liberation.

▶ Key Terms

child depravity theory (130)
naturalistic theory (130)
empiricism (133)
object lesson (139)
Social Darwinism (142)
utilitarian education (142)
scientific method (145)
socialized education (146)

Montessori schools (148)
sensorimotor stage (149)
preoperational stage (150)
concrete-operational period (150)
formal-operational period (150)
constructivism (151)
liberation pedagogy (151)

▶ Discussion Questions

1. How would you define an educational pioneer? Whom would you include in a chapter about educational pioneers?

2. In your personal philosophy of education, how do you define knowledge, education, and schooling? How do your conceptions agree with or differ from those of the pioneer educators in this chapter?

(3) Of the educators discussed in this chapter, whose ideas are most relevant to you as a prospective teacher? Whose are least relevant? Why?

(4) Identify a current educational trend such as whole-language learning, collaborative learning, constructivism, portfolio assessment, use of technology, and the standards movement. How might the educators discussed in this chapter react to your chosen trend?

(5) Reflect on Freire's argument that education should stimulate a person's critical consciousness. What does It mean to have a critical consciousness? How would the other educational pioneers discussed in this chapter react to Freire's argument?

(6) How did the educational pioneers discussed in this chapter define the teacher–student relationship?

► Suggested Projects for Professional Development

(1) To complement your reading about John Locke in the chapter, consult the "Victorian Web," **www.victorianweb.org/**. Click the Philosophy link to examine the educational implications of Locke's concepts of government and empiricism and his *Essay Concerning Human Understanding.*

(2) Explore Jane Addams's Hull-House by visiting the Web site of the Hull-House Museum at the University of Illinois at Chicago: **www.uic.edu/jaddams/hull/hull_house.html**. List the pros and cons of establishing close links between schools and social agencies such as Hull-House.

(3) Begin a search for information and sites related to Rousseau by visiting the Web site of the Rousseau Association at **www.wabash.edu/Rousseau**.

(4) Develop a listing of Web sites related to John Dewey's pragmatism by consulting the Center for Dewey Studies at Southern Illinois University at **www.siu.edu/~deweyctr**.

(5) Visit a kindergarten and record your observations. Did you find any evidence of Froebel's method?

(6) Visit a Montessori school and record your observations. What evidence did you find of Montessori's method?

(7) To explore connections between Piaget's developmental theory and constructivism, consult the following Web site: **http:www.piaget.org**.

(8) Research Freire. You can begin by consulting **http:www.infed.org/thinkers/et-freire.htm**. Conduct a critical dialogue, based on Freire's model, that examines the social, political, and economic conditions of your current educational situation. How do these conditions influence education?

► Suggested Resources

 Internet Resources

Short biographical sketches and information about Jean-Jacques Rousseau, Johann Heinrich Pestalozzi, Friedrich Froebel, and other educational pioneers can be found at **www.infed.org/thinkers**.

For a short biography of Herbert Spencer, consult the Internet Encyclopedia of Philosophy at **www.utm.edu/research/iep/s/spencer.htm**. Also, a discussion of Spencer's concept of progress can be found at the Modern History SourceBook at **www.fordham.edu/halsall/mod/spencer-darwin.html**.

For information on Maria Montessori, consult the "International Montessori Index" at **www.montessori.edu/** and Montessori Online at **www.montessori.org**.

Useful information related to Jean-Jacques Rousseau can be found at the following Web sites: the "Rousseau Association" at **www.wabash.edu/Rousseau**; the "lucid library" at **www.lucidcafe.com/library/library.html**; and the "Internet Encyclopedia of Philosophy" at **www.iep.utm.edu/**.

For information on Jane Addams, visit the Jane Addams Hull-House Museum at the University of Illinois at Chicago: **www.uic.edu/jaddams/hull/hull_house.html** and "Women in History" at **www.lkwdpl.org/wihohio/adda-jan.htm**.

For information about Piaget, consult resources for students at the Jean Piaget Society at **www.piaget.org**.

For essays on constructivism and education, consult **http:www.towson.edu/csme/ mctp/Essays.html**.

For information about Freire, consult **http//www.education.miami.edu/ep/contemporary ed/Paulo_Freire/paulo_Freire.html** and **niu.nl.edu/ace/Resources/Freire.html**.

Publications

Addams, Jane. *Twenty Years at Hull-House.* Edited by Victoria Bissell Brown. Boston: Bedford/St. Martin's, 1999. *A well-done edition of Jane Addams's story about her work at the famous settlement house.*

Brosterman, Norman. *Inventing Kindergarten.* New York: Harry N. Abrams, 1997. *Brosterman's beautifully illustrated book examines Froebel's kindergarten. The images provide excellent illustrations of kindergarten gifts, occupations, and activities in historical perspective.*

Comenius, John. *The Labyrinth of the World and the Paradise of the Heart.* Translated and introduced by Howard Louthan and Andrea Sterk. New York: Paulist Press, 1997. *This is a republication with a new introduction to Comenius's work on spirituality and ecumenism.*

Darder, Antonia. *Reinventing Paulo Freire.* Boulder, Colo.: Westview Press, 2002. *A recent appraisal of Freire's ideas.*

Davis, Allen F. *American Heroine: The Life and Legend of Jane Addams.* Chicago: Ivan Dee, 2000. *A well-done biography of Jane Addams, founder of Hull-House and proponent of multiculturalism and socialized education.*

Eldridge, Michael. *Transforming Experience: John Dewey's Cultural Instrumentalism.* Nashville, Tenn.: Vanderbilt University Press, 1998. *Eldridge examines Dewey's thought as a philosophy for dealing with life's problems.*

Freire, Paulo. *Pedagogy of the Oppressed.* Trans. Myra Bergman Ramos. New York: Continuum, 1996. *Freire's highly important work and key statement of his liberation pedagogy.*

Gutek, Gerald L. *Historical and Philosophical Foundations of Education: A Biographical Introduction.* Columbus, Ohio: Merrill, 2005. *Placing each educator in historical and cultural context, Gutek examines the educational ideas of Plato, Quintilian, Aquinas, Calvin, Rousseau, Pestalozzi, Froebel, Spencer, Montessori, Addams, Dewey, Du Bois, Gandhi, and Mao.*

Gutek, Gerald L. *Historical and Philosophical Foundations of Education: Selected Readings.* Columbus, Ohio: Merrill, 2001. *Contains selected primary source readings from Comenius, Rousseau, Pestalozzi, Froebel, Spencer, Dewey, Montessori, and other pioneering educational thinkers.*

Gutek, Gerald L. *Pestalozzi and Education.* Prospect Heights, Ill.: Waveland Press, 1999. *Gutek provides a biographical treatment and an analysis of the educational ideas of Johann Heinrich Pestalozzi.*

Martin, Jay. *The Education of John Dewey.* New York: Columbia University Press, 2002. *A thorough discussion of John Dewey's life and education with emphasis on how Dewey's emotional life influenced his philosophy.*

Menand, Louis. *The Metaphysical Club: A Story of Ideas in America.* New York: Farrar, Straus and Giroux, 2001. *An excellent and engaging narrative about the origins and development of pragmatism in American told through the intellectual engagement of Oliver Wendell Holmes, Charles S. Peirce, William James, and John Dewey.*

Montessori, Maria. *The Absorbent Mind.* New York: Holt, 1995. *A new edition of Montessori's important book on early childhood education.*

Morrow, Raymond A., and Torres, Carlos Alberto. *Reading Freire and Habermas: Critical Pedagogy and Transformative Social Change.* New York: Teachers College Press, Columbia University, 2002. *Relates Freire to the construction of critical pedagogy.*

Tanner, Laurel N. Dewey's *Laboratory School: Lessons for Today.* New York: Teachers College Press, 1997. *Tanner carefully examines the origins of Dewey's curriculum and methods at the University of Chicago Laboratory School and provides ideas of how such practices can find use in today's schools.*

Westbrook, Robert B. *John Dewey and American Democracy.* Ithaca, N.Y.: Cornell University Press, 1991. *Presents a definitive examination of the intellectual origins of John Dewey's thought.*

Zimmerman, Barry J., and Schunk, Dale H., ed., *Educational Psychology: A Century of Contributions.* Mahwah, N.J.: Lawrence Erlbaum, 2003. *This book, a project of the educational psychology division of the American Psychological Association, contains essays on Piaget and other leading educational psychologists of the twentieth century.*

CHAPTER 6

Historical Development of American Education

This chapter traces the history of American educational institutions and identifies formative contributions of individuals and groups to American education. The chapter examines (1) the colonial period, when European educational ideas and institutions were transported to America; (2) the creation of a uniquely American educational system during the revolutionary and early national eras; (3) the diffusion of universal education; (4) the development of secondary education from the Latin grammar school, through the academy, to today's comprehensive high school; (5) the development of institutions of higher learning; (6) the education of culturally diverse populations; and (7) trends in the history of American education such as educational technology development. As you read this chapter, consider the following questions:

FOCUS QUESTIONS

- How did the American environment transform European educational ideas and institutions?
- How did American democratic ideas contribute to public schooling in the United States?
- How does the American educational ladder differ from the European dual-track system?
- How did the United States become a culturally diverse society?
- What are the trends in the history of American education?

This chapter was written and revised by Dr. Gerald Gutek.

▶ The Colonial Period

■ Effect on Native Americans

■ Many ethnic groups among colonists

The colonization of North America in the seventeenth and eighteenth centuries produced complex cultural encounters and often violent conflicts between Europeans and indigenous peoples. Especially along the Atlantic coast, Europeans introduced diseases such as measles and smallpox, to which Native Americans had no immunity, and which decimated native populations.[1] The European colonists came from many ethnic and language backgrounds. The French established major European settlements in Canada and the Mississippi Valley; the Spanish in Mexico, Florida, and the Southwest; the Dutch in New Netherlands, now New York State; and the English in the original thirteen colonies that would constitute the United States after the War for American Independence. The English, who defeated the Dutch and the French, had the greatest impact on colonial politics, society, and education.

The colonists re-created the European socioeconomic-class–based **dual-track school system**. Lower-class boys and girls studied the primary-school curriculum, which included reading, writing, arithmetic, and religious instruction. Meanwhile, upper-class boys attended **Latin grammar schools**, preparatory schools that taught the Latin and Greek languages and literature required for admission to colonial colleges.

New England Colonies

The New England colonies of Massachusetts, Connecticut, and New Hampshire were a crucible for the development of American educational ideas and institutions. In fact, Massachusetts enacted the first formal education laws in British North America. (See Overview 6.1 for significant events in American education.)

■ Puritan schools

The Puritan Massachusetts colonists believed that educated persons who knew God's commandments as preached by Puritan ministers could resist the devil's temptations. Closely tied to the church, Puritan schools emphasized obedience to what was preached as divine law.

■ Schools for economic and social utility

Puritanism also gave education a Calvinist economic rationale. The Puritan work ethic defined good Puritans as those who read their Bibles and were industrious and thrifty business owners, farmers, and workers. To shape such enterprising individuals, schools stressed values of punctuality, honesty, and hard work. This tendency to relate school to economic productivity remains a strong influence on American education.

■ Child seen as sinful

Child Depravity. The Puritan concept of child nature shaped colonial New England's child-rearing and educational beliefs. Children were regarded as depraved, or at least inclined to evil. Children's play was seen as idleness and children's talk as gibberish. Following on the adage "Spare the rod and spoil the child," Puritan teachers used firm discipline and often corporal punishment.[2] The Puritan view of children dramatically contrasts with the attitudes of Comenius, Rousseau, Pestalozzi, and other educational pioneers discussed in the chapter on Pioneers in Education.

---

[1]For historical perspectives on English encounters with Native Americans, see Martin Daunton and Rick Halpern, *Empire and Others: British Encounters with Indigenous Peoples, 1600–1850* (Philadelphia: University of Pennsylvania Press, 1999).

[2]Ross W. Beale, Jr. "In Search of the Historical Child: Miniature Adulthood and Youth in Colonial New England," in N. Ray Hiner and Joseph H. Hawes, eds. *Growing Up in America: Children in Historical Perspective* (Urbana: University of Illinois Press, 1985), pp. 7–24.

■ A teacher for every town

"Old Deluder Satan." Even in Massachusetts' first years of settlement, the Puritans were establishing schools. In 1642, the Massachusetts General Court passed a law requiring parents and guardians to ensure that children in their care learned to read and understand the principles of religion and the commonwealth's laws. In 1647, the General Court enacted the "Old Deluder Satan" Act, a law intended to outwit Satan, who, the Puritans believed, tricked ignorant people into sinning. The law required every town of fifty or more families to appoint a reading and writing teacher. Towns of one hundred or more families were to employ a Latin teacher to prepare young men to enter Harvard College.

■ The three Rs, plus religion

The Town School. The New England colonists re-created the dual-track system, providing town schools for the majority of students and Latin grammar schools for upper-class boys. The New England **town school** was a locally controlled institution that educated both boys and girls ages six to thirteen or fourteen. Attendance was irregular, depending on weather conditions and the need for children to work on family farms. The school's curriculum included reading, writing, arithmetic, catechism, and religious hymns. Children learned the alphabet, syllables, words, and sentences by memorizing the **hornbook,** a sheet of parchment covered by transparent material made by flattening cattle horns. The older children read the *New England Primer,* which included religious materials such as the Westminster catechism, the Ten Commandments, the Lord's Prayer, and the Apostle's Creed. Arithmetic was primarily counting, adding, and subtracting.

■ Atmosphere of the town school

The New England town school was often a simple log structure, dominated by the teacher's pulpit-like desk at the front of the single room. Pupils sat on wooden benches and memorized their assignments until called before the schoolmaster to recite. The teachers were men, some of whom earned their living in this way while preparing for the ministry. Others took the job to repay debts owed for their voyage to North America. Some, unfortunately, were incompetents who controlled their pupils by corporal punishment.

■ Classics for upper-class boys

The Latin Grammar School. The sons of the upper classes attended the Latin grammar school, which prepared them for college entry. These boys generally had learned to read and write English from private tutors. Entering the Latin grammar school at age eight, the student would complete his studies at fifteen or sixteen. He studied such Latin authors as Cicero, Terence, Caesar, Livy, Vergil, and Horace. More advanced students studied such Greek authors as Isocrates, Hesiod, and Homer. Little attention was given to mathematics, science, or modern languages. The Latin masters who taught in these schools often held college degrees and enjoyed higher social status than elementary teachers. The Latin grammar school was one of colonial America's closest links to European education, resembling classical humanist schools of the Renaissance.

■ Harvard College

After completing Latin grammar school, New England upper-class young men sought admission to Harvard College, established in 1636. Harvard was founded on the Puritan belief that future ministers and other leaders needed a sound classical and theological education. Students had to demonstrate competency in Latin and Greek to be admitted to Harvard, where the curriculum consisted of grammar, logic, rhetoric, arithmetic, geometry, astronomy, ethics, metaphysics, and natural science. In addition, Hebrew, Greek, and ancient history were offered for their usefulness in studying the Bible and other religious works.

OVERVIEW 6.1 *Significant Events in the History of American Education*

Major Political Events		Significant Educational Events	
1630	Settlement of Massachusetts Bay Colony	1636	Harvard College founded, first English-speaking college in western hemisphere
		1642	First education law enacted in Massachusetts
		1647	Old Deluder Satan Act enacted in Massachusetts, requiring establishment of schools
		1751	Benjamin Franklin's Academy established in Philadelphia
1775–1783	American Revolution	1783	Noah Webster's *American Spelling Book* published
1788	U.S. Constitution ratified	1785	Northwest Ordinance, first national education law, enacted
		1821	First public high school in the United States opened in Boston
			Emma Willard's Female Seminary, a school of higher education for women, established in Troy, New York
		1823	First private normal school in the United States opened in Concord, Vermont
1824	Bureau of Indian Affairs established	1825	Webster's *American Dictionary* completed
		1827	Massachusetts law requiring public high schools passed
1830	Indian Removal Act	1837	Horace Mann appointed secretary of Massachusetts board of education
1846–1848	Mexican-American War; U.S. acquisition of southwestern territories	1839	First public normal school opened in Lexington, Massachusetts
1849	Gold Rush to California	1855	First German-language kindergarten in the United States established
		1860	First English-language kindergarten in the United States established
1861–1865	Civil War	1862	Morrill Land Grant College Act passed, establishing in each state a college for agricultural and mechanical instruction
		1865	Freedmen's Bureau established
		1872	*Kalamazoo* decision upheld public taxation for high schools
1887	Dawes Act divides tribal lands	1881	Tuskegee Institute established by Booker T. Washington
		1892	Committee of Ten established
1898	Spanish-American War; U.S. acquisition of Puerto Rico and the Philippines	1896	*Plessy v. Ferguson* decision upheld constitutionality of "separate but equal" schools for white and black students
		1909	First junior high school established in Berkeley, California

Major Political Events	Significant Educational Events
1914–1918 World War I	1917 Smith-Hughes Act passed, providing funds for vocational education, home economics, and agricultural subjects
	1918 *Cardinal Principles of Secondary Education* published
	1919 Progressive Education Association organized
1929 Beginning of the Great Depression	1930s New Deal programs during the Great Depression provided federal funds for education of the unemployed and for school construction
1939–1945 World War II	1944 G.I. Bill passed, providing federal funds for continuing education of veterans
1950–1953 Korean War	1954 *Brown v. Board of Education of Topeka* ended racial segregation of public schools
	1957 Soviet Union launched *Sputnik*, leading to criticism and reevaluation of American public education
	1958 National Defense Education Act passed, providing federal funds to improve science, math, and modern foreign language instruction and guidance services
	1964 Civil Rights Act authorizes federal lawsuits for school desegregation
1965–1973 Vietnam War	1965 Elementary and Secondary Education Act passed, providing federal funds to public schools, especially for compensatory education
	1968 Bilingual Education Act
	1972 Title IX Education Amendment passed, outlawing sex discrimination in schools receiving federal financial assistance
	1975 Education for All Handicapped Children (Public Law 94-142) passed
	1980 Department of Education established in federal government with cabinet status
	1983 Publication and dissemination of *A Nation at Risk* stimulated national movement to reform education
1990 End of Cold War	1994 *Goals 2000: The Educate America Act* outlines national education goals
1991 Gulf War	
2001 Terrorist attacks on New York City and Washington, D.C.	1996 The nation's first educational technology plan: *Getting Students Ready for the Twenty-first Century: Meeting the Technology Literacy Challenge*
2003 Iraq War	2001 No Child Left Behind Act

Middle Atlantic Colonies

■ Diverse cultures

The Middle Atlantic colonies—New York, New Jersey, Delaware, and Pennsylvania—differed from New England. Whereas New England had a common language and religion, the Middle Atlantic colonies had Dutch in New York, Swedes in Delaware, and Germans in Pennsylvania. Along with different languages came religious diversity. This cultural diversity influenced schooling. Whereas New England created town schools, the churches in the Middle Atlantic colonies established parochial schools.

■ Private schools

New York. New York was initially a Dutch colony. The Dutch Reformed Church continued to operate schools after the English seized New Netherlands. Dutch parochial schools taught reading, writing, and religion. With English rule, the Church of England established charity and missionary schools.

In New York City, a commercial port, private for-profit schools charged students fees to study navigation, surveying, bookkeeping, Spanish, French, and geography. For-profit private schools also operated in other colonies.

■ Quaker schools

Pennsylvania. Pennsylvania, a proprietary colony founded by William Penn, became a haven for the Society of Friends, or Quakers, a religious denomination. As conscientious objectors, Quakers refused to support war efforts or serve in the military. Quaker schools were open to all children, including blacks and Native Americans. (Philadelphia had a small African American community, and some Native Americans remained in the colony.) Quaker schools taught the reading, writing, arithmetic, and religion found in other colonial primary schools but were unique in including vocational training, crafts, and agriculture. Still another difference was that Quaker teachers rejected both the concept of child depravity and corporal punishment.[3]

Southern Colonies

The southern colonies—Maryland, Virginia, the Carolinas, and Georgia—had still another pattern of education. Except for flourishing cities in tidewater areas such as Charleston and Williamsburg, the southern population was generally more dispersed than those in New England or the Middle Atlantic colonies. Rural families struggled to bring children together at a single location to attend school. Moreover, culture, economics, and politics in the South were profoundly shaped by the use of enslaved Africans as the plantation labor force.

■ Private tutors

Because the population was so dispersed, the children of wealthy white plantation owners often studied with private tutors who lived in the manor house. Some families sent their children to private schools sponsored by the Church of England in towns such as Williamsburg or Charleston.

Although slavery existed throughout the colonies, the largest population of enslaved Africans was in the South. Africans were seized by force and brutally transported in slave ships to North America to work on southern plantations. The enslaved Africans were trained as agricultural field hands, craftspeople, or domestic servants, but generally were forbidden to learn to read or write. Some notable exceptions learned to read secretly. Over time, the African heritage became the foundation of African American religion and culture.[4]

---

[3]James D. Hendricks, "Be Still and Know: Quaker Silence and Dissenting Educational Ideals, 1740–1812," *Journal of the Midwest History of Education Society* (Annual Proceedings, 1975), pp. 14–40.
[4]Ira Berlin, *Many Thousands Gone: The First Two Centuries of Slavery in North America* (Cambridge, Mass.: Belknap Press, 1998).

■ Class bias in schooling

The slave system also affected economically disadvantaged, nonslaveholding whites. While wealthy plantation owners occupied the most fertile area, the poorer farmers settled in less fertile backcountry or mountainous areas. The wealthy and politically powerful plantation elite focused on the education of their own children but provided few schools for the rest of the population.

Colonial Education: A Summary View

■ Parallels among regions

Despite regional variations, certain educational similarities existed among New England, the Middle Atlantic colonies, and the South. All three were British colonies, and all, despite language and religious differences, inherited the Western European educational tradition. Religious belief shaped morality, and the family was a strong force in forming opinions, values, and skills.[5]

■ Gender discrimination

Educational opportunities were gender based in all three regions. Both girls and boys attended primary schools, but Latin grammar schools and colleges were restricted to boys and men. Women were forbidden to be ministers or lawyers, which, according to the educational philosophy of the time, eliminated the need for them to attend a Latin grammar school or college. Instead of Greek and Latin, they learned the basics (reading and writing) to fulfill their family and religious responsibilities. Many, especially men who controlled educational institutions, believed that women were intellectually incapable of higher studies.

■ Tracking by social class

This division into two tracks in colonial schools reflected European class prejudices. Primary schools, intended for lower-class children, provided basic literacy but discouraged upward social mobility. Few pupils who completed primary schools advanced to Latin grammar schools and colonial colleges. The sons of the upper classes, in contrast, attended the preparatory Latin grammar schools and, if successful, entered college. During the nineteenth century, frontier egalitarianism, political democratization, and economic change would erode these European-based educational structures, creating the American system of universal public education.

REFOCUS In what ways do you think the Puritan attitude to work and morality has influenced American culture and schools? What place does the Puritan ethic hold in your own philosophy of education? Why was the establishment of schools an important concern for the early colonists?

▶ The Early National Period

■ Northwest Ordinance

The American Revolution, which began in 1776, ended British rule in the thirteen colonies. Although the inherited vernacular and denominational elementary schools and Latin grammar schools continued for some time, the new republic's leaders sought to devise educational institutions appropriate to the self-governing citizens of the United States.

The earliest federal educational legislation was incorporated in the Northwest Ordinance of 1785, which required that a section of each thirty-six-square-mile township be reserved for education. The Northwest Ordinance established the precedent for financing education through **land grants** in the nineteenth century.

■ Tradition of local control

Although the U.S. Constitution made no mention of education, the Tenth Amendment's "reserved powers" clause (which reserves to the states all powers not

---

[5]Lawrence A. Cremin, *American Education: The Colonial Experience, 1607–1783* (New York: Harper and Row, 1970).

specifically delegated to the federal government or prohibited to the states by the Constitution) left responsibility for education with the individual states. The New England tradition of local school control and general opposition to centralized political power also contributed to a state rather than a national school system in the United States.

■ New educational ideas for the new nation

During the early national period, several political and intellectual leaders made educational proposals for the emergent republic. These plans generally argued that education (1) should prepare people for republican citizenship; (2) should include utilitarian and scientific emphases to aid in developing the nation's vast expanses of frontier land and abundant natural resources; and (3) should be divested of European cultural attitudes and create a uniquely American culture.[6] These general goals are evident in the proposals of Benjamin Franklin, Thomas Jefferson, and Noah Webster. The issue of a uniquely American culture is debated in the Taking Issue box.

Franklin: The Academy

■ Franklin's academy

Benjamin Franklin (1706–1790) founded an **academy**, a private secondary school, and described its rationale in his "Proposals Relating to the Education of Youth in Pennsylvania."[7] His academy's utilitarian curriculum differed notably from the traditional Latin grammar school. English grammar, composition, rhetoric, and public speaking replaced Latin and Greek as the chief language studies. Students could also choose a second language based on their future careers. For example, prospective clergy could choose Latin and Greek, and those planning on commercial careers could elect French, Spanish, or German. Mathematics was taught for its practical use in bookkeeping, surveying, and engineering rather than as an abstract subject. History and biography provided occasions for students to examine the ethical decisions made by famous historical personages.

■ Emphasis on science and practical skills

Prophetically, Franklin recognized the future importance of science, invention, and technology. His curriculum also incorporated utilitarian skills that schools had traditionally ignored, such as carpentry, shipbuilding, engraving, printing, and farming. By the mid-nineteenth century, many academies similar to Franklin's had been established.

Jefferson: Education for Citizenship

■ Education for citizenship

Thomas Jefferson (1743–1826) expressed his educational philosophy in his "Bill for the More General Diffusion of Knowledge," which he introduced in the Virginia legislature in 1779. Jefferson was also the principal founder of the University of Virginia. Education's major purpose, Jefferson stated, was to promote a democratic society of literate and well-informed citizens. Committed to separation of church and state, he believed that the state, not the churches, should play the primary educational role. State-sponsored schools, not private ones, would be funded by public taxes.[8]

---

[6]Jacqueline S. Reinier, *From Virtue to Character: American Childhood, 1775–1850* (New York: Twayne of Macmillan, 1996), p. xi.

[7]Walter Isaacson, *Benjamin Franklin: An American Life* (New York: Simon and Schuster, 2003), pp. 146–147. Other biographies of Franklin are Edmund S. Morgan, *Benjamin Franklin* (New Haven: Yale University Press, 2002); H. W. Brands, *The First American: The Life and Times of Benjamin Franklin* (New York: Anchor Books/Random House, 2000).

[8]Julius P. Boyd, ed., *The Papers of Thomas Jefferson*, vol. II (Princeton, N.J.: Princeton University Press, 1950), pp. 526–533. Also consult "The Publicly-Accessible Jefferson Collection" at the University of Virginia: **www.etext.virginia.edu/etcbin/ot2www?specific=/web/data/jefferson/texts/jefall.02w.**

taking issue

Question Should American public education transmit a distinctively American culture? In other words, should schools deliberately convey a specific cultural core?

Schools and American Culture

A long-standing issue in American education is the degree to which public schools should transmit a distinctively American culture. Some educators believe that all public schools should teach certain key cultural concepts and values. Others contend that schools should promote multiculturalism and respect for diversity. The issue over a common cultural core versus cultural diversity also relates to current controversies over bilingual and bicultural education.

Arguments PRO

1 As American leaders since Thomas Jefferson have recognized, a primary purpose of schooling is to educate responsible citizens. We need a basic knowledge of the ideas and values central to our national life to function as citizens.

2 The United States, which has always been a nation of immigrants, needs a core culture to bind diverse groups together. Noah Webster recognized this point, and it is even more important today. Without a shared culture to unite our different peoples and cultures, our society is in danger of splintering.

3 Schools bring diverse people together and can inculcate the basic values of our common culture. By doing so, schools would help solve problems that plague us such as violence and drug abuse.

4 Given the intense economic competition among countries, it is vital that American citizens share certain common purposes. Schools can promote shared goals by transmitting the values and concepts unique to American culture.

Arguments CON

1 From the earliest days of American history, the nation has been characterized by cultural pluralism. Beyond a basic knowledge of how American democracy works, no one set of ideas or values makes a responsible American citizen.

2 American society derives its strength from the creative diversity of its people, not from a core culture that makes everyone think alike. We will find real unity only if we appreciate diversity and respect what every group contributes to American life.

3 If schools try to impose a single set of values, they alienate many students. Instead, schools should encourage students to understand the cultural diversity in our society.

4 To succeed on the world scene, the United States needs a greater knowledge and appreciation of foreign cultures. Schools should focus on multiculturalism and internationalism, not on a rigidly defined Americanism.

■ Jefferson's plan

Jefferson's bill, though not passed, is important for the issues that it raised in the new nation. For example, it suggested establishing public schools and attempted to resolve conflicts between equity and excellence in education. It would have subdivided Virginia's counties into districts. Excluding enslaved children, the bill stipulated that free children, both girls and boys, could attend an elementary school in each district. Here they would study reading, writing, arithmetic, and history. Tuition would be free for the first three years. Jefferson's proposal also would have established twenty grammar schools throughout the state to provide secondary education to boys. In these grammar schools, students would study Latin, Greek, English, geography, and higher mathematics.

■ Scholarships based on merit

Jefferson's bill anticipated the idea of academic merit scholarships. In each district school, the most academically able male student who could not afford to pay tuition would receive a scholarship to continue his education at a grammar school.

The ten scholarship students of highest academic achievement would receive additional state support to attend the College of William and Mary.

Webster: Schoolmaster of the Republic

Noah Webster (1758–1843) was one of the early republic's leading cultural nationalists.[9] When the Constitution was ratified in 1789, Webster argued that the United States should have its own "language as well as government." Realizing that a distinctive national language and literature build a sense of national identity, Webster sought to create an American version of the English language.

■ Learning American culture through language

Webster believed that as children learned Americanized English they would acquire a uniquely American cultural identity. Textbooks would shape the teaching, and Webster spent his life writing spelling and reading books. His greatest work was his *American Dictionary*, completed in 1825 after twenty-five years of intensive research.

■ Webster's influence on Americanization

Called the "schoolmaster of the republic," Noah Webster helped to create a sense of American language, identity, and nationality. At the same time he encouraged a monolithic American cultural identity. In future years, immigrants were "Americanized" by learning what had become the standard form of American English. Today, educational efforts for multiculturalism and bilingualism seek to recognize American diversity and correct the excesses of cultural nationalism.

REFOCUS Think back to the questions at the beginning of the chapter: How did American democratic ideas contribute to public schooling in the United States? Examine how you believe the ideas of Franklin, Jefferson, and Webster contributed to these ideas.

▶ The Movement Toward Public Schooling

■ Sunday schools

Before public schools were established, several private voluntary alternatives to tax-supported schools were tried. Chief among them were Sunday and monitorial schools, both popular in the early nineteenth century. During that time, many children worked in the factories of the industrializing Northeast. Sunday schools opened in larger cities such as New York and Philadelphia to provide a minimal basic education. They met on the one day of the week when factories were idle and taught children writing, reading, arithmetic, and religion.

■ Students as assistant teachers

The **monitorial method** used monitors, older and more experienced pupils trained by a master teacher, to assist in teaching classes, taking attendance, and maintaining order. For example, the master teacher would train monitors in a particular skill, such as adding single-digit numbers. These monitors would then teach that skill to groups of less experienced pupils. Designed to teach basic skills to masses of students, monitorial schools received support from private philanthropists who wanted a large but inexpensive school system. Like Sunday schools, monitorial schools were popular in large eastern cities. For example, more than 600,000 children attended monitorial schools conducted by the New York Free School Society.[10]

■ Rise and fall of monitorial schools

---

[9]Harlow Giles Unger, *Noah Webster, The Life and Times of an American Patriot* (New York: Wiley, 1998).
[10]William R. Johnson, "'Chanting Choristes': Simultaneous Recitation in Baltimore's Nineteenth-Century Primary Schools," *History of Education Quarterly* (Spring 1994), pp. 1–12.

In the 1840s, monitorial schools were replaced by common schools, as people began to realize that they provided only rudimentary education.

The Common School

■ A school for all classes

The common school movement of the first half of the nineteenth century is highly significant in American education because it created publicly financed elementary education. The **common school**, today's public school, was an elementary educational institution that offered a basic curriculum of reading, writing, and arithmetic. It was called a "common" school because it was open to children of all social and economic classes. Historically, however, enslaved African children in the South did not attend until the Civil War ended slavery.

■ Differences among regions

Because the Tenth Amendment of the U.S. Constitution reserved education to the individual states, the United States did not create a national school system as did other countries such as France and Japan. Thus the patterns by which common schools were established differed from state to state and even within a given state. Especially on the western frontier, where many small school districts were created, resources and support for schooling varied from one district to another.

■ Growth of the common school

The common school movement gained momentum between 1820 and 1850. Common schools were first established in the New England states, where Massachusetts and then Connecticut were leading examples. In 1826, a Massachusetts law required every town to elect a school committee responsible for all the schools in the town. This began the policy of organizing public schools into a school system under a single authority. Ten years later, in 1836, Massachusetts established the first state board of education. Connecticut then followed its neighbor's example. Other northern states generally adopted New England's common school model. As the frontier moved westward and new states were admitted to the Union, they, too, established a common or public elementary school system. In the South, however, the establishment of common schools was generally delayed until after the Civil War.

Although varying from state to state, legislatures typically established common schools in the following sequence:

■ Three stages of legislation

- First, they permitted residents to organize local school districts with approval of local voters.

- Second, they deliberately encouraged, but did not mandate, establishing school districts, electing school boards, and levying taxes to support schools.

- Third, they made common schools compulsory by mandating the establishment of districts, election of boards, and raising taxes to support schools.

The common schools laid the foundation of the American public school system. Later in the nineteenth century, the public high school would complete the **educational ladder** that prepared students to enter state colleges and universities. Perhaps the most prominent American educator in the common school movement was Horace Mann.

Mann: The Struggle for Public Schools

Horace Mann (1796–1859) was a steadfast proponent of common schools.[11] When the Massachusetts legislature established a state board of education in 1837, Mann

---

[11]Jonathan Messerli, *Horace Mann: A Biography* (New York: Knopf, 1972).

was appointed its secretary. His *Annual Reports* contained his philosophy of education and his opinions on educational issues. As editor of the *Common School Journal*, moreover, Mann won national support for public schools. (For Mann's appointment and other events in American education, see Overview 6.1.)

■ Building support for common schools

Mann used his political acumen to mobilize support for public education. First, he had to convince taxpayers that it was in their self-interest to support public schools. To win support from the business community, Mann developed the *stewardship theory*. He argued that wealthy people had a special responsibility in providing public education. Those who had prospered, Mann asserted, were the guardians or stewards of wealth. In addition, their support of public education would create industrious men and women who would obey the law, be diligent in their work, and add to the state's economy. Thus tax support of public education was actually an investment that would yield high dividends in the form of public safety, progress, and prosperity. To the workers and farmers of Massachusetts, Mann argued that the common school would be a great social equalizer, giving children from lower socioeconomic classes the skills and knowledge to acquire better jobs and upward mobility.

■ Public schools as vital to democratic society

Mann, like Jefferson, saw a crucial relationship between public schooling and a democratic society. He argued that citizens must be literate to participate intelligently in representative political processes. He believed that the United States, a nation of immigrants, differed from the homogeneous western European nations. To develop a unifying common culture, the country needed a common elementary education that would promote a sense of national identity and purpose.

■ School taxes

According to Mann, the common, or public, school should be financed by state and local taxes. The public, which paid for the schools, would govern them. Following the New England tradition of local control, popularly elected officials would exercise ultimate authority. The common schools must also be nonsectarian and free of church control.

Normal Schools and Women's Education

In addition to providing publicly supported elementary education for the majority of American children, the common school movement had two important complementary consequences: (1) it contributed to establishing **normal schools** as teacher-preparation institutions, and (2) made elementary-school teaching an important career path for women.

■ Rise of normal schools

Normal schools took their name from the French *école normale* on which they were modeled. First established in New England in 1823 and encouraged by Horace Mann, normal schools were two-year institutions that provided courses in history and philosophy of education, methods of teaching, and practice or demonstration teaching for prospective teachers. By the end of the nineteenth century, however, many normal schools had become four-year teacher-education colleges.[12]

■ Expanding opportunities for women

The establishment of common schools created a demand for trained teachers, and many women were attracted to teaching careers in the expanding elementary school system. The normal schools prepared women for these careers and at the same time provided opportunities for higher education hitherto denied them. Although salaries were low and conditions demanding, teaching gave middle-class women a rare opportunity for a career outside the home.

---

[12]For the history of American teacher education, see Jurgen Herbst, *And Sadly Teach: Teacher Education and Professionalization in American Culture* (Madison: University of Wisconsin Press, 1989).

Until the Civil War, most rural schoolteachers were men. By 1900, however, partly as a result of the growth of normal schools, 71 percent of rural teachers were women. Among the leaders of this dramatic change in women's roles was Catharine Beecher.

Catharine Beecher: Preparing Women as Teachers

▪ Reform and women's rights

In the first half of the nineteenth century, feminist leaders such as Elizabeth Cady Stanton, Emma Willard, Susan B. Anthony, and Catharine Beecher spoke out for women's educational and political equality.

▪ A key role for women

Catharine Beecher (1800–1878) founded the Hartford Female Seminary in 1828 to prepare women for teaching careers. She also organized and led the American Women's Educational Association. Beecher advocated establishing special teacher-education institutions, or seminaries, for women's professional development as teachers. Like normal schools, each seminary would have a demonstration school where future teachers, supervised by experienced master teachers, did practice teaching. Professionally educated women, Beecher reasoned, could contribute to national development by bringing literacy, civility, and morality to the American frontier, in acute need of prepared teachers to staff the many one-room schools.[13]

The One-Room School

▪ Direct democracy in small districts

The local school district with its one-room school was almost a direct democracy in which an elected school board set the tax rate and hired and supervised the teacher.[14] Many of these small districts were consolidated into larger ones in the early twentieth century, as described in the chapter on Governing and Administering Public Education.

Teacher certification was simple but chaotic; each board issued its own certificates to its teachers, which other districts often refused to recognize. Today's more uniform state certification is a step toward greater professionalization for teachers.

▪ The typical schoolhouse

On the western frontier, the one-room log school was often the first community building constructed. By the 1870s, wood-frame schoolhouses, painted white or red, replaced the crude log structures. These improved buildings, heated by wood-burning stoves, had slate blackboards and cloakrooms. The teacher's desk stood on a raised platform at the front of the room. Many classrooms had large double desks that seated two pupils. Later, these often were replaced with single desks, each with a desktop attached to its back. The single desks had to be arranged in straight rows, one behind the other, so that a seat was behind each desktop.[15]

▪ Basic curriculum

The pupils, who ranged in age from five to seventeen, studied a basic curriculum of reading, writing, grammar, spelling, arithmetic, history, geography, and hygiene. Teachers used the recitation method, in which each pupil stood and recited a previously assigned lesson. Schools emphasized punctuality, honesty, and hard work. The rural one-room schoolteachers, expected to be disciplinarians as well as in-

---

[13]Barbara M. Cross, ed., *The Educated Woman in America: Selected Writings of Catharine Beecher, Margaret Fuller, and M. Carey Thomas* (New York: Teachers College Press, Columbia University, 1965), pp. 73–75.

[14]A Web presentation on the one-room school is "One Room Schools: Michigan's Educational Legacy," Clarke Historical Library, Central Michigan University: **www.lib.cmich.edu/ clarke/schoolsintro.htm.**

[15]Wayne E. Fuller, *One-Room Schools of the Middle West: An Illustrated History* (Lawrence: University of Kansas Press, 1994), pp. 7–19, 18–27, 30–40.

The one-room school represented a form of direct democracy in school government: the elected school board set the tax rate and hired and supervised the teacher. The small rural school also served as a cultural center for the community. *(© Art Resource)*

structors, had "to be their own janitors, record keepers, and school administrators."[16] For more about the one-room school, see the Technology @ School box.

The McGuffey Readers

■ 120 million copies

William Holmes McGuffey (1800–1873), clergyman, professor, and college president, is best known for the series of readers that bears his name. The McGuffey readers, which affirmed the values of literacy, hard work, diligence, and virtuous living, evoked a favorable response in nineteenth-century public schools. More than 120 million copies of McGuffey's readers sold between 1836 and 1920.[17]

■ Patriotism and moral values

McGuffey readers emphasized the moral values of white Anglo-Saxon Protestant rural America, as well as patriotism and heroism. Reading selections included the orations of Patrick Henry, Daniel Webster, and George Washington. McGuffey provided the first graded readers for our school systems and paved the way for a totally graded system, beginning in the 1840s.

REFOCUS Think back to the questions at the beginning of the chapter: How does the American educational ladder differ from the European dual-track system? Consider how the common school established a broad-based foundation for the American system as you know it today.

---

[16]*Ibid.*, p. 61.
[17]John H. Westerhoff, *McGuffey and His Readers: Piety, Morality, and Education in Nineteenth Century America* (Nashville, Tenn.: Abingdon, 1978). See also James M. Lower, "William Holmes McGuffey: A Book or a Man? Or More?" *Vitae Scholasticae* (Fall 1984), pp. 311–320.

Studying the One-Room School

As a prospective teacher, you may want to learn more about the one-room schools in American frontier days. Studying one-room schools can help your students make a personal connection to the lives of America's pioneer teachers. Following are several useful Web sites on one-room schools:

- The Kansas ORSH Project: **www.ukans.edu/heritage/orsh/133/**

- The Kansas State Historical Society: **www.kshs.org/features/feat996.htm**

- ColesCounty.Net—One-Room Schools: **www.colescounty.net/schools_history.html**

- Country Schools: **www.plainsfolk.com/bowman/schools.htm.**

- One Room Schools: Michigan's Educational Legacy, Clarke Historical Library, Central Michigan University: **clarke.cmich.edu/schoolsintro.htm**

- Rural Education in the Late 1800s: **www.cobleskill.edu/schools/mcs/CSBest/school.htm**

These sites examine one-room schools and provide information about their teachers, students, architecture, textbooks, and curriculum. You and your students can continue your research with a visit to your local or school library, where you can identify articles and books on this subject. Research these materials and create a bibliography about one-room schools.

You may also wish to arrange more direct experiences. Consult the local museums and history societies in your area. See if they have materials or collections on one-room schools and nineteenth- and early-twentieth-century education. You could arrange a class visit to the collections. In addition, people in your community or in students' families may have attended one-room schools. You and your students could conduct interviews with some of these individuals.

► The Development of American Secondary Schools

■ Completing the educational ladder

Common schools created the foundation for tax-supported and locally controlled public elementary education in the United States. After a period of evolution, public secondary schooling eventually completed the institutional rungs of the American educational ladder, on which students could progress to higher education.

The Academy: Forerunner of the High School

■ Academy replaces grammar school

Initiated by Benjamin Franklin, academies were the first replacements for colonial-period Latin grammar schools. The academy became the dominant secondary school during the first half of the nineteenth century. Serving middle-class educational needs, it offered a wide range of curricula and subjects. By 1855, more than 6,000 U.S. academies enrolled 263,000 students.

■ Broader curriculum and student body

Unlike Latin grammar schools, academies expanded their enrollment beyond students preparing for college; they also served students planning to complete their formal education at the academy. The academies' curriculum also included more than Latin and Greek. Programs varied considerably in quality and quantity but usually followed three patterns: (1) the traditional college preparatory curriculum

■ Academies for women

with emphasis on Latin and Greek; (2) the English-language program, a general curriculum for those planning to end formal education with completion of secondary school; and (3) the normal course, for prospective common school teachers. Students might also attend specialized military academies.

In contrast to Latin grammar schools, some academies enrolled women as well as men. Others were founded expressly for young women. Among the academies founded for women was the Troy Female Seminary in New York, established in 1821 by Emma Willard, a leader in the women's rights movement. Along with conventional domestic science programs, women's academies offered classical and modern languages, science, mathematics, art, and music. Teacher-preparation, or normal, curricula also were popular.

The academies generally were controlled by private boards of trustees. Occasionally, they might be semipublic and receive partial funding from cities or states. The era of the academies extended to the 1870s, when they declined and were replaced by public high schools. However, private academies still provide secondary education for a small percentage of the population.

The High School

■ Taxes for public high schools

Although a few **high schools** existed in the United States from the founding of the English Classical School of Boston in 1821, the high school did not become the dominant institution of American secondary education until the second half of the nineteenth century, when it gradually replaced the academy. In the 1870s the courts ruled in a series of cases (especially the Kalamazoo, Michigan, case in 1874) that school districts could establish and support public high schools with tax funds if they desired.[18] After that, the public high school movement spread rapidly. By 1890, public high schools in the United States enrolled more than twice as many students as private academies.

■ Compulsory attendance

Eventually the states passed compulsory school attendance laws. Provision of public secondary schools thereafter became a state obligation, rather than a voluntary matter. Students could attend approved nonpublic schools, but the states had the legal right to set minimum standards for all schools.

Urbanization and the High School.   The rise of the high school resulted from a variety of socioeconomic forces. The United States in the mid-nineteenth century experienced a dramatic transition from an agricultural and rural society to an industrial and urban nation. For example, New York City's population quadrupled between 1860 and 1910. By 1930, more than 25 percent of all Americans lived in seven great urban areas: New York, Chicago, Philadelphia, Boston, Detroit, Los Angeles, and Cleveland. Rapid urbanization also generated a need for more specialized occupations, professions, and services, a need to which high schools responded.[19]

■ Effort to standardize curriculum

Reshaping the High-School Curriculum.   In the high school's early years, educators sought to define its purpose and curriculum. Traditionalists saw it as a college preparatory school, but others wanted more immediately practical vocational and career programs. In some large cities, high schools, known as "people's colleges," of-

[18]See *Stuart v. School District No. 1 of Village of Kalamazoo*, 30 Mich. 69 (1874).
[19]Edward A. Krug, *The Shaping of the American High School, 1880–1920* (New York: Harper and Row, 1964); Edward A. Krug, *The Shaping of the American High School, 1920–1941* (Madison: University of Wisconsin Press, 1972); Jurgen Herbst, *The Once and Future School: Three Hundred Years of American Secondary Education* (New York: Routledge, 1996); and William J. Reese, *The Origins of the American High School* (New Haven, Conn.: Yale University Press, 1995).

Comprehensive high schools became the dominant institution of American secondary education in the early twentieth century. *(Corbis/Bettmann)*

fered liberal arts and science programs.[20] To resolve these issues, the National Education Association (NEA) in 1892 established the **Committee of Ten**, chaired by Harvard University president Charles Eliot. The committee made two important recommendations: (1) uniform teaching of subjects for both students continuing on to college and those planning to end formal education upon graduation; (2) eight years of elementary and four years of secondary education.[21] It identified four curricula as appropriate for the high school: classical, Latin-scientific, modern language, and English. However, each curriculum included foreign languages, mathematics, science, English, and history courses found in college preparatory programs. Although the committee recommended alternatives to the dominant Latin and Greek classical curriculum, its recommendations remained oriented to college preparatory rather than terminal students.

■ Rising diversity

By 1918, thirty states required full-time school attendance until age sixteen.[22] Increasing enrollments made high-school students more representative of the general population and more culturally varied than in the past. No longer only the children of the professional and business classes, high-school students came from the nation's adolescent population at large.

---

[20]Herbst, *The Once and Future School*, pp. 95–106.
[21]National Education Association, *Report of the Committee on Secondary School Studies* (Washington, D.C.: U.S. Government Printing Office, 1893).
[22]Krug, *The Shaping of the American High School, 1920–1941*, p. 7.

■ A comprehensive orientation

The high-school population's changing characteristics were recognized by the NEA's **Commission on the Reorganization of Secondary Education** in its 1918 report, *Cardinal Principles of Secondary Education*. Recognizing the needs of an urban and industrial society, the commission redefined the high school as a comprehensive institution serving the country's various social, cultural, and economic groups. They recommended differentiated curriculum to meet agricultural, commercial, industrial, and domestic as well as college preparatory needs without sacrificing its integrative and comprehensive social character.[23]

Secondary-School Organization

■ Varied programs for varied students

By the 1920s, high schools had developed four curricular patterns: (1) the college preparatory program, which included English language and literature, foreign languages, mathematics, natural and physical sciences, and history and social studies; (2) the commercial or business program with courses in bookkeeping, shorthand, and typing; (3) industrial, vocational, home economics, and agricultural programs; and (4) a general academic program for students whose formal education would end with graduation.

■ A four-year sequence

Despite variations, the typical high-school pattern followed a four-year sequence encompassing grades 9–12 and generally including ages fourteen to eighteen. Variations included reorganized six-year schools, where students attended a combined junior-senior high school after completing a six-year elementary school, three-year junior high schools, which comprised grades 7–9, and three-year senior high schools for grades 10–12.

■ Junior high schools

The **junior high school** was the product of educators who wanted a transitional institution between elementary and secondary education oriented to the needs of early adolescents. As they developed in the 1920s and 1930s, junior high schools were either two-year institutions that encompassed grades 7 and 8, or three-year institutions that also included the ninth grade. The junior high school curriculum extended beyond that of elementary schools by including some vocational and commercial courses. By 1920, there were 883 junior high schools in the United States. By the 1940s, the junior high school was so well established that more than 50 percent of young adolescents were attending junior high schools.[24]

■ Middle schools

In the 1960s, **middle schools** became another type of transitional institution between elementary and high school.[25] They generally include grades 6–8 (ages eleven through thirteen) and facilitate a gradual transition from childhood to adolescence by emphasizing programs oriented to preadolescent development and needs. New middle schools were designed; they often featured learning centers, language laboratories, and arts centers. Their numbers grew rapidly from 1,434 in 1971 to 9,750 in 2000.[26] Although most school districts today use the middle school model, a few districts retain the junior high school approach.[27]

---

[23]Commission on the Reorganization of Secondary Education, *Cardinal Principles of American Secondary Education,* Bulletin no. 35 (Washington, D.C.: U.S. Government Printing Office, 1918).
[24]Douglas MacIver and Allen Ruby, "Middle Schools," in James W. Guthrie, ed., *Encyclopedia of Education,* 2nd ed., vol. 5 (New York: Macmillan/Thomson Gale, 2003), p. 1630.
[25]For a discussion of middle-school education, see Thomas Dickinson, ed., *Reinventing the Middle School* (New York: Routledge Farmer, 2001).
[26]MacIver and Ruby, "Middle Schools," p. 1630.
[27]For recent developments in middle-school education, see Anthony W. Jackson and Gayle A. Davis, *Turning Points 2000: Educating Adolescents in the 21st Century* (New York: Teachers College Press, 2000). For trends see Jerry W. Valentine, "United States Middle Level Grade Organization Trends" at **www.mlle.org/docs/USMI**.

■ Frequent efforts to redefine the high school

Frequent efforts to redefine the high school's purpose and curriculum have included a 1957 attempt, when U.S. cold war adversary the Soviet Union successfully orbited space satellite *Sputnik*. The Soviet success and well-publicized American space failures generated a national crisis. Attempting to explain U.S. slippage in the space race, critics alleged that American students were deficient in mathematics and science in comparison with Soviet students. Congress responded by passing the National Defense Education Act (NDEA) in 1958, which provided federal funds to improve curricula and instruction in areas considered crucial to national defense: mathematics, science, and foreign languages. The NDEA illustrates how external forces can affect high schools. Later chapters in this book discuss more recent attempts to redefine high schools' organization and curriculum in response to perceived social and economic crises.

The Development of Educational Technology

■ Early technologies

Since the mid-twentieth century, America's schools have integrated educational technology into their classrooms. Using technology is also a key part of teacher education.

Educational technology entered the schools in the 1930s with the introduction of radio and motion pictures. Although these innovations were often add-ons rather than integrated into the curriculum, they infused instruction with dynamic audio and visual elements. A major development in educational technology, the advent of television, followed World War II. In the early 1950s, educators began experimenting with educational television. In 1957, Alexander J. Stoddard initiated the National Program in the Use of Television in the Schools.

■ Educational television

The 1960s, called a time of educational revolution, saw further developments in instructional technologies such as educational television, programmed learning, and computer-assisted instruction. In 1961, the six-state Midwest Program on Airborne Television Instruction began telecasting lessons to schools. Indiana University, in 1965, established a National Center for School and College Television.[28] Educational television has had a major and continuing impact on instruction. Today, many high schools have their own television studio and channel. Closed-circuit television frequently augments teacher education, providing teachers with an instant videotaped critique of their teaching.

■ Cultural impact of television

Although television has important educational possibilities, we also must consider it in terms of its total cultural impact. Many U.S. children and adolescents spend hours each day viewing commercial television, which carries many mixed messages about sex, violence, and other social mores. Network television and CNN can bring events to viewers in a rapid-fire and dynamic way. The television image, however, lacks the reflective element of the printed page.

■ Teaching machines and programmed instruction

The educational revolution also included "teaching machines" that used programmed and computer-assisted instruction. Programmed instruction was aimed at forming concepts through carefully graduated steps that provided students with instant self-evaluation. Students could recognize their successes and mistakes as quickly as they made them and proceed at their own learning rate. Programmed instruction proved especially adaptable to subjects such as grammar, foreign languages, logic, and mathematics that could be reduced to elemental steps.

■ Computers

The 1990s produced large-scale development and implementation of computer-based educational technology. Electronic data retrieval, the Internet, and computer-

---

[28]Gerald L. Gutek, *An Historical Introduction to American Education* (Prospect Heights, Ill.: Waveland Press, 1991), pp. 206–207.

assisted instruction marked a technological revolution in education.[29] In 1996, the U.S. Department of Education released "Getting America's Students Ready for the Twenty-first Century: Meeting the Technology Literacy Challenge," a national plan for using technology effectively. States and local school districts substantially increased the number of computers in classrooms, improved Internet access, and provided increased technical support and in-service professional development activities for teachers. The national technology plan featured the following goals:

Standards & Assessment ✓

- Access to information technology for all students and teachers.
- Effective technology use by teachers to help students achieve high academic standards.
- Technology and information literacy skills for all students.
- More research and evaluation to improve the application of technology to instruction.
- Digital content and networked applications to transform teaching and learning.[30]

Computers represent both continuity and change in education. While they are extensions of such historical technological breakthroughs as writing and the printing press, they represent a new technological dynamic that has dramatically increased the storage of information in readily accessible form. As described in the chapter on Motivation, Preparation, and Conditions of the Entering Teacher, knowledge and skill in the new educational technology, especially in using computers, is considered so essential to teachers that it is required in many teacher-education programs and in teachers' professional development.

▶ The American College and University

■ Colleges of the colonial period

The colonial colleges were established under religious auspices. Believing that an educated ministry was needed to establish Christianity in the New World, the Massachusetts General Court created Harvard College in 1636. By 1754, Yale, William and Mary, Princeton, and King's College (later Columbia University) had also been established by various denominations. Other colonial colleges were the University of Pennsylvania, Dartmouth, Brown, and Rutgers. The general colonial college curriculum included (year 1) Latin, Greek, Hebrew, rhetoric, and logic; (year 2) Greek, Hebrew, logic, and natural philosophy; (year 3) natural philosophy, metaphysics, and ethics; and (year 4) mathematics and a review of Greek, Latin, logic, and natural philosophy.[31]

■ Morrill Act and land-grant colleges

During the first half of the nineteenth century, states established colleges and universities. Many religious denominations also founded their own private colleges as revivalism swept the country. By the early 1850s, critics of traditional liberal arts colleges were arguing for colleges for agriculture and mechanical science established with support from federal land grants. Such institutions, they claimed, were essential for national development. They got their wish when the Morrill Act of 1862

---

[29]For an historical perspective, see Michael E. Hobart and Zachary S. Schiffman, *Information Ages: Literacy, Numeracy, and the Computer Revolution* (Baltimore, Md.: Johns Hopkins University Press, 1998).
[30]See **www.ed.gov/Technology/clearing/index.html** (03/27/2001).
[31]Frederick Rudolph, *The American College and University: A History* (Athens: University of Georgia Press, 1990).

granted each state 30,000 acres of public land for each senator and representative in Congress. The income from this grant was to support state colleges for agricultural and mechanical instruction.[32] **Land-grant colleges** provided agricultural education, engineering, and other applied sciences as well as liberal arts and professional education. Many leading state universities originated as land-grant colleges.

■ Community colleges

Today, one of the largest and most popular higher-education institutions is the two-year community college. Many two-year institutions originated as junior colleges in the late nineteenth and early twentieth centuries when several university presidents recommended that the first two years of undergraduate education take place at another institution rather than at a four-year college. After World War II, many junior colleges were reorganized into community colleges and numerous new community colleges were established with the broader function of serving their communities' educational needs. Important constituents in statewide higher-education systems, community colleges are exceptionally responsive in providing training for technological change, especially those related to the communications and electronic data revolutions.

■ G.I. Bill

■ Rising enrollments

The greatest growth in American higher education came after World War II with the 1944 passage of the Servicemen's Readjustment Act, known as the G.I. Bill. To help readjust society to peacetime and reintegrate returning military personnel into domestic life, the G.I. Bill provided federal funds for veterans for education. Tuition, fees, books, and living expenses were subsidized, and between 1944 and 1951, 7,800,000 veterans used the bill's assistance to attend technical schools, colleges, and universities. The effect was to inaugurate a pattern of rapid growth in higher education enrollments that has continued through the present day.[33]

REFOCUS Think back to the questions at the beginning of the chapter: How does the American educational ladder differ from the European dual-track system? Do you foresee any future changes in the organization and structure of the American educational system?

▶ Education in a Culturally Diverse Society

■ A history of diversity

Historically, the United States has been, just as it is today, a racially and ethnically diverse nation. With the exception of the Native Americans, American roots trace to other continents, especially to Europe, Africa, and Asia. So far, this chapter has focused on the European heritage; this section examines other groups that have contributed to the United States.

African Americans

The Civil War, Reconstruction, and the Thirteenth Amendment ended slavery in the United States. Emancipation brought with it the challenge of providing education for the freed men and women and their children, particularly in the defeated Confederate states.

■ Freedmen's Bureau

In 1865, Congress established the Freedmen's Bureau to assist in the economic and educational transition of African Americans from bondage to freedom in the

---

[32]Benjamin E. Andrews, *The Land Grant of 1862 and the Land-Grant College* (Washington, D.C.: U.S. Government Printing Office, 1918).
[33]Gerald L. Gutek, *American Education 1945–2000: A History and Commentary* (Prospect Heights, Ill.: Waveland Press, 2000), pp. 9–14.

South. Under the leadership of General O. O. Howard, the bureau established schools throughout the South. In 1869, its schools enrolled 114,000 African American students. The schools followed a New England common-school curriculum of reading, writing, grammar, geography, arithmetic, and music, especially singing. Many of the schools functioned until 1872, when bureau operations ended.[34]

■ Stereotypes limited teaching

Although a few African American teachers were trained by the Freedmen's Bureau, most schools were staffed by northern schoolteachers, who brought with them their educational philosophies and teaching methods. These northern white teachers had stereotypic notions about the education African Americans should receive. Rather than encouraging educational self-determination, educators such as Samuel C. Armstrong, the mentor of Booker T. Washington, emphasized industrial training and social control that kept African Americans in a subordinate economic and social position.[35]

Washington: From Slavery to Freedom. Booker T. Washington (1856–1915) was the leading educational spokesperson for African Americans in the half century after the Civil War. As illustrated in his autobiography, *Up from Slavery,* Washington was a transitional figure. Born a slave, he experienced the hectic years of Reconstruction and cautiously developed a compromise with the white establishment.[36]

■ "Uplift" through work

As a student at Hampton Institute, Washington learned the educational philosophy of General Samuel Armstrong, who established the institute to prepare African American youth for teaching, agriculture, and industry. Armstrong argued that industrial education would prepare African Americans to be competent workers. Washington subscribed to Armstrong's philosophy of moral and economic "uplift" through work.

■ Washington's influence at Tuskegee

In 1881, Washington was appointed principal of the educational institute that the Alabama legislature had established for African Americans at Tuskegee. Washington shaped the Tuskegee curriculum according to his perceptions of southern African Americans as a landless agricultural class. He wanted to create an economic base—primarily in farming but also in occupational trades—that would provide jobs. Thus Tuskegee's curriculum emphasized basic academic, agricultural, and occupational skills; the values of hard work; and the dignity of labor. It encouraged students to become elementary schoolteachers, farmers, and artisans, but discouraged involvement in law and politics. Professional education and political action, Washington believed, were premature and would cause conflict with the dominant white power structure in the South.

■ Theory of social separation

Washington, a dynamic and popular platform speaker, developed the theory that blacks and whites were mutually dependent economically but could remain separate socially. In 1885, Washington summed up his philosophy in an address at the Cotton Exposition in Atlanta, Georgia, when he said, "In all things that are purely social, we can be as separate as the fingers, yet one as the hand in all things essential to mutual progress."[37]

■ Controversy about Washington

Today, Washington is a controversial figure in history. Defenders say he made the best of a bad situation and that, although he compromised on racial issues, he preserved and slowly advanced African Americans' educational opportunities. Crit-

[34]Paul A. Cimbala, *Under the Guardianship of the Nation: The Freedmen's Bureau and the Reconstruction of Georgia, 1865–1893* (Athens: University of Georgia Press, 1997).
[35]Robert Francis Engs, *Educating the Disenfranchised and Disinherited: Samuel Chapman Armstrong and Hampton Institute, 1839–1893* (Knoxville: University of Tennessee Press, 1999).
[36]Booker T. Washington, *Up from Slavery* (New York: Doubleday, 1938).
[37]Booker T. Washington, *Selected Speeches of Booker T. Washington* (New York: Doubleday, 1932).

Under the leadership of Booker T. Washington, the Tuskegee Institute emphasized agricultural and vocational training. These students were learning scientific soil analysis. *(Corbis/Bettmann)*

ics see Washington as the head of a large educational network that he used to advance his own power rather than to improve the situation of African Americans in the United States. One of Washington's critics was W. E. B. Du Bois.

Du Bois: Challenger to the System.   W. E. B. Du Bois (1868–1963) was a sociological and educational pioneer who challenged the segregated system that severely limited the educational opportunities of African Americans.[38] Questioning Booker T. Washington's leadership, Du Bois urged a determined stand against segregation and racism.

■ Du Bois as a scholar

Unlike Washington, whose roots were in southern agriculture, Du Bois's career spanned both sides of the Mason-Dixon Line. Born in Massachusetts, he attended Fisk University in Nashville, did graduate work in Germany, earned his doctorate at Harvard University, and directed the Atlanta University Studies of Black American Life. His important book, *The Philadelphia Negro: A Social Study,* examined the social, economic, and educational problems of an urban African American community.[39] An academic sociologist and historian, he was also a determined civil rights activist.

■ Du Bois as a civil rights leader

In 1909 Du Bois helped organize the National Association for the Advancement of Colored People (NAACP). His editorials in *The Crisis,* the NAACP's major publication, argued that all American children and youth, including African Americans, should have genuine equality of educational opportunity. Du Bois and the NAACP were persistent adversaries of racially segregated schools, and his dedicated efforts helped outlaw racial segregation in public schools. (We discuss desegregation's progress in the chapter on Social Class, Race, and School Achievement.)

----

[38]For the definitive biography of Du Bois, see David Levering Lewis, *W.E.B. Du Bois: Biography of a Race, 1868–1919* (New York: Henry Holt, 1973); and David Levering Lewis, *W.E.B. Du Bois: The Fight for Equality and the American Century, 1919–1963* (New York: Henry Holt, 2000).
[39]W.E.B. Du Bois, *The Philadelphia Negro: A Social Study* (Philadelphia: University of Pennsylvania Press, 1998). See also Michael B. Katz and Thomas J. Segrue, eds., *W.E.B. Du Bois, Race, and the City: The Philadelphia Negro and Its Legacy* (Philadelphia: University of Pennsylvania Press, 1998).

■ Promoting social and educational change

Unlike Booker T. Washington, who took a compromising and accommodationist path on racial relations, Du Bois worked for deliberate social change. He believed that African Americans needed well-educated leaders, especially in the professions, and he articulated the concept of the "talented tenth," according to which 10 percent of the African American population would receive a higher education. Du Bois was adamant that a person's occupation should be determined by ability and choice, not by racial stereotyping. A prophetic leader, Du Bois set the stage for significant changes in American race relations since the mid-1950s.

Native Americans

■ Traditional tribal education

Education among pre-Columbian Native Americans was largely informal. Children learned skills, social roles, and cultural patterns from their group's oral tradition and direct experience with tribal life.

Marked by suspicion and violence, encounters among Native Americans and European colonists affected both cultures. As colonists attempted to re-create European culture in North America and Native Americans sought to preserve their culture, both changed.[40]

■ Missionary educational efforts

European colonists' efforts to "civilize" North American indigenous peoples rested on the Europeans' sense of their own cultural superiority. In the Mississippi Valley, French missionaries sought to convert the Native Americans to Catholicism as well as educate French colonists' children, in schools that introduced the French language and culture.

In the Spanish-controlled Southwest, Jesuit and Franciscan priests sought to alleviate exploitation of Native Americans by Spanish landlords by establishing missions to protect, control, and convert the tribes to Catholicism. Mission schools taught religion, reading, and writing.[41] The Moravians, religious followers of John Amos Comenius, in North America taught the Native American tribes and translated the Bible and religious tracts into Indian languages.

■ Cherokee alphabet

Among the early Native American educators was Sequoyah, a Cherokee, who devised an alphabet in his native language. His alphabet, completed in 1832, made the Cherokees the first Native American tribe to have a written language.

■ Assimilationist education

In the nineteenth century, the U.S. government forcibly relocated the majority of Native Americans to reservations west of the Mississippi River in remote areas of the Great Plains and Southwest. After 1870, the federal Bureau of Indian Affairs (BIA), encouraged by well-intentioned but misguided reformers, again attempted to "civilize" Native Americans by assimilating them into white society. These "reformers" sought to eradicate tribal cultures and instill "white" values through industrial training.[42]

■ Boarding schools

From 1890 to the 1930s, the BIA used **boarding schools** to implement the assimilationist educational policy. Boarding schools emphasized a basic curriculum of reading, writing, arithmetic, and vocational training. Native American youngsters were ruled by military discipline in these schools. They often were forbidden to speak their own native languages and forced to use English.[43]

---

[40]Colin G. Calloway, *New Worlds for All: Indians, Europeans, and the Remaking of Early America* (Baltimore: Johns Hopkins University Press, 1997), p. 42.

[41]For a discussion of mission culture, see Christopher Vecsey, *On the Padres' Trail* (Notre Dame, Ind.: University of Notre Dame Press, 1996).

[42]David W. Adams, "Fundamental Considerations: The Deep Meaning of Native American Schooling, 1880–1900," *Harvard Education Review* (February 1988), pp. 1–28. Also see Ruth Spack, *America's Second Tongue: American Indian Education and the Ownership of English, 1860–1900* (Lincoln: University of Nebraska Press, 2002), p. 75.

[43]David W. Adams, *Education for Extinction: American Indians and the Boarding School Experience, 1875–1928* (Lawrence: University Press of Kansas, 1995); and Brenda J. Child, *Boarding School Seasons: American Indian Families, 1900–1940* (Lincoln: University of Nebraska Press, 1998).

■ Students' reactions

Native American youngsters either resisted, passively accepted, or accommodated to the boarding schools' regimen. Active resisters repeatedly ran away from the boarding schools. Accommodationists tried to gain skill in using English without losing their tribal identities.[44] Parents often encouraged them to accept the boarding schools' program as a way to learn a trade in order to earn a living.[45] Many students suffered a loss of cultural identity, feeling trapped in a never-never land between two different cultures.

■ Contemporary schooling

After the boarding-school concept was discontinued in the 1930s, Native American education experienced significant change. Many Native Americans left reservations to live in urban centers, particularly inner cities. Children living on reservations attended a variety of schools: BIA schools, tribal schools, and public and private institutions. Those living in cities usually attended public schools.

In the 1970s, the assimilationist policy of the U.S. government yielded to one encouraging self-determination. The new direction officially began with the Indian Self-Determination and Education Assistance Act of 1975, which has continued to the present. Enactment of this legislation officially ended the federal government's assimilationist policy. The act encouraged and promoted Native Americans' right "to control their own education activities."[46]

■ Alienation from the system

Although assimilation is no longer an official government policy, Native Americans still suffer from a discrimination that alienates many youngsters from the educational system. Compared to the national population, a greater percentage of Native Americans is under twenty years of age, but their participation in schooling is far lower than the national average. An extremely high dropout rate leaves Native American high-school completion far below that of the U.S. population at large.

Latino Americans

■ Latino peoples and cultures

Latino Americans comprise the fastest-growing ethnic group in the United States. *Latino* is a collective term used to identify Spanish-speaking people whose ethnic origins can be traced to Mexico, Puerto Rico, Cuba, or other Latin American countries. Although Latino Americans may speak Spanish as a common language and share many Spanish traditions, each national group has its own distinctive culture.[47]

■ Assimilation in the Southwest

Mexican Americans are the largest Latino group in the United States.[48] The Treaty of Guadeloupe Hidalgo in 1848, which ended the Mexican War, forced Mexico to cede to the United States the vast territories that now comprise Arizona, California, Colorado, Nevada, New Mexico, and Utah. This territory, along with Texas, was home to a large Mexican population.[49] In these states, public schools followed

---

[44]Spack, *America's Second Tongue: American Indian Education and the Ownership of English,* p. 131.

[45]David W. Adams, "From Bullets to Boarding Schools: The Educational Assault on Native American Identity, 1878–1928," in Philip Weeks, ed., *The American Indian Experience* (Arlington Heights, Ill.: Forum Press, 1988), pp. 218–239.

[46]George Pierre Castile, *To Show Heart: Native American Self-Determination and Federal Indian Policy, 1960–1975* (Tucson: University of Arizona Press, 1998).

[47]For a discussion of terminology and textbooks, see Joseph A. Rodriguez and Vicki L. Ruiz, "At Loose Ends: Twentieth-Century Latinos in Current United States History Textbooks," *Journal of American History* 86 (March 2000), pp. 1689–1699.

[48]Victoria-Marie MacDonald, "Hispanic, Latino, Chicano, or 'Other'? Deconstructing the Relationship between Historians and Hispanic-American Educational History," *History of Education Quarterly* 41 (Fall 2001), pp. 368–369.

[49]Histories of Mexican Americans are Manuel G. Gonzales, *Mexicanos: A History of Mexicans in the United States* (Bloomington: Indiana University Press, 1999); and Richard Griswold del Castillo and Arnoldo De Leon, *North to Axtlan: A History of Mexican Americans in the United States* (New York: Twayne, 1996).

the "**Americanization**" assimilationist policy then used throughout the United States. Mexican American children were taught in English, rather than their vernacular Spanish, and their Latino cultural heritage was ignored. Consequently, schooling imposed a negative self-image, often portraying Mexican Americans as the conquered people of an inferior culture. Today, bilingual and multicultural education, replacing Americanization, contributes to developing a Mexican American historical consciousness.[50] (For more on bilingual and multicultural education, see the chapter on Providing Equal Educational Opportunity.)

■ Few educational opportunities

In later years, the Mexican American population increased as migrant workers crossed the U.S.-Mexican border to work in the United States. Since Mexicans provided cheap labor as ranch workers, railroad crews, and especially farm workers, employers encouraged their entry. Wages were low, housing frequently squalid, and working conditions harsh. Children of the migrant workers, even if not working in the fields with their parents, had few or no educational opportunities. Although many migrant workers returned to Mexico, others remained in the United States, either legally or illegally. Since World War II the Mexican American population has expanded from the Southwest to other states, often to the large Northeastern and Midwestern cities. Today, approximately 90 percent of Mexican Americans live in urban areas.[51]

■ Chicano movement

In the late 1960s, the *Chicano movimiento*, similar to the African American civil rights movement, pursued two goals: (1) uniting Mexican Americans to work for improved social, economic, and educational conditions; (2) preserving the Mexican American cultural heritage as a source of group identity.[52] Cesar Chavez organized the United Farm Workers to secure improved working conditions and higher wages for agricultural workers. The League of United Latin American Citizens (LULAC), organized in 1929 to promote Latino civil rights, attracted middle-class professionals. The Chicano movement encouraged Mexican American political activity, economic development, and educational participation. Despite increased Mexican American attendance in elementary and secondary education, higher-education enrollments fall below the national average.

■ Americanization of Puerto Ricans

The history of Puerto Rican Americans, another large Latino group, begins with the Spanish-American War of 1898, when defeated Spain ceded the island of Puerto Rico to the United States. Citizens of Puerto Rico, a U.S. possession, became U.S. citizens in 1917 and Puerto Rico attained Commonwealth status in 1952.[53]

Believing that Puerto Rico needed American-style social and economic development, U.S. officials overhauled the old Spanish school system.[54] They made school attendance compulsory, established American-style public schools, and employed English-speaking teachers trained by Americans in U.S. teaching methods. Although some classes continued to be taught in Spanish, English was made compulsory to

---

[50]Lisbeth Haas, *Conquests and Historical Identities in California, 1769–1930* (Berkeley and Los Angeles: University of California Press, 1995), p. 151.

[51]For the Mexican American urban experience, see George J. Sanchez, *Becoming Mexican American: Ethnicity, Culture, and Identity for Chicano Los Angeles, 1900–1945* (New York: Oxford University Press, 1993). Mexican American social and political consciousness is treated in David G. Gutierrez, *Walls and Mirrors: Mexican Americans, Mexican Immigrants, and the Politics of Ethnicity* (Berkeley and Los Angeles: University of California Press, 1995).

[52]F. Arturo Rosales, *Chicano!: The History of the Mexican American Civil Rights Movement* (Houston: University of Houston Arte Público Press, 1996).

[53]For the history of Puerto Rico as a U.S. possession, see Jose Trias Monge, *Puerto Rico: The Trials of the Oldest Colony in the World* (New Haven: Yale University Press, 1997).

[54]Gervasio Luis Garcia, "I Am the Other: Puerto Rico in the Eyes of North Americans, 1898," *Journal of American History* 38 (June 2000), p. 41.

promote Americanization. Students developed a kind of dual cultural identity—their island's Hispanic culture and the English-speaking American culture.

■ Dropout rates

Puerto Rican immigration to the U.S. mainland has been continuous since the early twentieth century. Today, more than two million Puerto Rican Americans live in the large urban centers such as New York, Chicago, and Philadelphia. Historically, their high-school dropout rates have been high and college attendance rates low. In recent years, however, Puerto Rican Americans have become more politically active, especially in New York and Chicago, and have improved their economic and educational position.

■ Varied educational backgrounds

The Cuban American experience in the United States represents a different pattern from that of other Latino groups in that its origins were those of a community in political exile from its native land. Several waves of immigration from Cuba combined to form the U.S. Cuban American community. The first exiles, 1959 to 1973, fled Fidel Castro's repressive Communist regime. Many were upper- and middle-class Cubans who brought with them the political, economic, and educational background and organizations needed to create a distinctive Cuban American cultural community. The Mariel immigrants of the 1980s came from Cuba's disadvantaged underclass. The Cuban American community, mirroring some aspects of the Cuba they left, has created a unique but adaptive culture.[55]

At the beginning of the twenty-first century, Latino Americans play a larger role in American social, political, and economic life and sustain growing and influential Latino professional and business middle classes. The concept of "permeable cultures" is useful in interpreting Latino American cultures. In an exchange of cultural elements immigrants and their children choose, borrow, retain, reject, and create their own cultural patterns.[56]

■ Bilingual education

Public schools have now abandoned the old assimilationist and Americanization policies. The 1968 Bilingual Education Act was a watershed for Latino Americans. That act, along with the 1974 Supreme Court decision in *Lau v. Nichols,* led to the establishment of bilingual education programs (see the chapter on Providing Equal Educational Opportunity). Recently, however, bilingual education has become politically controversial, including proposals to make English the official language. Led by California in 1998, several states have voted to end bilingual education programs. The In This Case box presents differing viewpoints on bilingual education that exist in the United States today.

Asian Americans

Whereas European immigrants entered the United States by way of the East Coast, principally New York City, Asian Americans generally came by way of the West Coast, especially Los Angeles and San Francisco. For these geographical reasons, the Asian American population concentrated historically in the western states bordering the Pacific Ocean. From there, Asian Americans moved eastward. The first Asian people to settle in the United States were Chinese and Japanese. More recent Asian immigrants include Filipinos, Indians, Thais, Koreans, Vietnamese, Laotians, and Cambodians.

■ Early Chinese immigrants

Chinese immigration began in California during the gold rush of 1848–49 and reached its peak between 1848 and 1882, when 228,945 Chinese were admitted to

---

[55]Maria Cristina Garcia, *Havana USA: Cuban Exiles and Cuban Americans in South Florida, 1959–1994* (Berkeley and Los Angeles: University of California Press, 1996), pp. 111–118.
[56]Rodriguez and Ruiz, "At Loose Ends: Twentieth-Century Latinos in Current United States History Textbooks," p. 1696.

IN THIS CASE

Differing Viewpoints

I have a real problem with those who wish to do away with the bilingual program," said Maria Manuel. "I could never have coped with school if I couldn't have used Spanish. I moved here in the fourth grade, when I was nine years old. I was the only child In my family. My mom and dad did not speak English. My friends spoke Spanish most of the time. At least I could learn English slowly, carefully, and correctly. If I'd had to sink or swim, I wouldn't be in the teacher education program now."

Another teacher education student, Nichole Knesek, responded, "When my parents immigrated to the United States from Czechoslovakia, there was no bilingual education. They had to learn to speak English or suffer the consequences. They tell me that they are glad they had to learn English quickly. Both of them have fine business careers now. Both want to end the bilingual program. After all, English is the language of this nation. All citizens and even residents should be able to speak Standard English."

A third student said he favored a middle approach. "Why not allow bilingual education but limit the ages we serve and their time in the program. I think we should allow bilingual education, but only through grade 2 or 3. Then students would know that they have to get serious and learn English if they want an education and to get ahead."

"What if a student comes into the country when she or he is in eighth grade?"

"Then I think that they are old enough to sink or swim. Just look at the Vietnamese. They came at all ages, and they have succeeded well."

A fourth student spoke up: "I think that recent initiatives to kill the bilingual program are money driven. Many states and school districts are in financial difficulty. Money seems to be the bottom line—not the educational results and not educational philosophies."

The professor intervened at this point to ask, "Do you know how bilingual education came to be? Do you know how it operates in most of the schools here? Do you know what research studies have found about student success in bilingual education programs or in English immersion programs? We can have an endless, although enlightening, discussion by sharing our own personal viewpoints, but I think each of you needs to develop a well-researched knowledge base about bilingual education. As teachers you must be able to articulate your position in a reasoned way. At this point, I am not sure that we can say positively which method is best for those whose primary language is other than English."

Questions

1. What would you need to know to better evaluate the viewpoints expressed by Maria and Nichole?

2. How may bilingual education be linked to the issue of multiculturalism?

3. What is your position on bilingual education? What facts support your stance?

4. What evidence can you find, if any, of correlation between funding problems and reducing bilingual programs?

the United States. Early Chinese immigrants worked as miners, farm workers, and railroad construction workers. Enterprising Chinese merchants operated small businesses, grocery stores, and laundries in West Coast cities. In San Francisco and Los Angeles, Chinese enclaves developed with social, religious, cultural, and educational societies.[57]

■ Japanese immigrants

■ Limited educational opportunity

Japanese immigration began later than Chinese immigration, between 1885 and 1924. Japanese immigrants came primarily from the agricultural area of south-

---

[57]Shifh-Shan Henry Tsai, *The Chinese Experience in America* (Bloomington: Indiana University Press, 1986), pp. 1–20.

western Japan where labor contractors recruited workers for Hawaiian sugar and pineapple plantations and Californian farms. Japanese immigration increased until 1910, when immigrant numbers declined because of economic and political issues between Japan and the United States.[58]

Between 1882 and 1924, the U.S. Congress enacted laws to prohibit further Chinese and Japanese immigration and to prevent Chinese and Japanese from becoming U.S. citizens. The Chinese Exclusion Act in 1882 made Chinese the first group to be officially excluded from immigrating to the United States.[59] Immigrants who arrived before these laws took effect often found educational and economic opportunities limited by racial discrimination. In 1906, for example, the San Francisco Board of Education began segregating students of Asian ethnicity from other pupils. Diplomatic protests from the Japanese government persuaded the board to rescind its segregationist policy.[60] Before World War II, few Chinese or Japanese Americans attained sufficient levels of education to enter the professions.

World War II brought racial prejudice against Japanese Americans to the surface.[61] Responding to fears that Japanese in the United States would aid the enemy, the U.S. government interned in relocation camps 110,000 people of Japanese heritage, many of whom were American citizens. The camps, sited in remote areas, lacked basic services and amenities. Although camp schools were eventually established for the young people, the internment experience produced both physical hardship and psychological alienation. The government based this repressive action on unfounded fears; not a single act of sabotage was committed by a Japanese American. Not until the 1980s did the federal government admit its wartime violation of civil liberties and compensate those interned. The Civil Liberties Act of 1988 provided a presidential letter of apology and monetary reparations for more than 82,000 persons of Japanese ancestry who had been interned without due process of law during World War II.[62]

A substantial number of Filipinos had migrated to the mainland by the start of World War II. Many Filipino men served in the U.S. Navy and later settled with their families on the West Coast. Others, especially in the 1930s, came to the mainland as farm workers.

After World War II the economic and educational status of Chinese, Japanese, and Filipino Americans improved substantially. The McCarran-Walter Act of 1952, while retaining limited quotas, repealed the ban on Asian immigration and citizenship. Asian immigration then increased dramatically and included many professionals with advanced education. Their arrival sparked a general rise in higher education among Asian Americans. The change has been particularly notable for Japanese Americans, whose participation in postsecondary education is higher than the European American majority or any other minority group. Nearly 90 percent of third-generation Japanese Americans attend colleges or universities.

---

[58]David J. O'Brien and Stephen S. Fugita, *The Japanese American Experience* (Bloomington: Indiana University Press, 1991), pp. 4–17.

[59]Andrew Gyory, *Closing the Gate: Race, Politics, and the Chinese Exclusion Act* (Chapel Hill: University of North Carolina Press, 1998). Later Chinese immigration is examined in Xiaojian Zhao, *Remaking Chinese American Immigration, Family, and Community* (New Brunswick, N.J.: Rutgers University Press, 2002).

[60]O'Brien and Fugita, *The Japanese American Experience*, p. 17.

[61]Lon Kurashige, "The Problem of Biculturalism: Japanese American Identity and Festival Before World War II," *Journal of American History* 86 (March 2000), pp. 1632–1654; and Charlotte Brooks, "In the Twilight Zone Between Black and White: Japanese American Resettlement and Community in Chicago, 1942–1945," *Journal of American History* 86 (March 2000), pp. 1655–1687.

[62]Mitchell T. Maki, Harry H. L. Kitano, and S. Megan Berthold, *Achieving the Impossible Dream: How Japanese Americans Obtained Redress* (Urbana: University of Illinois Press, 1999).

■ New Asian immigrants

After the 1960s, immigration increased among other Asian groups, especially Koreans and Indians. Following the collapse of American-supported governments in Southeast Asia in the 1970s, Vietnamese, Cambodians, Laotians, and Hmongs have arrived with differing educational backgrounds. For example, among the South Vietnamese are former military officers, government officials, businessmen, and professionals. The Hmongs, by contrast, come from a rural culture that lacks a written language.

Arab Americans

The designation "Arab," is a cultural and linguistic rather than a racial term and refers to those who speak Arabic as their first language. The majority of Arabs are Muslims, followers of Islam, but millions are Christian Arabs. An Arab American is an American of Arabic descent. The majority of Arab Americans are the descendants of immigrants from Lebanon, Syria, Palestine, Iraq, Jordan, and Egypt.

The early Arab immigrants came to the United States from the Turkish Ottoman empire in the late nineteenth century, especially between 1875 and 1915. Many of these early immigrants were from Lebanon and Syria and were Orthodox or Catholic Christians. They tended to settle largely in ethnic neighborhoods in the northeastern states. Many became small business owners, merchants, and restaurateurs. Like other immigrant groups, they established fraternal organizations and recreational societies such as the Syrian Brotherhood Orthodox Society, often under sponsorship of a church or mosque. One of the earliest Arabic newspapers, *Kawkab America, The Star of America,* was founded in 1892.[63]

A second wave of Arab immigration, especially from Palestine and Jordan, began after World War II and still continues.[64] More recent immigrants are predominately Islamic and generally have more formal education than the earlier immigrants.[65]

Arab Americans have much in common with other immigrant groups. Many older Arab Americans became assimilated by attending public schools, through membership in community and political organizations, and through work. While assimilating into the larger American society, they maintained their Arabic culture through language, customs, religion, music, literature, and storytelling.[66] Many immigrants were bilingual and often established Arabic language, culture, and religion classes, in churches or mosques.

The proportion of Arab Americans who attend college is higher than the national average, with many earning advanced degrees. Many Arab Americans are self-employed in family-owned businesses. About 60 percent of Arab Americans in the work force are executives, professionals, and office and sales staff.

After the terrorist attacks on September 11, 2001, concerns arose that Arab Americans might be victims of stereotyping and discrimination. Isolated instances of discriminatory acts have occurred, but the Arab American community took a proactive stance to educate the general population about their history and culture. Educators, too, have worked to include the Arab American community into the context of multicultural education.[67]

---

[63]Elizabeth Boosahda, *Arab-American Faces and Voices: The Origins of an Immigrant Community* (Austin: University of Texas Press, 2003), pp. 84–86.
[64]For the Palestinian experience and the forming of Arab American identity, see Edward Said, *Out of Place* (New York: Knopf, 1999).
[65]**http:www. freekp.com/jobspage/arabs/arab4.html** (12/23/03).
[66]Boosahda, *Arab-American Faces and Voices,* p. 9.
[67]For example, see Patty Adeed and G. Pritchy Smith, "Arab Americans: Concepts and Materials," in James Banks, ed., *Teaching Strategies for Ethnic Studies* (Boston: Allyn and Bacon, 1997).

REFOCUS Think back to the questions at the beginning of the chapter: How did the United States become a culturally diverse society? Reflect on the roles of African, Latino, Arab, and Asian Americans in American culture and their contributions.

▶ Recent Historical Trends

Though it is difficult to assess which trends in contemporary education will be lasting and historically significant, this section identifies some that seem important: movements toward gender equity, equal educational opportunities for students with disabilities, increased professionalism of education, reduction of violence in the schools, and school responses to national crises.

Gender Equity

■ Title IX

Title IX of the 1972 Education Amendments to the Civil Rights Act and the Women's Educational Equity Act of 1974 (WEEA) prohibited discrimination against women in federally aided education programs. Trends emerging from this legislation included increased participation of women in mathematics, science, athletics, and technology programs and careers. Despite these improvements in women's education opportunities, many educators believe more reforms are still needed.[68]

Educating Students with Disabilities

■ Education for All Handicapped Children Act

In 1975, Congress passed the Education for All Handicapped Children Act (PL 94-142), which improved opportunities for a group of children who had previously lacked full access to a quality education. The law established a national mandate that children with disabilities would receive an "appropriate public education." (We provide a full discussion of educating children with disabilities in the chapter on Providing Equal Educational Opportunity.)

The U.S. Department of Education

■ U.S. Department of Education

In 1979, Congress enacted legislation, promoted by President Carter, to establish a U.S. Department of Education whose secretary would be a member of the president's cabinet. Prior to this, the Office of Education was part of other federal agencies, such as the Department of Interior or Department of Health, Education, and Welfare. The department has promoted federal initiatives such as more educational technology in schools and using standardized tests to assess academic achievement as provided by the No Child Left Behind Act. (See the chapters on The Teaching Profession and Governing and Administering Public Education for more on educational governance.)

Reducing School Violence

A series of gun-related assaults on students by their classmates during the 1990s called attention to increasing violence in the schools. National attention focused dramatically on this issue in April 1999, when two students, armed with guns and

[68]Stan Crock and Michele Galen, "A Thunderous Impact on Equal Opportunity," *Business Week* (June 26, 1995), p. 37; and Daniel E. Tungate and Daniel P. Orie, "Title IX Lawsuits," *Phi Delta Kappan* (April 1998), pp. 603–604.

bombs, killed twelve classmates and a teacher at Columbine High School in Little-ton, Colorado. Columbine was not an isolated incident; similar situations have oc-curred in other school districts and states. As discussed in the Legal Aspects of Education chapter, many school districts have since inaugurated "zero tolerance" programs that prohibit students from bringing any kind of weapon on school prop-erty. Many violence-prevention programs were also established, and teachers have received in-service training on appropriate actions to ensure student safety.

War on Terrorism

On September 11, 2001, terrorists hijacked and deliberately crashed commercial air planes into the World Trade Center in New York and the Pentagon in Washington, D.C. The attack and resulting loss of life of 3,100 persons changed how Americans view the world and life in their own country. Although global terrorism poses chal-lenges dramatically different from earlier threats, a certain continuity with the past provides historical perspectives on these events.[69]

Schools Have Responded to Crises in the Past. Although the events of Septem-ber 11, 2001, and the subsequent war against terrorism have the unique feature of being waged in part on American soil, looking at past school responses to crises can help us determine how we should respond to current events. During World War I, schoolchildren raised funds for liberty loans and planted liberty gardens to raise vegetables. During World War II, schools and teachers conducted scrap metal drives, purchased war saving stamps and bonds, and planted victory gardens. These actions were a direct response to wartime, but the more important lesson taught and learned in schools was that sacrifice is necessary to protect the American way of life and American democracy.

Schools Can Promote Democratic Values and Multicultural Understanding in a Time of Crisis. Almost immediately after U.S. entry into World War I, the teach-ing of German virtually disappeared from high schools throughout the country. A strong reaction against Germany deprived many students of studying an important language and culture. As noted earlier in the chapter, World War II–era fears of spy-ing and sabotage led to the forced relocation of thousands of Japanese Americans into resettlement camps. To prevent repeating these past mistakes of racial and eth-nic stereotyping, schools, teachers, and students can avoid discriminating against Arabs and Muslims and respect democratic and multicultural values.

REFOCUS Think back to the questions at the beginning of the chapter: What are recent trends in the history of American education? Identify what trends you be-lieve will have the greatest impact on your own teaching career. Is it possible for schools to cultivate both a common and a culturally pluralistic culture?

---

[69]For a discussion of the terrorist attacks on America, see Allan C. Ornstein, *Teaching and Schooling in America: Pre– and Post–September 11* (Boston: Allyn & Bacon, 2003).

▶ Summing Up

1 When the English colonists settled in North America, they imported conventional European educational institutions based on a social-class pattern. Primary or vernacular schools for the lower socioeconomic strata of society provided a basic curriculum of reading, writing, arithmetic, and religion. Preparatory schools, such as the Latin grammar school and the colonial college, were reserved for upper-class boys and men, offering a classical curriculum to prepare them for leadership roles in church, state, and society.

2 After the United States won its independence, the common- or public-school movement led to the establishment of elementary schools throughout the country.

3 The emergence of the public high school in the nineteenth century contributed to the growing inclusiveness of public schooling in the United States. The rise of state colleges and universities and passage of the Morrill Act in 1862 created the final step of an educational ladder that replaced the vestiges of the exclusive European dual-track system. By the beginning of the twentieth century, the American public school system embraced elementary, secondary, and higher institutions.

4 At mid-twentieth century, the infusion of educational technology began to transform teaching and learning.

5 By the mid-twentieth century, concerted efforts were being made to provide equal educational opportunities to the children of minority groups, especially African Americans, Native Americans, and Latinos. Recent trends in American education have included more groups in the mainstream of American schooling and have emphasized greater academic achievement.

6 The Americanization ideology of the late nineteenth and early twentieth centuries stressed assimilation into a homogeneous cultural pattern. This idea was replaced by a pluralistic philosophy that values the multicultural contributions of all Americans.

▶ Key Terms

dual-track system (160)
Latin grammar school (160)
town school (161)
hornbook (161)
land grant (165)
academy (166)
monitorial method (168)
common school (169)
educational ladder (169)
normal school (170)

high school (174)
Committee of Ten (175)
Commission on the Reorganization of
   Secondary Education (176)
junior high school (176)
middle school (176)
land-grant colleges (179)
boarding schools (182)
"Americanization" (184)

▶ Discussion Questions

1 In what ways has American education become more inclusive over time? What do you believe you can do, as a teacher, to foster inclusiveness?

2 Is Jefferson's concept of civic education adequate for the needs of contemporary American society? What place does citizenship education have in your philosophy of education?

3 In terms of the history of American secondary education, why is the purpose of the high school often so controversial? What do you believe should be the purpose of secondary education?

4 Describe your opinion on "Americanization" and cultural pluralism. What is the basis for your opinion? How does it relate to your professional development as a teacher and your personal philosophy of education?

5 How is the history of American education, especially the treatment of minority groups, instructive for educational policies related to the war on terrorism?

▶ Projects for Professional Development

1 For sources on African American education, visit "African American Odyssey" at the Library of Congress's American Memories Collection, at **memory.loc.gov/ammem/aaohtml/aohome.html**. Review the sources in the collection and identify those that supplement this chapter's section on African Americans.

2 Booker T. Washington is a controversial historical figure. Visit the Web site of the Booker T. Washington National Monument at **www.nps.gov/bowa/home.htm**. How is Washington depicted? Do you agree or disagree with the presentation of Washington as a leader?

3 Invite representatives of African American, Latino, Asian American, and Arab American organizations to speak to your class about the educational issues facing the groups.

4 What is your opinion of the U.S. attempt to use schooling to assimilate Native American children? Visit "Native American Education: Documents from the Nineteenth Century," at **www.duke,edu/~exsl1/education/index.html**. Based on your research, revise or restate your opinion. What evidence have you used to form your opinion?

5 Reflect on the major historical developments treated in this chapter. Then develop a class project using oral interviews with experienced K–12 school administrators and classroom teachers that focus on major changes in their professional work. You might ask, "What was school like when you began your work as an administrator or teacher? What changes have occurred? How have you adapted to or worked to create change?"

6 Organize a group research project in which students examine representative books and materials used to teach elementary-level reading. Identify key periods such as the 1840s, 1850s, 1860s, and so on. You might begin with the McGuffey readers. Using historical research and interpretation, determine how stories, characters, and values in the books have changed over time.

7 Organize a panel discussion in which each presenter analyzes an author's educational experiences based on his or her autobiography. Autobiographies might include themes such as a Native American's experience at a boarding school, an African American's experience in segregated schools, a woman's experience in entering a male-dominated profession, or a Christian fundamentalist's rejection of cultural relativism.

▶ Suggested Resources

 Internet Resources

For a summary of government efforts to improve elementary and secondary education, consult "Government's 50 Greatest Endeavors" at **www.brookings.edu/gs/cps/50ge/endeavors/elementarysecondary.htm**.

For current as well as historical sources, especially statistical, consult the "U.S. Department of Education" at **www.ed.gov/**.

For a brief biography, a chronology, and material on Jefferson's home, consult "Monticello Resources" at **www.monticello.org/resources.html**.

An important source for Jefferson's writings is the Thomas Jefferson Digital Archive at the University of Virginia: **etext.lib.virginia.edu/jefferson/**.

For information about women's rights and education, consult the "National Women's History Project" at **www.nwhp.org/index.html**.

For "Lessons of a Century: Education Week's Review of One Hundred Years of American Education," visit **www.edweek.org/sreports/century.htm**.

For a biography and other information about W. E. B. Du Bois, visit the "W. E. B. Du Bois Virtual University" at **www.members.tripod.com/~Du Bois/index.htm**.

For historical representations and images of Native Americans, visit **bancroft.berkeley.edu/Exhibits/nativeamericans/index.html**.

For the disenfranchisement and segregation of African Americans from the Reconstruction period through the modern civil rights movement, visit "The History of Jim Crow" at **www.jimcrowhistory.org/home.htm**.

Publications

Adams, David W. *Education for Extinction: American Indians and the Boarding School Experience, 1875–1928*. Lawrence: University Press of Kansas, 1995. *Adams analyzes the policies, curriculum, and environments of federal Indian boarding schools. The title refers to efforts to assimilate Native American children into white culture by eradicating their tribal cultures.*

Beatty, Barbara A. *Preschool Education in America: The Culture of Young Children from the Colonial Era to the Present*. New Haven: Yale University Press, 1995. *Beatty provides a useful history of such early childhood institutions as infant schools, kindergartens, and nursery schools in the United States.*

Child, Brenda J. *Boarding School Seasons: American Indian Families, 1900-1940*. Lincoln: University of Nebraska Press, 1998. *Uses letters written by students in Indian boarding schools to reconstruct their educational experiences.*

Cutcliffe, Stephen H., and Terry S. Reynolds, eds. *Technology and American History: A Historical Anthology from Technology and Culture*. Chicago: University of Chicago Press, 1997. *A useful collection of articles on the cultural impact of technology on American society.*

Fontenot, Chester J., Jr., and Mary Alice, Morgan, eds. *W.E.B Du Bois and Race: Essays Celebrating the Centennial Publication of* The Souls of Black Folk. Macon, Ga.: Mercer University Press, 2001. *Provides essays commenting on the significance of Du Bois's* Souls of Black Folks *to African American and to general American history and education.*

Gonzales, Manuel G. *Mexicanos: A History of Mexicans in the United States*. Bloomington: Indiana University Press, 1999. *Gonzales provides a well-researched and useful general history of the Mexican American experience in the United States.*

Gutek, Gerald L. *American Education 1945–2000*. Prospect Heights, Ill.: Waveland Press, 2000. *Gutek provides a historical commentary on major educational events, movements, and trends since the end of World War II.*

Herbst, Jurgen. *The Once and Future School: Three Hundred and Fifty Years of American Secondary Education*. New York: Routledge, 1996. *Herbst examines the history of secondary education in the United States, with a special emphasis on the high school's one-time role as a "people's college."*

Hobart, Michael E., and Zachary S. Schiffman. *Information Ages: Literacy, Numeracy, and the Computer Revolution*. Baltimore: Johns Hopkins University Press, 1998. *A historical analysis that puts the new technology into historical perspective.*

Lewis, David Levering. *W. E. B. Du Bois: The Fight for Equality and the American Century 1919–1963*. New York: Holt, 2000. *In this second volume of his biographical study of Du Bois, Lewis examines the contributions of the great African American scholar and activist.*

MacDonald, Victoria-Maria. "Hispanic, Latino, Chicano, or 'Other': Deconstructing the Relationship between Historians and Hispanic-American Educational History." *History of Education Quarterly* 41 (Fall 2001), pp. 365–413. *MacDonald provides an excellent and detailed historiographic essay on Latino educational history from the colonial period to the present. It is highly recommended for students interested in and researching the education of Latinos.*

Marsden, William F. *The School Textbook: Geography, History and Social Studies.* Portland, Ore.: Woburn Press, 2001. *Provides a comparative analysis of American and British textbooks in history and geography from the late eighteenth century to the contemporary standards movement.*

Mowery, David C., and Nathan Rosenberg. *Paths of Innovation: Technological Change in 20th-Century America.* New York: Cambridge University Press, 1998. *Provides perspective on the impact of technology in generating change in the United States.*

Ornstein, Allan C. *Teaching and Schooling in America: Pre- and Post-September 11.* Boston: Allyn & Bacon, 2003. *A consideration and interpretation of educational foundations and issues from the perspective of the new reality caused by the terrorist attacks on New York City and Washington, D.C., on September 11, 2001.*

Patterson, James T. *Brown v. Board of Education: A Civil Rights Milestone and Its Troubled Legacy.* New York: Oxford University Press, 2001. *Patterson examines the highly significant case that ended legally sanctioned racial segregation in the United States.*

Ravitch, Diane. *Left Back: A Century of Failed School Reforms.* New York: Simon and Schuster, 2000. *Ravitch, a distinguished historian, examines the history of educational reform in the twentieth century and why reforms often failed.*

Reese, William J. *The Origins of the American High School.* New Haven: Yale University Press, 1995. *Reese uses examples to contextualize the history of the American high school in terms of significant cultural, economic, and political developments.*

Reinier, Jacqueline S. *From Virtue to Character: American Childhood, 1775–1850.* New York: Twayne of Macmillan, 1996. *The author analyzes adult beliefs and children's experience in the perspective of American history. The book is useful in developing insights into American conceptions of childhood.*

Staff of *Education Week. Lessons of a Century: A Nation's Schools Come of Age.* Bethesda, Md.: Editorial Projects in Education, 2000. *Written by the staff of* Education Week, *this highly attractive book provides a historical perspective on the persons, institutions, forces, and issues that shaped American education in the twentieth century.*

Spack, Ruth. *America's Second Tongue: American Indian Education and the Ownership of English, 1860–1900.* Lincoln: University of Nebraska Press, 2002. *Examines English language instruction in terms of federal policy and Indian schools.*

Vinovskis, Maris A. *Education, Society, and Economic Opportunity: A Historical Perspective on Persistent Issues.* New Haven: Yale University Press, 1995. *Vinovskis, a respected historian of education, examines such issues as the changing role of families, early childhood education, and secondary education in their relationship to socioeconomic participation and mobility.*

Zimmerman, Barry J., and Schunk, Dale J. *Educational Psychology: A Century of Contributions.* Mahwah, N.J.: Erlbaum, 2003. *Provides essays on the biographies and theories of leading educational psychologists of the twentieth century.*

PART THREE

Political, Economic, and Legal Foundations

CHAPTER 7

Governing and Administering Public Education

E
ducation in the United States is organized on four governmental levels—local, intermediate (in some states), state, and federal. Understanding the formal organization of schools and how they are governed can help you to make wise choices and realistic decisions about schools and to take appropriate political action. In this chapter, we examine the various governmental levels and how they affect education.

The United States does not have a national education system like those in Great Britain, France, or Japan. We have fifty different state educational systems and many differences among local school systems even within the same state.

The U.S. Constitution makes no mention of public education, but the Tenth Amendment to the Constitution reserves to the states all powers not specifically delegated to the federal government or prohibited to the states by the Constitution. This Amendment is the basis for allocating to the states primary legal responsibility for public education. However, the states have delegated responsibility for day-to-day school system operations to local districts. So we begin our discussion of how schools are governed and administered at the local level. As you read this chapter, think about the following questions:

FOCUS QUESTIONS

- How do local, state, and federal governments influence education?
- How does the local school board work with the district superintendent in formulating school policy?
- Why have many school districts consolidated or decentralized?
- What are the various roles and responsibilities of the governor, state legislature, state board of education, state department of education, and chief state school officer in determining school policy?
- How has the federal role in education changed in recent years?

This chapter was revised by Dr. James Lawlor, Towson University.

▶ Local Responsibilities and Activities

Every public school in the United States is part of a local school district. The district is created by the state. The state legislature, subject to the restrictions of the state constitution, can modify a local district's jurisdiction, change its boundaries and powers, or even eliminate it altogether. The local district encompasses a relatively small geographical area and operates schools for children within specific communities. However, because a school district operates for the state, local policies must be consistent with policies set forth in the state school code.

Characteristics of Local School Boards

■ Responsibilities of local boards

Despite the fact that the state limits their prerogatives, **local school boards** have assumed significant decision-making responsibility. Many school boards have the power to raise money through taxes. They exercise power over personnel and school property. Some states leave curriculum and student policy largely to local school boards, but others, by law, impose specific requirements or limitations.

■ Most school boards elected

Methods of selecting board members are prescribed by state law. The two standard methods are election and appointment. Election is thought to make for greater accountability to the public, but some people argue that appointment leads to greater competence and less politics. Election, by far the most common practice, accounts for about 95 percent of school board members nationwide.[1] A few states specify a standard number of board members, others specify a permissible range, and a few have no requirements. Most school boards fall within a seven-to-nine-member range, with the largest school board having nineteen members.

■ School board diversity: a continuing concern

Many educators are concerned about whether school boards adequately reflect the diversity of the communities they serve. Recent nationwide surveys indicate that the number of women on school boards has increased, from about 33 percent in 1981 to 40 percent in 2002 (see Figure 7.1). Minority representation increased slightly over the same period, from 8.5 percent to 14 percent, but continues to lag behind the rising proportion of minority students in U.S. public schools (39 percent in 2002).[2] The largest one hundred school systems (those enrolling sixty thousand or more students) tend to have more heterogeneous boards. A 2001 survey indicated that minority members constituted 22 percent of the school board membership in these systems; women made up 42 percent.[3]

School board members tend to be older than the general population (82 percent are over age forty); more educated (67 percent have had four or more years of college); and wealthier (24 percent have incomes of $50,000 or more, and 40 percent earn more than $75,000 annually). They are more likely to be professionals or managers (45 percent) or to own businesses. Thirty-four percent of school board members live in small towns, and an almost equal number live in suburban areas. Twenty-two percent live in rural communities, and almost 12 percent live in urban areas.

Interestingly, only 57 percent of school board members are parents, and almost 47 percent have no children in school. School districts are aware that whether or

[1]Donna Harrington-Leuker, "School Boards at Bay," *American School Board Journal* (May 1996), pp. 18–22; Steven Taylor, "Appointing or Electing the Boston School Committee," *Urban Education* (January 2000), pp. 4–26.
[2]*Digest of Education Statistics, 2002,* at **www.ed.gov**; Table 96.
[3]*Education Vital Signs, 2002* (Alexandria, Va.: National School Boards Association, 2002), pp. 32–47; and Allan C. Ornstein, "School Superintendents and School Board Members: Who They Are," *Contemporary Education* (Winter 1992), pp. 157–159.

not board members have children in the district's schools can affect the board members' policy-making agendas, although different districts react to this knowledge differently. Some school districts require board members to have school-age children; other districts permit children of board members to attend school *outside* the district.

Age and socioeconomic factors may contribute to board members' political views. Most board members see their political affiliation as conservative (55 percent), and 38 percent are liberal. Board members' general political views may, in turn, contribute to their votes on school issues in their districts.[4]

■ Types of board meetings

School boards hold three types of meetings: regular, special, and executive. The first two are usually open to the public. The third type, usually closed to the public, deals with personnel issues or serious problems. Open board meetings obviously enhance school–community relations and allow parents and other citizens to understand the problems of education as well as to air their concerns. The use of closed board meetings to reach major policy decisions is often criticized and is illegal in many states. The In This Case feature describes an open executive meeting.

■ Pressure on school boards

School board members experience considerable pressure as they listen to and weigh the competing demands of citizen advisory groups, the business community, parents with special concerns (such as students with disabilities, gifted and talented programs, school-based management committees), the teachers' association, and local and state politicians, who often are key in funding decisions. Some decisions

| Figure 7.1 | Diversity of Local and State School Board Members |

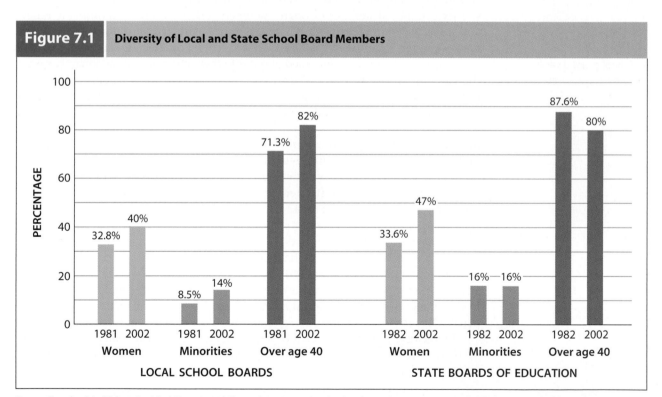

Source: "Leadership," *Education Vital Signs, 2002* (Alexandria, Va.: National School Boards Association, 2002); telephone interview with Brenda Welburn, director, National Association of State Boards of Education, October 1, 2003; and National Association of State Boards of Education, *Gender, Age, and Racial Demographics of the State Board Members* (Alexandria, Va.: Author, 1998), pp. 2, 4, 8.

---

[4]*Education Vital Signs, 1997* (Alexandria, Va.: National School Boards Association, 1997), p. A15; and Nora Carr, "The Toughest Job in America," at Education Vital Signs, **www.nsba.org**.

IN THIS CASE[5]

A Partnership in Decision-Making?

It was time for the school board executive session to start. Dr. Clore, superintendent of schools, nodded to the president of the school board that he was ready for the meeting to commence.

This would be a difficult meeting. They would be considering all administrative contracts, but special concerns had arisen about the contract of Tom Day, the principal of Westside Elementary-Middle School. Many parents and teachers thought him an incompetent administrator. These groups had generated a small mountain of documentation to support their point of view and had pushed their request for his termination through all of the school district's required steps up to tonight's announcement of the decision. Dr. Clore, too, had recommended that the board not renew Mr. Day's contract. He had worked with him for two years but had seen no improvement. In his mind, Principal Tom Day was not an instructional leader.

Other parents and former students, however, continued to support Principal Day and had been lobbying both publicly and privately with the board for his retention. Dr. Clore looked around. On one side of the room sat the parents and teachers who supported Tom Day, ready to raise their objections if—more like "when," thought Dr. Clore—the board announced Day's departure. On the other side sat those who had worked to remove him. It looked like a no-win situation. "Tonight," Dr. Clore thought, "we are all at a crossroad."

Dr. Clore sighed and wished, again, that the state's "sunshine laws," designed to encourage openness in governmental decision-making, permitted a little more privacy about personnel matters. Although most of the deliberation had been conducted behind closed doors, the announcement of contracts had to be made in an open meeting. At least he could be glad it wasn't a regular meeting, with the usual press corps and full board present, he thought. But no one, he thought, no matter how lacking in their leadership, deserved the public embarrassment about to be heaped upon Tom Day.

"Well," he thought to himself, "at least it will all finally be over with fairly quickly." The policy of this board was to allow a maximum of five minutes of citizen input on any agenda item. Each group with a similar view would have to select a representative to speak. Dr. Clore was certain that the pro and con groups of parents were prepared to have a representative speak before the board, although he was less sure about the teachers. That meant at least ten minutes of unpleasantness, perhaps twenty minutes.

He hoped nothing got out of hand. The school board president was relatively new to his position, and personnel considerations could become emotional. Dr. Clore knew that if the procedures were not followed exactly, a lawsuit could follow.

Questions

1. Ideally, school boards and superintendents work in partnership. How would you define the roles of the superintendent and school board in this situation?
2. Why would Dr. Clore think that the people attending the meeting were at a crossroad in life?
3. What role, if any, might teachers have in such personnel decisions?
4. In a larger district, how might central office staff other than the superintendent be involved in an issue such as this?
5. What might be a better way for the school board to handle this potentially explosive situation?

have winners and losers; high priorities take precedence over lower ones, and funding constraints frequently mean difficult (and occasionally unpopular) decisions.

■ More divisive school boards

School quality is an important factor in determining a community's reputation, property values, and the willingness of businesses to locate nearby. Yet, according to

---

[5]Dan C. Wertz, "The Resilient Superintendent," *American School Board Journal* (July 2002), pp. 21–25.

a recent survey of sixty-six Illinois school superintendents, school boards have become more political and divisive in recent years; newer board members seem more interested in the views of their electors than in the views of other board members or professional educators. This has caused educators and citizens to question the value of elected school boards and the politicization they often bring.[6]

School Board Responsibilities

■ Schools are big business

School administration and management is big business, and school board members must understand good business practices. Overall, U.S. school boards have fiscal responsibility for $373 billion each year and employ more than five million teachers, administrators, and support staff (such as guidance counselors, librarians, and nurses).[7] They constitute the largest nationwide employer. A typical school board member will spend more than twenty hours per week on school board business. Board members must be fair and mindful of the law when dealing with students, teachers, administrators, parents, and other community residents.

The powers and responsibilities of school boards may be classified as follows:

■ Responsibilities of school board members

1. *Policy.* School boards set the general rules about what is done in the schools, who does it, and how. The recent shift to school-based management has changed the what, who, and how, permitting greater involvement of teachers, school-based administrators, and parent groups in day-to-day school operation and direction.

2. *Staffing.* Technically the board is responsible for hiring all school district employees. In practice, however, school boards usually confine themselves to recruiting and selecting the school superintendent (the district's chief executive officer) and high-ranking members of the central office staff. Decisions on hiring and retaining principals and teachers are usually made lower in the hierarchy.

3. *Employee relations.* School board members are responsible for all aspects of employee relations, including collective bargaining with teacher unions. Large school districts rely on consultants or attorneys to negotiate with teachers, but small school districts may use the superintendent or a school board committee.

4. *Fiscal matters.* The board must keep the school district solvent and get the most out of every tax dollar. The school district usually has a larger budget than any other aspect of local government.

5. *Students.* The board addresses questions of student rights and responsibilities, requirements for promotion and graduation, extracurricular activities, and attendance.

Standards & Assessment ☑

6. *Curriculum and assessment.* The school board develops curriculum—especially development related to state law and guidelines—and approves textbook se-

[6]April Gresham, Frederick Hess, Robert Maranto, and Scott Milliman, "Desert Bloom: Arizona's Free Market in Education," *Phi Delta Kappan* (June 2000), pp. 751–757; Mel Heller and Edward Ransic, "Are We Turning Superintendents into Politicians?" *Illinois School Board Journal* (May–June 1992), pp. 12–13; and Rebecca Jones, "Schools and the Law: Legal Trouble Spots and How to Avoid Them," *American School Board Journal* (April 2000), pp. 24–30.
[7]*Digest of Education Statistics, 2002* (Washington, D.C.: U.S. Government Printing Office, 2002), at National Center for Education Statistics, **www.nces.ed.gov**, Table 157; Education Vital Signs, 2003, at **www.nsba.org**.

lections. Likewise, the board must implement and report on state assessment requirements such as those of the federal No Child Left Behind Act.

7. *Community relations*. The school board must respond not only to parents but also to other members of the community.

8. *Intergovernmental requirements*. Federal and state agencies establish a variety of requirements for local schools, and the school board is responsible for seeing that these mandates are carried out.[8]

Board members are expected to govern the school system without encroaching on the superintendent's authority. Members, in theory, have no authority except during a board meeting and while acting as a collective group or board. They also must be politically prudent: eventually someone will ask for a favor, and they must be able to resist this pressure.

The School Superintendent and Central Office Staff

■ Executive officer of school system

One of the board's most important responsibilities is to appoint a competent **superintendent of schools**.[9] The superintendent is the chief executive officer of the school system, whereas the board is the legislative policy-making body. Sometimes, the superintendent literally is a CEO. Although the vast majority of superintendents are educators, in recent years a few larger school districts, most notably New York, have hired business professionals as superintendents.

As with school boards, concerns have emerged that superintendents fail to reflect the diversity of the districts they serve. Currently, 86 percent of school superintendents are men and 14 percent are women, and only 5 percent are members of minority groups.

The school board, which consists of laypeople rather than experts in school affairs, is responsible for seeing that schools are properly run by professional personnel. The board of education often delegates many of its own legal powers to the superintendent and staff, especially in larger districts, although the superintendent's policies are subject to board approval.

■ Board reliance on superintendent

A major function of the school superintendent is to gather and present data so that school board members can make intelligent policy decisions. The superintendent advises the school board and keeps members abreast of problems; generally, the school board refuses to enact legislation or make policy without the school superintendent's recommendation. However, in cases of continual disagreement or major policy conflict between the school board and the superintendent, the latter is usually replaced. The average tenure of superintendents is about three to four years. In large urban districts, the average is even lower, less than three years.[10] An early 1990s survey reported that in the largest one hundred school districts 24 percent of the superintendents had served in their current positions for one year or less.[11]

---

[8]"NSBA and AASA Sketch Your Roles," *American School Board Journal* (June 1994), pp. 20–21; Paul Houston and Anne Bryant, "The Roles of Superintendents and School Boards in Engaging the Public with the Public Schools," *Phi Delta Kappan* (June 1997), pp. 756–759; Council of Great City Schools, "Urban School Superintendents: Characteristics, Tenure and Salary" at **www.cgcs.org**; and Nora Carr, "Leadership: The Toughest Job in America," *American School Board Journal* (Supplement 2003), pp. 14, 15, 18–20.

[9]Education Vital Signs at **www.nsba.org**, 2003.

[10]William E. Eaton, *Shaping the Superintendency* (New York: Teachers College Press, Columbia University, 1990); and Kathleen Vail, "Teamwork at the Top," *American School Board Journal* (November 2001), pp. 23–25.

[11]Ornstein, "School Superintendents and School Board Members"; and Peter J. Negroni, "A Radical Role for Superintendents," *School Administrator* (September 2000), pp. 16–19.

The reasons most superintendents give for losing their jobs are communication breakdowns and micromanagement (interference in school administration) by the board. What would Dr. Clore's feelings be about school board interference and micromanagement?

■ Duties of the superintendent

Besides advising the board of education, the superintendent usually is responsible for many other functions, including the following:

1. *Management of professional and nonteaching personnel* (for example, custodians and cafeteria workers)

2. *Curriculum and instruction leadership*

3. *Administrative management,* including district organization, budgeting, long-range planning, and complying with directives from state and federal agencies

In addition, the superintendent oversees day-to-day operation of the district schools and serves as the major spokesperson for the schools.

■ Community pressure on superintendents

Superintendents often experience strong pressure from various segments of the community such as disgruntled parents or organized community groups with their own agendas (sometimes overt, sometimes covert). Much of the superintendent's effectiveness depends on his or her ability to deal with such pressure groups. Only a confident school leader can balance the demands and expectations of parents and community groups with the needs of the students. Experts agree that the key to success as a superintendent is communication—with school board members, citizen groups, teachers, parents, unions, and elected officials. Failure to build citizen, legislative, and political support quickly leads to a superintendent's downfall.[12]

■ Central office organization

A **central office staff** assists the superintendent (see Figure 7.2).[13] Large districts of 25,000 or more students may have many levels in the staff hierarchy: a deputy superintendent, associate superintendents, assistant superintendents, directors, department heads, and coordinators and supervisors, each with their own support staffs. Small school districts usually have a less bureaucratic central office.

■ Critique of bureaucracy

Critics charge that the many-layered bureaucracies of large school districts are inefficient—a waste of the taxpayers' money. Actually, in terms of administrator-to-student ratios, the largest districts are not necessarily the least efficient. Nevertheless, like large corporations, many school districts consider the benefits of streamlining in this era of limited resources and school reform.

The Principal and the School

Most schools have a single administrative officer, a **principal**, who is responsible for school operations. In small schools, the principal may teach part time as well; large schools may have one or more assistant or vice principals. Interestingly, 87 percent of school administrators (principals and vice principals) are men. The administrative hierarchy may also include department chairpersons, discipline officers (for instance, a dean of students), and guidance counselors. Each of these individuals works closely with the school principal and under his or her direction. Furthermore,

---

[12]Thomas Shannon, "The People's Choice: A Blueprint for Involving the Community in Superintendent Selection," *American School Board Journal* (March 1997), pp. 29–32; Matthew King and Irwin Blumer, "A Good Start," *Phi Delta Kappan* (January 2000), pp. 356–360; and Deborah King, "The Changing Shape of Leadership," *Educational Leadership* (May 2002), pp. 61–63.

[13]Kathleen Vail, "The Changing Face of Education," Education Vital Signs, 2003, at **www.nsba.org**.

Figure 7.2 Typical Medium-Sized School District (5,000 to 25,000 Students)

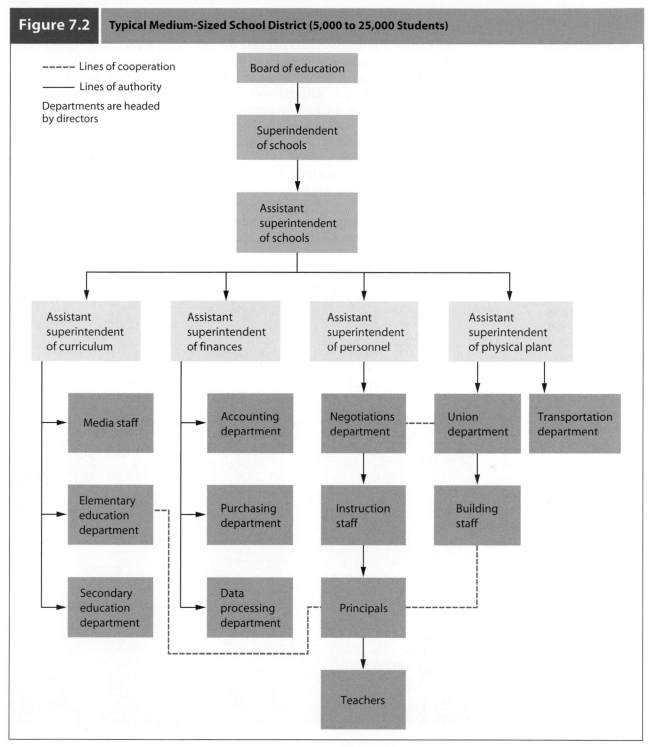

This figure shows an organizational chart of a medium-sized school district with 5,000 to 25,000 students, representative of almost 12 percent of school districts nationwide. Small school districts, with one thousand to five thousand students—about 37 percent of all districts nationally—have much simpler organizational structures. The organizational hierarchy of larger school districts is cumbersome; a chart of those with 100,000 or more students would extend off the page. *Source: Digest of Educational Statistics, 2002,* Table 88.

■ The principal's role

most principals work with a community-based school improvement group, often a parent-teacher association or, more recently, a school-based management team.

Probably the most important aspect of the principal's job is the role of manager: dealing with day-to-day school operations, meetings, paperwork, phone calls, and everyday tasks. However, principals are also expected to exert leadership in curriculum and instruction. Some authorities recommend that principals spend from 50 to 75 percent of their time focusing on curriculum and instruction (for example, math, English, social studies, art, and music).[14] However, principals point out that their numerous managerial tasks often make this impossible.

In general, secondary-school principals tend to see themselves primarily as general managers, whereas elementary school principals view themselves as leaders in curriculum and instruction.[15] This may in part be because larger secondary schools create more managerial work for the principal. Moreover, secondary-school principals usually have chairpersons who handle curriculum and instructional activities in various subject areas, whereas elementary-school principals rarely have such assistance.

As a teacher, how will you interact with your principal? In large secondary schools a teacher's interaction with the principal might be minimal, consisting of primarily formal observations; faculty meetings; cafeteria, hall, and bus duty; and conversations in the main office. In contrast, many elementary-school teachers have frequent, almost daily, contact with the principal, and these meetings cover a wide range of school- and student-related issues.

■ Influence of school-based management

Traditionally, authority concerning school policies has proceeded from the top down, from the school board through the superintendent and central office staff to

In general, secondary-school principals tend to see themselves primarily as general managers, whereas elementary-school principals view themselves as leaders in curriculum and instruction. (© Jeffrey Dunn/Stock Boston)

[14]Charles Majkowski, "The Essential Role of Principals in Monitoring Curriculum Implementation, *NASSP Bulletin* (February 2000), pp. 76–83; and Thomas J. Sergiovanni, *The Principalship: A Reflective Practice Perspective,* 2nd ed. (Needham Heights, Mass.: Allyn and Bacon, 1991).
[15]Laura A. Cooper, "The Principal as Instructional Leader," *Principal* (January 1989), pp. 13–16; and Allan C. Ornstein, "Leaders and Losers," *Executive Educator* (August 1993), pp. 28–30.

the principal. In some districts, however, as explained in the chapter on The Teaching Profession, *school-based management* has brought more decision-making power to individual schools. This gives principals and teachers increased responsibility for such matters as curriculum, staff development, teaching assignments, and even hiring and budgeting. Collaborations with teachers and other school staff to create school policies call for a more participatory governance style among school principals.[16]

REFOCUS What would be the ideal relationship between you, as a new teacher, and the principal at your school? Do you think you would ever like to serve as a principal?

Parent and Community Involvement

Many programs for school-based management go beyond collaboration among principals and teachers by giving important roles to parents and other community members as well. In doing so, they build on a movement for increased parent and community involvement evident since the 1970s.

■ Reasons for parent involvement

Many educators have promoted parent involvement for the most basic of reasons: research indicates that it pays off in higher student test scores, better grades, and improved attitudes toward learning,[17] particularly for inner-city and minority students.[18] Across the nation, polls indicate that the public overwhelmingly supports the idea of parent involvement and believes that parents play a major role in children's education.[19]

■ Uninvolved parents

Nevertheless, relatively few parents take full advantage of existing opportunities to involve themselves with their children's schooling. In a Department of Education survey of parents, only 32 percent of parents with eighth-grade children reported that they belonged to a parent-teacher organization, and only 36 percent had attended one or more school meetings.[20] According to another survey, most parents had nei-

---

[16]Jerome Delaney, "Principal Leadership: A Primary Factor in School-Based Management and School Improvement," *NASSP Bulletin* (February 1997), pp. 107–111; Alan B. Hankin, Peter Cistone, and Jay Dee, "Conflict Management Strategies of Principals in Site-Based Management Schools," *Journal of Educational Administration* (February 2000), pp. 142–158; Lynn K. Bradshaw, "The Changing Role of Principals in School Partnerships." *NASSP Bulletin* (May 2000), pp. 86–96; Gerald N. Tirozzi, "The Artistry of Leadership: The Evolving Role of the Secondary School Principal," *Phi Delta Kappan* (February 2001), pp. 434–439; Neil Dempster, "Guilty or Not: The Impacts and Effects of Site-Based Management in Schools," *Journal of Educational Administration* 39 (2000), pp. 47–63.

[17]Lloyd Campbell, "Parents and Schools Working for Student Success," *NASSP Bulletin* (April 1992), pp. 1–4; David A. Squires and Robert D. Kranyik, "The Comer Program," *Educational Leadership* (December 1995–January 1996), pp. 29–33; and Lynn G. Beck and Joseph Murphy, "Parental Involvement in Site-Based Management: Lessons from One Site," *International Journal of Leadership in Education* (April–June 1999), pp. 81–102.

[18]James P. Comer, "Empowering Black Children's Educational Environment," in H. P. McAdoo and J. L. McAdoo, eds., *Black Children* (Beverly Hills, Calif.: Sage, 1985), pp. 114–139; James Comer, *Waiting for a Miracle* (New York: Penguin, 1998), pp. 442–446; Barbara L. Jackson and Bruce S. Cooper, "Involving Parents in Urban Schools," *NASSP Bulletin* (April 1992), pp. 30–38; and Christina Ramirez-Smith, "Stopping the Cycle of Failure," *Educational Leadership* (February 1995), pp. 14–19.

[19]Laura Pappano, "In Parent-Teacher Conferences, 'Enemies' Can Be Friends." *Boston Sunday Globe,* September 28, 2003, p. B6; Rob McPhee, "Orchestrating Community Involvement," *Educational Leadership* (December 1995–January 1996), pp. 71–75; and Debbie Price, "Students Who Succeed Have Parents Who Care," *Baltimore Sun,* May 20, 1998, pp. A1, 12.

[20]*Digest of Education Statistics, 2002,* Table 25; "Parent Involvement," *NEA Today* (March 1991), p. 12; and Gill Crozier, "Uninvolved Parents," *Race, Ethnicity and Education* (December 2001), pp. 329–341.

ther the time nor the inclination to participate deeply in school matters. Only 35 percent of parents reported helping their children with homework once or twice per week and 63 percent of parents never helped teachers in the classroom or participated in school functions. Many parents, according to recent research, avoid school involvement because of feelings of inadequacy, negative experiences in schools as students and negative perceptions of administrator and teacher attitudes.[21]

■ Types of community involvement

Despite such lack of participation from individual parents, the pressure for reform has produced formal arrangements that give parents and other community members a voice in local educational decisions. Usually the community members merely offer advice, but in a few cases they have been granted substantial control over the schools. For purposes of discussion, we can divide community involvement into three broad categories: community participation, community control, and community education.

■ Areas of community participation

Community Participation. The usual form of **community participation** involves advisory committees at either the neighborhood school or central board level. These committees are commonly appointed by school officials and offer the school board help and advice. Citizen groups provide advice and assistance in many areas: (1) identification of goals, priorities, and needs; (2) selection and evaluation of teachers and principals; (3) development of curricula and extracurricular programs; (4) support for financing schools; (5) recruitment of volunteers; and (6) assistance to students in school and in "homework hotline" programs.[22]

■ Shared power

Community Control. In a system of **community control**, an elected community council or board does more than offer advice—it shares decision-making power with the central school board.

■ Experience in Chicago

In 1990 Chicago instituted a form of community control as part of local educational reform. Parent and community groups provided significant input on recruitment and retention of school principals, curriculum, and budgets, and such. Yet a recent examination showed that on three important reform indicators—student achievement, attendance, and dropout rate—Chicago public schools have either remained the same or declined. Though Chicago teachers, administrators, and local school councils generally felt positive about the administrative changes, the larger community of businesspeople, citizens, parents, and legislators did not.[23]

■ Operation of charter schools

Perhaps the newest major development in community involvement in education is the establishment of **charter schools** (discussed in more detail in the chapter on Financing Public Education). In this arrangement, the local school board or state board of education grants a community group a "charter" (a contract listing

[21]A. Y. Ramirez, "High School Teachers View of Parent Involvement," *American Secondary Education* (Summer 2000), pp. 27–32; and A. Y. Ramirez, "Survey on Teachers' Attitudes Regarding Parents and Parental Involvement," *School Community Journal* (Fall–Winter 1999), pp. 21–39.
[22]U.S. Department of Education, *Strong Families, Strong Schools: Building Community Partnerships for Learning* (Washington, D.C.: U.S. Government Printing Office, 1994); Kenneth Leithwood and Theresa Menzies, "A Review of Research Concerning the Implementation of Site-Based Management," *School Effectiveness and School Improvement* (September 1998), pp. 233–285; and June B. Huffman, "One School's Experience as a Professional Learning Community," *Planning and Changing* 31 (2000), pp. 84–94.
[23]Herbert J. Walberg and Richard P. Niemiec, "Is Chicago School Reform Working?" *Phi Delta Kappan* (May 1994), pp. 713–715; Thomas E. Hogueisson, "Chicago Public School Teachers' Opinions of the Reform School Board of Trustees," ERIC Document Number ED 398332, 1996; Alfred G. Hess, "Community Participation or Control? From New York to Chicago," *Theory into Practice* (Autumn 1999), pp. 217–224; and Pauline Lipman, "Making the Global City, Making Inequality: The Political Economy and Cultural Politics of Chicago School Policy," *AERA Journal* (Summer 2002), pp. 379–418.

specific rights, privileges, and expectations) that permits the group to establish and operate a public school. Specific arrangements about finance, school operation, student enrollment, and accountability are negotiated. If the charter school fails to meet prescribed accountability standards, its charter is revoked and the school is closed. Charter schools are an opportunity for both community involvement in local schools and community *control* over the fate of those schools.[24] See the Taking Issue feature for a discussion of the pros and cons of charter schools.

■ School system serving all ages

Community Education. Since the early 1980s, the school has come to be seen as only one of the educational agencies within the community. Under this concept—called **community education**—the school serves as a partner, or coordinating agency, in providing educational, health, social, legal, recreational, and cultural activities to the community.[25] In Baltimore, Maryland, for example, schools offer a variety of services to local citizens, such as preschool programs for three- and four-year-olds and their parents, as well as adult sports and drama, exercise, recreational, and vocational programs. All of this has occurred in response to changes in society. Programs such as these are especially helpful for low-income families.

■ Schools sharing with other agencies

As part of the community education plan, schools share their personnel and facilities with other community agencies or even businesses. In return, schools may expect to share facilities, equipment, and personnel with other community agencies, local businesses, and area universities. This type of sharing is especially important in a period of retrenchment and school budget pressures.

Size of Schools and School Districts

■ Debate about school size

Educators have long debated the question of size: How large should a school be? How many students should be enrolled in a single district? Four decades ago, James Conant argued that the most effective high schools were the ones large enough to offer comprehensive and diversified facilities. More recently, however, other educators have contended that small schools are more effective.[26]

■ Problems of large schools

In 1987, after reviewing several studies, two researchers concluded that high schools should have no more than 250 students. Larger enrollments, according to this analysis, result in a preoccupation with control and order, and the anonymity of a large school makes it harder to establish a sense of community among students, teachers, and parents.[27] For example, a 1994 study of thirty-four large high schools in New York City showed that when students were organized into "houses" of approximately 250 students, attendance improved, student responsiveness in school increased, and grades went up.[28]

---

[24]Judith Saks, *The Basics of Charter Schools: A School Board Primer* (Alexandria, Va.: National School Boards Association, 1997); Bob Stein, "O'Farrell Community School: Center for Advanced Academic Studies: A Charter School Prototype," *Phi Delta Kappan* (September 1996), pp. 28–29; Louann A. Bierlein, "Catching On, but the Jury's Still Out," *Educational Leadership* (December 1995–January 1996), pp. 90–91; Mike Kennedy, "Charter Schools: Threat or Boon to Public Schools," *American School and University* (December 2002), pp. 18–26.

[25]Mario D. Fantini, Elizabeth L. Loughren, and Horace B. Reed, "Toward a Definition of Community Education," *Community Education Journal* (April 1980), pp. 11–33; and Richard B. Riley and Vincent Ferrandino, "The 21st Century Principal: Opportunities and Challenges," *Principal* (September 2000), pp. 6, 10, 12.

[26]James B. Conant, *The American High School Today* (New York: McGraw-Hill, 1959).

[27]Thomas B. Gregory and Gerald R. Smith, *High Schools as Communities: The Small School Reconsidered* (Bloomington, Ind.: Phi Delta Kappa, 1987); see Hanna Skandera and Richard Sousa, "Why Bigger Isn't Better," *Hoover Digest* (Summer 2001).

[28]Rosalind Eichenstein et al., *Project Achieve, Part I: Qualitative Findings, 1993–94* (Brooklyn: New York City Board of Education, 1994).

taking issue

Question Are charter schools a better way to educate students?

Charter Schools as Public School Reform

As the pressure for school reform increased in the 1980s and 1990s, so did the public's wish for greater participation in its schools. Some parents sought even greater control by requesting that school boards grant them charter-school status, a controversial issue in many states.

Arguments PRO

1 Charter schools provide an alternative vision of schooling not realized in the traditional public school system.

2 Charter schools have increased autonomy from state and local school district regulations.

3 Special populations of students, often "at-risk" students, are served by charter schools.

4 Students, teachers, and parents participate by choice and are committed to making charter schools work.

5 Charter schools are generally smaller and more manageable in size.

6 Parental involvement and overall communication are increased in charter schools.

Arguments CON

1 Accountability goals frequently are not clearly spelled out by sponsors in charter schools, leading to misunderstanding and confusion.

2 Features and regulations of many federal education programs that apply to charter schools are ill-suited to their operation.

3 Charter schools often receive inadequate funding for start-up and operating expenses, especially if they serve special populations that require high expenditures.

4 Charter schools have difficulty finding staff, and this problem is exacerbated by the teacher shortage. In addition, teachers' unions often withhold support and attempt to restrict charter schools in their operation.

5 Inadequate school buildings and facilities affect classroom learning.

6 Insufficient planning time for charter school boards, principals, and staff makes for management and communication problems later on. Assertive and demanding parents can erode a charter school's effectiveness.

More recent studies indicate that learning is best in high schools of 600 to 900 students; learning declines as school size grows and is considerably less in high schools with more than 2,100 students. Not surprisingly, studies showed that more affluent communities had effective student learning even with larger schools, whereas low socioeconomic neighborhoods, or schools with high concentrations of minority students, needed small schools for students to learn.[29]

■ Ideal size of districts

The debate about school size parallels similar disputes about the optimum size of school districts. Larger school districts, according to their proponents, offer a broader tax base and reduce the educational cost per student; consequently, these

---

[29]See "Size of High Schools" at National Center for Education Statistics, **www.nces.gov/ programs/coe/2003/section4**.

districts can better afford high-quality personnel, a wide range of educational programs and special services, and good transportation facilities. Most studies of this subject over the past sixty years have placed the most effective school district size as between 10,000 and 50,000 students.[30]

■ Advantages of small districts

Today, however, small is often considered better in school districts as well as in individual schools. In a 1993 study of school board members, 78 percent of those surveyed believed that smaller districts were more manageable and promoted citizen involvement but saw large systems as administrative nightmares.[31]

■ Trend toward larger districts

Arguments and counterarguments aside, the trend in American education has been toward larger school districts. By 2000, one-quarter of all public school students were in the 100 largest districts, each serving 60,000 or more students.[32] In most cases, the larger school systems are located in or near cities, the largest being the New York City system with approximately 1,075,710 students, followed by Los Angeles with 710,000 students, and Chicago with 431,750. Two other large school systems, Puerto Rico (613,000) and Hawaii (186,000), span an entire territory and state, respectively.[33]

■ Combining school districts

Consolidation. School districts grow through population growth and through **consolidation**, when several smaller school districts combine into one or two larger ones. As Figure 7.3 illustrates, consolidation dramatically reduced the overall number of districts from more than 130,000 in 1930 to slightly less than 15,000 in 2002, with the bulk of the decline taking place in the thirty years between 1930 and 1960.[34]

School districts consolidate for a variety of reasons; chief among them are the following:

■ Reasons for consolidation

- *Size.* Larger schools, especially high schools, permit broader curriculum offerings and specialized faculty.

- *Services.* Larger schools justify hiring counselors, deans of students, assistant principals, team leaders, and specialists not normally found in smaller schools.

- *Economics.* Purchasing decisions (for example, books, paper, and art supplies) yield significant cost savings when ordering in bulk. Consolidation also permits older buildings to be retired at considerable cost savings. Redundant high-salaried central-office positions may also be cut when school districts combine.

---

[30]Howard A. Dawson, *Satisfactory Local School Units,* Field Study no. 7 (Nashville, Tenn.: George Peabody College for Teachers, 1934); Steven B. Mertens, "School Size Matters in Interesting Ways," *Middle School Journal* (May 2001), pp. 51–55; and Herbert J. Walberg, "Losing Local Control," *Educational Researcher* (June–July 1994), pp. 19–26.

[31]Craig Howley and Robert Bickel, "The Influence of Scale," *American School Board Journal* (March 2002), pp. 28–30; Matthew Andrews et al., "Revisiting Economies of Size in American Education: Are We Any Closer to Consensus? *Economics of Education Review* (June 2002), pp. 245–262; and Leonard Pellicer, "When Is a School District Too Large? Too Small? Just Right? Lessons from Goldilocks and the Three Bears," *School Business Affairs* (November 1999), pp. 4–6, 8–10, 26–29.

[32]See "Characteristics of the 100 Largest," at National Center for Education Statistics, **www.nces.gov/pubs2001/100_largest/table03.asp**.

[33]Look for a list of the largest school systems in *Digest of Education Statistics, 2000.* You'll find varied information regarding big-city districts by searching the Internet for "Great Cities Schools" and "State Education Agencies" at National Center for Education Statistics **(http:nces.ed.gov/pubs2001/100_largest/table01.asp)**.

[34]*Digest of Education Statistics, 2002,* Tables 87 and 89.

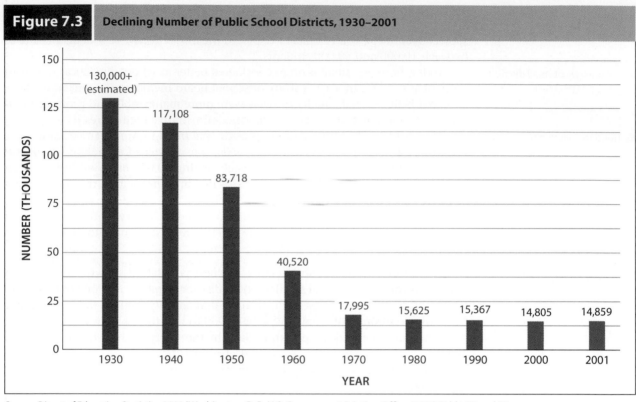

Figure 7.3 | Declining Number of Public School Districts, 1930–2001

Source: Digest of Education Statistics, 2002 (Washington, D.C.: U.S. Government Printing Office, 2002), Table 87 and 89.

■ Options for consolidation

Consolidating districts usually means closing schools, and this has proved to be a serious and emotional matter, especially in small and rural districts where the local school may be a focal point of community identity. A less drastic method of consolidation is for neighboring districts to share programs and personnel. For example, in 1995, sixty-seven Iowa school districts were sharing superintendents, seventy-one were involved in *whole-grade sharing* (programs in which all students in a certain grade from participating districts are assigned to a single district).[35]

REFOCUS As you read newspapers and magazines and listen to news broadcasts, what educational issues are discussed at the local school district level, the state level, and in Washington, D.C.? How do these issues affect the local district in which you teach or have field experiences?

▶ Intermediate Units

■ Coordination and supplementary services

The term **intermediate unit** or **regional educational service agency** (RESA) refers to an office or agency in a middle position between the state department of education and local school districts. This agency provides coordination and supplementary services to local districts and links local and state educational authorities. The

---

[35]Miles Bryant, "Rural School District Reorganization on the Great Plains," *Rural Educator* (Spring 2002), pp. 14–18; and Mary Anne Raywid and Thomas Shaheen, "In Search of Cost Effective Schools," *Theory into Practice* (Spring 1994), pp. 67–74.

intermediate unit is usually a legal and political extension of the state department of education created by the state legislature. By 2001 twenty-nine states had some form of intermediate unit. The average intermediate unit comprises twenty to thirty school districts and covers about fifty square miles. Approximately 1,282 intermediate or regional agencies currently provide services in the United States.[36]

■ Services provided

In recent years, intermediate units have provided school districts widely varied consulting services and resource personnel in curriculum, instruction, evaluation, in-service training, and other general areas of education. Intermediate units have also provided services in more specialized areas such as bilingual education, prekindergarten education, vocational education, education of the gifted and talented and children with disabilities, and data processing and technology education. Many educators believe that an intermediate unit covering several districts can economically provide services that many small or financially strapped school districts could not afford on their own.

 Does your state have intermediate units or regional educational service agencies? If so, how do they directly affect local schools? Cite two examples.

▶ State Responsibilities and Activities

■ Legal responsibility of state

Each state has legal responsibility for supporting and maintaining the public schools within its borders. The state:

- enacts legislation
- determines state school taxes and financial aid to local school districts
- sets minimum standards for training and recruiting personnel
- provides curriculum guidelines (some states also establish "approved" textbook lists)
- makes provisions for accrediting schools
- provides special services such as student transportation and free textbooks.

■ State laws

The **state school code** is the collection of laws that establish ways and means of operating schools and conducting education in the state. The state, of course, cannot enact legislation that conflicts with the federal Constitution. Many states have quite detailed laws concerning methods of operating the schools. The typical organizational hierarchy, from state to local levels, is shown in Figure 7.4.

The Governor and State Legislature

■ Powers of the governor

Although gubernatorial powers vary widely, authority on educational matters is spelled out in law. Typical aspects of the governor's role in education are summarized in Overview 7.1. Usually a governor is charged with making educational budget recommendations to the legislature. In many states, the governor has legal access to any accumulated balances in the state treasury, and these monies can be used for school purposes. The governor can generally appoint or remove school personnel at the state level. But these powers often carry restrictions, such as approval by the legislature. In most states, the governor can appoint members of the state board of education and, in a few states, the chief state school officer. Governors can

---

[36]*Digest of Education Statistics, 2002*, Table 89.

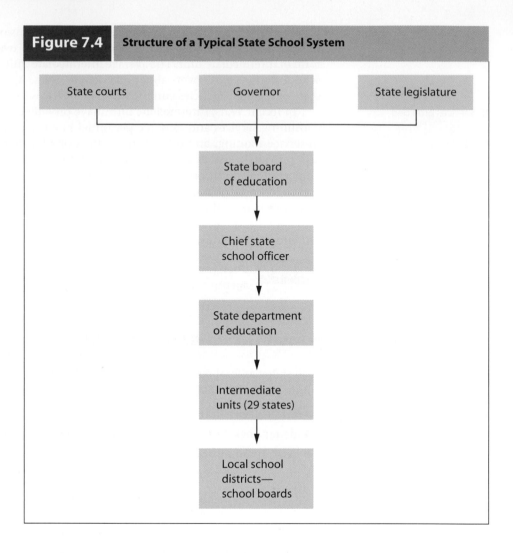

Figure 7.4 Structure of a Typical State School System

State courts   Governor   State legislature

State board of education

Chief state school officer

State department of education

Intermediate units (29 states)

Local school districts— school boards

veto educational measures or threaten to veto to discourage the legislature from enacting opposed educational laws.

■ Powers of the legislature

In most states, the legislature is primarily responsible for establishing and maintaining the public schools and has broad powers to enact laws pertaining to education. These powers are limited by restrictions in the form of federal and state constitutions and court decisions. The state legislature usually determines the aspects of the basic structure and functions of the educational system summarized in Overview 7.1.

The legislature also usually decides major financial matters, including the nature and level of state taxes for schools and the taxing powers of local school districts. It may also determine basic parameters of teaching and instruction, including (1) what may or may not be taught, (2) how many years of compulsory education will be required, and (3) the length of the school day and school year. In addition, the legislature may establish testing and assessment procedures, authorize school programs, and set standards for building construction. Where the legislature does not enact these policies, they are usually the responsibility of the state board of education, which we describe below.

Standards & Assessment ☑

■ New state legislation

As a teacher, you will need to comply with various state laws. Since the 1980s, state legislatures have become active in school reform by making more use of their powers over education. Nationwide, more than twelve hundred state statutes pertaining to school reform were enacted between 1983 and 1990 alone.[37] The new statutes have addressed matters ranging from curriculum to teaching qualifications, from class size to graduation requirements. Not since the wave of school reform that followed the 1957 Soviet launch of Sputnik have state legislatures played such a prominent role in educational policy.

The State Board of Education

The **state board of education** is usually the most influential and important state education agency. With the exception of Wisconsin, all states have some sort of state board of education, which depends on the state legislature for appropriations and authority and serves an advisory function for the legislature. (New York's Board of Regents is perhaps the strongest and most respected state board of education.) In addition, most states have a separate governing board for state colleges and universities. The precise duties and functions of state boards of education vary, but Overview 7.1 lists duties common to most state boards.

■ Selection of state board members

As of 2002, governors appointed board members in thirty-two states. The state legislature appointed board members in three states, and thirteen states elected members by popular vote (a method increasingly prevalent in recent decades). The remaining states used either legislative appointment or a combination of appointed members and elected members. The number of members on state boards ranges from seven to nineteen, with an eleven-member board the most popular.[38] (An odd number of members eliminates tie votes.)

■ Increasing diversity of board members

As with local boards, women are more often becoming state board members. In 1982, about 34 percent of board members were women; by 2002 the percentage had risen to 47 percent. Ethnic composition of state school boards, however, has changed little. In both 1982 and 2002, 16 percent were members of minority groups.[39] (See Figure 7.1 on page 198.) These trends are important because heterogeneity broadens the perspectives of board members and increases the likelihood that boards reflect a wide range of social and educational concerns.

The State Department of Education

■ Functions of state education departments

As a teacher, you are most likely to encounter in day-to-day work the **state department of education**. State departments of education usually operate under the direction of the state board of education and are administered by the chief state school officer. Traditionally, state departments of education primarily collected and disseminated statistics about the status of education within the state. Since the 1950s, however, state departments have taken on many other functions, such as those listed in Overview 7.1.[40] In short, they carry out the laws of the state legislature and the regulations of the state board.

---

[37]Linda Darling-Hammond and Barnett Berry, *The Evolution of Teacher Policy* (Santa Monica, Calif.: Rand, 1988); Allan C. Ornstein, "Reforming American Schools: The Role of the States," *NASSP Bulletin* (October 1991), pp. 46–55; and Thomas B. Timar and David Kirp, *Managing Educational Excellence* (New York: Falmer Press, 1988).

[38]"State Education Governance at a Glance," (2002), **www.nasbe.org**; *Digest of Education Statistics,* 2002.

[39]Telephone interview with Brenda Welburn, director, National Association of State Boards of Education, July 15, 1998, and April 20, 2001; and Dinah Wiley, *State Boards of Education* (Arlington, Va.: National Association of State Boards of Education, 1983), Tables 1–2, pp. 15–16.

[40]Fred C. Lunenburg and Allan C. Ornstein, *Educational Administration: Concepts and Practices* (Belmont, Calif.: Wadsworth, 1991).

■ Recent issues

During recent decades, state departments of education have had to grapple with controversial issues such as desegregation, compensatory education, student rights and unrest, school finance reform and fiscal crisis, aid to minority groups, collective bargaining, accountability, student assessment, and competency testing. Accordingly, the departments, once nearly invisible, have grown significantly in size. Larger states (including California, Michigan, New Jersey, New York, and Texas) have professional staffs approaching 1,000.[41]

The Chief State School Officer

■ Chief executive

The **chief state school officer** (sometimes known as the state superintendent or commissioner of education) heads the state department of education and is also the chief executive of the state school board. He or she is usually a professional educator.

■ Increasing numbers of women

The office is filled in one of three ways: in 2001, twelve states filled the position through appointment by the governor, twenty-four states through appointment by the state board of education, and thirteen states by popular election. As of 2002, two chief state school officers were African American; however, sixteen chief officers were women (32 percent)—a notable increase from earlier decades and double the figure in 1990.[42] The greater number of women in the position represents a departure from the "good-old-boy network" that once dominated the upper echelons of educational administration.

■ Duties of the chief state school officer

The duties of chief state school officers and relationships between that position and state boards and state departments vary widely. Generally an elected chief officer has more independence than one who is appointed. See Overview 7.1 for the basic responsibilities of chief state school officers.

R E F O C U S   Talk to teachers and administrators in local schools. In what ways do they see state board of education and state department of education policies affecting day-to-day school operations? Do they see this impact as positive or negative?

▶ The Federal Role in Education

We'll consider the federal government's role in four parts: (1) the federal agencies that promote educational policies and programs; (2) the trend that has moved many educational decisions from the federal government to the state governments; (3) federal financing of education; and (4) the Supreme Court's decisions concerning education. In this chapter we focus on the first two parts. Federal spending is examined in the chapter on Financing Public Education and court decisions are discussed in the chapter on Legal Aspects of Education.

Federal Educational Agencies

■ Desire for federal leadership

In most of the nation's first 150 years, between 1787 and 1937, Congress enacted only fourteen significant educational laws. In the past seven decades, however, we

---

[41]Fenwick W. English, *Educational Administration: The Human Science* (New York: HarperCollins, 1992); Thomas J. Sergiovanni et al., *Educational Governance and Administration,* 2nd ed. (Needham Heights, Mass.: Allyn and Bacon, 1992); and telephone conversation with Barbara Clements, staff specialist in statistics, Council of Chief State School Officers, July 16, 1998.

[42]*The Council, 2002,* available at **http:publications.ccsso.org**.

Individual or Group	Typically Responsible For
Governor	• Making educational budget recommendations to the legislature; may have access to accumulated general funds for educational use • Appointing or removing school personnel at state level • Appointing members of state board of education; may appoint chief state school officer • Holding veto power over school measure from legislature
State Legislature	Establishing basic structure of state educational system, including • The selection process for, and duties of, the state board of education and the chief state school officer • The functions of the state department of education • The types of local and regional school districts • Whether the state will provide community colleges, adult schools, and vocational schools • The selection methods and powers of local school boards • Deciding on major financial matters: tax formulas for schools, taxing powers of local districts • Determining basic parameters of teaching and instruction
State Board of Education	• Adopting and enforcing policies, rules, and regulations necessary to implement legislative acts related to education • Establishing qualifications and appointing personnel to the state department of education • Setting standards for teaching and administrative certificates • Establishing standards for accrediting schools • Managing state funds earmarked for education • Keeping records and collecting data needed for reporting and evaluating • Adopting long-range plans for development and improvement of schools • Creating advisory bodies as required by law • Acting as a judicial body in hearing disputes arising from state policies • Representing the state in determining policies on all matters pertaining to education that involve relationships with other agencies (including the federal government) • Advising the governor or legislature on educational matters • In some states, appointing the chief state school officer • Setting minimum salary schedules for teachers and administrators • Adopting policies regulating institutions of higher learning
Chief State School Officer	• Serving as the chief administrator of the state department of education and of the state board of education • Selecting personnel for the state department of education • Recommending improvements in educational legislation and in educational budgets • Ensuring compliance with state educational laws and regulations • Explaining and interpreting the state's school laws • Impartially settling controversies involving administration of the state's schools • Arranging studies, committees, and task forces as deemed necessary to identify problems and recommend solutions • Reporting on the status of education within the state to the governor, legislature, state board of education, and the public
State Department of Education	• Collecting and disseminating education statistics • Certifying teachers • Developing curriculum standards and accountability measures • Overseeing student transportation and safety • Monitoring compliance with federal regulations • Evaluating existing education programs and issuing reports • Developing programs to meet the needs of special students (including bilingual students and students with disabilities)

have passed more than 170 significant laws.[43] Traditionally, the major organizations of teachers and administrators, such as the American Federation of Teachers, the National Education Association, and the National School Boards Association, have preferred that the federal government offer financial aid and special services but refrain from interfering in educational policy. Many educators now believe, however, that the federal government should provide a clear statement of mission and specific kinds of guidance—curriculum frameworks as well as funds—to state and local agencies struggling to improve the schools.[44]

■ Evolution of the department

The U.S. Department of Education. Although many different federal agencies now encompass educational programs or activities, the **U.S. Department of Education** is the primary federal educational agency. When the Department of Education was founded in 1867, as the Office of Education, its commissioner had a staff of three clerks and a total of $18,600 to spend. From its humble beginnings, the agency has grown to about 4,700 employees, and in 2002 its annual expenditures exceeded $129 billion.[45] The department currently administers more than 120 separate programs.[46]

Over time, the Office of Education assumed the responsibilities of (1) administering grant funds and contracting with state departments of education, school districts, and colleges and universities; (2) engaging in educational innovation and research; and (3) providing leadership, consultative, and clearing-house services related to education.

■ Cabinet-level status

In 1979, after much congressional debate and controversy, the Office of Education was changed to the Department of Education. A secretary of education was named, with full cabinet-level status, and the department officially opened in 1980.

■ Role of the secretary of education

The secretary of education has widespread visibility and influence. Besides managing educational policies and promoting programs to carry out those policies, the secretary can exert persuasion and pressure in political and educational circles. Recent heads of the department, including William Bennett, Lamar Alexander, Richard Riley, and Roderick Paige, have used the limelight to push their own brands of reform. Although many conservatives have argued to cut back its activities and eliminate its cabinet-level status, the department has grown more visible than ever in the past few years. The Technology @ School feature discusses Internet sources of information on the Department of Education and other levels of school governance.

Standards & Assessment ✓

Returning Responsibility to the Federal Government

George W. Bush made educational reform a key goal of his presidency. In 2002, Congress approved President Bush's educational reform initiative, the No Child Left Behind Act (NCLB). NCLB aims to improve low-performing schools and to hold states and local school districts accountable for students meeting high standards, measured by annual performance tests in reading and mathematics. We discuss NCLB's specific provisions in the chapters on Motivation, Preparation, and Condi-

[43]*Digest of Education Statistics, 2002,* available at National Center for Education Statistics, **www.nces.ed.gov**.
[44]Lawrence Handy, "Main Events: the Year of NCLB," *Education Vital Signs, American School Board Journal* (Supplement 2003); Allan C. Ornstein, "The National Reform of Education: Overview and Outlook," *NASSP Bulletin* (September 1992), pp. 89–101; and Ronald Anderson, "Curriculum Reform: Dilemmas and Promise," *Phi Delta Kappan* (September 1995), p. 35.
[45]See "Summary of the 2003 Budget at President's Budget Request for the U.S. Department of Education" at **www.ed.gov**.
[46]*Digest of Education Statistics, 2002,* Table 364; Kenneth A. Doyle, "Coming of Age," *Phi Delta Kappan* (May 2002), pp. 674–676.

School Governance Information Available on the Internet

As a prospective teacher, you can learn more about the different levels of school government through research on the Web. Start with a visit to your state department of education Web site (find your state's department at **www.nasbe.org/SEA_links.html**).

From your state department's site, select two or three local district Web sites. Compare and contrast information on these Web sites. For example, which state board of education programs are mentioned on local board sites? Do local Web sites include vision, mission, and belief statements? If so, how do they compare or contrast with each other? What reference do you find to either state-mandated testing or indicators of student achievement? What information on each local school district Web site makes you want or not want to teach in that district?

Examine the Web sites of national school organizations listed below and look for the following: policy statements, areas of advocacy, federal and state legislative positions, No Child Left Behind, and special projects and news releases. How do these national organizations further the aims of local school districts? Which ones would you, as a teacher, visit to keep up to date on policy developments?

■ National School Boards Association (**www.nsba.org**)

■ National Association of State Boards of Education (**www.nasbe.org**)

■ Council of Chief State School Officers (**www.ccsso.org**)

■ Education Commission for the States (**www.ecs.org**)

tions for the Entering Teacher and School Effectiveness and Reform in the United States. States and local school districts that fail to improve student performance, especially for underachieving students, will receive fewer federal dollars.

In the 1980s and 1990s, the federal government sought to reduce monetary outlays and shift program responsibility to local governments. The Bush administration, however, through No Child Left Behind, exerted more federal influence on local public schools than at any time in the previous thirty years. Accountability pressure at both state and local school levels has superintendents, principals, and teachers scrambling to show increased test scores in reading and math, as well as demonstrating that every child has a "highly qualified teacher." Despite No Child Left Behind's far-reaching implications and somewhat increased funding levels, critics fault the Bush administration for leaving the NCLB an "unfunded mandate," and for usurping the authority of state and local educational agencies.

REFOCUS How does No Child Left Behind affect you as a beginning teacher?

► Nonpublic Schools

■ State aid for nonpublic schools

Although this chapter has focused on public education, nonpublic schools are not exempt from governmental influences. In particular, many state education laws apply to private and parochial schools as well as to public institutions—laws pertaining to health standards, building codes, child welfare, student codes, and so forth. In addition, legislative bodies in many states have passed laws to help private schools and to provide public-funded aid in such areas as student transportation,

Private schools are organized differently from public schools but remain influenced by governmental regulations in many ways. (© *Philip Gould/CORBIS*)

health services, dual enrollment or shared-time plans, school lunch services, book and supply purchases, student testing services, teacher salary supplements, student tuition, and student loans.

■ Enrollment in nonpublic schools

As indicated in Motivation, Preparation, and Conditions for the Entering Teacher, nonpublic schools now account for more than 11 percent of total enrollments in U.S. elementary and secondary schools. Catholic schools still enroll the most private-school students, although their numbers have declined from 85 percent of all private-school students in 1969 to 49 percent in 2001. Nonreligious, independent schools have increased their share of students from 8 percent of private-school enrollments in 1969 to 16 percent by 2002. Evangelical and fundamentalist Christian school numbers and enrollments have also grown dramatically, reflecting the increased influence of conservative Protestants who seek schools that emphasize God, discipline, and faith in community and country.[47]

Private schools typically operate differently from public schools. They have a principal or headmaster but generally lack the cadre of support people mentioned earlier in this chapter. They usually derive their authority from a board of directors or school committee, which, unlike a public school board, addresses the operation of one particular private school.

■ Competition or cooperation?

Many commentators see public and private sectors as competing for students and for funds. Other educators, however, prefer to envision cooperation between public and private schools. In fact, certain distinctions between public and private schools are becoming blurred.[48] For example, programs of *school choice* sometimes

---

[47]*Digest of Education Statistics, 2002, Table 59,* at National Center for Education Statistics, **www.nces.ed.gov**; Allan C. Ornstein, "The Growing Popularity of Private Schools," *Clearing House* (January 1990), pp. 210–213; Sister Dale McDonald, "A Chronology of Parental Choice in Education," *Momentum* (April–May 2001), pp. 10–15.

[48]Lamar Alexander, "A Horse-Trade for K–12 Education," *Phi Delta Kappan* (May 2002), pp. 698–699; Dennis P. Doyle, "The Role of Private Sector Management in Public Education," *Phi Delta Kappan* (October 1994), pp. 128–132; and Paul D. Houston, "Making Watches or Making Music?" *Phi Delta Kappan* (October 1994), pp. 133–135.

blend the public and private by allowing students to apply public funds to a private education. (Privatization is discussed in detail in the chapter on School Effectiveness and Reform in the United States, and school choice in the chapter on Financing Public Education.)

▶ Summing Up

1 The governance of education is organized on four governmental levels: local, intermediate (in some states), state, and federal.

2 Schools are organized into school districts; approximately 15,000 public school systems currently operate in the United States.

3 At the local level, the school board, the school superintendent, the central office staff, and school principals all take part in governing and administering the schools.

4 Educators have attempted to increase parent and community involvement in the schools. School-based management programs often include greater roles for parents and community members. Other forms of public involvement include community participation, community control, community education, and charter schools.

5 Educators have long debated the optimum size for schools and school districts. Many believe that increases in size do not necessarily mean increases in efficiency or effectiveness and may result in the opposite.

6 Whereas small and rural school districts have undergone significant consolidation since the 1930s, some large urban districts have followed the contrary trend to decentralize.

7 More than half of the states have one or more intermediate units that support local school districts and exercise limited regulatory powers.

8 In most states, the legislature is primarily responsible for establishing and maintaining public schools and has broad powers to enact laws pertaining to school education.

9 All states except Wisconsin have state boards of education. The state boards oversee state departments of education headed by the chief state school officer.

10 Overall, the federal role in education has dramatically expanded since the 1930s. Recent decades, however, have witnessed a movement toward reduced federal involvement.

11 Nonpublic schools account for more than 11 percent of total enrollments in U.S. elementary and secondary schools, with Catholic schools comprising almost 50 percent of these enrollments and nonreligious, independent schools 16 percent.

▶ Key Terms

local school boards (197)
superintendent of schools (201)
central office staff (202)
principal (202)
community participation (206)
community control (206)
charter school (206)
community education (207)
consolidation (209)

intermediate unit (210)
regional educational service agency
  (RESA) (210)
state school code (211)
state board of education (213)
state department of education (213)
chief state school officer (214)
U.S. Department of Education (216)

▶ Discussion Questions

1 What do you consider the advantages and disadvantages of elected, rather than appointed, local school boards? Do the same arguments apply to state boards of education? Would you rather work where school boards are elected or where they are appointed? Explain.

2 React to the following statement made by Ernest Boyer, president of the Carnegie Foundation, when critiquing the 1983 presidential report *A Nation at Risk:* "If indeed the nation is at risk, then where is the federal government's effort to address the problem?"

3 What are some reasons for and against shifting educational responsibilities from the federal government to the states?

4 How, as a teacher, can you influence educational change at the local level? At the state level?

▶ Projects for Professional Development

1 Interview classmates who went to large high schools (more than a thousand students) and those who went to smaller high schools (less than a thousand students). Where would you rather teach and why?

2 Make a chart listing the advantages and disadvantages of consolidation of school districts. Share your chart with a classmate.

3 Interview teachers and administrators in local schools regarding issues of teacher empowerment and school governance. You might ask the following questions: (a) To what extent are teachers involved in school governance and management? Does this school use true school-based management? If so, how does that function? (b) How do teachers regard their involvement in running the school? and (c) How do principals and other administrators regard teacher involvement in school governance? Analyze your interview responses. What can you conclude about teacher involvement in school governance? Is school-based management worthwhile or just another educational fad?

4 Talk with teachers and administrators in local schools about ways in which parents and the school community participate in the schools. Prepare a plan that would reach out to and/or involve students' parents in meaningful ways in your classroom and in the school community.

5 Visit the Web site of your local school district or a district in which you are especially interested. (See **www.nasbe.org**; click on links to "state education agencies," then click on "school boards" or "school districts." You may need to browse the site map.) What can you learn from this site about school board activities, such as curriculum issues, state assessment programs, board priorities, and policy issues? How would this information be useful to you if you were teaching in the school district? Now that you have preliminary information about a school district, attend a school board meeting. Examine the meeting agenda. What agenda items reinforce what you learned from the Web site? What individuals or community groups were present, and what views did they express? Did any individuals or groups express differing or alternative views? How did the school board respond to these different viewpoints? What decisions did the school board make, and how were these reached? Summarize what you learned about school district governance from your visit to the Web site and attendance at the meeting.

▶ Suggested Resources

 Internet Resources

Visit the U.S. Department of Education's home page at **www.ed.gov** to evaluate the scope of the federal government's involvement in education. The "Education-Related Toll-Free Numbers and Hotlines" page offers toll-free telephone numbers for government offices, agencies, and hotlines that deal with educational issues (**http:www.ed.gov/searchResults**). A good starting point for finding online sites of individual school districts is the Education K–12 category on the Yahoo home page (**www.yahoo.com**). In addition, you'll find useful information on topics addressed in this chapter with a general net search for NCREL (the North Central Regional Educational Laboratory) at **www.ncrel.org**, CPRE (the Center for Research in Educational Policy) at **www.people.memphis.edu/~coe_crep/**, AERA (the American Educational Research Association) at **/www.aera.net**, or other education-related organizations such as the American Federation of Teachers (**www.aft.org**) and the National Education Association (**www.nea.org**).

Publications

Bracey, Gerald. *The War Against America's Public Schools.* Boston: Allyn and Bacon, 2002. *A thoughtful essay on the negative aspects of privatizing America's public schools.*

Calabrese, Raymond L. *The Leadership Assignment: Creating Change.* Boston: Allyn and Bacon, 2002. *A primer for school administrators interested in fostering change.*

Donmoyer, Robert, Michael Imber, and James J. Scheurich, eds. *The Knowledge Base in Educational Administration.* Albany: State University of New York Press, 1995. *An excellent book on school organization and management, particularly concerning interactions with the community.*

Finn, Chester E., Louann Bierlein, and Bruno Manno. *Charter School Accountability: Findings and Prospects.* Bloomington, Ind.: Phi Delta Kappa, 1997. *This is an excellent book in PDK's Fastback Series (#425). It gives comprehensive coverage of the charter school movement, types of charter schools, start-up problems, accountability, and reasons for failure.*

Gregory, Thomas B., and Gerald R. Smith. *High Schools as Communities: The Small School Reconsidered.* Bloomington, Ind.: Phi Delta Kappa, 1987. *A powerful discussion of the need for small schools and the importance of school ethos and school-community relations.*

Poston, William K. *Making Governance Work.* Thousand Oaks, Calif.: Corwin Press, 1994. *An excellent discussion of school boards, school leadership, school-based management, and total quality management.*

Ravitch, Diane. "Different Drummers: The Role of Nonpublic Schools in America Today." *Teachers' College Record* (Spring 1991), pp. 409–414. *An excellent essay on the role of and growth of nonpublic schools in America, particularly in response to growing dissatisfaction with public schools.*

Rochester, J. Martin. *Class Warfare: Besieged Schools, Bewildered Parents, Betrayed Kids, and the Attack on Excellence.* San Francisco: Encounter Books, 2002. *A description of the clash between excellence and equality and their implications for American education.*

Sarason, Seymour B. *Parental Involvement and the Political Principle.* San Francisco: Jossey-Bass, 1995. *An excellent book focusing on school management and organization, parental involvement, the politics of education, school boards, and educational change.*

Sergiovanni, Thomas. *Leadership for the Schoolhouse: How Is It Different?* San Francisco: Jossey-Bass, 1996. *A fresh look at the importance of principal leadership behavior and management.*

Spring, Joel. *Conflict of Interests: The Politics of American Education.* New York: Longman, 1993. *An essay on the politics of education at the national, state, and local levels.*

Wilson, John. *Key Issues in Education and Teaching.* London: Cassell, 2000. *A concise focus on key issues in public education such as charter schools, accountability, student achievement, and teaching methods.*

U.S. Department of Education. *No Child Left Behind: A Parent's Guide.* Washington, D.C.: U.S. Department of Education, 2003. *Simply written to inform parents of specific aspects of No Child Left Behind and their implications for them and their children.*

CHAPTER 8

Financing Public Education

E ducation in the United States is big business. By 2002, public education (K–12) cost more than $373 billion annually, and elementary and secondary education represented 7.3 percent of the nation's annual gross domestic product.[1] The three major sources of revenue for public schools are local, state, and federal governments. As Figure 8.1 shows, revenues from federal sources have increased from less than half a percent in 1929–30 to 7.3 percent currently (achieving a high of almost 10 percent in 1979–80). State contributions also rose from less than 17 percent in 1929–30 to almost 50 percent by 2001. As state and federal contributions have risen, local revenues have fallen in proportion, from more than 80 percent to 43 percent.[2]

Although the percentages of funds provided by these three sources have changed, the *total* amount of money for schools concerns most local school districts. Because most school-related cost increases have outpaced inflation in recent years, the business of schooling is in serious financial trouble. Since the mid-1980s, school board members have consistently ranked "lack of financial support" as the number one challenge they face.[3]

This chapter explores the reasons for both the overall changes in school financing and the current climate of uncertainty. Today's educators must deal with budget constraints, equity in school financing, taxpayer resistance, and various plans to restructure the system of financial support. As you read, think about the following questions:

This chapter was revised by Dr. James Lawlor, Towson University.

[1]*Digest of Education Statistics, 2002* (Washington, D.C.: U.S. Government Printing Office, 2002), Table 157.
[2]*Vital Signs, 1994*, p. A-25; and *Digest of Education Statistics, 2002*, Table 159.
[3]*Education Vital Signs, 2003* at **nasb.org**; and Rebecca Jones, "The Kids Are Coming," *American School Board Journal* (April 1997), pp. 20–25. See also Daniel M. Seaton, "The Burden School Board Presidents Bear," *American School Board Journal* (January 1992), pp. 32–36.

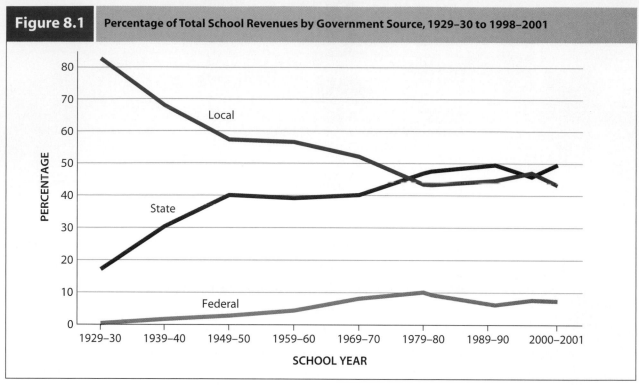

| Figure 8.1 | Percentage of Total School Revenues by Government Source, 1929–30 to 1998–2001 |

Source: The Condition of Education, 1987 (Washington, D.C.: U.S. Government Printing Office, 1987), Table 1.13, p. 36; *Digest of Education Statistics, 1982* (Washington, D.C.: National Center for Education Statistics, 1982), Table 66, p. 75; *Digest of Education Statistics, 2000*), Table 159; and *Estimates of School Statistics, 1994–95* (Washington, D.C.: National Education Association, 1995), Table 9, p. 39; see "Percent Distribution of Revenue for Public Elementary Schools by Source and State: School Year: 2000–2001 at **http:nces.ed.gov/edfin/graphs/topic.asp?INDEX=4**.

FOCUS QUESTIONS

- What proportion of school revenues do local, state, and federal governments contribute?
- What is wrong with relying on property taxes as school revenue sources?
- What particular fiscal problems characterize urban schools?
- Why do significant differences in education spending occur among and within states? How does public opinion affect spending?
- What major steps have been taken to reform school finance?
- What financial considerations will most affect school management?

▶ Tax Sources of School Revenues

■ Criteria for evaluating taxes

Public school funding relies primarily on revenues generated from taxes, especially local property taxes and state sales and income taxes. Certain taxes are considered better than others. Most people today accept the following criteria for evaluating taxes:

1. *A tax should not cause unintended economic distortions.* It should not change consumer spending patterns or cause the relocation of business, industry, or people.

■ Progressive versus regressive

2. *A tax should be equitable.* It should be based on the taxpayer's ability to pay. Those with greater incomes or with greater property worth should pay more taxes. Taxes of this sort are called **progressive taxes.** Inequitable taxes and those that require lower-income groups to pay a higher proportion of their income than higher-income groups are called **regressive taxes.**

3. *A tax should be easily collected.*

■ Elastic versus inelastic

4. *The tax should respond to changing economic conditions,* rising during inflation and decreasing in a recession.[4] Responsive taxes are *elastic;* those not responsive are *inelastic.*

▶ Local Financing for Public Schools

Although states are responsible for education, traditionally much of this responsibility has fallen to local school districts. Overview 8.1 summarizes governmental income sources and spending patterns for education at local, state, and federal levels. As indicated earlier, local contributions to school financing have decreased over the past several decades, but still amount to more than 40 percent of the total.

Property Tax

The **property tax** is the main source of revenue for local school districts, accounting for 77 percent of local funding nationwide. In eleven states, including all six

OVERVIEW 8.1 *Other Income Sources by Level and Spending Pattern*

Level	Income Sources	Spending Patterns
Local	• Property tax • Product rights • Special taxes and user fees	Funding goes to local schools in the district. Districts vary widely in their ability to fund their schools and state aid does not always equalize the discrepancies.
State	• Personal income tax • Sales tax • Other taxes: excise taxes, severance taxes • Lotteries	States vary in ability to finance education. Local districts are funded using combinations of four plans: flat grant, foundation, power-equalizing, or weighted student. Many states are working to make their distribution plans more equitable.
Federal	• U.S. Treasury	Funding is distributed primarily to states for designated purposes, such as reading improvement and special education. Current No Child Left Behind regulations require states to show adequate yearly progress in student achievement and provision of highly qualified teachers in every district.

---

[4]James Guthrie and Rodney J. Reed, *Education Administration and Policy,* 2nd ed. (Needham Heights, Mass.: Allyn and Bacon, 1991); and Donald E. Orlosky et al., *Educational Administration Today* (Columbus, Ohio: Merrill, 1984).

New England states, property taxes make up more than 98 percent of local school revenues.[5]

■ How property tax is calculated

Property taxes are determined by first arriving at the *market value* of a property—the probable selling price for the property. The market value is converted to an *assessed value* using a predetermined index or ratio, such as one-fourth or one-third; for example, a property with a market value of $200,000 might have an assessed value of only $50,000. The assessed value is always less than the market value. Finally, the local tax rate, expressed in mills, is applied to the assessed value. A **mill** represents one-thousandth of a dollar; thus a tax rate of 25 mills amounts to $25 for each $1,000 of assessed value (or $25 × 50 = $1,250 tax).

■ Problems with property tax

The property tax is not an equitable tax. Differing assessment practices and lack of uniform valuation may lead people owning equivalent properties to pay different taxes. Also, the property tax may fail to distribute the tax burden according to ability to pay. A retired couple may have a home whose market value has increased substantially, along with their taxes, but because they live on a fixed income, they cannot afford the increasing taxes. In this respect, the property tax is regressive.

In addition, the property tax is not immediately responsive to changing economic conditions. Some states reassess properties every one to two years, but others reassess only every three to four years. Thus a property's assessed value and actual tax are often based on outdated market conditions.

Other Sources of Local Funding

In addition to the property tax, school districts can gather revenues through special income taxes and other taxes or fees. Some municipalities, especially small villages and towns, depend on such sources as traffic fines and building permits to help raise money for schools.

■ Rise in user fees

User fees—fees charged to use a certain facility or service—are the most common type of special assessment. User fees can be levied on bus service, textbooks, athletic and recreational activities, preschool classes, and after-school centers. By 2002, more than thirty states permitted schools to assess user fees on students, and many school districts did so.[6] Because they are not based on ability to pay, user fees are considered a regressive tax.

■ Exclusive product rights

Recently some school boards have signed lucrative contracts with corporations for **exclusive product rights**. For example, Jefferson County (Colorado) schools signed an exclusive product contract with Pepsi estimated to bring the district $7.3 million in revenue over seven years. Other school districts have developed multimillion-dollar fund-raising campaigns with corporate sponsors, generating everything from cash donations to new stadiums, auditoriums, scoreboards, and equipment purchases. Nevertheless, these contracts are negotiated on a district-by-district basis, with some districts benefiting handsomely while others struggle to fund their school district budgets.[7] The Taking Issue box debates school–corporation contracts.

---

[5]*Significant Features of Fiscal Federalism, 1995* (Washington, D.C.: U.S. Advisory Commission on Intergovernmental Relations, 1995), Table 13, pp. 34–35; Edward C. Keller and William T. Hartman, "Prevailing Wage Rates: The Effects on School Construction Costs, Levels of Taxation, and State Reimbursements," *Journal of Education Finance* (Fall 2001), pp. 713–728.
[6]Robert W. Wassmer and Ronald C. Fisher, "Interstate Variation in the Use of Fees to Fund K–12 Public Education," *Economics of Education Review* (February 2002), pp. 87–100; and Claudette Bauman and David Brown, "Public School Fees as Hidden Taxation," *Educational Administration Quarterly* (December 1996), pp. 665–685.
[7]Alex Molnar, "Corporate Branding of Our Schools," *Education Leadership* (October 2002), p. 59.

Taxes are major sources of both local and state school funding. Property taxes, personal income taxes, and sales taxes provide much school funding, although since the 1970s, citizens in many parts of the country have resisted tax increases. *(Bob Daemmich)*

Local Resources and Disparities

■ Wealthy versus poor districts

Despite state and federal aid, some school districts have greater difficulty supporting education than others do. A school district located in a wealthy area or an area with a broad **tax base** (for example, residential neighborhoods, shopping centers, businesses, and industry) generates more revenue than a poor school district. As a result, in most states, the five wealthiest school districts often spend two to four times more per student than the five poorest school districts do.[8] As we discuss later in this chapter, state courts and legislatures have attempted to reduce these disparities through reforms in the system of educational finance. In most states, however, substantial disparities in funding persist.

■ Municipal overburden

Although financial problems affect many rural and suburban districts, the greatest financial troubles are usually found in large cities. Cities are plagued by what is commonly called **municipal overburden**, a severe financial crunch caused by population density and a high proportion of disadvantaged and low-income groups. The additional spending needed for social services prevents large cities from devoting as great a percentage of their total tax revenues to schools as suburban and rural districts can.

■ Educational overburden

Another problem is that city schools have a greater proportion of special-needs students—namely, bilingual and low-income students and students with disabilities. These students require programs and services that often cost 50 to 100 percent more per student than basic programs.[9]

---

[8]Bruce Biddle and David C. Berliner, "Unequal School Funding in the U.S.," *Educational Leadership* (April 2002), p. 48. Robert E. Slavin, "After the Victory: Making Funding Equity Make a Difference," *Theory into Practice* (Spring 1994), pp. 98–103; and Howard Wainer, "Does Spending Money on Education Help?" *Educational Researcher* (December 1993), pp. 22–24.

[9]Harold Hodgkinson, "Reform Versus Reality," *Phi Delta Kappan* (September 1991), pp. 8–16; Mary Jean LeTendre, "Improving Chapter 1 Programs: We Can Do Better," *Phi Delta Kappan* (April 1991), pp. 576–581; Lawrence Hardy, "Overburdened, Overwhelmed," *American School Board Journal* (April 2003), pp. 18–23.

taking issue

Question Should schools and school boards establish special financial relationships with corporations and businesses?

Expanding Funding for Public Education

Funding public education is a serious problem in America. As school populations have increased, support for public education has declined. Local governments and school boards have sought new taxes and creative ways to meet pressing financial needs. One innovative yet controversial approach to funding is the emergence of corporate–school relationships. For example, Channel One, a cable news network that broadcasts exclusively in public and private schools, offers its advertisers a captive audience of students. Although both schools and businesses stand to gain, these relationships present thorny issues for teachers and administrators, as well as for the public.

Arguments PRO

1 Corporations provide direct financial support to schools and school districts for exclusive use of their product(s), which include soft drinks, snack foods, movies, and cosmetics.

2 Some corporations provide free television sets, VCRs, satellite receivers, and computers.

3 Local corporate sponsors contribute to fund-raising campaigns, build stadiums, install scoreboards, and build auditoriums.

4 Channel One broadcasts a twelve-minute daily news report. Students view international stories, politics, and special issues affecting teenagers.

5 Eight million students, grades 6 through 12, watch Channel One news each day.

Arguments CON

1 Payment for exclusive product use favors one business over others. In addition, many parents and educators worry that food product placement, especially, contributes to unhealthy student eating habits.

2 The school pays for "free" equipment with access to the student body to sell corporations' products. Pandering to advertisers in schools is neither in students' best interests nor in the mission of public schools.

3 Schools and school districts that have access to generous local sponsors receive favored treatment, while others struggle to fund their school district budgets.

4 Critics say Channel One is like network news, especially because it includes advertisements. Students are exposed daily to ads for soft drinks, movies, video games, skin creams, and clothing for teens.

5 Some educators and critics such as Ralph Nader call Channel One "little more than junk news in an MTV wrapper," suggesting that the content fails to focus strongly on "hard news" stories.

■ Urban cycle of financial strain

Despite their dire need for more revenues, cities often cannot realistically raise taxes. Ironically, tax increases contribute to the decline of urban schools because they cause businesses and middle-income residents to depart for the suburbs. Thus the city's tax base is undermined. Declining services also cause residents to leave—a no-win situation.

R E F O C U S   **What are the primary sources of tax revenue in your local school district? How do these sources measure up against the criteria for evaluating taxes? Which tax or taxes do you see as fairest? Why?**

▶ State Financing of Public Schools

Although the states have delegated many educational powers and responsibilities to local school districts, each state remains legally responsible for educating its children and youth, and states' portion of funding increased steadily until the 1990s (see Figure 8.1). In this section we look at the principal types of state taxes used to finance education, variations in school funding from state to state, methods by which state aid is apportioned among local districts, and the role of state courts in promoting school finance reform.

State Revenue Sources

Sales taxes and **personal income taxes** are the two major state revenue sources. Because states currently pay almost 50 percent of the cost of public elementary and secondary education (see Figure 8.1), these two taxes are important elements in the overall support of public schools.

Sales Tax.   As of 2003, forty-five states had statewide sales taxes, with such taxes making up one-third of state revenues. The median rate was 5.16 percent, and fifteen states had rates of 6 percent or higher.[10]

▪ Sales tax evaluated

The sales tax compares favorably to other possible fund-raising taxes. For example, the sales tax meets the criterion of equity if the tax base does not include food and medical prescriptions. (If not, however, low-income groups are penalized because they spend a large portion of their incomes on basic goods such as food and medicine.) The sales tax is easy to administer and collect; it does not require periodic valuations or entail legal appeals (as the property tax does). The sales tax is also elastic, because the revenue derived from it tends to parallel the economy. When the state is in a recession, however, as happened in the early to mid-1990s and again in 2001–2002, sales tax revenues decrease sufficiently to reduce the state's income. Still, the tax is useful because relatively small increases in the rate result in large amounts of revenue.

Personal Income Tax.   The personal income tax is the second largest source of state tax revenue, representing about 32 percent of state revenues. Only eight states do not levy a personal state income tax.[11] Just as the sales tax rate varies among states—from 3 to 8 percent—the state income tax, based on a percentage of personal income, also varies.

▪ Income tax evaluated

A properly designed income tax should cause no economic distortions. Assuming no loopholes, it rates high in terms of equity, reflecting the taxpayer's income and ability to pay. The income tax is also more equitable than other taxes because it

---

[10]See the Sales Tax Clearinghouse, **www.theSTC.org**, "State Sales Tax Rate"; *Recent Changes in State, Local, and State-Local Tax Levels* (Denver: National Conference of State Legislatures, 1991); see David W. Harvey and Mark Schmidt, "Support for School Construction: Blending Sales Tax with Property Tax." School Business Affairs (December 2002), pp. 34–37.

[11]See the Sales Tax Clearinghouse, **www.theSTC.org**, "State Individual Income Tax Rates"; *Significant Features, 1995,* Table 13, pp. 34–35.

usually considers special circumstances of the taxpayer, such as dependents, illness, moving expenses, and the like. In general, state income taxes have become more progressive because of increased standard deductions and personal exemptions, and fifteen states have eliminated taxes on poor families altogether.[12]

The personal income tax is easy to collect, usually through payroll deductions. It is also highly elastic, allowing state government to vary rates according to the economy. However, its elasticity makes it vulnerable to recession, which drives income revenue down.

Other State Taxes.   Other state taxes contribute limited amounts to education. These include (1) excise taxes on motor fuel, liquor, and tobacco products; (2) estate and gift taxes; (3) severance taxes (on the output of minerals and oils); and (4) corporate income taxes.

◼ State lotteries

Another trend has emerged to establish state lotteries to support education. Although this was a major purpose of the early lotteries, funds have been diverted to meet other social priorities such as health care, social welfare agencies, and road construction. As a result, in most of the forty states where lotteries currently exist, the lottery contributes less than 2 percent of the state's total revenue for education.[13] Lotteries are somewhat regressive because relatively more low-income individuals play the lottery than do high-income individuals and they spend larger percentages of their annual income on it.

States' Ability to Finance Education

◼ State variations in spending

Some students are more fortunate than others, simply by geographic accident. State residence has a lot to do with the type and quality of education a child receives. In 2000–2001, Alaska, Connecticut, New Jersey, New York, and the District of Columbia spent more than ten thousand dollars per student. In contrast, Alabama, Arizona, Arkansas, Idaho, Mississippi, Nevada, Tennessee, and Utah spent less than $5,500 per student (see Figure 8.2).

◼ What can states afford?

Do these figures mean that some states set their education priorities more than twice as high as other states do? No, they reflect what states can afford, which has much to do with the personal incomes of their inhabitants. We must consider what the states spend on all other services and functions, such as housing, transportation, and medical care.

For example, in 1998, Mississippi spent $4,575 per student—the second-lowest figure nationwide and far short of the national average of $6,662—yet this amount represented 3.8 percent of Mississippi's per capita income (average income for each person living in the state). The national average was 2.9 percent of per capita income.[14]

◼ Aging population

Educational Support and the Graying of America.   Another factor that diminishes states' abilities to finance public education is an aging population. The median age of the U.S. population has risen steadily since 1900. The proportion of people

---

[12]*State Deficit Management Strategies; State Fiscal Conditions,* Legislative Finance Paper No. 55 (Denver: National Conference of State Legislators, 1986); Richard J. Fenton et al., "Rethinking Cuts in Public Education: An American Example," *Education Economics* (April 2001), pp. 53–68; O. Homer Erekson et al., "Fungibility of Lottery Revenues and Support of Public Education," *Journal of Education Finance* (Fall 2002), pp. 301–312.
[13]See **www.musl.com/lotterylinks/shtm,** "Lottery Links."
[14]*Estimates of School Statistics, 1994–95* (West Haven, Conn.: National Education Association, 1995), Table 11, p. 41; see also **nces.ed.gov/fastfacts/display.asp?id=66(2001);** and Gerald Bracey, "The Misery Index," *Phi Delta Kappan* (April 2000) pp. 633–634.

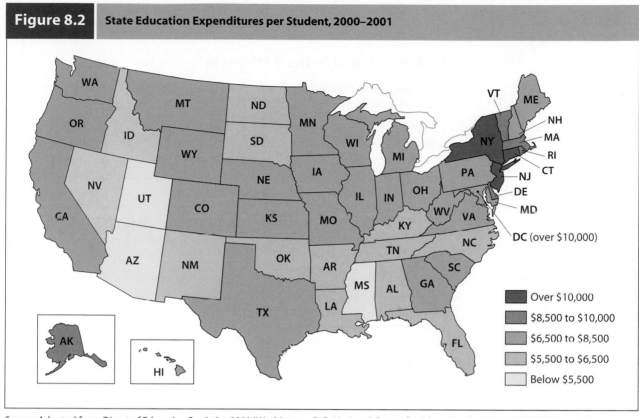

Figure 8.2 State Education Expenditures per Student, 2000–2001

Legend:
- Over $10,000
- $8,500 to $10,000
- $6,500 to $8,500
- $5,500 to $6,500
- Below $5,500

DC (over $10,000)

Source: Adapted from *Digest of Education Statistics, 2000* (Washington, D.C.: National Center for Education Statistics, 2000), Table 168. State expenditures are based on average daily attendance and include federal, state, and local revenues; see "Current Per-Pupil Expenditures for Elementary and Secondary Schools: School Year: 2000–2001" at **http:nces.ed.gov/edfin/graphs/topic.asp?INDEX = 2 and INDEX = 4**.

■ Effect on school budgets

older than sixty-five increased from 4.1 percent in 1900 to 17 percent by 2003 and will likely reach 20 percent or more by 2020.[15] Older people who no longer have children in school are generally more resistant to increased taxes for schools. Recent changes in government spending patterns reflect this attitude. Through the 1980s, educational spending per student outpaced inflation by about 30 percent, yet, by the late 1980s it began to decline. At the same time, government medical and health expenditures—a large proportion of which go to older people—increased.[16]

■ Graying of the Frostbelt

The increase in average age is a nationwide trend; however, some parts of the country are "graying" faster than others. In the 1970s and 1980s, Frostbelt states, such as New York, Pennsylvania, Illinois, Iowa, and Michigan, lost sizable numbers of young people to the Sunbelt. In many areas of the Northeast and Midwest the graying population is increasingly reluctant to provide financial and political support for

---

[15]Harold G. Shane, "Improving Education for the Twenty-first Century," *Educational Horizons* (Fall 1990), pp. 11–15; see also "Projected Resident Population of the United States as of July 1, 2025" and "Projected Resident Population of the United States as of July 1, 2003" at **www.census.gov/population/www/projections**.

[16]*Digest of Education Statistics, 1997*, Table 34, p. 37; John Sikula, "Why Our Educational System is Not Working," *Action in Teacher Education* (Spring 2003), pp. 89–92; Erik Bush, "The Effects of Local Limitations on General State Aid in Illinois," *Journal of School Business Management* (Spring 2002), pp. 36–42.

schools.[17] In contrast, areas with a boom in student enrollments, such as the South-east and Southwest, can offset the growing influence of older age groups.

State Aid to Local School Districts

States use four basic methods to finance public education. Some states have financial strategies that combine methods.

◼ The oldest, most unequal method

1. *Flat grant model.* This is the oldest and most unequal method of financing schools. State aid to local school districts is based on a fixed amount multiplied by the number of students in attendance. This fails to consider students with special needs (bilingual students cost more to educate than do native English speakers), special programs (vocational and special education), or the wealth of school districts.

   The remaining three methods each pursue greater equality of educational opportunity by allocating more funds to school districts in greatest need of assistance.

◼ A minimum per student

2. *Foundation plan.* This most common approach guarantees a foundation, or minimum annual expenditure per student, to all school districts in the state, irrespective of local taxable wealth. However, reformers usually consider the minimum level too low, and wealthy school districts easily exceed it. School districts with a high percentage of children from low-income families suffer with this plan.

◼ Inverse ratio to wealth

3. *Power-equalizing plan.* Many states have adopted some form of this more recent plan. Each school district retains the right to establish its own expenditure levels, but the state pays a percentage of local school expenditures based on district wealth. Wealthier school districts receive fewer matching state dollars and poorer districts more.

◼ Students weighted by characteristics

4. *Weighted student plan.* Students are weighted in proportion to their special characteristics (that is, disabled, disadvantaged, and so forth) or special programs (for example, vocational or bilingual) to determine the cost of instruction per student. For example, a state may provide four thousand dollars for each regular student, 1.5 times that amount (six thousand dollars) for vocational students, and 2 times that amount (eight thousand dollars) for students with disabilities.

The Courts and School Finance Reform

◼ *Serrano v. Priest*

Efforts to equalize educational opportunities among school districts within a state have been spurred by a series of court decisions that have fundamentally changed the financing of public education in most states. The 1971 landmark decision in *Serrano v. Priest* radically altered the way California allocated education funds. California, like nearly all the states, depended on local property taxes to support the schools, and plaintiffs argued that this system of financing resulted in unconstitutional disparities in expenditures between wealthy and poor school districts. The California Supreme Court agreed.

◼ *San Antonio v. Rodriguez*

After the *Serrano* decision, the Supreme Court ruled in 1973 in *San Antonio v. Rodriguez* that expenditure disparities based on differences in local property taxes between school districts in a state were not unconstitutional under the federal con-

---

[17]Albert R. Crenshaw, "So Long Sunbelt," *Philadelphia Inquirer,* March 4, 1994, p. A-2.

stitution but might be unconstitutional under state constitutions. The *Rodriguez* decision placed the issue of inequities in school finance in the hands of the state courts and legislatures, where many believed it belonged.

■ The Kentucky plan

Since *Rodriguez,* certain state courts have ruled that school financing arrangements are unconstitutional if they result in large disparities in per-pupil expenditures based on wealth differences among school districts. For example, in *Rose v. Council for Better Education* (1989), the Kentucky Supreme Court declared the entire state educational system, including the method of funding schools with property taxes, unconstitutional. This decision prompted the legislature to hike average education spending some 30 percent and to undertake an extensive plan of educational reform (described in the chapter on School Effectiveness and Reform in the United States.[18] After the Kentucky case, similar suits were filed in thirty states, and the

■ Disparities remain

problem of unequal funding is being revisited again and again in state legislatures.[19] The In This Case box shows how teachers might be affected by their states' distribution of money to local school districts.

■ Court decisions

Recent court decisions have focused on both adequacy, a minimum state contribution, and equity, the belief that students in poor school districts "have the right to the same educational opportunity that money buys for others."[20] In short, states need to close the gap between the best- and worst-financed education systems. Some states may also need to factor private schools into their distribution plans. In June 2003, the U.S. Supreme Court issued a ruling on the Cleveland (Ohio) voucher program. This program provides state money in the form of educational vouchers for low-income/minority students in private schools. The Court declared the voucher program constitutional as long as equivalent remedial services were provided for low-income/remedial students in public schools. This decision could significantly change the flow of public funds away from public schools to private schools.[21]

■ Does money alone make a difference?

Yet some critics of school finance reform have argued that money alone makes little difference in the quality of education.[22] They contend that educational improvement demands commitment and responsibility on the part of students, teachers, and parents. Moreover, unless we address a variety of social and cognitive factors, especially family structure, reform efforts may be useless. With all of these issues unresolved, school finance reform will be hotly debated for years to come.

REFOCUS How responsive are the sales tax and the personal income tax in times of recession and economic downturn? Which do you believe has the greater responsibility in funding public education: state or local government? Explain your reasoning.

---

[18]Ronald Henkoff, "Four States: Reform Turns Radical," *Fortune,* October 21, 1991, pp. 137–144; Robert Rothman, "KERA: A Tale of One School," *Phi Delta Kappan* (December 1997), pp. 272–275; and Jane C. Lindle, "Lessons from Kentucky About School-Based Decision Making," *Educational Leadership* (December 1995–January 1996), pp. 20–23.

[19]David Ritchey, "The Disparities in Public School Financial Support," *School Business Affairs* (September 2000), pp. 29–30, 32–36; Denise Lindjord, "Unequal Funding: Leveling the Playing Field for Families in the Poorest School Districts," *Journal of Early Education and Family Review* (January–February 2002) pp. 35–36.

[20]Joseph T. Viteritti, "Will the Supreme Court's Decision in Zellman End the Debate?" *Education Next* (Summer 2002) pp. 24–33.

[21]Verstegen, "New Wave," pp. 243–250; and Chris Pipho, "The Scent of the Future," *Phi Delta Kappan* (September 1994), pp. 10–11; Kenneth Howe, Margaret Eisenhart, and Damian Bettebenner, "School Choice Crucible: A Case Study of Boulder Valley," *Phi Delta Kappan* (October 2001). pp. 137–146.

[22]Gerald W. Bracey, "The Eleventh Bracey Report on the Condition of Public Education," *Phi Delta Kappan* (October 2001), pp. 157–169; and Sikula, "Why Our Educational System Is Not Working," pp. 89–92; Bruce J. Biddle and David C. Berliner, "Unequal School Funding in the U.S." *Educational Leadership* (May 2002) pp. 48–59.

IN THIS CASE

Funding Woes

"Why did *our* school district lose state money this fall?" Karen said. "We live and work in a property-poor school district, Lemuel! We should be getting more state money per pupil than the wealthy districts. That's what the equity lawsuits were all about!"

"You're right, Karen, it's not fair. But that's the way it is. We both chose to work here," replied Lemuel, "but I know that loss of low-income families has decreased our state money. The new housing development for seniors is nice, but it certainly has caused our student enrollment to decline. My principal, Mr. Schoebel, says that we've lost more than two hundred students."

"We'll also lose federal money," he went on. "Many of these students qualify for free and reduced lunches and Title I programs. Other federal programs that bring money to this district link to low-income students as well. I think disabled students and bilingual students benefit from federal funds, but I'm not sure if there is any link between these groups and the low-income group."

Karen sighed, "I just wish that education received the priority it needs to serve all students well. I know that the money comes from local, state, and federal sources, but it seems that in this state, local government is paying more and more as time goes on."

"Homeowners here are carrying a large share of the budget through the property tax, too," noted Lemuel.

"That affects us renters. My landlord just sent around a letter telling his tenants that his property taxes had increased 12 percent. That's a huge increase, and he says he has to pass along the costs by raising our rent. Most of the increase comes with the new school district tax rate. The hospital and utility districts increased their taxes, too, but not much compared to the school district."

"Even with more from local taxes," noted Karen, "I think our school district still has less than other area schools. How will the administration respond to all of this? I'm guessing they'll increase class sizes in the upper grades and maybe postpone or cancel building renovations."

"I'll bet you're right, Karen," agreed Lemuel. "Wealthy districts have figured out ways to generate local money beyond property taxes. Several of them have established foundations. The millionaires that live in the community contribute heavily each year and get a tax write-off."

"Too bad we don't have a few more generous millionaires!" laughed Karen. Then, turning serious, she asked, "Do you think the revenue loss will affect us, as beginning teachers?"

"Probably not this year, but it may in the future. Most of a school's budget is in personnel. That's you and me. In the meantime, I guess the best thing we can do is just keep focusing on the students."

Questions

1. Why is it important for beginning teachers like Karen and Lemuel to have a basic understanding of school finance?

2. How does student enrollment relate to school financing in your state?

3. How does school district wealth relate to school financing in your state?

4. What percentages of your local school district's money are derived from local sources? From state sources? From federal sources? If you don't know, estimate the amounts. Then check to see how close your estimates are.

▶ Federal Education Funding

■ The changing federal role

Until the middle of the twentieth century, the federal government gave states (or local schools) little financial assistance in educating American students (see the Historical Development of American Education chapter). This attitude aligned with the majority belief that the federal government should have little to do with education, which was a state responsibility. Although certain national laws and federal programs had a significant impact on how education developed in the United States, these programs and acts were neither systematic nor part of a broadly conceived national plan for education. After the Soviet Union launched the *Sputnik* satellite in 1957, national policy became more closely linked to education and federal funding dramatically increased and focused on specific, targeted areas. Increased federal monies were allocated for improvement of science, mathematics, foreign language instruction, and for teacher education.

■ Civil Rights Act

From the mid-1960s through the 1970s, the full force of the federal government came into play to enforce U.S. Supreme Court decisions on school desegregation. The impetus came from the Civil Rights Act of 1964, which provided that all programs supported by federal funds must be administered and operated without discrimination, or all federal funds were to be withheld.

■ Programs for diverse groups

In addition to these desegregation efforts, the educational needs of minority groups and women received considerable attention and funding from the mid-1960s to the late 1970s. Diverse groups such as bilingual students, African Americans, Native Americans, low-income students, and students with disabilities were targeted for special programs.

Current Trends in Federal Aid to Education

The 1980s brought a new conservatism at the federal level, and the federal contribution since then has represented a smaller percentage of total school financing (compare Table 8.1 with Figure 8.1). During the 1980s, school funding methods also changed. **Categorical grants** (funds for specific groups and designated purposes) gave way to **block grants** (funds for a general purpose without precise categories). This move was part of a "new federalism" that shifted responsibility for many federal social and educational programs from the national to state governments.

Standards & Assessment ✔

More recently, the trend has again shifted. Since the advent of No Child Left Behind in 2002, block grants to states have been eliminated in favor of federal funding specifically targeted to student academic achievement and teacher quality. States must document increases in student academic performance yearly at elementary and middle-school levels, using accepted achievement tests (such as the Iowa Test of Basic Skills, California Achievement Test, and Competency Test of Basic Skills). Additionally, principals must notify parents if their child is not being taught by a "highly qualified teacher." Federal funding to states has lagged behind states' needs to cover the costs of identifying and administering achievement tests and developing criteria to determine highly qualified teachers. This delay in funding has been frustrating to school officials at both state and local levels. Some critics call NCLB an "unfunded mandate," that is, a costly federal requirement that either partly or totally lacks sufficient federal funding.

■ Predictions for federal funding

As we move further into the new century, the federal government's role will probably increase in the area of technology (specifically computers) as well as in support for the infrastructure necessary to upgrade aging and deteriorating schools. Federal support has increased for national achievement tests in content disciplines, which, if enacted, could drive national curriculum standards. Other plans being considered or enacted at the federal level include:

- more emphasis on reading and mathematics achievement through No Child Left Behind, and the naming of a "reading czar";
- increased Head Start programs for disadvantaged preschoolers;

Table 8.1	Federal Funds for Elementary, Secondary, and Higher Education, 1970–2002	
Year	Amount (billions)	Amount adjusted for inflation (billions)
1970	$ 9.2	$ 6.8
1972	11.9	7.7
1974	13.1	8.7
1976	19.6	11.8
1978	21.6	12.0
1980	27.5	13.1
1982	26.8	11.6
1984	30.5	12.3
1986	33.7	13.9
1988	37.5	14.4
1990	45.3	15.3
1994	64.0	16.7
1997	73.0	17.4
2000	90.6	18.8
2002	102.2	19.8

Note: As a result of the Education Consolidation and Improvement Act in 1981, many programs and funds were shifted among various federal departments; the base of comparison has not been exactly the same since then.

Source: Digest of Education Statistics, 1980 (Washington, D.C.: National Center for Education Statistics, 1980), Table 160, pp. 184–186; *Digest of Education Statistics, 1982* (Washington, D.C.: National Center for Education Statistics, 1982), Tables 153–154, pp. 171–172; and *Digest of Education Statistics, 1990* (Washington, D.C.: National Center for Education Statistics, 1990), Table 327, p. 343. Amounts adjusted for inflation have been calculated by the authors on the basis of *Consumer Price Index: 1913–1990* (Washington, D.C.: Bureau of Labor Statistics, U.S. Department of Labor, 1990), pp. 1–3. See also *Digest of Education Statistics, 2002,* Table 349, pp. 370–373; and *Digest of Education Statistics, 2002,* Table 359.

- federal money to hire additional teachers to meet the teacher shortage; and
- money to improve the quality of teaching.[23]

Federal grants funding magnet schools will continue as a way to address racial imbalance within school districts. Concern is increasing at local, state, and federal levels regarding school violence and how to restore moral authority to America's public schools. Finally, as we discuss later in the chapter, school choice and vouchers remain popular alternative funding concepts with legislators, the public, and increasingly the courts. Pressure is increasing for choice between public education and private school alternatives by parents dissatisfied with public schools and by economically disadvantaged students living in subpar (often urban) school districts. In Milwaukee, Wisconsin, and Cleveland, Ohio, for example, state money pays parochial school tuition for low-income students. Now that the U.S. Supreme Court

---

[23]Mike Bowler, "President Concedes Loss on Vouchers," *The Sun,* May 2, 2001, pp. A1, 9; Thomas McDonald and William Bainbridge, "No Child Left Behind: Facts and Fallacies," *Phi Delta Kappan* (June 2002), pp. 781–782.

has approved vouchers for private-school students, less public money may be available for public education.[24]

R E F O C U S Do you believe that the federal government contributes sufficient support to public education in the United States? Explain your position.

▶ School Finance Trends

Financial crises in education sometimes make the headlines. For example, national recessions in the early 1990s and again in the early 2000s triggered state revenue shortfalls. Coupled with rising costs and other budgetary problems, the loss of state revenue placed many local school districts in a bleak fiscal situation. Although such crises may come and go with changes in the economy and in federal and state budgets, several long-lasting concerns about school finance remain. As we examine current trends, keep in mind that educators today are being asked to show proof that they are spending public money wisely. To find out more about current school funding, see the Technology @ School box.

Taxpayer Resistance

■ Taxpayer initiatives

Beginning in the late 1970s, a tax revolt swept the country, putting a damper on the movement for school finance reform. In California a 1978 taxpayer initiative called Proposition 13 set a maximum tax of 1 percent on the fair market value of a property and limited increases in assessed valuation to 2 percent a year. By 2003, forty-five more states had imposed property tax limitations or direct controls on school spending.[25]

■ Results of taxpayer resistance

As a result of this **taxpayer resistance**, thirty-five states have introduced *circuit-breaker* programs that give selected populations (such as older persons and first-time homeowners) a credit for property taxes paid.

■ The current climate

The late twentieth-century educational reform movement emphasized the need to improve the quality of education. Taxpayers seem willing to support increased education spending for that purpose, yet wary. They show much interest in results: what are we getting for the dollars we spend? This concern has led to increased educator accountability for the use of public funds.

Standards & Assessment ✓

The Accountability Movement

■ Responsibility for results

Although definitions of **accountability** vary, the term generally refers to the notion that teachers, administrators, school board members, and even students themselves must be held responsible for the results of their efforts. Teachers must meet some standard of competency, and schools must devise methods of relating expenditures to outcomes.

---

[24]Ronald Stephens, "Ten Steps to Safer Schools," *American School Board Journal* (March 1998), p. 30; Pete DuPont, "Wisconsin Ruling Gives Poor Students a Victory," *The Sun*, July 6, 1998, p. A9; Kenneth Howe et al., "The Price of Public School Choice," *Phi Delta Kappan* (April 2002) p. 20.

[25]John Augenblick, *School Finance: A Primer* (Denver: Education Commission of the States, 1991); and Richard McAdams, "Mark, Yen, Buck, Pound: Money Talks," *American School Board Journal* (July 1994), pp. 35–36; see also the Sales Tax Clearinghouse (2003) at **http:theSTC.com/STrates.stm**.

Finding School Financing Information on the Web

As a teacher you should remain informed about issues and trends in school financing. As discussed in this chapter, financing decisions at every level of government can affect daily activities in your classroom.

Visit your local school district Web site. (See **www.nasbe.org**; click on "links to state education agencies" and select your state. From your state agency's site, click on "county" or "school district" or "find a school.") Although not all school district Web sites include district budget information, educational goals are usually tied to fiscal goals. Look for information about priority educational issues, such as student testing, technology initiatives, special education, gifted and talented programs, and building construction and maintenance. How do these initiatives or programs affect local district budgets?

Check your state education agency site. (Go to **www.nasbe.org**; click on "links to state education agencies" and select your state.) Look for Web page headings such as "budget" or "funding" or a search feature that will let you use these key terms. What funding priorities do you see at the state department of education level? How do these priorities resemble and differ from local budget priorities and issues?

Examine the U.S. Department of Education Web site at **www.ed.gov**. Click on "site map" and explore links such as "President and Secretary's priorities," "news and events," "programs and services," "No Child Left Behind," and "state education agencies." In addition, consult the Web site of the nonpartisan Education Commission for the States at **www.ecs.org** for "daily news roundup," "e-clips and e-connections," "Congress and Bush education plan," "education issues," "early learning," and "K–12." Another good source for school finance information is the OERI (Office of Educational Research and Improvement) at **http:www.ed.gov/offices/OERI**. How do federal funding priorities and issues resemble and differ from state and local priorities and issues? Of all these fiscal priorities and issues, which do you believe are most important to educating children, and why?

■ Reasons for the accountability movement

The accountability movement stems from various factors. In recent years, more parents have realized that schooling is important for success and that their children are failing to learn sufficiently well. As the cost of education has increased, parents demand to know what they are paying for. Taxpayers, who want to keep the lid on school spending, wish to hold educators responsible for the outcomes of instruction.[26]

■ Federal and state measures

In addition, federal funding is now contingent upon evidence of satisfactory educational progress. The No Child Left Behind Act requires statewide assessment programs in reading and mathematics for all children in grades 3 through 8. In addition, many states and districts have introduced testing programs in other content areas and at other grade levels to measure students' performance and the cost-effectiveness of teaching.[27] Some states have declared underachieving schools as "failed" and subject to reconstitution (complete reorganization) or actual takeover by either the state or private groups such as universities or private businesses. Other states are

[26]Liz Bowie and Stephen Henderson, "Pupils Lose Ground in City Schools," *The Sun*, November 12, 1997, pp. A1, 12; Tony Weaver, "Reinventing America's Schools," *Phi Delta Kappan* (May 2003) pp. 665–668.

[27]Telephone conversation with Steven Gorman, project director, National Assessment of Educational Progress, November 7, 1991; Allan Odden, "The New School Finance," *Phi Delta Kappan* (September 2001), pp. 85–91.

comparing school district test scores and using the results to cut funding or reward districts with additional monies.[28] States are also developing stringent criteria to determine highly qualified teachers. Parents who object to having their child taught by a less than qualified teacher may have their child transferred to another school in the district. These changes have drastic implications for school funding at both the state and local district level.

Many educators fear a simplified concept of accountability that places responsibility solely on the teacher or principal, ignoring the roles of parents, community residents, school board members, taxpayers, and the students themselves. No Child Left Behind has both positive and negative potential. It can foster accountability and bring parents, teachers, school administrators, and the community into meaningful discussions of student performance. Unfortunately, it also might foster a bureaucracy that will consume funding dollars and allow the federal government or states to withhold needed monies for school reform. The next few years will tell.

Tuition Tax Credits, Educational Vouchers, and School Choice

■ Tuition tax credits

Tuition tax credits allow parents to claim a tax reduction for part of tuition fees paid to private schools. In the early 1990s, Minnesota became the first state to employ tuition tax credits; other states now have tax credits or tax deductions under consideration.[29] The tax credit movement reflects the public's desire for increased choice in schools as well as the continuing quest of nonpublic schools for support. The issue has been brought to the fore, however, by wavering faith in the public schools.

■ Educational vouchers

Use of **educational vouchers** is another trend in school finance reform. Under a voucher system, the state or local school district gives parents of school-age children a voucher or flat grant representing their children's estimated educational cost. Children then use this voucher to attend a school of the family's choosing. Some plans allow choice only within the public school system, as is currently the case in Minnesota, Wisconsin, California, Massachusetts, and ten other states.[30] Other plans permit the use of vouchers in private schools. U.S. Supreme Court approval of the Cleveland voucher plan for low-income students, discussed earlier in this chapter, is certain to increase use of vouchers in private schools.[31]

■ Arguments against tax credit and voucher programs

Debates over tuition tax credits and voucher programs have been vigorous and emotional. The NEA, the AFT, and other educational organizations contend that vouchers or tax credits increase segregation, split the public along socioeconomic lines, and reduce financial support for the public schools.[32] Opponents have also

---

[28]Maryland State Department of Education, *MSDE Bulletin,* February 8, 2001, p. 1.
[29]Louis Fischer, David Schimmel, and Leslie Stellman, *Teachers and the Law,* 6th ed. (White Plains, N.Y.: Longman, 2003), p. 427; Joe Nathan and William L. Boyd, "Lessons About School Choice from Minnesota: Promise and Challenges," *Phi Delta Kappan* (January 2003), pp. 350–355.
[30]Joe Nathan and James Ysseldyke, "What Minnesota Has Learned About School Choice," *Phi Delta Kappan* (May 1994), pp. 682–688; U.S. Department of Education, National Center for Educational Statistics, *State Indicators in Education, 1997,* Washington, D.C.: National Center for Educational Statistics, 1997, p. 40.
[31]Fischer, Schimmel, and Kelly, *Teachers and the Law,* pp. 427–428; Benjamin Dowling-Sendor, "The Voucher Decision," *American School Board Journal* (October 2002), pp. 52–54; Charles J. Russo and Ralph D. Mawdsley, "The Supreme Court and Vouchers Revisited," *School Business Affairs* (January 2003), pp. 41–44
[32]Timothy McDonald, "The False Promise of Vouchers," *Educational Leadership* (April 2002) p. 33; Joanna Richardson, "Order Blocks Nonsectarian Expansion of Voucher Program," *Education Week* (September 13, 1995), p. 3.

argued that such programs provide unconstitutional support for church-related schools, undermine the public-school system by supporting and encouraging the movement of students to nonpublic schools, and produce a large drain on public-school budgets or state treasuries.[33]

■ Choice and the "marketplace"

Proponents of tuition tax credits and vouchers generally link the issue with the concept of **school choice**, which is discussed in detail in the chapter on School Effectiveness and Reform in the United States. By widening the average person's choices for schooling, supporters contend, we can increase competition among schools and raise the overall level of educational quality. The idea is to depend on education to follow the laws of the marketplace: if students and parents can choose schools, the effective schools will stay in operation and the less desirable ones will either go out of business or improve.[34]

■ Arguments in favor

In addition, supporters of tuition tax credits and voucher programs argue that such credits are not unconstitutional and do not seriously reduce federal revenues or hamper public-school tax levy efforts. They also argue that these programs provide wider opportunity for students to attend schools outside the inner city; thus tax credits or vouchers do not contribute to, and might even reduce, racial and socioeconomic isolation. Many supporters also believe that tax credits or vouchers, besides providing parents with a choice in selecting schools, stimulate public-school improvement, particularly when families have choices within the public-school district.[35]

■ Charter schools

A variation on the school choice theme is the concept of *charter schools,* discussed in the chapter on Governing and Administering Public Education. In exchange for freedom from hundreds of rules and regulations, charter schools are held accountable for specific academic results and risk losing their charter if they fail to attain their academic goals.[36] Most charter-school organizers face significant budget challenges. Many school boards are frugal in allocating operating funds for charter schools, fearing a financial drain on already tight budgets.

Streamlining School Budgets

■ School budget scrutiny

In an era of taxpayer wariness, accountability demands, and strain on state budgets, school boards are being pressed to eliminate unnecessary spending before recommending tax increases. Not only must school outcomes measure up to expected standards, but the budget must stand up to close scrutiny. Corporate leaders often serve on school boards, and the gospel of streamlining and efficiency—so prevalent in the business community—has had considerable impact on American education. We should continue to see the following significant trends.

■ New research on class size

1. *Class size.* Research on class size, conducted by the Department of Education's Office of Educational Research and Improvement, shows that "smaller is bet-

[33]Daniel U. Levine and Rayna F. Levine, *Society and Education,* 9th ed. (Needham Heights, Mass.: Allyn and Bacon, 1996); Carol A. Langdon, "The Third Phi Delta Kappa Poll of Teachers' Attitudes Toward the Public Schools," *Phi Delta Kappan* (November 1996), pp. 244–250; and Kathleen M. S. Caire, "The Truth About Vouchers," *Educational Leadership* (April 2002), p. 38.

[34]See, for instance, William L. Boyd and Herbert J. Walberg, eds., *Choice in Education* (Berkeley, Calif.: McCutchan, 1990); Joseph Murphy, ed., *The Educational Reform Movement of the 1980s* (Berkeley, Calif.: McCutchan, 1990); and David Osborne, "Schools Got Scary," *Mother Jones* (January–February 1996), pp. 47–48.

[35]John Weisman, "Revolutionary Steps to Better Education," *Fortune,* October 21, 1991, pp. 128–129; and Michael Bowler, "Vouchers," *The Sun,* May 2, 2001, pp. A1, 9.

[36]Carol Ascher and Arthur Greenberg, "Charter Reform and the Education Bureaucracy," *Phi Delta Kappan* (March 2002), pp. 506–512.

tcr," and that smaller classes in the early grades lead to higher student achievement. These significant effects on achievement occur when class size is reduced to a point between fifteen and twenty students. This may lead to a nationwide concerted effort to reduce class size.[37]

■ Maintaining old facilities

2. *Modernization of older buildings.* Rather than build new schools, many districts are choosing to save money by maintaining and modernizing their older buildings. As we will see, however, in the next section, old buildings can cause budgetary strains of their own.[38]

■ Smaller, more efficient buildings

3. *Smaller schools.* In many areas the trend is toward smaller school buildings, which make more efficient use of space, require less fuel and lighting, are easier to maintain, and require fewer administrators.[39]

■ Adding more teachers

4. *Need for teachers.* Whereas selected areas of the country may be laying off teachers because of population decline, other areas, particularly suburban areas and Sunbelt states, are experiencing a population boom in the schools. Add to this an aging teaching corps, and projections are that schools will need more than 2.2 million new teachers by 2010.

■ Streamlining central staffs

5. *Administrative reductions.* Many districts are finding it possible to operate with smaller central office staffs. These reductions cause much less public outcry than when the teaching force is cut.

■ Reducing energy costs

6. *Energy economies.* Some schools dial down temperatures, delay warming up the school each morning, reduce heat in the hallways, and buy energy directly from gas and oil distributors.

School Infrastructure and Environmental Problems

■ Deteriorating facilities

The nation's **school infrastructure** is in critical disrepair. By infrastructure we mean the basic physical facilities of the school plant (plumbing, sewer, heat, electric, roof, carpentry, and so on). Building experts estimate that schools in the United States are deteriorating faster than they can be repaired and faster than most other public facilities. Plumbing, electrical wiring, and heating systems in many schools are dangerously out of date; roofing is below code; and exterior brickwork, stone, and wood are in serious disrepair. In the mid-1990s, the Government Accounting Office estimated the accumulated cost to repair public schools at $112 billion, a staggering increase over earlier projections.[40] Some of the largest school districts reported that an average of 85 percent of their schools needed repairs to bring them up to "good condition."[41]

---

[37]Jean Johnson, "Will Parents and Teachers Get on the Bandwagon to Reduce School Size," *Phi Delta Kappan* (January 2002), pp. 353–356; Robert Hampel, "Historical Perspectives on Small Schools," *Phi Delta Kappan* (January 2002), pp. 357–363.
[38]"Clinton Stands Firm on U.S. School Fixes," *The Sun*, October 1, 2000, p. A3; David Haney and Mark Schmidt, "Support for School Construction," pp. 34–37: Theodore J. Kowalski and Robert Schmielau, "Potential for States to Provide Equality in Funding School Construction," *Equity and Excellence in Education* (September 2001), pp. 54–61.
[39]Thomas Sergiovanni, "Small Schools, Great Expectations," *Educational Leadership* (November 1995), pp. 48–52; Hempel, "Historical Perspectives," pp. 357–363; Sandy Catshall, "Is Smaller Better? When It Comes to Schools, Size Does Matter," *Techniques: Connecting Education and Careers* (March 2003), pp. 22–25.
[40]Allan C. Ornstein, "School Finance and the Condition of Schools," *Theory into Practice* (Spring 1994), pp. 118–125; Catherine Sielke, "Funding School Infrastructure: Needs Across the States," *Journal of Education Finance* (Fall 2001), pp. 653–662.
[41]Government Accounting Office, *School Facilities: Profiles of School Condition by State* (Washington, D.C.: U.S. Government Printing Office, 1996).

School boards are being pressed to eliminate unnecessary spending, and school budgets must stand up to close scrutiny. Many districts are trying to "do more with less," in spite of demands for smaller classes, teacher shortages, and deteriorating old school buildings. (© Kevin Horan/Stock Boston)

■ Asbestos cleanup

Environmental hazards in school buildings are a special problem. For example, the Environmental Protection Agency (EPA) has ordered government and commercial property owners, including school districts, to clean up buildings laden with asbestos. Although the costs are hard to calculate, one estimate placed the bill for schools at $3.1 billion, which would cover some 45,000 schools in 3,100 districts.[42]

■ Additional hazards

Additional hazards such as radon gas, lead paint, and seismic upgrades also represent drains on school monies in many districts.

■ More classrooms will be needed

Even as school boards struggle to meet the needs of an aging infrastructure, the U.S. Census Bureau has modified its projections for the growth of the school-age population. Using 2000 census figures as a baseline, the bureau now expects the school-age population to remain steady through 2010. Public secondary-school enrollment is expected to rise by 4 percent during the same decade. This prediction is based on current fertility and immigration rates. Repairs aside, concern is growing about where the money will come from to build the additional classrooms we continue to need.[43]

 **REFOCUS** How do you feel about plans to link student progress on yearly achievement tests to federal funding? What are the pros and cons of this funding approach?

---

[42]Catherine C. Sielke, "Financing School Infrastructure: What Are the Options? *School Business Affairs* (December 2001), pp. 12–15; Julie Wakefield, "Learning the Hard Way: The Poor Environment of America's Schools," *Environmental Health Perspectives* (June 2002), pp. A298–A305.

[43]*Digest of Educational Statistics, 2000,* Table 3; Faith Crampton and David C. Thompson, "The Condition of America's Schools: A National Disgrace," *School Business Affairs* (December 2002), pp. 12–15.

▶ Summing Up

1 Schools are financially supported by state and local governments and to a lesser extent by the federal government. Overall, since the early twentieth century, state support has increased dramatically and local support has declined; the percentage of federal support grew until the 1980s and then declined.

2 Although the property tax is the main local source of school revenue, it is considered a regressive tax.

3 There is wide variation in the financial ability among states and within states (at the local district level) to support education. Poorer school districts tend to receive more money from the state than do wealthier school districts, but the amount rarely makes up for the total difference in expenditures.

4 School finance reform, initiated by the courts and carried forward by state legislatures, has attempted to reduce or eliminate funding disparities between poorer and wealthier districts. The basic goal is to equalize educational opportunities and give poorer districts the means to improve their performance.

5 Since the *Sputnik* era, federal funding of education has become increasingly linked to national policy. But since the 1980s, some responsibility for educational funding has shifted from the federal government back to the individual states.

6 Controversies over accountability, tuition tax credits, educational vouchers, charter schools, and school choice reflect increasing public dissatisfaction with the educational system.

7 Taxpayer resistance, especially to increases in property taxes, results in strong pressure to streamline school budgets.

8 Deteriorating school infrastructure and environmental dangers pose significant problems for many schools.

▶ Key Terms

progressive taxes (225)
regressive taxes (225)
property tax (225)
mill (226)
user fees (226)
exclusive product rights (226)
tax base (227)
municipal overburden (227)
sales tax (229)

personal income tax (229)
categorical grants (235)
block grants (235)
taxpayer resistance (237)
accountability (237)
tuition tax credits (239)
educational voucher (239)
school choice (240)
school infrastructure (241)

▶ Discussion Questions

1 How could school boards and local elected officials design a tax structure that is fair and equitable and capable of keeping abreast of changing economic conditions? What specific elements would make up this tax code?

2 State your reasons for or against the following types of financial support for school choice:

(a) Government vouchers that any student can use to pay tuition in any accredited school, public or private

(b) Vouchers as in (a), but issued only to students whose families demonstrate financial need

(c) No vouchers for private or parochial schools, though students are free to choose any *public* schools they like

3 What do you see as the pros and cons of corporate/school partnerships, such as educational Channel One and curriculum materials with advertisements?

▶ Suggested Projects for Professional Development

1 Survey taxpayers (parents, neighbors, classmates, coworkers) about their attitudes toward school taxes. To what extent do they resist such taxes? For what reasons, or under what conditions, might they be willing to pay more? Do you notice any differences of opinion among various age groups, ethnic groups, income groups, or social classes? Summarize your findings for the class.

2 In your visits to schools this term, be alert to infrastructure concerns. What specific problems do you see, and what do the students and faculty complain about? Are circumstances significantly better or worse in neighboring districts? If so, how do people account for these differences? Keep notes on your findings in a journal.

3 Examine several weeks' worth of the state and local news section of your daily paper (hard copy or via the Web) for articles relating to school finance. Do these articles support or criticize the current system? Do they agree with any of the points of view presented in this chapter, or do they take a different approach? Share your findings with the class.

4 Visit your state department of education Web site (see **bcol02.ed.gov/Programs/EROD/ org_list.cfm?category_ID=SEA**) to discover how public education is financed in your state. Look for charts or tables that specify local, state, and federal contributions. Does your state have a school assessment plan based on student performance outcomes? Does it have a means for taking control of districts that fail to meet state standards?

5 Gather position papers and policy statements from several agencies concerned with school finance: for instance, the local teacher's association or union, the state department of education, and local citizens' organizations. Supplement the written materials by interviewing representatives from at least two of the groups. List the main themes that emerge.

6 Interview a local school board member regarding the following:

- Concerns about funding and the budget process

- His or her most important budget priorities

- Creative ways to address budget problems

- How public support for the budget is built, once the budget is established

7 Visit the U.S. Census Bureau Web site and examine "Model-Based Income and Poverty Estimates for Baltimore City, Maryland, in 1999"(**www.census.gov/hhes/www/saipe/ stcty/estimate.html**) and "Montgomery County, Maryland, in 1999." Each of these is a Maryland school district and among the largest school districts in the United States. Note the following:

- Percentage of all ages in poverty

- Percentage of people under age eighteen in poverty

- Percentage of related children ages five to seventeen of families in poverty

- Median household income

What do these statistics tell you about these two school districts in terms of taxpayer ability to support schools, need for special education services, and programs for disadvantaged students? Does your state include two counties with which you can compare these statistics?

▶ Suggested Resources

 Internet Resources

Many up-to-date statistics on school finance are available in the yearly federal publications *The Condition of Education* and the *Digest of Education Statistics,* both of which are available through the U.S. Department of Education's Web site (**http:www.ed.gov**). Also consult the National Center for Educational Statistics at **nces.ed.gov/programs/digest/**. In addition, several topics in this chapter—such as "education vouchers," "school choice," and "tuition tax credits,"—can be researched at federal government Internet sites, particularly **www.ed.gov**. Also consult the nonpartisan site of the Education Commission for the States at **www.ecs.org**.

Publications

Augenblick, John. *School Finance: A Primer.* Denver: Education Commission of the States, 1991. *Examines various existing approaches to financing schools and proposes alternatives.*

Bosworth, Matthew. *Courts as Catalysts: State Supreme Courts and Public School Finance Equity.* Albany: State University of New York Press, 2001. *An examination of recent state supreme court decisions regarding school financing.*

Guthrie, James W., Walter I. Garms, and Lawrence C. Pierce. *School Finance and Education Policy.* Englewood Cliffs, N.J.: Prentice-Hall, 1988. *A comprehensive examination of various methods for distributing resources and services for public schools.*

Howard, Nelson. *Venturesome Capital: State Charter School Finance Systems.* Jessup, Md.: U.S. Office of Educational Research and Improvement, 2000. *A comprehensive examination of the states' financing of charter schools in the United States.*

Mulholland, Lori A., and Louann A Bierlein. *Understanding Charter Schools.* Bloomington, Ind.: Phi Delta Kappa Educational Foundation, 1995. *An excellent book on the emerging concept of charter schools in the United States.*

Odden, Allen R., and Lawrence O. Picus. *School Finance: A Policy Perspective,* 2nd ed. New York: McGraw-Hill, 2000. *An examination of school productivity formulas, fiscal policy, and fiscal federalism.*

Ravitch, Diane. *City Schools: Lessons from New York.* Baltimore: Johns Hopkins University Press, 2000. *A conservative examination of the financial and socioeconomic aspects of New York City public and charter schools.*

Rotberg, Iris C., James J. Harvey, Kelly E. Wormer, and Nancy Rizor. *Federal Policy Options for Improving the Education of Low-Income Students.* Santa Monica, Calif.: Rand, 1994. *Examines the inequalities in school finance and their impact on poor children in public-school districts.*

Swanson, Austin D., and Richard A. King. *School Finance: Its Economics and Politics.* New York: Longman, 1991. *Discusses the hows and whys of school finance decisions.*

Uchitelle, Susan. "School Choice," in Donovan R. Walling, ed., *Hot Buttons: Unraveling 10 Controversial Issues in Education.* Bloomington, Ind.: Phi Delta Kappa Educational Foundation, 1997. *Features many of the arguments behind school choice and issues such as vouchers and tuition tax credits.*

Ward, James G., and Patricia Anthony. *Who Pays for Student Diversity?* Newbury, Calif.: Sage/Corwin Press, 1992. *Argues that school finance policy can be a source of social justice and equity funding for students at risk.*

Chapter 9

Legal Aspects of Education

During the past fifty years, the courts have increasingly been asked to resolve issues relating to public education in the United States. This rise in educational litigation reflects the fact that education has assumed a greater importance in our society than it had a few decades ago. The growth in litigation has been paralleled, and to some extent spurred on, by an enormous increase in state and federal legislation affecting education.

This chapter presents a general overview of the U.S. court system and examines the legal topics and court decisions that have most affected today's schools and teachers. The major topics considered are the rights and responsibilities of both teachers and students, and religion and the schools.[1] Questions to consider as you read this chapter include the following:

FOCUS QUESTIONS

- What legal rights and responsibilities do teachers have?
- What are the legal rights of students?
- Can religious activities be conducted in public schools?
- Can the government assist nonpublic schools?

---

[1]Other chapters of this book also discuss selected legal issues in education. For court decisions regarding school finance, see the chapter on Financing Public Education. Desegregation law and legislation regarding special education are considered in the chapter on Providing Equal Educational Opportunity.

▶ The Court System

Cases involving education-related issues can be heard either in federal or state courts, depending on the allegations of the **plaintiffs** (the persons who sue). Federal courts decide cases that involve federal laws and regulations or constitutional issues. State courts adjudicate cases that involve state laws, state constitutional provisions, school board policies, or other nonfederal problems. Most cases pertaining to elementary and secondary education are filed in state courts. However, to keep from overburdening court calendars, both federal and state courts usually require that prospective **litigants** (the parties in a lawsuit) exhaust all administrative avenues available for resolution before involving the court system.

State Courts

State court organization has no national uniformity. The details of each state's judicial system are found in its constitution. At the lowest level, most states have a court of original jurisdiction (often called a municipal or superior court) where cases are tried. The facts are established, evidence is presented, witnesses testify and are cross-examined, and appropriate legal principles are applied in rendering a verdict.

The losing side may appeal the decision to the next higher level, usually an intermediate appellate court. This court reviews the trial record from the lower court and additional written materials submitted by both sides. The appellate court is designed to ensure that appropriate laws were properly applied, that they fit with the facts presented, and that no deprivation of constitutional rights occurred.

If one side remains unsatisfied, another appeal may be made to the state's highest court, often called its supreme court. A state supreme court decision is final unless a question involving the U.S. Constitution has been raised. The side wishing to appeal further may then petition the U.S. Supreme Court to consider the case.

Federal Courts

Federal courts are organized into a three-tiered system: district courts, circuit courts of appeals, and the Supreme Court. The jurisdiction and powers of these courts are set forth in the Constitution and are subject to congressional restrictions. The lowest level, the district court, holds trials. For appeals at the next federal level, the nation is divided into twelve regions called circuits. Each circuit court handles appeals only from district courts within its particular geographic area. Unsuccessful litigants may request that the U.S. Supreme Court review their case. If four of the nine justices agree, the Supreme Court will take the case; if not, the appellate court ruling stands.[2]

Decisions of a court below the U.S. Supreme Court have force only in the geographic area served by that particular court. For this reason, it is possible to find conflicting rulings in different circuits. Judges often look to previous case law for guidance in rendering decisions, and they may find precedent for a variety of legally defensible positions on a single issue.

The First and the Fourteenth Amendments.   Although education is considered a state responsibility, it has produced an abundance of federal litigation, particularly in connection with the First and Fourteenth Amendments to the U.S. Constitution.

---

[2]Some case citations in this chapter include the term *cert. denied.* This means that the losing parties petitioned the U.S. Supreme Court for review, but their request was denied.

The First Amendment concerns freedom of religion, speech, press, and assembly and the right "to petition the government for redress of grievances." Many First Amendment cases have dealt with the role of religion in public education and with the extent of protection guaranteed to freedom of expression by students and teachers. Two First Amendment clauses are frequently cited in lawsuits: the **establishment clause**, which prohibits the establishment of a government-sanctioned religion, and the **free exercise clause**, which protects rights of free speech and expression. To interpret these clauses, the courts generally use the criteria or "tests" shown in Figure 9.1.

■ Fourteenth Amendment

Court cases involving the Fourteenth Amendment often focus on the section declaring that no state shall "deprive any person of life, liberty, or property, without due process of law; nor deny to any person within its jurisdiction the equal protection of the law." The first part of this passage is known as the **due process clause**, and the second part as the **equal protection clause**. Fourteenth Amendment cases have addressed the issue of school desegregation as well as the suspension and expulsion of students. Litigants citing the Fourteenth Amendment must show that a "liberty" or a "property" interest is a major element in the case. A liberty interest is involved if "a person's good name, reputation, honor or integrity is at stake." A property interest may arise from legal guarantees granted to tenured employees; for instance, teachers beyond the probationary period have a property interest in continued employment. Similarly, students have a property interest in their education. If either a liberty or a property interest is claimed, a school district must provide due

■ Liberty and property interests

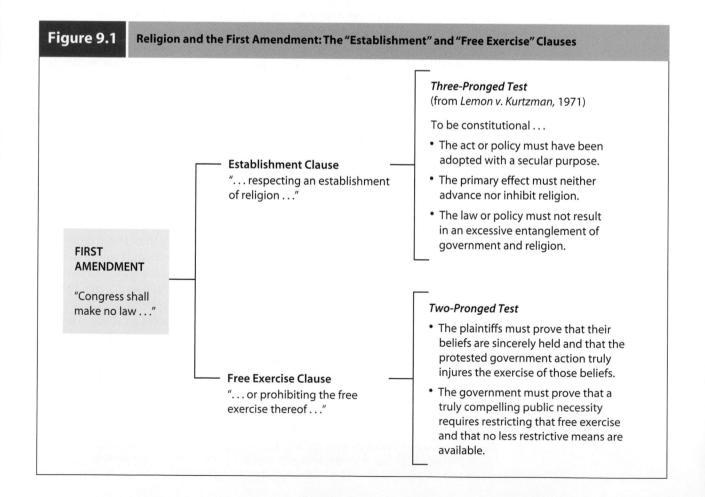

| **Figure 9.1** | Religion and the First Amendment: The "Establishment" and "Free Exercise" Clauses |

FIRST AMENDMENT

"Congress shall make no law . . ."

Establishment Clause
". . . respecting an establishment of religion . . ."

Three-Pronged Test
(from *Lemon v. Kurtzman,* 1971)

To be constitutional . . .

- The act or policy must have been adopted with a secular purpose.
- The primary effect must neither advance nor inhibit religion.
- The law or policy must not result in an excessive entanglement of government and religion.

Free Exercise Clause
". . . or prohibiting the free exercise thereof . . ."

Two-Pronged Test

- The plaintiffs must prove that their beliefs are sincerely held and that the protested government action truly injures the exercise of those beliefs.
- The government must prove that a truly compelling public necessity requires restricting that free exercise and that no less restrictive means are available.

process to the people involved. The rest of this chapter will explore the use of these and other legal concepts in actual school settings.

▶ Teachers' Rights and Responsibilities

As pointed out in the chapter on The Teaching Profession, teachers historically were vulnerable to dismissal by local boards of education for virtually any reason and without recourse. Collective negotiation statutes, tenure laws, mandatory due-process procedures, and other legal measures have been established to curb such abuses and to guarantee teachers certain rights. Along with rights come responsibilities, and many of these, too, have been written into law.

Testing and Investigation of Applicants for Certification or Employment

■ Background checks

Almost everywhere in the United States, individuals who wish to teach in grades K–12 must possess teaching certificates, which are usually granted by the state. In recent years many states have passed legislation requiring thorough background checks of prospective teachers, and some extend this requirement to currently employed teachers seeking recertification. For example, New York now requires that all candidates for certification be fingerprinted as part of a check for criminal histories. Some states share background information about candidates for government positions electronically.[3]

This trend has been fueled by two complementary developments. On the one hand, technology has made it more feasible to use fingerprints and other information sources in checking with local, state, and federal law enforcement agencies. On the other hand, the public has become increasingly concerned about dangers posed by child molesters and potential school employees with other criminal records.

Standards & Assessment ☑

■ Nondiscrimination requirements

As described in the chapter on Motivation, Preparation, and Conditions for the Entering Teacher, states require, in addition to background checks, that prospective teachers pass one or more competency tests for certification. In some cases, current teachers also must pass competency tests for continued employment. States where minority candidate passing rates are considerably lower than those for nonminorities have faced several lawsuits charging that specific tests discriminate against minority applicants. To answer such a lawsuit, employers must be able to specify the characteristics a test measures, establish that these characteristics are necessary in carrying out the job, and demonstrate that the test correlates with the work behavior in question.

Most lawsuits charging that teacher tests are discriminatory have either failed or been withdrawn because the available data did not demonstrate a clear pattern of discrimination or an intent to discriminate. On the other hand, worries about possible legal challenges, particularly from minority candidates, undoubtedly have occasionally led states to keep passing scores low. For example, concerns regarding a legal challenge alleging discrimination in part led the Massachusetts State Board of Education to substantially reduce the minimum score required to pass a proposed certification test in that state.[4]

---

[3]"Collecting Criminal Background Information From More Than One State" (2002), paper posted at the Commerce Clearing House Internet site, available at **www.hr.cch.com:** search for "background check."

[4]Kevin C. McDowell, "Teacher Competency Tests," *State Educator Standard* (Winter 2000), available at **www.nasbe.org/Standard**; and Diana Pullin, "Key Questions in Implementing Teacher Testing and Licensing," *Journal of Law and Education* (July 2001), pp. 383–429.

Employment Contracts and Tenure

In choosing which teachers to hire, local school boards must comply with laws that prohibit discrimination with respect to age, sex, race, religion, or national origin. Upon appointment, the teacher receives a written contract to sign. The contract may specify that the teacher must adhere to school board policies and regulations. If the school district has negotiated with a teacher organization, the provisions of that agreement apply as well.

■ Breach of contract

Contracts are binding on both parties. When one side fails to perform as agreed—called a **breach of contract**—the contract is broken. In such instances, the party that breached the contract may be sued for damages. Some states permit a teacher's certificate to be revoked if the teacher breaches the contract. If a school district breaks a contract, teachers may be awarded payments for damages or be reinstated to their former positions.

■ Terms of tenure

Nearly every state also has some type of tenure law. **Tenure** provides job security for teachers by preventing their dismissal without cause. Each state defines "cause"; the usual reasons include incompetency, immorality, insubordination, and unprofessional conduct. In addition, as explained in the next section, the school district must follow due process if it wishes to dismiss a tenured teacher.

■ History of tenure

From its inception, the notion of tenure has been controversial. Arguments for and against tenure are presented in this chapter's Taking Issue box.

■ Continuing employment

Once granted tenure, rather than sign an annual contract, many teachers are employed under a **continuing contract**. The term means that their reemployment for the next year is guaranteed unless school officials give notice by a specific date that the contract will not be renewed.

■ Probationary period

Most states have a probationary period before teachers achieve tenure. Moreover, many tenured teachers who change districts lose their tenure and must serve another period of probation. The probationary period often consists of three years of consecutive, satisfactory service, but some states have been moving to establish much shorter periods, at the end of which new teachers can be quickly removed from their jobs.

Probationary contracts in some states allow the teacher to be discharged at the end of the contract term for any reason and without explanation—no due process is required, unless the teacher can demonstrate that his or her dismissal involves a constitutionally guaranteed liberty or property interest. (See the next section for information on the meaning of due process.) In other states, probationary teachers have general due-process rights, but the process may be streamlined to expedite dismissal of candidates rated as incompetent.[5]

Due Process in Dismissal of Teachers

■ "Fairness" in teacher dismissal

Due process refers to the use of legal rules and principles established to protect the rights of the accused. These principles are especially important to a teacher being dismissed from the job. The core element of due process is "fairness." Although re-

---

[5]Perry A. Zirkel, "Old-Fashioned Teaching," *Phi Delta Kappan* (February 1996), pp. 449–451; Susan B. Reis, "Teacher Tenure in Pennsylvania" (2000), paper prepared for the Pennsylvania Education Policy Center, available at **www.ed.psu.edu/pepc/TenurePart2.html**; and Richard Vacca, "Teacher Tenure Under Fire," *CEPI Education Law Newsletter* (February 2003), available at **www.cepi.vcu.edu/newsletter**. For sample material, see "Non-renewal of Teacher Contracts," undated posting at the Association of Texas Professional Educators Internet site, available at **www.atpe.org**: search for "non-renewal."

taking issue

Question Should the tenure system for teachers continue?

Tenure for Teachers

At one time, many teaching positions in large cities were controlled by political patronage. In some cities, principalships were available for a price at the ward committeeman's office, and teaching jobs were won or lost on the basis of precinct work. In general, teachers were afraid to contradict an administrator or an influential parent. Tenure was introduced partly to stop these abuses and to give teachers independence in and out of the classroom. However, some educators now contend that the tenure system has outlived its usefulness.

Arguments PRO

1 Teaching is, by its nature, controversial. A good teacher cannot help but offend someone at some level. Teachers can do their jobs properly only with the academic freedom that tenure helps to protect.

2 A tenure system does not protect incompetence. Procedures exist for removing a teacher who is clearly ineffective. The responsibility for teacher incompetence lies with lax state licensing procedures and with administrators who are too reluctant to dismiss teachers during probationary periods.

3 Teachers must cope with pressure from a bewildering array of sources, including parents, other community members, administrators, and legislators. A complaint from any one of these parties might lead to a teacher's dismissal. For this reason, teachers need—and deserve—the special protection offered by tenure.

4 Tenure was originally a response to serious political and administrative abuses, especially in large cities. The same forces that caused these problems still exist, and they will create similar abuses if the protection of tenure is ever removed.

Arguments CON

1 Some teachers use their positions to advance personal, social, or political views under the guise of controversial discussion. Other teachers are simply lazy or incompetent. Often these marginal teachers—not the good teachers—benefit from tenure protection.

2 The procedures for removing a tenured teacher are often so complex and arouse so much resentment among other teachers that administrators are discouraged from trying. Furthermore, even with upgraded screening methods, many ineffective teachers will continue to slip through. The only solution is to give school officials, like private employers, the right to fire an unproductive employee.

3 The many sources of pressure actually enhance a teacher's security. Active parents and community members often use their influence to protect good teachers. The layers of school administration offer avenues of appeal if a teacher's position is threatened. Thus, even without a tenure system, competent teachers will be secure in their jobs.

4 Teachers now have powerful professional organizations that shield them from undue political and administrative interference. With these organizations looking after teachers' rights, the tenure system has become an anachronism.

■ Assistance for struggling teachers

quirements vary from state to state, the rules shown in Table 9.1 are generally recognized in cases of teacher dismissal.

Firing a teacher for incompetence requires documentation of efforts to help that person improve. Obtaining this documentation can be burdensome for everyone involved, and few tenured teachers are dismissed using formal legal procedures. Instead,

Table 9.1	Due-Process Rules for Dismissing a Tenured Teacher

1. The teacher must be given timely, detailed, written notice of the charges.
2. The teacher must be accorded a hearing and sufficient time to prepare.
3. The teacher has a right to be represented by legal counsel.
4. The teacher may present written and oral evidence, including witnesses.
5. The teacher may cross-examine witnesses and challenge evidence.
6. The hearing is to be conducted before an impartial body. The U.S. Supreme Court has ruled (in *Hortonville District v. Hortonville Education Association*) that under the U.S. Constitution a school board may be that impartial body unless bias can be proven.
7. The teacher is entitled to a written transcript of the proceedings.
8. The teacher has the right to appeal an adverse ruling to a higher legal authority, usually the state court system.

Source: *See* Hortonville District v. Hortonville Education Association, *426 U.S. 482 (1976); Janine M. Bernard, "Ethical and Legal Dimensions of Supervision," ERIC Digest (April 1994), pp. 1–4; Richard Rothstein, "Some Fair Steps to Take Before Firing Teachers," New York Times, June 26, 2002; and Richard S. Vacca, "Teacher Evaluation and the Courts," CEPI Education Law Newsletter (December 2003), available at* **www.cepi.vcu.edu/newsletter**.

■ Other procedures for removing teachers

administrators sometimes use less formal procedures for excluding incompetent teachers from their school districts. These procedures include counseling incompetent teachers out of the profession and suggesting and financing early retirement.[6]

Negotiation and Strikes

■ Most states allow negotiation

Teachers have the right to form and belong to unions and other professional organizations. Since the 1960s, such teacher groups have lobbied for state legislation to permit school boards to negotiate agreements with them. This effort has been successful in most states; however, a few continue to prohibit negotiations between teachers and school boards. Although the laws enacted vary widely, they usually allow the two sides to bargain collectively or at least to "meet and confer." Some states specify the procedure that must be followed if the two sides fail to agree (for example, fact-finding in Kansas; binding arbitration in Maryland).[7]

■ Penalties for striking

Because education is considered a vital public service, the law generally prohibits employee strikes. (A few states allow teachers to withhold services under specific conditions written into state law.) However, teachers sometimes do strike despite legal prohibitions. In such instances, school officials can seek court injunctions ordering teachers to return to their classrooms. Defiance of a court order can result in penalties. Florida and Minnesota, for example, prohibit striking teachers from receiving salary increases for one year after a strike; New York law allows striking teachers to be penalized two days' pay for each day on strike; and Michigan permits dismissal of striking teachers.

---

[6]Edwin M. Bridges, *Managing the Incompetent Teacher,* 2nd ed. (Eugene, Ore.: ERIC Clearinghouse on Educational Management, 1990). See also Steve Permuth and Robert Egley, "Letting Teachers Go—Legally," *Principal Leadership* (September 2002).

[7]Tom Loveless, ed., *Conflicting Missions* (Washington, D.C.: Brookings Institution, 2000); and Dan Weissmann, "Bargaining Rights Deal Key in Contract Talks," *Catalyst* (October 2002).

Protection Against Assault

■ Physical assault

In recent decades, physical assault on teachers and administrators has become an important problem at some schools, particularly secondary schools in big cities. In such cases, courts generally have convicted defendants who violated either educational statutes or state criminal codes. Some analysts have concluded that educators can help protect themselves and their fellow employees by vigorously pressing criminal charges and initiating civil suits for assault and battery. In addition, many school districts have developed policies that stress punishment of students who assault teachers and also assist teachers in pursuing legal responses. For example, the Cincinnati Board of Education has incorporated the following provisions in its contractual agreement with the district's teachers:[8]

■ Contractual protection

- A teacher may use such force as shall be reasonable and necessary to protect himself/herself from attack, to prevent school property from damage and/or destruction and/or to prevent injury to another person.

- A student who physically assaults a teacher who is performing a duty in the line of employment, including extracurricular activities, shall be immediately suspended.

Freedom of Expression

Courts have tended to uphold teachers' rights to express themselves in public or in school (see Overview 9.1). However, in determining whether the expression is "protected" under the First Amendment, the court considers the effects on school operation, teacher performance, teacher–superior relationships, and coworkers, as well as the appropriateness of the time, place, and manner of the teacher's remarks.

■ *Pickering:* protection of free expression

An example is the case of Marvin Pickering, a tenured high-school teacher who published a letter to the editor of the local newspaper criticizing the board and superintendent about bond proposals and expenditures. The letter resulted in his termination. In *Pickering v. Board of Education,* the U.S. Supreme Court held that publishing the letter did not impede the "proper performance of his daily duties in the classroom or . . . [interfere] with the regular operation of schools generally." For this reason, Pickering's dismissal was found to be improper.[9]

■ Impaired teacher effectiveness

On the other hand, two teachers in Alaska were dismissed for writing a letter that was highly critical of their superintendent and contained many false allegations. Reaction to the letter was immediate and prolonged. The Alaska Supreme Court held that the teachers' effectiveness had been impaired by their remarks and that their ability to work closely with colleagues had been diminished.[10]

■ Three-step analysis

A comparison of these cases shows that the decision rested not just on the behavior itself but also on its results. The courts have developed a three-step analysis for assessing teachers' rights to freedom of expression: (1) Did the teacher's

---

[8]Perry A. Zirkel and Ivan B. Gluckman, "Assaults on School Personnel," *NASSP Bulletin* (March 1991), p. 10; Kevin Bushweller, "The Return of Laura Marks," *Teacher Magazine* (November/December 2001), pp. 22–29; and "Cincinnati Federation," undated Internet posting at **www.aft.org/research/models/contracts/conindex.htm**.

[9]*Pickering v. Board of Education,* 391 U.S. 563 (1968). See also John Rukavina, "Pickering Still Rules Roost in First Amendment Law," *Fire Chief,* June 1, 2002, available at **www.firechief.com:** search for "Pickering."

[10]*Watts v. Seward School Board,* 454 P. 2d 732 (Alaska 1969), cert. denied, 397 U.S. 921 (1970). See also "Appellate Rulings Threaten Creative Teaching," *Censorship News Online* (Winter 1998–1999), available at **www.ncac.org**.

OVERVIEW 9.1 Selected U.S. Supreme Court Decisions Affecting Teachers' Rights and Responsibilities

Case	Summary of Decision
Pickering v. Board of Education (1968)	Teachers may speak their opinions as long as the school's regular operation is not disrupted.
Board of Regents of State Colleges v. Roth (1972)	After the probationary period, teachers have a property interest in continued employment.
Cleveland Board of Education v. LeFleur (1974)	Boards of education may establish leave policies for pregnant teachers, but these policies may not contain arbitrary leave and return dates.
Hortonville District v. Hortonville Education Association (1976)	In a due-process hearing a school board may be the impartial body conducting the hearing.
Washington v. Davis (1976)	Underrepresentation of a group in the work force does not, in itself, prove unconstitutional employment discrimination, but the employer in this situation must prove that hiring has not been discriminatory.
School Board of Nassau County v. Arline (1987)	Dismissing a teacher because of a physical impairment or contagious disease is unconstitutional.
Lehnert v. Ferris Faculty Association (1991)	Employees who are not union members cannot be required to pay dues used for political purposes unrelated to collective bargaining agreements.

expression of opinion involve a public matter of political, social, or other concern to the community? (2) If yes, courts still must weigh First Amendment rights against the employer's responsibility to promote a productive and harmonious climate for the delivery of education. Finally, (3) the teacher is entitled to judicial relief only if his or her expression of opinion can be shown to be a motivating factor in dismissal or other punitive action.[11]

■ Nonpublic teachers not necessarily protected

Pickering and similar decisions would not be applicable to teachers in schools not publicly funded. The civil rights of private- and parochial-school teachers—tenure, freedom of expression, due process, and the like—depend primarily on the terms of their individual contracts with the school.

■ Verbal abuse not condoned

Verbal and Emotional Abuse of Students.   Teachers' rights to freedom of expression do not extend, of course, to verbal or emotional abuse of students. Teachers can be sued and/or suspended or dismissed for engaging in such behavior. A teacher who also served as a basketball and football coach was accused of using terms (while coaching) such as "Tontos" in dealing with Native American students and "jungle bunnies" in referring to African American students. Although allowed to continue teaching science and physical education, he was suspended from coaching for unprofessional conduct. Other teachers have had their employment terminated or in-

---

[11]Benjamin Dowling-Sendor, "Is Speaking Out Cause for Dismissal?" *American School Board Journal* (March 1990), pp. 8, 46; "Academic Freedom and the Rights of Religious Faculty" (1999), paper posted at the Leadership U Internet site, available at **www.leaderu.com:** search for Whitehead; and Mark Walsh, "High Court Declines to Hear Two School Free-Speech Cases," *Education Week*, October 16, 2002.

terrupted for directing obscene curses at students they perceived as troublesome or for persistently using sarcasm and ridicule to pressure or embarrass students. Teachers also can be sued personally under civil liability or criminal statutes by parents who believe their children have been injured by verbal or emotional abuse.[12]

Academic Freedom

■ Challenges to books and other materials

Academic freedom refers to the teacher's freedom to choose subject matter and instructional materials relevant to the course without interference from administrators or outsiders. Recent years have witnessed hundreds of incidents in which parents or others have tried to remove or restrict use of public-school materials, including allegedly immoral or unwholesome works such as *Little Red Riding Hood*, the Harry Potter series, *Snow White, Huckleberry Finn*, and the *Goosebumps* series. Several courts have ruled that materials can be eliminated on the basis of vulgarity but not on censorship of ideas. Although the U.S. Supreme Court has not provided definitive rulings, it has emphasized that school officials must take account of the First Amendment. Teachers should consider the objections of parents who do not want their children to study specific materials, but they also must work with administrators to ensure that legitimate materials are not removed entirely from classrooms and libraries.[13]

■ Teachers upheld

Appeals courts have upheld a high-school teacher's right to assign a magazine article containing "a vulgar term for an incestuous son"; another teacher's use of a film in which citizens of a small town randomly killed one person each year; and elementary teachers' use of a literary anthology in which students were instructed to pretend they were witches and write poetic chants.[14]

■ Restrictions upheld

On the other hand, decisions of school officials to restrict teachers' academic freedom have sometimes been upheld. For example, a West Virginia art teacher was suspended for (unwittingly) distributing sexually explicit cartoons, an Ohio English teacher was prohibited from assigning the books *One Flew over the Cuckoo's Nest* and *Manchild in the Promised Land* to juvenile students unless their parents consented, and a North Carolina teacher was disciplined after her students performed a play containing adult language in a state drama competition.

■ Issues courts consider

In general, courts have considered the following issues: (1) students' age and grade level, (2) the relevancy of the questioned material to the curriculum, (3) the duration of the material's use, (4) the general acceptance of a disputed teaching method within the profession, (5) the prior existence of board policy governing selection of materials and teaching techniques, (6) whether the materials are required or optional, and (7) whether actions against the teacher involved retaliation for free expression.[15]

---

[12]Perry A. Zirkel and Ivan B. Gluckman, "Verbal Abuse of Students," *Principal* (May 1991), pp. 51–52; Mark Walsh, "'Slave Ship' Case Settled," *Education Week,* July 8, 1998; and James K. Daly, Patricia L. Schall, and Rosemary W. Skeele, eds., *Protecting the Right to Teach and Learn* (New York: Teachers College Press, 2001).

[13]*Board of Education v. Pico,* 102 S. Ct. 2799 (1982); and Mark Clark and Larra Clark, "Harry Potter Again Tops List of Most Challenged Books" (2001), press release posted at the American Library Association Internet site, available at **www.ala.org/bbooks:** search for "Harry Potter."

[14]*Keefe v. Geanakos,* 418 F. 2d 359 (1st Cir. 1969); *Pratt v. Independent School District* No. 831, 670 F. 2d 771 (8th Cir. 1982); and *Brown v. Joint Unified School District,* 42-15772 (9th Cir. 1994). See also David A. Splitt, "Respecting a Review Process," *Executive Educator* (January 1996), pp. 9, 31; and Richard S. Vacca, "Academic Freedom," *CEPI Education Law Newsletter* (April 2003), available at **www.cepi.vsu.edu/newsletter**.

[15]*DeVito v. Board of Education,* 317 S.E. 2d 159 (W. Va. 1984). See also Jack L. Nelson, Kenneth Carlson, and Stuart B. Palonsky, *Critical Issues in Education* (New York: McGraw-Hill, 1996); and Benjamin Dowling-Sendor, "Who Has the Right to Choose?" *American School Board Journal* (March 2002), available at **www.asbj.com**.

Teacher as Exemplar or Role Model

■ Morality standards

The chapter on The Teaching Profession described rules governing teacher conduct in Wisconsin. Teachers' lives were regulated because communities believed they should be exemplars—that is, examples to their students of high moral standards and impeccable character, conservative dress and grooming, and polished manners. Although these standards have relaxed, in some places teachers may still be dismissed under immorality statutes for a drunk-driving incident, homosexuality, or for living unmarried with a member of the opposite sex. Seemingly less weighty behaviors have also become grounds for dismissal, such as engaging in a water fight in which a student suffered mild skin irritations or joking about testes and menstrual periods when these topics were not part of the curriculum being taught by a science teacher.[16]

■ Renewed emphasis on "role model" responsibilities

Recent years have seen a movement toward reemphasizing teachers' responsibilities as "moral exemplars" in and out of school. Many parents have demanded that schools reinforce traditional values among students, and many schools have introduced "character education" programs. School district policies generally still require that teachers serve as "positive role models." Based in part on such requirements, Indiana courts upheld the dismissal of a teacher who drank beer in the presence of students at a local restaurant and then drove them home. According to attorneys for the National School Boards Association, misbehavior outside the school that reduces teachers' capacity to serve as positive role models can justify reprimands or dismissals as long as rights to free speech and free association (with friends or acquaintances of one's choice) are not violated.[17]

■ Prohibiting gay discrimination

Moral standards are also subject to changing social mores. In the past few years, for example, some states and numerous jurisdictions have passed laws prohibiting discrimination against gay or lesbian individuals. Several courts have cited such laws in rejecting job termination and other actions that may have been directed against gay or lesbian teachers (or students).[18]

■ Dress and grooming cases

Courts also have decided cases in which teachers' dress and grooming conflicted with school district policies or traditions. One California court ruled that women teaching at "back-to-basics" schools in Pomona could not be required to wear dresses if they preferred to wear outfits with pants. Another California court ruled that Paul Finot's wearing of a beard was symbolic expression protected by the First Amendment as well as a liberty protected under the Fourteenth Amendment. On the other hand, when Max Miller's contract was not renewed because of his beard and long sideburns, the circuit court upheld the dismissal. "As public servants in a special position of trust," the judges stated, "teachers may properly be subjected to many restrictions in their professional lives which would be invalid if generally applied."[19]

Tort Liability and Negligence

■ Student injuries

Torts are civil wrongs. Under tort law, individuals who have suffered through the improper conduct of others may sue for damages. For example, educators may be found

---

[16]*Everett Area School District v. Ault,* 548 A. 2d 1341 (Pa. Cmwlth. 1988); Perry A. Zirkel, "Weeding Out Bad Teachers," *Phi Delta Kappan* (January 1992), pp. 418–421; and *Baldrige v. Board of Trustees,* No. 97-230 (Washington, 1997).
[17]Laurel S. Walters, "Value Ed Also Tests Teachers," *Christian Science Monitor,* November 5, 1997.
[18]Michael D. Simpson, "Big Legal Victories for Gay Students and Teachers," *NEA Today* (January 2003), available at **www.nea.org/neatoday**.
[19]*Miller v. School District No. 167 of Cook County, Illinois,* 495 F. 2d 65 (7th Cir. 1974); *Finot v. Pasadena City Board of Education,* 58 Cal. Rptr. 520 (1976); and Bess Keller, "Keep Your Pants On," *Teacher Magazine* (April 1997).

guilty of negligence when students are injured during classes, on the playground, or elsewhere if the injury resulted from failure to take appropriate preventive action. Of course a case won't be filed every time a child is accidentally injured, but when injury results from negligent or intentional action, legal remedies can be pursued.

■ Decline of immunity

A generation ago, nearly every school district was immune from tort liability. This immunity had its origins in English common law, under which the king, as sovereign, could not be sued. Since 1960, most states have eliminated or modified this view of governmental immunity. In states that permit suits, the parties sued may include the school district as well as specific school administrators, teachers, and other staff. For example, school districts can be held liable for their employees' negligent or malicious actions (such as sexual abuse, neglect of hazing among students, or failure to report students' suicidal intentions) if school officials have provided little or no supervision or ignored persistent complaints. These responsibilities even extend to malicious or neglectful action or inaction by volunteers who donate time to work with a school.[20]

■ Standards of proper care

Teachers are required by law to protect their students from injury or harm. In nearly all states, the traditional standard of care is what a reasonable and prudent person would do under similar circumstances. In one case, a kindergarten teacher was charged with negligence when a child fell from a playground structure while the teacher was attending to other children. The court ruled that the teacher was not required to have all children in sight at all times. Her presence in the immediate area was sufficient to establish that the teacher was fulfilling her duty. The New York State Supreme Court reached a similar conclusion in overturning a jury award to an injured high-school athlete, on grounds that school officials had exercised "reasonable care" in operating their school's football program. In other cases, however, school districts or their employees have been found partially or wholly responsible for students' injuries that a reasonable person should have been able to foresee.[21]

■ Can danger be foreseen?

An important principle is whether the injury could have been foreseen and thus prevented. An overweight student expressed concern to her physical education teacher about a class requirement to perform a back somersault. The teacher insisted the somersault be done, and the student's neck snapped in the attempt. The court said the teacher showed utter indifference to the student's safety, and the jury awarded $77,000 in damages. Similarly, a high school student in an introductory chemistry class blew away his hand while completing an assignment to make gunpowder. The court ruled that the injury was foreseeable and the teacher was negligent.[22]

■ Parental consent forms

School districts require parents to sign consent forms when students are involved in activities such as field trips or athletic competition. The form generally has two purposes: to inform parents of their children's whereabouts and to release school personnel from liability in case of injury. However, because parents cannot waive a child's right to sue for damages if an injury occurs, these forms actually

---

[20]David A. Splitt, "Drawing a Line on Liability," *Executive Educator* (March 1992), pp. 13, 42; Perry A. Zirkel, "Student Suicide," *Principal* (May 1996), pp. 45–46; Rebecca Jones, "Schools and the Law," *American School Board Journal* (April 2000), available at **www.asbj.com**; and Scott Rosner and R. Brian Crow, "Institutional Liability for Hazing in Interscholastic Sports," *Houston Law Review* (Summer 2002).

[21]*Clark v. Furch,* 567 S.W. 2d 457 (Mo. App. 1978); "Ellipses," *Executive Educator* (May 1995), p. 13; and William R. Mason Jr., "CAUTION: Litigation May Lie Ahead," *Best Practices* (May/June 2002), available at **www.schoolmatch.com/articles/bpmay_june02.htm**.

[22]*Landers v. School District No. 203, O'Fallon,* 383 N.E. 2d 645 (Ill. App. Ct. 1978). See also Michael D. Richardson et al., "Science Lab Liability for Teachers," *Journal of Chemical Education* (August 1994), pp. 689–690; and Sam Blank, "Teacher Rights, Responsibilities and the Law" (undated), paper posted at the Guidance Channel Internet site, available at **www.guidancechannel.com:** click on "Resources," then "SC Archives."

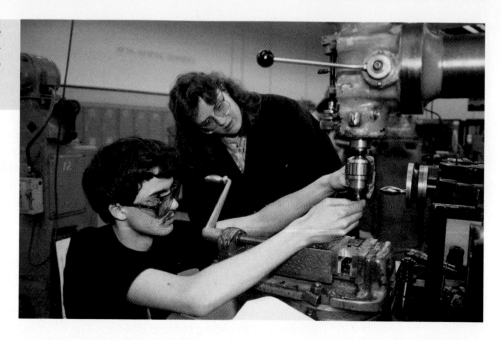

Teachers must try to foresee potentially dangerous situations and prevent injuries to their students. *(Dennis Mac-Donald/PhotoEdit)*

serve only the first purpose. Obtaining a parental waiver does *not* release teachers from their legal obligations to protect the safety and welfare of students.

◼ Rise of strict liability

Recent years have brought what some observers describe as an "explosion" in litigation related to liability and negligence. In addition, rather than accepting the exercise of reasonable precautions as a defense against negligence, recent judicial decisions have frequently emphasized "strict liability." In this situation, teachers cannot be too careful, for negligence might occur in numerous school settings. Physical education instructors, sponsors of extracurricular activities, and shop and laboratory teachers must take special care. Prudent safeguards include a clear set of written rules, verbal warnings to students, regular inspection of equipment, adherence to state laws and district policies regarding hazardous activities, thoughtful planning, and diligent supervision.[23]

Reporting Child Abuse

◼ Laws require reporting abuse

Because a high percentage of abuse is directed at school-age children, schools play an important role in protecting them. In most states, laws require educators to report suspected cases of child abuse to authorities or designated social service agencies. As a result, increasing numbers of school districts have written policies describing how teachers should proceed when they suspect abuse. Warning signs that may indicate a child is being abused are shown in Table 9.2.

Copyright Laws

◼ Fair use guidelines

A *copyright* gives authors and artists control over the reproduction and distribution of works they create; consequently, permission for reproduction usually must be ob-

[23]Jonathan Schorr, "A Trust Betrayed," *Teacher Magazine* (February 1996), pp. 37–41; Christopher J. Zirkle, "A Primer on Teacher Liability," *Tech Directions* (August 1999), pp. 32–34; and Robert J. Shoop, "Identifying a Standard of Care," *Principal Leadership* (March 2002).

Table 9.2	Selected Physical and Behavioral Indicators of Physical Abuse and Neglect, Sexual Abuse, and Emotional Abuse
Physical Indicators	**Behavioral Indicators**

Physical Abuse—nonaccidental injury to a child that may involve some beatings, burns, strangulation, or human bites

■ Unexplained bruises, swollen areas	■ Self-destructive
■ Welts, bite marks, bald spots	■ Withdrawn and/or aggressive extremes
■ Unexplained burns, fractures, abrasions	■ Complaints of soreness or discomfort
■ Evidence of inappropriate treatment of injuries	■ Bizarre explanation of injuries

Physical Neglect—failure to provide a child with basic necessities

■ Unattended medical need, lice, poor hygiene	■ Regularly displays fatigue, listlessness
■ Consistent lack of supervision	■ Steals food, begs from classmates
■ Consistent hunger, inadequate nutrition	■ Frequently absent or tardy
■ Consistent inappropriate clothing	■ Reports no caretaker at home

Sexual Abuse—sexual exploitation, including rape, incest, fondling, and pornography

■ Torn, stained, or bloody underclothing	■ Withdrawal, chronic depression
■ Pain, swelling, or itching in genital area	■ Hysteria, lack of emotional control
■ Venereal disease	■ Inappropriate sex play, premature sex knowledge
■ Frequent urinary or yeast infections	■ Excessive seductiveness

Emotional Abuse—a pattern of behavior that attacks a child's emotional development such as name calling, put-downs, terrorization, isolation

■ Speech disorders	■ Habit disorders (sucking, rocking, biting)
■ Delayed physical development	■ Emotional disturbance
■ Substance abuse	■ Neurotic traits (sleep disorders, play inhibition)
■ Ulcer, asthma, severe allergy	■ Antisocial, destructive, delinquent

Note: SOC-UM emphasizes the following advice: "Symptoms, or indications of abuse, vary greatly from child to child. . . . Possibly only one or a few, or none of these symptoms . . . will be readily apparent in a child who IS being abused. Absence of any or all . . . does NOT mean that a child is NOT being abused. If you suspect there is a problem, do NOT try to diagnose or determine the extent of the problem on your own; please contact a professional immediately."

Source: Adapted from guidelines posted by Safeguarding Our Children—United Mothers (SOC-UM), at **www.soc-um.org**. Reprinted with permission. Also see material at **www.childabuse.com**, and Felicia F. Romeo, "The Educator's Role in Reporting the Emotional Abuse of Children," *Journal of Instructional Psychology* (September 2000).

tained from the owner. Beginning in the 1970s, widespread use of copying machines bred serious and regular violations of copyright laws. To address this problem, in 1976 Congress amended the original 1909 copyright laws to include photocopying and the educational use of copyrighted materials. In addition, a committee of librarians, publishers, authors, and educators developed "fair use" guidelines. **Fair use** is a legal principle that allows use of copyrighted materials without permission from the author under specific, limited conditions. Table 9.3 summarizes fair use restrictions on copying for classroom use or other educational purposes.[24]

[24]Kenneth T. Murray, "Copyright and the Educator," *Phi Delta Kappan* (March 1994), pp. 552–555. See also Linda Starr, "Copyrights and Copying Wrongs" (2000), paper posted at the Education World Internet site, available at **www.educationworld.com/a_curr/curr280a.shtml**; and U.S. copyright legislation and practices, updated for 2003, at **www.loc.gov/copyright**.

Table 9.3	Guidelines on Copying Materials for Educational Use

- Copying of prose is limited to excerpts of no more than 1,000 words.

- Copies from an anthology or encyclopedia cannot exceed one story or entry, or 2,500 words.

- A poem may be copied if it is less than 250 words, and an excerpt of no more than 250 words may be copied from a longer poem.

- Distribution of copies from the same author more than once a semester or copying from the same work or anthology more than three times during the semester is prohibited.

- Teachers may make one copy per student for class distribution; if charges are made, they may not exceed actual copying costs.

- It is illegal to create anthologies or compilations by using photocopies as a substitute for purchasing the same or similar materials.

- Consumable materials, such as workbooks, may not be copied.

- Under the fair use doctrine, single copies of printed materials may be made for personal study, lesson planning, research, criticism, comment, and news reporting.

- Most magazine and newspaper articles may be copied freely. However, items in weekly newspapers and magazines designed for classroom use by students may not be copied without permission.

- Individual teachers must decide, independently, to copy material; they may not be directed to do so by higher authorities.

- There are three categories of material for which copies may be freely made: writings published before 1978 that have never been copyrighted, published works for which copyrights are more than seventy-five years old, and U.S. government publications.

- New restrictions on use of copyrighted materials are emerging in connection with the Internet and other digital media.

■ Plays and musicals

Authors usually copyright plays and musical productions, and schools must obtain permission from the author or the author's agent before presenting such works. Often a royalty fee is charged to secure permission, the amount of which may depend on whether or not admission is charged.

■ Video recordings

Videotapes and DVDs also fall within the fair use guidelines of the copyright laws. These guidelines specify that educational institutions may not keep the recordings they make of copyrighted television programs for more than forty-five days without a license. During the first ten days, an individual teacher may use the recorded program once, and may show it once again after that period when "instructional reinforcement is necessary." After forty-five days the tape or DVD must be erased. Video recording may occur only when a faculty member requests it in advance; thus it may not be done on a regular basis in anticipation of faculty requests.

■ Software

Computer software is subject to the same fair use restrictions as other copyrighted materials. For example, teachers may not copy protected computer programs and distribute them for use on school computers. Downloading computer files from another source may require permission and/or fees. For example, after it was found that a Los Angeles school allegedly possessed pirated copies of hundreds of software programs, district officials agreed to pay $300,000 to rectify this infringement and to develop a multimillion-dollar plan to pay for violations at other schools.[25]

---

[25]Information on the complex issues involving copyright of digital materials is provided at **www.wustl.edu/policies/computinghtml**.

■ Internet

Copyright issues involving the Internet have become an important concern for teachers, students, and administrators. Copyright holders have taken action to prohibit unauthorized use of text or images, to correct or restrict posting of incomplete or erroneous materials, or otherwise to reduce or eliminate potentially illegal publication of their materials on the World Wide Web and other platforms. Business and commercial groups led by the entertainment and software industries worked with federal legislators to develop the No Electronic Theft Act of 1997, which provides hefty penalties for possessing or distributing illegal electronic copies, and the Digi-

■ Digital Millennium Act

tal Millennium Copyright Act of 1998. The latter law includes provisions that allow copyright owners to prevent downloading of their material without permission and/or to require recipients to pay a fee. These laws also protect the copyrights of teachers whose material is posted online.[26]

> **REFOCUS** What areas of caution did the preceding material suggest to you as a teacher? What topics might require further study to make sure you do not violate the law but can also defend your rights as a teacher?

▶ **Students' Rights and Responsibilities**

■ Decline of *in loco parentis*

During the 1960s, students increasingly began to challenge the authority of school officials to control student behavior. Before these challenges, students' rights were considered limited by their status as minors and by the concept of *in loco parentis*, according to which school authorities assumed the powers of the child's parents during the hours the child was under the school's supervision. Use of this concept has declined, however, and the courts have become more active in identifying and upholding students' constitutional rights. Student responsibilities have been increasingly recognized as well—that is, understanding that students' educational rights are tied in with responsibilities on the part of both students and educators to ensure effective operation of the school.

■ Nonpublic-school students not necessarily protected

The following sections and Overview 9.2 summarize some of the most important court decisions involving students' rights and responsibilities. These apply primarily to public schools. As with teachers, students in nonpublic schools may not enjoy all the constitutional guarantees discussed in this chapter. Unless a substantial relationship between the school and the government can be demonstrated, private-school activity is not considered action by the state and therefore does not trigger state constitutional obligations. However, the movement toward voucher plans (see the chapter on Financing Public Education) and other school choice arrangements (discussed in the chapter on School Effectiveness and Reform in the United States) that provide public funds for students attending nonpublic schools has begun to blur this distinction.

---

[26]Wendy A. Grossman, "Downloading as a Crime," *Scientific American* (March 1998); Michael D. Simpson, "Cyber Threats on the Rise," *NEA Today Online* (January 2001), available at **www.nea.org/neatoday**; and Linda Howe-Stiger and Brian C. Donohue, "Technology Is Changing What's Fair Use in Teaching—Again," *Education Policy Analysis Archives*, January 12, 2002, available at **http:epaa.asu.edu**.

OVERVIEW 9.2 *Selected U.S. Supreme Court Decisions Affecting Students' Rights and Responsibilities*

Case	Summary of Decision
Tinker v. Des Moines Independent Community School District (1969)	Students are free to express their views except when such conduct disrupts class work, causes disorder, or invades the rights of others.
Goss v. Lopez (1975)	Suspension from school requires some form of due process for students.
Ingraham v. Wright (1977)	Corporal punishment is not cruel or unusual punishment and is permitted where allowed by state law.
New Jersey v. T.L.O. (1985)	To be constitutional, searches of students and students' property must meet a two-pronged test.
Bethel School District No. 403 v. Fraser (1986)	Schools need not permit offensive or disruptive speech.
Hazelwood School District v. Kuhlmeier (1988)	A school newspaper is not a public forum and can be regulated by school officials.
Honig v. Doe (1988)	Disabled students who are disruptive must be retained in their current placement until official hearings are completed.
Gebser v. Lago Vista Independent School District (1998)	School districts are not legally at fault when a teacher sexually harasses a student unless the school acted with "deliberate indifference" in failing to stop it.

Freedom of Expression

■ *Tinker:* guarantees of free speech

In 1965, John Tinker, fifteen, his sister Mary Beth, thirteen, and friend Dennis Eckhardt, sixteen, were part of a small group planning to wear black armbands to school as a silent, symbolic protest against the war in Vietnam. Hearing of this plan and fearing problems, administrators responded by adopting a policy prohibiting the wearing of armbands; the penalty was suspension until the armbands were removed. The Tinkers and Eckhardt wore the armbands as planned, refused to remove them, and were suspended. Their parents filed suit. In finding for the plaintiffs, the U.S. Supreme Court outlined the scope of student rights, so that this case, *Tinker v. Des Moines Independent Community School District,* became the standard for examining students' freedom of speech guarantees.[27]

■ *Bethel/Fraser:* limits of free speech

To justify prohibition of a particular expression of opinion, the Court ruled, school officials must be able to show that their actions were caused by "something more than a mere desire to avoid the discomfort and unpleasantness that always accompany an unpopular viewpoint." Student conduct that "materially disrupts classwork or involves substantial disorder or invasion of the rights of others" could be prohibited. In the absence of such good reasons for restraint, the students' constitutional guarantees of free speech would apply. But as the preceding statements sug-

---

[27]*Tinker v. Des Moines Independent Community School District,* 393 U.S. 503 (1969). See also Dorianne Beyer, "School Safety and the Legal Rights of Students," *ERIC Clearinghouse on Urban Education Digest* (May 1997), pp. 1–4; and Benjamin Dowling-Sendor, "See Red over Speech," *American School Board Journal* (March 2003), available at **www.asbj.com**.

gest, free expression in public schools has limits. In *Bethel School District No. 403 v. Fraser,* the U.S. Supreme Court confirmed that students may be punished for offensive or disruptive speech.[28]

■ *Hazelwood/Kuhlmeier:* regulating student publications

Student publications may also raise problems. For example, in one case school policy required the principal to review each proposed issue of *The Spectrum,* the school newspaper written by journalism students at Hazelwood East High School in St. Louis County, Missouri. The principal objected to two articles scheduled to appear in one issue. The principal claimed the articles were deleted not because of the subject matter but because he considered them poorly written and there was insufficient time to rewrite them before the publication deadline.

Three student journalists sued, contending that their freedom of speech had been violated. This case, *Hazelwood School District v. Kuhlmeier,* reached the U.S. Supreme Court, which upheld the principal's action. The justices found that *The Spectrum* was not a public forum but rather a supervised learning experience for journalism students. As long as educators' actions were related to "legitimate pedagogical concerns," they could regulate the newspaper's contents in any reasonable manner. The ruling further stated that a school could disassociate itself not only from speech that directly interfered with school activities but also from speech that was "ungrammatical, poorly written, inadequately researched, biased, prejudiced, vulgar or profane, or unsuitable for immature audiences." This decision was a clear restriction on student rights as previously understood.[29]

■ Legitimate regulation

Controversies concerning publications written or distributed by students have prompted many school boards to develop written regulations that can withstand judicial scrutiny. Generally, these rules specify a time, place, and manner of distribution; a method of advertising the rules to students; a prompt review process; and speedy appeal procedures. Students may not distribute literature that is by legal definition obscene or libelous, or that is likely to cause the substantial disruption specified in *Tinker.* School boards also have considerable leeway in determining whether nondisruptive material will be published in school newspapers and yearbooks. This chapter's case study involves a teacher concerned about her responsibilities as the school newspaper adviser.

■ "Acceptable use" policies for Internet use

Student Internet Use. The Internet has generated legal issues that educators will be contending with for a long time to come. Like businesses and other organizations, most schools have "acceptable use policies" that govern the online behavior of students and staff provided that statutory and constitutional requirements protecting free speech and other rights are not thereby violated. Developments include the following:[30]

---

[28]*Bethel School District No. 403 v. Fraser,* 106 S. Ct. 3159 (1986). See also "NRA Sues School for Not Letting Student Wear Shirt," *School Law News,* September 27, 2002, p. 10; David L. Hudson Jr. and John E. Ferguson Jr., "The Court's Inconsistent Treatment," *John Marshall Law Review* (Fall 2002), pp. 181–210; and Perry A. Zirkel, "The Case of the Purloined Letter," *Phi Delta Kappan* (April 2003), pp. 628–630.

[29]*Hazelwood School District v. Kuhlmeier,* 86-836 S. Ct. (1998). See also "Ask Sybil Liberty About Your Right to Free Expression" (2000), paper posted at the American Civil Liberties Union Internet site, available at **www.aclu.org/students:** search for "Sybil"; Mark J. Fiore, "Trampling the Marketplace of Ideas," *University of Pennsylvania Law Review* (June 2002), pp. 1915–1974; and Richard S. Vacca, "Student Speech and Expression 2004," *CEPI Education Law Newsletter* (February 2004), available at **www.cepi.vcu.edu/newsletter**.

[30]Linda Lindroth, "How to Improve Online Safety," *Teaching PreK–8* (April 1998); Andrew Trotter, "High Tech High Jinks," *Teacher Magazine* (August–September 1998); and "Website Wrangling: Do You Have Any Options?" *School Principal's Legal Alert* (April 2003), pp. 2–3. Information and illustrations regarding school "acceptable use policies" are easily found by using this term to search the Internet.

IN THIS CASE

A Difficult Start

Sara Jones could hardly believe that she had been assigned to be the faculty adviser for the student newspaper. After all she was just a beginning teacher. Sara had written for her high school and university student newspapers, but she had never been in charge of such a project. Now Sara found herself supervising and directing eighteen-year-old students, just three years her junior.

Sara, twenty-one, had recently graduated with an English major and journalism minor. She would be teaching English II and English III, and the student newspaper would be an extracurricular activity.

Bob Cartwright, the student editor, seemed rather offbeat and different to Sara. She was uncertain how she would handle him if a ticklish situation arose. Sara did not have long to wait. Just one month into the school year, all students attended a required assembly for an anti-drug program. The next day, Bob came to her and said that he was going to write an editorial emphasizing student rights. He was tired of being forced to attend boring presentations when he had more important things to do with his time.

The next day Sara found this editorial written by Bob on her desk.

Student Rights Ignored!
Drug-free schools! Just say no!

Slogans without meaning were once again presented to an audience that was more knowledgeable about drugs than any of the presenters. Every year we have to submit to this inane practice. What a colossal waste of time and energy! If the presenters were knowledgeable, they would already know that some drugs are being grown right on this very campus.

This editor just says NO to more assemblies about drug-free schools. Students are encouraged to walk out should another of these so-called educational opportunities present itself as a requirement. Let's stand up for our right to have a voice in determining what we must suffer. Write letters to this paper. Write to the principal and to the superintendent. Let them know what you think about this assembly and demand to have students involved in the planning process for all assemblies in the future.

Sara decided she must respond quickly, yet she did not want to cause a problem where there was none. She wondered if this editorial would cause real trouble. She thought she had better seek assistance from the principal. Her English classes were going well, but she wondered if problems serving as student newspaper adviser might jeopardize her chances for tenure or a continuing contract. She wondered if her evaluation might even depend on how she handled this situation.

Questions

1. What responsibilities and authority does Sara have as faculty adviser for the student newspaper?
2. What should Sara have determined before accepting such a position?
3. Should the student editor's action affect her evaluation?
4. What rights and responsibilities does the student newspaper editor have?

- Schools have installed software to inhibit access to Internet sites that programmers have classified as pornographic, obscene, or otherwise undesirable for children or youth.

▪ Suspension for digital ridicule

- Some students have been punished for sending e-mail or posting Web pages that school officials considered threatening, defamatory, obscene, or potentially disruptive or destructive. Such punishment may be legal even if the computers involved are off school property. However, electronic materials that might fit in these categories have the same legal standing as printed documents, which may require finding a delicate balance between legally protected individual rights on the one hand, and prohibitions on harming individuals and institutions on the other. For example, an Ohio school district had to pay thirty thousand dollars to a high-school student after it lost a court case in which he challenged his suspension for posting material that ridiculed his band teacher.

- Libraries, including school libraries, have been sued for using filtering software to screen out sexually oriented Internet sites. Libraries also have been sued for not using such software. Libraries that receive federal funding are currently required to use such software.

This chapter's Technology @ School feature offers more information on legal issues involved with student computer use.

■ Mixed rulings

Dress Codes and Regulations.   Many courts have had to determine whether dress codes and regulations constitute an unconstitutional restriction on students' rights to free expression. In some instances, as in a Louisiana case dealing with requirements that football team members shave their mustaches, judges have ruled that the Constitution allows school boards to impose dress and grooming codes to advance their educational goals. Similarly, a U.S. district court upheld a ban on boys' earrings as part of a policy prohibiting display of gang emblems.

In other cases, however, judges have ruled that prohibitions against long hair were arbitrary and unreasonable, and that girls' wearing of pantsuits or slacks could not be prohibited. Much depends on the arguments and evidence regarding the educational purposes served by such restrictions, the likelihood that violations will be disruptive, and the extent to which dress codes and restrictions are intended to accomplish a valid constitutional goal.[31]

■ A "rational basis"

In general, school officials must demonstrate a "rational basis" for prohibiting language or symbols they think may contribute to school problems. Applying this test, several courts also have ruled that public schools can require students to wear a designated uniform if school officials present evidence indicating that uniforms could help make schools safer or more productive. In several cases dress codes have been upheld under this standard, but in some cases dress codes have been challenged successfully on the grounds that they were arbitrary or capricious.[32]

Suspension and Expulsion

The issue of expulsion is illustrated in the case of nine students who received ten-day suspensions from their Columbus, Ohio, secondary schools for various alleged acts of misconduct. The suspensions were imposed without hearings but in accordance with state law; the school board had no written procedure covering suspensions. The students filed suit, claiming deprivation of their constitutional rights. In defense, school officials argued that without a constitutional right to education at public expense, the due process clause of the Fourteenth Amendment did not apply.

■ Minimum due process

When this case, *Goss v. Lopez,* reached the Supreme Court in 1975, a majority of the Court disagreed with the school officials, reasoning that students had a legal

---

[31]Benjamin Dowling-Sendor, "A Matter of Disruption, Not Dress," *American School Board Journal* (August 1998), available at **www.asbj.com**; Kerry A. White, "Do School Uniforms Fit?" *School Administrator* (February 2000); and Wendell Anderson, "School Dress Codes and Uniform Policies," *Policy Report* (Fall 2002), available at **www.eric.uoregon.edu**.
[32]Perry A. Zirkel and Ivan Gluckman, "Regulating Offensive T-Shirts," *Principal* (May 1995), pp. 46–48; Perry A. Zirkel, "A Uniform Policy," *Phi Delta Kappan* (March 1998), pp. 550–551; and Linda Lumsden and Gabriel Miller, "Dress Codes and Uniforms," *NAESP Research Roundup* (Summer 2002), available at **www.naesp.org**.

TECHNOLOGY @School

Legal Issues Involving Technology in Schools

The widespread and still growing emphasis on using technology in education increases the likelihood that you, as a teacher, will face legal issues involving your students' use of computers. Some of these issues are spelled out at the EnGauge Web site sponsored by the North Central Regional Educational Laboratory (**www.ncrel.org/engauge/framewk/pro/issues/proisspr.htm**).

Designed to help schools and school districts use technology more effectively, the EnGauge Web site lists six "essential conditions" of a comprehensive technology program in schools. One of these conditions addresses "proficiency" of operation, and several indicators of proficiency level involve helping students understand legal (as well as social and ethical) issues in using technology. The authors point out that teachers should model and guide students toward "legal and ethical practices related to technology use," and should "facilitate student investigations of the legal and ethical issues related to technology and society." Their examination of these issues includes a listing of "Ten Commandments for Computer Ethics," examples of lesson topics for developing students' skills and understandings, and advice on key legal considerations in student use of the Internet.

The sponsors of EnGauge emphasize their intention to expand the site regularly. You may want to check out new postings from time to time.

right to public education. In other words, students had a property interest in their education that could not be taken away "without adherence to the minimum procedures" required by the due-process clause. Further, the justices said that students facing suspension "must be given some kind of notice and afforded some kind of hearing," including "an opportunity to explain [their] version of the facts." Also, "as a general rule notice and hearing should precede removal of the student from school." Applying these principles to suspensions of up to ten days, the Court added that longer suspensions or expulsions might require more elaborate due-process procedures.[33]

■ Written policies

In response to such court decisions, most school districts have developed written policies governing suspensions and expulsions. These policies usually distinguish between short- and long-term suspensions. Short-term suspension rights typically include oral or written notice describing the misconduct, the evidence on which the accusation is based, a statement of the planned punishment, and an opportunity for the student to explain his or her version or refute the stated facts before an impartial person. Expulsions require full procedural due process similar to that necessary for teacher terminations.[34]

■ Rights of students with disabilities

Controversy Regarding Students with Disabilities. Recent court decisions have limited school officials' authority to suspend or expel disabled students who are dis-

---

[33]*Goss v. Lopez,* 419 U.S. 565 (1975). See also Perry A. Zirkel, "Supporting Suspenders," *Phi Delta Kappan* (November 1994), pp. 256–257; Perry A. Zirkel and Ivan B. Gluckman, "Due Process in Student Suspensions and Expulsions," *Principal* (March 1997), pp. 62–63; and Benjamin Dowling-Sendor, "Policy and Tragedy," *American School Board Journal* (December 2002), available at **www.asbj.com**.
[34]Perry A. Zirkel and Ivan B. Gluckman, "Due Process for Student Suspensions," *NASSP Bulletin* (March 1990), pp. 95–98; "Ask Sybil Liberty About Your Right to Fair Treatment" (1997), paper posted at the American Civil Liberties Union Internet site, available at **www.aclu.org:** search for "Sybil"; and Patrick Jonsson, "Before You Suspend Me, Can I Call a Lawyer?" *Christian Science Monitor,* March 4, 2003.

ruptive or violent. In the case of *Honig v. Doe,* the Supreme Court ruled that such students must be retained in their current placement pending the completion of lengthy official hearings. The Individuals with Disabilities Education Act (IDEA) of 1990 specified additional rights that make it difficult to suspend or expel students with disabilities, including those who may be severely disruptive or prone to violence. As a result, educators are seeking new ways to guarantee the rights of students while dealing with disruptive pupils who are classified as disabled. In 1997 Congress passed legislation aimed at making it less cumbersome for administrators to suspend disabled students who violate school discipline rules, but several years later educators reported that practical issues were still murky.[35]

Protection from Violence

■ Schools may be liable for violence

Educators have a duty to protect students against violent actions that occur at school or at school-sponsored events, which frequently extends to off-campus events such as graduations, proms, and parties. Depending on the circumstances, the courts may find school districts or their employees legally liable for failing in this duty. For example, a Louisiana court held a school district partly responsible for the gunshot wound suffered by a student after a school security guard warned the student of trouble but refused to escort him to his car. By contrast, an Illinois appellate court held Chicago high-school officials not liable for the shooting of a student because they did not know that the weapon had been brought into school. In general, if the chance of harm to students is highly foreseeable, the educator's "duty to care" becomes a "duty to protect." Of course, regardless of questions involving legal culpability, educators should do everything possible to protect their students from violence.[36]

■ Gun-Free Schools Act

■ "Zero tolerance"

Zero Tolerance and Its Effects on Schools. Although school laws and policies dealing with school safety are primarily the responsibility of state and local governments (including public-school districts), growing national concern with violence in and around schools helped stimulate passage of the federal Gun-Free Schools Act of 1994. This legislation prohibits districts from receiving federal grants to improve performance among disadvantaged students unless their respective state governments have legislated "zero tolerance" of guns and other potentially dangerous weapons. By 1995, all fifty states had introduced such legislation, which in general provides for automatic suspension of students who possess objects that school officials decide are dangerous. Most districts have policies specifying how the legislation will be implemented and any additional grounds, such as possession of illegal substances, for automatic suspension.[37]

---

[35]Mitchell L. Yell, "*Honig v. Doe*," *Exceptional Children* (September 1989), pp. 60–69; Perry A. Zirkel, "Manifest Determination?" *Phi Delta Kappan* (February 2001), pp. 478–479; Pam and Pete Wright, *From Emotions to Advocacy* (Hartfield, Va.: Harbor House Law Press, 2002); and Lisa Goldstein, "Discipline Split at Heart of IDEA Overhaul Debate," *Education Week*, June 18, 2003.

[36]Perry A. Zirkel, "Safe Promises?" *Phi Delta Kappan* (April 2000), pp. 635–636; and Richard S. Vacca, "The Duty to Protect Students from Harm," *CEPI Education Law Newsletter* (November 2002), available at **www.cepi.vcu.edu/newsletter**.

[37]Caroline Hendrie, "One Strike, You're Out," *Teacher Magazine* (February 1998); Chris Pipho, "Living with Zero Tolerance," *Phi Delta Kappan* (June 1998), pp. 725–726; Jennifer A. Sughrue, "Zero Tolerance for Children," *Educational Administration Quarterly* (April 2003), pp. 238–259; and Sara Rimer, "Unruly Students Facing Arrest, Not Detention," *New York Times*, January 4, 2004.

■ Zero tolerance sometimes out of control

Zero-tolerance laws and policies have made schools safer than before, but have also had negative effects. A study by the Harvard University Civil Rights Project found that zero-tolerance practices frequently had "spun out of control" in dishing out "harsh punishments" for minor infractions. For example, certain items considered dangerous have generated a great deal of public ridicule of school districts, including a kitchen knife in a lunch box, a belt buckle with a sharp edge, the finger of a kindergarten student who used it as a play gun during recess, a strong rubber band that could make a powerful sling shot, and a drawing of a student attacking a teacher. A more serious problem, according to the Advancement Project, headquartered in Washington, is that many disadvantaged students are "derailed" from schooling into incarceration by minor infractions of zero-tolerance policies. To avoid such outcomes and improve school climate through actions involving safety in schools, analysts urge educators to[38]

- Make sure students have opportunities to talk with and connect with caring adults.
- Provide flexibility and consider alternatives to expulsion.
- Clearly define what constitutes a weapon, a misbehavior, or a drug.
- Comply with due-process laws.
- Tailor policies to local needs and review them annually.

Search and Seizure

■ Fourth Amendment rights

A legal search usually requires a lawfully issued search warrant. But rising drug use in schools and accompanying acts of violence have led some school officials (particularly in big-city high schools) to install metal detectors or x-ray machines to search for weapons. They have banned beepers and cell phones (sometimes used in drug sales), required students to breathe into alcohol-analysis machines, searched students' book bags, and systematically examined lockers. Court challenges of such practices have usually centered on the Fourth Amendment, which states: "The right of the people to be secure in their persons, houses, papers, and effects, against unreasonable searches and seizures, shall not be violated, and no warrants shall issue, but upon probable cause, supported by oath or affirmation, and particularly describing the place to be searched, and the person or things to be seized."

■ Reasonable cause

Legal terms express suspicion in differing degrees. The "probable" cause mentioned in the Fourth Amendment means that searchers believe it is more probable than not that evidence of illegal activity will be found. This is the degree of suspicion required for police searches. In contrast, where school searches have been upheld, courts have said "reasonable" cause was sufficient for school officials to act. Searches usually are conducted because administrators have reason to suspect that illegal or dangerous items are on the premises.

■ *T.L.O.:* searching a purse

These principles were considered in a case involving a teacher who discovered two girls in a school restroom smoking cigarettes. This was a violation of school rules, and the students were taken to the vice principal's office and questioned. One of the girls admitted smoking, but T.L.O., age fourteen, denied all charges. The vice principal opened T.L.O.'s purse and found a pack of cigarettes. While reaching for

---

[38]"Preventing School Shootings," *NIJ Journal* 248 (2002); Judith A. Browne, *Derailed: The Schoolhouse to the Jail Track* (Washington, D.C.: Advancement Project, 2003), available at **www.advancementproject.org/bpublications.html**; "The Untolerated," *NEA Today Online* (April 2003), available at **www.nea.org/neatoday/0304**; and "Walking the Fine Legal Line," *School Principal's Legal Alert* (April 2003), pp. 4–5.

the cigarettes he noticed some rolling papers and decided to empty the purse. The search revealed marijuana, a pipe, some empty plastic bags, a large number of dollar bills, and a list entitled, "People who owe me money." T.L.O.'s mother was called, and the evidence was turned over to the police. T.L.O. confessed to the police that she had been selling marijuana at school.

■ Two-pronged standard

After she was sentenced to one year's probation by the juvenile court, T.L.O. appealed, claiming the vice principal's search of her purse was illegal under the Fourth Amendment. In finding for school authorities in *New Jersey v. T.L.O.*, the U.S. Supreme Court set up a two-pronged standard to be met for constitutionally sanctioned searches. Courts consider (1) whether the search is justified at its inception, and (2) whether the search, when actually conducted, is "reasonably related in scope to the circumstances which justified the interference in the first place." Using these criteria, the Court found the search of T.L.O.'s purse justified because of the teacher's report of smoking in the restroom. This information gave the vice principal reason to believe that the purse contained cigarettes. T.L.O. denied smoking, which made a search of her purse necessary to determine her veracity. When the vice principal saw the cigarettes and came across the rolling papers, he had reasonable suspicion to search her purse more thoroughly.[39]

■ Drug-sniffing dogs

Courts have also ruled that the suspicions of school officials were not sufficiently reasonable to justify the searches that followed. The use of trained dogs to sniff student lockers and cars for evidence of drugs has been accepted because it occurred when the lockers and cars were unattended and in public view. The use of such dogs with students, however, can raise problems. In Highland, Indiana, 2,780 junior- and senior-high students waited for hours in their seats while six officials using trained dogs searched for drugs. A school official, police officer, dog handler, and German shepherd entered the classroom where Diane Doe, thirteen, was a student. The dog went up and down the aisles sniffing students, reached Diane, sniffed her body, and repeatedly pushed its nose on and between her legs. The officer interpreted this behavior as an "alert" signaling the presence of drugs. Diane emptied her pockets as requested, but no drugs were found. Finally, Diane was taken to the nurse's office and strip-searched. No drugs were found. Before school, Diane had played with her own dog, which was in heat, and this smell remaining on her body had alerted the police dog.

■ Strip-search unconstitutional

The Does filed suit. Both the district court and the appeals court concluded that although the initial procedures were appropriate, the strip-search of Diane was unconstitutional. The court of appeals said, "It does not require a constitutional scholar to conclude that a nude search of a thirteen-year-old child is an invasion of constitutional rights of some magnitude. More than that: It is a violation of any known principle of human decency." Diane was awarded $7,500 damages.[40]

■ Guidelines for searches

In sum, when searches are conducted without a specific warrant, the following guidelines seem appropriate:[41]

---

[39]*New Jersey v. T.L.O.*, 105 S. Ct. 733 (1985). See also Andrew Trotter, "The Perils of Strip Searches," *Executive Educator* (June 1995), pp. 29–30; Benjamin Dowling-Sendor, "Is This Search Necessary?" *American School Board Journal* (September 2000); "Searching for the Right Answer," *American School Board Journal* (May 2003); and "Searching for Security," *American School Board Journal* (May 2004), all available at **www.asbj.com**.

[40]*Doe v. Renfrou*, 635 F. 2d 582 (7th Cir. 1980), cert. denied, 101 U.S. 3015 (1981). See also Karen M. Blum, "11th Circuit Is Out of Step," *National Law Journal* (April 2003).

[41]Perry A. Zirkel and Ivan B. Gluckman, "Search of Student Automobiles Revisited," *NASSP Bulletin* (November 1993), pp. 101–104; Benjamin Dowling-Sendor, "Discipline on the Road," *American School Board Journal* (February 2000), available at **www.asbj.com**; and Kate Ehlenberger, "The Right to Search Students," *Educational Leadership* (December 2001/January 2002), pp. 31–36.

- Searches must be particularized. Reasonable suspicion should exist that *each student* being searched possesses specific contraband or evidence of a particular crime.

- Lockers are considered school property and may be searched if reasonable cause exists.

- Dogs may be used to sniff lockers and cars. Generalized canine sniffing of students is permitted only when the dogs do not touch them.

- Strip-searches are unconstitutional and should never be conducted.

- School officials may perform a "pat-down" search for weapons if they have a reasonable suspicion that students are bringing dangerous weapons to school.

- School officials may conduct searches on field trips, but the usual standards for searches still apply.

- School officials' judgments are protected by government immunity if the search is not knowingly illegal.

■ Testing athletes for drugs

Drug Testing as a Form of Search. Some school board members and other policy makers have urged administrators to introduce random testing of student athletes' urine to detect marijuana, steroids, and other illegal substances. Such testing generally has been viewed as a potentially unconstitutional search. However, in 1995 the U.S. Supreme Court ruled that this type of drug search is not unconstitutional even without specific reason to suspect a particular individual. A majority of the justices concluded that school officials have reasonable grounds to be especially concerned with drug use among athletes, who presumably set an example for other students. Since then, the Supreme Court has also permitted drug testing of students engaged in other extracurricular activities.[42]

Standards & Assessment

Academic Testing of Students

As student testing has become a major phenomenon in elementary and secondary education, legal issues related to testing have grown more prominent and contentious. The most important of these issues has involved the use of test scores as a requirement for graduation.

■ Florida case

The first major challenge to testing for graduation was settled in the 1980s when a federal appeals court ruled that Florida could impose a high-school graduation test because the state government had a proper interest in upholding standards, had used a test that examined what actually had been taught, and had provided appropriate remedial opportunities. The court also ruled that students' due-process rights were not violated because adequate notice (four years) had been given of the requirements.

■ Texas case

In 2000, a federal district court came to similar conclusions regarding a legal challenge to tests required for graduation in Texas. The Mexican American Legal Defense and Educational Fund argued that the test was unconstitutionally discriminatory because failure rates for minority students were greater than for nonminority students; nearly 90 percent of failing students were minority. Judge Edward Prado ruled, however, that rather than the test discriminating against minorities, evidence

[42]Samantha Shutler, "Random, Suspicionless Drug Testing of High School Athletes," *Journal of Criminal Law and Behavior* (Summer 1996), pp. 1265–1304; Benjamin Dowling-Sendor, "Second Thoughts on Drugs," *American School Board Journal* (November 2000), available at **www.asbj.com**; and Mark Walsh and Linda Jacobson, "Supreme Court Allows Expansion of Schools' Drug-Testing Policies," *Education Week*, July 10, 2002.

indicated that the test helped to identify and eradicate educational disparities. He also found that the test had been developed to address high-school curriculum and content in a scientifically acceptable manner.[43]

Classroom Discipline and Corporal Punishment

■ "Time out" arrangements

Classroom discipline was the issue in a case involving a sixth grader who was placed in a "time out" area of the classroom whenever his behavior became disruptive. The student had a history of behavioral problems, and the teacher had tried other methods of discipline without success. While in "time out" the boy was allowed to use the restroom, eat in the cafeteria, and attend other classes. His parents sued, charging that the teacher's actions (1) deprived their son of his property interest in receiving a public education; (2) meted out punishment disproportionate to his offense, in violation of his due-process rights; and (3) inflicted emotional distress.[44]

The district court said that school officials possess broad authority to prescribe and enforce standards of conduct in the schools, but this authority is limited by the Fourteenth Amendment. In this case, the student remained in school and thus was not deprived of a public education. "Time out" was declared to be a minimal interference with the student's property rights. The court noted that the purpose of "time out" is to modify the behavior of disruptive students and to preserve the right to an education for other students in the classroom. All of the student's charges were dismissed.

■ Use of corporal punishment

A particularly controversial method of classroom discipline is corporal punishment, which has a long history in American education dating back to the colonial period. It is unacceptable to many educators, although it enjoys considerable support within some segments of the community and is administered more frequently than educators like to admit. Recent surveys indicate that nearly half a million children are spanked or paddled each school year, and thousands sustain injuries that require medical attention.[45]

■ Variations in state law and local policies

Certain state legislatures have prohibited all corporal punishment in public schools. In states where the law is silent on this issue, local boards have wide latitude and may ban physical punishment if they choose. However, where a state statute explicitly permits corporal punishment, local boards may regulate but not prohibit its use. In this context, many school boards have developed detailed policies restricting the use of corporal punishment. Violations of policy can lead to dismissal, and legal charges are possible for excessive force, punishment based on personal malice toward the student, or unreasonable use of punishment.

■ Paddling of students

Florida is an example of a state that allows corporal punishment. In 1977 the U.S. Supreme Court, in *Ingraham v. Wright,* ruled on the constitutionality of this law from two federal perspectives: (1) whether use of corporal punishment was a violation of the Eighth Amendment barring cruel and unusual punishment, and

---

[43]*GI Forum v. Texas Education Agency,* 87 F. Supp. 2d 667 (2000). See also "Giving All Students a Fair Shot," *Achieve Policy Brief* (Fall 2000), available at **www.achieve.org:** search for "fair shot"; Roger Clegg, "Passing the Test" (2000), paper prepared for the Center for Equal Opportunity, available at **www.ceousa.org/html/clegg.html**; and "High-Stakes Tests Spawn High-Stakes Lawsuits," *NEA Today Online* (May 2003), available at **www.nea.org/ neatoday/0305**.

[44]*Dickens v. Johnson County Board of Education,* 661 F. Supp. 155 (E.D. Tenn. 1987). See also Brooke Grone, "School Discipline: What Process Is Due?" *American Journal of Criminal Law* (Spring 2000), pp. 233–247.

[45]Daniel Gursky, "Spare the Child?" *Teacher Magazine* (February 1992), pp. 17–19; Perry A. Zirkel and David W. Van Cleaf, "Is Corporal Punishment Child Abuse?" *Principal* (January 1996), pp. 60–61; and "Corporal Punishment in U.S. Public Schools" (2003), available at **www.stophitting.com:** click on "Discipline in Schools."

■ Eighth Amendment not
applicable

(2) whether prior notice and some form of due process were required before administering punishment.

In this case, James Ingraham and Roosevelt Andrews were junior-high students in Dade County, Florida. Because Ingraham had been slow to respond to the teacher's instructions, he received twenty paddle swats administered in the principal's office. As a consequence, he needed medical treatment and missed a few days of school. Andrews was also paddled, but less severely. Finding that the intent of the Eighth Amendment was to protect those convicted of crimes, the justices said it did not apply to corporal punishment of schoolchildren. As to due process, the Court said, "We conclude that the Due Process clause does not require notice and a hearing prior to the imposition of corporal punishment in the public schools, as that practice is authorized and limited by common law."[46]

■ Possible liability

Despite this ruling, the Court also commented on the severity of the paddlings. In such instances, the justices stated, school authorities might be held liable for damages to the child. Moreover, if malice is shown, the officials might be subject to prosecution under criminal statutes. In a later action the Court also indicated a role for the due-process clause discussed earlier in this chapter. By declining to hear *Miera v. Garcia,* the Court let stand lower-court rulings that "grossly excessive" corporal punishment may constitute a violation of students' due-process rights. Thus teachers can be prosecuted in the courts for using excessive force and violating students' rights.[47]

■ No excessive force

Indeed, lower courts have ruled against teachers or administrators who have used cattle prods to discipline students, slammed students' heads against the walls, or spanked students so hard they needed medical attention, and the Supreme Court will probably continue to uphold such rulings. Overall, recent judicial decisions, together with the ever-present possibility of a lawsuit, have made educators cautious in using corporal punishment.

Sexual Harassment or Molestation of Students

■ Unwelcome sexual advances

The Supreme Court's decision in *Ingraham v. Wright* regarding physical punishment and a later decision in *Franklin v. Gwinnett* strengthened prohibitions against sexual harassment and sexual molestation. Definitions of these terms vary, but for interactions between students and teachers the terms generally include not only sexual contact that calls into question the teacher's role as exemplar but also unwelcome sexual advances or requests for favors, particularly when the recipient may believe that refusal will affect his or her academic standing. Recent years have seen a dramatic increase in court cases involving school employees accused of sexually harassing students. Although the courts have been unclear on what constitutes illegal

---

[46]*Ingraham v. Wright,* 430 U.S. (1977). See also Perry A. Zirkel, "You Bruise, You Lose," *Phi Delta Kappan* (January 1990), pp. 410–411; Perry Zirkel and Ivan B. Gluckman, "Is Corporal Punishment Child Abuse?" *Principal* (January 1996), pp. 60–61; Benjamin Dowling-Sendor, "A Shock to the Conscience," *American School Board Journal* (April 2001), available at **www.asbj.com**; and Linda Starr, "Punishment," *Education World,* November 12, 2002, available at **www.educationworld/a_issues**.
[47]*Miera v. Garcia,* 56 USLW 3390 (1987); Mitchell L. Yell and Reece L. Peterson, "Disciplining Students with Disabilities and Those at Risk for School Failure," *Clearing House* (July–August 1996), pp. 365–370; Benjamin Dowling-Sendor, "When Teachers Get Too Tough?" *American School Board Journal* (May 2000), available at **www.asbj.com**; and Patricia H. Hinchey, "Corporal Punishments: Legalities, Realities, and Implications," *Clearing House* (January/February 2003), pp. 127–132.

sexual harassment of students, clearly both staff members and the districts that employ them can be severely punished if found guilty in court.[48]

■ **Proactive action against sexual harassment**

School officials' legal responsibilities regarding teachers' sexual harassment of students were clarified in a 1998 Supreme Court decision (*Gebser v. Lago Vista Independent School District*) that involved a ninth grader who was seduced by a science teacher but never informed administrators about this sexual relationship. Her parents sued for damages from the school district using the argument that Title IX of the Education Amendments of 1972 requires schools to proactively take action to identify and eliminate sexual harassment. The Supreme Court ruled that school officials are not legally liable unless they know of the harassment and then proceed with "deliberate indifference." Some analysts were unhappy because they believed this decision allowed officials to avoid identifying and combating harassment, but others believed it reinforced administrators' resolve to implement policies that demonstrate their concern about harassment.[49]

■ **Touching students unlawful?**

Despite the relief from liability that *Gebser* provides for school officials, individual staff members must be wary of any action a student or parent might interpret as sexual harassment or assault. Given the numerous allegations brought against teachers in recent years, many teacher organizations have been advising their members to avoid touching students unnecessarily. They also recommend that teachers make sure that doors are open and/or that other persons are present when they meet with a student. Legal advisers recognize the necessity for or benefits of touching or even hugging a student, as when a kindergarten teacher helps students put on coats or comforts a distressed pupil, but many advise teachers to avoid physical contact as much as possible, particularly with older students.

■ **Guidelines for dealing with potential harassment**

Sexual abuse or harassment of one student by another is also a serious problem. As in the case of students allegedly harassed by teachers, the law regarding harassment by other students is poorly defined and murky. Name calling and teasing with sexual overtones have been interpreted as illegal harassment that educators have a legal obligation to suppress, but in certain situations school staff have been absolved of legal responsibility. Some school districts' antiharassment policies have prohibited "unwelcome" statements about gays and lesbians, but a federal appeals court prevented punishment of students who made such statements when it ruled they were exercising First Amendment rights to religious expression. On the other hand, several districts have paid settlements to gay or lesbian students who were harassed by peers. The following guidelines have been suggested for educators who think sexual harassment may be occurring:[50]

---

[48]Carol Shakeshaft and Audrey Cohan, "Sexual Abuse of Students by School Personnel," *Phi Delta Kappan* (March 1995), pp. 513–519; Martha M. McCarthy, "The Law Governing Sexual Harassment in Public Schools," *Phi Delta Kappa Research Bulletin* (May 1998), pp. 15–18; Wendy Schwartz, "Preventing Student Sexual Harassment," *ERIC Clearinghouse on Urban Education Digest* (December 2000); Benjamin Dowling-Sendor, "What Did They Know?" *American School Board Journal* (August 2002), available at **www.asbj.com**; Caroline Hendrie, "States Target Sexual Abuse by Educators," *Education Week*, April 30, 2003; and Matthew D. Olson and Gregory Lawler, *Guilty—Until Proven Innocent* (Stillwater, Okla.: New Forums, 2003).

[49]*Gebser v. Lago Vista Independent School District*, 98-1866 S. Ct. (1998). See also *Revised Sexual Harassment Guidance* (Washington, D.C.: U.S. Department of Education Office of Civil Rights, 2001), available at **www.ed.gov/offices/OCR**; and Michael D. Simpson, "Big Legal Victories for Gay Students and Teachers," *NEA Today Online* (January 2003), available at **www.nea.org/neatoday:** search for "legal victories."

[50]Perry A. Zirkel, "Student-to-Student Sexual Harassment," *Phi Delta Kappan* (April 1995), pp. 448–450; Kelley R. Taylor, "Protecting Our Students from Harassment," *Education Digest* (April 2003); and Perry A. Zirkel, "Gay Days," *Phi Delta Kappan* (January 2003), pp. 412–413.

1. Don't ignore the situation or let it pass unchallenged.

2. Don't overreact; find out exactly what happened.

3. Don't embarrass or humiliate any party to an incident.

4. Initiate steps to support the alleged victim.

5. Apply consequences in accordance with school behavior codes.

6. Don't assume that the incident is an isolated occurrence.

7. Provide comprehensive awareness programs for students.

Student Records and Privacy Rights

■ FERPA curbs abuses

Until 1974, although students or their parents could not view most student records kept by schools, prospective employers, government agencies, and credit bureaus could. As might be guessed, abuses occurred. In 1974, Congress passed the **Family Educational Rights and Privacy Act** (also called either FERPA or the **Buckley Amendment**) to curb possible abuses in institutions receiving federal funds.

■ Parents' rights

The Buckley Amendment requires public school districts to develop policies allowing parents access to their children's official school records. The act prohibits disclosure of these records to most third parties without prior parental consent. Districts must have procedures to amend records if parents challenge the accuracy or completeness of the information they contain. Hearing and appeal mechanisms regarding disputed information must also be available. Parents retain rights of access to their child's school records until the child reaches age eighteen or is enrolled in a postsecondary institution.

■ Certain records exempt

However, the Buckley Amendment allows several exceptions. Private notes and memoranda of teachers and administrators (including grade books) are exempt from view. In addition, records kept separate from official files and maintained for law enforcement purposes (for example, information about criminal behavior) cannot be disclosed. Nothing may be revealed that would jeopardize the privacy rights of other pupils. Last, schools may disclose directory-type information without prior consent; however, students or their families may request that even this information be withheld.[51]

■ Hatch Amendment

Student privacy policies also are affected by the Hatch Amendment to the federal General Education Provisions Act of 1978. The Hatch Amendment specified that instructional materials used in connection with "any research or experimentation program or project" must be "available for inspection" by participating students' parents and guardians. In addition, no student can be required to participate in testing, psychological examination, or treatments whose "primary purpose is to reveal information" concerning political affiliations, sexual behaviors or attitudes, psychological or mental problems, income, and other personal matters. It has been difficult to define terms such as "instructional materials" and "research program," and many parents have used the Hatch Act to object to school activities that probe students' feelings or beliefs. Consequently, teachers must consider carefully

---

[51]Peter A. Walker and Sara J. Steinberg, "Confidentiality of Educational Records," *Journal of Law and Education* (July 1997), pp. 11–27; Perry A. Zirkel, "A D-Grading Experience?" *Phi Delta Kappan* (November 2000), pp. 253–254; Gareth Parry, "Privacy in the Classroom," *Education and the Law* (September 2002), pp. 173–181; and Richard S. Vacca, "Student Records 2004," *CEPI Education Law Newsletter* (May 2004), available at **www.cepi.vcu.edu/ newsletter**.

whether collecting information on students' background or beliefs serves a legitimate goal.[52]

Compulsory Attendance and Home Schooling

Every state has a law requiring children to attend school, usually from age six or seven to age sixteen or seventeen. In the past two decades, these compulsory attendance laws have received increased attention because of a revival of interest in home schooling. A growing number of parents who object to subject matter taught in public schools, the teaching methods used, or the absence of religious activities have chosen to teach their children at home. State governments allow for home schooling, but depending on state legislation, they impose regulations dealing with hours of study, testing, whether home-schooled children can participate in extracurricular activities at nearby public schools, and other matters.[53]

Standards & Assessment ☑
■ Requirements for home schooling

Home-schooling parents brought to court for violating compulsory attendance laws have usually been asked to demonstrate the home program's essential equivalence to public-school offerings with respect to subject matter covered, adequacy of texts used, and hours of daily instruction. In some states, they also must show test results indicating that their children's education is comparable to that of school-educated peers. Parents have often prevailed in such cases, but courts have consistently upheld the right of state legislatures to impose restrictions and requirements.[54]

Need for Balance Between Rights and Responsibilities

■ Critique of courts

During the past several decades, as courts have upheld the constitutional rights of students and placed restrictions on school officials, many educators and parents have decided that the legal process is out of balance. They believe that the courts place too much emphasis on student rights and too little on the need for school discipline. The result, said former AFT president Albert Shanker, "is schools where little or no learning goes on because teachers have to assume the role of warden."[55]

■ Focus on reasonableness

However, some scholars believe that since the mid-1980s the Supreme Court has moved to redress the balance. In this view, the Court's decisions in *T.L.O.* (1985), *Bethel v. Fraser* (1986), and *Hazelwood v. Kuhlmeier* (1988) place less burden on school officials than the 1969 *Tinker* decision. Rather than demonstrating that

---

[52]Edward B. Jenkinson, *Student Privacy in the Classroom* (Bloomington, Ind.: Phi Delta Kappa, 1990); *Protecting the Privacy of Student Education Records* (Washington, D.C.: National Center for Education Statistics, 1996), available at **www.ed.gov**; and "Recent Changes Affecting FERPA and PPRA" (2002), paper posted at the Center for Positive Practices Internet site, available at **www.positivepractices.com**.

[53]J. Gary Knowles, Stacey E. Marlow, and James Muchmore, "From Pedagogy to Ideology," *American Journal of Education* (March 1991); Robert S. Bluey, "Massachusetts Homeschoolers Survive Custody Threat," *CNSNEWS.com*, June 18, 2003, available at **www.cnsnews.com**; and information from the Home School Legal Defense Association, available at **www.hslda.org**.

[54]Naomi Gitins, ed., *Religion, Education, and the U.S. Constitution* (Alexandria, Va.: National School Boards Association, 1990); Perry A. Zirkel, "Home Sweet...School," *Phi Delta Kappan* (December 1994), pp. 332–333; and Rhea R. Borja, "Oregon Mulls Relaxing Test Mandate for Home Schoolers," *Education Week*, April 30, 2003.

[55]Albert Shanker, "Discipline in Our Schools," *New York Times*, May 19, 1991, p. E7. See also Perry A. Zirkel, "The Right Stuff," *Phi Delta Kappan* (February 1998), pp. 473–474; and Benjamin Dowling-Sendor, "Balancing Safety with Free Expression," *American School Board Journal* (December 2001), available at **www.asbj.com**.

certain rules are necessary, school officials now need to show only that the rules are reasonable. This emphasis on reasonableness indicates that the Court "is placing considerable confidence in school officials," trusting those officials to maintain a proper balance between student rights and the school's needs.[56]

▶ Religion and the Schools

■ Government "neutral"

The framers of our Constitution were acutely aware of religious persecution and sought to prevent the United States from experiencing the serious and often bloody conflicts that had occurred in Europe. As noted at the beginning of this chapter, the First Amendment, adopted in 1791, prohibits the establishment of a nationally sanctioned religion (the establishment clause) and government interference with individuals' rights to hold and freely practice their religious beliefs (the free exercise clause). Judge Alphonso Taft succinctly stated the position of government toward religion more than one hundred years ago: "The government is neutral, and while protecting all, it prefers none, and it disparages none."[57]

Prayer, Bible Reading, and Religious Blessings and Displays

■ State-written prayer unconstitutional

Students in New Hyde Park were required to recite daily this nondenominational prayer composed by the New York State Board of Regents: "Almighty God, we acknowledge our dependence upon thee, and we beg thy blessings upon us, our parents, our teachers and our Country." Although exemption was possible upon written parental request, the U.S. Supreme Court in *Engle v. Vitale* (1962) ruled the state-written prayer unconstitutional. According to the Court, "Neither the fact that the prayer may be denominationally neutral nor the fact that its observance on the part of students is voluntary can serve to free it from the limitations of the Establishment Clause."[58]

The decision created a storm of protest that has barely subsided to this day. A year later, the Court again prohibited religious exercises in public schools. This time, the issue involved oral reading of Bible verses and recitation of the Lord's Prayer. These were clearly religious ceremonies and "intended by the State to be so," even when student participation was voluntary. In 2000, the Court excluded student-led prayer at a football game because the game and therefore the prayer were officially sponsored by the school. On the other hand, the courts have ruled that students can

---

[56]Lowell C. Rose, "Reasonableness—The Court's New Standard for Cases Involving Student Rights," *Phi Delta Kappan* (April 1988), pp. 589–592. See also Lawrence F. Rossow and Janice A. Hiniger, *Students and the Law* (Bloomington, Ind.: Phi Delta Kappa, 1991); Yong S. Lee, "Theory of a 'Reasonable' Public Servant" (2002), paper posted at the Bush School Internet site, available at **www.tamu.edu:** search for "public servant"; and Marjorie Coeyman, "Are Schools More Afraid of Lawsuits Than They Used to Be?" *Christian Science Monitor,* May 27, 2003.

[57]Quoted by Justice Tom Clark in *School District of Abington Township v. Schempp,* 374 U.S. 203 (1963). See also "Religious Liberty, Public Education, and the Future of American Democracy," *Educational Leadership* (May 1995), pp. 92–93; S. L. Guerke, "The Supreme Court and Religious Exercise in the Public Schools" (2000), paper posted at the Apathia Internet site, available at **www.apathia.org:** click on "Library"; and Benjamin Dowling-Sendor, "Trouble in Paradise," *American School Board Journal* (June 2002), available at **www.asbj.com**.

[58]*Engle v. Vitale,* 370 U.S. 421 (1962). See also "A Matter of Conscience," *Church and State* (March 1995), pp. 10–12; and "Guidelines on Constitutionally Protected Prayer" (2003), paper posted at the U.S. Department of Education Internet site, available at **www.ed.gov/inits/religionandschools**.

lead or participate in prayers at commencement ceremonies, as long as decisions to do so are made by students without the involvement of clergy.[59]

■ Invocations and benedictions

The Supreme Court also has ruled against invocations and benedictions in which a clergyman opens or closes a public-school ceremony by invoking blessings from a deity. In a 1992 decision, the Court concluded that such blessings violate the standards established in *Lemon v. Kurtzman* (see Figure 9.1), which prohibit the government from advancing religion. However, Justice Anthony Kennedy's majority opinion noted that state actions implicating religion are not necessarily unconstitutional because some citizens may object to them, and that the decision was not meant to require a "relentless and pervasive attempt to exclude religion from every aspect of public life."

■ "Moment of silence" policies

One effect of the decision was to postpone full constitutional review of several important questions, such as whether schools can implement "moment of silence" policies that allow voluntary silent prayer in classrooms, whether a school choir can perform clearly Christian songs at a graduation ceremony, and whether private groups can distribute free Bibles on school premises.

■ A "secular" atmosphere

Displaying religious symbols (such as a cross or a menorah) in public schools in a manner that promotes a particular religion is clearly unconstitutional. However, the Supreme Court has ruled that religiously oriented artifacts such as a Nativity scene can be displayed in public settings if the overall atmosphere is largely secular. The interpretation of this ruling is controversial. In one nonschool case, the Court banned a Nativity scene in front of the Allegheny County (Pa.) Courthouse because it had not been "junked up" (in the words of a county official) with Santa Claus figures or other secular symbols. After that decision, a federal judge required the removal of a crucifixion painting from the Schuylerville (N.Y.) School District, on the grounds that the painting lacked any "meaningful" secular features. In 2002, an Ohio school district was prohibited from posting the Ten Commandments in front of four high schools.[60]

Access to Public Schools for Religious Groups

■ School meetings of religious groups

Bridget Mergens, an Omaha high-school senior, organized a group of about twenty-five students who requested permission to meet on campus before school every week or so to read and discuss the Bible. Although similar Bible clubs were allowed to meet at other schools, administrators refused the request, partly to avoid setting a precedent for clubs of Satanists, Ku Klux Klanists, or other groups the school would find undesirable. Bridget's mother brought suit, and in 1990 the U.S. Supreme Court found in her favor. Public high schools, the Court ruled, must allow students' religious, philosophical, and political groups to meet on campus on the same basis as other extracurricular groups. Permitting such meetings, the Court stated, does not mean that the school endorses or supports them.[61]

---

[59]*School District of Abington Township v. Schempp* and *Murray v. Curlett,* 374 U.S. 203 (1963). See also Benjamin Dowling-Sendor, "A Defeat for Pregame Prayer," *American School Board Journal* (August 2000), available at **www.asbj.com**; and Richard S. Vacca, "Graduation Prayer," *CEPI Education Law Newsletter* (May 2003), available at **www.cepi.vcu.edu/newsletter**.
[60]Rob Boston, "The Klan, a Cross, and the Constitution," *Church and State* (March 1995), pp. 7–9; "City-Sponsored Religious Display Struck Down by Court," *Church and State* (April 1997), p. 3; and "'Thou Shalt Not...'" (March 2003), paper posted at the National Education Association Internet site, available at **www.nea.org/neatoday/0303**.
[61]*Board of Education of the Westside Community Schools v. Mergens,* 88 S. Ct. 1597 (1990). See also "The Federal Equal Access Act" (2003), at the OCRT Internet site, available at **www. religioustolerance.org:** search "this site" for "equal access."

■ Options for schools

Implications of the *Mergens* case have aroused great uncertainty. Schools apparently must choose between allowing practically any student group to meet or dropping all extracurricular activities. A third option would be to permit meetings only by groups whose activities relate directly to the curriculum, but difficult problems arise in defining such activities. Recent Supreme Court cases have failed to fully clarify the issue, but it is clear that religious groups and activities must satisfy criteria such as the following:[62]

- The activity must be student initiated.

- The school may not sponsor the activity, but its employees may attend meetings and it may pay incidental costs such as heating.

- Outsiders may not direct the group or regularly attend meetings.

Pledge of Allegiance

■ Religious objections to pledge

The separation of church and state also applies to statements of allegiance to the state. In one case, several Jehovah's Witnesses went to court over a West Virginia requirement that their children recite the pledge of allegiance at school each morning. The parents based their objection on religious doctrine. The court ruled that the children could be exempted from this requirement because it conflicted with their religious beliefs. Using this ruling as precedent, federal judges have concluded that students who refuse to stand and recite the pledge cannot be compelled to do so if participation violates their religious or other personal beliefs. Recent decisions have provided further support for this conclusion.[63]

In 2002, a federal court of appeals ruled the Pledge of Allegiance unconstitutional because it includes the words "under God." This decision predictably sparked nationwide controversy; whether or not the ruling can be implemented is yet to be determined by the Supreme Court and other courts.[64]

Religious Objections Regarding Curriculum

■ Basal readers challenged

In Tennessee in the mid-1980s, fundamentalist Christian parents brought suit against the Hawkins County School District charging that exposure of their children to the Holt, Rinehart and Winston basal reading series was offensive to their religious beliefs. The parents believed that "after reading the entire Holt series, a child might adopt the views of a feminist, a humanist, a pacifist, an anti-Christian, a vegetarian, or an advocate of a one-world government." The district court held for the parents, reasoning that the state could satisfy its compelling interest in the literacy of Tennessee schoolchildren through less restrictive means than compulsory use of the Holt series. However, an appellate court reversed this decision, stating that no evidence had been produced to show that students were required to affirm their belief or disbelief in any idea mentioned in the Holt books. The textbook series, the

---

[62]Benjamin Dowling-Sendor, "Opening Your Schools," *American School Board Journal* (May 1999); and "A Question of Equity," *American School Board Journal* (February 2003), both available at **www.asbj.com**.
[63]*West Virginia State Board of Education v. Barnette,* 319 U.S. 624 (1943); *Lipp v. Morris,* 579 F. 2d 834 (3rd Cir. 1978); Perry A. Zirkel and Ivan B. Gluckman, "Pledge of Allegiance," *NASSP Bulletin* (September 1990), pp. 115–117; and Christopher Clausen, "Opening Exercises," *American Scholar* (Winter 2003), pp. 35–44.
[64]Scott Holleran, "Restore the Pledge of Allegiance to Its Original Meaning," *Capitalism Magazine,* March 2, 2003, available at **www.capmag.com:** search for "pledge."

Federal judges have concluded that students who refuse to stand and recite the pledge of allegiance cannot be compelled to do so if participation violates their religious or other personal beliefs. *(© Russell D. Curtis/ Photo Researchers)*

court said, "merely requires recognition that in a pluralistic society we must 'live and let live.'"[65]

■ Secular humanism

In somewhat similar cases, district judges upheld a group of parents in Alabama who contended that school textbooks and activities advanced the religion of secular humanism[66] and a New York group that contended the Bedford Public Schools were promoting pagan religions when students recited a liturgy to the Earth or sold worry dolls. The first decision was reversed by a federal appeals court, which held that the textbooks did not endorse secular humanism or any other religion, but rather attempted to instill such values as independent thought and tolerance of diverse views. The appeals court noted that if the First Amendment prohibited mere "inconsistency with the beliefs of a particular religion there would be very little that could be taught in the public schools." The second case also was resolved in favor of the schools. Similar conclusions have been reached by courts in California and several other states.[67]

■ The evolution controversy

In 1987 the U.S. Supreme Court considered *Edwards v. Aguillard,* a case that challenged Louisiana's Balanced Treatment for Creation-Science and Evolution-Science Act. Creation science, or creationism, is the belief that life has developed through divine intervention or creation rather than through biological evolution. The Louisiana act required that creation science be taught wherever evolution was taught, and that appropriate curriculum guides and materials be developed. The Supreme Court ruled this law unconstitutional. By requiring "either the banishment

[65]*Mozert v. Hawkins County Board of Education,* 86-6144 (E.D. Tenn. 1986); *Mozert v. Hawkins County Board of Education,* 87-5024 (6th Cir. 1987); and Rob Reich, "Opting Out of Education," *Educational Theory* (Fall 2002), pp. 445–461.
[66]The secular humanism philosophy de-emphasizes religious doctrines and instead emphasizes the human capacity for self-realization through reason.
[67]*Smith v. Board of School Commissioners of Mobile County,* 87–7216, 11th Cir. (1987); David A. Splitt, "Sorting Out What Is and Isn't Religious," *Executive Educator* (March 1995), pp. 13, 47; Perry A. Zirkel, "Good Faith Efforts—Part 2," *Phi Delta Kappan* (March 2000), pp. 553–554; and Jim Allison, "Secular Humanism in U.S. Supreme Court Cases" (undated), paper available at **http:members.tripod.com/~candst/sec-hum3.htm**.

of the theory of evolution . . . or the presentation of a religious viewpoint that rejects evolution in its entirety," the Court reasoned, the Louisiana act advanced a religious doctrine and violated the establishment clause of the First Amendment.[68]

■ School-district responses

The controversy has continued. The California and Kansas boards of education have tried to compromise, for example, by referring to evolution as a theory rather than a fact. In line with creationist beliefs, some school districts have introduced books that assert life is too complex to be formed through evolution, but avoid explicit references to divine creation. In other districts, comparable controversies have arisen when parents have objected to certain materials designed to improve students' thinking skills, contending that the materials reflected "New Age" religious practices. Some school districts have responded by eliminating such materials.[69]

Teaching About Religion

■ Promoting understanding of religious traditions

Guarantees of separation between church and state do not prohibit public schools from teaching *about* religion. Some states and school districts have been strengthening approaches for developing an understanding of religious traditions and values while neither promoting nor detracting from any particular religious or nonreligious ideology. In addition, many scholars have been preparing materials for such constitutionally acceptable instruction.[70]

■ Federal guidelines

According to guidelines issued in 1995 and reissued in 1998 by the U.S. Department of Education, schools can teach subjects such as "the history of religion, comparative religion, the Bible (or other scripture) as literature, and the role of religion in the history of the United States and other countries." These federal guidelines, which also touched on many other controversies concerning religion and schools, are summarized in Overview 9.3. However, courts may not necessarily support what the executive branch deems correct.[71]

Government Guidelines Regarding Prayer and Religion in Schools

■ Teachers may neither encourage nor discourage

In 2003, the Department of Education issued more detailed guidelines involving prayer and related activities in public schools. Guidelines and commentary included the following:[72]

---

[68]*Edwards v. Aguillard,* 197 S. Ct. 2573 (1987); Eugene C. Scott, "Monkey Business," *Policy Review* (January–February 1996), pp. 20–25; Daniel J. Kelves, "Darwin in Dayton," *New York Review of Books,* November 19, 1998, pp. 61–63; Francis Beckwith, *Law, Darwinism and Public Education* (Lanham, Md.: Rowman and Littlefield, 2003); and "Religion and Public Schools" (undated), posted at the Pew Forum Internet site, available at **www.pew-forum.org/ issues**.

[69]Tim Beardsley, "Darwin Denied," *Scientific American* (July 1995), pp. 12–13; Leon Lynn, "The Evolution of Creationism," *Rethinking Schools* (Winter 1997/1998), available at **www.rethinkingschools.org**; and Amy J. Binder, *Contentious Curricula* (Princeton, N.J.: Princeton University Press, 2002). Internet sites dealing with creationism and evolution are easily found by using search engines to investigate "creationism."

[70]For example, see Charles C. Haynes and Oliver Thomas, eds., *Finding Common Ground* (Nashville, Tenn.: Freedom Forum First Amendment Center, 2001), available at **www. firstamendmentcenter.org:** click on "First Amendment publications"; "Navigating Religion in the Classroom" (2002), paper posted at the National Education Association Internet site, available at **www.nea.org/neatoday/0211**; and Susan Black, "Teaching About Religion," *American School Board Journal* (June 2003), available at **www.asbj.com**.

[71]Charles C. Hayne, "Religion in the Public Schools," *School Administrator* (January 1999); James M. Banner Jr., "Teaching About Religion," *Basic Education Online* (October 2002), available at **www.c-b-e.org**; and information at **www.teachingaboutreligion.org**.

[72]Rod Paige, "Guidance on Constitutionally Protected Prayer in Public Elementary and Secondary Schools" (2003), paper posted at the U.S. Department of Education Internet site, available at **www.ed.gov/inits/religionandschools**.

OVERVIEW 9.3 *Guidelines on Religion in the Schools, from the U.S. Department of Education*

Student prayer and religious discussion: [The U.S. Constitution] does not prohibit purely private religious speech by students. Students therefore have the same right to engage in individual or group prayer and religious discussion during the school day as they do to engage in other comparable activity.

Generally, students may pray in a nondisruptive manner when not engaged in school activities or instruction, and subject to the rules that normally pertain in the applicable setting.

Graduation prayer: Under current [U.S.] Supreme Court decisions, school officials may not mandate or organize prayer at graduation nor organize religious baccalaureate ceremonies.

Official neutrality: Teachers and school administrators . . . are prohibited by the [Constitution] from soliciting or encouraging religious activity and . . . from discouraging activity because of its religious content.

Teaching about religion: Public schools may not provide religious instruction, but they may teach about religion . . . , the history of religion, comparative religion, the Bible (or other scripture) as literature, and the role of religion in the history of the United States and other countries are all permissible public school subjects.

Although public schools may teach about religious holidays . . . and may celebrate the secular aspects of holidays, schools may not observe holidays as religious events or promote such observance by students.

Student assignments: Students may express their beliefs about religion in the form of homework, artwork, and other written and oral assignments . . . . Such home and classroom work should be judged by ordinary academic standards.

Religious literature: Students have a right to distribute religious literature to their schoolmates on the same terms as they are permitted to distribute other literature that is unrelated to school curriculum or activities.

Religious exemptions: Schools enjoy substantial discretion to excuse individual students from lessons that are objectionable to the student or the student's parents on religious or other conscientious grounds.

Released time: Schools have the discretion to dismiss students to off-premises religious instruction, provided that schools do not encourage or discourage participation . . . . Schools may not allow religious instruction by outsiders on school premises during the school day.

Teaching values: Though schools must be neutral with respect to religion, they may play an active role with respect to teaching civic values and virtue.

Student garb: Students may display religious messages on items of clothing to the same extent that they are permitted to display other comparable messages.

The Equal Access Act: Student religious groups have the same right of access to school facilities as is enjoyed by other comparable student groups.

Source: Richard W. Riley, "Secretary's Statement on Religious Expression" (Statement released by the U.S. Department of Education, Washington, D.C., 1998).

- Students may organize prayer groups, religious clubs, and 'see you at the flagpole' gatherings before school to the same extent that students are permitted to organize other noncurricular student activities groups. . . .

- Teachers may . . . take part in religious activities where the overall context makes clear that they are not participating in their official capacities. Before school or during lunch, for example, teachers may meet with other teachers for prayer or Bible study to the same extent that they may engage in other conversation or nonreligious activities. . . .

- If a school has a 'moment of silence' or other quiet periods during the school day, students are free to pray silently, or not to pray. . . . Teachers and other school employees may neither encourage nor discourage students from praying during such time periods. . . .

- Students may express their beliefs about religion in homework, artwork, and other written and oral assignments free from discrimination based on the religious content of their submissions. Such home and classroom work should be judged by ordinary academic standards of substance and relevance and against other legitimate pedagogical concerns.

Government Regulation and Support of Nonpublic Schools

■ States can regulate

In 1925, *Pierce v. Society of Sisters* established that a state's compulsory school attendance laws could be satisfied through enrollment in a private or parochial school. Attention then turned to the question of how much control a state could exercise over the education offered in nonpublic schools. A 1926 case, *Farrington v. Tokushige,* gave nonpublic schools "reasonable choice and discretion in respect of teachers, curriculum and textbooks." Within that framework, however, states have passed various kinds of legislation to regulate nonpublic schools. Some states have few regulations; others require the employment of certified teachers, specify the number of days or hours the school must be in session, or insist that schools meet state accreditation standards. One current controversy involves the application of state standards for special education.[73]

■ State aid for transportation

On the other side of the coin, states have offered many types of support for nonpublic schools, including transportation, books, and health services. In the 1947 case *Everson v. Board of Education of Erving Township,* the Supreme Court considered a provision in the New Jersey Constitution that allowed state aid for transportation of private and parochial students. The Court held that where state constitutions permitted such assistance, they did not violate the U.S. Constitution. (Transportation aid for private-school students has been ruled unconstitutional in only Idaho and Hawaii.) Since then, the distinction between permissible and impermissible state aid to nonpublic schools has usually been based on the **child benefit theory**: aid that directly benefits the child is permissible, whereas aid that primarily benefits the nonpublic institution is not.[74]

■ *Wolman:* permissible state aid

In *Wolman v. Walter* (1977), *Agostini v. Felton* (1997), *Mitchell v. Helms* (2000), and *Zelman v. Simmons-Harris* (2002), the Supreme Court went further. Addressing state support for nonpublic schools permitted by the Ohio and New York Constitutions, the Court decided each specific question by applying the three-pronged *Lemon v. Kurtzman* test illustrated in Figure 9.1. The Court's decisions were as follows:[75]

- Providing for the purchase or loan of secular textbooks, standardized tests, and computers is constitutional.

- Providing speech, hearing, and psychological diagnostic services at the nonpublic-school site is constitutional.

- Providing for the purchase and loan of other instructional materials and equipment, such as projectors, science kits, maps and globes, charts, record

[73]*Pierce v. Society of Sisters,* 268 U.S. 510 (1925); and *Farrington v. Tokushige,* 273 U.S. 284 (1926). See also Sarah Wildman, "Credit Is Due," *New Republic,* February 26, 2001, pp. 15–16; and David F. Salisbury, "Lessons From Florida," *Cato Institute Briefing Papers,* March 20, 2003, available at **www.cato.org**.

[74]*Everson v. Board of Education of Erving Township,* 330 U.S. (1947); and Stewart J. Douglas, "A Comparative Analysis of Funding Non-Government Schools," *Education and the Law* (March 2001).

[75]*Wolman v. Walter,* 433 U.S. 229 (1977); *Agostini v. Felton,* 96 S. Ct. 552 (1997); *Mitchell v. Helms,* 98 S. Ct. 1648 (2000); Gene Straughan, "The Supreme Court, Religious Liberty, and Parochial School Aid" (2001), paper posted at the Lewis-Clark State College Internet site, available at **www.lcsc.edu/gtstraughn**; *Zelman v. Simmon-Harris et al.,* No. 00-1751 S. Ct. (2002); and Clint Bolick, "The Promise of Choice," *Hoover Digest* (Spring 2003), available at **www.hoover.stanford.edu**.

players, and so on, was ruled unconstitutional because this involves excessive government entanglement with religion.

■ Providing funds for field trips is unconstitutional because "where the teacher works within and for a sectarian institution, an unacceptable risk of fostering religion is an inevitable byproduct."

■ Providing Title 1 remedial services from public-school staff located at neutral facilities does not constitute excessive entanglement of church and state.

■ Providing students with vouchers used to pay for tuition at nonpublic schools is constitutional if no financial incentives skew the program toward religious schools.

■ A legal muddle

The conclusions outlined above show why many legal scholars believe that constitutional law regarding religion and the schools is something of a muddle. Why should government purchase of textbooks, tests, and computers for nonpublic schools be constitutional but not purchase of maps, globes, charts, and record players? Why can government-supported psychological services be provided at nonpublic schools, whereas remedial services must be provided at a neutral site? Questions as convoluted as these help explain why Court attempts at clarification have been only partly successful.[76]

> **REFOCUS** Do you think controversies involving church and state will affect you directly as a teacher? Which aspects are most relevant in your subject field? What difficulties or challenges that relate to religion might arise in schools in your community?

► Summing Up

1 Education-related court cases have significantly increased in the past few decades. Such cases can be heard in both federal and state courts, depending on the issues involved. Only decisions of the U.S. Supreme Court apply nationally.

2 Tenure protects teachers from dismissal except on such specified grounds as incompetence, immorality, insubordination, and unprofessional conduct. Teachers accused of such conduct are entitled to due-process protections.

3 Teachers have the right to form and belong to unions and other professional organizations, but most states prohibit teachers from striking.

4 Teachers' rights regarding freedom of expression and academic freedom depend on a balance between individual and governmental interests. Teachers have rights guaranteed to individuals under the Constitution, but school boards have obligations to ensure the "proper" and "regular" operation of the schools, taking into account the rights of parents, teachers, and students.

5 Restraints on teachers' behavior outside school and on their dress and grooming are not as stringent as they once were in the United States, but teachers still are expected to serve as role models and to behave in an exemplary manner.

---

[76]Clint Bolick, "Blocking the Exits," *Policy Review* (May–June 1998), available at **www. heritage.org:** search for "Blocking the Exits"; R. Craig Wood and Michael C. Petko, "Assessing *Agostini v. Felton* in Light of *Lemon v. Kurzman*," *BYU Education and Law Journal*, vol. 2000, no. 1, available at **www.byu.edu**; Andrew Stark, "The Contradiction at the Core of Constitutional Discourse Over State Aid to Parochial Schools," *William and Mary Law Review* (April 2001); and James E. Ryan, "The Neutrality Principle," *Education Next* (Fall 2003), available at **www.educationnext.org**.

6 Schools must uphold definite safety standards to avoid legal suits charging negligence when students are injured. In addition, teachers must obey copyright laws.

7 The courts have clarified and expanded such students' rights as freedom of expression, due process in the case of suspension or expulsion, prohibition against bodily searches in the absence of specific grounds, limitations on corporal punishment, and privacy of records.

8 Organized and mandated prayer and Bible reading are not allowed in public schools. School curricula do not automatically constitute unconstitutional discrimination against religion when they ignore religious points of view or explanations.

9 The legal basis for government support for nonpublic schools is mixed. For example, government may provide textbooks, tests, and psychological services for students at nonpublic schools, but providing funds for field trips, projectors, science kits, or maps is thought to entangle church and state.

▶ Key Terms

plaintiffs (247)	due process (250)
litigants (247)	academic freedom (255)
establishment clause (248)	torts (256)
free exercise clause (248)	fair use (259)
due process clause (248)	*in loco parentis* (261)
equal protection clause (248)	Family Educational Rights and Privacy Act
breach of contract (250)	(Buckley Amendment) (274)
tenure (250)	child benefit theory (282)
continuing contract (250)	

▶ Discussion Questions

1 Should teachers be required to meet higher or different standards of personal morality than other citizens? Why or why not?

2 Debate the pros and cons of prayer, Bible reading, and religious observances in public schools. Should current laws change regarding these activities?

3 Should students' due-process rights differ from those of adults outside the school? Why or why not? What differences may be most justifiable?

4 To what extent are academic freedom issues in elementary schools different from those in secondary schools? How might this distinction be important for you as a teacher?

5 Think of a situation in which your personal views might conflict with your school's policies regarding corporal punishment, student dress codes, or some other legal issue. To what extent would you find it difficult to comply with official policies? If you refused to comply, might this make it difficult to work with colleagues, students, or parents? What might you do to modify the policies or otherwise resolve the problem?

▶ Suggested Projects for Professional Development

1 Research the teacher tenure regulations in your state and in one or two nearby states. Do the states differ with respect to probationary period, cause for dismissal, or other matters? Are teachers in your community aware of these policies?

2 From a nearby school district, collect and analyze information about teachers' responsibilities for identifying and reporting child abuse. What are the district's explicit policies? Have any teachers been released or otherwise disciplined for failure to meet these responsibilities?

3 Survey several nearby school districts regarding their policies on student and teacher dress codes. Find out whether and how these policies have changed in the past ten or fifteen years. Do you expect to see further changes in the near future?

4 For your portfolio, prepare a lesson plan dealing with religious holidays in a manner that neither unconstitutionally promotes nor inhibits religion.

5 Go to **http:library.lp.findlaw.com/education_1html**, then search for and download the Department of Education's report "Discipline of Students with Disabilities." What conclusions and responsibilities are likely to be most important and perhaps most problematic to you as a teacher?

► Suggested Resources

 Internet Resources

You can find useful sources dealing with material in this chapter at **www.findlaw.com**. Hear sound clips of arguments in Supreme Court cases at **www.oyez.org** (click on "Hear ye, Hear Ye"). Most Supreme Court cases can be examined at **www.thisnation.com/index.html**.

The American Civil Liberties Union at **www.aclu.org** gives considerable attention to education-related cases.

A wealth of law-related material involving school safety and student discipline is available at **www.keepschoolsafe.org**.

"School Law Topics" is a useful site that the Missouri Department of Elementary and Secondary Education updates at **www.dese.state.mo.us/schoollaw**.

Publications

Alexander, Kern, and David M. Alexander. *American Public School Law.* 5th ed. Belmont, Calif.: Wadsworth, 2002. *This venerable text has been providing solid and reliable information and analysis regarding school law for decades.*

Bailey, Kirk A. *School Policies and Legal Issues Supporting Safe Schools.* Washington, D.C.: National Criminal Justice Reference Services, 2002. *This publication is available at* **www.ncjrs.org***, by searching "Full-Text Publications" for "School Policies and Legal Issues."*

Osborne, Allan G., and Charles J. Russo. *Special Education and the Law.* Thousand Oaks, Calif.: Corwin, 2003. *Topics considered in this book have great relevance for classroom teachers.*

Provenzo, Eugene F., Jr. *Religious Fundamentalism and American Education.* Albany: State University of New York Press, 1990. *Describes and analyzes major Supreme Court decisions dealing with church and state censorship, family rights and education, and related issues.*

Rossow, Lawrence F., and Janice A. Hiniger. *Students and the Law.* Bloomington, Ind.: Phi Delta Kappa, 1991. *This slim "Fastback" includes chapters on freedom of speech, student publications, search and seizure, drug testing, religious activity, discipline in special education, and expulsions and suspensions.*

PART FOUR

Social Foundations

Chapter 10

Culture, Socialization, and Education

We are all aware that the world is changing rapidly. Communications and the economy are becoming globalized, career success requires increasingly advanced skills, immigration has accelerated in the United States and many other countries, and family patterns today differ greatly from those thirty years ago. Each such change has a major impact on education from elementary school through university.

Nevertheless, certain underlying imperatives and influences regarding how we rear children and youth necessarily remain important. Student development still is strongly influenced by families, neighborhoods, and friends, and by wider cultural and social forces such as the mass media, just as it was thirty or sixty or ninety years ago.

On the other hand, the specific ways in which such forces exert their influence on children and youth change over time. For example, you, as a teacher, may have increasing difficulty capturing students' attention in a digitized world that offers myriad competing stimuli. To respond adequately, you must understand what is happening in the family, the mass media, and the peer group, and how cultural and social trends are influencing the behaviors and ideas that students bring to the classroom.

As you read the chapter, keep these questions in mind:

FOCUS QUESTIONS

- What cultural patterns influence instruction in schools?
- How does school culture socialize the young?
- How have television and other mass media affected students?
- Do sex roles and sex differences influence learning and achievement? If so, how?
- How do aspects of youth culture affect the schools?

■ Aspects of culture

A society ensures its unity and survival by means of culture. The term *culture* has been broadly defined to encompass all the continually changing patterns of acquired behavior and attitudes transmitted among the members of a society. Culture is a way of thinking and behaving; it is a group's traditions, memories, and written records, its shared rules and ideas, its accumulated beliefs, habits, and values. No individual, group, or entire society can be understood without reference to culture. Habits of dress, diet, and daily routine—the countless small details of ordinary life that seem to require little reflection—all constitute cultural identity. Together, **acculturation**, which teaches children the concepts, values, and behavior patterns of their common culture, and **socialization**,which prepares them to function first as young people and then as adults, transmit culture and allow society to function satisfactorily.

■ School as cultural agent

Many individuals and institutions play a part in acculturating and socializing children and youth. The family, of course, is most important for young children, but in modern societies formal institutions also help determine what a child learns and how well he or she is prepared to function in society. The school serves as perhaps the major institution (other than the family) devised by the adult generation for maintaining and perpetuating the culture. It supplies the tools necessary for survival and ensures the transmission of knowledge and values to future generations. Schools uphold and pass on the society's values, beliefs, and **norms** (rules of behavior), not only in lesson subject matter but also through the very structure and operation of the educational system.

In a diverse society such as our own, schools are responsible for helping young people learn to participate in a national culture, but they also must be sensitive to cultural differences and make sure that students from minority groups have equal opportunities to succeed in education. We discuss the challenges posed by this imperative in the multicultural education sections of the chapter on Providing Equal Educational Opportunity.

▶ Agents of Socialization

■ Major socializing institutions

Various social institutions help to transmit culture to children and youth. For many societies, the most important historically have been the church, peer group, school, and, of course, family. Some of these institutions, such as the church, have become less influential in Western societies while others, such as the mass media, have emerged as a socializing force. In this section we discuss several issues concerning the influence of family patterns on education. We then go on to consider the peer group's socializing role and educational implications, school culture, and the influences of television and other mass media. Overview 10.1 summarizes the socializing contributions of each of these institutions.

The Family

■ Early influence of family

Although its organization varies, the family is the major early socializing agent in every society. As such, it is the first medium for transmitting culture to children. Because the family is the whole world to young children, its members teach a child what matters in life, often without realizing the enormous influence they wield. The behaviors adults encourage and discourage and the ways in which they provide discipline also affect a child's orientation toward the world.

■ Home environment and preparation for school

Many children do well in school because their family environment has provided them with good preparation for succeeding in the traditional classroom. Others do

OVERVIEW 10.1 *Effects of Major Socializing Institutions*

Institution	Trends and Characteristics	Socializing Effects
Family	• Poverty • Single-parent families • Increase in working mothers • Latchkey children • Pressures on children • OverIndulged children • Homelessness	Some trends, such as increasing numbers of working mothers and expanding options for before- and after-school activities hold positive potential, but most put children at risk for difficulty in school.
Peers	• Popularity, athletics, attractiveness more important than academics • Extracurricular activities with peers • Bullying	Cooperative activities can reduce bullying and foster peer relationships that promote academics. Extracurricular activities tend to promote academic achievement.
School Culture	• Active learner role carries risks • Hidden curriculum has diverse and frequently important impacts • Classroom cultures stress order • Accommodations, bargaining, compromise • Teacher overload leads to rationing attention	School often teaches students to reduce their enthusiasm and to prefer passive learning.
Television and Digital Media	• Unclear relationship of television to achievement • Television may socialize aggression, undesirable attitudes • Internet may hold promise for active learning	Television and other media can contribute to academic achievement, but their content and use must be carefully planned or they can become agents of negative socialization.

poorly in part because they have been poorly prepared and the schools generally have failed to help them overcome this disadvantage. (We'll describe possibilities for modifying instruction and other ways of helping unsuccessful students in later chapters.) Recent changes in the nature of the family have important implications for children's educational development and success in school. This section discusses several of the most important changes affecting families, including increases in poverty, single-parent families, and working mothers. We'll also discuss how families may create educational difficulties by pressuring or overindulging children. Finally, we'll examine the severe problems some children face in their home situations, including abuse and homelessness.

Children in Poverty. Poverty is a major problem for many families. More than 15 percent of American children live in poverty. Poverty rates are particularly high for children from minority groups; approximately 30 percent of African American and Latino children and youth are growing up in families below the poverty line. Poor children often face educational difficulties. We'll discuss the relationship between social class and educational achievement in more detail in the chapter on Social Class, Race, and School Achievement.

■ Single-parent families

Single-Parent Families. Many observers connect the substantial poverty rates among children and youth with the high incidence of single-parent families. Recent decades have seen a large increase in the percentage of households with a single parent, usually a never-married, divorced, or separated woman. Overall, single-parent families now constitute almost 30 percent of all households with children under age eighteen. About 40 percent of female-headed families are below the poverty line, compared with 8 percent for two-parent families.[1]

Some observers conclude that modern marriage is a roulette game, as likely as not to land children in single-parent families. For example, of all non-Hispanic white children, only 70 percent were living in two-parent households in 2002, compared with more than 90 percent in 1960. The figures for African American children and youth are even more startling: less than 35 percent were living in two-parent households in 2002. Overall, more than half of all young people younger than eighteen live in a single-parent family for some part of their childhood.[2]

■ Impact on children

Much research has concentrated on the specific effects of growing up in a home where the father is absent. A few studies assess little measurable impact on children, but most others find a variety of negative effects, including a greater likelihood that families will fall into poverty and that children will suffer serious emotional and academic problems. The major reason this research lacks conclusiveness is the difficulty in controlling for the effects of social class. A large percentage of families that "lost" a father also declined in social class, and this change in status makes it difficult to identify the separate effects of each factor.[3]

To help you, as a teacher, respond to the trend toward single-parent families, analysts have recommended steps like the following:[4]

■ Recommendations for schools

- Do not assume that all or even most children from single-parent families have unusual problems.

- Send copies of communications to the noncustody parent.

- Include representation of single-parent families in the curriculum and add library materials that show varied lifestyles and help children cope with divorce.

---

[1]Thomas Davey, "Considering Divorce," *American Prospect,* January 1–15, 2000, pp. 42–44; James Q. Wilson, *The Marriage Problem* (New York: HarperCollins, 2002); and Jason Field, "Children's Living Arrangements and Characteristics," *Current Population Reports* (June 2003).
[2]Linda J. Rubin and Sherry B. Borgers, "The Changing Family: Implications for Education," *Principal* (September 1991), pp. 11–13; Jesse McKinnon, "The Black Population of the United States," *Current Population Reports* (April 2003); and Kristin F. Seefeldt and Pamela J. Smock, "Marriage on the Public Policy Agenda," *Poverty Research Insights* (Winter 2004), available at **www.npc.umich.edu**.
[3]Stephanie Coontz, "The American Family and the Nostalgia Trap," *Phi Delta Kappan* (March 1995), pp. K1–K10; Maggie Gallagher and David Blankenhorn, "Family Feud," *American Prospect* (July–August, 1997), pp. 12–15; Sara L. McLanahan, "Life Without Father" (2001), paper prepared for the Princeton University Center for Research on Child Wellbeing, available at **http:crcw.princeton.edu/workingpapers/WP01-21-McLanahan.pdf**; and William Jeynes, *Divorce, Family Structure, and the Academic Success of Children* (Binghamton, N.Y.: Haworth, 2002).
[4]Adele M. Brodkin and Melba Coleman, "Teachers Can't Do It Alone," *Instructor* (May–June 1995), pp. 25–26; Peter Benson and Eugene Roehlkepartain, "Making a Difference" (1999), paper posted at the Connect for Kids Internet site, available at **www.connectforkids.org:** search for "Peter Benson," and Jody Seidler, "Single Parent Support" (undated), posting at the Digital Women Internet site, available at **www.digital-women.com/howto01d.htm**.

- Cooperate with other agencies in improving child-care arrangements before and after school.
- Conduct workshops to help teachers avoid any negative expectations they may have developed for children from single-parent families.
- Serve as advocates in providing appropriate help for individual students.
- Schedule meetings and events at times convenient for single parents.
- Form school-sponsored support groups for single parents and their children.

■ Mothers who work

Increase in Working Mothers.   The percentage of U.S. working mothers with children under age eighteen has increased steadily since 1950. Several reasons account for this increase: better employment opportunities for women, rising divorce rates, family financial pressures that require a second income, increase in the age at first marriage, and changes in traditional cultural attitudes dictating that mothers stay home. Schools, which traditionally relied on unemployed mothers for volunteer help, need to adjust their expectations of when their students' parents will be available for meetings and volunteering. Most schools have also adjusted their programs to help address the need to supervise children of working parents after the end of the regular school day.

Latchkey Children and Community Learning Centers.   The situation of **latchkey children** who return to unsupervised homes after school is particularly problematic because many of these children spend much of their time watching television or roaming the streets. National data indicate that as many as seven million latchkey children return to empty homes or go to community locations such as malls or street corners. Partly for this reason, many school officials as well as civic and political leaders have taken action to expand opportunities for children and youth to participate in extended-day programs at school or recreational and learning activities at community centers after school. After-school programs thus have become an important aspect of services for young people in many locations, and you are likely to find that many of the students you teach will attend before- or after-school programs. However, an overemphasis on academics in after-school or other out-of-school programs can make for "hurried children," described in the next section.[5]

■ "Superbabies"

■ School responses to "hurried" children

Pressures on Children.   Awareness of the growing importance of education in contemporary society has stimulated many parents to overemphasize early learning. The desire to raise so-called superbabies appears particularly prevalent among middle-class parents, for whom the "ABCs" of childhood frequently center on "Anxiety, Betterment, [and] Competition." To meet the demands of such parents, many preschool and primary classrooms may focus so systematically on formal instruction that they harm children in a misplaced effort to mass-produce "little Einsteins." The concern that many youngsters feel excessive pressure to excel at an early age also extends to art, music, and other educational areas. Some developmental psychologists characterize such parental pressure as a type of "miseducation" that creates **hurried children** and deprives young people of childhood. Responses to this problem include raising the age for enrolling in kindergarten and

[5]Penelope Leach, *Children First* (New York: Viking, 1995); Suzie Boss, "The Barefoot Hours," *NW Education* (Summer 2002), pp. 2–7, available at **www.nwrel.org/nwedu**; and Michael A. Rebell and Joseph J. Wardenski, "Of Course Money Matters" (2004), paper prepared for the Campaign for Fiscal Equity, available at **www.cfequity.org**. See also information available at **www.afterschoolalliance.org**.

retaining five-year-olds not ready to advance to first grade for an additional year in kindergarten.[6]

■ An "epidemic" of overindulgence

Overindulged Children. Whereas many children may be pressured to meet parental demands for early learning, others are overindulged by parents who provide them with too many material goods or protect them from challenges that would foster emotional growth. (Of course, some children may be simultaneously overpressured and overindulged.) Many observers believe that overindulgence is a growing tendency, particularly among young middle-class parents trying to provide their children with an abundance of advantages. Some psychologists argue that overindulgence is an epidemic afflicting as many as 20 percent of the children in the United States. These "cornucopia kids" may find it hard to endure frustration, and thus may present special problems for their teachers and classmates.[7]

■ Reports of abuse and neglect increasing

Child Abuse. Children from any social class may suffer abuse by their parents or other household members. As we noted in the chapter on Legal Aspects of Education, as a teacher, you will have a major responsibility to report any evidence that a student has been abused. Our society has become more aware of the extent and consequences of child abuse, and the number of children reported as victims of abuse and neglect has increased by nearly 90 percent since 1980. More than half these cases involved neglect of such needs as food, clothing, or medical treatment; about one-seventh involved sexual mistreatment; and approximately one-fourth involved beatings or other physical violence. Many child-welfare agencies have been overburdened by the extent of the problem. Although they work to keep families together when safe for children, such agencies often must remove children from their homes and place them in foster care.[8]

■ Subsequent problems of abused children

Research on child abuse indicates that its victims tend to experience serious problems in emotional, intellectual, and social development. As adults they have relatively high rates of alcohol and drug abuse, criminal behavior, learning disorders, and psychiatric disturbance. However, this research is difficult to interpret because a relatively large proportion of abuse victims are low-income children. The links between poverty and developmental problems and delinquent or criminal behavior make it harder to separate out the influence of abuse. The relationship is by no means simple; in fact, many abused children manage to avoid serious emotional and behavioral problems.[9]

■ School and teacher responses

In any case, educators must recognize that abused or seriously neglected students may not only have a difficult time learning but may also behave in ways that interfere with other students' learning. For this reason, organizations such as the

[6]David Elkind, *The Hurried Child: Growing Up Too Fast Too Soon,* 3rd ed. (Cambridge, Mass.: Perseus, 2001); Walter Kirn and Wendy Cole, "What Ever Happened to Play?" (2001), paper at the *Time* Internet site, available at **www.hyper-parenting.com/time.htm**; and Jan Jewett and Karen Peterson, "Stress and Young Children," *ERIC Digest* ED471911 (December 2002), available at **www.ericfacility.net/databases/ERIC_Digests/ed471911.html**.
[7]Bruce A. Baldwin, *Beyond the Cornucopia Kids* (New York: Direction Dynamics, 1988); and Lauren Bradway, "Cornucopia Kids" (2000), posting at **www.atozkidsstuff.com/article20.html**.
[8]Enrique Garcia, "Visible but Unreported," *Child Abuse and Neglect* (September 1995), pp. 1083–1094; and various articles in "Children, Families, and Foster Care," *The Future of Children* (Winter 2004), available at **www.futureofchildren.org**. See also material at **www.childabuse.com** and **http:nccanch.acf.hhs.gov**.
[9]Mary P. Larner, Carol S. Stevenson, and Richard E. Behrman, "Protecting Children from Abuse and Neglect," *The Future of Children* (Spring 1998), pp. 4–22; and "Child Abuse" (2003), paper at the Jim Hopper Internet site, available at **www.jimhopper.com/abstats**.

Children's Television Workshop and the National Education Association have developed materials to help teachers deal with abused children, and they are working with other agencies to alleviate abuse and neglect.[10]

■ More children homeless

Homelessness.   Periods of economic recession, rising real estate values and prices, "deinstitutionalization" of mentally ill persons, and other factors have led to a significant increase in the homeless population in the United States. In particular, more families and children are homeless now than in the past. In fact, in some smaller metropolitan areas, families with children may constitute one-third of the homeless population.

■ Implications for the schools

Several studies indicate that homeless children disproportionately suffer from child abuse and physical ill health. As we would expect, they also are relatively low in school attendance and achievement. The federal government has done relatively little to provide for homeless adults and children, and many local governments have been unwilling or unable to provide much assistance. However, many schools are striving to provide appropriate help. Some districts and schools, for instance, hire additional counselors, sponsor after-school programs, employ a full-time person to coordinate services with shelters for homeless families, or try to avoid transferring homeless children from one school to another.[11]

■ Overall effects on children

Assessment of Trends Related to the Family.   The various interrelated trends we have been discussing have produced a significant change in the structure and function of families in the United States. Research does not conclusively establish that all the results are damaging to children; in some respects, maternal employment and other related trends lead to gains for children. However, many studies indicate that maternal employment and life in a single-parent or divorced family have detrimental effects for many children. Trends such as the rise in homelessness and poverty are obviously even more damaging.

■ Decline of the nuclear family

Historically, according to many analysts, our system of universal education drew support from the development of the **nuclear family** (two parents living with their children), which grew to prominence in Western societies during the past two centuries. The nuclear family has been described as highly child centered, devoting many of its resources to preparing children for success in school and later in life. With the decline of the nuclear family since World War II, the tasks confronting educators appear to have grown more difficult.[12]

■ Difficulties for schools magnified

■ The "postnuclear" family

David Popenoe, examining family trends in highly industrialized countries such as Sweden and the United States, concluded that these trends are creating the "postnuclear" family, which emphasizes "individualism" (individual self-fulfillment, pleasure, self-expression, and spontaneity), as contrasted with the nuclear family's child-centered "familism." Adults, Popenoe further concluded, "no longer need chil-

[10]Lisa Feder-Feitel, "Teachers Against Child Abuse," *Creative Classroom* (January–February 1992), pp. 55–62; and "Prevention Information" (undated), posting at the Prevent Child Abuse, Missouri, Internet site, available at **www.pcamo.org/info.htm**.
[11]Yvonne Rafferty, "Meeting the Educational Needs of Homeless Children," *Educational Leadership* (January 1998), pp. 48–52; John H. Holloway, "Addressing the Needs of Homeless Students," *Educational Leadership* (December 2002/January 2003); and Kathleen Vail, "Where the Heart Is," *American School Board Journal* (June 2003), available at **www.asbj.com**.
[12]Edward Shorter, *The Making of the Modern Family* (New York: Basic Books, 1975). See also Lawrence Stone, *Road to Divorce: England 1537–1987* (New York: Oxford University Press, 1991); Diana Schaub, "Marriage Envy," *Public Interest* (Winter 1996), pp. 99–102; David Popenoe, "Sex Without Strings, Relationships Without Rings" (2000), paper at the "National Marriage Project" Internet site, available at **http:marriage.rutgers.edu/publications/ pubsexwostrings.htm**; and Joan Acocella, "Little People," *New Yorker,* August 18 and 25, 2003, pp. 138–143.

dren in their lives, at least not in economic terms. The problem is that children . . . still need adults . . . who are motivated to provide them with . . . an abundance of time, patience, and love." Many social scientists also worry about the "total contact time" between parents and children. Some research indicates that this time has declined as much as 40 percent during the past few decades.[13]

■ Agencies overloaded

In the context of these family changes and the problems they create, social agencies established to help children and youth sometimes become too overloaded to provide services effectively. William Zinsmeister has described how "many child-protection agencies are now doing little more than preventing murder, and sometimes they fail even to do that." For example, one Maryland social worker, when asked why a six-year-old had not been removed from a known crack house run by his mother, responded that he had "twenty similar cases on his desk, and that he didn't have time to go through the time-consuming process of taking a child from a parent" unless there was an immediate emergency.[14]

■ Many children in jeopardy

In the words of the National Commission on Children, though most American children remain "healthy, happy, and secure," many are now "in jeopardy." Even those children free from extreme misfortune may confront difficult conditions. "They too attend troubled schools and frequent dangerous streets. The adults in their lives are often equally hurried and distracted. . . . The combined effects are that too many children enter adulthood without the skills or motivation to contribute to society."[15] In This Case describes the efforts of two teachers to motivate children with difficult home lives.

 **What steps might you take as a teacher to work effectively with children whose families differ from the traditional nuclear family?**

▶ The Peer Group

■ Peer group influence

Whereas family relationships may constitute a child's first experience of group life, peer-group interactions soon begin to make their powerful socializing effects felt. From play group to teenage clique, the peer group affords young people many significant learning experiences—how to interact with others, how to be accepted by others, and how to achieve status in a circle of friends. Peers are equals in a way parents and their children or teachers and their students are not. A parent or a teacher sometimes can force young children to obey rules they neither understand nor like, but peers do not have formal authority to do this; thus children can learn the true meaning of exchange, cooperation, and equity more easily in the peer setting.

Peer groups increase in importance as the child grows, and they reach maximum influence in adolescence, by which time they sometimes dictate much of a young person's behavior both in and out of school. Some researchers believe that

[13]David Popenoe, *Disturbing the Nest* (New York: Aldine de Gruyter, 1988), pp. 329–330; and David Popenoe, "Where's Papa?" *Utne Reader* (September–October 1997), pp. 68–71, 104–106. See also Leon Cass, "The End of Courtship," *Public Interest* (Spring 2001).
[14]William Zinsmeister, "Growing Up Scared," *Atlantic Monthly* (June 1990), p. 67; and Jennifer McGee, "Study Finds High Concentration of Welfare Cases in Cities," *Nation's Cities Weekly* (October 7, 2002), p. 12.
[15]National Commission on Children, *Beyond Rhetoric: A New American Agenda for Children and Families* (Washington, D.C.: U.S. Government Printing Office, 1991), pp. xvii–xviii. See also Laura D. Lindberg, Scott Boggess, Laura Porter, and Sean Williams, "Teen Risk-Taking" (2000), paper posted at the the Urban Institute Internet site, available at **www.urban.org**: search by author for "Lindberg."

IN THIS CASE

Tuning In

Mark and Claudia have students in their classes with difficult home lives and other issues. The two teachers are discussing ways to motivate these children and support their learning.

Mark: Claudia, help me understand what I can do to motivate these kids. I have tried everything we were taught in our methods class. What do you do to attract and hold the students' attention?

Claudia: Early in the year I try and find out what their favorite TV programs are. Then I use the programs' dilemmas and our discussions of the characters to introduce major units. It seems to work, but you have to do your homework on the students first. You might give that a try, Mark.

Mark: How do I even begin to figure out their favorite TV programs? What do you do, have them fill out a survey form on the first day of class?

Claudia: No, I just talk to them as they come in and ask if they saw this or that program last night. They tell me what programs they watched, and in a week, I have a pretty good list of programs that most of the kids watch. Just talk to them and ask them. They'll tell you.

Mark: I wonder how much TV they actually watch. I hardly have time to turn my TV on, but if I'm going to use this approach, I guess I'd better start making it part of my own homework assignment. What else do you think would help, Claudia?

Claudia: By now you should know which students are your potential troublemakers. Find out what they like. And ask their guidance counselor what he or she can share about the student. Many of our students come from troubled families, families in poverty, homeless families. As the economy worsens, we're seeing more qualifiers for free and reduced-price breakfast and lunches. That's just one small indicator that we are dealing with many students who lack the advantages we had when we were growing up.

Mark: Some of my students want to sleep most of the time. Do you think drugs have much to do with their inattention in class?

Claudia: Maybe in a few cases, but there's no single answer. I'm betting some of your students have bad home situations and possibly poor nutrition, and others are overscheduled with sports and jobs, besides school. They get less sleep than they need for many reasons. Plus, I've read recent research that suggests the brain chemistry of adolescents changes their sleep schedules. Teachers deal with all of this. Also, I don't want to make you feel bad, but when *all* of my students seem sleepy, the first thing I check is whether *I* could be boring them.

Mark: Okay, I'll make sure it isn't me! But I'll talk to the counselor about some of these kids, and the athletic director, too. She and the other coaches have a pretty good handle on students who go out for sports. Maybe some of my underachievers or troublemakers are playing volleyball or football this fall. Maybe between us we can benefit everyone—the students, the coaches, and the teacher.

Questions

1. Do you think teachers should use television programs to help promote attention to concepts they teach? Explain your answer.

2. Why is it important that teachers understand the background of students in their classrooms?

3. What other steps do you think Mark should take to help his effectiveness as a teacher?

peer groups are more important now than in earlier periods—particularly when children have little close contact with their parents and few strong linkages with the larger society.[16]

---

[16]Janis B. Kupersmidt et al., "Childhood Aggression and Peer Relations in the Context of Family and Neighborhood Factors," *Child Development* (April 1995), pp. 361–375; Lawrence Steinberg, *Adolescence,* 4th ed. (New York: McGraw-Hill, 1996); Frank E. Furstenberg, "The Sociology of Adolescence and Youth in the 1990s," *Journal of Marriage and the Family* (November 2000), pp. 896–911; and Karen F. Osterman, "Preventing School Violence," *Phi Delta Kappan* (April 2003), pp. 622–623.

■ Qualities that students esteem

Peer Culture and the School.   Educators are particularly concerned with the characteristics of student culture within the school. **Peer culture** frequently works against academic goals at school. For example, a landmark 1961 study by James Coleman found that high-school students gained the esteem of their peers by a combination of friendliness and popularity, athletic prowess, an attractive appearance and personality, or possession of valued skills and objects (cars, clothes, records). Scholastic success was not among the favored characteristics; in general, the peer culture hindered rather than reinforced the school's academic goals.[17]

■ Importance of friends, looks, athletics

More than two decades later, John Goodlad and his colleagues asked more than seventeen thousand students, "What is the one best thing about this school?" As shown in Table 10.1, the most frequent response by far was "my friends." Respondents also were asked to identify the types of students they considered most popular. Only 10 percent of respondents in junior and senior high schools selected "smart students"; instead, 70 percent of students selected either "good-looking students" or "athletes." Pondering these data, Goodlad concluded that "physical appearance, peer relationships, and games and sports" are more than mere concerns students carry into the school; these phenomena "appear to prevail" there. Noting that Coleman and others reported similar findings in earlier decades, he further wondered "why we have taken so little practical account of them in schools."[18]

Teachers should help students develop positive peer relationships conducive to learning. (© *Michael Newman/ Photo Edit*)

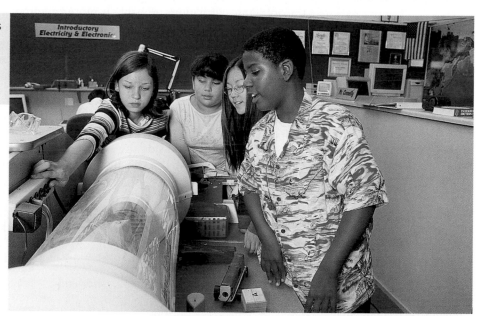

[17]James S. Coleman, *The Adolescent Society* (New York: Free Press, 1961); and James S. Coleman, "Reflections on Schools and Adolescents," in Derek L. Burleson, ed., *Reflections* (Bloomington, Ind.: Phi Delta Kappa, 1991), p. 64. See also Stanford T. Gotto, "Nerds, Normal People, and Homeboys," *Anthropology and Education Quarterly* (March 1997), pp. 70–84; and A. D. Pellegrini, "Bullying, Victimization, and Sexual Harassment During the Transition to Middle School," *Educational Psychologist* (Fall 2002), pp. 151–164.
[18]John I. Goodlad, *A Place Called School* (New York: McGraw-Hill, 1984), p. 75. See also Heather Voke, "Motivating Students to Learn," *ASCD Infobrief* (February 2002), available at **www.ascd.org/readingroom:** search for "motivating"; and Julian R. Betts, Andrew C. Zau, and Lorien A. Rice, *Determinants of Student Achievement* (San Francisco: Public Policy Institute of California, 2003).

■ Suggestions for teachers

To foster peer relationships that support rather than impede learning, some educators recommend conducting activities that encourage students to learn cooperatively. In addition, teachers should promote children's interaction with peers, teach interpersonal and small-group skills, assign children responsibility for the welfare of their peers, and encourage older children to interact with younger children. Such steps may help counteract peer pressure for antisocial behavior.[19]

Participation in Extracurricular Activities.   Polls continually show that students consider their cooperation and interaction with peers in extracurricular activities a highlight of their school experience. Many educators believe this participation is a positive force in the lives of students, but the effect has been difficult to measure. The difficulty lies in determining whether participation in extracurricular activities is a cause or an effect of other aspects of students' development. It is known, for example, that students who participate in many extracurricular activities generally have higher grades than those who do not participate, other things being equal. It may also be true, however, that students with higher grades are more likely to participate than are those with lower grades.

■ Positive impact on educational aspirations

Despite these difficulties, research suggests that participation—especially in athletics, service, leadership activities, and music—fosters students' aspirations to higher educational and occupational attainment (for example, more years of school completed later). The research also suggests that positive effects are more likely in small schools than in large schools.[20]

■ Importance for teachers

These conclusions have great significance for educators. Participation outside the academic curriculum probably is more "manipulable" (alterable by the school) than most other factors related to educational outcomes. For example, home environments may cause problems, but educators can rarely change a student's home environment. But teachers and administrators can promote student participation in extracurricular activities, and this may be one of the most effective ways to improve students' performance.

■ Causes and prevention of bullying

Research on Bullying and Its Prevention.   In recent years, research has begun to address the problems caused by "bullies"—youngsters who severely harass their peers either inside or outside the school. Factors frequently cited as causing some children to behave as bullies include neglect and abuse in their homes, the influ-

Table 10.1	Secondary Students Responses to the Question "What Is the *One* Best Thing About This School?"						
	My Friends	**Sports**	**Good Student Attitudes**	**Nothing**	**Classes I'm Taking**	**Teachers**	**Other**
Junior high respondents	37%	15%	10%	8%	7%	5%	18%
Senior high respondents	34	12	12	8	7	3	24

Source: Compiled from data in John I. Goodlad, *A Place Called School* (New York: McGraw-Hill, 1984), pp. 76–77.

---

[19]David W. Johnson, Roger T. Johnson, and Edythe J. Holubec, *The New Circles of Learning* (Alexandria, Va.: Association for Supervision and Curriculum Development, 1994); and David W. Johnson, Roger T. Johnson, and Karl A. Smith, "Constructive Controversy," *Change* (January–February 2000), pp. 28–37.

[20]Alyce Holland and Thomas Andre, "Participation in Extracurricular Activities in Secondary Schools," *Review of Educational Research* (Winter 1987), pp. 437–466; and Susan Black, "The Well-Rounded Student," *American School Board Journal* (June 2002), available at **www.asbj.com**.

ence of television, and a lack of social skills that leads to a cycle of aggressive behavior. Educators are concerned about not only the harm bullies do to others but also the tendency of bullies to exhibit criminal behavior as adults. Approaches you might apply to modify bullying behaviors include behavioral contracts, instruction in peaceful conflict resolution, classroom activities designed to reduce teasing, and enlisting parental involvement in supervising behavior.[21]

REFOCUS How might you, as a teacher, shape your students' peer relationships in positive directions?

▶ School Culture

■ Aspects of school culture

Education in school, compared with learning experiences in family or peer-group contexts, occurs in relatively formal ways. Group membership is not voluntary but determined by age, aptitudes, and frequently gender. Students are tested and evaluated; they are told when to sit, when to stand, how to walk through hallways, and so on. The rituals of school assemblies, athletic events, and graduation ceremonies—as well as the school insignia, songs, and cheers—all convey the school culture and socialize students. Less ritualized activities and teacher behaviors also acculturate students to the school.[22]

Student Roles and the Hidden Curriculum. Gita Kedar-Voivodas has examined teacher expectations for student roles—that is, desired student behaviors and characteristics—in the elementary classroom. She identified three main types of expected student role: the pupil role, the receptive learner role, and the active learner role.

■ Three major student roles

The *pupil role* is one in which teachers expect students to be "patient, docile, passive, orderly, conforming, obedient and acquiescent to rules and regulations, respectful to authority, easily controllable, and socially adept." The *receptive learner role* requires students to be "motivated, task-oriented, . . . good achievers, and as such, receptive to the institutional demands of the academic curriculum." In the *active learner role,* according to Kedar-Voivodas, students go "beyond the established academic curriculum both in terms of the content to be mastered and in the processes" of learning. Traits of the active learner include "curiosity, active probing and exploring, challenging authority, an independent and questioning mind, and insistence on explanations." Kedar-Voivodas noted that many educational philosophers, among them John Dewey and Maria Montessori, have stressed the value of active learning.[23]

■ Rejecting the active learner

Kedar-Voivodas also found, however, that students exemplifying the active learner role sometimes are rejected by teachers. That is, many teachers respond negatively to active, independent, and assertive children. The difference is large, Kedar-Voivodas said, between the school's "academic" curriculum, which demands

---

[21]Peter Smith and Sonia Sharp, *School Bullying* (New York: Routledge, 1995); Ron Banks, "Bullying in Schools," *ERIC Review* (Spring 2000), pp. 12–13; "Addressing Bullying as Part of Violence Prevention," *Health and Health Care in Schools* (May 2001), available at **www.healthinschools.org**; and Julie Blair, "New Breed of Bullies Torment Their Peers on the Internet," *Education Week* (February 5, 2003). Also see material at **www.bullyonline.org**.

[22]Ralph Parish and Frank Aquila, "Cultural Ways of Working and Believing in the School," *Educational Leadership* (December 1996), pp. 298–305; and Barbara B. Tye, *Hard Truths* (New York: Teachers College Press, 2000).

[23]Gita Kedar-Voivodas, "The Impact of Elementary Children's School Roles and Sex Roles on Teacher Attitudes: An Interactional Analysis," *Review of Educational Research* (Fall 1983), p. 417.

successful mastery of cognitive material, and its "hidden" curriculum, which demands "institutional conformity."[24]

■ Effects of the hidden curriculum

The **hidden curriculum**—a term used by many critics of contemporary schools—is what students learn, other than academic content, from what they do or are expected to do in school. In addition to teaching children to passively conform in the classroom, the hidden curriculum may be preparing economically disadvantaged students to be docile workers later in life. It can communicate negative racial and sexual stereotypes through material included in (or omitted from) textbooks. Excessive emphasis on competition for grades may create a hidden curriculum teaching students that "beating the system" is more important than anything else.[25]

■ Routine classroom activities

Classroom Culture. In his study of classroom processes in elementary schools, Philip Jackson found a diversity of specific subjects but few different types of classroom activity. The terms *seatwork, group discussion, teacher demonstration,* and *question-and-answer period* described most of what happened in the classroom. Further, these activities were performed according to well-defined rules such as "no loud talking during seatwork" and "raise your hand if you have a question." The teacher served as a "combination traffic cop, judge, supply sergeant, and timekeeper." In this cultural system, the classroom often becomes a place where events happen "not because students want them to, but because it is time for them to occur."[26]

■ Stress on order, obedience

The "rules of order" that characterize most elementary school classrooms, Jackson concluded, focus on preventing disturbances. Thus the prevailing socialization pattern in the culture of the school and classroom places its greatest emphasis on what Kedar-Voivodas called the obedient "pupil" role. Other studies have reached essentially the same conclusion. For example, "A Study of Schooling" conducted by John Goodlad and his colleagues described the following widespread patterns:[27]

1. The classroom is generally organized as a group that the teacher treats as a whole. This pattern seems to arise from the need to maintain "orderly relationships" among twenty to thirty people in a small space.

■ Enthusiasm controlled

2. "Enthusiasm and joy and anger are kept under control." As a result, the general emotional tone is "flat" or "neutral."

3. Most student work involves "listening to teachers, writing answers to questions, and taking tests and quizzes." Textbooks and workbooks generally constitute the "media of instruction."

4. These patterns become increasingly rigid and predominant as students proceed through the grades.

---

[24]Ibid., p. 418. See also Michael Apple, *Education and Power,* 2nd ed. (New York: Routledge, 1995); Chris Richards, "Popular Culture, Politics, and the Curriculum," *Educational Researcher* (June–July 1998), pp. 32–34; and John Ramsey, "Savor the Slump," *Education Week,* April 16, 2003.
[25]Maggie Rosen, "The Hidden Curriculum," *Principal* (September 1995), p. 60; Annette Lareau, *Unequal Childhoods* (Berkeley: University of California Press, 2003); and Rodney P. Riegle, "Everything You Learned in School" (undated), posting available at **www.coe.ilstu.edu/rpriegle/wwwdocs/hidden.htm**.
[26]Philip W. Jackson, *Life in Classrooms* (New York: Holt, 1968), pp. 8–9, 13. See also Philip W. Jackson, *The Practice of Teaching* (New York: Teachers College Press, 1986); and Fritz K. Oser, "Ethnographic Inquiries into the Moral Complexity of Classroom Interaction," *Educational Researcher* (April 1995), pp. 33–34.
[27]John Goodlad, *A Place Called School,* pp. 123–124, 236, 246. See also Donald J. Willower and William L. Boyd, *Willard Waller on Education and Schools* (Berkeley, Calif.: McCutchan, 1989); and Thomas Armstrong, *Awakening Genius in the Classroom* (Alexandria, Va.: Association for Supervision and Curriculum Development, 1998).

■ Curiosity not encouraged

5. Instruction seldom goes beyond "mere possession of information." Relatively little effort is made to arouse curiosity or to emphasize thinking.

In summary, Goodlad wrote, students "rarely planned or initiated anything, read or wrote anything of some length, or created their own products. And they scarcely ever speculated on meanings."[28]

■ Passive learning in working-class schools

As we discuss elsewhere in this book, such systematic emphasis on passive learning by rote is in opposition to most contemporary ideas of what education should accomplish. Much has changed since Goodlad and his colleagues collected their data, but many classrooms still exemplify passive, rote learning. In particular, passive, rote learning is more likely to be emphasized in schools with low-achieving, working-class students than in schools with high-achieving, middle-class students. To study this topic, Jean Anyon examined five elementary schools that differed markedly in social class. In the two predominantly working-class schools, Anyon found that instruction emphasized mostly mechanical skills such as punctuation and capitalization. In contrast, instruction in the schools she categorized as predominantly middle-class or "affluent professional" emphasized working independently and developing analytical and conceptual skills. Similar patterns have been reported by other researchers.[29]

■ Why so much passive learning?

Why do classrooms so often function in this way? This is an important question, and many analysts have addressed it. Reasons they have offered include the following:

■ Institutional realities

1. *Institutional requirements to maintain order.* As Jackson points out, a multitude of routines seek to govern interactions between twenty or thirty students and a teacher. Researchers use terms such as *institutional realities* and *organizational dynamics* to describe the forces that translate a need for order into an emphasis on passive learning.[30]

■ Students hold back

2. *Student preferences for passive learning.* We should not underestimate the degree to which many students resist active learning. As Walter Doyle writes, students may "restrict the amount of output they give to a teacher to minimize the risk of exposing a mistake." By holding back, students can also persuade other students or the teacher to help them. As one older student said, "Yeah, I hardly do nothing. All you gotta do is act dumb and Mr. Y will tell you the right answer. You just gotta wait, you know, and he'll tell you."[31]

■ Making a deal for low standards

3. *Accommodations, bargains, and compromises between students and teachers.* In a context that combines institutional requirements for order with student preference for passive learning, the teacher and students may reach an *accommodation or bargain* by which they *compromise* on a set of minimal standards. For

---

[28]John I. Goodlad, "A Study of Schooling: Some Findings and Hypotheses," *Phi Delta Kappan* (March 1983), p. 468. See also Ronald E. Comfort and Jacqueline Giorgi, "In a Different Voice," *High School Journal* (February–March 1997), pp. 178–183; and Edgar H. Schuster, "The Persistence of the 'Grammar of Schooling,'" *Education Week*, April 30, 2003.

[29]Jean Anyon, "Social Class and the Hidden Curriculum of Work," *Journal of Education* (Winter 1980), pp. 67–92, reprinted in Gerald Handel, ed., *Childhood Socialization* (New York: Aldine de Gruyter, 1990); and Jean Anyon, *Ghetto Schooling* (New York: Teachers College Press, 1997).

[30]Goodlad, "A Study of Schooling," pp. 469–470; Barbara B. Tye, "The Deep Structure of Schooling," *Phi Delta Kappan* (November 1987), pp. 281–284; and Max Angus, *The Rules of School Reform* (London: Falmer, 1998).

[31]Walter Doyle, "Academic Work," *Review of Educational Research* (Summer 1983), pp. 184–185. See also David Tyack and William Tobin, "The 'Grammar' of Schooling," *American Educational Research Journal* (Fall 1994); and Larry Cuban, *How Can I Fix It?* (New York: Teachers College Press, 2001).

example, Martin Haberman has observed what he calls "the Deal" in many urban classrooms: students are nondisruptive as long as the teacher ignores the fact that they are not diligent in their classwork. The widespread existence of such "ABCs" has been documented in major studies. Michael Sedlak and his colleagues called such an arrangement "a complex, tacit conspiracy to avoid rigorous, demanding academic inquiry."[32]

■ Which students get attention?

4. *Teachers' allocation of attention.* Many teachers feel compelled to give most of their time and attention to a few students. In some cases, these will be the slowest students—whomever the teacher believes most need help. In many other cases, however, attention goes primarily to the brightest students, who teachers frequently believe will benefit the most from extra attention. This attitude is particularly prevalent when teachers have so many "slow" students that helping them all seems impossible.

Helen Gouldner and her colleagues found these dynamics in an inner-city, all-black elementary school with a large proportion of students from low-income home environments that failed to prepare them to function well in the classroom. The few well-prepared students (generally from relatively high-status families) were the "pets"—those whom teachers helped throughout their school careers. The largest group of students (the "nobodies") received relatively little teacher attention and generally were neither disruptive nor particularly successful. The remaining students, a small group of "trouble-makers," were unable or unwilling to conform to the routine demands of the classroom. These patterns were well in line with the school's "sorting and selecting" function because the teachers, most of whom were African American, could feel they were promoting success for at least some black students in a difficult learning environment.[33]

■ Conformity as a social demand

5. *Society's requirement that students learn to conform.* Underlying schools' emphasis on passive learning is the reality that young people must learn to function in social institutions outside the school. Because most people in contemporary society must cope with large economic, political, and social institutions, children must be socialized to follow appropriate routines and regulations. Philip Jackson summarizes this part of a school's socialization mission as follows: "It is expected that children will adapt to the teacher's authority by becoming 'good workers' and 'model students.' The transition from classroom to factory or office is made easily by those who have developed 'good work habits' in their early years." This goal of schooling is part of the "hidden curriculum" mentioned earlier.[34]

■ Burdens on teachers

6. *Teacher overload.* It is difficult for teachers to provide active, meaningful learning experiences when they must cope with the demands of large classes and

---

[32]Michael W. Sedlak et al., *Selling Students Short* (New York: Teachers College Press, 1986), p. 13; Martin Haberman, "The Ideology of Nonwork in Urban Schools," *Phi Delta Kappan* (March 1997), pp. 499–503; and Martin Haberman, "The Pedagogy of Poverty Versus Good Teaching" (undated), posting at the Eisenhower National Clearinghouse Internet site, available at **www.enc.org**.

[33]Helen Gouldner, *Teachers' Pets, Troublemakers, and Nobodies* (Westport, Conn.: Greenwood, 1978), pp. 133–134. This self-fulfilling prophecy and the way it operated at the school studied by Gouldner and her colleagues are described at greater length in Ray C. Rist, *The Urban School: A Factory for Failure* (Cambridge, Mass.: MIT Press, 1973). See also John E. Chubb and Tom Loveless, eds., *Bridging the Gap* (Washington, D. C.: Brookings, 2002).

[34]Jackson, *Life in Classrooms*, p. 32. See also Ann A. Ferguson, *Bad Boys* (Ann Arbor: University of Michigan Press, 2000); and David Schimmel, "The Bill of Rights and the School Curriculum," *Insights on Law and Society* (Fall 2002), available at **www.rutherford.org**.

class loads, a variety of duties and tasks outside their classrooms, pressures to "cover" a wide range of material and skills, and other such responsibilities.[35] As we document elsewhere in this book, recognition is growing of the heavy burdens on teachers, and many reformers are working to reduce teacher overload.

We can offer many additional reasons why classroom instructional patterns have been relatively unaffected by contemporary learning theory, but most of them in some way involve institutional constraints that favor passive, rote learning.[36] Overcoming such constraints requires significant innovations in school organization and pedagogy, as we will see in the chapter on School Effectiveness and Reform in the United States.

■ Positive aspects

Our focus in this section on negative aspects of school culture merits a reminder regarding the many positive aspects of elementary and secondary schools in the United States. Most schools provide an orderly learning environment, and most students learn to read and compute at a level required to function in our society. Relationships among teachers, students, and parents are generally positive. Most students receive a high-school diploma, and many proceed to various postsecondary educations. We describe in greater detail many successful aspects of the U.S. education system in the chapters on Historical Development of American Education; Social Class, Race, and School Achievement; International Education; School Effectiveness and Reform in the United States; and elsewhere in this book.

REFOCUS To what extent did your high-school teachers emphasize active learning? Do you recall any obvious obstacles to active learning that emphasized higher-order goals?

▶ Television and Digital Media

■ More television time than school time

Some social scientists refer to television as the "first curriculum" because it appears to affect the way children develop learning skills and orient themselves toward acquiring knowledge and understanding. Because watching television requires little of the viewer in the way of effort and skills, educators face a formidable challenge in maintaining students' interest and motivation in schoolwork. The average eighth grader spends more than three times as much time viewing television and playing video games as doing homework and reading outside school. In addition, a large proportion of children and youth believe their peers' values are significantly influenced by what they see in the media. For more on the influence of television, see the Taking Issue box.

■ Television and school achievement

Although research shows a relationship between school achievement and television viewing, the nature of this relationship is not entirely clear. Some studies suggest that viewing television may reduce students' reading activities, but this conclusion is not well documented, and international studies show that students in

---

[35]Linda M. McNeil, *Contradictions of School Reform* (New York: Routledge, 2000); and Evans Clinchy, *The Rights of All Our Children* (Portsmouth, N.H.: Heinemann, 2002).
[36]Other frequently cited reasons include the tendency for teachers to teach the way they were taught, the high costs involved in introducing new approaches, and lack of adequate preservice and in-service training. See Leon Lederman, "Blackboard Bungle," *Sciences* (January–February 1995), pp. 16–20; and Elizabeth Duffrin, "Winning Students' Hearts and Minds," *Catalyst* (March 2001), available at **www.catalyst-chicago.org**.

taking issue

Question Does television's influence on students generally benefit the teacher?

The Influence of Television

Television is a fixture in almost every home; its influence is so pervasive that it has been called another parent. Because most children spend more time watching television than attending school, debate continues over television's effect on student learning and behavior.

Arguments PRO

1 Television enriches students' background knowledge so that they can understand much instruction more readily. Teachers who take advantage of what students already have learned from television can accelerate subject matter presentation.

2 In addition to providing useful information, television awakens interest in a wide range of topics. Teachers can draw on the interests that television arouses and involve students more deeply in many parts of the curriculum.

3 Television assists teachers by making learning palatable at an early age. Programs such as *Sesame Street* have increased student achievement in the early years by showing children that learning can be fun.

4 Television provides a catharsis for feelings of hostility and anger. Children who watch television dramas can work out potentially violent impulses that might otherwise be directed at classmates, parents, or teachers.

5 Television can provide a good socializing experience. Research has shown that programs like *Sesame Street* can increase cooperative behavior among children. Furthermore, many children's shows offer their viewers a welcome relief from the world of adults.

Arguments CON

1 Most often, the information students gain from television is a superficial collection of facts, not useful background knowledge. Moreover, television may delude students into thinking that these scattered facts represent genuine understanding.

2 Television viewing creates mental habits that teachers must try to counteract. Although television may provoke a fleeting interest in a topic, it accustoms students to learning through passive impressions rather than thoughtful analysis. In addition, extensive television viewing by children is associated with a reduced attention span.

3 Early exposure to "fun" learning often raises false expectations about school. The teacher cannot be as entertaining as Big Bird. The need to compete with such television shows makes the teacher's job more difficult.

4 Research on modeling indicates that many children, confronted with a situation parallel to one they have seen on television, respond with the same behavior used by the television characters. In other words, violent television programs often encourage violent behavior.

5 For every *Sesame Street,* dozens of television programs tend to alienate children from the values of the school and the wider society. For example, some programs reinforce negative peer attitudes toward social institutions; some present simplistic or distorted notions of right and wrong; and many encourage dangerous fantasies.

some countries that rank high on television viewing among children also have relatively high achievement scores. It is difficult to separate cases in which television "causes" reduced attention to reading from those in which low-performing students turn to television for escape. Nevertheless, many educators are concerned that watching television may lower achievement for many students, particularly because surveys indicate that millions of children watch television late into the night and then yawn their way through school the next day.[37]

■ General mass media effects

Apart from their possibly negative effects on school achievement, television and other media, such as movies, video games, and the music industry, deeply influence the acculturation and socialization of children and youth. The media both stimulate and reflect fundamental changes in attitudes and behaviors that prevail in our society, from recreation and career choices to sexual relationships, consumerism, and drug use. Unfortunately, no conclusive data determine just how much the media affect children and youth or whether overall effects are positive or negative (depending, of course, on what one values as positive or negative). For example, twenty-four-hour-a-day rock-music programming on cable television has been viewed both as a means to keep young people off the streets and as the beginning of the end of Western civilization.[38]

■ Correlation with aggression

Many adults are particularly worried that television and other media may encourage aggressive or violent behavior. The average child now witnesses thousands of simulated murders and tens of thousands of other violent acts by the time he or she completes elementary school. The effects depend in part on situational factors: for example, the child's degree of frustration or anger, potential consequences such as pain or punishment, and opportunity to perform an act of violence. Overall, however, according to a committee of behavioral scientists, "television violence is as strongly correlated with aggressive behavior as any other behavioral variable that has been measured." The American Academy of Pediatrics and the American Psychological Association also have concluded that repeated exposure to violence on television and in other media promotes violent behavior.[39]

■ Positive uses of television

It also is true, however, that television can be an important force for positive socialization. For example, research shows that the program *Sesame Street* has helped both middle-class and working-class youth academically, and that children can become more cooperative and nurturant after viewing programs emphasizing these behaviors. Research also indicates that programs like *Cyberchase* can help elementary students improve in mathematics.[40]

---

[37]*Survey of Sixth Grade School Achievement and Television Viewing Habits* (Sacramento: California State Department of Education, 1982); Barbara F. Mates and Linda Strommen, "Why Ernie Can't Read: Sesame Street and Literacy," *Reading Teacher* (December 1995–January 1996), pp. 300–307; Angela T. Clark and Beth Kurtz-Costes, "Television Viewing, Educational Quality of the Home Environment, and School Readiness," *Journal of Educational Research* (May–June 1997), pp. 279–286; Steven S. Schlozman, "To View or Not to View," *Educational Leadership* (December–January 2003), pp. 87–88; and Ron Kaufman, "The Impact of Television and Video Entertainment on Student Achievement in Reading and Writing" (undated), posting at the "Kill Your Television" Internet site, available at **www.turnoffyourtv.com**.
[38]Robert Hughes, "Why Watch It, Anyway?" *New York Review of Books*, February 16, 1995, pp. 37–42; and David Walsh, "Whoever Tells the Stories Defines the Culture," Statement to the U.S. Senate Committee on Commerce, Science, and Transportation (March 21, 2000), available at **www.mediafamily.org/press**.
[39]U.S. Department of Health and Human Services, *Television and Human Behavior: Ten Years of Scientific Progress and Implications for the Eighties,* vol. 1, Summary Report (Washington, D.C.: U.S. Government Printing Office, 1982), pp. 6, 38–39; Ed Donnerstein et al., *National Television Violence Study* (Santa Barbara: University of California at Santa Barbara, 1998); and "What Goes In Must Come Out" (2003), paper at **www.mediafamily.org/research/index. shtml**.
[40]David A. England, *Television and Children* (Bloomington, Ind.: Phi Delta Kappa, 1984); Daniel R. Anderson, "Educational Television Is Not an Oxymoron," *Annals of the American Academy of Political and Social Science* (May 1998), pp. 24–38; and "Children, Adolescents, and Television," *Pediatrics* (February 2001), pp. 423–426.

■ Reform efforts

Recognizing both the good and the damaging effects media can have on children and youth, many people are working for improvements. The Parent-Teacher Association has made television reform—particularly reductions in sex, commercialism, and violence during prime time—one of its major national goals, and organizations such as the National Citizens Committee for Broadcasting have lobbied for change.

However, progress has been slow. A typical afternoon of "kidvid" still can be a mind-numbing march of cartoon superheroes, and many programs insistently instruct children to demand another trip to the nearest toy store. In 1996 the federal government introduced a requirement that television stations broadcast at least three hours per week of "educational and informational" programs for children, but much of this programming has few viewers, and programs emphasizing sex and/or violence continue mostly unabated.[41]

■ Different from television

The Net Generation in the Digital Age.   Some analysts have begun to examine possible changes as children and youth grow up in an environment permeated by digital communications and information sources such as interactive video and the increasingly ubiquitous Internet. One of the first books to address these developments is Don Tapscott's *Growing Up Digital*. Tapscott, who refers to young people growing up in the emerging digital age as the "net generation," believes the Internet is quite different from television—it stimulates interactive participation rather than passive viewing. Tapscott predicts that the Internet will produce "a generation which increasingly questions the implicit values contained in information . . . [and in so doing forces children] to exercise not only their critical thinking but their judgment . . . [and thus contributes] to the relentless breakdown of the notion of authority."[42]

■ Liberating and productive

Tapscott believes that the digital revolution's primary effects will be liberating for individuals and productive for society. Individuals will find information and knowledge easily accessible and opportunities vastly expanded. In addition, familiarity with digital media is preparing young people to function effectively at "multitasking" required in complicated jobs. Society will find that a knowledge-based economy improves efficiency and productivity, and that technology will enable the educational system to function successfully in preparing young persons for skilled employment. Like other analysts, however, Tapscott is concerned that digital media and learning will increase the already troublesome gap between the haves and the have-nots, that is, between middle-class youth who have good access to new technologies and low-income youth who have relatively poor access and thus may be further disadvantaged.

■ Concern for have-nots

Questions and Implications for Educators.   Many observers are more cautious than Tapscott in assessing socialization problems that may be associated with emerging digital media. For example, educators and media specialists at the Center for Media Education have identified a series of questions that should be attended to if emerging technologies are to be a positive force in children's development:

■ What are the unique characteristics of new interactive technologies, and how can they be integrated with the child's development?

---

[41]Ron Kaufman, "How Television Images Affect Children" (undated), posting at the Kill Your Television Internet site, available at **www.turnoffyourtv.com**.

[42]Don Tapscott, *Growing Up Digital* (New York: McGraw-Hill, 1998), p. 26. See also Simon Garfinkel, "The Net Effect," *Technology Review*, August 8, 2003, available at **www.techreview .com**; Jennifer A. Hendricks, "The Net Generation," *Current Issues in Education* 7, no. 1 (2004), available at **http:cie.asu.edu**; and information at **www.growingupdigital.com**.

- Can any applications become successful models for enhancing children's "natural eagerness to learn, to create, and to communicate"?

■ What role for educators?

- What roles should educators, parents, and technology advocates play in shaping evolution of the interactive media market?

■ Positive interactive learning

Staff of the Center for Media Education have described their investigations involving these and related questions in their online publication titled *InfoActive Kids*. One issue reviewed projects under way at media labs where developers are devising interactive learning experiences that can foster students' skills in constructing meaning, solving problems, and generally learning to learn. Projects described in such publications have great potential for shaping children's growth in a positive direction.[43] See the Technology @ School box for more on "media literacy."

▶ Gender Roles and Sex Differences

■ Early reinforcement of gender roles

Not only does society demand conformity to its fundamental values and norms; it also assigns specific roles to each of its members, expecting them to conform to certain established behavioral patterns. Socialization is particularly forceful regarding

TECHNOLOGY @ School

Helping Students Develop Media Literacy

"Media literacy" involves skill in learning from and critically evaluating different forms of electronic and print media. Helping students develop media literacy will be an important part of your job as a teacher. Most of your students will not only spend time watching television, they also will play computer and video games and use the Internet for many purposes. One way to avoid negative outcomes such as potential school achievement problems, unfavorable socialization, and unquestioning acceptance of media values, is to encourage active listening, viewing, and surfing.

You can find information to improve your own media literacy and that of your students at **www.medialit.org**. For a wide range of readings on many facets of media literacy, start with **http://interact.uoregon.edu/MediaLit/mlr/home/index.html** and follow the screens and links relevant to your special interests.

For example, you might help your students understand how commercial television functions. You can discuss points raised in the article "Key Concepts for Teaching Television" at **http://interact.uoregon.edu/MediaLit/mlr/readings/articles/key.html**. Renee Hobbs offers more suggestions in the article "Teaching Media Literacy: YO! Are You Hip To This?" at **http://interact.uoregon.edu/MediaLit/mlr/readings/articles/hobbs/teachingml.html**. You'll find guidelines for evaluating Web sites that you can adapt or share with your students at **www.school.discovery.com/schrockguide/eval.html**.

Standards & Assessment ✓

Media literacy is part of many state and district standards. The chart at **www.med.sc.edu:1081/statelit.htm** will help you locate the standards in your state that deal with media literacy. The article "Educational Standards and Media Literacy" at **www.medialit.org/reading_room/article458.html** provides advice for implementing media literacy instruction that addresses a wide range of curriculum standards.

---

[43]"Out of the Lab and into the Market," *InfoActive Kids* (Winter 1998), available at **www.cme.org/publications/infoactive.html**. See also Joan Almon, ed., *Fools' Gold: A Critical Look at Computers and Childhood* (College Park, Md.: Alliance for Childhood, 2000), available at **www.allianceforchildhood.net/projects/computers**; and Steve Goodman, *Teaching Youth Media* (New York: Teachers College Press, 2003).

gender roles—ideas about the ways boys and girls and men and women are "supposed" to act. Gender roles vary from culture to culture, but within a given culture they are rather well defined, and children are socialized in them through an elaborate schedule of selective reinforcement. For example, a preschool boy may be ridiculed for playing with dolls, and young girls may be steered away from activities considered too physically rough. By age three, as Robert Havighurst has remarked, there is already a "noticeable difference in behavior between boys and girls." Even at such an early age, boys are more "active," girls more "dependent" and "nurturant."[44]

■ Gender roles and school problems for boys

When children go to school, they discover that it is dominated by traditional norms of politeness, cleanliness, and obedience. Teachers generally suppress fighting and aggressive behavior. This can be a problem for boys because, as research indicates, on the average they are more aggressive than girls almost from the time they are born, probably because of hormone differences. Some scholars believe that teachers' tendency to reward passive behavior and discourage aggressiveness helps account for boys' relatively high rates of alienation and violation of school rules. Boys receive many more reprimands from teachers than do girls, and by the time students enter the secondary grades, boys greatly outnumber girls in remedial classes and in classes for those with emotional disturbances.[45]

■ Gender roles and school problems for girls

By way of contrast, the problems that girls encounter in the educational system generally reflect their socialization for dependence rather than assertiveness. Historically, most girls were not encouraged to prepare for high-status fields such as law or medicine or high-paying technical occupations. Instead, they were expected to prepare for roles as wives and homemakers. The few occupations women were encouraged to consider, such as elementary teacher, social worker, and nurse, tended to have relatively low pay and low status. This type of socialization did not motivate girls to acquire skills useful for later economic success. Furthermore, verbal skills of the kind in which girls tend to excel failed to prepare them for success in mathematics and science. As a result, many girls were excluded from educational opportunities.[46]

■ Girls not encouraged in competition or leadership

Although socialization in the elementary school frequently intends to make boys obedient and cooperative, in high school the emphasis placed on athletics means that boys have often received more opportunities than girls have to learn leadership and competitive skills useful in later life. Girls, expected to be cooperative and even docile, traditionally have had relatively little encouragement to learn such skills, and those who did were perceived as violating "proper" norms for female behavior in American society.

■ Boys' versus girls' peer groups

Raphaela Best found that school peer groups also help communicate traditional expectations for boys and girls. Best reported that boys' peer groups stress "canons" such as "always be first" and "don't hang out with a loser," whereas girls' peer groups place relatively more emphasis on having fun rather than winning and on cooperation rather than competition. Best also reported that as the students she

---

[44]Robert J. Havighurst, "Sex Role Development," *Journal of Research and Development in Education* (Winter 1983), p. 61. See also Timothy J. Lensmire, "Learning Gender," *Educational Researcher* (June–July 1995), pp. 31–32; Andrew Sullivan, "Mother Nature Strikes Back," *Independent Women's Quarterly* (Summer 2000), available at **www.iwf.org/pubs/twq**; and Amy Benfer, "One for the Lads" (2002), posting at the Salon.com Internet site, available at **www.salon.com:** search for "laddism."
[45]Christina H. Sommers, *The War Against Boys* (New York: Simon and Schuster, 2000); and Thomas Newkirk, "The Quiet Crisis in Boys' Literacy," *Education Week*, September 10, 2003.
[46]Susan L. Gabriel and Isaiah Smithson, eds., *Gender in the Classroom* (Urbana: University of Illinois Press, 1990); and Helen L. Parks and Joe Parks, "Society Cannot Continue to Exclude Women From the Fields of Science and Mathematics," *Education* (Spring 2000), pp. 529–538.

studied grew older, they made some progress in overcoming stereotypes that limited the aspirations of girls and restricted the emotional growth of boys. Similarly, Barrie Thorne studied elementary-school students and concluded that gender roles are "socially constructed" at an early age. She also concluded that teachers should try to counteract gender stereotypes by facilitating cooperative behaviors and enhancing opportunities to participate in diverse activities.[47]

Sex Differences in Achievement and Ability

■ Reading and mathematics

Recent studies in the United States indicate that sex differences in achievement are relatively small. For example, data on the reading performance of nine-, thirteen-, and seventeen-year-olds indicate that girls score only a little higher than boys. Conversely, among seventeen-year-olds, boys score higher than girls in higher-order mathematics achievement, but this difference is smaller than it was in 1970, nine- and thirteen-year-olds show little meaningful difference in mathematics scores for girls and boys. Research also indicates that female gains in mathematics probably are partly due to greater participation in math courses during the past few decades.[48]

■ Innate differences?

Though sex differences in achievement are narrowing, much controversy remains about possible differences in innate ability. These arguments often focus on whether a larger proportion of boys than girls have unusually strong innate ability for higher-order mathematics or abstract thinking in general. Research on this topic shows more variability in ability among boys than among girls: boys are more likely to be either markedly high or markedly low in ability.[49]

■ Different brain functioning

Those who believe that ability differences between the sexes are present at birth point to differences in the brain functioning of boys and girls. For most people, the left hemisphere of the brain specializes in verbal tasks, whereas the right hemisphere specializes in nonverbal ones, including spatial functions important in mathematics. In this respect, brain research suggests some differences associated with sex hormones that begin to function at birth or even earlier. Among right-handed people (the majority), women handle spatial functions more with the *left* hemisphere than do men. Women also use the *right* hemisphere more in verbal functions.[50]

■ "Math anxiety" and fear of success

Other observers, however, argue that differences in experience and expectations account for most or all of the learning and related differences between boys and girls, including brain differences. Particular attention has been paid to "math

---

[47]Raphaela Best, *We've All Got Scars: What Boys and Girls Learn in Elementary School* (Bloomington: Indiana University Press, 1983); and Barrie Thorne, *Gender Play* (New Brunswick, N.J.: Rutgers University Press, 1993). See also Cathrine E. Matthews et al., "Challenging Gender Bias in Fifth Grade," *Educational Leadership* (January 1998), pp. 54–57; and "Some Practical Ideas for Confronting Curricular Bias" (undated), posting at the David Sadker Internet site, available at **www.american.edu/sadker**.

[48]Yupin Bae et al., *Trends in Educational Equity of Girls and Women* (Washington, D.C.: National Center for Education Statistics, 2000), available at **www.nces.ed.gov:** search for "Bae"; and Marshall Poe, "The Other Gender Gap," *Atlantic* (January–February 2004), available at **www.theatlantic.com**.

[49]Elizabeth Fennema et al., "New Perspectives on Gender Differences in Mathematics," *Educational Researcher* (June–July, 1998), pp. 19–21; Doreen Kimura, *Sex and Cognition* (Cambridge, Mass.: MIT Press, 2000); and Doreen Kimura, "Sex Differences in the Brain," *Scientific American* (June 2002).

[50]Richard M. Restak, "The Other Difference Between Boys and Girls," *Educational Leadership* (December 1979), pp. 232–235; Doreen Kimura, "Male Brain, Female Brain: The Hidden Difference," *Psychology Monthly* (March 1988), pp. 77–82; Michael Gurian and Patricia Healey, *Boys and Girls Learn Differently* (San Francisco: Jossey-Bass, 2001); and Simon D. Cohen, *The Essential Differences* (New York: Basic Books, 2003).

Though sex differences in achievement are narrowing, much controversy remains about possible sources of sex differences and ways to address them. *(Gabe Palmer/CORBIS)*

anxiety" among women—the possibility that the relatively poor performance of certain women in math (and therefore in science and other fields dependent on math) stems from socialization practices that make them anxious and fearful about mathematical analysis. A related line of argument is that women fear success in traditionally male activities and occupations because succeeding would violate sex stereotypes, thereby inviting ridicule. Still other analysts believe that girls tend to divert their attention more toward social relationships as they enter adolescence. But the situation is complex, and few large-scale generalizations can be made.[51]

Educational and Occupational Attainment of Women

■ Educational gains for women

Throughout most of U.S. history, women completed fewer years of schooling than did men. In 1979, however, women for the first time outnumbered men among college freshmen. Since 1992, more than half of all bachelor's and master's degrees have been awarded to women, compared with 40 percent in 1962. Women have continued to increase their proportions in higher education in the past decade, and they now constitute nearly 60 percent of college enrollment.[52]

■ Occupational gains

Related gains have also been registered in the occupational status of women. For example, in 1950 only 15 percent of accountants were women, compared to nearly 60 percent in 2000; the comparable percentages for female lawyers were 4 percent in 1950 and about one-third in 2000. Large recent increases in the percentages of female students in medicine, business administration, and other profes-

[51]Lynn Friedman, "The Space Factor in Mathematics: Gender Differences," *Review of Educational Research* (Spring 1995), pp. 22–50; Andrew S. Latham, "Gender Differences on Assessments," *Educational Leadership* (January 1998), pp. 88–89; Lesley Rogers, *Sexing the Brain* (New York: Columbia University Press, 2001); and "The Theory Behind the Research" (undated), posting at the Girls Tech Internet site, available at **www.girlstech.douglass.rutgers.edu**.
[52]Brenda Feigen, *Not One of the Boys* (New York: Knopf, 2000); Cathy Young, "Where the Boys Are," *Reason Online* (February 2001), available at **www.reason.com:** search for "Cathy Young"; and Renee L. Spraggins, "Women and Men in the United States: March 2002," *Current Population Reports* (March 2003).

sional fields will increase the number of women employed in high-status positions in the future. Both schools and the wider society are seeing the effects of efforts to eliminate sexism from school curricula, encouraging girls to attend college and prepare for the professions, support for girls and women to enter scientific fields and computing, and other actions to equalize opportunity.[53]

■ Much to be accomplished

Nevertheless, much remains to be achieved. Despite recent gains, women still are concentrated in low-paying, low-status occupations. Although the number of female scientists and engineers with doctoral degrees more than doubled between 1973 and 1995, they still constitute less than one-quarter of the total.

■ Ways to improve gender equity in education

The increase in women's educational and occupational attainments is associated with growth in the percentage of working mothers and single-parent families. As we saw earlier, these trends may have a negative impact on children and schools, but they signify greater equalization of opportunity, and they may improve the social class and income of many families. Researchers' suggestions for further improving educational opportunities and equity for girls and women include the following:[54]

- Increase teacher training dealing with gender issues.

- Attend more closely to gender equity in vocational education.

- Eliminate any bias in standardized tests and reduce the role of these tests in college admissions.

- Improve educational programs dealing with health and sexuality.

- Reduce sex stereotyping and further increase the representation of females in instructional materials.

- Protect the rights of pregnant girls and teenage parents.

- Introduce "gender-fair" curricula that accommodate learning-style differences.

- Introduce special programs to encourage girls to participate in math, computing, and science programs.

- Work to counteract the decline in self-esteem that many girls experience as they become concerned with their appearance.

 **What might you do as a teacher to encourage girls, or boys, for that matter, to overcome overly passive tendencies?**

▶ Adolescent and Youth Problems

In many traditional, nonindustrialized cultures, the young are initiated into adult life after puberty. This initiation sometimes takes place through special rituals

---

[53]Pamela Mendels, "Who's Managing Now?" *Working Woman* (October 1995), pp. 44–45; Jonathan D. Glater, "Women Are Close to Being Majority of Law Students," *New York Times*, March 26, 2001; and "20 Leading Occupations of Employed Women," undated posting at **www.infoplease.com:** search for "employed women."
[54]*How Schools Shortchange Women: The A.A.U.W. Report* (Washington, D.C.: American Association of University Women, 1992); Eileen V. Hilke and Carol Conway-Gerhardt, *Gender Equity in Education* (Bloomington, Ind.: Phi Delta Kappa, 1994); Kaaren Stabiner, "Speaking Out," *Principal* (November/December 2002), available at **www.naesp.org**; Denise E. Agosto, "Girls and Gaming" (2003), paper posted at the Girls Tech Internet site, available at **www.girlstech.douglass.rutgers.edu**; and Susan K. Dyer, ed., "Under the Microscope" (2004), paper posted at the American Association of University Women Internet site, available at **www.aauw.org/research/microscope.cfm**.

designed to prove the young person's worthiness to assume adult roles. In such societies one is either a child or an adult; only a brief gap—if any gap at all—separates the two.

■ Adolescence as a modern phenomenon

In modern technological societies the young are forced to postpone their adulthood for a period of time called adolescence or youth. A major reason is that modern society no longer has an economic need for young people in this age group. One unfortunate result is that youth have become more and more isolated from the rest of society. In recent decades, this isolation has intensified many youth-centered problems, such as drug use, drinking, suicide, early pregnancy, and delinquency. At the same time, the isolation of youth hampers efforts of schools and other social institutions to prepare young people for adulthood.[55]

Drugs and Drinking

■ Patterns of use

General usage of drugs and alcohol among youth has grown markedly over the past half-century, and recently, after a decade or more of decline, the use of certain drugs has begun to rise again. Parents, educators, and others who work with youth remain deeply concerned with the effects of drug use and abuse. The following list summarizes some recent patterns:[56]

Cigarettes. The percentage of high-school seniors who smoked cigarettes within the previous month averaged about 30 percent throughout the 1980s and 1990s, then increased to almost 40 percent in 1997. Anti-smoking efforts and a growing general intolerance of smoking helped bring the rate back down to less than 25 percent in 2003.

Marijuana. The percentage of high-school seniors who had used marijuana during the previous year declined from 50 percent in 1978 to 22 percent in 1992, but then increased to the mid-30s in the late 1990s and early 2000s.

Heroin. In 2003, less than 1 percent of seniors had used heroin or other opiates within the previous year.

Cocaine. Annual use of cocaine among seniors increased from 6 percent in 1975 to 13 percent in 1985, but then declined to 5 percent in 2003. Past-year use of crack was reported by 2 percent of seniors in 2003.

Methamphetamine. Formerly called "speed" and now referred to by various names such as "ice" and "crank," methamphetamines were used during the previous year by less than 4 percent of seniors in 2003.

Hallucinogens/LSD. Past-year use of hallucinogens and LSD was reported by 6 percent and 2 percent, respectively, of seniors in 2003.

MDMA (Ecstasy). Past-year use of MDMA declined from 8 percent of seniors in 2000 to less than 5 percent in 2003.

Alcohol. Regular use of alcohol has remained fairly stable, but research indicates that alcohol use has been increasing among students younger than fifteen years old, that many teenagers have driven an automobile while intoxi-

---

[55]James S. Coleman, "Families and Schools," *Educational Researcher* (August–September 1987), pp. 32–38; and James E. Cote, *Arrested Adulthood* (New York: New York University Press, 2000).

[56]Data are summarized largely from annual surveys conducted by the University of Michigan Institute for Survey Research. Search the Internet for "Monitoring the Future." For information on organized efforts to deal with youth substance abuse problems, visit **www. jointogether.org**.

cated, and that an alarming number of teenagers frequently drink alone when they are bored or upset.

■ Implications of drug and alcohol use

Educators worry that young people's use of alcohol, marijuana, and other relatively mild drugs may reinforce or stimulate alienation from social institutions or otherwise impede the transition to adulthood. This is not to say that problems such as low academic performance, rebelliousness, and criminal activity are *caused* by drug use; it is just as likely that the problems arise first and lead to the drug use. Many young people are using drugs and alcohol to escape from difficulties they encounter in preparing for adult life. But whatever the sequence of causation, usage rates among U.S. youth remain higher than in any other industrialized nation. Moreover, contrary to much earlier opinion, some authorities now believe that mild drugs such as marijuana are often a steppingstone to stronger drugs such as cocaine and heroin. Young people themselves believe that drugs and alcohol are a negative influence in their lives. National surveys consistently show that most high-school students cite either drugs or alcohol as the "single worst influence" in their lives.[57]

Suicide

■ Rise in suicide rate

Educators have become increasingly concerned about suicide among young people. The suicide rate among children and youth has nearly quadrupled since 1950, and some surveys suggest that as many as one in ten school-age youth may attempt suicide. Reasons for this increase appear to include a decline in religious values that inhibit suicide, influence of the mass media, perceived pressures to excel in school, failed relationships with peers, and pressures or despondency associated with divorce or other family problems.[58]

■ Teachers should learn warning signs

Teachers and other school personnel need to be alert to the suicide problem. Warning signs include the following: withdrawal from friends, family, and regular activities; violent or rebellious behavior; running away; alcohol or drug abuse; unusual neglect of personal appearance; radical change in personality; persistent boredom; difficulty in concentrating; decline in schoolwork quality; and emotional or physical symptoms such as headaches and stomachaches. Teachers also should keep in mind a U.S. District Court ruling that found school officials partly responsible for a student's suicide when they failed to provide "reasonable" care and help for a young man who had displayed suicidal symptoms.[59]

Teenage Pregnancy

■ Rise in births out of wedlock

Among teenagers as a whole, the number and rate of births have fallen substantially during the past half-century, partly because of the availability of contraceptives and abortion and the success of abstinence campaigns in some communities. On the other hand, the percentage of births to teenage mothers that occur out of wedlock has skyrocketed from 15 percent in 1960 to almost 90 percent in the past decade.

[57]Adrienne D. Coles, "Proms, Graduations Spur Schools to Redouble Anti-Drinking Efforts," *Education Week,* June 10, 1998; and "RAND: Early Alcohol Use Linked to Adult Behavior Problems," *Alcoholism and Drug Abuse Weekly,* May 12, 2003, pp. 2–3.

[58]Jessica Portner, "Complex Set of Ills Spurs Rising Teen Suicide Rate," *Education Week,* April 12, 2000; and Victor M. Parachin, "Teen Suicide: A Preventable Tragedy," *Scouting* (May–June 2002), available at **www.scoutingmagazine,org**.

[59]Melissa Etlin, "How to Help a Suicidal Student," *NEA Today* (May–June 1990), p. 6; and Rebecca Jones, "Suicide Watch," *American School Board Journal* (May 2001), available at **www.asbj.com**. See also "Teen Suicide Theme Page" and links provided at **www.cln.org/ themes/suicide.html**.

■ Associated problems

Researchers have linked this trend to various social problems. For example, families headed by young mothers are much more likely than other families to live below the poverty line, and teenage mothers are much less likely to receive prenatal care than are older mothers. Not surprisingly, then, children of teenage mothers tend to have poor health and to perform poorly in school. Moreover, society spends billions of dollars each year to support the children of teenage mothers.[60]

■ Reasons for increase

Teenage births constitute a substantially higher percentage of births in the United States than in most other industrialized nations. According to social scientists who have analyzed fertility data, high incidence of out-of-wedlock births among teenagers results from such interrelated factors as social acceptance of teenage sexuality, earlier and more frequent sexual intercourse, a decrease in early marriages, lack of potential marriage partners, a decline in community and parental influence over the young, and the assumption by social agencies of responsibility for helping younger mothers.[61]

■ School responses

Many schools have responded by establishing school-based clinics for pregnant teenagers and new mothers, and expanding courses that focus on sex education, health, personal development, and family life. Although early data on these activities were generally negative, recent studies indicate that they can be effective in preventing or at least alleviating problems associated with teenage pregnancy. Positive results also have been reported for a variety of approaches implemented since 1996 as part of the federally sponsored National Campaign to Prevent Teen Pregnancy. In addition, organizations such as Girls, Inc. have conducted projects that provide girls with a combination of assertiveness training, health services, communications skills, personal counseling, and information about sexuality. Recent data show that these efforts appear to have substantially reduced the incidence of teenage pregnancies.[62]

Delinquency and Violence

■ Overall trends

Juvenile delinquency has increased in recent decades, paralleled by related increases in single-parent families, peer culture influence, drug and alcohol use, and the growth of low-income neighborhoods in big cities. Problems connected with violence and delinquency are particularly acute among young African American males, whose rate of death from homicide has more than tripled since 1985. Even among young white males, however, homicide rates are more than twice as high as in any other industrialized country.[63]

---

[60]Janet B. Hardy and Laurie S. Zabin, *Adolescent Pregnancy in an Urban Environment* (Washington, D.C.: Urban Institute Press, 1991); Jane Mauldron and Kristin Luker, "Does Liberalism Cause Sex?" *American Prospect* (Winter 1996), pp. 80–85; Kay S. Hymowitz, "It's Morning After in America," *City Journal* (Spring 2004), available at **www.city-journal.org**; and "Teen Birth Rates Continue to Decline" (undated), posting at the Family Education Network Internet site, available at **www.infoplease.com:** search for "teen birth."

[61]Kingsley Davis, "A Theory of Teenage Pregnancy in the United States," in Catherine S. Chilman, ed., *Adolescent Pregnancy and Childbearing* (Washington, D.C.: U.S. Government Printing Office, 1980); and Nigel Baeber, "Marital Opportunity, Parental Opportunity, and Teen Birth Rates," *Cross-Cultural Research* (August 2001), pp. 263–279.

[62]Dean F. Miller, *The Case for School-Based Health Clinics* (Bloomington, Ind.: Phi Delta Kappa, 1990); "American Academy of Pediatrics Reports on School Health Centers," *Health and Health Care in Schools* (February 2001), available at **www.healthinschools.org:** click on "e-journal"; and Priscilla Pardini, "A Supportive Place for Teen Parents," *Rethinking Schools* (Summer 2003).

[63]John J. DiIulio Jr., "Liberalism's Last Stand?" *Public Interest* (Winter 1995), pp. 119–124; John Hagan, "Defiance and Despair," *Social Forces* (September 1997), pp. 119–134; Mike Males, "Kids and Guns," *Youth Today* (April 2000); and John P. Hoffmann, "A Contextual Analysis of Differential Association, Social Control, and Strain Theories of Delinquency," *Social Forces* (March 2003), pp. 753–785.

Research on delinquency and violence among youth supports several generalizations:[64]

- Significant delinquency rates appear among youth of all social classes. However, violent delinquency is much more frequent among working-class than among middle-class youth.

- Although a large proportion of crimes are committed by people under age twenty-five, most delinquents settle down to a productive adult life.

- An increase in gangs has helped generate greater violence among youth.

■ Unemployment

- Delinquency is associated with unemployment. From this point of view, delinquency is a partial response to the restricted opportunities available to some young people in modern society.

- Family characteristics related to delinquency include lack of effective parental supervision, lack of community cohesiveness, and lack of a father.

■ Delinquency among girls

- Delinquency and violent crime rates for girls have increased much more rapidly than those for boys. However, community delinquency rates for females and males are highly correlated: communities that have high rates for one sex also tend to have high rates for the other.

■ School performance

- Delinquency is related to learning disabilities and low school achievement.

■ Influence of peers

- One of the strongest predictors of delinquency is peer influence, but this influence interacts with the family, the neighborhood, and other factors.

- Violent youth crime has increased substantially in suburban and rural areas.

Effects on Schools

■ Major consequences for schools

As we have seen, young people do not simply leave larger cultural patterns behind when they enter the schoolhouse door. Like the other topics discussed in this chapter, the characteristics of youth culture have enormous consequences for the U.S. educational system. The most direct problems are drugs and alcohol in the schools, and violence, theft, and disorder on school grounds. Indicators of antisocial behavior in and around the schools have been a continuing topic of debate during the past thirty years. In 2002, 63 percent of respondents in a national poll said that "fighting, violence, and gangs" constituted a serious problem facing public schools in their communities.[65]

Although violence and vandalism are most common at low-income schools in big cities, they are serious problems at many schools outside the inner city, especially when the schools are afflicted by teenage and young-adult gangs, by crime connected with substance abuse and drug sales, and by trespassers who infiltrate school buildings. Nearly two hundred students have been killed in or around schools during the past ten years, some of them in the highly publicized shootings at Columbine and Santee High Schools. In recent years, elaborate security plans have been put in place, zero-tolerance policies (described in the chapter on Legal

[64]Christopher Jencks, *Rethinking Social Policy* (Cambridge, Mass.: Harvard University Press, 1992); Paul V. McNulty, "Natural Born Killers," *Policy Review* (Winter 1995), pp. 84–87; Jeanne Weiler, "Girls and Violence," *ERIC Review* (Spring 2000), pp. 14–15; and Jill S. Williams, "Grouping High-Risk Youths for Prevention May Harm More Than Help," *NIDA Notes* (January 2003).

[65]Lowell C. Rose and Alec M. Gallup, "The 34th Annual Phi Delta Kappa Gallup Poll," *Phi Delta Kappan* (September 2002), pp. 41–56.

Aspects of Education) have been introduced, and schools have implemented multiple programs to reduce bullying and intergroup hostilities.[66]

■ Social service personnel in schools

In response to youth problems in general, schools now employ many more counselors, social workers, and other social service personnel than they did in earlier decades. Urban high schools, for example, use the services of such specialized personnel as guidance and career counselors, psychologists, security workers, nurses, truant officers, and home-school coordinators. Many of these specialists help conduct programs that target alcohol and drug abuse, teenage sex, school dropout, suicide, intergroup relations, and parenting skills.

In addition, many schools are cooperating with other institutions in operating school-based health clinics and/or in providing coordinated services that help students and families receive assistance with mental and physical health problems, preparation for employment, and other preoccupations that detract from students' performance in school. Thousands of schools also are implementing programs to improve schoolwide discipline, teach students conflict resolution skills, develop peer-mediation mechanisms, and control gang activities. Later chapters of this book provide additional information on efforts to improve school climates and environments.[67]

> R E F O C U S How do you think your teaching will be affected by problems of adolescence such as violence, drug use, and pregnancy? What kind of help might you need in dealing with such problems?

▶ Summing Up

1 Changes in family composition may be detrimentally influencing children's behavior and performance in school. Although the situation is complicated, increases in single-parent families and in the number of working mothers appear to be having a negative effect on many students.

2 The peer culture becomes more important as children proceed through school, but it has an important influence on education at all levels of schooling. Educators should be aware of the potentially positive effects of participation in extracurricular activities.

3 The school culture (that is, "regularities" in school practice) appears to stress passive, rote learning in many elementary and secondary schools, particularly in working-class schools and mixed-class schools with relatively large numbers of low-achieving students. This happens in part because schools, as institutions, must maintain orderly environments; because many students prefer passive learning; because teachers generally cannot adequately attend to the learning needs of all students; and because society requires that students learn to function within institutions.

4 Television probably increases aggressiveness and violent behavior among certain children and youths, and it may tend to detract from achievement, particularly in reading.

---

[66]Linda Lantieri, "Waging Peace in Our Schools," *Phi Delta Kappan* (January 1995), pp. 386–388; Mike Males, "Leave the Kids Alone," *In These Times*, June 12, 2000; Lottie L. Joiner, "Life-Saving Lessons," *American School Board Journal* (March 2002), available at **www.asbj.com**; and Susan Black, "Angry at the World," *American School Board Journal* (June 2003), available at **www.asbj.com**.

[67]The May 2003 issue of *Psychology in the Schools* is mostly devoted to the topic of school-based health centers. See also "Youth Violence Prevention and Intervention" (undated), posting at the National Association of School Psychologists Internet site, available at **www.nasponline.org/advocacy/youth_violence.html**.

Some analysts have also begun studying the social and cultural effects of digital technologies.

5 Girls traditionally have not been encouraged to seek education that prepares them for full participation in the larger society, and both girls and boys have experienced gender-role pressures in the school. Even so, educational and occupational opportunities for women have been improving rapidly. Although gender differences in school achievement have been declining, certain differences in ability may persist in verbal skills (favoring females) and advanced mathematics (favoring males).

6 Youth has become a separate stage of life marked by immersion in various subcultures. Teenage drug use and drinking, suicide, pregnancy, delinquency, and violence raise serious concerns about the development of adolescents and youth both inside and outside the school.

▶ Key Terms

culture (289)
acculturation (289)
socialization (289)
norms (289)
latchkey children (292)

hurried children (292)
nuclear family (294)
peer culture (297)
hidden curriculum (300)
gender roles (308)

▶ Discussion Questions

1 How do adolescents' socialization experiences differ in urban and rural communities? Are such differences declining over time, and if so, why?

2 How does "schooling" differ from "education"? As a prospective teacher, what implications do you see in this line of analysis?

3 In your experience, which types of students are most popular? Do you believe that popularity patterns have changed much in recent decades? If so, why?

4 What might the schools do to alleviate problems of drug use, violence, and teenage pregnancy? What *should* they do? Do you believe the "might" and "should" are different? Why or why not?

▶ Suggested Projects for Professional Development

1 Write a description of the "regularities" of schooling as you remember them at the high school you attended. Compare your description with those of your classmates. Do these patterns seem to vary much from one school to another? If so, how?

2 Contact local government officials in a nearby city, or use the Internet to obtain data on changes occurring in family life and family composition. Does the city have any data showing how such changes have affected the schools? What can you learn or predict from the data?

3 Interview local school district officials to determine what their schools are doing to reduce drug use and abuse. Cite any evidence that these efforts have been effective. What might be done to make them more effective?

4 Based on library and Internet sources cited in this chapter, develop a plan that could help a school or a teacher respond effectively and appropriately to challenges posed by students who have difficult home situations. Consider including this plan in your personal portfolio.

▶ Suggested Resources

Internet Resources

The federal government's *Preventing Drug Use Among Children and Adolescents: A Research-Based Guide* is available online at **www.nida.nih.gov/Prevention/prevopen.html**.

Possibilities for improving media literacy among children and youth are explored at **http://interact.uoregon.edu/MediaLit/mlr/home/index.html**.

"Weaving Gender Equity into Math Reform" is the theme of a site at **www.terc.edu/wge**. A bibliography on school-based health centers is available at **www.healthinschools.org**.

Conclusions from more than three hundred studies involving teens' academic success are summarized in a 2002 paper at **www.childtrends.org/PDF/k4brief.pdf**.

Vast resources for teachers are available at the Media Literacy Clearinghouse at **www.med.sc.edu:1081**.

Trends involving the family and youth, particularly positive recent developments, are described in "It's Morning After in America" by Kay S. Hymowitz, *City Journal* (Spring 2004), available at **www.city-journal.org**.

Publications

Best, Raphaela. *We've All Got Scars: What Boys and Girls Learn in Elementary School.* Bloomington: Indiana University Press, 1983. *Gives detailed observations of gender-related behaviors in the elementary grades, analyzes why relatively more boys than girls are poor readers, and examines differences in boys' and girls' participation in the academic curriculum and the hidden curriculum.*

Borman, Kathryn, and Barbara Schneider, eds. *The Adolescent Years.* Chicago: University of Chicago Press, 1998. *Chapters in this wide-ranging volume focus on the problems of adolescence, socialization of girls, extracurricular activities, and other related topics and issues.*

Lareau, Annette. *Unequal Childhoods.* Berkeley: University of California Press, 2003. *An ethnographic study of family cultures and parenting practices in low-income, working-class, and middle-class families.*

Lortie, Dan C. *Schoolteacher.* Chicago: University of Chicago Press, 1975. *A seminal analysis of the role and functioning of teachers within elementary- and secondary-school cultures.*

Sedlak, Michael W., Christopher W. Wheeler, Diana C. Pullin, and Philip Cusick. *Selling Students Short.* New York: Teachers College Press, 1986. *Evaluates classroom "bargains" that result in low-level learning and analyzes the weaknesses of bureaucratic school reform that takes little account of these classroom realities.*

Spindler, George, and Louise Spindler. *The American Cultural Dialogue and Its Transmission.* New York: Falmer, 1990. *The authors summarize their decades of observation and analysis on topics relating to culture and education.*

Waite, Linda J., and Maggie Gallagher. *The Case for Marriage.* New York: Doubleday, 2000. *A systematic description and critique of social and cultural trends affecting the family.*

CHAPTER 11

Social Class, Race, and School Achievement

We begin this chapter by briefly explaining social class and examining relationships among students' social class, racial and ethnic background, and performance in the educational system. Then we discuss why students with low social status, particularly disadvantaged minority students, typically rank low in educational achievement and attainment. We conclude the chapter by examining the implications of these relationships in the context of our nation's historic commitment to equal educational opportunity.

This chapter, like the one on Culture, Socialization, and Education, offers no easy answers; but we hope it will provide you with a deeper understanding. We will show how inadequate achievement patterns have become most prevalent among students with socioeconomic disadvantages, especially if those students also belong to minority groups that have experienced widespread discrimination. Other chapters will look at efforts to change the prevailing patterns and improve the performance of disadvantaged students. First, however, we must focus on the multiple root causes of the problem and their implications for teaching and learning. As you read this chapter, think about these questions:

FOCUS QUESTIONS

- What is the relationship between social class and success in the educational system?
- After accounting for social class, are race and ethnicity associated with school achievement?
- How do environment and heredity affect low achievement levels?
- What are the major reasons for low achievement among students with low socioeconomic status?
- What roles do home and family environment play in encouraging or discouraging high achievement?

■ How does the relationship between social class and school achievement affect the national goal of providing equal educational opportunities for all students?

▶ Social Class and Success in School

American society is generally understood to consist of three broad classes: working, middle, and upper. A well-known and strong relationship exists between social class and educational achievement. Traditionally, working-class students have performed less well than middle- and upper-class students. As you read the analysis in this section, you should ask yourself why it has been so difficult to improve the achievement of working-class students and what can be done to improve their achievement in the future.

Categories of Social Class

■ Class and SES

In the 1940s W. Lloyd Warner and his colleagues used four main variables— occupation, education, income, and housing value—to classify Americans and their families into five groups: upper class, upper middle class, lower middle class, upper lower class, and lower lower class. Individuals high in occupational prestige, amount of education, income, and housing value ranked in the higher classes. Such people are also said to be high in **socioeconomic status (SES)**; that is, others see them as upper-class persons and they are influential and powerful in their communities. Conversely, people low in socioeconomic status are considered low in prestige and power.[1]

■ Social classes defined

Today, the term *working class* is more widely used than *lower class,* but social scientists still identify three to six levels of SES, ranging from upper class at the top to lower working class at the bottom. The **upper class** is usually defined as including wealthy persons with substantial property and investments. The **middle class** includes professionals, managers, and small-business owners (upper middle) as well as technical workers, technicians, sales personnel, and clerical workers (lower middle). The **working class** is generally divided into upper working class (including skilled crafts workers) and lower working class (unskilled manual workers). Skilled workers may be either middle class or working class, depending on their education, income, and other considerations such as the community in which they live.[2]

■ Intergenerational poverty

In recent years, observers have identified an **underclass** group within the working class. The underclass generally resembles the lower working class, but many of its members are the third or fourth generation to live in poverty and depend on public assistance to sustain a relatively meager existence. Usually concentrated in the inner slums of cities or in deteriorated areas of rural poverty, many members of

---

[1]W. Lloyd Warner, Marcia Meeker, and Kenneth Eells, *Social Class in America* (Chicago: Science Research Associates, 1949). See also Delbert C. Miller, *Handbook of Research Design and Social Measurement,* 5th ed. (Newbury Park, Calif.: Sage, 1991); and William G. Domhoff, *Who Rules America?* (New York: McGraw-Hill, 2002).

[2]William A. Galston and Elaine C. Kamarck, "Five Realities That Will Shape 21st Century Politics," *Blueprint* (Fall 1998), available at **www.dlc.org/blueprint**. A bibliography is at **www.pbs.org/peoplelikeus**. At the latter site you can also participate in an interactive game to characterize your home furniture preferences in social-class terms.

the underclass frequently have little hope of improving their economic and social situation.[3]

Also, some analysts have gone still further and have identified an "establishment" (or "overclass") that they believe is prospering in a competitive international economy at the same time that much of our population is stagnating economically. As do observers studying underclass development, these analysts generally emphasize the importance of education in determining one's social status and income.[4]

Research on Social Class and School Success

■ "Middletown" study

One of the first systematic studies investigating the relationship between social class and achievement in school was Robert and Helen Lynd's study of "Middletown" (a small midwestern city) in the 1920s. The Lynds concluded that parents, regardless of social class, recognize the importance of education for their children; however, many working class children come to school unequipped to acquire the verbal skills and behavioral traits required for success in the classroom. The Lynds' observations of social class and the schools were repeated by W. Lloyd Warner and his associates in a series of studies of towns and small cities in New England, the Deep South, and the Midwest. Hundreds of studies have since documented the close relationship between social class and education in the United States and, indeed, throughout the world.[5]

Standards & Assessment ☑
■ NAEP

For example, we have a clear picture of this relationship from the **National Assessment of Educational Progress (NAEP)** and other agencies that collect achievement information from nationally representative samples of students. As shown in Table 11.1, mathematics and reading proficiency scores of groups of students vary directly with their social class. Students with well-educated parents (one primary measure of social class) score much higher than students whose parents have less education. This holds to such an extent that nine-year-olds whose parents had at least some college had average scores not far below those for thirteen-year-olds whose parents had not completed high school.

Standards & Assessment ☑
■ Achievement correlated with community

School achievement also correlates with type of community, which reflects the social class of people who reside there. As shown in Table 11.1, the average mathematics and reading scores of students in "urban fringe/large town" areas (with a relatively high proportion of residents in professional or managerial occupations) are much higher than those of students in "central city" areas (with a high proportion of residents who receive public assistance or are unemployed). Only 26 percent of the eighth graders in central cities were proficient in reading in 2002.[6]

---

[3]Christopher Jencks and Paul E. Peterson, eds., *The Urban Underclass* (Washington, D.C.: The Brookings Institution, 1991); Martin M. Wooster, "Inside the Underclass," *American Enterprise* (May–June 1998), pp. 83–84; and Lisa Finnernan and Morgan Kelly, "Social Networks and Inequality," *Journal of Urban Economics* (March 2003), pp. 282–299.
[4]David Brooks, *Bobos in Paradise* (New York: Simon and Schuster, 2000).
[5]Robert S. Lynd and Helen M. Lynd, *Middletown: A Study in American Culture* (New York: Harcourt, Brace and World, 1929); Doris R. Entwistle and Nan M. Astone, "Some Practical Guidelines for Measuring Youth's Race/Ethnicity and Socioeconomic Status," *Child Development* (December 1994), pp. 1521–1540; and OECD/UNESCO, *Literacy Skills for the World of Tomorrow* (Paris: Organisation for Economic Cooperation and Development, 2003).
[6]Wendy S. Grigg et al., *The Nation's Report Card: Reading 2002* (Washington, D.C.: U.S. Department of Education, 2003).

Standards & Assessment ✓

Table 11.1	Percentages of Eighth Graders Performing at or above Proficient Levels, 2000 and 2002	
	Mathematics 2000	Reading 2002
Parental Education		
Not graduated high school	08	14
Graduated high school	16	21
Some education after high school	27	34
Graduated college	39	44
Type of Community		
Central city	23	26
Urban fringe/large town	31	37
Rural/small town	26	33

Note: The National Assessment of Educational Progress defines community type as follows: *"Central city"* includes central cities in metropolitan areas. *"Urban fringe/large town"* generally includes other locations in metropolitan areas. A *"large town"* is a place with at least 25,000 people outside metropolitan areas.
Source: James S. Braswell et al., *The Nations' Report Card. Mathematics 2000* (Washington, D.C.: U.S. Department of Education, 2001); and Wendy S. Grigg et al., *The Nation's Report Card: Reading 2002* (Washington, D.C.: U.S. Department of Education, 2003).

■ Concentrated poverty schools

Further evidence of the relationship between social class and school achievement can be found in studies of poverty neighborhoods in large cities. For example, Levine and his colleagues examined sixth-grade achievement patterns at more than a thousand predominantly low-income schools (which they called concentrated poverty schools) in seven big cities and reported that all but a few had average reading scores more than two years below the national average. They also pointed out that at least one-fourth of the students at these schools cannot read well enough when they enter high school to be considered functionally literate. This pattern can be found at concentrated poverty schools in big cities throughout the United States.[7]

■ Rural poverty

Many educators also are concerned about the achievement of rural students, especially those who live in low-income regions and pockets of rural poverty. Although rural students generally achieve near the national average, research indicates that poverty and inequality can hamper their progress, and that two-thirds of rural educators believe the academic performance of their low-income students is in either "great need" or "fairly strong need" of improvement.[8]

---

[7]Daniel U. Levine and Rayna F. Levine, *Society and Education,* 9th ed. (Needham Heights, Mass.: Allyn and Bacon, 1996). See also Richard D. Kahlenberg, "Socioeconomic Integration," *Principal* (May 2000), available at **www.naesp.org:** search for "Kahlenberg"; Richard D. Kahlenberg, "The New Brown," *Legal Affairs* (May–June, 2003), available at **www.legalaffairs .org**; and Gary Orfield and Chungmei Lee, "Brown at 50" (2004), paper posted at the Harvard University Civil Rights Project Internet site, available at **www.civilrightsproject .harvard.edu/research/reseg04/resegregation04.php**.
[8]Alan J. DeYoung and Barbara K. Lawrence, "On Hoosiers, Yankees, and Mountaineers," *Phi Delta Kappan* (October 1995), pp. 104–112; Helen Silvis, "Forget Isolation, We're Online Now," *NW Education* (Winter 2000), pp. 43–44, available at **www.nwrel.org:** search for "Silvis"; and Anne C. Lewis, "Rural Schools," *Education Digest* (April 2003), pp. 69–72.

■ Effective schools

We also should emphasize, however, that methods exist for improving the achievement of students with low socioeconomic status. In particular, the "effective schools" movement that came to prominence in the 1980s showed that appropriate schoolwide efforts to enhance instruction can produce sizable gains in the performance of disadvantaged students, even in concentrated poverty schools in big cities and rural schools in poor areas. It is easier today than only ten or fifteen years ago to find schools that have improved achievement among their low-income students. We describe the effective schools movement and other efforts to improve performance among disadvantaged students in other chapters, particularly the chapter on School Effectiveness and Reform in the United States.

■ Percentages attending college

Social Class, College Participation, and National Problems. Social class is associated with many educational outcomes in addition to achievement in reading, math, and other subjects. On the average, working-class students not only have lower achievement scores but also are less likely than middle-class students to complete high school or to enroll in and complete college. Only about 25 percent of high-school graduates from the lowest two socioeconomic quartiles (the lowest 50 percent of students measured in terms of family income) enter college and attain a postsecondary degree, compared with more than 80 percent of high-school graduates in the highest quartile. (Each "quartile" contains one-quarter of the population.)[9] Researchers find that social class relates to college attendance and graduation even when they compare students with similar achievement levels. For example, one study showed that low-status high-school seniors were nearly 50 percent less likely to enter a postsecondary institution than were high-status seniors with similar reading achievement scores. Limitations in federal financial aid, among other reasons, have caused this discrepancy to grow in recent years.[10]

One team of researchers studying international literacy patterns recently concluded that "inequality is deeply rooted in the education system and in the workplace in the United States.... our nation concentrates on producing and rewarding first-class skills and, as a result, is world class at the top; however it ... accepts in fact, if not in rhetoric, a basic skills underclass." These patterns also led a senior researcher at the Educational Testing Service to observe that the U.S. has not adequately "recognized the need to eliminate barriers to achievement that arise in the family, and how lack of resources affect achievement."[11]

REFOCUS Have you visited schools where many students were from a different social class from most students in schools you attended? What differences did you observe? How do you think these differences would affect achievement?

---

[9]Stephanie Cuccaro-Alamin, *Postsecondary Persistence and Attainment* (Washington, D.C.: U.S. Department of Education, 1997); Thomas G. Mortenson, "The Challenge of Broadening Opportunity through Public Policy" (2003), paper posted at the Postsecondary Education Opportunity Internet site, available at **www.postsecondary.org**; and Jennifer Washburn, "The Tuition Crunch," *Atlantic* (January–February 2004), available at **www.theatlantic .com**.

[10]Thomas G. Mortenson, "The Crisis of Access in Higher Education," *Academe* (November–December 2000), pp. 1–5; and Paul E. Barton, "The Closing of the Education Frontier," *ETS Policy Information Center Reports* (September 2002), available at **www.ets.org/research/pic**.

[11]Paul E. Barton, "Toward Inequality," *ETS Policy Information Center Report* (October 1997), no page number provided; and Andrew Sum, Irwin Kirsch, and Robert Taggart, "The Twin Challenges of Mediocrity and Inequality," *ETS Policy Information Center Report* (February 2002), pp. 31–32. Both reports are available at **www.ets.org/research/pic**. See also Michael Lind, "Are We Still a Middle-Class Nation?" *Atlantic* (January–February 2004), available at **www.theatlantic.com**; and Sandra S. Ruppert, "Closing the College Participation Gap" (2003), paper prepared for the Education Commission of the States, available at **www .ecs.org**.

▶ Race, Ethnicity, and School Success

■ Race and ethnicity defined

Patterns of social class and educational achievement in the United States are further complicated by the additional factors of race and ethnicity. *Race* identifies groups of people with common ancestry and physical characteristics. *Ethnicity* identifies people who have a shared culture. Members of an **ethnic group** usually have common ancestry and share language, religion, and other cultural traits. Because no "pure" races exist, some scholars avoid referring to race and instead discuss group characteristics under the heading of ethnicity.

■ Status of minority groups

As we saw in the chapter on Historical Development of American Education, the U.S. population is a mix of many races and ethnicities. Some racial and ethnic minority groups in this country have experienced social and economic oppression *as a group* despite the accomplishments of many individuals. For example, African Americans have a lower average socioeconomic status than that of the white majority, even though many individual African Americans may be of higher SES than many whites. Other major ethnic minority groups, such as Mexican Americans and Puerto Ricans, are also disproportionately low in socioeconomic status. (These two groups, combined with Cuban Americans and citizens with Central and South American ancestry, constitute the Hispanic/Latino population, which is growing rapidly and will soon outnumber the African American population. This chapter uses the term *Hispanic* in reporting data from government publications employing this terminology and generally uses *Latino* elsewhere.) An ongoing concern for educators is the fact that these racial and ethnic minority groups are correspondingly low in academic achievement, high-school and college graduation rates, and other measures of educational attainment.[12]

Standards & Assessment ☑

■ Eighth-grade samples

We can see the close association among social class, race or ethnicity, and school performance in Figure 11.1, which presents average math and reading scores attained by nationally representative samples of eighth graders. African American students have the lowest SES scores (as reflected by higher percentages in poverty). They also have the lowest math scores and the lowest reading scores. In contrast, non-Hispanic whites are highest in SES and in math and reading. In general, school achievement scores parallel scores on socioeconomic status; the higher the SES score, the higher the achievement scores.[13]

■ Gains by minorities

Data collected by the NAEP indicate that the gap between African American and Latino students on the one hand and white students on the other may be narrowing. African American and Latino students have registered gains in reading, math, and other subjects. Some observers attribute these improvements partly to the federal Title 1 program and/or to increases in desegregation. (See the chapter on Providing Equal Educational Opportunity for discussions of Title 1 and desegregation.) The gap is by no means closed, however. African American and Latino students still score far below whites in reading and other subjects, and black and Latino

---

[12]Roberto Suro, *America's Racial Divide and the Latino Challenge* (New York: Knopf, 1998); "White/Latino Achievement Gap," *No Excuses Notes* (June 2003), available at **www.noexcuses.org**; and Brian Grow, "Is America Ready?" *Business Week*, March 15, 2004, pp. 59–70.

[13]Further analysis of these and other data also indicates considerable variation within broad racial and ethnic classifications. For example, among Hispanics, Cuban Americans have much higher SES and achievement scores than do Mexican American and Puerto Rican students. Among Asian American subgroups, Hmong and Vietnamese students tend to be relatively low in status and achievement.

Standards & Assessment

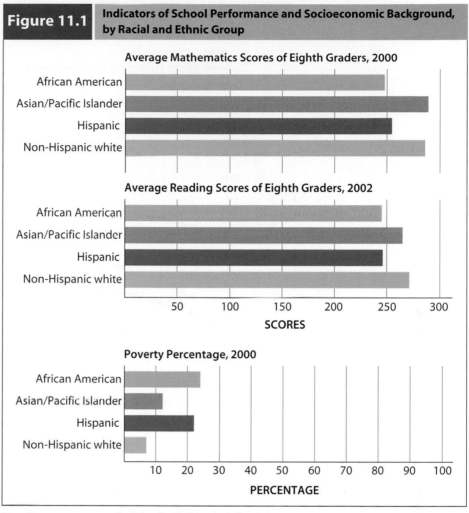

Figure 11.1 Indicators of School Performance and Socioeconomic Background, by Racial and Ethnic Group

Note: Poverty percentage for Asian/Pacific Islander is for 1998.
Source: Statistical Abstract of the United States 2003 (Washington, D.C.: U.S. Government Printing Office, 2003); James S. Braswell et al., *The Nation's Report Card: Mathematics 2000* (Washington, D.C.: U.S. Department of Education, 2001); and Wendy S. Grigg et al., *The Nation's Report Card: Reading 2002* (Washington, D.C.: U.S. Department of Education, 2003).

seventeen-year-olds still have approximately the same average reading scores as white thirteen-year-olds.[14]

■ Dropout rates

As you might expect from the achievement data shown in Figure 11.1, non-Hispanic white and Asian students (other than Vietnamese Americans) are more likely to complete high school than are African American and Latino students. Figure 11.2 shows that the high-school completion rate for African American students has been rising since 1975, but it remains significantly below the rate for whites, and the rate

[14]Samuel S. Peng, DeeAnn Wright, and Susan T. Hill, *Understanding Racial-Ethnic Differences in Secondary School Science and Mathematics Achievement* (Washington, D.C.: U.S. Department of Education, 1995); James S. Jackson and Nicholas A. Jones, "New Directions in Thinking About Race in America," *African American Research Perspectives* (Winter 2001), pp. 1–36; and Jens Ludwig, "Educational Achievement and Black–White Inequality," *Education Next* (Summer 2003), available at **www.educationnext.org**.

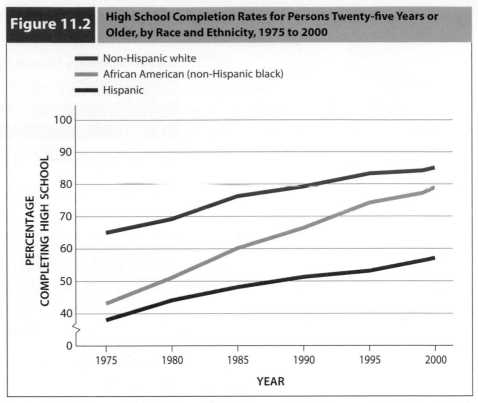

Figure 11.2 **High School Completion Rates for Persons Twenty-five Years or Older, by Race and Ethnicity, 1975 to 2000**

Source: Statistical Abstract of the United States 2003 (Washington, D.C.: U.S. Government Printing Office, 2003).

for Latinos has remained so low that national leaders are gravely concerned about the future of Latino youth. In addition, high-school dropout rates are still extremely high among African American and Latino students in big-city poverty areas. Knowledgeable observers estimate that dropout rates range from 40 to 60 percent in some big cities and may exceed 75 or 80 percent at schools enrolling mostly underclass students.[15]

■ College attendance

African American and Latino students are also less likely to enter and complete college and other postsecondary institutions. Postsecondary enrollment rates for African American and Latino high-school graduates rose substantially in the 1960s and early 1970s but have increased only slightly since then. As a result, African American and Latino students constitute less than 20 percent of enrollment in higher education, well below their percentage in the college-age population. The causes cited for these patterns include rising tuition, reductions in federal funds, and cuts in special recruiting and assistance programs. Some educators also note that participation in drug cultures may have disabled many minority youth. Reports from major educational agencies have referred to the rate of minority enrollment in higher education as "shockingly low" and "intolerable." The reports generally con-

[15]Sonia M. Perez, *Latino Education: Status and Prospects* (Washington, D.C.: National Council of La Raza, 1998); and *From Risk to Opportunity* (Washington, D.C.: President's Advisory Commission on Educational Excellence for Hispanic Americans, 2003), available at **www.yic .gov/paceea/final.html**.

■ Calls for improvement

clude that colleges, universities, and government officials should take steps to increase minority enrollment.[16]

The Special Problem of Minority Status Plus Urban Poverty

■ Segregated inner cities

As we have documented, educational achievement generally is distressingly low at schools in poor inner-city neighborhoods. We have also pointed out that although high-school completion rates for African American students have been rising nationally, the dropout problem remains severe in big cities. These problems reflect the fact that the inner cores of many large U.S. urban areas have become segregated communities populated by working-class and underclass African American and Latino residents. Causes and results of this socioeconomic and racial/ethnic stratification include the following:

■ Polarization among African Americans

1. *The African American population of the United States has become more economically polarized.* The overall socioeconomic status and income of this population have increased substantially since 1950. For example, the average income (in real dollars) of married couples among African Americans has approximately doubled since 1950, and the number of black families earning $50,000 or more has nearly quadrupled. However, many other African Americans still live in urban poverty, in neighborhoods where most families are headed by single women and where rates of crime, delinquency, drug abuse, teenage pregnancy, and other indicators of social disorganization remain extremely high.[17]

    We can make somewhat similar statements concerning the Hispanic or Latino population. A substantial split divides a growing middle-class segment and a large segment residing in big-city poverty neighborhoods. Rates of social disorganization in these latter neighborhoods are high.[18] The In This Case feature in this chapter shows challenges that face teachers in these neighborhoods.

■ Increasing concentration in urban poverty areas

2. *Both the number and the percentage of low-income minority people living in urban poverty areas have increased substantially.* Although the overall population of the fifty largest cities in the United States has declined since 1970, the number of low-income African Americans living in poverty areas has increased by more than one-third. Despite the fact that concentrations of urban poverty decreased in the past decade, big city neighborhoods and schools still tend to have large low-income populations. More than two-thirds of the students in many big-city school districts such as Chicago, Detroit, and New York, are

[16]The agencies mentioned include the Education Commission of the States, the State Higher Education Executive Officers, the United States Commission on Civil Rights, and the American Council on Education. See, for example, *Equal Educational Opportunity and Nondiscrimination for Students with Limited English Proficiency* (Washington, D.C.: United States Commission on Civil Rights, 1997); and *Empty Promises* (Washington, D.C.: Advisory Committee on Student Financial Assistance, 2002).
[17]Bart Landry, *The New Black Middle Class* (Berkeley: University of California Press, 1987); William J. Wilson, *The Truly Disadvantaged* (Chicago: University of Chicago Press, 1987); Henry L. Gates Jr., "The Two Nations of Black America," *Brookings Review* (Spring 1998), pp. 4–7; and William J. Wilson et al., *The Roots of Racial Tension* (New York: Knopf, 2003).
[18]Peter Dreier and David Moberg, "Moving from the 'Hood,'" *American Prospect* (Winter 1996), pp. 75–79; Michael B. Teitz and Karen Chapple, "The Causes of Inner-City Poverty," *Cityscape* 3, no. 3 (1998) available at **www.huduser.org**: click on "Periodicals"; and David Pacchioli, "Not by Jobs Alone," *Penn State Online* (January 2003), available at **www.rps .psu.edu/0301**.

IN THIS CASE

Hoping for Success

David Rusciatti looked over his first class in eighth-grade English. He had agreed to teach in this inner city school because that's where he began his own schooling, but the neighborhood was a different place now from just a few years ago when he had lived here.

David knew that this would be a challenging first year. In fact, a couple of the more experienced teachers had told him that they wouldn't like to be in his shoes. His schedule was full, with five classes of eighth-grade English. This first class seemed to have a mix of students of differing ethnicities and vastly different backgrounds. According to the guidance counselor, most of the students were low achievers. He knew that at least four of the boys and two of the girls had attended eighth grade last year.

David heard quite a bit of giggling and chatting. As he took role call, he noted back and hand slapping as each student raised his or her hand to indicate they were present. He remembered what his supervising professor had told him last year, "Remember, David, the first day and the first week are all-important. You must set the pace and lay down the rules then or you are finished for the year."

David had prepared the first day's class with his professor's advice about setting the tone in mind. Following the premise that he must involve the students in their own active learning, he had developed a series of questions and activities. Before he could implement his plan of action, however, the assistant principal came in and took him aside. He whispered, "Don't rile Thomas Davis, over there. I've been told that he has a small pistol concealed under his shirt. I've called the campus police, and they'll nab him as soon as class is dismissed. He's upset about something to do with his girlfriend. If you have trouble before then, you can call me at the office using that phone on the wall. Think you'll be okay?"

"I'll be okay. I have the day well planned."

As the assistant principal left, David wondered if he actually would be okay. All went well until he asked the students to write a short paragraph telling about their best experiences of the summer. Several students began commenting to each other, joking and laughing. David was unsure how much of this he should allow, so he smiled and encouraged those who were writing to continue. At the same time, he began to walk around the class to talk to each student not writing.

He scanned the class, noting the different levels of involvement. He would have to learn more about how to teach a group of students with such varying backgrounds. And about each individual, too. Maybe that should come first.

Questions

1. Should first-year teachers be assigned difficult classes such as this one? Justify your answer.
2. What obstacles must David hurdle to be considered an effective teacher?
3. How would you prepare for and handle a class such as this?
4. What instructional policies might David want to introduce?

now from low-income families, and more than 80 percent are minority students.[19]

■ Dysfunctional institutions

3. *Social institutions such as the family, the school, and the law enforcement system often appear to have collapsed in the inner city.* Parents find it difficult to control

---

[19]Craig St. John, "Interclass Segregation, Poverty, and Poverty Concentration," *American Journal of Sociology* (March 1995), pp. 1325–1333; Matthew R. Lee, "Concentrated Poverty, Race and Homicide," *Sociological Quarterly* (Spring 2000); and G. Thomas Kingsley and Kathryn L. S. Pettit, "Concentrated Poverty: A Change in the Course," *Neighborhood Change in America* (May 2003), available at **www.urban.org**.

their children, and law enforcement agencies are unable to cope with high rates of juvenile delinquency and adult crime.[20]

■ Rising social isolation

4. *The concentration of low-income minority populations in big-city poverty areas has increased their isolation from the larger society.* In contrast to the urban slums and ghettos of fifty or one hundred years ago, today's concentrated poverty areas are larger geographically, and in many cases their residents are more homogeneous in (low) socioeconomic status. Unskilled and semiskilled jobs are more difficult to obtain, and many jobs have been moved overseas or to the suburbs, where they are practically inaccessible to central-city residents. Andrew Hacker observed that the contemporary "mode of segregation, combining poverty and race, is relatively new. To reside amid so many people leading desultory lives makes it all the harder to break away."[21]

■ Problems for young black males

5. *The problems experienced by young black males have escalated enormously.* Some knowledgeable observers believe that the plight of young males in inner-city poverty areas is at the root of a series of other serious problems: high rates of out-of-wedlock births, the persistence of welfare dependency, and violent crime and delinquency. The growth in female-headed families in urban poverty areas relates directly to the high rates at which young African American men drop out of the labor force, are incarcerated in prisons or placed on parole, or otherwise are excluded or exclude themselves from mainstream institutions. The result is a great reduction in the pool of men available to participate in stable families and accumulate resources for upward mobility.[22]

Comparing the Influence of Social Class and Ethnicity

■ Social class as the primary factor

The close interrelationship between social class, race and ethnicity, and school achievement leads researchers to frequently ask whether race and ethnicity are associated with performance in the educational system even after one takes into account the low socioeconomic status of African Americans and other disadvantaged minority groups. In general, the answer has been that social class accounts for much of the variation in educational achievement by race and ethnicity. That is, if you know the social class of a group of students, you can predict with a good deal of accuracy whether their achievement, ability scores, and college attendance rates are high or low. Information about their racial or ethnic group generally does relatively little to improve such a prediction. This also means that working-class white students as a group are low in achievement and college attainment, whereas middle-class minority students, as a group, rank relatively high on these variables.[23]

---

[20]Carl L. Bankston and Stephen J. Caldas, "Race, Poverty, Family Structure and the Inequality of Schools," *Sociological Spectrum* (January–March, 1998), pp. 55–74; Sheldon Danziger and Ann C. Linn, "Coping with Poverty," *African American Research Perspectives* (Fall 2000), pp. 41–53;and Craig Burnett, "Is Blade Runner in Our Future?" *Law and Society Review* 2 (2002–2003), available at **www.lawso.ucsb.edu/projects/review**.

[21]Andrew Hacker, "American Apartheid," *New York Review of Books,* December 3, 1987, pp. 32–33; Andrew Hacker, *Two Nations* (New York: Ballantine, 1995); and Narayan Sastry and Anne R. Pebley, "Neighborhoods, Poverty and Children's Well-Being" (2003), paper prepared for Rand, available at **www.rand.org/labor**.

[22]Glenn Loury, "The Impossible Dilemma," *New Republic,* January 1, 1996, pp. 21–25; Rodger Doyle, "Bad Things Happen," *Scientific American* (June 2002), pp. 26–27; and Katharine Boo, "The Marriage Cure," *New Yorker,* August 17 and 25, 2003, pp. 102–120.

[23]Ian McCallum and Feyisa Demie, "Social Class, Ethnicity and Educational Performance," *Educational Research* (Summer 2001), pp. 147–159; and Derek Neal, "Resources and Educational Outcomes Among Black Children" (2004), paper prepared for the Harvard University conference on "50 Years After Brown," available at **www.ksg.harvard.edu/pepg/pdf/ BrownConf/PEPG_04-06Neal.pdf**.

Disadvantaged minorities in the United States remain disproportionately working class and underclass and their children remain much less successful in the educational system than are the children of the middle class. Moreover, because education is an important channel for gaining access to the job market, minority students with low socioeconomic status have relatively less opportunity for economic success later in their lives. From this point of view, the schools' ineffectiveness in educating students from working-class homes helps to perpetuate the current class system—and the burden of poverty and low achievement falls disproportionately on the nation's racial and ethnic minority groups.

■ A divided population

For educators, the challenge is to improve the performance of all low-status students, from whatever ethnic group. The U.S. population as a whole has become more divided, with a growing high-income segment, a growing low-income segment, and a shrinking middle segment. Many commentators share the alarm of former Secretary of Labor Robert Reich: "If we lose our middle class and become a two-tiered society, we not only risk the nation's future prosperity but also its social coherence and stability. As the economy grows, people who work the machines and clean the offices and provide the basic goods and services are supposed to share in the gains, but that hasn't been happening."[24]

REFOCUS If the middle-income segment of the population is shrinking, and the low-income segment is growing, chances are good that, as a teacher, you will have low-income students in your classes. What are you doing to prepare yourself to effectively teach children from all social classes?

▶ Reasons for Low Achievement Among Low-Status Students

Over the past forty years, much research has been aimed at understanding and overcoming the academic deficiencies of low-achieving students in general and low-achieving students from working-class or poor families in particular. Although the explanations are not necessarily mutually exclusive, we will group them under the following major factors: home environment, heredity versus environment, and obstacles in the classroom, also summarized in Overview 11.1.

Home Environment

The chapter on Culture, Socialization, and Education points out that families are the most important agent in children's early socialization and education. We also noted that characteristics of the home environment closely reflect the family's social class. Thus social-class differences in home environment associate with educational performance and student attainment. Many working-class students grow up in homes that fail to prepare them well for school. Even though their parents may stress the importance of education, these students tend to function poorly in the typical classroom.

---

[24]Quoted in Keith Bradsher, "Productivity Is All, But It Doesn't Pay Well," *New York Times,* June 25, 1995, p. 4E. See also Christopher Jencks and Joseph Swingle, "Without a Net," *American Prospect,* January 3, 2000; and Michael Hout, "Money and Morale" (2003), paper posted at the University of California Berkeley Survey Research Center Internet site, available at **www.unc.edu/depts/soc/Morale_Working_Paper.pdf**.

OVERVIEW 11.1 *Obstacles to Achievement for Working-Class Students by Area of Influence*

Area of Influence	Potential Obstacles to Achievement for Working-Class Students
Home	Disadvantages in home environment of some working-class students, especially in first few years of life, may leave children unprepared to learn in school. Specifically: • *Knowledge and Understandings.* Lack of exposure to cultural and technological world may limit understandings needed in school. • *Cognitive and Verbal Skills.* Restricted language does not help prepare children for school. • *Values and Attitudes.* Focus on control does not encourage higher-order thinking or independent problem-solving skills needed in school.
Heredity versus Environment	Working-class children average lower scores on intelligence tests, which may be related to low achievement in school. Debate over why scores are low includes at least three views: • *Heredetarian.* Differences in intellectual capacity are inborn, affected little by environment. • *Environmentalist.* Family, school, and cultural environment are major factors in determining IQ test performance. • *Synthesis.* Both environment and heredity contribute to IQ and school performance. Teachers and parents should provide the best possible environment for each child to make the most of their inherited abilities.
Classroom	Obstacles in the classroom that can contribute to low achievement by working-class students include the following: • Inappropriate curriculum and instruction • Lack of previous success in school • Ineffective fixation on low-level learning • Difficult teaching conditions in working-class schools • Teacher perceptions of student inadequacies • Ineffective homogeneous grouping • Delivery-of-service problems • Overly large classes • Lack of teacher preparation and experience • Negative peer pressure • Differences between teacher and student backgrounds • Incompatibility between classroom expectations and students' behavioral patterns/learning styles

■ Knowledge and understandings

Children's home environments cultivate three key sets of characteristics important to their school achievement: (1) knowledge and understandings, (2) cognitive and verbal skills, and (3) values and attitudes. Regarding *knowledge and understandings,* middle-class children are more likely than working-class children to acquire a wide knowledge of the world outside the home through access to books and cultural institutions (for example, museums), parental teaching, and exploration of diverse environments. Knowledge and understandings acquired through exposure to the

Development of cognitive skills relates to home environment quality during the preschool years. *(Michael Keller/CORBIS)*

■ Cognitive and verbal skills

■ Values and attitudes

wider world are helpful to children when they enter school. Working-class students today may experience even greater disadvantages than in earlier eras because they tend to have less access to computers at home than do middle-class students.[25]

Students' *cognitive and verbal skills* also reflect social-class differences in family language environments. Basil Bernstein has found that both middle- and working-class children develop adequate skills with respect to "ordinary" or "restricted" language, but middle-class children are superior in the use of "formal" or "elaborated" language. Ordinary, restricted language is grammatically simple, relying on gestures and further explanations to clarify meaning. Elaborated, formal language is grammatically complex and provides greater potential for organizing experience within an abstract meaning system. Many scholars believe that facility in using elaborated language helps middle-class children excel in cognitive development.[26]

Regarding *values and attitudes*, socialization practices in many working-class homes ill-prepare children to function independently in the school and classroom. Many children from lower socioeconomic backgrounds are at a disadvantage because their socialization appears to emphasize obedience and conformity, whereas middle-class families tend to stress independent learning and self-directed thinking. After an intensive study of seven hundred families in Nottingham, England, John and Elizabeth Newson summarized these different socialization patterns as follows:[27]

---

[25]Annette Lareau, "Social Class Differences in Family–School Relationships: The Importance of Cultural Capital," *Sociology of Education* (April 1987), pp. 73–85; Betty Hart and Todd R. Risley, "The Early Catastrophe," *American Educator* (Spring 2003), available at **www.aft .org/american_educator**; and Annette Lareau, *Unequal Childhoods* (Berkeley: University of California Press, 2003).

[26]Basil Bernstein, *The Structuring of Pedagogic Discourse* (New York: Routledge, 1990); James Atherton, "Language Codes" (2002), paper posted at the Doceo Internet site, available at **www.doceo.co.uk/background**; and Jeanne S. Chall and Vicki A. Jacobs, "Poor Children's Fourth-Grade Slump," *American Educator* (Spring 2003), available at **www.aft.org/ american_educator**.

[27]John Newson and Elizabeth Newson, *Seven Years Old in the Home Environment* (London: Allen and Unwin, 1976), p. 406. See also Jeanne Brooks-Gunn, "Do You Believe in Magic?" *Social Policy Report* 17, no. 1 (2003).

Parents at the upper end of the social scale are more inclined on principle to use democratically based, highly verbal means of control, and this kind of discipline is likely to produce personalities who can both identify successfully with the system and use it for their own ends later on. At the bottom end of the scale . . . [many] parents choose on principle to use a highly authoritarian, mainly non-verbal means of control, in which words are used more to threaten and bamboozle the child into obedience than to make him understand the rationale behind social behavior. . . . Thus the child born into the lowest social bracket has everything stacked against him including his parents' principles of child upbringing.

Differences in child-rearing practices reflect the fact that many working-class environments are relatively dangerous for children, and parents use methods that do not help at school but do prepare their children to function in this hostile environment. Other differences arise from parents' own limits in education, resources, and knowledge of what practices help children develop intellectually.

■ Stimulation by home environment

The importance of the home and family environment for general intellectual development has also been documented in studies by J. McVicker Hunt, Martin Deutsch, and other researchers. These studies generally indicate that environmental stimulation in working-class homes is less conducive to intellectual development, on the average, than it is in middle-class homes. Deutsch outlined factors, such as lack of productive visual and tactile stimulation, that limit learning readiness in many disadvantaged children. Deutsch and others developed indexes of environmental disadvantage that correlate even more closely with IQ scores and school success than do social-class indicators.[28]

■ Early cognitive development

The environmental disadvantage theory holds that early developmental years are more important than later years. As pointed out by Benjamin Bloom, David Hamburg, and others, the most rapid development of many human characteristics, including cognitive skills, occurs during the preschool years. Furthermore, the child's intellectual development is affected even during the prenatal stages by the mother's general health, her diet, her alcohol intake and drug usage, and stress and other emotional factors. Although we can counteract learning deficits that arise from disadvantaged early environments, it is, as this implies, more difficult to produce changes for older children; we need a more powerful environment to bring about these changes. It further implies that as a society we should use more of our resources to address early environmental problems and disadvantages. These understandings helped lead to the development of *compensatory education,* which, as described in the chapter on Providing Equal Educational Opportunity, tries to remedy the effects of environmental disadvantages by providing preschool education and improved instruction in elementary and secondary schools.[29] We will further describe compensatory education in the next chapter.

---

[28]Martin Deutsch, "The Role of Social Class in Language Development and Cognition," in A. H. Passow, M. I. Goldbery, and A. J. Tannenbaum, eds., *Education of the Disadvantaged* (New York: Holt, 1967), pp. 214–224; Jack Shonkoff et al., *From Neurons to Neighborhoods* (Washington, D.C.: National Academy of Sciences Press, 2000); Richard J. Colcy, "An Uneven Start" (2002), paper prepared for the Educational Testing Service, available at **www.ets.org/research/pic**; and Richard Rothstein, *Class and Schools* (New York: Teachers College Press, 2004).

[29]Benjamin S. Bloom, *Stability and Change in Human Characteristics* (New York: Wiley, 1964); Benjamin S. Bloom, *Human Characteristics and School Learning* (New York: McGraw-Hill, 1976); J. Larry Brown and Ernesto Pollitt, "Malnutrition, Poverty, and Intellectual Development," *Scientific American* (February 1996), pp. 38–43; Arthur J. Reynolds, *Success in Early Intervention* (Lincoln: University of Nebraska Press, 2000); and Harold L. Hogkinson, "Leaving Too Many Children Behind" (2003), paper posted on the Institute for Educational Leadership Internet site, available at **www.iel.org/manychildren.pdf**.

■ Early brain development

Concern is growing regarding the negative effects on cognitive performance that impoverished environments can produce as scientists learn more about how the brain develops and what this knowledge may mean for educators. In general, neurologists and other investigators have reinforced Bloom's conclusions about the importance of a positive home environment in the first two or three years of life, when the brain is growing rapidly and establishing billions of neural connections. In addition to emphasizing the value of good preschools, many educators are exploring the implications for devising instructional methods that take into account how the brain works. However, it may be some time before we know enough to anticipate substantial improvements in curriculum and instruction based on an understanding of how the brain functions and develops.[30]

■ Average differences are not universal patterns

Socialization differentials like those we have discussed in this section reflect *average* differences across social-class groups. As a teacher, you must remember that no universal patterns distinguish all middle-class families and students from all working-class families. Many children from working-class families do well in school, and many middle-class children do not. Many families with low socioeconomic status do provide a home environment conducive to achievement, and the great majority of low-income parents try to offer their children a positive learning environment. It also appears that the child-raising methods of working-class families probably are becoming more like those of middle-class families. Nevertheless, children from low-income, working-class homes are still disproportionately likely to grow up in an environment that inadequately prepares them to succeed in contemporary schools.

REFOCUS How could you, as a teacher, make low-income parents feel comfortable talking to you about things they could do at home to support their child's school achievement?

Standards & Assessment

The Heredity-Versus-Environment Debate

■ Early IQ tests

The past century has seen heated controversy about whether intelligence, which relates strongly to school achievement, is determined primarily by heredity or by environment.

Hereditarian View. When IQ tests were undergoing rapid development early in the twentieth century, many psychologists believed that intelligence was determined primarily by heredity. Those who took this **hereditarian view of intelligence** thought that IQ tests and similar instruments measured innate differences, present from birth, in people's capacity. When economically disadvantaged groups and some minority groups, such as African Americans, scored considerably below other groups, the hereditarians believed that the groups with the lower scores were innately inferior in intellectual capacity.

The hereditarian view underwent a major revival in the 1970s and 1980s, based particularly on the writings of Arthur Jensen, Richard Herrnstein, and a group of researchers conducting the Minnesota Study of Twins. Summarizing previous research as well as their own studies, these researchers identified heredity as the major factor

[30]Justine C. Baker and Frances G. Martin, *A Neural Network Guide to Teaching* (Bloomington, Ind.: *Phi Delta Kappan,* 1998); Janelle Miller, *Brain Research and Education* (Denver Education Commission of the States, 1998); Barbara K. Given, *Teaching to the Brain's Natural Learning Systems* (Alexandria, Va.:Association for Supervision and Curriculum Development, 2002); Sally Shaywitz, *Overcoming Dyslexia* (New York: Knopf, 2003); and Gerald Coles, "Danger in the Classroom," *Phi Delta Kappan* (January 2004), pp. 344–352.

in determining intelligence—accounting for up to 80 percent of the variation in IQ scores.[31]

■ Jensen and his critics

Jensen published a highly controversial study in the *Harvard Educational Review* in 1969. Pointing out that African Americans averaged about 15 points below whites on IQ tests, Jensen attributed this gap to a genetic difference between the two races in learning abilities and patterns. Critics countered Jensen's arguments by contending that a host of environmental factors that affect IQ, including malnutrition and prenatal care, are difficult to measure and impossible to separate from hereditary factors. IQ tests are biased, they said, and do not necessarily even measure intelligence.[32]

After his 1969 article, Jensen continued to cite data that he believed link intelligence primarily to heredity. His critics continue to respond with evidence that environmental factors, and schooling in particular, have a major influence on IQ.[33]

■ Stress on compensatory help

Environmentalist View. By the middle of the twentieth century, numerous studies had contradicted the hereditarian view, and most social scientists took the position that environment is as important as or even more important than heredity in determining intelligence. Social scientists who stress the **environmentalist view of intelligence** generally emphasize the need for continual compensatory programs beginning in infancy. Many also criticize the use of IQ tests on the grounds that these tests are culturally biased. Many attribute the differences in IQ scores between African Americans and whites, for example, to differences in social class and family environment and to systematic racial discrimination.

■ IQ gains

Sandra Scarr and Richard Weinberg studied differences between African American children growing up in their biological families and those growing up in adopted families. They concluded that the effects of environment outweigh the effects of heredity. Thomas Sowell, after examining IQ scores collected for various ethnic groups between 1920 and 1970, found that the scores of certain groups, including Italian Americans and Polish Americans, have substantially improved. Other studies indicate that the test scores of African Americans and Puerto Ricans have risen more rapidly than scores in the general population in response to improvements in teaching and living conditions.[34]

■ Cause of IQ gains

James Flynn, who collected similar data on other countries, found that "massive" gains in IQ scores in fourteen nations have occurred during the twentieth century. These improvements, according to Flynn's analysis, largely stemmed not from

[31]Arthur R. Jensen, "How Much Can We Boost IQ and Scholastic Achievement?" *Harvard Educational Review* (Winter 1969), pp. 1–123; Arthur R. Jensen, *Bias in Mental Testing* (New York: Free Press, 1980); Richard J. Herrnstein and Charles Murray, *The Bell Curve* (New York: Free Press, 1994); Linda S. Gottfredson, "What Do We Know About IQ?" *American Scholar* (Winter 1996), pp. 15–30; and Frank Miele and Arthur R. Jensen, *Intelligence, Race, and Genetics* (Boulder, Colo.: Westview, 2002).

[32]Jensen, "How Much Can We Boost IQ and Scholastic Achievement: A Discussion," *Harvard Educational Review* (Winter 1969), pp. 273–356; Howard Gardner, "Cracking Open the IQ Box," *American Prospect* (Winter 1995), pp. 71–80; and H. Nyborg, ed., *The Scientific Study of Human Intelligence* (New York: Pergamon, 2003).

[33]Arthur R. Jensen, "g: Artifact or Reality?" *Journal of Vocational Behavior* (December 1986), pp. 330–331; Elaine Mensh and Harry Mensh, *The IQ Mythology* (Carbondale: Southern Illinois University Press, 1991); Arthur R. Jensen, *The g Factor* (Westport, Conn.: Praeger, 1998); Arthur R. Jensen, "Race Differences, G, and the 'Default Hypothesis,'" *Psychology,* January 1, 2000; and Robert J. Sternberg and Elena L. Grigorenko, eds., *The General Factor of Intelligence* (Mahwah, N.J.: Erlbaum, 2002).

[34]Sandra Scarr and Richard A. Weinberg, "I.Q. Test Performance of Black Children Adopted by White Families," *American Psychologist* (July 1976), pp. 726–739. See also Robert Howard, "Bright Young Things," *New Scientist,* May 13, 2000, p. 45; and Thomas Sowell, "Race and IQ," *Capitalism,* October 18, 2003.

genetic improvement but from environmental changes that led to gains in the kinds of skills assessed by IQ tests. Torsten Husen and his colleagues also have concluded, after reviewing large amounts of data, that improvements in economic and social conditions, and particularly in the availability of schooling, can produce substantial gains in average IQ from one generation to the next. In general, educators committed to improving the performance of low-achieving students find these studies encouraging.[35]

■ A middle position

Synthesizers' View. Certain social scientists have taken a middle, or "synthesizing," position in this controversy. The **synthesizers' view of intelligence** holds that both heredity and environment contribute to differences in measured intelligence. For example, Christopher Jencks, after reviewing a large amount of data, concluded that heredity is responsible for 45 percent of the IQ variance, environment accounts for 35 percent, and interaction between the two ("interaction" meaning that particular abilities thrive or wither in specific environments) accounts for 20 percent. Robert Nichols reviewed all these and other data and concluded that the true value for heredity may be anywhere between 0.40 and 0.80, but that the exact value has little importance for policy.

■ Interaction of heredity and environment

In general, Nichols and other synthesizers maintain that heredity determines the fixed limits of a range; within those limits, the interaction between environment and heredity yields each individual's actual intelligence. This view has been supported by recent studies indicating that in impoverished families much of the IQ variation correlates with quality of environment, whereas in wealthier families (which presumably provide an adequate environment) heredity exerts a greater influence on children's intelligence. In this view, even if interactions between heredity and environment limit our ability to specify exactly how much of a child's intelligence reflects environmental factors, teachers (and parents) should provide each child with a productive environment in which to realize her or his maximum potential.[36]

 **REFOCUS** How might you, as a teacher, establish a classroom environment that can facilitate full development of a broad range of student abilities?

Obstacles in the Classroom

We have noted that the home and family environment of many working-class students lacks the kind of educational stimulation needed to prepare students for success in the classroom. However, certain school and classroom dynamics also foster low achievement. The following list highlights some of the most important classroom obstacles to achievement working-class students face.

[35]Marguerite Holloway, "Flynn's Effect," *Scientific American* (January 1999); James R. Flynn, *How to Defend Humane Ideals* (Lincoln: University of Nebraska Press, 2000); William T. Dickens and James R. Flynn, "Great Leap Forward," *New Scientist,* April 21, 2001; and Tomoe Kanaya, Matthew H. Scullin, and Stephen H. Cecci, "The Flynn Effect and U. S. Policies," *American Psychologist* (October 2003), available at **www.apa.org/journals/amp.html**.
[36]Robert C. Nichols, "Policy Implications of the IQ Controversy," in Lee S. Shulman, ed., *Review of Research in Education* (Itasca, Ill.: Peacock, 1978); John Rennie, "Outsmarting Our Genes," *Scientific American* (May 1998); Steve Olson, "The Genetic Archeology of Race," *Atlantic* (April 2000), pp. 69–80, available at **www.theatlantic.com**; William T. Dickens and James R. Flynn, "Heritability Estimates Versus Large Environmental Effects," *Psychological Review* (April 2001), pp. 346–369; Linda Jacobson, "IQ Study Weighs Genes, Environment," *Education Week*, September 10, 2003; and Eric Turkheimer et al., "Socioeconomic Status Modifies Heritability of IQ in Young Children," *Psychological Science* (November 2003), pp. 623–628, available at **www.people.virginia.edu/~ent3c/papers2/papers.htm**.

■ Concepts increasingly abstract

1. *Inappropriate curriculum and instruction.* Curriculum materials and instructional approaches in the primary grades frequently assume that students are familiar with vocabulary and concepts to which working-class students have had little or no exposure. After grade 3, much of the curriculum requires advanced skills that many working-class students have not yet acquired; hence they fall further behind in other subject areas.[37]

■ Students' perceptions of inadequacy

2. *Lack of previous success in school.* Lack of academic success in the early grades not only detracts from learning more difficult material later; it also damages a student's perception that he or she is a capable learner who has a chance to succeed in school and in later life. Once students believe that they are inadequate learners and lack control over their future, they are less likely to work vigorously at overcoming learning deficiencies.[38]

■ Insufficient higher-order instruction

3. *Ineffective fixation on low-level learning.* When a student or group of students functions far below grade level, teachers tend to concentrate on remediating basic skills in reading, math, and other subjects. This reaction is appropriate for some achievers who need intensive help in acquiring initial skills, but it is damaging for those who could benefit from more challenging learning experiences and assignments. Although helping low-achieving students master higher-order learning skills presents a difficult challenge to teachers, certain instructional strategies make it possible to move successfully in this direction.[39]

■ Problems for teachers

4. *Difficulty of teaching conditions in working-class schools.* As students fall further behind academically and as both teachers and students experience frustration and discouragement, behavior problems increase in the classroom. Teachers have more difficulty providing a productive learning environment. Some give up trying to teach low achievers or leave the school to seek less frustrating employment elsewhere.[40]

■ Gaps in language and culture
■ Self-fulfilling prophecy

5. *Teacher perceptions of student inadequacy.* Teachers in working-class schools may see low achievement in their classrooms and conclude that many of their students cannot learn. This view easily becomes a self-fulfilling prophecy because teachers who question their students' learning potential are less likely to work hard to improve academic performance, particularly when improvement requires an intense effort that consumes almost all of a teacher's energy.[41]

[37]Michael S. Knapp and Patrick M. Shields, eds., *Better Schooling for the Children of Poverty* (Berkeley, Calif.: McCutchan, 1991); and Yvette Jackson, "Comprehension and Discipline Literacy," *New Horizons for Learning* (December 2002), available at **www.newhorizons.org**.
[38]Bernard Weiner, "Integrating Social and Personal Theories of Achievement Striving," *Review of Educational Research* (Winter 1994), pp. 557–563; Richard D. Kahlenberg, *All Together Now* (Washington, D.C.: Brookings, 2000); and Marvin Marshall, "Metacognition," *Teachers Net Gazette* (June 2003), available at **www.teachers.net/gazette/JUN03**.
[39]Julia B. Smith, Valerie E. Lee, and Fred M. Newmann, *Instruction and Achievement in Chicago Elementary Schools* (Chicago: Consortium on Chicago School Research, 2001), available at **www.consortium-chicago.org**; Martin Haberman, "The Pedagogy of Poverty Versus Good Teaching" (1991), paper posted at the Eisenhower National Clearinghouse Internet site, available at **www.enc.org/topics/equity/articles**: click on "urban"; James P. Spillane, "Challenging Instruction for 'All Students'" (2002), paper posted by the Joint Center for Poverty Research, available at **www.jcpr.org**; and Richard Rothstein, "Testing Our Patience," *American Prospect* (February 2004), available at **www.prospect.org**.
[40]Stanley Pogrow, "Making Reform Work for the Educationally Disadvantaged," *Educational Leadership* (February 1995), pp. 20–24; Dennis Sparks, "Low Incomes, High Hurdles," *Journal of Staff Development* (Summer 2000); and Richard D. Kahlenberg and Bernard Wasow, "What Makes Schools Work?" *Boston Review* (October–November 2003), available at **www .bostonreview.net**.
[41]Charles M. Payne, *Getting What We Ask For* (Westport, Conn.: Greenwood, 1984); Lisa Delpit, *Other People's Children* (New York: New Press, 1995), pp. 173–174; and Eric J. Cooper, "Quality Counts But Just Counting Doesn't Reveal All the Qualities that Count," 2002 paper posted at the National Urban Alliance Internet site, available at **www.nuatc.org**.

■ Separate groups for "slow" learners

6. *Ineffective homogeneous grouping.* Educators faced with large groups of low achievers frequently address the problem by setting them apart in separate classes or subgroups where instruction can proceed at a slower pace without detracting from the performance of high achievers. Unfortunately, both teachers and students tend to view concentrations of low achievers as "slow" groups for whom learning expectations are low or nonexistent.

■ Less support for the "slow"

Ray Rist studied this type of arrangement, called **homogeneous grouping**, at a working-class school in St. Louis. A kindergarten class was divided into groups, the "fast learners" and the "slow learners." The fast group received "the most teaching time, rewards, and attention from the teacher." The slow group was "taught infrequently, subjected to more control, and received little if any support from the teacher." Naturally, by the end of the year, differences had emerged in how well prepared these children were for first grade, and the first-grade teacher grouped the students on the basis of their "readiness."[42]

■ Instructional alternatives

Situations like the one Rist described might benefit from keeping the students in heterogeneous classes (that is, groups with a diversity of previous achievement) but giving them individualized instruction so that each can progress at his or her own rate. However, individualization is extremely difficult to implement and often requires such system-wide change in school practices that it becomes almost an economic impossibility. Thus teachers in schools with mostly low-income students, confronted with heterogeneous classes, generally have failed to work effectively with their numerous low achievers.

One solution is to group low achievers homogeneously for blocks of reading and language instruction but to make sure that the groups are small and are taught by highly skilled teachers who work well with such students. This alternative aligns with research indicating that "restrictive" settings (that is, separate arrangements for low achievers) may have either positive or negative outcomes, depending on what educators do to make instruction effective. We further discuss the issue of homogeneous grouping in the chapter on School Effectiveness and Reform in the United States and in this chapter's Taking Issue box.[43]

---

[42]Ray C. Rist, *The Urban School: A Factory for Failure* (Cambridge, Mass.: MIT Press, 1973), p. 91. See also Elizabeth G. Cohen and Rachel A. Lotan, *Working for Equity in Heterogeneous Classrooms* (New York: Teachers College Press, 1997); Ray C. Rist, "Student Social Class and Teacher Expectations," *Harvard Education Review* (Fall 2000), pp. 257–266; Sharon Cromwell, "Homogeneous or Heterogeneous: Which Way to Go?" (1999), paper with links prepared for "Education World," available at **www.educationworld.com/a_admin/admin095 .html**; Kevin G. Welner, *Legal Rights, Local Wrongs* (Albany: State University of New York Press, 2001); and Carol C. Burris, "When Excellence and Equity Thrive," *Education Week*, January 28, 2004.

[43]Michael Scriven, "Problems and Prospects for Individualization," in Harriet Talmage, ed., *Systems of Individualized Education* (Berkeley, Calif.: McCutchan, 1975), pp. 199–210; Gaea Leinhardt and Allan Pallay, "Restrictive Educational Settings: Exile or Haven?" *Review of Educational Research* (December 1982), pp. 557–558; Yiping Lou et al., "Within-Class Grouping," *Review of Educational Research* (Winter 1996), pp. 423–458; Richard D. Kahlenberg, ed., *A Nation at Risk* (New York: Century Foundation, 2000), available at **www.equaleducation .org/Notion**; Judith Ireson and Susan Hallan, *Ability Grouping in Education* (London: Paul Chapman, 2001); and Ronald F. Ferguson and Jal Mehta, "An Unfinished Journey," *Phi Delta Kappan* (May 2004), pp. 656–669.

taking issue

Question Is placing students in homogeneous groups by ability a generally effective approach for classroom instruction?

Homogeneous Grouping

Many schools and classrooms group students by ability in specific subjects, separating the slower learners from the faster ones or the more advanced from the less advanced. Advocates of homogeneous grouping argue that it is both fair and effective, but critics have charged that it harms students, particularly low achievers.

Arguments PRO

1 In a large, heterogeneous class with students at many different levels, the teacher cannot give the slowest learners the special attention they need. In fact, teachers may begin to see students who struggle to master the lesson as "problems," and quicker students as favorites. Therefore, it makes sense to separate students into ability groups for specific subjects.

2 It is unfair to high-achieving students who are capable of learning quickly to slow the pace of instruction to suit average students. The high achievers may become bored and discouraged unless they are separated into groups that can proceed at a faster rate.

3 Homogeneous grouping encourages the growth of an esprit de corps among group members. With cooperation and friendly competition, students at similar levels can spur each other forward.

4 Many teachers are more effective with certain kinds of students than with others. Homogeneous grouping allows teachers to spend more time with groups they enjoy teaching and are best suited to teach.

5 Homogeneous grouping indicates to parents that the school recognizes differences in learning styles. The school is seen as making a commitment to each child's individual needs.

Arguments CON

1 Research has shown that ability grouping tends to stereotype slower learners and hamper their progress. The instruction offered to such groups is often inferior. Because little is expected of them, they are seldom challenged, and thus they fall further behind the more advanced students. In general, slower learners will do better in heterogeneous classes.

2 Although high-achieving students may be hindered somewhat in a heterogeneous setting, they will remain motivated as long as they sense that the teacher appreciates their talents. Moreover, it is important for them to learn that students of all academic levels have something of value to contribute.

3 A group spirit may develop among high achievers who feel a special honor in being placed together, but low achievers will feel stigmatized, often leading to negative group attitudes. They may become increasingly alienated from school and society.

4 Only a few extraordinary teachers have the necessary skill, patience, and enthusiasm to work effectively with an entire group of low achievers. Other teachers assigned to such groups may become frustrated and demoralized.

5 Parents of low achievers are rarely pleased at seeing their children separated from others. A heterogeneous setting is the best indication that the school cares about all its students.

■ Overload on teachers and schools

7. *Service-delivery problems.* The problems we have described suggest the great difficulty in delivering educational services effectively in classes or schools with a high percentage of low achievers. For example, a teacher in a working-class school who has ten or twelve low-achieving students in a class of twenty-five has a many times more difficult task of providing effective instruction than does a teacher who has only four or five low achievers in a middle-class school. Not only may teachers in the former situation need to spend virtually all their time overcoming low achievers' learning problems, but the negative dynamics that result from students' frustration and misbehavior make the task much more demanding. Administrators, counselors, and other specialized personnel in working-class schools experience the same predicament: the burden of addressing learning and behavior problems may leave little time for improving services for all students. The serious problems endemic in such **overloaded schools** make it difficult for educators to function effectively.[44]

8. *Overly large classes.* As suggested above, classes too large for teachers to provide sufficient help to overcome learning problems often lead to ineffective instruction for low-achieving students. Teachers of large classes find it particularly hard to help low achievers master complex skills such as critical thinking, reading comprehension, mathematics problem solving, and other higher-order skills.[45]

■ Benefits of small classes

The effects of class size were assessed in a major study of students in Tennessee. The researchers found that students in small classes scored substantially higher in reading and math in kindergarten and first grade than did students in average-sized classes. They also maintained their advantage in later grades. Effects were particularly impressive at schools that enrolled large proportions of students from low-income minority backgrounds. Several subsequent smaller studies have arrived at similar conclusions.[46]

9. *Teacher preparation and experience.* Studies of high-poverty schools in big cities have shown that teachers at schools with concentrations of low-SES students tend to have less preparation and experience in teaching their subjects than teachers at schools with mostly middle-class students. For this reason, many analysts believe that upgrading teacher training and preparation and hiring

---

[44]Clara Claycomb, "High-Quality Urban School Teachers," *State Education Standard* (Winter 2000), available at **www.nasbe.org/Standard**; and Mike Schmoker, "Planning for Failure?" *Education Week,* February 12, 2003.

[45]Bryan Goodwin, "Raising the Achievement of Low-Performing Students," *McREL Policy Briefs* (May 2000), available at **www.mcrel.org**; Barbara A. Nye, "Do the Disadvantaged Benefit More From Small Classes?" *American Journal of Education* (November 2000), pp. 1–25; Christopher Jepsen and Steven Rivken, "Class Size Reduction, Teacher Quality, and Academic Achievement in California Public Elementary Schools" (2002), paper prepared for the Public Policy Institute of California, available at **www.ppic.org**; Wendy Schwartz, "Class Size Reduction and Urban Students," *ERIC Digest* (February 2003), available at **www.ericfacility.net/databases/ERIC_Digests/ed472486.html**; and Michael A. Rebell and Joseph J. Wardenski, "Of Course Money Matters" (2004), paper prepared for the Campaign for Fiscal Equity, available at **www.cfequity.org**.

[46]Jeremy D. Finn and Charles M. Achilles, "Answers and Questions About Class Size: A Statewide Experiment," *American Educational Research Journal* (Fall 1990), pp. 557–577; and Alex Molnar, "2001 Results of the Student Achievement Guarantee in Education (SAGE) Program Evaluation" (2001), paper by the Sage Evaluation Team, available at **www.uwm.edu/Dept/CERAI**; and materials available at **www.heros-inc.org**.

Conditions such as over-crowded classes, inexperienced teachers, or mismatches between the expectations of schools and teachers and the backgrounds and learning styles of students all can contribute to lower achievement. *(Spencer Ainsley/The Image Works)*

teachers with appropriate experience should be priority goals in efforts to improve the achievement of low-income and working-class students.[47]

■ Ridiculing high achievers

10. *Negative peer pressure.* Several researchers have reported that academically oriented students in predominantly working-class schools are often ridiculed and rejected for accepting school norms. John Ogbu and Signithia Fordham, among others, have described negative peer influences as being particularly strong among working-class African American students. At inner-city schools where significant numbers of students react in this way, high achievers who work hard are often labeled "brainiacs" and accused of "acting white."[48] Commenting on these phenomena, an African American professor concluded that

[47]Linda Darling-Hammond, "Teacher Quality and Student Achievement," *Education Policy Analysis Archives* (January 2000), available at **http://epaa.asu.edu**; and Cynthia D. Prince, "The Challenge of Attracting Good Teachers and Principals to Struggling Schools" (2002), paper prepared for AASA, available at **www.aasa.org/issues_and_insights/issues_dept**.
[48]Paul Willis, *Learning to Labour* (Westmead, England: Saxon House, 1977); Robert Everhardt, *Reading, Writing and Resistance* (Boston: Routledge and Kegan Paul, 1983); Signithia Fordham, "Racelessness as a Factor in Black Students' School Success," *Harvard Educational Review* (February 1988), pp. 54–84; John H. McWhorter, *Losing the Race* (New York: Free Press, 2000); and John U. Ogbu, *Black American Students in an Affluent Suburb* (Mahwah, N.J.: Erlbaum, 2003).

the "notion that someone with a hunger for knowledge would be regarded as a 'traitor to his race' . . . would seem like some kind of sinister white plot. In a society where blacks had to endure jailings, shootings, and lynchings to get an education, it seems utterly unbelievable that some black youngsters now regard . . . academic failure as a sign of pride."[49]

■ Recognizing education's importance

Some researchers have reported that such attitudes appear to be much less prevalent or nonexistent among middle-class black students or those who attend desegregated schools. In addition, research by Lois Weis and her colleagues suggests that antischool peer pressures among working-class students lessen as they realize that education is important for future success. Although working-class adolescents historically tended to view academic learning as irrelevant to their future employment, the high-school boys in her study perceived schooling as offering "utilitarian opportunities" for acquiring skilled jobs and thus were willing to "put in their time" in school and even go to college.[50]

■ Middle-class expectations for behavior

11. *Differences in teacher and student backgrounds.* Teachers from middle-class backgrounds may have difficulty understanding and motivating disadvantaged pupils. Particularly in the case of white teachers working with disadvantaged minority students, differences in dialect, language, or cultural background may make it difficult for the teachers to communicate effectively with their students.[51]

12. *Incompatibility between classroom expectations and students' behavioral patterns and learning styles.* Teachers may also be unprepared for diversity in their students' learning styles and behavior. Numerous analysts have concluded that the behavioral patterns and learning styles of many working-class students and some groups of minority students differ from those of middle-class or nonminority students. When teachers gear their classroom expectations to the learning styles and behavior of high-achieving, middle-class students, such style differences can lead to school failure.

For example, some researchers suggest that the following patterns of behaviors exist, and they recommended the following ways for teachers to adapt their instruction to help students who have these styles:[52]

■ Many African American students tend to be energetic (a pattern researchers refer to as having high "activation" levels). These students do not perform well if teachers require them to sit in one place for extended periods of time or prohibit impulsive responses. If, as a

[49]Prudence L. Carter, "A Review: The Role of Race and Culture in the Academic and Social Attainment of African American Youth," *African American Research Perspectives* (Fall 2000), pp. 65–73; and Pedro A. Noguera, "How Racial Identity Affects School Performance," *Harvard Education Letter* (March/April 2003), available at **www.edletter.org/past**.
[50]Maxine Seller and Lois Weis, *Beyond Black and White* (Albany: State University of New York Press, 1997). See also Cathy Young, "Where the Boys Are," *Reason Online* (February 2001), available at **www.reason.com**: search for "Cathy Young."
[51]Ricardo D. Stanton-Salazar, "A Social Capital Framework for Understanding the Socialization of Racial Minority Children and Youth," *Harvard Educational Review* (Spring 1997), pp. 1–40; and Armando Laguardia, "Toward a More Equitable Future," *NW Education* (Fall 2002), pp. 32–33, available at **www.nwrel.org/nwedu**.
[52]Jacqueline J. Irvine, *Black Students and School Failure* (Westport, Conn.: Greenwood, 1990); Diana T. Slaughter-Defoe, "Revisiting the Concept of Socialization," *American Psychologist* (April 1995), pp. 276–286; Lisa Delpit and Joanne Dowdy, eds., *The Skin That We Speak* (New York: New Press, 2002); and LaVonne Neal et al., "The Effects of African American Movement Styles," *Journal of Special Education* (Spring 2003), pp. 49–58.

teacher, you have highly active students, you should plan learning activities that allow students some physical movement.

- Some low-income African American students tend to become confused when teachers fail to act forcefully and "authoritatively." Researchers therefore suggest that as a teacher you maintain authority and avoid treating students as "buddies."

- African American and Latino students may tend to be "field dependent"—that is, they learn poorly when instruction begins with abstract, "decontextualized" concepts. You can help field-dependent students by presenting concrete material before moving to abstract analysis. Providing opportunities for students to learn in pairs or cooperative groups may also help.

We should emphasize that research has not conclusively established the existence of such distinctive behavioral patterns or learning styles among working-class or minority students. Learning differences between low-income African American, Latino, or other minority students and nonminority students may stem mostly from socioeconomic status rather than from race or ethnicity. Nevertheless, numerous studies do support the conclusion that you can help improve performance among your low-achieving students if you adjust for the various behavioral and learning styles of *all* your students. We'll discuss such alternative teaching practices in the next chapter's section on multicultural education.[53]

Our analysis so far makes it clear that many students are economically disadvantaged and also experience educational disadvantages in schools and classrooms. Recent research indicates that disadvantaged students can increase their success in the educational system with outstanding teachers and appropriate instructional strategies.[54] But the discouraging facts of achievement and social class have raised questions about whether or not schools do indeed make a difference—if they help in any significant way in countering the disadvantages students experience. The rest of this chapter confronts this issue. Later chapters, particularly "School Effectiveness and Reform in the United States," will discuss ways to bolster student achievement by improving the organization and delivery of instruction.

REFOCUS   Which reasons for low achievement among many low-income students seem most important to you? Can you identify other possible explanations not listed in this chapter? (Hint: Many low-income parents move around a lot.)

[53]Madge G. Willis, "Learning Styles of African American Children: A Review of the Literature and Interventions," *Journal of Black Psychology* (Fall 1989), pp. 47–65; Ronnie Hopkins, *Educating Black Males* (Stony Brook, N.Y.: SUNY Press, 1997); A. Wade Boykin and Caryn T. Bailey, "The Role of Cultural Factors in School Relevant Cultural Functioning" (2000), paper prepared for the Center for Research on Students Placed at Risk, available at **www.csos.jhu .edu/crespar/reports.htm**; and Deborah Moffit, "Success by Design"(2003), paper posted at the New Horizons for Learning Internet site, available at **www.newhorizons .org/strategies/styles/front_styles.htm**.

[54]Daniel U. Levine and Beau Fly Jones, "Mastery Learning," in Richard Gorton, Gail Schneider, and James Fischer, eds., *Encyclopedia of School Administration and Supervision* (Phoenix, Ariz.: Oryx, 1988); Samuel C. Carter, *No Excuses* (Washington, D.C.: Heritage, 2000), available at **www.noexcuses.org**; Stanley Pogrow, "Teacher Feature," *Teachers.Net Gazette* (January 2002), available at **www.teachers.net/gazette/JAN02**; and Robert J. Marzano, *What Works in Schools* (Alexandria, Va.: Association for Supervision and Curriculum Development, 2003).

▶ Do Schools Equalize Opportunity?

■ Coleman's study

The research discussed in the preceding sections indicates that disproportionate numbers of students from low-income backgrounds enter school poorly prepared to succeed in traditional classrooms and in later years rank relatively low in school achievement and other indicators of success. If we define equal opportunity in terms of overcoming disadvantages associated with family background so that students on the average perform equally well regardless of socioeconomic status, one must conclude that the educational system has failed to equalize opportunity.

Equal educational opportunity has received considerable attention since the 1966 publication of a massive national study conducted by James Coleman and his colleagues. Titled *Equality of Educational Opportunity,* this federally supported study collected data on approximately six hundred thousand students at more than four thousand schools. Its congressional sponsors expected it to show that low achievement among low-socioeconomic students stemmed from low expenditures on their education, thus justifying increased school funding.

■ Influence of school spending versus social class

As expected, Coleman and his colleagues reported that achievement related strongly to students' socioeconomic background and that schools with high proportions of working-class and underclass students generally received less funding than did middle-class schools. However, they also found that expenditures for reduced class size, laboratories, libraries, and other aspects of school operation were fundamentally unrelated to achievement after one took into account (1) a student's personal socioeconomic background and (2) the social-class status of other students in the school. Many readers incorrectly interpreted the data to mean that schools cannot improve the performance of economically disadvantaged students. In reality, the results supported two conclusions: (1) simply spending more on education for disadvantaged students was unlikely to substantially improve their achievement, and (2) moving students from mostly working-class schools to middle-class schools *could* improve achievement.[55]

■ Jencks's conclusions

In the next decade, two influential books by Christopher Jencks and his colleagues bolstered this analysis. After examining a great deal of data, Jencks and his colleagues reached the following conclusions:[56]

1. School achievement depends substantially on students' family characteristics.

2. Family background accounts for nearly half the variation in occupational status and up to 35 percent of the variation in earnings.

3. The schools accomplish relatively little in terms of reducing the achievement gap between students with higher and lower socioeconomic status.

---

[55]James S. Coleman et al., *Equality of Educational Opportunity* (Washington, D.C.: U.S. Government Printing Office, 1966); Frederick Mosteller and Daniel P. Moynihan, eds., *On Equality of Educational Opportunity* (New York: Random House, 1972); and James S. Coleman, *Equality and Achievement in Education* (Boulder, Colo.: Westview, 1990). See also Gregory J. Fritzberg, "Schools Can't Do It Alone" (2003), paper posted at the New Horizons for Learning Internet site, available at **www.newhorizons.org/strategies/multicultural/fritzberg.htm**.
[56]Christopher Jencks et al., *Inequality* (New York: Basic Books, 1972); and Christopher Jencks et al., *Who Gets Ahead?* (New York: Basic Books, 1979). See also Daniel P. McMurrer and Isabel V. Sawhill, *Getting Ahead* (Washington, D.C.: Urban Institute, 1998); Bahash Mazdumder, "Analyzing Income Mobility Over Generations," *Chicago Fed Letter* (September 2002), available at **www.chicagofed.org/other/publications.cfm**; and "Christopher Jencks Interview," undated Internet posting by the Public Broadcasting System, available at **www.pbs.org/fmc/interviews/jencks.htm**.

■ International parallels

Studies from many other countries support similar conclusions. For example, scholars at the World Bank, after reviewing several decades of international research, reported that family background has an "early and apparently lasting influence" on achievement. Likewise, a review of studies in Great Britain concluded that schools there have served as "mechanisms for the transmission of privileges from one generation of middle-class citizens to the next."[57]

This does not mean, however, that all or even most students from low-income families will be unsuccessful as adults or that the schools should be viewed as mostly unsuccessful in helping provide opportunities for students with diverse socioeconomic backgrounds. Research supports the following general conclusions:

■ Significant socioeconomic mobility

1. *Although students with low socioeconomic status tend to perform poorly in school and later have restricted employment opportunities, a substantial proportion of working-class children and some from families living in poverty do eventually attain middle-class status.* For example, although nearly two-thirds of men in the U.S. labor force grew up in working-class families or on a farm, more than 50 percent are in middle- or high-status jobs; nearly 40 percent are in upper-middle-class jobs even though less than 25 percent were raised in upper-middle-class families. Socioeconomic mobility of this kind has been present throughout U.S. history.[58]

■ Role of education

2. *The educational system has helped many people surpass their parents' status.* Its role in promoting socioeconomic mobility has grown more central as middle- and high-status jobs have become more complex and dependent on specialized educational skills and credentials and technological and economic changes have eliminated many unskilled jobs.[59]

■ College as the dividing line

3. *As education increasingly determines socioeconomic status and mobility, college attendance and graduation constitute a kind of "dividing line" between those likely to attain high socioeconomic status and those not.* One hundred years ago, enrollment in high school probably was the best educational indicator of socioeconomic status. As of fifty or sixty years ago, high-school graduation was the clearest dividing line. Today, postsecondary education is almost a prerequisite for middle- or high-status jobs.

■ Continuing disadvantages of underclass

4. *Despite the success of many working-class students, opportunities—educational, social, and economic—are too few to overcome the disadvantages of the underclass.* Children who attend low-achieving poverty schools remain disproportionately likely to stay low in socioeconomic status.

---

[57]Marlaine E. Lockheed, Bruce Fuller, and Ronald Nyirongo, *Family Background and School Achievement* (Washington, D.C.: World Bank, 1988), p. 23; Yossi Shavit and Hans-Peter Blossfeld, eds., *Persistent Inequality* (Boulder, Colo.: Westview, 1993); Richard Hatcher, "Class Differentiation in Education," *British Journal of Sociology of Education* (March 1998), pp. 5–24; and OECD/UNESCO, *Literacy Skills for the World of Tomorrow* (Paris: Organisation for Economic Cooperation and Development, 2003), available at **www.pisa.oecd.org**.

[58]David L. Featherman and Robert M. Hauser, *Opportunity and Change* (New York: Academic Press, 1978); Michael Hout, "More Universalism, Less Structural Mobility: The American Occupational Structure in the 1980s," *American Journal of Sociology* (May 1988), pp. 1358–1400; Isabel V. Sawhill, "Still the Land of Opportunity?" (1999), paper prepared for the Urban Institute, available at **www.urban.org**; and Robert M. Hauser, "Meritocracy, Cognitive Ability, and the Sources of Occupational Success," *CDE Working Paper* No. 98-07, August 17, 2002.

[59]Hout, "More Universalism"; Nancy Birdsall and Carol Graham, eds., *New Markets, New Opportunities?* (Washington, D.C.: Brookings Institution Press, 2000); and Gueorgui Kambourov and Iourii Manovskii, "Rising Occupational and Industry Mobility in the United States: 1968–1993" (2004), paper posted at the Penn State University Internet site, available at **www.econ.upenn.edu/~manovski**.

Traditional Versus Revisionist Interpretations

■ Opposite views of U.S. schools

Growing recognition of the strong relationship between social class and school achievement has led to a fundamental disagreement between two groups of observers of U.S. education. According to the **traditional view of schools**, the educational system succeeds in providing economically disadvantaged students with meaningful opportunities for social and economic advancement. The **revisionist view of schools**, in contrast, holds that the schools fail to provide most disadvantaged students with a meaningful chance to succeed in society. You may hear *critical theory* or *critical pedagogy* used as synonyms for the revisionist view. The following sections explore the ramifications of these two arguments.[60]

The Traditional View

■ Education as balancing excellence with opportunity

Proponents of the traditional view acknowledge the relationships among social class, educational achievement, and economic success, but they emphasize existing opportunities and data indicating that many working-class youth do experience social mobility through schools and other institutions. Most traditionalists believe that our educational and economic institutions balance a requirement for excellence with provision of opportunity. From this perspective, each individual who works hard, no matter how disadvantaged, has the opportunity to succeed in elementary and secondary schools and to go to college.

■ Multiple chances

Traditionalists point out that the U.S. educational system gives the individual more chances to attend college than do the educational systems of most other countries (see the chapter on International Education). Students in this country do not, as in some nations, face an examination at age eleven or twelve that shunts them into an almost inescapable educational track. Even if American students do poorly in high school, they can go to a community college and then transfer to a university. Furthermore, admission standards at many four-year colleges permit enrollment of all but the lowest-achieving high-school graduates.

■ Schools as screening devices

Traditionalists admit that schools serve as a screening device to sort different individuals into different jobs, but they do not believe that this screening is systematically based on race, ethnicity, or income. Instead, they believe, better educated people obtain better jobs primarily because schools have made them more productive. Additional years of schooling are an indication of this greater productivity. The employer needs criteria to guide hiring choices, and in a democratic society that values mobility and opportunity, quality of education counts, not the applicant's family connections, race, ethnic origin, or social class.

The Revisionist View and Critical Pedagogy

■ Education as maintaining elite dominance

Revisionists contend that elite groups control the schools and thus channel disadvantaged students into second-rate secondary schools and programs, third-rate community colleges, and fourth-rate jobs. Many critical pedagogists also believe that the educational system has been set up specifically to produce disciplined workers at the bottom of the class structure. This is accomplished in part by emphasizing dis-

---

[60]Revisionists are often referred to as neo-Marxists if they believe that the capitalist system must be abolished or fundamentally changed if schools are to provide truly equal opportunity for all students.

cipline in working-class schools, just as the working-class family and the factory labor system emphasize discipline.[61]

▪ Why students "resist"

Much analysis in critical pedagogy has been referred to as **resistance theory**, which attempts to explain why some students with low socioeconomic status refuse to conform to school expectations or to comply with their teachers' demands. The students' resistance, in this view, arises partly because school norms and expectations contradict the traditional definitions of masculinity and femininity these students hold. In addition, an "oppositional peer life" stimulates students to resist what they perceive as the irrelevant middle-class values of their teachers. As described in the chapter on Philosophical Roots of Education, resistance theorists have further concluded that the traditional curriculum marginalizes the everyday knowledge of such students, thereby reinforcing anti-intellectual tendencies in working-class cultures.[62]

▪ What teachers should do

Critical theorists have been devoting considerable attention to ways educators can improve the situation. Using a variety of related terms such as *critical discourse, critical engagement,* and *critical literacy,* they have emphasized the goal of teachers becoming "transformative intellectuals" who work to broaden schools' role in developing a democratic society. For example, Pauline Lipman believes that teachers should promote not just the "personal efficacy" but also the "social efficacy" of working-class and minority students, and should help them prepare to become leaders in their local communities. She also believes that teachers should pursue this type of goal as part of a larger effort to reform public schools. Jennifer Hendricks believes that teachers can use young people's familiarity with the Internet and technology to help them become politically informed and active.[63] As the Technology @ School box discusses, however, students from some groups lack sufficient access to this technology.

An Intermediate Viewpoint

This chapter began by providing data indicating that working-class students as a group underperform middle-class students. After examining reasons offered to account for this difference, we summarized several decades of research concluding

---

[61]Major writings of the revisionist scholars and critical pedagogists include the following: Martin Carnoy, ed., *Schooling in a Corporate Society* (New York: McKay, 1975); Joel H. Spring, *The Sorting Machine* (New York: McKay, 1976); Samuel Bowles and Herbert Gintis, *Schooling in Capitalist America* (New York: Basic Books, 1976); Michael W. Apple and Lois Weis, eds., *Ideology and Practice in Schooling* (Philadelphia: Temple University, 1983); Henry A. Giroux, *Cultural Workers and the Politics of Education* (New York: Routledge, 1991); Michael Apple, *Education and Power,* 2nd ed. (New York: Routledge, 1995); Henry A. Giroux, *The Abandoned Generation* (New York: Palgrave Macmillan, 2003); and Samuel Bowles, Herbert Gintis, and Melissa Osborne-Groves, eds., *Unequal Chances* (Princeton: Princeton University Press, 2004). See also Susan Ohanian, "Capitalism, Calculus, and Conscience," *Phi Delta Kappan* (June 2003), pp. 729–735, available at **www.pdkintl.org**.
[62]Robert W. Connell et al., *Making the Difference* (Boston: George Allen and Unwin, 1982); Henry A. Giroux, "Youth and the Politics of Representation," *Educational Researcher* (May 1997), pp. 27–30; Kathleen K. Abowitz, "A Pragmatist Revisioning of Resistance Theory," *American Educational Research Journal* (Winter 2000), pp. 877–907; and Michelle Fine and Lois Weis, *Silenced Voices and Extraordinary Conversations* (New York: Teachers College, 2003).
[63]Henry A. Giroux, *Teachers as Intellectuals* (Granby, Mass.: Bergin and Garvey, 1988); Pauline Lipman, *Race, Class, and Power in School Restructuring* (Albany: State University of New York Press, 1998); Henry A. Giroux, "Public Time and Educated Hope" (2003), paper posted by The Initiative Anthology, available at **www.units.muohio.edu/eduleadership/ anthology**; Peter McLaren, "Critical Pedagogy and Class Struggle," *Democracy and Nature* (March 2003), pp. 65–80; and Jennifer A. Hendricks, "The Net Generation," *Current Issues in Education* 7, no. 1 (2004), available at **http://cie.asu.edu**.

TECHNOLOGY @School

Dealing with the Digital Divide

Recent years have brought much attention to the extent and implications of the digital divide—the gap between advantaged and disadvantaged Americans in access to digital media. For example, a 2003 report on children's Internet use from the Corporation for Public Broadcasting, called *Connected to the Future* stated that 66 percent of high-income children had Internet access at home, compared with only 29 percent of low-income children. The report is available at **www.cpb.org/ed/resources/connected**. Similarly, a 2003 federal government report, available at **http://nces.ed.gov/pubsearch/pubsinfo.asp? pubid=2004011**, states that 41 percent of black and Latino students use a computer at home, compared to 77 percent of whites.

As a teacher, you will encounter students who have had extensive computer exposure and other students with little, if any. You will need ways to help all of them become more proficient with computers, just as you address other individual differences. Your school may or may not have widespread and fast access to the Internet, but in either case you should help all your students use the Web and other digitized resources to improve their learning.

You'll find discussion and proposals regarding possibilities for narrowing the digital divide in society in a report titled "Falling Through the Net: Toward Digital Inclusion" at **www.ntia.doc.gov/ntiahome/fttn00/contents00.html**. You also can locate plenty of information and thoughtful discussion to help you deal with the digital divide in your classroom. Download the free teacher's guide that accompanied the 2000 PBS series, "The Digital Divide," at **www.pbs.org/digitaldivide**. You may want to pay particular attention to the "Tech Tips" included with the guide. The guide also includes suggested classroom activities that can help students investigate the digital divide. Useful information and ideas also are available from the Network of Regional Technology in Education Consortia (**www.rtec.org**), a program established to help successfully integrate technologies into K–12 classrooms and schools.

that elementary and secondary schools frequently fail to overcome the disadvantages that working-class students bring to school. Although recent studies have pointed to various more successful schools, the overall pattern offers support for some of the revisionists' conclusions.

■ Schools' failures versus successes

On the other hand, not all working-class students and minority students fail in the schools, and not all middle-class students succeed. An accurate portrayal of the relationships between social class and achievement lies somewhere between the revisionist and the traditional views. Schools do not totally perpetuate the existing social-class structure into the next generation; but neither do they provide sufficient opportunity to break the general pattern in which a great many working-class students perform at a predictably low level. Levine and Levine, reviewing the research on each side of the debate, have offered an intermediate view that stresses the following:[64]

[64]Levine and Levine, *Society and Education.* See also Michael W. Apple, "Are Markets and Standards Democratic?" *Educational Researcher* (August–September 1998), pp. 24–27; and Paul Skilton-Sylvester, "Less Like a Robot," *American Educational Research Journal* (Spring 2003), pp. 3–42.

■ Lowest class positions most "frozen"

- Research on status mobility in the United States indicates that people at the bottom level most tend to "freeze" into their parents' status. Despite considerable intergenerational movement up the socioeconomic ladder and some movement down, large proportions of Americans with the lowest social-class backgrounds do not progress beyond the status of their parents.

■ Minorities and concentrated poverty schools

- Social and demographic trends have concentrated many children in low-income urban and rural communities in schools extremely low on achievement measures. A disproportionately high percentage of students in these schools are from racial or ethnic minority groups.

■ Equal opportunity, past and present

- Although many working-class students attend predominantly working-class schools that reinforce their initial disadvantages through ineffective instruction, many others attend mixed-status schools with teaching and learning conditions more conducive to high performance. In addition, a growing number of working-class schools appear to be emphasizing higher-order learning.

■ Schools promote mobility

- Although we cannot pinpoint the exact percentage of working-class students who succeed in the schools or who use their education to advance in social status, the schools do serve as an important route to mobility for many economically disadvantaged children.

Historically, educational leaders such as Horace Mann worked to establish and expand the public school system partly because they believed this would help give all American children an equal chance to succeed in life, regardless of the circumstances of their birth. The data cited in this chapter suggest that the traditional public-school function of providing equal educational opportunity has taken on a more charged meaning. Provision of equal opportunity in society now depends on improving the effectiveness of instruction for children—particularly those from minority backgrounds—who attend predominantly poverty schools. This issue will be discussed further in succeeding chapters.

REFOCUS Where does your position on equality of opportunity best fit—with a traditionalist, revisionist, or intermediate viewpoint? Why?

▶ Summing Up

① Social class relates both to achievement in elementary and secondary schools and to entry into and graduation from college. Students with low socioeconomic status tend to rank low in educational attainment; middle-class students tend to rank high. Low achievement is particularly a problem in poverty areas of large cities.

② Low-income minority groups generally are low in educational achievement, but little or no independent relationship exists between race or ethnicity and achievement after taking account of social class.

③ Major reasons for low achievement include the following: (a) students' home and family environments poorly prepare them for success in the traditional school; (b) genetic considerations (that is, heredity) may interact with environment in some cases to further hamper achievement; and (c) traditionally organized and operated schools have failed to provide effective education for economically disadvantaged students.

④ Many problems in the schools tend to limit achievement: inappropriate curriculum and instruction, lack of previous success in school, difficult teaching conditions, teacher perceptions of student inadequacy, ineffective homogeneous grouping, delivery-of-service problems, overly large classes, negative peer pressures, differences in teacher and student backgrounds, and incompatibility between classroom expectations and students' behavioral patterns.

5 Research on social class and education has somewhat supported the revisionist view that schools help perpetuate the existing social-class system. This contrasts with the traditional view that U.S. society and its educational system provide children and youth with equal opportunity to succeed regardless of their social-class background.

6 Because recent research indicates that the schools can be much more effective, we may move closer to the ideal of equal educational opportunity in the future.

▶ Key Terms

socioeconomic status (SES) (320)
upper class (320)
middle class (320)
working class (320)
underclass (320)
National Assessment of Educational
    Progress (NAEP) (321)
race (324)
ethnicity (324)
ethnic group (324)

hereditarian view of intelligence (334)
environmentalist view of intelligence
    (335)
synthesizers' view of intelligence (336)
homogeneous grouping (338)
overloaded schools (340)
traditional view of schools (346)
revisionist view of schools (346)
critical theory (critical pedagogy) (346)
resistance theory (347)

▶ Discussion Questions

1 What can teachers and schools do to overcome each of the school-related obstacles and problems that contribute to low achievement among economically disadvantaged students? What might you accomplish in working to overcome these obstacles and solve these problems?

2 Which revisionist arguments are the most persuasive? Which are most vulnerable to criticism?

3 Imagine that you have been hired as a new teacher in a school with a racial, economic, and linguistic composition quite unlike your own background. What can you do to improve your chances to succeed, and whom might you ask for assistance?

4 What was your own experience with homogeneous and heterogeneous grouping in high school? Were these arrangements beneficial for both high- and low-achieving students? What might or should have been done to make them more effective?

5 To what extent would you be willing to contact parents of low-achieving students when you become a teacher? Do you think this should be part of the classroom teacher's responsibilities?

▶ Suggested Projects for Professional Development

1 For your portfolio, prepare an analysis of unusually effective schools, those whose students achieve more than students with similar social background at most other schools. What are the characteristics or "correlates" of these unusually effective schools? Searching the Internet for "effective schools" will give you access to sites that focus on effective schools.

2 Contact a nearby elementary school to determine what steps teachers are taking to improve achievement among low-income and/or minority students. Compare your findings with those of your classmates. You may wish to work together in identifying ideas and approaches to use in your own classroom.

3 Interview someone from a low-income background who has been successful in the educational system. To what does he or she attribute this success? What special obstacles did the person encounter, and how were they overcome?

4 Compile articles from newspapers, magazines, and the Internet discussing low achievement in the public schools. Do these sources consider the kinds of material presented in this chapter? How? What solutions do the authors propose? What is your assessment of the likely effectiveness of these solutions?

► Suggested Resources

 Internet Resources

Useful sites to explore regarding topics in this chapter include home pages of professional organizations such as the American Psychological Association (**www.apa.org**) and the National Education Association (**www.nea.org**). Sites sponsored by the Brookings Institution (**www.brook.edu**), the Institute for Research on Poverty (**www.ssc.wisc.edu/irp**), the Rand Organization (**www.rand.org**), and other organizations concerned with public policy also provide information on relevant topics.

Several papers portraying patterns of racial/ethnic segregation and socioeconomic stratification in the United States are available at **http://mumford1.dyndns.org/cen2000/report.html**.

An extensive analysis of the "Tracking and Ability Grouping Debate" is available at **www.edexcellence.net/foundation/publication/publication.cfm?id=127**.

Several papers by critical theorist Henry Giroux are available at **www.popcultures.com/theorists/giroux.html**.

Problems involved in retaining good teachers at high-poverty schools in big cities are described in "High-Quality Urban School Teachers" by Carla Claycomb, available at **www.nasbe.org/ Standard** (go to "past issues" and click on "Winter 2000").

Educational Testing Service (ETS) offers information on equality of educational, economic, and social opportunity at its Policy Information Center, **www.ets.org/research/pic**.

Find resources on the black versus white racial educational achievement gap at **www.ncrel.gap.smartlibrary.info**.

Publications

Brooks, David. *Bobos in Paradise.* New York: Simon and Schuster, 2000. *Brooks describes how the countercultural "bohemians" of the 1960s entered the middle class and thereby changed cultural attitudes and practices. An excerpt is available at* **www.pbs.org/peoplelikeus/essays**.

Herndon, James. *The Way It Spozed to Be.* New York: Bantam, 1968. *A classic account of the way education works, or doesn't work, in inner-city schools.*

Kahlenberg, Richard D., ed. *A Nation at Risk.* New York: Century Fund, 2000. *Incisive discussion and analysis of educational matters involving social class, race/ethnicity, and other topics in this chapter. The full text is available at* **www.equaleducation.org/Nation**.

McQuilan, Patrick J. *Educational Opportunity in an Urban American High School.* Albany: State University of New York Press, 1998. *Much of the analysis describes a project to improve instruction for low-achieving students.*

Presseisen, Barbara Z., ed. *Teaching for Intelligence I: A Collection of Articles.* Arlington Heights, Ill.: Skylight, 1999. *Chapters in this collection analyze and provide suggestions for possible solutions of problems involved in teaching low-income students with unsatisfactory academic achievement.*

CHAPTER 12

Providing Equal Educational Opportunity

U.S. schools were the world's first to aim at providing all students with educational opportunity through high school and postsecondary levels. Nonetheless, as the chapter on Social Class, Race, and School Achievement indicated, effective education all too rarely extends to economically disadvantaged and minority students. Stimulated by the civil rights movement, many people have recognized the need to improve educational opportunity not just for disadvantaged students but also for students with disabilities.

In this chapter, we examine desegregation, compensatory education for economically disadvantaged students, multicultural education (including bilingual education), and education for students with disabilities. These topics reflect four significant movements that have attempted to enlarge and equalize educational opportunities for our students. You may agree that our schools should provide equal opportunity but consider this a matter for the government, the school board, and civil rights groups. How would it affect you in the classroom? Several ways:

- First, wherever you teach, you will find yourself professionally and morally obligated to furnish specific help for low-achieving students.
- Second, the increasing racial and ethnic diversity in student populations means that you will probably need to accommodate students from a variety of ethnic groups, cultural backgrounds, and different languages.
- Third, more students than ever before are being classified as having disabilities, and increasingly these students are included in regular classrooms. As a teacher, you will be at least partly responsible for addressing their special needs.

To begin formulating your own philosophy and approach to equal educational opportunity, think about the following questions as you read this chapter:

- What are the rationales for desegregation, compensatory education, multicultural education, and education of children with disabilities?
- What are the major obstacles and approaches in desegregating the schools?
- What are the major approaches to compensatory education?
- What is multicultural education? What forms does it take in elementary and secondary schools? What are its major benefits and dangers?
- What does the law say about providing education for students with disabilities? What are the major issues in their education?

▶ Desegregation

■ Desegregation and integration

Desegregation of schools is the practice of enrolling students of different racial groups in the same schools. **Integration** generally means more: not only that students of different racial groups attend schools together, but also that effective steps are taken to accomplish two of the underlying purposes of desegregation: (1) overcoming the achievement deficit and other disadvantages of minority students and (2) developing positive interracial relationships. During the past four decades, attention has turned increasingly from mere desegregation to integration, with the goal of providing equal and effective educational opportunity for students of all backgrounds. However, we have much to do to fully achieve either of these goals.

A Brief History of Segregation in American Education

■ Slavery and the Constitution

Discrimination and oppression by race were deeply embedded in our national institutions from their very beginning. The U.S. Constitution, for example, provided for representation of the free population but allowed only three-fifths representation for "all other persons," generally meaning slaves. ("Representation" refers to distribution of seats in the U.S. House of Representatives.) In most of the South before the Civil War, it was a crime to teach a slave to read and write.

■ Segregated facilities

After the Civil War, the Thirteenth, Fourteenth, and Fifteenth Amendments to the Constitution attempted to extend rights of citizenship irrespective of race. During Reconstruction, African Americans made some gains, but after 1877 legislative action segregated blacks throughout the South and in other parts of the country. They were required to attend separate schools, were barred from competing with whites for good employment, and were denied the right to vote.[1] Victimized by "Jim Crow" laws, African Americans were required to use separate public services and facilities (for instance, transportation, recreation, restrooms, drinking fountains) and frequently had no access at all to private facilities such as hotels, restaurants, and theaters. Many were lynched or severely beaten by members of the Ku Klux Klan and other extremist associations.

Asian Americans, Latinos, Native Americans, and other minority groups experienced similar though generally less virulent discriminatory practices. For example,

---

[1]In this chapter the term *whites* refers to non-Latino whites, that is, citizens not classified as members of a racial or ethnic minority group for the purposes of school desegregation.

Since 1957, when the National Guard escorted African American students to a formerly all-white public high school in Little Rock, Arkansas, considerable progress has been made in desegregating the country's public schools in medium-sized cities and towns in rural areas. (© UPI/ Corbis-Bettmann)

some states by law excluded Chinese Americans from many well-paid jobs and required their children to attend separate schools.[2]

■ Separate, unequal schools

On any measure of equality, schools provided for African Americans seldom equaled schools attended by whites. As an example, in the early 1940s school officials in Mississippi spent $52.01 annually per student in white schools but only $7.36 per student in black schools. In many cases, African American students had to travel long distances at their own expense to attend the nearest black school, and often black senior high schools were a hundred miles or more away.[3]

■ The *Brown* case

Legal suits challenged segregation in elementary and secondary schools in the early 1950s. The first to be decided by the U.S. Supreme Court was a case in which lawyers for Linda Brown asked that she be allowed to attend white schools in Topeka, Kansas. Attacking the legal doctrine that schools could be "separate but equal," the plaintiffs argued that segregated schools were inherently inferior, even if they provided equal expenditures, because forced attendance at a separate school automatically informed African American students that they were second-class citizens and thus destroyed many students' motivation to succeed in school and in society. In May 1954, in a unanimous decision that forever changed U.S. history, the Supreme Court ruled in *Brown v. Board of Education* that "the doctrine of separate but equal has

---

[2]Gwen Kin Kead, "Chinatown-1," *New Yorker,* June 10, 1991, pp. 45–83; Christopher Vasillopulos, "Prevailing upon the American Dream," *Journal of Negro Education* (Summer 1994), pp. 289–298; James A. Ferg-Cadima, "Black, White, and Brown" (2004), paper prepared for the Mexican American Legal Defense and Educational Fund, available at **www.maldef.org/ pdf/LatinoDesegregation.pdf**; and Mary A. Zehr, "A Long Struggle for Equality," *Education Week*, March 10, 2004.
[3]U.S. Commission on Civil Rights, *Fulfilling the Letter and Spirit of the Law: Desegregation of the Nation's Public Schools* (Washington, D.C.: U.S. Government Printing Office, 1976); National Research Council, *Common Destiny* (Washington, D.C.: National Academy Press, 1989); "Revisiting Our Past," *Brown Quarterly* (Winter 2001), available at **http://brownvboard.org**; Gaston Caperton, "Justice Redressed," *College Board Review* (Fall 2003); and "The Ruling that Changed America," *American School Board Journal* (April 2004), available at **www.asbj.com**.

■ Civil rights movement

no place" in public education. Such segregation, the Court said, deprived people of the equal protection of the laws guaranteed by the Fourteenth Amendment.[4]

Effects of the *Brown* decision soon were apparent in many areas of U.S. society, including employment, voting, and all publicly supported services. After Mrs. Rosa Parks refused in December 1955 to sit at the back of a bus in Montgomery, Alabama, protests against segregation were launched in many parts of the country. Dr. Martin Luther King Jr. and other civil rights leaders emerged to challenge deep-seated patterns of racial discrimination. Fierce opposition to civil rights demonstrations made the headlines in the late 1950s and early 1960s as dogs and fire hoses were sometimes used to disperse peaceful demonstrators. After three civil-rights workers were murdered in Mississippi, the U.S. Congress passed the 1964 Civil Rights Act and other legislation that attempted to guarantee equal protection of the laws for minority citizens.[5]

■ Resistance to desegregation

Initial reaction among local government officials to the *Brown* decision was largely negative. The Supreme Court's 1955 *Brown II* ruling that school desegregation should proceed with "all deliberate speed" met massive resistance. This resistance took such forms as delaying reassignment of African American students to white schools, opening private schools with tuition paid by public funds, gerrymandering school boundary lines to increase segregation, suspending or repealing compulsory attendance laws, and closing desegregated schools. In 1957, Arkansas governor Orval Faubus refused to allow school officials at Central High in Little Rock to admit five African American students, and President Dwight Eisenhower called out the National Guard to escort the students to school. As of 1963, only 2 percent of African American students in the South were attending school with whites.

The Progress of Desegregation Efforts

■ Types of segregation

After the early 1960s, school districts in medium-sized cities and towns and in rural areas made considerable progress in combating both **de jure segregation** (segregation resulting from laws, government actions, or school policies specifically designed to bring about separation) and **de facto segregation** (segregation resulting from housing patterns rather than from laws or policies). In response to court orders, school officials have reduced African American attendance in racially isolated minority schools (often defined as either 50 percent or more minority, or 90 percent or more minority).[6] As shown in Figure 12.1, the national percentage of African American students attending schools 90 percent or more minority decreased from 64 percent in 1969 to 37 percent in 2000. Progress has been greatest in the South, where the percentage of African American students in schools 90 percent or more

■ Reducing desegregation for African Americans

---

[4]William L. Taylor, "The Role of Social Science in School Desegregation Efforts," *Journal of Negro Education* (Summer 1998), pp. 196–203; James T. Patterson, *Brown v. Board of Education* (New York: Oxford, 2001); Charles T. Clotfelter, *After Brown* (Princeton: Princeton University Press, 2004); and O. L. Davis Jr., "Fifty Years Past . . . and Still Miles to Go," *Journal of Curriculum and Supervision* (Winter 2004).

[5]Frank Brown, "*Brown* and Educational Policy Making at 40," *Journal of Negro Education* (Summer 1994), pp. 336–348; John R. Wachtal, "We'll Never Turn Back," *American Educational Research Journal* (Summer 1998), pp. 167–198; Louis Menand, "Civil Actions," *New Yorker*, February 12, 2001, pp. 91–96; and Brian Willoughby, "Brown v. Board: An American Legacy," *Teaching Tolerance* (Spring 2004), available at **www.tolerance.org**.

[6]The term *minority* in this context refers to African Americans, Asians, Latinos, Native Americans, and several other smaller racial or ethnic groups as defined by the federal government.

minority decreased from 78 percent in 1969 to less than 30 percent beginning in the 1980s. The South is now the most integrated region of the United States.[7]

■ Increasing segregation for Latinos

For Latino students, however, the percentage attending predominantly minority schools has increased since 1969 (see Figure 12.1). In that year, 55 percent of Latinos attended schools more than 50 percent minority; by 2000, 76 percent of Latino students attended such schools. This trend reflects the movement of Latino people into inner-city communities in large urban areas, particularly the migration of Mexicans into cities in California and Texas and of Puerto Ricans into New Jersey, New York, Chicago, and other eastern and midwestern cities.[8]

■ Big-city segregation remains

At the same time that small-town and rural districts have desegregated, segregation in large metropolitan regions has increased. The main cause seems to be increasingly pronounced housing segregation in those areas. Today, the large majority of public-school students in big cities such as Atlanta, Chicago, Detroit, New York, and Philadelphia are minority students, and most attend predominantly minority schools. A major stumbling block to desegregation of schools has been the desire of most whites, and of many minority parents, to maintain neighborhood schools. Highly segregated residential patterns in most metropolitan areas produce highly segregated neighborhood schools.

■ Middle-class withdrawal

In many instances, predominantly minority neighborhoods also have high poverty rates and rank extremely low in socioeconomic status. Opposition to desegregation is strong in school districts where a high percentage of minority students are from low-income families. As noted in the chapter on Social Class, Race, and School Achievement, schools in these neighborhoods struggle with the effects of concentrated poverty, and most have failed to provide effective education. White parents and middle-class parents generally are quick to withdraw their children from schools in which desegregation has substantially increased the proportion of low-income students. The net result is that city school districts and schools have become increasingly low income and minority in their student composition.[9]

■ Trend toward cessation

In the 1990s and 2000s, many school districts ceased all or part of the desegregation plans they had introduced in previous decades. They cited various reasons for their decisions:

- Some urban districts had predominantly minority enrollment in all their schools and found it difficult to maintain desegregated schools even with substantial student busing.

- In some districts, courts ruled that the district had accomplished enough to overcome discriminatory effects attributable to the original constitutional violations.

---

[7]Gary Orfield, "Our Resegregated Schools," *Principal* (May 2000), available at **www.naesp .org**; Erica Frankenberg, Chungmei Lee, and Gary Orfield, "A Multiracial Society with Segregated Schools" (2003), paper posted at the Harvard University Civil Rights Project Internet site, available at **www.civilrightsproject.harvard.edu/research/reseg03/ AreWeLosingtheDream.pdf**; and Gary Orfield and Erica Frankenberg, "Brown v. Board: Where Are We Now?" *Teaching Tolerance* (Spring 2004), available at **www.tolerance.org**.
[8]Luis M. Laosa, "School Desegregation of Children Who Migrate to the United States from Puerto Rico," *Education Policy Analysis Archives,* January 1, 2001, available at **http://epaa .asu.edu**; and Gary Orfield and Chungmei Lee, "Brown at 50" (2004), paper posted at the Harvard University Civil Rights Project Internet site, available at **www.civilrightsproject .harvard.edu/research/reseg04/resegregation04.php**.
[9]Bruce Katz, and Amy Liu, "Moving Beyond Sprawl," *Brookings Review* (Spring 2000), pp. 31–34; and Debra Viadero, "In U.S. Schools, Race Still Counts," *Education Week,* January 21, 2004.

Figure 12.1	Percentages of African American and Hispanic Students in Racially Segregated Public Schools, 1969 to 2000

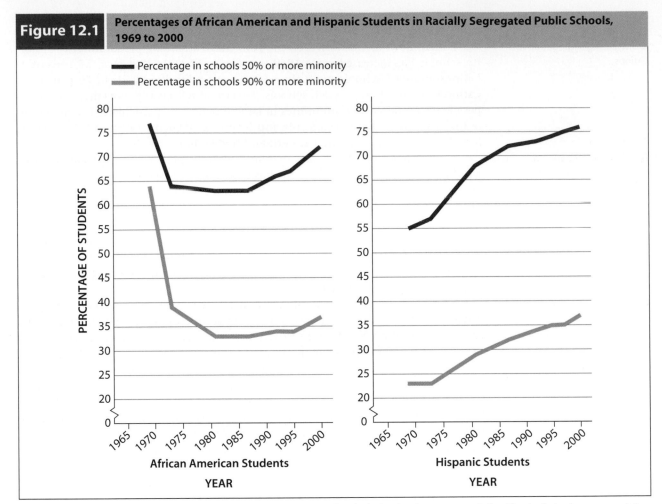

Note: "Minority" refers to Asian, African American, Latino, and other racial and ethnic minority groups as defined by the federal government. As in the previous chapter, we use the term *Hispanic* in reporting data from government publications employing this terminology, and generally use *Latino* elsewhere.

Source: Data adapted from Erica Frankenberg, Chungmei Lee, and Gary Orfield, "A Multiracial Society with Segregated Schools" (2003), paper posted at the Harvard University Civil Rights Project Internet site, available at **www.civilrightsproject.harvard.edu/research/reseg03/ AreWeLosingtheDream.pdf**.

■ In other districts, public and school officials concluded that desegregation efforts did little to actually help minority students.

Desegregation Plans

■ Components of desegregation plans

Plans to accomplish desegregation usually involve one or more of the following actions:

- Alter attendance areas to include a more desegregated population.
- Establish **magnet schools**—schools that use specialized programs and personnel to attract students throughout a school district.
- Bus students involuntarily to desegregated schools.

- Pair schools, bringing two schools in adjacent areas together in one larger zone. For example, School A enrolls all students from grades one through four; School B enrolls all students from grades five through eight.
- Allow **controlled choice**, a system in which students may select the school they wish to attend as long as such choice does not result in segregation.
- Provide voluntary transfer of city students to suburban schools.

■ Milwaukee as a desegregation example

Means such as these have led to substantial school desegregation in many small or medium-sized cities. A good example is Milwaukee. At a time when African American students made up approximately 40 percent of the city's school population, Milwaukee increased the number of its desegregated schools (defined as 25 to 50 percent black) from 14 in 1976 to 101 in 1978. Most of this increase was achieved through (1) establishing magnet schools, (2) implementing a voluntary city-suburban transfer plan, and (3) redrawing school boundaries. The number of desegregated students fell greatly when the city-suburban program ended, but the pattern illustrates what voluntary desegregation can accomplish in all but the largest, most segregated cities.[10]

■ Big-city obstacles

Large central-city districts—especially those with 50 percent or higher minority enrollment—find desegregated schooling extremely difficult to attain. For example, in a big city with 80 percent minority students, action to eliminate predominantly single-race schools may involve hour-long bus rides and transporting students from one largely minority school to another. For these and similar reasons, desegregation plans in many big cities generally concentrate on trying to improve the quality of instruction.

■ Emphasizing quality of instruction

■ Magnet schools

According to research, even large and heavily segregated cities can produce more desegregation by expanding magnet schools than through large-scale, involuntary busing that transports students to predominantly minority schools. The most frequently used themes include arts, business, foreign languages, health professions, international studies, Montessori early childhood, science and mathematics, and technology. Districts that operate or have operated a substantial number of magnet schools include Buffalo, Houston, Jacksonville, and Minneapolis.[11] The Taking Issue box explores the effectiveness of magnet schools.

Nonblack Minorities

■ What is a minority group?

Another aspect of desegregation that deserves special attention is the status of non-black minority groups. Depending on regional and local circumstances and court precedents, various racial minority groups may or may not be counted as minority for the purposes of school desegregation. For example, in the 1970s, the courts determined that Mexican American students in the Southwest were victims of the same kinds of discrimination as were African American students. However, in some cities, the courts did not explicitly designate Mexican American and other Latino students to participate as minorities in a desegregation plan, even though many or most attend predominantly minority schools.[12]

---

[10]Robert S. Peterkin, "What's Happening in Milwaukee?" *Educational Leadership* (January 1991), pp. 50–52; and Peter W. Cookson Jr. and Sonali M. Shroff, "Recent Experience with Urban School Choice Plans," *ERIC Clearinghouse on Urban Education Digest* no. 127 (1997), available at **www.ericfacility.net/databases/ERIC_Digests/ed413388.html**.
[11]Christine H. Rossell, "The Desegregation Efficiency of Magnet Schools," *Urban Affairs Review* (May 2003).
[12]However, federal data collection activities are standardized and have required that student enrollments be reported separately for the following groups: "Black," "American Indian," "Spanish-Surnamed American," "Portuguese," "Asian," "Alaskan Natives," "Hawaiian Natives," and "Non-Minority."

taking issue

Question Are magnet schools an effective means of promoting desegregation and achieving related school-improvement goals?

Magnet Schools and Desegregation

In recent years, many city school districts have established desegregation plans that rely in part on magnet schools. Magnet schools offer a specialized program in a particular field of interest to attract students from all parts of a city or region, thereby creating a mix of ethnic and racial groups. Critics have argued, however, that magnet schools often cause more problems than they solve.

Arguments PRO

1 Research in various cities has shown that a coordinated plan involving magnet schools can lead to substantial gains in desegregation. Milwaukee and Buffalo, for example, are using magnet schools effectively.

2 Magnet schools' specialized, high-level programs attract middle-class and college-bound students to the public school system, thus helping reverse the white, middle-class exodus that has long plagued desegregation efforts.

3 In addition to attracting various ethnic and racial groups, magnet schools create a mixture of socioeconomic classes. Working-class and middle-class students gather in a setting that encourages beneficial socialization.

4 Concentration of resources allows magnet schools to offer a better education than a system of non-specialized schools. Most important, they make this high-quality education available to everyone, regardless of racial, social, or cultural background.

5 As students gain recognition for academic excellence at the magnet schools, community pride will grow. The schools will become a means of promoting community identity, bringing together all races and classes in a common endeavor.

Arguments CON

1 Only limited evidence supports the idea that magnet schools make a significant contribution to desegregation. Because magnets frequently are expensive to develop and maintain, they may well become unjustifiable financial burdens for school districts.

2 Magnets often "drain away" the best students, leaving other public schools in the district with high concentrations of low achievers. These other schools find it increasingly difficult to maintain teacher and student morale and deliver a good education.

3 Converting a local school into a magnet has sometimes led to increased tension between socioeconomic groups. Local students distrust the "outsiders" (generally of a different social class) who come into the neighborhood to attend the school.

4 Many magnet schools are in fact not for everyone. Instead, they are selective: students must meet certain achievement standards to be admitted. Thus low-achieving students—the ones most in need of help—are less likely to benefit from magnet schools than are other students.

5 Their elitist nature prevents magnet schools from fostering a sense of community. They are more likely to provoke resentment among parents whose children are excluded—especially when taxes are raised to support the magnet program.

The situation is further complicated by the relatively large number of Asian American groups in many big cities. With a rapidly growing population of Filipino, Korean, and Vietnamese students added to the many students of Chinese and Japanese ancestry, city school districts face considerable uncertainty in devising multiethnic desegregation plans. The court order for San Francisco, for example, required multiethnic enrollment and busing of four groups: Asian American, African American, Hispanic, and non-Hispanic white.

▪ **Difficult issues**

Questions regarding the desegregation of nonblack minority groups will multiply in the future as more Asian and Latino students move into many localities. Many of these students need bilingual services, which are easiest to deliver to a group of students together. Grouping them together, however, will conflict with desegregation goals that emphasize dispersal and multiethnic enrollment.

Effects on Student Performance and Attitudes

▪ **Inconsistent data**

To what extent do students benefit from integrated schools? The voluminous research on this subject is somewhat contradictory. Some studies show a positive relationship between desegregation and academic achievement, but other studies show little or no relationship. Several analysts have concluded that desegregation seldom detracts from the performance of white students and frequently contributes to achievement among minority students. Achievement among low-income minority students is most likely to improve when they attend schools with middle-income nonminority students. This can only happen, however, when desegregation plans are well implemented (see below) and schools take substantial action to improve the effectiveness of instruction.[13]

▪ **Importance of implementation**

What about students' attitudes toward people from other racial and ethnic groups? As with achievement, some data show that desegregation has positive effects on interracial attitudes, while other studies indicate no effect or even a negative effect. Positive intergroup relationships develop only if desegregation is implemented well and if educators promote equal-status contact between minority and nonminority students.

Studies on students' aspirations are much more consistent, indicating that desegregation frequently improves the educational aspirations and college enrollment of minority students by making those aspirations more realistic and better informed. Several studies also indicate that desegregated schooling helps minority students enter the mainstream "network" of social and cultural contacts needed for success in later life.[14]

---

[13]Ronald A. Krol, "A Meta Analysis of the Effects of Desegregation on Academic Achievement," *Urban Review* (December 1980), pp. 211–224; Daniel U. Levine, "Desegregation," in Torsten Husen and T. Neville Postlethwaite, eds., *International Encyclopedia of Education*, 3rd ed. (Oxford: Pergamon, 1994), pp. 1483–1486; Gary Orfield, "Does Desegregation Help Close the Gap?" *Journal of Negro Education* (Summer 1997), pp. 241–254; Richard D. Kahlenberg, "The New Brown," *Legal Affairs* (May–June 2003), available at **www.legalaffairs.org**; Ronald F. Ferguson and Jal Mehta, "An Unfinished Journey," *Phi Delta Kappan* (May 2004), pp. 656–669; and Richard Kahlenberg, "Post-Brown Schooldays," *Slate,* May 11, 2004, available at **http://slate.msn.com/id/2100282**.

[14]Janet Schofield, "School Desegregation and Intergroup Relations," in Gerald Grant, ed., *Review of Research in Education* 17 (Washington, D.C.: American Education Research Association, 1991), pp. 335–412; Amy Stuart Wells, "Re-examining Social Science Research on School Desegregation," *Teachers College Record* (Summer 1995), pp. 691–706; William T. Trent, "Outcomes of School Desegregation," *Journal of Negro Education* (Summer 1997), pp. 255–257; Richard D. Kahlenberg, *All Together Now* (Washington, D.C.: Brookings, 2000); and Willis D. Hawley, "Who Knew? Integrated Schools Can Benefit All Students," *Education Week,* May 5, 2004.

■ Implications for minority students at poverty schools

The complexities of desegregation and its effects on achievement and attitudes leave many people perplexed: what does desegregation imply for minority students who attend predominantly minority, low-achieving schools in low-income neighborhoods? Assigning such students to a desegregated school with a substantially higher percentage of high-achieving students places them in a potentially much less dysfunctional educational environment. Provided that they receive appropriate support and teaching, their academic performance can substantially improve. We emphasize elsewhere—particularly in the chapter on School Effectiveness and Reform in the United States—that some high-poverty schools are unusually successful, and that many more should be equally successful. Until that happens, effective instruction at desegregated schools is an important alternative for helping low-achieving minority students.

■ Characteristics of well-desegregated schools

Unfortunately, only a few studies focus on schools in which desegregation seems to have worked. One of the most comprehensive of such studies evaluated the Emergency School Aid Act, which provided hundreds of millions of dollars between 1972 and 1982 to facilitate desegregation. This study indicated that desegregation aided African American students' achievement in schools in which (1) resources were focused on attaining goals, (2) administrative leadership was outstanding, (3) parents were more heavily involved in the classroom, and (4) staff systematically promoted positive interracial attitudes.[15]

■ Moral and political imperatives

Despite the mixed evidence, perhaps the most compelling reasons for integration are moral and political. Morally, our national education policy must reflect a commitment to American ideals of equality. Politically, two separate societies, separately educated, cannot continue to exist in America without serious harm to the body politic. In the words of Federal Appeals Court Judge Gerald Heaney, because minority students must "compete in an integrated society, they must, to the extent possible, be educated in an integrated school system."

REFOCUS Were the schools you attended well integrated, or did one racial or ethnic group predominate? Do you want to teach in a school with enrollment similar to that where you attended, or with differing enrollment? Why?[16]

▶ Compensatory Education

Another aspect of our nation's commitment to equal educational opportunity is the **compensatory education** movement, which has sought to overcome (that is, "compensate" for) disadvantaged background and thereby improve the performance of low-achieving students, particularly those from low-income families. Stimulated in part by the civil rights movement in the 1960s, compensatory education was expanded and institutionalized as part of President Lyndon Johnson's War on Poverty. Although it has been funded largely by the federal government, some states and local school districts also have set aside funds for this purpose.

■ Title 1

The Elementary and Secondary Education Act (ESEA), passed in 1965, among other provisions immediately provided one billion dollars to improve the education

---

[15]J. E. Coulson, *National Evaluation of the Emergency School Aid Act* (Washington, D.C.: System Development Corporation, 1976). See also Richard D. Kahlenberg, "An Unambitious Legacy," *Education Week,* February 21, 2001.
[16]Gerald W. Heaney, "School Desegregation: Results and Prospects," *Metropolitan Education* (Spring 1987), pp. 79–85. See also Richard D. Kahlenberg, ed., *A Notion at Risk* (New York: Century Foundation, 2000), available at **www.equaleducation.org/notion**.

of economically disadvantaged children. (A disadvantaged student was defined as a student from a family below the government's official poverty line.) The moneys are known as **Title 1** funds, named after the portion of the ESEA that describes them. The federal government distributes the funds to the states, which, along with school districts, identify schools with sufficient disadvantaged students to receive a share. More than $140 billion were spent on Title 1 between 1965 and 2003. By 2004, Title 1 funding of more than $12 billion annually provided assistance to more than five million students, and many additional students participated in other compensatory programs. Schools and districts have used the money to establish substantial compensatory education programs to provide early childhood education, bilingual education, and other services. Some of the important services of compensatory education are listed below. The Technology @ School box also tells you how to learn more about successful Title 1 schools.

■ Compensatory education services

1. *Parental involvement and support.* Programs emphasizing parental involvement and support have ranged from helping parents learn to teach their children to improving family functioning and parents' employability.

2. *Early childhood education.* **Head Start** and **Follow Through** have been the largest programs of this kind. Head Start generally attempts to help disadvantaged four- and five-year-olds achieve "readiness" for the first grade. Follow Through has concentrated on improving achievement in the primary grades.

3. *Reading, language, and math instruction.* Most Title 1 projects have concentrated on improvement in reading, language, and math.

4. *Bilingual education.* Latino children constitute the largest group in bilingual programs, but nationwide, bilingual programs have been provided in more than sixty languages. Bilingual programs are discussed in the following section on multicultural education.

5. *Guidance, counseling, and social services.* Various psychological and social services have been provided for disadvantaged students.

6. *Dropout prevention.* Services that include vocational and career education have aimed at keeping students from dropping out of school.

7. *Personnel training.* Many preservice and in-service training programs have been funded to help teachers improve instruction.

8. *After-school programs.* These provide academic-improvement services or general enrichment activities, or both.

9. *Computer laboratories and networks.* In recent years, Title 1 and other compensatory education funds have helped many schools establish computer laboratories and in-school computer networks.

Early Childhood Compensatory Education

■ Discouraging early results

During the first decade of compensatory education, most interventions appeared to be relatively ineffective in raising student achievement levels and cognitive development. Despite the expenditure of billions of dollars per year, students generally were not making long-range academic gains.

■ Improved procedures and funding

This discouraging start led to corrections. The federal and state governments improved monitoring procedures, required more adequate evaluation, and sponsored studies to improve compensatory education. Some states also began to provide additional money for compensatory programs. By the early 1980s, research suggested that

TECHNOLOGY @School

An Internet Location About Successful Title 1 Schools

Go to the URL **www.ed.gov/pubs/urbanhope** to read a study of "high-performing, high-poverty" urban schools. Select a school from the list and read the description of developments and outcomes at the school. As you read, ask yourself questions such as the following:

1. What seems to have improved achievement the most?
2. Are the described practices "transportable," that is, easy to use at other schools?
3. How were special education and/or bilingual programs and teachers involved?
4. How were Title 1 funds spent?
5. Would you want to teach at this school?

You may also want to share your conclusions and material with classmates who selected other schools.

---

compensatory education in preschool and the primary grades could indeed improve the cognitive development and performance of disadvantaged students.[17]

■ **Exemplary early childhood programs**

In particular, several studies of outstanding early childhood education programs demonstrated that such efforts can have a long-lasting effect if they are well conceived and effectively implemented. Positive long-range achievement results have been reported for disadvantaged students in outstanding preschool programs in Ypsilanti, Michigan; Syracuse, New York; and several other locations. Compared with nonparticipants, students who participate in such programs are less likely to be placed later in special education or to repeat grades (both costly). Participants are also more likely to graduate from high school and to acquire the skills and motivation needed for rewarding employment, thereby increasing tax revenues and reducing reliance on public assistance.[18]

■ **Overall pluses and minuses**

These impressive results, however, usually come from programs that researchers consider exemplary. The vast majority of preschool programs have been less well funded or less well implemented and have produced fewer gains. In addition, Title 1 programs in elementary and secondary schools still fail to ensure that most low-achieving students will acquire the academic and intellectual skills necessary to obtain good jobs in a modern economy.

---

[17]Thomas W. Fagan and Camilla A. Heid, "Chapter 1 Program Improvement: Opportunity and Practice," *Phi Delta Kappan* (April 1991), pp. 582–585; Robert E. Slavin, "Making Money Make a Difference," *Rethinking Schools* (Summer 1995), pp. 10, 23; Sherri Odden, Lawrence J. Schweinhardt, and David Weikart, *Into Adulthood: A Study of the Effects of Head Start* (Ypsilanti, Mich.: High/Scope, 2000); Jennifer Park-Jadotte and Toni Bickart, "Head Start" (2003), paper prepared for Teaching Strategies, available at **www.teachingstrategies.com**; and Michael A. Rebell and Joseph J. Wardenski, "Of Course Money Matters" (2004), paper prepared for the Campaign for Fiscal Equity, available at **www.cfequity.org**.
[18]W. Steven Barnett and Colette M. Escobar, "The Economics of Early Educational Intervention: A Review," *Review of Educational Research* (Winter 1987), pp. 387–414; "Long-Term Outcomes of Early Childhood Programs," *The Future of Children* (Winter 1995), available at **www.futureofchildren.org**; and Ron Haskins, "Competing Visions," *Education Next* (Winter 2004), available at **www.educationnext.org**.

Comprehensive Ecological Intervention

Improved school programs cannot be expected to overcome the extreme disadvantages of students who grow up in particularly harmful environments, such as concentrated poverty neighborhoods. For this reason, policy makers and educators increasingly support **ecological intervention**—comprehensive efforts to improve the family environment of young children.[19]

■ Importance of early family environment

Advocates of ecological intervention point to research on the important cognitive development that occurs during infancy, as well as to the frequently disappointing results of Head Start interventions that do not begin until age four or five. Comprehensive psychological, social, and economic support can be successful, the research indicates, if it begins when children are younger than two or three years old. Some effective programs of this type enroll young children in educationally oriented day care or preschool classes. The successful programs also typically include nutrition and health care, and capable staff members often provide individualized guidance on parenting.[20]

■ Features of successful programs

Standards & Assessment ✓   ## The No Child Left Behind Act

■ Reauthorization of ESEA

In 2001, Congress reauthorized the ESEA and Title I, but in so doing, established sweeping new requirements for all elementary and secondary schools. The new version of the law, known as the **No Child Left Behind Act (NCLB)**, has affected not just schools that receive Title 1 funding, but all public schools. NCLB includes regulations in the following key areas:[21]

■ Challenging standards and annual tests

■ *Standards and Testing.* States and school districts are required to develop challenging academic content and achievement standards for all students in reading/language arts and mathematics, with the goal of having all students attain specified levels of proficiency by the 2013–2014 school year.

To assess progress toward standards, states must test students, beginning with annual tests for students in grades 3–8 in reading/language arts and mathematics, and at least one test for students in grades 10–12. Science standards and tests are being added after these initial tests. At least 95 percent of students overall and in each special-needs subgroup (see below) must be tested.

■ Disaggregated data

■ *Special Needs Students.* States, districts, and schools must identify English Language Learner (ELL) students and develop instructional benchmarks and a proficiency test to assess their progress in learning English. Schools and districts must also include ELL students and students with disabilities in the annual testing required of all other students, although educators may provide

[19]Lizbeth Schorr, *Within Our Reach* (New York: Anchor Doubleday, 1989); Edna W. Comes and Mark W. Fraser, "Evaluation of Six-Family-Support Programs," *Families in Society* (March–April, 1998), pp. 134–148; Arthur J. Reynolds, *Success in Early Intervention* (Lincoln: University of Nebraska Press, 2000); David J. Armor, "Environmental Effects on IQ," *Education Week*, November 19, 2003; and "Cost-Benefit Analysis of the Chicago Child-Parent Centers," *Focus* (Winter 2004), available at **http://www.ssc.wisc.edu/irp/focus/foc231h.pdf**.
[20]National Commission on Children, *Beyond Rhetoric* (Washington, D.C.: U.S. Government Printing Office, 1991); David J. Armor, *Maximizing Intelligence* (New Brunswick, N.J.: 2003); Richard Rothstein, *Class and Schools* (Washington, D.C.: Teachers College Press, 2004); and Lizbeth Schorr, "The O'Connor Project," *American Prospect,* January 1, 2004.
[21]Jack Jennings, "Stricter Federal Demands, Bigger State Role," *State Education Standard* (Spring 2002); Eric Robelen, "An ESEA Primer," *Education Week*, January 9, 2002; Michael Casserly, "Driving Change," *Education Next* (Summer 2004), available at **www.educationnext.org**, and material available at **www.ed.gov/nclb**.

reasonable adaptations and accommodations for them, such as tests in the first language of ELL students. Scores of different special-needs subgroups of students (including ELL students, disabled students, poverty students, and racial/ethnic minorities) must be *disaggregated*, or reported separately from the total for all students at a school.

■ Schools needing improvement

■ *Adequate Yearly Progress.* A key provision of NCLB is that all schools and districts must make **adequate yearly progress** (AYP) toward their 2013–2014 goals. Schools and districts that fail to make sufficient progress are designated as "needing improvement." The school is identified as needing improvement if the school as a whole or any disaggregated subgroup has achievement scores below those the state government has determined are required in moving forward to meet its 2013–2014 goals. Because many schools compile scores for fifty or more subgroups, it is easy for a school to be identified as "needing improvement." (For example, a school may have four or five racial/ethnic subgroups at each grade tested.)

By 2004, nearly 30 percent of U.S. schools had received this designation, and the percentage is likely to rise in the future because NCLB requires that an increasing percentage of students score at the proficient level until 100 percent do so by 2014. One particularly widespread problem has involved the fact that higher-achieving ELL students frequently are quickly moved to regular classrooms, thus lowering the average scores of students remaining in future ELL subgroups.

■ Supplemental services and restructuring

Schools needing improvement are to receive special help from their district or state, such as consultants, professional development, or other additional resources. Students at Title 1 schools needing improvement also are to receive "supplemental services" such as tutoring, after-school help, or summer school. If, after several years, a school still fails to meet yearly progress goals, its students are eligible to transfer to another public school in the district. Still further failure to make adequate progress subjects schools to "corrective action" or "restructuring," which may include replacing the faculty and administration, conversion to charter-school status, or takeover by an outside organization.[22]

■ *Teachers and staff.* As described in the chapter on Motivation, Preparation, and Conditions for the Entering Teacher, states must ensure that all teachers of core academic subjects and all teachers and paraprofessionals in Title I programs meet state standards as "highly qualified."

■ Confusion and uncertainty

States, school districts, teachers, students, and parents have all experienced a great deal of confusion and uncertainty concerning how to implement NCLB requirements. (The NCLB involves nearly seven hundred pages of law and thousands of pages of regulations.) Part of the confusion involves the fact that states create their own definitions of most terms and concepts in the Act. States decide not only on the skills and concepts to be tested and the tests to be administered, but also on the definition of what is proficient or acceptable achievement. These definitions vary widely from state to state and even within states. For example, one study indicated

■ Variation in defining proficiency

---

[22]Diane S. Rentner et al., "From the Capital to the Classroom" (2003), report prepared for the Center on Education Policy, summary available at **www.cep-dc.org/nclb**; Jamal Abedi and Ron Dietel, "Challenges in the No Child Left Behind Act for English-Language Learners," *Phi Delta Kappan* (June 2004), pp. 782–785; and Diane S. Rentner et al., "From the Capital to the Classroom" (2004), report prepared for the Center on Education Policy, available at **www.cep-dc.org/nclb**.

that eighth graders with the same skills would be at the thirty-sixth percentile in Montana but the eighty-ninth percentile in Wyoming. The same study showed that in Washington the fourth-grade proficiency level in reading was set at the fifty-third percentile, but at the seventy-sixth percentile in mathematics.

■ States define and decide

The states also determine what type and how much yearly progress is "adequate" for schools. Some states define acceptable achievement in terms of closing gaps among different subgroups of students, others in terms of absolute performance levels. Some states define adequacy as involving equal increments of gain each year until 2014, but others require smaller gains in the initial years and larger amounts as we approach 2014. States must also decide what to do with schools not making adequate yearly progress and even whether to apply the same rules and policies to all schools, or just those receiving Title I funding.[23]

■ Many schools "failing"

Media depictions of schools not making adequate yearly progress may also create confusion. Newspapers and other mass media have been prone to report that such schools, and even whole school districts, are "failing" to educate U.S. children. Statisticians point out, however, that the yearly progress of an entire school can be affected by the test performances of even small groups of students. In addition, small schools often experience widespread variation from year to year in students' ability at a given grade level. In fact, some schools identified as "failing" according to AYP criteria have recently or simultaneously received rewards for high student performance from other external sources.

■ Gaming the system

The desire to avoid being labeled as failures may be leading school officials and educators to try to "game the system," or find ways to increase the likelihood that their schools and districts will attain AYP. Many analysts assert that students are hurt by such practices, which include the following:

■ Possibly lowered standards

■ Some critics believe that NCLB has occasionally resulted in lowering standards and student performance. Several states, for example, have reset scores needed to achieve proficiency at levels lower than before NCLB.

■ Unidentified disabilities

■ A subgroup must generally include a minimum of students—say, thirty or fifty—before test scores of those students are counted in determining a school's AYP. This is leading some school officials to identify fewer students with disabilities to keep this subgroup below the minimum number. Students with unidentified learning disabilities may not receive the help they need.

■ Encouraging dropouts

■ Other schools and districts may be encouraging or facilitating dropouts or transfers out among students whose low achievement might detract from AYP status, or retaining many students in middle school or the ninth grade if their promotion might damage high schools' classification on AYP.

---

[23]Robert L. Linn, Eva L. Baker, and Damian W. Betebenner, "Accountability Systems," *Educational Researcher* (August/September 2002), available at **www.aera.net/pubd/er**; Sam Dillon, "States Cut Test Standards to Avoid Sanctions," *New York Times*, May 22, 2003; G. Gage Kingsbury, et al., "The State of State Standards" (2003), report published by the Northwest Evaluation Association, summary available at **www.young-roehr.com/nwea/ NWEA-State-of-Stndrds.4.pdf**; Monty Neill, "Leaving Children Behind," *Phi Delta Kappan* (November 2003), pp. 225-228; Bruce Buchanan, "Defining 'Adequate Yearly Progress,'" *Education Vital Signs* (February 2004), available at **www.asbc.com/evs**; Lawrence Hardy, The High Cost of NCLB," *Education Vital Signs* (February 2004), available at **www.asbc .com/evs**; Stan Karp, "Taming the Beast," *Rethinking Schools* (Summer 2004), available at **www.rethinkingschools.org**; Thomas Newkirk, "False Positives," *Education Week*, March 3, 2004; Lynn Olson, "Enveloping Expectations," *Education Week*, January 8, 2004; Richard Rothstein, "Testing Our Patience," *American Prospect* (February 1, 2004), available at **www.prospect.org**; and Peter Schrag, "Bush's Education Fraud," *American Prospect* (February 1, 2004), available at **www.prospect.org**.

■ Clinging to the gifted

■ Faculty have been reported to be discouraging gifted students from attending (beneficial) special schools or programs elsewhere, because their withdrawal would reduce AYP scores.

■ Overly concentrating on the nearly proficient

■ Many schools and teachers are accused of concentrating teaching resources on students with scores near the proficient level and thereby neglecting or reducing efforts to help their lowest and highest achievers.

■ Teaching to the test

■ Some analysts also believe that more teachers and schools are emphasizing low-level skills of the kind likely to be tested on state assessments since passage of the NCLB.

All these patterns have long been reported as constituting problems associated with state accountability systems, but some observers believe NCLB has significantly exacerbated them.

■ Treatment of ELL and disabled students

Many educators and observers have expressed particular dissatisfaction concerning policies and regulations for treating ELL students and students with disabilities. They are concerned that holding these students to the same standards as regular students can be impractical, or even counterproductive. In many cases, these critics assert, this policy results in teaching and testing with materials that students do not understand, thereby resulting in demoralizing failure for both staff and students. States have been required to allow accommodations, such as changes in test materials and procedures, to provide more valid assessment of special education and LEP students, but the cost of modifying tests is more than many schools can reasonably afford.

■ Failure to support tutoring and transfers

Many students and their families are also disappointed with NCLB. They point out that requirements to provide students tutoring and transfer opportunities have not been met. In many cases such opportunities have been made available to only a small percentage of eligible students, and even smaller percentages have made use of them. Many caregivers are uninterested in such services for their students. Other reasons for low availability and utilization have included failure to notify students and parents about alternatives; reluctance of schools to divert Title 1 resources to tutoring (especially private tutors); shortages of qualified tutors; and lack of space at other schools to which students might transfer.

■ Funding and control complaints

In the face of these and other complaints, some states have considered ending their efforts to meet the requirements of NCLB, even though doing so would mean the loss of millions of dollars in federal assistance.

Questions About Compensatory Education

Although data collected since the 1980s suggest that compensatory education can help disadvantaged students, many questions remain about its nature and effectiveness.

■ Ineffective "pullout"

1. *How can we make Title 1 more effective?* Research indicates that Title 1 has been relatively ineffective in many schools partly because most programs have used a **pullout approach**—that is, they take low achievers out of regular classes for supplementary reading or math instruction. Pullout approaches generally have struggled because they tend to generate much movement of students and therefore confusion throughout the school. In addition, they usually have overemphasized the acquisition of "mechanical" subskills, such as word recognition in reading and simple computation in math, rather than broader and

more functional skills, such as reading comprehension, math problem solving, and "learning-to-learn" strategies.[24]

■ Recent improvements

In recent years, federal legislation, including NCLB, has made it much easier to replace Title 1 pullout with schoolwide approaches that allow for coordinated, in-class assistance for low achievers. In addition, expanded staff development has helped teachers learn how to broaden compensatory instruction beyond mechanical subskills. Partly for this reason, more Title 1 schools are reporting impressive achievement gains, but we know relatively little about how to make these gains more widespread.[25]

■ Behavioristic versus cognitive approaches

2. *What type of early instruction should we provide?* Much uncertainty in early compensatory education surrounds whether programs should use a behavioristic direct-instruction approach, which focuses on basic skills such as decoding of words or simple computation in math, or instead should emphasize conceptual development and abstract thinking skills. Some direct-instruction programs have had excellent results through the third grade, but performance levels often fall when participating children enter the middle grades. Results in cognitive-oriented programs stressing independent learning and thinking skills generally have been less successful in terms of mastery of "mechanical" skills in the primary grades, but some of the best cognitive approaches have resulted in gains that show up later.[26]

■ Uncertainty about secondary schools

3. *What should we do in high schools?* High schools have achieved moderate success in individual classrooms and in "schools within a school" in which a selected group of teachers work intensively with relatively few low-achieving students. However, researchers still know little about the best compensatory approaches for secondary-school students.[27]

■ High costs

4. *Is it financially feasible to include the most economically disadvantaged students in effective compensatory education programs?* Effective programs for the most economically disadvantaged students tend to be expensive because they require prolonged intervention in the home and school environments. But many disadvantaged students now receive only one or two years of compensatory services and therefore achieve less.

■ The basic question: Can it really work?

5. *Can compensatory education spur permanent, meaningful gains for most disadvantaged students?* This, of course, is the fundamental question about compensatory

[24]Michael S. Knapp and Patrick M. Shields, eds., *Better Schooling for the Children of Poverty* (Berkeley, Calif.: McCutchan, 1991); Stanley Pogrow, "What Is an Exemplary Program, and Why Should Anyone Care?" *Educational Researcher* (October 1998), pp. 22–30; and Kenneth Wong, "Title I as a Reform Strategy in Urban Schools," *ERIC Digest* EDO-UD-03-0, November 2003, available at **http://iume.tc.columbia.edu**.

[25]For examples of Title 1 schools reporting gains in student performance, see articles in the Winter 2004 issue of *New Horizons for Learning*, available at **www.newhorizons.org**: click on "Quarterly Journal."

[26]Sharon L. Kagan, "Early Care and Education," *Phi Delta Kappan* (November 1993), pp. 184–187; Rebecca A. Marcon, "Doing the Right Thing for Children," *Young Children* (November 1994), pp. 8–20; and Martha A. MacIver and Elizabeth Kemper, "Research on Direct Instruction in Reading," *Journal of Education for Students Placed at Risk* 7, no. 2 (2002), pp. 107–116.

[27]Daniel U. Levine, "Educating Alienated Inner City Youth: Lessons from the Street Academies," *Journal of Negro Education* (Spring 1975), pp. 139–149; Daniel U. Levine, "Implementation of an Urban School-Within-a-School Approach," in Hersholt C. Waxman et al., eds., *Students at Risk in At-Risk Schools* (Newbury Park, Calif.: Sage Corwin, 1992); Michael C. Rubenstein and Jessica C. Wodatch, *Stepping Up to the Challenge* (Washington, D.C.: U.S. Department of Education, 2000); and Erik W. Robelen, "Bush Outlines Plan to Help Older Students," *Education Week*, January 28, 2004.

education. Data indicate that many disadvantaged students entering secondary schools still show unacceptably low performance regardless of whether they have been in Title 1 or other compensatory programs.

In view of such findings, some educators question whether compensatory education, even if designed for maximum effectiveness, can significantly improve a student's chances of succeeding in school and in later life—especially a minority student living in a neighborhood of concentrated poverty. As described in the chapter on Social Class, Race, and School Achievement, revisionist critics argue that U.S. public schools have failed to provide equal opportunity and, in the absence of fundamental reforms in society as a whole, will continue to marginalize disadvantaged students. Thus some observers believe that we may need to improve parents' economic opportunities before children's school achievement will rise significantly. It remains to be seen whether efforts to improve education for disadvantaged students can be sufficiently effective to disprove these skeptics' pessimism.[28]

 **Do you think you are or will be well prepared to teach students who receive or should receive compensatory services? What might you do to be better prepared?**

▶ Multicultural Education

■ Multicultural goals for all students

Multicultural education refers to the various ways in which schools can take productive account of cultural differences among students and improve opportunities for students with cultural backgrounds distinct from the U.S. mainstream. Certain aspects of multicultural education focus on improving instruction for students who have not learned Standard English or who have other cultural differences that place them at a disadvantage in traditional classrooms. As a teacher, you should also be concerned with the larger implications of multicultural education that make it valuable for *all* students. By fostering positive intergroup and interracial attitudes and contacts, multicultural education may help *all* students function in a culturally pluralistic society. (From this point of view, the movement toward desegregation can be considered a part of multicultural education.)

■ Historical emphasis on assimilation

Although the U.S. population always has been pluralistic in composition, the emphasis throughout much of our history (as noted in the chapter on Pioneers in Education) has been on assimilating diverse ethnic groups into the national mainstream rather than on maintaining group subcultures, mixing them into the "melting pot" of America. In educating diverse groups of immigrants, the public school system has stressed the development of an American identity. Students learned how "Americans" were supposed to talk, look, and behave, sometimes in classes of fifty or sixty pupils representing the first or second generation of immigrants from ten or fifteen countries.[29] Although this approach succeeded in Americanizing and allow-

[28]John Ogbu, "Racial Stratification and Inequality in the United States," *Teachers College Press* (Winter 1994), pp. 264–298; John Ogbu and Herbert D. Simons, "Voluntary and Involuntary Minorities," *Anthropology and Education Quarterly* (June 1998), pp. 155–188; Sheldon H. Danziger and Ann C. Lin, eds., *Coping with Poverty* (Ann Arbor: University of Michigan Press, 2000); and Paul Tough, "The Harlem Project," *New York Times Magazine*, June 20, 2004.
[29]T. Alexander Aleinikoff, "A Multicultural Nationalism?" *American Prospect* (January–February 1998), pp. 80–86; and "Assimilation? If So, to What Degree?" (undated), posting of the Academy for the Advancement of Science and Technology, available at **www.bergen.org/ AAST/Projects/Immigration**.

ing social mobility for many immigrants, observers have pointed out that African Americans, Asian Americans, Latinos, Native Americans, and certain European ethnic groups were systematically discriminated against in a manner that revealed the shortcomings of the melting pot concept.[30]

■ Valuing diversity

In the 1960s, civil rights leaders fought to reduce the exclusion of minority groups and to shift emphasis from assimilation to diversity and cultural pluralism. In place of the melting pot metaphor, **cultural pluralism** introduced new metaphors such as a "tossed salad" or a "mosaic," that allow for distinctive group characteristics within a larger whole. According to the American Association of Colleges for Teacher Education (AACTE), "to endorse cultural pluralism is to endorse the principle that there is no one model American." From this viewpoint, the differences among the nation's citizens are a positive force.[31]

■ Between assimilation and separation

Remember, emphasizing cultural pluralism does not mean you support a philosophy aimed at cultural, social, or economic separation. Depending on how we define cultural pluralism, it may or may not stress integration in cultural, social, or economic matters. Generally it lies somewhere between total assimilation and strict separation of ethnic or racial groups. Cultural pluralism, particularly in education, is more important than ever before as the United States becomes transformed into what observers call the first "universal nation."

Multicultural Instruction

One key area in multicultural education concerns instructional approaches for teaching students with differing ethnic and racial backgrounds. Several of the most frequently discussed approaches address student learning styles, recognition of dialect differences, bilingual education, and multiethnic curriculum.

■ Accommodating cultural learning patterns

Student Learning Styles.   In the preceding chapter we briefly described behavioral patterns and **learning styles** that appear to correlate with students' socioeconomic status and, perhaps, with their race or ethnicity. We also mentioned attempts to modify instruction to accommodate different learning styles. One good example of research on this subject was provided by Vera John-Steiner and Larry Smith, who worked with Pueblo Indian children in the Southwest, concluding that schooling for these children would be more successful if it emphasized personal communication in tutorial (face-to-face) situations. Other observers of Native American classrooms have reported that achievement rose substantially when teachers interacted with students in culturally appropriate ways: that is, social control was mostly indirect, and teachers avoided putting students in competitive situations. Similarly, several researchers have reported that cooperative learning arrangements are particularly

---

[30]Ilan Stavans, *The Hispanic Condition* (New York: HarperCollins, 1995); K. Anthony Appiah, "The Multiculturalist Misunderstanding," *New York Review of Books,* October 9, 1997; Min Zhou and Carl L. Bankston III, *Growing Up American* (New York: Russell Sage, 1998); Amy Goldstein and Robert Suro, "A Journey in Stages," *Washington Post,* January 16, 2000; and "Native Education: Bitter Past, Hopeful Future," *NW Education* (Spring 2004), available at **www.nwrel.org/nwedu**.

[31]"No One Model American: A Statement of Multicultural Education" (Washington, D.C.: American Association of Colleges for Teacher Education, 1972), p. 9. See also Nathan Glazer, *We Are All Multiculturalists Now* (Cambridge, Mass.: Harvard University Press, 1997); John J. Miller, *The Unmaking of Americans* (New York: Free Press, 1998); and Christopher Clausen, *Faded Mosaic* (Chicago: Ivan R. Dee, 2000).

effective with some Mexican American students whose cultural background de-emphasizes competition.[32]

■ The KEEP program

Another approach that modifies instruction to fit students' cultural learning styles is the Kamehameha Early Education Program (KEEP) in Hawaii. The KEEP approach combines whole-group direct instruction with individualized work in learning centers. The program addresses students' cultural backgrounds by emphasizing student-produced stories in language arts, instant feedback, no penalty for "wrong" answers, and discussion of students' responsibilities as group members. According to the research, this attempt to capitalize on the informal interaction characteristic of native Hawaiian culture has improved student achievement. Educators working with Navajo students and other culturally distinctive groups are adapting the KEEP approach at other locations.[33]

■ Model minority stereotype

Analysts also have examined research on the performance of Asian American students. Several observers believe that certain subgroups of Asian students (for example, Koreans and Vietnamese) tend to be nonassertive in the classroom, and that this reluctance to participate may hinder their academic growth, particularly with respect to verbal skills. (However, research suggests that such behavioral patterns diminish or disappear as Asian American students become more assimilated within U.S. society.) In addition, Asian American students can be harmed by a stereotype indicating that they are all part of a "model minority" who have no serious problems in school.[34]

■ Black English

Recognition of Dialect Differences. Teachers generally have tried to teach "proper" or Standard English to students who speak nonstandard dialects. Frequently, however, a simplistic insistence on proper English has caused students to reject their own cultural background or else to view the teachers' efforts as demeaning and hostile. In recent years, educators have been particularly concerned with learning problems among students who speak Black English. Research shows that Black English is not simply a form of slang; it differs systematically from Standard English in grammar and syntax. Because Black English seems to be the basic form of English spoken by many low-income African American students who are floundering academically, educators have proposed that schools use Black English as the language of instruc-

[32]Vera John-Steiner and Larry Smith, "The Educational Promise of Cultural Pluralism" (1978), paper prepared for the National Conference on Urban Education, St. Louis, Mo.; Kay M. Losey, "Mexican American Students and Classroom Interaction," *Review of Educational Research* (Fall 1995), pp. 283–318; Roland Tharp et al., *Teaching Transformed* (Scranton, Pa.: Westview, 2000); Beverly J. Klug and Patricia Whitfield, *Widening the Circle* (New York: Routledge/Falmer, 2002); and Paulette Running Wolf and Julie A. Rickard, "Talking Circles," *Journal of Multicultural Counseling & Development* (January 2003), pp. 39–43.
[33]Kathryn H. Au and Alice J. Kawakami, "Research Currents," *Language Arts* (April 1985), pp. 406–411; Kathryn H. Au and Jacqueline H. Carroll, "Improving Literary Achievement through a Constructivist Approach," *Elementary School Journal* (January 1997), pp. 203–221; and Kathryn H. Au, "Culturally Responsive Instruction as a Dimension of New Literacies" (2001), paper prepared for Reading Online, available at **www.readingonline.org**: click on "New Literacies," then "Archives."
[34]Ester Lee Yao, "Asian-Immigrant Students' Unique Problems That Hamper Learning," *NASSP Bulletin* (December 1987), pp. 82–88; Don T. Nakanishi and Tinya Y. Nishida, eds., *The Asian American Educational Experience* (New York: Routledge, 1995); Angela Kim and Christine J. Yeh, "Stereotypes of Asian American Students," *ERIC Digest* EDO-UD-02-1 (February 2002), available at **http://iume.tc.columbia.edu**; and Wenju Shen and Weimin Mo, "Reaching Out to Their Cultures" (undated), paper posted by NCELA, available at **www.ncela.gwu .edu/pathways/asian/cultures.htm**.

tion for these students until they learn to read. Although this approach seems logical, research has provided little support for it.[35]

■ Ebonics in Oakland

Analysis of the dialect of many African American students (that is, Black English) frequently is referred to as **Ebonics**. An important controversy regarding Ebonics and its possible use in improving instruction for African American students arose in 1997 after the Oakland, California, school board declared that Black English is a distinctive language. The board requested state and federal bilingual education funds to help teachers use Black English in implementing approaches for improving black students' performance with respect to Standard English and reading. After television sound bites allowed for the interpretation that Oakland schools were abandoning the goal of teaching "good" English, numerous national figures (including Reverend Jesse Jackson) criticized the board for its policies regarding the use of Ebonics in teaching. Although the Linguistic Society of America declared that Oakland's policy was "linguistically and pedagogically sound," the Oakland Board of Education responded by removing terminology involving Ebonics from its policies and setting aside $400,000 for a "Standard English Proficiency" program designed to help teachers understand and build on dialect characteristics in instructing students whose language patterns strongly emphasize Black English.[36]

■ *Lau v. Nichols* requirements

Bilingual Education. **Bilingual education**, which provides instruction in their native language for students not proficient in English, has been expanding in U.S. public schools as immigration has increased. In 1968, Congress passed the Bilingual Education Act, and in 1974 the Supreme Court ruled unanimously in *Lau v. Nichols* that the schools must take steps to help students who "are certain to find their classroom experiences wholly incomprehensible" because they do not understand English. Congressional appropriations for bilingual education increased from $7.5 million in 1969 to more than $400 million in 2001. Although the federal and state governments fund bilingual projects for more than sixty language groups speaking various Asian, Indo-European, and Native American languages, the majority of children served by these projects are native speakers of Spanish. Overview 12.1 summarizes several approaches for helping children whose first language is not English.

■ Rise of bilingual programs

The Supreme Court's unanimous decision in the *Lau* case, which involved Chinese children in San Francisco, did not focus on bilingual education as the only remedy. Instead, the Court said, "Teaching English to the students of Chinese ancestry is one choice. Giving instruction to this group in Chinese is another. There may be others." In practice, early federal regulations for implementing the *Lau* decision tended to focus on bilingual education as the most common solution for English Language Learner (ELL) students. The regulations generally suggested that school districts initiate bilingual programs if they enrolled more than twenty students of a

---

[35]J. R. Harber and D. N. Bryan, "Black English and the Teaching of Reading," *Review of Educational Research* (Summer 1976), pp. 397–398; Jane W. Torrey, "Black Children's Knowledge of Standard English," *American Educational Research Journal* (Winter 1983), pp. 627–643; Charles J. Fillmore, "A Linguist Looks at the Ebonics Debate" (1997), posting at the Center for Applied Linguistics Internet site, available at **www.cal.org/ebonics**; Abha Gupta, "What's Up wif Ebonics, Y'All?" (1999), posting at Reading Online, available at **http://readingonline .org/articles/gupta**; and Sandra Stein, "Student Diversity," *Teachers College Record* (February 2002), pp. 109–127.

[36]Wayne O'Neill, "If Ebonics Isn't a Language, Then Tell Me, What Is?" *Rethinking Schools* (Fall 1997), available at **www.rethinkingschools.org**; John H. McWhorter, "Throwing Money at an Illusion," *Black Scholar* (January 1997); Johnnie J. Hafernik, "The Ebonics Controversy and the Education of African American Children," *Educational Researcher* (November 2000), pp. 23, 40; and Geneva Smitherman and John Baugh, "The Shot Heard from Ann Arbor," *Howard Journal of Communications* (January–March 2002), pp. 20–24.

OVERVIEW 12.1 *Pros and Cons of Alternatives for Teaching English Language Learners*

Approach	Variations	Pros	Cons
Bilingual Education	First Language Mainte-nance—emphasis on teaching in the native language over a long time	• May sustain a construc-tive sense of identity among ethnic or racial minority students. • Can provide a better basis for learning higher-order skills such as read-ing comprehension while they acquire basic English skills.	• Requires many speakers of native languages as teachers. • Separates groups from one another. • May discourage students from mastering English well enough to function successfully in the larger society. • Students may not suffi-ciently master English before moving to regular classes, hurting their ability to learn other subjects.
	Transitional Bilingual Education (TBE)—providing intensive Eng-lish instruction and then proceeding to teach all subjects in English as soon as possible.	• Supported by federal and most state govern-ments. • Moves students rela-tively quickly into regu-lar classes. • Requires relatively few native language speak-ers as teachers.	
	Universal Bilingual Education—instruction in two languages for all students, native and non-native English speakers.	• All students learn more than one language, increasing their compe-tence in a global society	
English Language Instruction	Submersion—Placing ELL students in regular class-rooms with no modifica-tions.	No or little extra cost to school.	Students generally may fail to learn English or other subjects.
	Structured Immersion—placement in regular classes with special assis-tance provided inside and outside of class.		
	Sheltered Immersion—using principles of second-language learning in regular classrooms.		

given language group at a particular grade. Bilingual programs proliferated accord-ingly.

Since 1983, however, the federal government has begun to accept, and even en-courage, English-as-a-second-language (ESL) instruction or other nonbilingual ap-proaches for providing help to ELL students. Researchers agree that ELL students should be given special help in learning to function in the schools. "Submersion" approaches, which simply place ELL students in regular classrooms without any special assistance or modifications in instruction, frequently result in failure to learn. Data collected by the Council of Chief State School Officers and other organizations indicate, moreover, that significant numbers of ELL students are receiving little specialized assistance to help them learn English and other subjects.[37]

■ Controversies: how much English, how soon?

Controversies over bilingual education have become increasingly embittered. As in the case of teaching through dialect, arguments erupt between those who would "immerse" children in an English-language environment and those who believe initial instruction will be more effective in the native language. Educators and laypeople concerned with ELL students also argue over whether to emphasize teaching in the native language over a long period of time, called **first-language maintenance,** or provide intensive English instruction and teach all subjects in English as soon as possible, called **transitional bilingual education (TBE).** Those who favor maintenance believe that this will help sustain a constructive sense of identity among ethnic or racial minority students and provide a better basis for learning higher-order skills such as reading comprehension while they acquire basic English skills. Their opponents believe that maintenance programs are harmful because they separate groups from one another or discourage students from mastering English well enough to function successfully in the larger society.[38] TBE has been supported by federal guidelines and by legislation in certain states. Studies indicate that approximately 75 percent of Latino students and nearly 90 percent of other groups such as Asian and Russian students exit transitional programs within three years. NCLB regulations generally are pushing schools toward fewer years outside the regular classroom.

■ Staffing disputes

Adherents and opponents of bilingual education also differ on staffing issues. Those who favor bilingual and bicultural maintenance tend to believe that the schools need many adults who can teach ELL students in their own language. Advocates of transitional or ESL programs, on the other hand, tend to believe that a legitimate program requires only a few native language or bilingual speakers. Some critics of bilingual education go so far as to claim that bilingual programs are primarily a means of providing teaching jobs for native language speakers who may not be fully competent in English.

■ How much improvement?

Educators are particularly concerned with how well bilingual education improves performance among low-achieving students. Among scholars who believe that bilingual education has produced little if any improvement, several have reviewed the research and concluded that "structured immersion" (placement in regular classes with special assistance provided inside and outside of class) and "sheltered immersion" (using principles of second-language learning in regular classrooms) are

[37]Cynthia G. Brown, *The Challenge and State Response* (Washington, D.C.: Council of Chief State School Officers, 1990); Eugene E. Garcia and René Gonzalez, "Issues in Systemic Reform for Culturally and Linguistically Diverse Students," *Teachers College Record* (Spring 1995), pp. 418–430; *Meeting the Needs of Students with Limited English Proficiency* (Washington, D.C.: U.S. Government Accounting Office, 2001); and Carlos J. Ovando, "Bilingual Education in the United States," *Bilingual Research Journal* (Spring 2003), available at **http://brj.asu.edu**.
[38]Noel Epstein, *Language, Ethnicity, and the Schools* (Washington, D.C.: George Washington University Institute for Educational Leadership, 1977); Rosalie P. Porter, *Forked Tongue* (New York: Basic Books, 1990); Linda Chavez, *Out of the Barrio* (New York: Basic Books, 1991); Christine Rossell, *Different Questions, Different Answers* (Washington, D.C.: Institute for Research in English Acquisition and Development, 2000); Carlos Ovando, "Beyond 'Blaming the Victim,'" *Educational Researcher* (April 2001), pp. 29–31, 39, available at **www.aera.net/pubs/er**; and Jill K. Mora, "A Road Map to the Bilingual Education Controversy" (2003), paper prepared at San Diego State University, available at **http://coe.sdsu.edu/people/jmora**.

more successful than TBE.[39] Other scholars disagree, arguing that well-implemented bilingual programs do improve achievement, and several reviews of research have reported that bilingual education worked significantly better than immersion or other mostly monolingual programs.[40] Part of the reason for these differences in conclusions involves disagreements about which studies should be reviewed and the criteria for selecting them.

■ California and Arizona restrict bilingual education

The arguments are not confined to academic researchers. In recent years, voters in California, Arizona, and Massachusetts supported legislation designed to reduce or eliminate bilingual education. The new laws in those states restrict non-English-speaking students to one year or less of bilingual instruction in their native language while they develop their English skills. Each vote was accompanied by heated debate. Supporters of the legislation argued that, although bilingual education was attractive in theory, it generally was not working in practice. Opponents emphasized the difficulties that ELL students experience when taught in a language they do not understand. After the new laws were passed, educators in many school districts in these states sought waivers that would exempt their students from the regulations, and some decided to challenge the laws in the courts. Time will tell how successful the new laws prove. Meanwhile these developments appear to be having minimal influence on bilingual programming in most other states.[41]

■ Uncertain future

■ Marks of good programs

Various researchers have concluded that programs for ELL students should (1) be taught or assisted by adults who speak students' native language, (2) enroll students continually rather than intermittently, (3) frequently monitor students' progress, and (4) offer open-ended assistance rather than an arbitrary ending point. Bilingual programs in particular are more likely to succeed when teachers can (1) engage students in active learning of challenging content, (2) communicate high expectations to their students, (3) coordinate English-language development with other academic studies, and (4) relate curriculum to students' family and community experiences.[42] In addition, numerous researchers report that it is critically

---

[39]Rosalie P. Porter, "Language Choice for Latino Students," *Public Interest* (Fall 1991), pp. 48–60; Rosalie P. Porter, "The Case Against Bilingual Education," *Atlantic* (May 1998), pp. 28–38; *The ABC's of English Immersion* (Washington, D.C.: Center for Equal Opportunity, 2000); and Seth Stern, "Conversion to Immersion," *Christian Science Monitor*, November 5, 2002.
[40]Ann C. Willig, "A Meta-Analysis of Selected Studies on the Effectiveness of Bilingual Education," *Review of Educational Research* (Fall 1985), pp. 269–317; Stephen Krashen, "Bilingual Education Works," *Rethinking Schools* (Winter 2000/2001), pp. 3, 9, 258; Shelly Rappaport, "Beyond Bilingual Education" (2002), report prepared for the Puerto Rican Legal Defense and Education Fund, available at **www.prldef.org/lib/Beyond_Bilingual_Education1.pdf**; and Robert E. Slavin and Alan Cheung, "Effective Reading Programs for English Language Learners" (2003), report prepared for the Center for Research on the Education of Students Placed At Risk, available at **www.csos.jhu.edu/crespar/techReports/Report66.pdf**.
[41]Lynn Schnaiberg, "In Battle over Prop. 227, Both Sides Command Armies of Statistics," *Education Week,* April 29, 1998; Don Terry, "Latino Community Remains Divided over Future of Bilingual Education," *New York Times,* June 5, 1998; Keith Baker, "Structured English Immersion," *Phi Delta Kappan* (November 1998), pp. 199–204; James Crawford, "Bilingual Education: Strike Two," *Rethinking Schools* (Winter 2000–2001), pp. 3, 8; and Mary A. Zehr, "Boston Schools Adjust to Bilingual Education Restrictions," *Education Week*, December 10, 2003.
[42]William J. Tikinoff, *Applying Significant Bilingual Instruction Features in the Classroom* (Roslyn, Va.: Inter-America Research Association, 1985); Thomas P. Carter and Michael L. Chatfield, "Effective Bilingual Schools," *American Journal of Education* (November 1986), pp. 200–232; Maria R. Montecel and Josie D. Cortez, "Successful Bilingual Education Programs," *Bilingual Research Journal* (Spring 2002), pp. 1–21, available at **http://brj.asu.edu**; and "Observing the Five Standards in Practice," *CREDE Research Briefs* (March 2004), available at **www.crede.ucsc/products/print/research_briefs.html**.

important to stress cognitive development and higher-order skills in education for ELL students.[43]

■ Bilingual education for everyone

Many scholars believe that all students, regardless of their ethnic group, should receive bilingual education. In part this argument stems from the international economic advantages of a nation's citizens knowing more than one language. Programs that provide education in both English and another language for all students at a multiethnic school are sometimes referred to as "two-way" or "dual" bilingual immersion. To make this type of education a positive force in the future, several groups of civic leaders have recommended stressing multilingual competence, rather than just English remediation, as well as insisting on full mastery of English.[44]

■ New multiethnic materials and methods

Multiethnic Curriculum and Instruction. Since the mid-1960s, educators have been striving to take better account of cultural diversity by developing multiethnic curriculum materials and instructional methods. Many textbooks and supplemental reading lists have been revised to include materials and topics relating to diverse racial and ethnic groups. In-service training has helped teachers discover multiethnic source materials and learn to use instructional methods that promote multicultural perspectives and positive intergroup relations.

■ Approaches for Native Americans

Efforts to implement multiethnic curricula have been particularly vigorous with respect to Native American students. For example, educators at the Northwest Regional Education Laboratory have prepared an entire Indian Reading Series based on Native American culture. Mathematics instruction for Native American students sometimes uses familiar tribal symbols and artifacts in presenting word and story problems, and local or regional tribal history has become an important part of the social studies curriculum in some schools. Many observers believe that such approaches can help Native American students establish a positive sense of identity conducive to success in school and society.[45]

However, multiethnic curricula are not intended merely to bolster the self-image and enhance the learning of minority students. A crucial purpose is to ensure that all students acquire knowledge and appreciation of other racial and ethnic groups. Guidelines for attaining this goal typically stress helping students build skills and understandings such as the following:[46]

---

[43]Kenji Hakuta, *Mirror of Language* (New York: Basic Books, 1986); Kenji Hakuta and Lois J. Gould, "Synthesis of Research on Bilingual Education," *Educational Leadership* (March 1987), pp. 38–45; and Mary A. Zehr, "Early Bilingual Programs Found to Boost Test Scores," *Education Week*, September 4, 2002.

[44]Nancy Cloud, Fred Genesee, and Else Hamayan, *Dual Language Instruction* (Boston: Heinle and Heinle, 2000); and Elizabeth R. Howard, Julie Sugarman, and Donna Christian, "Trends in Two-Way Immersion Education" (2003), report prepared for the Center for Research on the Education of Students Placed at Risk, available at **www.csos.jhu.edu/crespar/ techReports/report63.pdf**.

[45]Lee Little Soldier, "The Education of Native American Students," *Equity and Excellence* (Summer 1990), pp. 66–69; *Indian Reading Series* (Portland, Oreg.: Northwest Regional Educational Laboratory, 1990); Lee Little Soldier, "Is There an Indian in Your Classroom?" *Phi Delta Kappan* (April 1997), pp. 650–653; Buffy Sainte-Marie, "Beyond Autumn's Stereotypes," *Education Week*, October 27, 1999, pp. 37, 39; Teresa L. McCarty, *A Place to Be Navajo* (Mahwah, N.J.: Erlbaum, 2002); and Mindy Cameron, "In the Language of Our Ancestors," *NW Education* (Spring 2004), available at **www.nwrel.org/nwedu**.

[46]Ellen Wolpert, "Using Pictures to Combat Bias," *Rethinking Schools* (Summer 1995), p. 25; Deirdre A. Almeida, "Countering Prejudice Against American Indians and Alaska Natives Through Antibias Curriculum and Instruction," *ERIC Digest* EDORC-96-4 (October 1996), Harriett D. Romo, "Improving Ethnic and Racial Relations in the Schools," *ERIC Review* (Spring 2000), pp. 25–26; Geneva Gay, "The Importance of Multicultural Education," *Educational Leadership* (December 2003/January 2004); and Rhonda Barton, "Nets & Paddles," *NW Education* (Spring 2004), available at **www.nwrel.org/nwedu**.

■ Components for building
multicultural understanding

- *Human relations skills* involving development of students' self-esteem and interpersonal communications

- *Cultural self-awareness* developed through students' research on their ethnic or racial group, family history, and local community

- *Multicultural awareness* derived in part from historical studies and literary or pictorial materials incorporating diverse racial and ethnic points of view

- *Cross-cultural experiences* including discussions and dialogue with students and adults from different ethnic and racial groups

■ Reducing Eurocentrism

Recent Controversies.   In recent years, particular attention has been given to ensuring that curriculum and instruction are not overwhelmingly *Eurocentric* (reflecting the culture and history of ethnic groups of European origin) but incorporate the concerns, culture, and history of ethnic and racial groups of different origins. Such approaches not only introduce materials dealing with the history and status of minority groups, but also involve activities such as community service assignments and cooperative learning tasks designed to acquaint students with minority cultures.

Standards & Assessment ✓

Most such curricula include the contributions of many groups; others focus on a single group. For example, *Afrocentric* programs focus on the history and culture of African Americans. Efforts to introduce Afrocentric and other minority-oriented themes have provoked controversy in California, New York, and other states, as well as in individual school districts. Critics suggest that such programs reject Western culture and history, leaving students lacking knowledge common in U.S. society. Some also suggest that many such curricula include historical inaccuracies. Another concern is that minority-oriented curricula can encourage divisiveness by focusing on problems with European traditions, ignoring other racial and ethnic groups, and stereotyping beliefs and attitudes of minority racial and ethnic groups. Another criticism is that emphasis on minority culture and history sometimes becomes a substitute for other difficult actions required to improve minority students' academic performance.[47]

■ Responses to the critiques

Supporters of Afrocentric and other minority-oriented themes respond by pointing out that few advocates of these approaches want to eliminate Western culture and history from the curriculum. Molefi Asante argues that the Afrocentric movement strives to de-bias the curriculum by adding appropriate Afrocentric materials, not by eliminating Western classics. In addition, they note that few, if any, supporters of Afrocentric or related approaches minimize the importance of academic achievement or advocate its de-emphasis in the curriculum.

■ Initial reports promising

Indeed, some initial reports suggest that Afrocentric and related approaches may help improve the performance of low-achieving students. For example, educators in certain big cities have concluded that including materials on minority history and culture can help raise students' motivation to learn. Both attendance and reading scores appear to have improved at some schools that introduced Afrocentric

---

[47]Molefi Asante, *The Afrocentric Idea* (Philadelphia: Temple University Press, 1987); Charles Devarics, "Afro-centric Program Yields Academic Gains," *Black Issues in Higher Education,* December 6, 1990, pp. 1, 34; Molefi Asante, "Afrocentric Curriculum," *Educational Leadership* (January 1992), pp. 28–31; Maulana Karenga, "An Idea Worth Considering," *Black Issues in Higher Education* (June 11, 1998), p. 25; Eleanor Brown, "Black Like Me? 'Gangsta' Culture, Clarence Thomas, and Afrocentric Academies," *New York University Law Review* (May 2000), available at **www.nyu.edu/pages/lawreview/75/2/brown.pdf**; Charles C. Verhaven, "Philosophy's Roles in Afrocentric Education," *Journal of Black Studies* (January 2002), pp. 295–321; and Lisa Delpit, "Educators as 'Seed People' Growing a New Future," *Educational Researcher* (October 2003), available at **www.aera.net/pubs/er**.

themes, and an assessment of college students who participated in an Afrocentric studies program for one year found that their grades improved substantially.

Multiculturalism for the Future

■ Continuing controversies

The controversies about multicultural education as a whole follow lines similar to the specific arguments about Afrocentric and other minority-oriented curricula. Critics worry that multicultural education may increase ethnic separatism, fragment the curriculum, and reinforce the tendency to settle for a second-rate education for economically disadvantaged or minority students. To avoid such potential dangers, the director of an institute for civic education has provided useful guidelines for you, as a teacher, to use in multicultural programs:

■ Guidelines for multicultural programs

- *Find out what positive aspects of Western civilization are being taught.* If students are not learning that constitutional government, the rule of law, and the primacy of individual rights are among the hallmarks of Western civilization, then they are not learning the essential features of their heritage . . . .

- *Find out if students are being taught that racism, sexism, homophobia, and imperialism are characteristics of all cultures and civilizations at some time—not culture-specific evils . . . .* America's failings should not be taught in isolation from the failings of other countries—no double standard.

- *Insist that all students study both Western and non-Western cultures.* Students need solid academic courses in Latin American, African, and Asian history, in addition to European history.[48]

■ School as an extension of community

Despite the controversies, most influential educators believe there is an urgent need for comprehensive multicultural approaches that give attention to minority experiences. "If children are to do well academically," says former New York State Commissioner of Education Thomas Sobol, "the child must experience the school as an extension, not a rejection, of home and community." We believe that, for years to come, the goal of attaining equal opportunity through multiculturalism will continue as a prominent theme in U.S. education. A central goal, Sobol contends, should be to "develop a shared set of values and a common tradition" while also helping "each child find his or her place within the whole."[49]

REFOCUS In what ways are you preparing to work with students from a variety of cultural and linguistic backgrounds? How might you benefit as a teacher from knowing more about the cultural background of students different from yourself?

▶ **Education for Students with Disabilities**

■ Growth of special education

Major developments in education in the past twenty years have involved schooling for children with disabilities. Large gains have been made in providing and improving special-education services for these students. (Placement in "special education"

---

[48]Mary S. Hanley, "The Scope of Multicultural Education" (2002), paper prepared for New Horizons for Learning, available at **www.newhorizons.org/strategies/multicultural/ hanley.htm**; and Jynotsa Pattnaik, "Learning About the 'Other,'" *Childhood Education* (Summer 2003), pp. 204–211.

[49]Thomas Sobol, "Understanding Diversity," *Educational Leadership* (February 1990), pp. 27–30. See also Michael Lind, *The Next American Nation* (New York: Free Press, 1995); and Geneva Gay, "Beyond Brown," *Journal of Curriculum and Supervision* (Spring 2004).

usually means that a disabled student receives separate, specialized instruction for all or part of the day in a self-contained class or a resource room.) Table 12.1 shows the numbers of students with selected disabilities served in or through public education in 2001. Analysis conducted by the U.S. Department of Education indicates that almost three-quarters of students with disabilities receive most or all of their education in regular classes (with or without assignment to part-time resource rooms); approximately 25 percent are in self-contained classes; and the rest are in special schools or facilities. Since 1988, the proportion of students with disabilities who spend 80 percent or more of their time in regular education classrooms has increased from less than one-third to nearly half.[50]

■ PL 94-142 and IDEA

Federal requirements for educating students with disabilities have been enumerated through a series of federal laws, including the **Education for All Handicapped Children Act** of 1975 (often known by its public law number, PL 94-142), the **Individuals with Disabilities Education Act (IDEA)** of 1990, and the 1997 Reauthorization of the IDEA. The basic requirements spelled out in these acts, as well as by other laws and judicial interpretations, are as follows:

■ Basic requirements for special services

1. Children cannot be labeled as disabled or placed in special education on the basis of a single criterion such as an IQ score; testing and assessment services must be fair and comprehensive.

2. Parents or guardians must have access to information on diagnosis and may protest decisions of school officials.

3. Every student eligible for special education services must be taught according to an **individualized education program (IEP)** that includes both long-range and short-range goals. Because it is an agreement in writing regarding the resources the school agrees to provide, the IEP is a cornerstone of a school's efforts to help students with disabilities. It must specify special and related services that will be provided in accordance with the needs of the student. The IEP must be prepared within thirty days of when the child is declared eligible for special services, by a committee that must include the student's teacher, parent or guardian, and an administrator's designee.

4. Educational services must be provided in the **least restrictive environment**, which means that children with disabilities should be in regular classes to the extent possible. They may be placed in special or separate classes only for the amount of time judged necessary to provide appropriate services. If a school district demonstrates that placement in a regular educational setting cannot be achieved satisfactorily, the student must be given adequate instruction elsewhere, paid for by the district.

■ Mainstreaming and inclusion

As a result of these legal mandates, school districts throughout the country have made efforts to accommodate students with disabilities in regular class settings for all or most of the school day. The term *mainstreaming* was originally used to describe such efforts. More recently, the term *inclusion* has been applied. Inclusion usually denotes an even more strenuous effort to include disabled students in regular classrooms as much as is possible and feasible. Even if a disability is severe and a child needs to spend a substantial amount of time away from the regular classroom,

---

[50]U.S. Department of Education, *To Assure the Free Appropriate Education of All Handicapped Children* (Washington, D.C.: U.S. Department of Education, 1996); Lynne A. Weikart, "Segregated Placement Patterns of Students with Disabilities," *Educational Policy* (July 1998), pp. 432–448; and Thomas D. Snyder and Charlene M. Hoffman, *Digest of Education Statistics 2002* (Washington, D.C.: U.S. Government Printing Office, 2003).

Table 12.1	Number of Students Receiving Public Special-Education Services in 2001, by Type of Disability
Type of Disability	**2001**
Speech or language impaired	1,084,000
Mentally retarded	599,000
Learning disabled	2,842,000
Other health impaired	292,000
Hearing impaired	70,000
Orthopedically impaired	72,000
Visually handicapped	25,000
Total	6,293,000

Note: Numbers do not add to the total because not all categories are shown.
Source: Thomas D. Snyder and Charlene M. Hoffman, *Digest of Education Statistics, 2002* (Washington, D.C.: U.S. Government Printing Office, 2003).

he or she can still be encouraged to take part in activities open to other children, such as art or music.

Neither mainstreaming nor inclusion approaches are necessarily intended to eliminate special services or classes for children with exceptional needs. Children in these arrangements may receive a wide range of extra support, from consultation by specialists skilled in working with a particular disability to provision of special equipment.[51]

■ Studies ambiguous

Research on mainstreaming and inclusion has produced ambiguous results. Early studies generally failed to find evidence that placement of disabled students in regular classes for most or all of the day consistently improved their academic performance, social acceptance, or self-concept. Few classrooms examined in that early research, however, provided a fair test because too little had been done to train teachers, introduce appropriate teaching methods, provide a range of suitable materials, or otherwise ensure that teachers could work effectively with heterogeneous groups of disabled and nondisabled students. Reflecting such criticism, several recent studies were limited to districts and states considered outstanding in providing mainstreamed or inclusive opportunities for disabled students. Again, results generally were disappointing: relatively few indications emerged that mainstreaming or inclusion has been consistently beneficial for disabled students.[52]

[51]Christine L. Salisbury and Barbara J. Smith, "The Least Restrictive Environment: Understanding the Options," *Principal* (September 1991), pp. 24–27; Reinhard Nickisch, "Strategies for Integrating Handicapped Students," *Principal* (January 1992), pp. 20–21; Maike Philipsen, ed., *Assessing Inclusion* (Bloomington, Ind.: Phi Delta Kappa, 2000); and "Q&A About Inclusive Education" (undated), posting by TASH, available at **www.tash.org/inclusion/ qainclusion.htm**.

[52]Andrew R. Brulle, "Appropriate, with Dignity," *Phi Delta Kappan* (February 1991), p. 487; Justine Maloney, "A Call for Placement Options," *Educational Leadership* (December 1994–January 1995), p. 31; Kenneth A. Kavale and Steven R. Forness, "History, Rhetoric, and Reality," *Remedial and Special Education* (September/October 2000), pp. 279–310; Naomi Zigmond, "Where Should Students with Disabilities Receive Special Education Services?" *Journal of Special Education* (Fall 2003), pp. 193–199; and Ann C. Dybvik, "Autism and the Inclusion Mandate," *Education Next* (Spring 2004), available at **www.educationnext.org**.

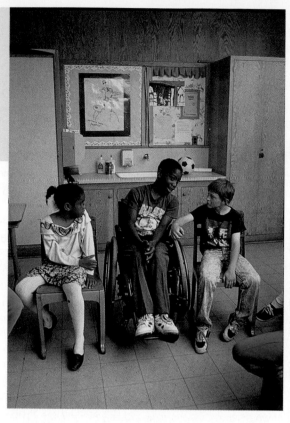

Effective mainstreaming of students with disabilities into regular classroom settings requires a variety of special resources, relatively small classes, and educators skilled in and dedicated to creating an effective learning environment and acceptance for all students. (© *Elizabeth Crews*)

■ Model efforts based on systematic reforms

On the other hand, several recent assessments of individual schools are more promising. In general, these schools have been described as models of restructuring: they made systematic reforms to prepare teachers to work with heterogeneous groups; they provided special resources to assist both students and teachers who need help; and they kept class size relatively small. In addition, teachers were effective at individualizing instruction and introducing cooperative learning. The researchers tend to agree that successful mainstreaming or inclusion on a national basis will require similar effective restructuring of schools throughout the United States.[53] The In This Case feature presents concerns that you and others entering the teaching profession might have about inclusion.

The legal requirements for educating students with disabilities create several challenges for teachers and administrators, beginning with determining who qualifies. Once an appropriate determination has been made, schools must assess which services children need and how well they can fulfill those needs. We'll explore these challenges, as well as other questions about special education.

---

[53]Allan Gartner and Dorothy Kerzner Lipsky, "Beyond Special Education: Toward a Quality System for All Students," *Harvard Educational Review* (November 1987), pp. 367–395; Ray Van Dyke, Martha A. Stallings, and Kenna Colley, "How to Build an Inclusive School Community," *Phi Delta Kappan* (February 1995), pp. 475–485; Wesley Sharpe, "Special Education Inclusion: (Part 2)" (2001), paper posted at the Education World Internet site, available at **www.educationworld.com/a_curr/curr320a.shtml**; and Pat Steinberg and Suzie Baier, "Alderwood Middle School Makes a Difference," *New Horizons for Learning* (Winter 2004), available at **www.newhorizons.org**: click on "Quarterly Journal."

IN THIS CASE

Meeting All Needs

Bob and Don are graduating this year and heading for their first year of classroom teaching. Bob looks over at Don. "I don't know about you, Don, but I'm pretty overwhelmed by what we're expected to do with and for special-needs students in an inclusion program. I know it's important for special-needs students to spend as much time as possible in the least restrictive environment, but just dealing with the requirements for normal students will be plenty of responsibility for me in my first year of teaching."

Don nods. "I agree. I suspect that inclusion helps the school district's financial situation. Look at the state formula for funding special education. More money comes to the districts that practice inclusion. But I'm not at all sure that inclusion is the best practice for most students with disabilities. I certainly don't have the training to deal with emotionally disabled students. If a disabled student becomes disruptive, how does a teacher proceed normally?" Don taps his finger on the table. "I am also really wondering how all of this affects learning for regular students. We'll have to follow Individual Education Plans for all disabled students. Couldn't following the IEP sometimes lead regular students to suspect unfairness? Before I took Overview of Special Education this year, even I kind of thought special education students could get away with doing almost nothing and call it 'adapting the curriculum.' How can I explain the differences to my class?"

Bob sighs. "I was only worried about meeting the special ed needs. But I can see potential problems in developing or maintaining effective education for regular students, too. In the effort to serve disabled students, I might be tempted to ease up on my preparation for regular students, and vice-versa. And behavior problems of just one student can easily distract a whole class, causing all of us to waste valuable time. I wonder how new teachers feel about this after their first year."

Don makes a note on a notepad. "Let's ask Professor Goodwin if we could have a panel discussion. She would know which of last year's graduates are teaching in a school using full inclusion. Then we could ask all our questions about this issue."

Bob looks over at the notepad. "I think we should include teachers who have lots of experience and who have seen how other arrangements work, as well. I remember the old resource rooms where they used to send most of the disabled students. That set-up may have worked better for some kids, but I also remember the disruption in class when they gathered up their stuff to go for their special sessions.

"Maybe the working teachers can talk about team teaching," Bob adds. "We don't necessarily have to work alone, you know. I've heard of shared teaching responsibilities, where a special education teacher teams with the regular teacher. I would definitely like to learn more about that. And there are always aides. Some of them serve as teachers even though they're not certified. Let's ask about these—and more."

Questions

1. What arrangements do local schools use to provide services to special education students?

2. What do you see as the most effective way to serve disabled students?

3. Do you have concerns about working with certain classes of disabled students?

4. Arrange to talk to regular and special education teachers. What arrangements do special ed teachers believe serve special education students best? How do regular classroom teachers answer the same question?

Classification and Labeling of Students

■ Classification difficulties

Educators face many difficulties in identifying students who require special education services. It is hard to be certain, for example, whether a child is mentally retarded and could benefit from special services or is simply a slow learner who requires more time and guidance to learn. Similarly, it is difficult to determine whether a child who is working below capacity has a learning disability or is performing poorly because he or she is poorly motivated, poorly taught, or culturally unprepared for assessment materials. (Of course, all these reasons may apply to the same child.) Although "learning disability" is currently the most used label—covering students with specific deficits in reading, math, writing, listening, or other abilities—experts disagree among themselves not only on what constitutes such a disability but also on what services should be provided to ameliorate it. Similar problems are encountered in distinguishing between severe and mild emotional disturbances or between partial and complete deafness. Children who appear borderline in disability status (a potentially fuzzy borderline) are especially difficult to classify.[54]

■ Growth of the vague "LD" category

Many analysts have suggested that the vagueness of the learning disabilities (LD) category has encouraged school districts to use this classification as a way to obtain federal funds to improve their educational services for low-achieving students. Because most LD students spend much of their time in regular classes but receive extra assistance in resource rooms, LD services often provide compensatory education for disadvantaged or low-achieving students who do not qualify for Title 1 services. This may help to explain why the number of U.S. students classified as learning disabled has more than tripled since the 1970s. Research indicates that half or more LD students may not meet criteria commonly accepted by special education experts.

■ Dangers in labeling

Effects of Labeling. Critics also are concerned that classification may become a self-fulfilling prophecy. Students labeled as "disturbed," for example, may be more inclined to misbehave because the label makes unruly behavior acceptable and expected. Researchers have tried to determine whether placement in a special class or program has either a positive or a detrimental effect on students. Among the variables they have considered are peer acceptance and effects on self-concept. On the

■ Inconclusive research

whole, the research is inconclusive. (Difficulties in conducting this type of research include defining terms, measuring program effects, and allowing for students' differing reactions to a given program.) Although some researchers report that special education classes limit the progress of many students, others have found that special-class placement can be beneficial when instruction is well planned and appropriate.[55]

---

[54]Maynard C. Reynolds, "Classification of Students with Handicaps," in Edmund W. Gordon, ed., *Review of Research in Education* (Washington, D.C.: American Educational Research Association, 1984), p. 89. See also James J. Gallagher, "New Patterns in Special Education," *Educational Researcher* (June–July 1990), pp. 34–36; Perry A. Zirkel, "Sorting Out Which Students Have Learning Disabilities," *Phi Delta Kappan* (April 2001), pp. 639–641; and Debra Viadero, "Disparately Disabled," *Education Week*, January 8, 2004.

[55]Gaea Leinhardt and Allan Pallay, "Restrictive Educational Settings: Exile or Haven?" *Review of Educational Research* (Winter 1982), pp. 557–578; Douglas Fuchs and Lynn S. Fuchs, "Sometimes Separate Is Better," *Educational Leadership* (December 1994–January 1995), pp. 22–26; Kenneth A. Kavale and Mark P. Mostert, "River of Ideology, Islands of Evidence," *Exceptionality* 11, no. 4 (2003), pp. 191–208; and Naomi Zigmond et al., "Special Education in Restructured Schools" (undated), paper posted at the New Horizons Internet site, available at **www.newhorizons.org/spneeds/inclusion/systems/jenkins.html**.

Disproportionate Placement of Minority Students

■ Use of "retarded" label for minorities and poor

Data on special education placement show that students from some racial minority groups are much more likely to be designated for mental retardation programs than are non-Latino white students. African American students, for example, are nearly three times as likely as white students to be in "educable mentally retarded" classes. In addition, black students in special education are approximately twice as likely to spend 60 percent or more of their time outside regular classrooms than are white students with disabilities. Placement in mental retardation categories also correlates highly with students' socioeconomic background and poverty status.

■ Causes and effects

Many analysts believe that placement in classes for the retarded has been too dependent on intelligence tests, which have been constructed for use with middle-class whites. Some also believe that disproportionate numbers of minority students are shunted into classes for emotionally disturbed or retarded children mainly to alleviate teachers' problems in dealing with culturally different children and youth. Many educators and parents worry that such placements may constitute a new version of segregation and discrimination, by which minority students are sentenced to special classes with low or nonexistent educational expectations.[56]

■ Court intervention

Several courts, sympathetic to this criticism, have issued rulings to make it less likely that students will be misassigned to special education classes. In the 1970 case *Diana v. Board of Education,* for example, a California court ruled that (1) all children whose primary language is not English must be tested in both their primary language and English; (2) the tests cannot depend solely on vocabulary, general information, or other experience-based items; and (3) districts with a disparity between the percentage of Mexican American students in regular classes and in special education classes must be able to show that valid classification methods account for this disparity. In another case, *Larry P. v. Riles,* a California court heard evidence indicating that the dialect and family environment of many African American students produced invalid scores on IQ tests. The court then ruled that these students could not be placed in classes for the educable mentally retarded on the basis of IQ tests "as currently administered." Like the other controversies concerning special education, this one will continue in the future.[57]

Issues and Dilemmas

We have touched on several issues involved in special education, mainstreaming, and inclusion. In this section we focus on four issues or dilemmas that may have particular prominence in the next several years. How we resolve these issues will affect your day-to-day life as a teacher.

■ Financial dilemmas

1. *How will we handle the costs?* Legal rulings that schools must provide an "appropriate" free education for children with disabilities have often been interpreted to mean that schools must provide the services necessary to help

---

[56]James Lytle, "Is Special Education Serving Minority Students?" *Harvard Educational Review* (February 1988), pp. 116–120; Kate Zernike, "Study Points to Racial Slant in Special Education," *New York Times,* March 3, 2001; and M. Suzanne Donovan and Christopher T. Cross, eds., *Minority Students in Special and Gifted Education* (Washington, D.C.: National Academy Press, 2002).

[57]Betsy B. Waterman, "Assessing Children for the Presence of a Disability" (2000), paper posted at the Kids Source Online Internet site, available at **www.kidsource.com/ NICHCY/assessing.1.html**; and Eileen M. Ahearn, "Specific Learning Disability" (2003), paper prepared for the National Association of Directors of Special Education, available at **http://nasdse.org/FORUM/specific_learning_disabilities.pdf**.

children with special needs derive as much benefit from education as do other students—perhaps establishing an optimal learning environment for every student who requires special assistance. However, providing an optimal learning environment for students with severe disabilities (or, perhaps, for any student) can be expensive. The federal government, while raising academic standards for disabled students under the No Child Left Behind Act, has provided only a fraction of the funds needed to support these services. Upon studying this issue, one congressman confessed that federal failure to fully fund implementation of disability regulations "has to be the mother of all unfunded mandates in this country."[58]

■ Rights versus expenses

Arguments have arisen between school officials, who claim they cannot afford to provide maximally effective education for all students with disabilities, and parents or other advocates who believe that such students have a constitutional right to whatever services ensure maximum educational gains. Administrators face a series of dilemmas here. Although key court cases have suggested that schools must provide only the level of services that give disabled students "a basic floor of opportunity," federal laws seem to require increasing levels of support. Administrators must not only determine their legal obligations, they must also decide whether additional services beyond the minimal obligations—and additional costs—are worth the educational payoff for the child. Then they must decide how to pay those costs.

One possible response is to divert local funds. Another is to classify more students as learning disabled in order to receive additional federal funding. Still another possibility involves including disabled students in regular classes *without* providing costly additional services there or undertaking systematic restructuring. Although any of these approaches can compromise education for both students with disabilities and without, such responses have been common in many school districts.[59]

Standards & Assessment ☑

2. *How should special education students prepare for state testing?* Until recently, most states allowed testing exemptions for special education students, but this has changed as decision makers realized that many schools increased enrollment in disabled categories to protect their scores and as the No Child Left Behind Act began to penalize schools for not testing or reporting scores of disabled students. However, as we discussed earlier in this chapter, many educators are concerned that applying statewide standards may prove disastrous for learning disabled and other students in special education.[60]

■ Potential effects on nondisabled students

3. *To what extent do arrangements and services for educating disabled students detract from education of nondisabled students?* If school officials divert substantial amounts of money from regular budgets to pay for separate placements or special services for disabled students, or if school officials assign students with severe disabilities to regular classes where teachers cannot address their problems efficiently, will classroom conditions for nondisabled students suffer?

---

[58]"What the Numbers Say," *Curriculum Review* (April 1998), p. 2; and "Special Education and the Individuals with Disabilities Education Act" (2003), statement posted by the National Education Association, available at **www.nea.org/specialed**.

[59]Jordan Cross, "25 Years Without Paying the Bills," *School Administrator* (November 2000), available at **www.aasa.org/publications/sa**; "Special Staff for Special Kids," *PRSP Reporter* (Winter 2003), available at **www.aft.org/publications**; and Joetta Stack, "The Funding Fix," *Education Week*, January 8, 2004.

[60]Rick Allen, "Learning Disabilities at the Assessment Crossroads," *ASCD Curriculum Update* (Fall 2000); and "'No Child Left Behind' After Two Years" (2004), statement posted by Fair Test, available at **www.fairtest.org**.

Observers disagree. Some believe that mainstreaming and inclusion have not substantially detracted from opportunities and outcomes for nondisabled students. Other observers believe that because regular classroom teachers often receive little or no help in dealing with students who have severe mental or emotional problems, some now have more difficulty delivering effective instruction for all students.[61]

■ Many questions about implementation

4. *What services should we provide for which students, where, when, and how?* Posing this omnibus question indicates that many issues we've discussed remain unresolved. For example, to what extent should we make differing arrangements for severely and mildly disabled students, or for differing students within either category? To what extent should schools implement "full inclusion" arrangements for all or most of the day, as contrasted with "partial inclusion" that assigns students to resource rooms or separate schools for significant amounts of time? To what extent should such decisions rest with parents, who may have little understanding of their schoolwide effects, or by professionals, who may lack sensitivity to the particular problems of an individual student? To what extent is it desirable—and feasible—to provide regular classroom support services, such as a sign language interpreter for deaf students or a nurse to assist incontinent students? Does using resource rooms complicate and disrupt the operation of the school as a whole—or is it more disruptive to bring a range of support services into the regular classroom? Will schoolwide restructuring carried out partly to accommodate full inclusion result in substantially improved schooling for all students, or is it unreasonable and unrealistic to expect effective widespread restructuring in the foreseeable future? These are a few of the questions for which educators still need good answers.

■ Suggested policies and guidelines

School officials struggling with the uncertainties of providing equal opportunity for students with disabilities could benefit from policies and guidelines for deciding what to do. Many informed observers believe that successfully educating students with disabilities will require changes at all levels of the U.S. educational system, including the following:[62]

- Congress should provide more funds to help schools implement its mandates.
- Legislation should require that teachers receive adequate training.
- States and school districts should find ways to quickly identify classrooms or schools where full inclusion or other arrangements are not working well.
- States should pass legislation to expedite quick removal from regular classes of disabled students who are violent or extremely disruptive.
- Schools opting to pursue full inclusion should receive whatever technical help is necessary.
- Teachers and staff in inclusive classrooms should receive training and support in using appropriate instructional strategies that will help all of their students

[61]Wesley Sharpe, "Special Education Inclusion" (2001), paper posted at the Education World Internet site, available at **www.educationworld.com/a_curr/curr320.shtml**; and Jennifer Katz and Pat Mirenda, "Including Students with Developmental Disabilities in General Education Classrooms," *International Journal of Special Education* 17, no. 2 (2002), available at **www.internationaljournalofspecialeducation.com/articles.cfm**.
[62]Pete Idstein, "Swimming Against the Mainstream," *American Educator* (Winter 1995–1996), pp. 28–31, 46; Joyce S. Choate and Thomas A. Rakes, *Inclusive Instruction for Struggling Readers* (Bloomington, Ind.: Phi Delta Kappa, 1998); and Diana L. Ryndak and Douglas Fisher, eds., *Foundations of Inclusive Education*, 2nd ed. (Baltimore: TASH, 2003).

master basic and advanced learning skills, including peer-mediated instruction, mastery learning, differentiated instruction, and cooperative teaching.

 **REFOCUS** What aspects of working with inclusion students do you believe will be most
challenges? challenging for you, as a teacher? What are you doing now to prepare for the
challenges?

▶ Summing Up

1 Concern for equal educational opportunity has been expanding to emphasize issues
involving racial and ethnic desegregation, achievement levels of students from low-
income families, introduction of bilingual education and other aspects of multicultural
education, and inclusion of students with disabilities in regular classrooms. Each of these
and related sets of issues involve sizable expenditures to enlarge opportunities and
ensure that the benefits of education are realistically available to all students. As you
enter the education field in the next decade, you will play an important role in determining the extent to which such efforts succeed or fail.

2 Although much desegregation has occurred in smaller school districts, big-city districts,
with their concentration of minority students and economically disadvantaged students, have found stable desegregation difficult.

3 Compensatory education seemed unsuccessful until evidence accumulating in the
1980s began to justify a more positive conclusion. However, many serious questions
remain concerning the degree to which compensatory education can have large-
scale, substantial, and lasting results. The No Child Left Behind Act (NCLB) has caused
sweeping changes not only in compensatory education, but also in public schooling for
all students.

4 Efforts toward constructive cultural pluralism through education include multicultural
education approaches that take account of student learning styles, recognize differences in dialect, provide for bilingual education, and introduce methods and materials
involving multiethnic curriculum and instruction. These approaches can help improve
the performance of economically disadvantaged minority students and otherwise promote a productive pluralistic society.

5 Legislative and court mandates have led to large expansions in education for students
with disabilities. As part of this process, educators are trying to mainstream these students as much as possible to avoid the damaging effects of labeling and separation.
Research, however, is unclear concerning the overall gains and losses associated with
mainstreaming or inclusion, and many questions remain.

▶ Key Terms

desegregation (354)
integration (354)
de jure segregation (356)
de facto segregation (356)
magnet school (358)
controlled choice (359)
compensatory education (362)
Title 1 (363)
Head Start (363)
Follow Through (363)

ecological intervention (365)
No Child Left Behind Act (NCLB) (365)
adequate yearly progress (366)
pullout approach (368)
multicultural education (370)
cultural pluralism (371)
learning styles (371)
Ebonics (373)
bilingual education (373)
first-language maintenance (375)

transitional bilingual education
(TBE) (375)
Education for All Handicapped Children
Act (380)
Individuals with Disabilities Education Act
(IDEA) (380)

individualized education program (IEP)
(380)
least restrictive environment (380)
mainstreaming (380)
inclusion (380)

▶ Discussion Questions

1 What actions and policies are most important in bringing about successful desegregation? In what situations is it most difficult to implement desegregation effectively?

2 Why is compensatory education an important national issue? What approaches are most promising for improving the achievement of low-income students?

3 What are some major goals and components of multicultural education? What can teachers in predominantly nonminority schools do to advance its goals?

4 How can you, as a regular classroom teacher, help disabled students in your classes? What difficulties are they likely to encounter? How might you help overcome these difficulties? If you are planning to become a special education teacher, how can you help your students who are included, fully or partially, in regular classrooms?

▶ Suggested Projects for Professional Development

1 Interview teachers in nearby elementary schools to determine whether they are using or considering inclusion arrangements. What are their attitudes toward inclusion? What can you learn from them that may be useful in your own career?

2 Talk with administrators in nearby schools to find out what school districts are doing to implement Title 1 and No Child Left Behind. Are improvements occurring? What changes have taken place during the past few years? Are similar changes taking place in districts in which you may apply for a position?

3 If a nearby school district operates magnet schools, visit one of them. Ask students and faculty what the magnet school is accomplishing and how it differs from a regular, non-magnet school. Ask administrators how the school district defined the school's goals. Does the school seem to be successful in meeting these goals? Do you think you would enjoy working there? Why or why not?

4 Organize and participate in a debate about the desirability of bilingual education. As part of your preparation for the debate, identify articles and books that help you reach valid conclusions. Good Internet starting points are **www.ncela.gwu.edu** and **www.ceousa.org**.

5 For your portfolio, begin preparing a section that will show your experience and studies with respect to topics considered in this chapter.

▶ Suggested Resources

 Internet Resources

In addition to federal government and ERIC sites and other more specialized Internet locations identified elsewhere in this text, you can research the important policy issues introduced in this chapter at the Web sites of organizations that conduct public-policy analysis.

These include the Brookings Institution (**www.brook.edu**), the Heritage Foundation (**www.heritage.org**), the Rand Corporation (**www.rand.org**), and the Electronic Policy Networks (**www.movingideas. org**). Electronic journals such as *Educational Policy Analysis Archives* also address issues reviewed in this chapter. You can also visit many sites related to specific chapter topics.

Desegregation

The April 2004 edition of the *American School Board Journal* at **www.asbj.com** is devoted to historical and current material on desegregation.

Multicultural Education

Internet sites dealing with multicultural resources are enumerated in the June 2002 *NCCSR Bookmark,* available at **www.goodschools.gwu.edu/pubs**. Relevant research centers located on the Internet include the Center for Multilingual, Multicultural Research at **www-rcf.usc.edu/~cmmr**. A series of essays addressing multicultural education is available in the "Teaching and Learning" section at **www.newhorizons.org**. Much of the Fall 2000 issue of *Rethinking Schools,* available at **www.rethinkingschools.org**, is devoted to multicultural education. Numerous research reports dealing with bilingual and multicultural education can be accessed at **www.ncela.gwu.edu**.

The Spring 2004 edition of *NW Education* at **www.nwrel.org/nwedu** includes a series of articles dealing with educating Native American students. Research on the education of Native Americans is available at **www.indianeduresearch.net**.

 Special Education

Abundant information about relevant laws, policies, and practices can be found by searching for "special education" at **www.ecs.org**. Despite its title, *Bright Futures for Exceptional Learners,* available at **www.cec.sped.org/spotlight/cond**, documents and analyzes major problems such as "overwhelming paperwork" and "ambiguous responsibilities" in the implementation of special education. Step-by-step strategies for teaching disabled students in inclusive classrooms are presented in "She Will Succeed," by Mary Prater, available at **http://journals.sped.org/EC/Archive_Articles/VOL.35NO.5MAYJUNE2003_TEC_Article-8.pdf**.

Publications

Banks, James A., and Cheryl A. M. Banks, eds. *Handbook of Research on Multicultural Education.* New York: Macmillan, 1995. *A wide variety of research-based chapters deal with cultural diversity and learning, effective instruction for low-income students, desegregation, the history and performance of minority groups, multicultural instruction, and related topics.*

Clausen, Christopher. *Faded Mosaic.* Chicago: Ivan R. Dee, 2000. *Clausen provides evidence and reasons to support his conclusion that although Americans draw from cultural "bits and pieces" everywhere, the past century brought about "postculturalism" marked by assimilation into a national culture.*

Gibson, Margaret A., and John U. Ogbu, eds. *Minority Status and Schools.* New York: Garland, 1991. *In addition to analyzing the experience of minority students in several countries, this book deals specifically with African American, Korean, Latino, Sikh, Ute Indian, and West Indian students in the United States.*

Kahlenberg, Richard D. *All Together Now.* Washington, D.C.: Brookings, 2000. *Includes current and historical data dealing with desegregation, school choice, concentrated poverty, and related topics.*

Klug, Beverly J., and Patricia T. Whitfield. *Widening the Circle.* New York: Routledge/Falmer, 2002. *Subtitled "Culturally Relevant Pedagogy for American Indian Children," this book provides a comprehensive description of problems and possible improvements in educating American Indian students.*

Levine, Daniel U., and Rayna F. Levine. *Society and Education,* 9th ed. Needham Heights, Mass.: Allyn and Bacon, 1996. *This text on the sociology of education provides detailed analysis of topics discussed in this chapter.*

Lind, Michael. *The Next American Nation.* New York: Free Press, 1995. *Provides detailed descriptions and discussions of topics involving immigration, multiculturalism, desegregation, affirmative action, sex equity, social class, and related issues.*

PART FIVE

Curricular
Foundations

CHAPTER 13

The Purposes of Education

Contemporary society changes fundamentally and rapidly. As it changes, we must fit ourselves into the present and project ourselves into the future. We look to the schools to help us cope with the climate of change. As a society, we react to change and social pressures by revising our educational purposes, and the schools respond by changing their programs.

Where *are* we going? As teachers and educators, what are our real purposes, and how should they be guiding our work?

This chapter will begin to focus your thinking on important education issues. As you read, think about the following questions:

FOCUS QUESTIONS

- How do social forces combine with philosophies of education to shape our educational purposes?
- How do we formulate our goals and objectives?
- What groups of students have been targeted for special treatment in recent decades?
- What are the major themes of recent policy reports on education?
- What goals will be most important in the future?

In this continual revision of educational priorities, the basic philosophies and theories examined in the chapter on Philosophical Roots of Education, play a strong role. People respond differently to the same events; they appraise, reflect on, and react to the tendencies of the times according to their own philosophies and values. Moreover, certain eras in American education have been dominated by particular philosophical approaches. As times change, the dominant philosophy or theory often changes, and the impact is felt in classrooms across the country—classrooms like yours. As a new teacher you will need to look for a "fit" between your philosophy of education and the educational values of the school district in which you teach. Examine your school district goals as well as those of your school. How do these goals translate into curriculum and teaching methods, and, most importantly, how comfortable are you philosophically with the answers to these questions?

This chapter was revised by Dr. James Lawlor, Towson University.

This chapter shows how philosophies and theories of education interact with social forces to influence the purposes of American education. After describing the purposes that have prevailed at different times in the history of American education, we examine the important changes of recent years. First, however, the chapter shows how we define educational purposes in terms of goals and objectives.

REFOCUS What current examples of changes in society, knowledge, or beliefs about the nature of learners do you believe will affect your goals as a teacher?

▶ Establishing Goals and Objectives

Standards & Assessment ☑
■ Levels of educational purpose

When we talk about the purposes of education, we may be referring to purposes at one or more of the following levels: nation, state, school district, school, subject/ grade, unit plan, or lesson plan. Despite mixed opinions, most educators use the terms *goals* and *objectives* to distinguish among levels of purpose, with goals being broader and objectives being more specific. Both terms describe a direction—what we are seeking to accomplish. Many educators refer to goals and objectives as "ends" or "endpoints" of education.

■ Effect of social forces and philosophies

All endpoints, however, feel the influences of social forces and prevailing philosophies or theories of education. Social forces and philosophies combine to shape the goals adopted at the national or state level; these goals in turn affect the more specific goals and objectives adopted in particular schools and classrooms. Over time, changes in social forces can also lead to modifications in prevailing philosophies and theories. The three main types of influential forces are society in general, developments in knowledge, and beliefs about the nature of the learner.[1]

■ Three influential forces

Changes in *society* include shifts in emphasis among the various influences examined in the chapter on Culture, Socialization, and Education and the chapter on Social Class, Race, and School Achievement, such as the family, peer groups, social class, and the economy. Changes in *knowledge* include new developments in science and technology, new methods of processing and storing information, and new methods of defining or organizing fields of study. Finally, changes in beliefs about the nature of the *learner,* such as new theories of the learning process, may also produce changes in educational theories and purposes.

Goals

■ Goals as broad statements of purpose

Although goals are important guides in education, we cannot directly observe or evaluate them; rather, they are broad statements that denote a desired and valued competency, a theme or concern that applies to education in general. The most general goals are often called *aims.*

■ National or state goals

Goals or aims are formulated at national and state levels, often by prestigious commissions or task forces. Here is one example of a goal at the national level, from the *National Education Goals Panel Report*: "All children in America will start

---

[1]The concept of three sources of change is rooted in the ideas of Boyd Bode and John Dewey, who wrote approximately eighty years ago. These ideas, popularized by Ralph Tyler in 1949, have been developed by contemporary curriculum theorists such as Allan Ornstein, J. Galen Saylor, and Robert Zais; Jerry Paquette, "Cross-Purposes and Crossed Wires in Education: Policy Making on Equity," *Journal of Curriculum Studies* (January–February 2001), pp. 89–112.

school ready to learn."[2] Another national or state goal might be to prepare students for democratic citizenship. Although these are admirable goals, it is unclear how local school districts might achieve them. They merely suggest a general direction to follow.

■ District goals

Goals at the school district level begin to narrow in focus. For example, a school district goal related to the national goal of school readiness might be "all children will have access to high-quality and developmentally appropriate preschool programs that help prepare children for school." A more sharply focused example of the national citizenship goal might be "students will participate actively in the political and social life of the community." Each of these goals helps to point teachers, principals, and superintendents toward certain general ends.

■ School goals

Goals at the school level usually narrow in focus even more, translating national, state, and district goals into statements that coincide more closely with the philosophy and priorities of the local school community.[3] School-level goal statements often appear in documents known as *school improvement plans.* These goal statements flow from an overall school *mission statement,* which articulates the school's role in educating the community's youth.[4] An example of a school-level goal related to the national goal of school readiness might be "kindergarten will be expanded from a half-day program to a full-day program."

In the late 1940s, Ralph Tyler developed an outline for school goals that remains influential today. Tyler identified four fundamental questions to consider:

■ Tyler's four questions

1. What educational purposes should the school seek to attain?

2. What educational experiences can be provided to help attain these purposes?

3. How can these educational experiences be effectively organized?

4. How can we determine whether [and to what extent] the purposes have been attained?[5]

■ Goodlad's twelve major goals

A generation later, another influential educator, John Goodlad, studied lists of school goals published by local boards of education across the country and identified a cluster of twelve that represented the spirit of the total list. Each of the twelve is further defined by a rationale statement in Table 13.1. These goals have changed little since then; rather, the emphasis varies depending on a school district's or school's philosophy and the way it interprets the forces of social change.

■ Citizen input

The process of developing goals for a school district or individual school should permit citizens, parents, and, at times, students meaningful input. Working in partnership with professional educators who understand child development and the

---

[2]National Education Goals Panel, *The National Education Goals Panel Report,* 1998, at **www .ed.gov/MailingLists/EDInfo/Archive/msg00410.html**; Margaret E. Goertz, "Redefining Government Roles in an Era of Standards-Based Reform," *Phi Delta Kappan* (September 2001), pp. 62–66; Lauro F. Cavazos, "Emphasizing Performance Goals and High Quality Education for All Students," *Phi Delta Kappan* (May 2002), pp. 690–697.
[3]Randall B. Parsons, "Ten Principles for Principals," *Principal* (March 2001), pp. 49–51.; and Allan C. Ornstein and Francis P. Hunkins, *Curriculum: Foundations, Principles, and Issues,* 3rd ed. (Boston: Allyn and Bacon, 1998).
[4]Maryland State Department of Education, *Maryland Earns "A" in Standards and Accountability,* at **www.msde.state.md.us** (2003); Patricia George, "Breaking Ranks in Action," *Principal Leadership* (December 2000), pp. 56–61; Charles Willis, "Confidence, Trust and Respect: the Preeminent Goals of Education Reform," *Journal of Negro Education* (Fall 2000), pp. 255–262.
[5]Ralph W. Tyler, *Basic Principles of Curriculum and Instruction* (Chicago: University of Chicago Press, 1949), p. 1.

Table 13.1	Major Goals of American Schools

1. *Mastery of basic skills or fundamental processes.* In our technological civilization, an individual's ability to participate in the activities of society depends on mastery of these fundamental processes.

2. *Career or vocational education.* An individual's satisfaction in life will be significantly related to satisfaction with her or his job. Intelligent career decisions will require knowledge of personal aptitudes and interests in relation to career possibilities.

3. *Intellectual development.* As civilization has become more complex, people have had to rely more heavily on their rational abilities. Full intellectual development of each member of society is necessary.

4. *Enculturation.* Studies that illuminate our relationship with the past yield insights into our society and its values; further, these strengthen an individual's sense of belonging, identity, and direction for his or her own life.

5. *Interpersonal relations.* Schools should help every child understand, appreciate, and value persons belonging to social, cultural, and ethnic groups different from his or her own.

6. *Autonomy.* Unless schools produce self-directed citizens, they have failed both society and the individual. As society becomes more complex, demands on individuals multiply. Schools help prepare children for a world of rapid change by developing in them the capacity to assume responsibility for their own needs.

7. *Citizenship.* To counteract the present human ability to destroy humanity and the environment requires citizen involvement in the political and social life of this country. A democracy can survive only through the participation of its members.

8. *Creativity and aesthetic perception.* Abilities for creating new and meaningful things and appreciating the creations of other human beings are essential both for personal self-realization and for the benefit of society.

9. *Self-concept.* The self-concept of an individual serves as a reference point and feedback mechanism for personal goals and aspirations. Facilitating factors for a healthy self-concept can be provided in the school environment.

10. *Emotional and physical well-being.* Emotional stability and physical fitness are perceived as necessary conditions for attaining the other goals, but they are also worthy ends in themselves.

11. *Moral and ethical character.* Individuals need to develop the judgment that allows us to evaluate behavior as right or wrong. Schools can foster the growth of such judgment as well as a commitment to truth, moral integrity, and moral conduct.

12. *Self-realization.* Efforts to develop a better self contribute to the development of a better society.

Source: Adapted from John I. Goodlad, *What Are Schools For?* (Bloomington, Ind.: Phi Delta Kappa, 1979), pp. 44–52. Reprinted with permission.

learning process, citizens can provide a valuable perspective in helping to decide what public schools are to teach.[6]

■ Goals are not behavioral

Whether formulated at the national, state, school district, or school level, goals are usually written in nonbehavioral terms, not tied to particular content or subject matter. They are intended to be long-lasting guides. Goals provide a direction by describing what schooling is intended to accomplish, but they are too vague and long-term for teachers and students to apply them directly in the classroom. Thus for classroom use, goals must be translated into more specific objectives.

[6]Ronald S. Brant and Ralph W. Tyler, "Goals and Objectives," cited in Allan C. Ornstein and Linda S. Behar-Horenstein, *Contemporary Issues in Curriculum.* Boston: Allyn and Bacon, 2003; "School Boards and Student Achievement: A Comparison of Governance in High- and Low-Achieving Districts," *ERS Spectrum* (Winter 2001), pp. 38–40.

Objectives

Objectives are generally written at three levels of instruction: subject/grade level, unit plan level, and lesson plan level.[7] They usually have a shorter accomplishment time than goals. Although objectives are more specific than goals, educators disagree about how detailed they ought to be. Some prefer fairly general objectives; others advocate objectives precise enough to be measured in behavioral terms or performance—that is, by the observable behavior of the student.

■ Classroom objectives

In practice at the classroom level, you will most likely organize instruction with a combination of general and specific objectives in mind. General objectives are characterized by "end" terms such as to *know, learn, understand, comprehend,* and *appreciate.* Such objectives will help you develop a sequenced curriculum for a grade level or a unit.

■ Lesson plan objectives

At the level of the individual lesson plan, objectives usually become specific, as recommended by Robert Mager. They use precise wording (often action words) such as *discuss, describe in writing, state orally, list, role-play,* and *solve.* Sometimes called *behavioral* or *performance objectives,* these statements are content or skill specific, require particular student behavior or performance, and are observable and measurable. Both teacher and learner can evaluate the amount or degree of learning.[8] The In This Case feature gives one example of how teachers and their students can benefit from preparing clear objectives.

Standards & Assessment ☑

As a prospective teacher, you have probably already heard a lot about state standards. Many states are now developing state-level standards called "indicators of achievement" and requiring both local school districts and teachers to align curricula with these state indicators.[9]

■ Examples of objectives

An example of a general unit objective might be that "students will understand why American colonists wanted to separate from Great Britain in the 1770s." Transposing this general objective into a specific lesson objective, we might obtain "Students will describe in writing three reasons American colonists gave in favor of separation from Great Britain." This objective refers to a specific kind of knowledge, states what is expected of students, and gives a precise criterion of three reasons.

Overview 13.1 summarizes the differences among the various levels of goals and objectives. As we move from national goals to lesson objectives, the examples become more specific—that is, easier to observe and/or measure.

REFOCUS   **How will you find out about the goals of your state and school district when you, as a teacher, plan your classroom goals and lesson objectives?**

▶ Historical Perspective

We live in an era when educators and the public at large are questioning the purposes of American education. What should our schools be trying to do? The answers are varied, and the debate has often been heated. To understand this debate, we

---

[7]George J. Posner and Alan N. Rudnitsky, *Course Design: A Guide to Curriculum Development for Teachers,* 5th ed. (New York: Longman, 2001); and Hilda Taba, *Curriculum Development: Theory and Practice* (New York: Harcourt, Brace, 1962).

[8]Robert F. Mager, *Preparing Instructional Objectives,* rev. 3rd ed. (Atlanta: Center for Effective Performance, 1997); Matt DeLong and Dale Winter, "An Objective Approach to Student-Centered Instruction," *Primus* (March 2001), pp. 27–52; and W. James Popham, *Modern Educational Measurement,* 2nd ed. (Englewood Cliffs, N.J.: Prentice-Hall, 1990).

[9]National Association of State Boards of Education. "Assessing the State of State Education Assessments," *State Education Standard* (Spring 2000), p. 5.

IN THIS CASE

Goals and Objectives

"What was the point of the lesson I just observed, Jane?" asked Professor Yates. "I was with you from start to finish, but still I am not sure I have learned what you want me to learn. I am not sure the students are learning what you want them to learn either."

"In this case, Dr. Yates, I would like to have all students learn to appreciate the many different ways that birds adapt to various environments," Jane replied. "Then I would like them to apply the concept of adaptation to one or more of our local birds. If they can do that, they ought to be able to understand adaptation of almost any sort."

"What came across to me," Professor Yates said, "is that birds are found in many sizes, colors, and places. Adaptation didn't seem to be a main point. Perhaps you could write your objective for the lesson on the board at the start of the lesson. What skills and attitudes did you want to link with this knowledge?"

"Well," said Jane. "I want them to learn to observe, to reflect on what they observe, and to appreciate nature's remarkable variety of adaptations, particularly in birds. I can start tomorrow's lesson with a review and ask some pointed questions about today's lesson. That should tell me pretty quickly if the kids didn't understand the concept of adaptation in birds. What do you think of that, Professor Yates?"

Professor Yates nodded. "That might be one strategy to try. I would also like you to talk with your mentor teacher here at the school. Ms. Butler may have ideas to help you. You need to know what specific objectives you have in mind when preparing a lesson. Know what learning you expect from students. And you'll be sure the class is following your thought pattern as you teach the lesson if you ask questions as you go along." He smiled. "Now I have some more leading questions for you to consider about your lesson. With which school or district goal or goals does this objective align?"

"Gosh, I haven't gotten that far." Jane said, a little disconcerted. "I thought it was enough to try to prepare the lesson with the specifics on the birds. I guess I need to expand my vision about how all of this ties together. This semester of practice teaching has really been tough for me, but I can see that having a vision of how everything fits together might help me keep on target. I want to rethink my lesson for tomorrow. Can you give me some leads, Professor Yates?"

"I could, but I won't," replied Mr. Yates. "I want you to work with Ms. Butler and think out these things for yourself. Your students' responses will tell you if you are successful or not. Be sure that you know your general curriculum objectives and the specific objectives for the lesson. I'll be back to observe another lesson in two weeks. Concentrate on objectives as you prepare your lessons these next two weeks."

Questions

1. Why is Professor Yates pushing Jane to consider specific objectives as well as links to school and district goals?

2. What national goals may be linked to Jane's teaching area? To your own teaching area? Explain.

3. If schools are particularly concerned with helping students adapt to changing life conditions, how might Jane expand her lesson beyond biology?

---

need to know how educational purposes have developed and changed over the years. As the following sections illustrate, the goals of American education have undergone many transformations.

Before the twentieth century, the perennialist theory generally dominated American education. Subject matter was organized and presented as a mere accounting of information. Proponents of the **mental discipline approach** believed that the mind is strengthened through mental activities, just as the body is strengthened by exercising. Traditional subjects, such as languages (Latin, Greek, French, and German), mathematics, history, English, physics, chemistry, government, and

■ Mental discipline: exercising the mind

OVERVIEW 13.1 *Goals and Objectives of Education*

Ends	Level of Direction	Developed by	Example(s)
National and state goals	Nation, state	Commissions, task force groups, broad professional associations	Improving basic literacy skills
Local goals	School district, school	Groups of administrators, teachers, and/or community members; broad professional associations	Acquiring information and meaning through reading, writing, speaking, and mathematical symbols
General objectives	Subject/grade	Subject-centered professional associations; curriculum departments or committees of state departments of education; large school districts	Improving reading comprehension; Appreciating the reading of whole books
	Unit plan	Textbook authors; teachers	Developing word recognition skills; Listening to stories read
Specific objectives	Lesson plan	Textbook authors; teachers	Identifying the main ideas of the author; Writing ten new vocabulary words

biology, were valued for their cultivation of the intellect; the more difficult the subject and the more the student had to exercise the mind, the greater the value of the subject.[10]

■ Progressive demands for reform

Gradually demands were made for various changes in schooling to meet the needs of a changing social order. The pace of immigration and industrial development led a growing number of educators to question the classical curriculum and the emphasis on mental discipline and repetitive drill. Adherents of the new pedagogy represented the progressive voice in education. They emphasized schoolwork and school subjects designed to meet the needs of everyday life for all children. By the early twentieth century, the effort to reform the schools along more progressive lines was well under way.

■ Concern for the whole child

In contrast to the perennialist philosophy and mental discipline approach that prevailed before World War I, the period from World War I to after World War II was dominated by the philosophy of progressivism and the science of child psychology. These emphasized the **whole-child concept** and life adjustment. The prevailing view held that schools must be concerned with the growth and development of the entire child, not just with certain selected mental aspects. Goals related to cognitive or mental growth had to share the stage with other important purposes of education such as goals involving social, psychological, vocational, moral, and civic development. Table 13.2 describes the two most important statements of goals of this era.

---

[10]Ellwood P. Cubberley, *Public Education in the United States,* rev. ed. (Boston: Houghton Mifflin, 1947), p. 543.

Educational approaches influenced by progressive philosophies emphasize focusing on educating the "whole child," rather than strictly on academic purposes. Which approach is closer to your personal philosophy of education? *(Bob Rowan/ CORBIS)*

The whole-child concept and the corresponding growth of child psychology had a tremendous impact on the schools that we still feel today.

During the era of the cold war and the Soviet *Sputnik* flight (1957), international events gave major impetus to the U.S. movement to reexamine academic disciplines as the focus of schooling. The country was appalled at the notion of losing technological superiority to the Soviets; national pride was challenged, and national goals were threatened.

■ **Return to academic essentials**

■ **National legislation**

Influenced by the perennialist and essentialist theories of education, critics called for a return to academic essentials and mental discipline. Thus, hard on the heels of *Sputnik* came national legislation to support training, equipment, and programs in fields considered vital to defense. The National Defense Education Act singled out science, mathematics, modern languages, and guidance (often considered a way to steer youth into the three former fields and into college). The scientific community, university scholars, and curriculum specialists were called upon to reconstruct subject-matter content, especially on the high-school level, while government and foundation sources provided the funds.[11] The new educational climate also included an increasing emphasis on providing topnotch education for the academically talented child.

■ **Concern for non-college-bound students**

The 1960s saw this change, as increased concern about poverty, racial discrimination, and equal educational opportunity brought new educational priorities, often related to the progressive and social reconstructionist theories of education. Educators noted that most students did not go on to college and that many dropped out of school or graduated as functional illiterates. Under those circumstances, serious

---

[11]William Van Til, "In a Climate of Change," in E. F. Carlson, ed., *Role of Supervisor and Curriculum Director in a Climate of Change,* 1965 ASCD Yearbook (Washington, D.C.: Association for Supervision and Curriculum Development, 1965), p. 21.

Table 13.2	Goals of Education: Two Major Statements of the Progressive Approach
Cardinal Principles of Secondary Education (1918)	**Ten Imperative Needs of Youth (1944)**
1. *Health:* provide health instruction and a program of physical activities; cooperate with home and community in promoting health. 2. *Command of fundamental processes:* develop fundamental thought processes to meet needs of modern life. 3. *Worthy home membership:* develop qualities that make the individual a worthy member of a family. 4. *Vocation:* equip students to earn a living, to serve society well through a vocation, and to achieve personal development through that vocation. 5. *Civic education:* foster qualities that help a person play a part in the community and understand international problems. 6. *Worthy use of leisure:* equip people to find "recreation of body, mind, and spirit" that will enrich their personalities. 7. *Ethical character:* develop ethical character both through instructional methods and through social contacts among students and teachers.	Develop skills and/or attitudes that enhance the following: 1. Productive work experiences and occupational success 2. Good health and physical fitness 3. Rights and duties of a democratic citizenry 4. Conditions for successful family life 5. Wise consumer behavior 6. Understanding of science and the nature of man 7. Appreciation of arts, music, and literature 8. Wise use of leisure time 9. Respect for ethical values 10. The ability to think rationally and communicate thoughts clearly

Source: Commission on the Reorganization of Secondary Education, *Cardinal Principles of Secondary Education,* Bulletin no. 35 (Washington, D.C.: U.S. Government Printing Office, 1918), pp. 11–15; and Educational Policies Commission, *Education for All American Youth* (Washington, D.C.: National Education Association, 1944).

problems could be anticipated if educational goals continued to be narrowly directed toward the most able students.[12]

■ Multicultural and bilingual programs, and students with disabilities

The focus on disadvantaged students extended into the 1980s and expanded to include multicultural and bilingual students and students with disabilities. The nation's multicultural and bilingual efforts were characterized by increased federal funding for Hispanic, Asian American, and Native American students, and by legal support for students with limited English skills (*Lau v. Nichols,* U.S. Supreme Court, 1974).

During the 1980s and 1990s, much concern also surfaced for special education, especially for students with learning disabilities or other special needs. Two important pieces of legislation, the Education for All Handicapped Children Act (1975) and the Individuals with Disabilities Education Act (IDEA, 1991), detailed policies and procedures for including students with disabilities in regular classrooms, to the extent possible.

■ Ongoing controversies

In the 1990s, however, conservative reactions against these trends increased. As noted in the chapter on Social Class, Race, and School Achievement, multicultural and bilingual programs have been heavily criticized as contributing to fragmentation and separatism rather than cultural unity. Educators have also split into fac-

---

[12]See, for example, John W. Gardner, *Excellence: Can We Be Equal and Excellent Too?* (New York: Harper and Row, 1961), pp. 28–29, 77; Peter Teitlebaum and Philip Kaufman, "Labor Market Outcomes of Non-College Bound High School Graduates," *Education Statistics Quarterly* (Spring 2002), pp. 73–74.

tions over the most effective way to conduct special education. Some want full inclusion (elimination of self-contained classrooms for special-education students and assignment of special-education teachers to coteach regular classrooms). Others support partial inclusion (whereby students with learning disabilities are placed in general-education classrooms as much as possible). Still others favor maintaining mostly separate classes for special-education students.[13]

■ Focus on outcomes

The end of the twentieth century also brought increased demands for educational accountability (demands expressed by elected officials and business leaders as well as by laypeople). Many argued that education should focus more clearly on *outcomes* or outputs—that is, on meaningful, measurable academic results—rather than on inputs such as money, programs, efforts, and intentions. According to some of these critics, mere completion of a curriculum means little if students cannot use their education in real-life contexts. As a result of this new focus, twenty-five states have developed or implemented an **outcomes-based education (OBE)** approach, and eleven others have made outcomes part of the state assessment process. Of course, although many educators believe the focus on student outcomes is a sensible way to look at educational goals, OBE is not without its critics. Some fear that it emphasizes affective outcomes and critical thinking to the detriment of religious faith and family values. Others claim that OBE promotes minimal academic standards, "dumbing down" the curriculum. Still other critics claim that OBE involves higher costs without corresponding results.[14]

Standards & Assessment ✓

■ State standards

While some educators focused on student performance outcomes, the first decade of the twenty-first century found other educators calling for clear **state standards** to which all students would be taught. Advocates for state standards wanted to develop authentic methods of assessing progress and mastery. Such clear standards and assessment of progress would help hold students, teachers, schools, and school districts accountable for learning. The federal 2002 **No Child Left Behind Act (NCLB)** emphasizes standards and yearly assessment of student progress (known as "adequate yearly progress").

■ "High stakes" testing

As a teacher, your state's standards are likely to heavily influence your instructional planning. Forty-nine states created standards, accompanied by accountability systems to affix praise and censure to those who would be affected by the standards. One concern expressed by many observers of the state standards movement is that the assessments are linked to "high stakes" outcomes for those taking the tests. Test results in many states help make decisions about promotion, graduation, and college scholarships, and they are related to a range of consequences for the school districts and professionals preparing students for those exams, including school accreditation, pay raises, and bonuses.

In spite of these and other stumbling blocks confronting states, standards are worth sustaining. For the first time in the history of American public education, lofty goals have been established for all children, and the notion that even one

---

[13]Douglas Fuchs and Lynn S. Fuchs, "What's 'Special' About Special Education?" *Phi Delta Kappan* (March 1995), pp. 522–529; James William Noll, cd., "Is Full Inclusion of Disabled Students Desirable?" in *Taking Sides: Clashing Views on Educational Issues* (Guilford, Conn.: Dushkin/McGraw-Hill, 1999), pp. 224–238; Devery R. Mock and James M. Kauffman, "Preparing Teachers for Full Inclusion: Is it Possible?" *Teacher Educator* (Winter 2002), pp. 202–215.

[14]Bruno V. Manno, "The New School Wars: Battles over Outcome-Based Education," *Phi Delta Kappan* (May 1995), pp. 720–726; James O. Lee, "State v. Local Control of Educational Standards: Effects on Teaching," *Educational Forum* (Fall 2002), pp. 36–46; Linda Matlock, Kay Fielder, and Dawn Walsh, "Building the Foundation for Standards-Based Instruction for All Students," *Teaching Exceptional Children* (May–June 2001), pp. 68–72.

child can be left behind is no longer acceptable. One point apparently not carefully considered is the notion that children learn at different paces and in different ways, and thus might need to be tested at different levels and through different means.[15]

REFOCUS | Over the decades, educational goals have targeted different groups of students, such as the academically talented or at-risk students. Which group of students now appears the target of most educational goals?

▶ The Call for Excellence

■ National reports call for reform

Keeping in mind how American educational goals have changed over time, we can look more closely at the contemporary demand for reform in the schools. How do various recent proposals reflect important changes in American educational purposes? How well do particular reforms fit your own ideas about the purpose of education?

Overview of Policy Reports

By the early 1980s national attention began to focus on the need for educational excellence and higher academic standards for all students—particularly the neglected "average" student—and not just the disadvantaged or the talented. In the years since then, national policy reports, most of which reflected a so-called neo-essentialist perspective, have urged reforms to improve the quality of education in the United States. Six of the most influential of these were as follows:

- *Action for Excellence* (1983)
- *Educating Americans for the 21st Century* (1983)
- *High School* (1983)
- *A Nation at Risk* (1983)
- *First Lessons: A Report on Elementary Education in America* (1986)
- *The National Education Goals* (1990, 1994, 1997)

To support their proposals, the reports have presented devastating details and statistics indicating a serious decline in American education. For example:

■ Declining achievement and competency

1. Average achievement scores on the Scholastic Aptitude Test (SAT—now called the Scholastic Assessment Test) declined steadily from 1963 to 1990. Average verbal scores fell 34 points (466 to 432), and mathematics scores dropped 10 points (492 to 482). In recent years both scores have rebounded, but not significantly (verbal increased 5 points to 437 and math increased 13 points to 495).[16]

2. Little change occurred in eighth-grade mathematics and science achievement between 1995 and 1999, despite concerted federal, state, and local efforts to increase math and science achievement scores.[17]

---

[15]Brenda Welburn, "Executive Summary," *State Education Standard* (Spring 2000), p. 5; Andrew Porter, "Doing High-Stakes Assessment Right," *School Administrator* (December 2000), pp. 28–31; Gerald Bracey, "The 13th Annual Bracey Report on the Condition of Public Education," *Phi Delta Kappan* (October 2003), pp. 148–164.
[16]*Digest of Education Statistics, 1997* (Washington, D.C.: U.S. Government Printing Office, 1997), Table 129, p. 133; and *Digest, 2002*, Table 132.
[17]See **http://isc.bc.edu/**. Substitute "science" for "math" in URL for science report.

Recent shifts in educational goals have brought a new emphasis on assessment and accountability for students, teachers, and schools, including the use of controversial "high stakes" testing used to make decisions about outcomes such as graduation and promotion. *(© A. Ramey/Stock Boston)*

■ International comparisons

3. As we looked into the new century, U.S. eighth-grade students still performed below their peers in fourteen other industrialized nations—hardly the performance at "world class standards" called for in the *National Education Goals.*[18] (See the chapter on International Education for further discussion of international comparisons.)

■ Functional illiteracy

4. About 21 percent of 192 million U.S. adults are functionally illiterate by the simplest tests of everyday reading and writing. Moreover, about 13 percent of all seventeen-year-olds in the United States are considered functionally illiterate, and this illiteracy rate jumps to 40 percent among minority youth.[19] More alarming is that the average literacy skills of both elementary- and secondary-school students remained unchanged from 1993 through 2001, with improved scores of high-performing students (75th to 90th percentile) being offset by declining scores for low-performing students (those at the 10th percentile level).[20]

■ Student–teacher ratios

5. These problems have occurred despite a relatively good student–teacher ratio: approximately sixteen students per teacher in the United States, compared to ratios above twenty-five to one in Japan and Korea. Moreover, our per-pupil expenditures for K–12 education have been the second highest in the world (second only to Finland).[21]

---

[18]*The Condition of Education, 2000* (Washington, D.C.: U.S. Government Printing Office, 2000), p. 84; *Digest of Education Statistics, 2002,* Tables 398 and 400.
[19]See "Human Development Indicators" at **www.undp.org/hdr2003/indicator/indc_29_/_/.html**.
[20]National Education Goals Panel, *Data Volume for the National Goals Report, Volume I, National Data, 1994* (Washington D.C.: U.S. Government Printing Office, 1994), pp. 92–94. See also "The Nation's Report Card" at **http:nces.ed.gov/nationsreportcard/**.
[21]*Digest of Education Statistics, 2002,* Table 4; Mark David Milliron and Cindy Miles, "Education in a Digital Democracy: Leading the Charge for Learning About, with, and Beyond Technology," *Educause Review* (November–December 2000), pp. 50–62.

Standards & Assessment ☑

▪ Reports' common themes
▪ Importance of technology

▪ Higher standards, more rigorous requirements

▪ Schools play too many roles

All of these reports emphasize the need to strengthen the curriculum in the core subjects of English, math, science, foreign language, and social studies. Technology and computer courses are mentioned often, and at the beginning of the twenty-first century the need to improve students' technology skills and to upgrade schools technologically is almost a "mantra"—the fourth "R," as some call it. (For more information, see the Technology @ School box.) High-level cognitive and thinking skills are also stressed. Although certain reports also address programs and personnel for disadvantaged students and students with learning disabilities, this message is not always loud and clear.

The reports further emphasize tougher standards and tougher courses, and a majority propose that colleges raise their admission requirements. Most of the reports also talk about increasing homework, time for learning, and time in school, as well as instituting more rigorous grading, testing, homework, and discipline. They mention upgrading teacher certification, increasing teacher salaries, increasing the number of science and math teachers and paying higher salaries, and providing merit pay for outstanding teachers. Overall, the reports stress academic achievement, not the whole child, and increased productivity, not relevancy or humanism.

Most of the reports express concern that the schools are pressed to play too many social roles; that the schools cannot meet all these expectations; and that the schools are in danger of losing sight of their key purpose—teaching basic skills and core academic subjects, new skills for computer use, and higher-level cognitive skills for the world of work and technology. Many of the reports, concerned not only with academic productivity but also with national productivity, link human capital with economic capital. Investment in schools would be an investment in the economy and in the nation's future stability. If education fails, so do our work force and nation. Hence business, labor, and government must work with educators to help educate and train the U.S. population.

In the following sections, we will look more closely at the two most popularized and influential reports: *A Nation at Risk,* published in 1983, and *The National Education Goals,* a 1994 revision of a report first published in 1990. The Taking Issue box deals with the question of whether national reports are useful.

▪ Rising tide of mediocrity

▪ Recommendations of *A Nation at Risk*

A Nation at Risk.   The report by the National Commission on Excellence in Education, compiled by a panel appointed by the U.S. Department of Education, indicates that a "rising tide of mediocrity" is eroding the well-being of the nation.[22] This mediocrity is linked to the foundations of our educational institutions and is spilling over into the workplace and other sectors of society. The report lists several aspects of educational decline that were evident to educators and citizens alike in the late 1970s and early 1980s: lower achievement scores, lower testing requirements, lower graduation requirements, lower teacher expectations, fewer academic courses, more remedial courses, and higher illiteracy rates. It states that the United States has compromised its commitment to educational quality as a result of conflicting demands placed on the nation's schools and concludes that the schools have attempted to tackle too many social problems that the home and other agencies of society either will not or cannot resolve.

The report calls for, in part, tougher standards for graduation, including more courses in science, mathematics, foreign language, and the "new basics" such as

[22]National Commission on Excellence in Education, *A Nation at Risk: The Imperative for Educational Reform* (Washington, D.C.: U.S. Department of Education, 1983); Gerald W. Bracey, "April Foolishness: The 20th Anniversary of *A Nation at Risk,*" *Phi Delta Kappan* (April 2003), pp. 16–21; Diane Ravitch, "The Testing of Time," *Education Next* (Spring 2003), pp. 32–38.

Finding and Assessing National, State, and Local School District Goals

Teachers, both new and experienced, must be well informed about national, state, and local educational goals and how these goals will affect their work in the classroom. To this end, you can review the eight national goals at **www.ed.gov/G2K/GoalsRpt/**. Ask yourself how worthy these are as "national goals" at the beginning of the twenty-first century. What goals would you add? Examine the most recent data related to achieving the national goals at the National Education Goals Panel's Interactive Data Site, **www.negp.gov/datasystemlinks.html**. Here you can examine ten years of data on individual state progress, national progress, states compared with the nation, and even international comparisons on the eight national goals. In your opinion, what progress has been made in meeting the national goals?

For state goals, you can visit your state department of education Web site (go to **www.nasbe.org** and click on "links to state education agencies.") How do state-level outcomes and goals differ from the national goals? For example, you might visit the state of Maryland site at **www.marylandpublicschools.org/MSDE** and search for "goals." How do "Maryland School Performance and Assessment Program" (MSPAP) outcomes and learning goals for grades 3, 5, and 8 differ from the national goals?

It is also important to find out whether your state department of education Web site refers to technology standards for students and teachers. What technology knowledge and skills do you believe students and teachers should have in this fast-paced, changing world? Examine the "National Educational Technology Standards for Students" (NETS) at **http://cnets.iste.org/Students** and click on "standards for students." How helpful are these six standards as guidelines for planning technology-based activities in the classroom? Also click on "performance profiles for teachers." How do these standards differ from the "standards for students"? For additional information on technology standards for teachers, use Google to search "standards projects" and "NCATE standards project."

computer skills; a longer school day and school year; far more homework; improved and updated textbooks; more rigorous, measurable, and higher expectations for student achievement; higher teacher salaries based on performance, and career ladders that distinguish among the beginning, experienced, and master teacher; demonstrated entry competencies and more rigorous certification standards for teachers; accountability from educators and policy makers; and greater fiscal support from citizens.

Reports such as *A Nation at Risk* and Educational Policies Commission reports often spring from a broad-based concern about the quality of public education in changing times. The goal of these reports is to make practical recommendations for educational improvement and, as such, provide guidance to state and local boards of education, school districts, and ultimately teachers as they plan for instruction. The impact of *A Nation at Risk* has been substantial, driving increases in high school graduation requirements, increases in mathematics and science courses, a return to academic basics, changes in technology, and increased college entrance requirements. Most of these changes occurred at the local school district level, and you may have felt them if you were a student in the public schools during this time.

The federal government's current No Child Left Behind initiative continues in the tradition of national reports in its concern about the general quality of public education in changing times and its practical recommendations for educational

taking issue

Question   Given public concern about the decline of education in America, do national reports on education provide appropriate guidance and direction to shape school reform?

National Reports: Are They Useful?

The 1980s and 1990s saw a plethora of national reports criticizing public education in the United States, be it educational goals, student performance and achievement, academic rigor, teaching methods, or the preparation of teachers. Replacing words with action is the necessary next step for educators, politicians, and the public as we set goals for educational reform and school improvement for the twenty-first century.

Arguments PRO

1 National reports help focus attention on the problems and criticisms of public education. Today, the fear about educational decline in America touches far more people than ever before, and school reform has received increasing political and financial support from legislators, politicians, and the public.

2 The recommendations of the national reports can help build consensus among government, corporate, and educational groups, as well as parents and the public, regarding priorities for a core set of educational reform efforts.

3 National reports drive efforts to raise educational standards, particularly at state and national levels. This is reflected in the educational programs of the two most recent presidents: Bill Clinton and George W. Bush, both of whom have supported greater federal involvement and investment in education, as well as national testing and yearly assessment of student achievement.

4 Some reformers believe sweeping changes in public education are needed, and the political climate is ripe to support this change.

Arguments CON

1 Despite guarded willingness on the part of the American public to spend additional money for education, they want substantive results for their investment, that is, genuine accountability. Legislators and politicians echo this demand for accountability from students and educators.

2 Seasoned educators have learned, sometimes the hard way, that there are no "magic bullets" for reforming schools, and, as David Cohen notes, "America is awash with competing schemes to save the schools." This causes confusion rather than clarity of purpose.

3 National reports, and subsequent government mandates, often tend to be idealistic in scope, emphasizing excellence at the expense of equity, and are expensive to implement. Regarding national testing, educators, politicians, and the public disagree about who should be tested, what should be tested, what tests should be used, and when and how often students should be tested. Even more controversy surrounds what test scores mean.

4 Reports ignore a basic fact about school change and improvement: the process is complex and involves the cooperation of teachers, administrators, parents, community members, and politicians, all of whom have different ideas about reform.

improvement. It differs in that it provides explicit directives, partially supported by federal funds, to state and local boards of education, and school districts.

■ "Sweeping changes" demanded

The National Education Goals.   In 1994 Congress passed the **Goals 2000:** Educate America Act. The complete set of goals, published as *The National Education Goals* and often referred to simply as Goals 2000, is listed in Table 13.3. The overriding theme of those goals was the push for an educated citizenry, well trained and re-

Table 13.3	The National Education Goals

Goal 1   School Readiness
By the year 2000, all children in America will start school ready to learn.

Goal 2   School Completion
By the year 2000, the high school graduation rate will increase to at least 90 percent.

Goal 3   Student Achievement and Citizenship
By the year 2000, all students will leave grades 4, 8, and 12 having demonstrated competency over challenging subject matter including English, mathematics, science, foreign languages, civics and government, economics, arts, history, and geography, and every school in America will ensure that all students learn to use their minds well, so they may be prepared for responsible citizenship, further learning, and productive employment in our Nation's modern economy.

Goal 4   Teacher Education and Professional Development
By the year 2000, the Nation's teaching force will have access to programs for the continued improvement of their professional skills and the opportunity to acquire the knowledge and skills needed to instruct and prepare all American students for the next century.

Goal 5   Mathematics and Science
By the year 2000, United States students will be first in the world in mathematics and science achievement.

Goal 6   Adult Literacy and Lifelong Learning
By the year 2000, every adult American will be literate and will possess the knowledge and skills necessary to compete in a global economy and exercise the rights and responsibilities of citizenship.

Goal 7   Safe, Disciplined, and Alcohol- and Drug-free Schools
By the year 2000, every school in the United States will be free of drugs, violence, and the unauthorized presence of firearms and alcohol and will offer a disciplined environment conducive to learning.

Goal 8   Parental Participation
By the year 2000, every school will promote partnerships that will increase parental involvement and participation in promoting the social, emotional, and academic growth of children.

Source: Goals 2000: Educate America Act (March 31, 1994); *The National Education Goals* (Washington, D.C.: U.S. Department of Education, 1994).

sponsible, capable of adapting to a changing world, knowledgeable of its cultural heritage and the world community, and willing to accept and maintain America's leadership position in the twenty-first century. Educators must be given greater flexibility to devise teaching and learning strategies that serve all students, regardless of abilities or interests; at the same time, they should be held responsible for their teaching. Parents must become involved in their children's education, especially during the preschool years. Community, civic, and business groups all have a vital role to play in reforming education. Finally, students must accept responsibility for their education, and this means they must work hard in school.

■ Developing national standards

In 2001, the National Education Goals Panel made its final major report on the progress on the eight goals and twenty-six "indicators" in Goals 2000. Although the nation as a whole did not meet the national goals by the year 2000 and, in fact, is unlikely to ever fully reach the eight ambitious goals, many states made remarkable progress. With the suspension of The National Educational Goals Panel in 2002 and the advent of No Child Left Behind, America's educational expectations changed to a more specific focus on improved student performance in reading and math, having highly qualified teachers in every classroom, and identifying and improving schools where students are not meeting these goals (see **www.ed.gov/**). Future reports will chart the states' progress toward these NCLB goals.

The national reports emphasized core curriculum subjects, tougher standards, and accountability. Which of these do you believe has most affected your career as a student? Which will be of most importance to you as a teacher?

▶ Swings of the Pendulum

■ Old themes reemerge

In examining educational goals from the turn of the twentieth century until today, we see considerable change but also old ideas reemerging in updated versions. For example, a stress on rigorous intellectual training, evident in the early twentieth century, reappeared in the 1950s during the Cold War, and again from the 1980s through the early twenty-first century, as a result of concern over economic competition with foreign countries. Similarly, as the social ferment of the 1960s and 1970s brought increasing concern for the rights and aspirations of low-income and minority groups, the ideas of the early progressive educators resurfaced, and a renewed stress was placed on educating the disadvantaged. Although this concern for disadvantaged or at-risk students remains, the pendulum has now swung closer to the center: our current priorities are more diffuse, and there is growing concern for various kinds of students, including average and academically talented groups.

■ Too much expected of schools?

In looking at the broad sweep of American educational purposes, you may ask yourself whether schools are expected to do more than is feasible. The schools are often seen as ideal agencies to solve the nation's problems, but can they do so? Many people throughout society refuse to admit their own responsibility for helping children develop and learn. Similarly, parents and policy makers often expect teachers and school administrators to be solely responsible for school reform. In fact, without significant cooperation from parents and community members, schools cannot do a good job, and reform efforts will fail.

■ Coping with change

Unquestionably, the goals of education must be relevant to the times. If the schools cannot adapt to changing conditions and social forces, how can they expect to produce people who do? Today we live in a highly technical, automated, and bureaucratic society, and we are faced with pressing social and economic problems—aging cities, the effects of centuries of racial and sexual discrimination, an aging population, economic dislocations, terrorism, and the pollution of the physical environment. Whether we allow the times to engulf us, or whether we can cope with our new environment, will depend to a large extent on what kinds of skills are taught to our present-day students—and on the development of appropriate priorities for education.[23]

What is your top goal as a teacher? Ask this same question of several other educators and prospective educators. Compare and contrast your answer with theirs.

---

[23]Charles Nevi, "Saving Standards," *Phi Delta Kappan* (February 2001), pp. 460–461.

▶ Summing Up

1 The purposes of education are influenced by changing social forces as well as by educational philosophies and theories.

2 Broad statements of educational purpose, generated at the national or state level, are usually translated into more specific goals by the school district or individual school. These goals, in turn, are developed into even more specific objectives at the subject/grade, unit plan, and lesson plan levels.

3 Since the turn of the century, the goals of American education have gone through at least five periods, each with a different focus of attention: academic rigor and mental discipline; the whole child; academically talented students; disadvantaged and minority students and children with disabilities; and, from the 1980s through the early twenty-first century, tougher academic standards for all students.

4 Most of the major reports released since 1983 have emphasized the need for educational excellence and higher standards. Although educators disagree about many of the reports' recommendations, most states have already implemented changes based on these reports.

5 We must learn to live with some disagreement about the purposes of schooling. Various groups of people need to work together in formulating future educational priorities.

6 We often expect schools to be a key instrument for solving our technological or social problems and preparing our work force for the future. The years ahead will severely test this expectation.

▶ Key Terms

goals (395)
objectives (395)
National Education Goals Panel Report (395)
mental discipline approach (399)
whole-child concept (400)

outcomes-based education (OBE) (403)
state standards (403)
No Child Left Behind Act (NCLB) (403)
A Nation at Risk (406)
The National Education Goals (406)
Goals 2000 (408)

▶ Discussion Questions

1 In terms of the various types and levels of educational goals, why is the question "What are schools for?" so complex?

2 Are the goals of the Educational Policies Commission, as summarized in the right-hand column of Table 13.2, desirable for education today? Based on your personal philosophy of education, how might you modify them?

3 Who should have educational priority: below-average students, average students, or above-average students? Why? What philosophical leanings and social forces influence your answer to the question?

4 What is your opinion of No Child Left Behind? Discuss your thinking with other students in class. Is NCLB an improvement over Goals 2000? How do these goals align with your emerging philosophy of education?

5 What argument could you make for or against computer technology and skills as a "new basic" or "fourth R"?

▶ Suggested Projects for Professional Development

1 As you visit schools, ask to examine any available goal statements such as position papers, mission statements, and school improvement plans. How do teachers and administrators believe the goals will be implemented? How would you implement them?

2 Select a school with yearly goals and ask to see its goal statements. Talk with teachers and administrators to find out the following: the process for developing the goals, who developed them, how parents and the community participated in the process, and how goals assessment takes place. How would you feel about this process if you were participating? What would you see as your role?

3 Write Goals 2020. Be as idealistic as you like, but also realistic. How do you believe you, as a teacher, would work toward your Goals 2020?

4 Select one national goal and visit your state department of education Web site (see **www.nasbe.org**; click on "links to state education agencies"). How does your state education agency address this goal? Click on "school boards" or "school districts" and select one or two local school districts in which you are particularly interested. How do they address this goal? In general, what references do you see to the national goals at the state board and local district Web sites? Are other goals evident? If so, how do you think these goals will provide direction for school boards, curriculum developers, and teachers?

▶ Suggested Resources

 Internet Resources

Access the U.S. Department of Education's Web site (**www.eric.ed.gov**) for the full texts of the Goals 2000: Educate America Act, the Improving America's Schools Act of 1994, The National Educational Goals Panel Report of 2002, and No Child Left Behind. One starting point for general information about educational reform is a search at **www.fedworld.gov/**. Search the U.S. Department of Education's sites for topics such as "accountability" and "gifted students." General Internet searches for key terms such as *educational technology, school reform,* and *national/ state standards* can also be useful.

Publications

Baum, Howell. *Community Action for School Reform.* Albany: State University of New York Press, 2003. *A look at community schools and school improvement/reform in Baltimore, Maryland.*

Bracey, Gerald. *The War Against America's Public Schools.* Boston: Allyn and Bacon, 2002. *Describes competing visions Americans have about their public schools.*

Conant, James B. *The American High School Today.* New York: McGraw-Hill, 1959. *A classic written during the Sputnik era, this book offers many recommendations for upgrading the high-school curriculum.*

Duke, Daniel, and Robert L. Canady. *School Policy.* New York: McGraw-Hill, 1991. *A compact book on federal, state, and local school policy—and on how to formulate, evaluate, and revise goals of education.*

Gardner, John W. *Excellence: Can We Be Equal and Excellent Too?* New York: Harper and Row, 1961. *Another classic text, this book remains relevant today. The questions and issues it raises are still of deep concern in American schools and society.*

Gordon, David. *A Nation Reformed? American Education 20 Years After* A Nation at Risk. Cambridge, Mass.: Harvard Education Press, 2003. *A comprehensive look at the impact of* A Nation at Risk. *Did it really engender school reform?*

National Commission on Excellence in Education. *A Nation at Risk: The Imperative for Educational Reform.* Washington, D.C.: U.S. Department of Education, 1983. *Among recent reports on American education, this one has had the most political impact.*

Ravitch, Diane, and Maris A. Vinovskis, eds. *Learning from the Past: What History Teaches Us About School Reform.* Baltimore: Johns Hopkins University Press, 1995. *An excellent work on standards in American education; issues of federal, state, and local control; equity and the changing conception of multiculturalism; and school reform strategies.*

Spring, Joel. *American Education.* 8th ed. Hightstown, N.J.: McGraw-Hill, 1998. *A concise look at the purposes of public schooling and multicultural education issues.*

Spring, Joel. *Wheels in the Head: Educational Philosophies of Authority, Freedom, and Culture from Socrates to Human Rights.* 2nd ed. New York: McGraw-Hill, 1999. *A wonderful little book dealing with philosophies of schooling and critical questions educators need to think about as they shape teaching and learning in classrooms, school districts, and society.*

CHAPTER 14

Curriculum and Instruction

Perhaps more than the citizens of any other country, Americans have demanded the utmost from their schools. We ask the schools to teach children to think, to socialize them, to alleviate poverty and inequality, to reduce crime, to perpetuate our cultural heritage, and to produce intelligent, patriotic citizens. Inevitably, American schools have failed to meet all of these obligations. Nonetheless, the demands persist, focusing on curriculum—planned experiences provided through instruction—and curriculum is continuously modified as education goals are revised, student populations change, social issues are debated, and new interest groups emerge.

We describe in the chapter on The Purposes of Education how the goals of education have shifted with changing national priorities and social pressures. In this chapter we will look at several major curricular approaches used in recent decades to help meet our changing national goals. You will see that the curriculum approaches also relate closely to the philosophies and theories discussed in the chapter on Philosophical Roots of Education.[1] Reflect on how these curricular approaches relate to your own emerging philosophy of education.

As we examine curriculum, we will also examine instructional activities that relate to curriculum. This chapter will help you answer the following questions:

FOCUS QUESTIONS

- How does curriculum content reflect changes in society?
- In what ways is curriculum organized?
- How might the use of cooperative learning or mastery learning influence your work as a teacher?

This chapter was revised by Dr. James Lawlor, Towson University.

[1]See R. Freeman Butts, *The Revival of Civic Learning* (Bloomington, Ind.: Phi Delta Kappa, 1980); Lawrence A. Cremin, *American Education: The National Experience* (New York: Harper and Row, 1980); and Lawrence A. Cremin, *The Transformation of the School* (New York: Random House, 1964).

■ How can you use computers and other electronic resources in the class-room to improve instruction?

■ What trends seem likely to affect curriculum and instruction in the future?

▶ Curriculum Organization

■ Subject matter versus student needs

We can view the various types of curriculum organization in American schools from two perspectives. One emphasizes the subject to be taught; the other emphasizes the student. The first perspective views curriculum as a body of content, or subject matter, that leads to certain achievement outcomes or products. The second defines curriculum in terms of student needs and attitudes; it is most concerned with process—in other words, how the student learns and the classroom or school climate. Few schools employ pure subject-centered (cognitive) or pure student-centered (psychological) approaches in the teaching–learning process. You will find that even though most teachers tend to emphasize one approach over the other, they incorporate both choices in the classroom.

■ Curriculum blends

Subject-Centered Curricula

■ Organization by subjects

Subject matter is both the oldest and most contemporary framework of curriculum organization. It is also the most common—primarily because it is convenient, as you can tell from the departmental structure of secondary schools and colleges. Even in elementary schools, where self-contained classrooms force the teachers to be generalists, curricula are usually organized by subjects.

■ Arguments pro and con

Proponents of **subject-centered curricula** argue that subjects present a logical basis for organizing and interpreting learning, that teachers are trained as subject-matter specialists, and that textbooks and other teaching materials are usually organized by subject. Critics claim that subject-centered curricula often are a mass of facts and concepts learned in isolation. They see this kind of curriculum as de-emphasizing life experiences and failing to consider the needs and interests of students. In subject-centered curricula, the critics argue, the teacher dominates the lesson, allowing little student input.

The following sections discuss several variations of subject-centered approaches to curricula, such as the subject-area approach, back-to-basics, and the core curriculum. These represent neither the only possible variations nor hard-and-fast categories. Many schools and teachers mix these approaches, drawing from more than one of them.

■ Drawing on the classical tradition

Subject-Area Approach to Curriculum. The subject-area approach is the most widely used form of curriculum organization. This long-standing approach has its roots in the seven liberal arts of classical Greece and Rome: grammar, rhetoric, dialectic, arithmetic, geometry, astronomy, and music. Modern subject-area curricula trace their origins to the work of William Harris, superintendent of the St. Louis school system in the 1870s. Steeped in the classical tradition, Harris established a subject orientation that has virtually dominated U.S. curricula from his day to the present. For example, consider Table 14.1, which shows the recommendations of the Committee of Fifteen in 1895. Although the committee's proposal is more than a century old, the subject categories are quite recognizable. As a student, you were most likely introduced to "algebra" and "English grammar," "reading" and "writing," as well as "geography" and "history."

| Table 14.1 | The Elementary School Curriculum Proposed by the Committee of Fifteen in 1895 | | | | | | | |

Branches	1st year	2nd year	3rd year	4th year	5th year	6th year	7th year	8th year
Reading	10 lessons a week		5 lessons a week					
Writing	10 lessons a week		5 lessons a week		3 lessons a week			
Spelling lists				4 lessons a week				
English grammar	Oral with composition lessons				5 lessons a week with textbook			
Latin								5 lessons a week
Arithmetic	Oral, 60 minutes a week		5 lessons a week with textbook					
Algebra							5 lessons a week	
Geography	Oral, 60 minutes a week		*5 lessons a week with textbook				3 lessons a week	
Natural science and hygiene	60 minutes a week							
U.S. history							5 lessons a week	
U.S. Constitution								*5 lessons a week
General history	Oral, 60 minutes a week							
Physical culture	60 minutes a week							
Vocal music	60 minutes a week divided into 4 lessons							
Drawing	60 minutes a week							
Manual training or sewing and cooking							One-half day each	
Total hours of recitation (reciting/answering questions	12	12	11	13	16¼	16¼	17½	17½

Questions

1 If your major is early childhood or elementary education, study the Committee of Fifteen's proposals for grades 1–5. How do the suggested subjects and their treatment compare with curriculum treatment you believe students should receive today? List specific additions and deletions.

2 If your major is secondary education, do the same as in question 1 for grades 6, 7, and 8. How do the committee's suggested subjects and treatment compare with the curriculum treatment you feel students should receive today? List specific additions and deletions.

3 Which theories of education described in the chapter on Philosophical Roots of Education best fit the Committee of Fifteen's proposals? What evidence in Table 14.1 supports your choice of theories?

*Begins in second half of year.

Source: Committee of Fifteen, "Report of the Sub-Committee on the Correlation of Studies in Elementary Education," *Educational Review* (March 1895), p. 284.

■ Categories of subjects

The modern **subject-area curriculum** treats each subject as a specialized and largely autonomous body of knowledge. Subjects referred to as the "basics" are considered essential for all students; these usually include the three Rs at the elementary level and English, history, science, and mathematics at the secondary level. Other specialized subjects develop knowledge and skills for particular vocations or professions—for example, business mathematics and physics. Finally, elective content affords the student optional offerings, often tailored to student interests and needs.

■ Exploratory subjects

A newer term, *exploratory subjects,* refers to subjects that students may choose from a list of courses designed to suit a wide range of learning styles, needs, and interests. These courses, which can include such subjects as study skills, computer science, creative writing, and drama, allow the school to diversify its offerings. They appear most often in middle school and late elementary school curricula.[2] Schools that include exploratory subjects in the curriculum tend to be more progressive in outlook than schools that still favor the traditional core academic subjects.

■ Perennialism: the best of the past

Perennialist and Essentialist Approaches to Curriculum. Two of the educational theories described in the chapter on Philosophical Roots of Education are fundamentally subject centered: perennialism and essentialism.[3] Believing that the main purpose of education is the cultivation of the intellect and of certain timeless values concerning work, morality, and family living, the perennialists concentrate their curriculum on the three Rs, Latin, and logic at the elementary level, adding study of the classics at the secondary level. The assumption of the **perennialist approach to curriculum,** according to Robert Hutchins, is that the best of the past—the so-called permanent studies, or classics—remains equally valid for the present.[4]

■ Essentialism: major disciplines, cultural literacy

Essentialists believe that the elementary curriculum should consist of the three Rs, and the high-school curriculum of five or six major disciplines: English (grammar, literature, and writing), mathematics, the sciences, history, foreign languages, and geography.[5] Adherents of the **essentialist approach to curriculum** believe these subject areas constitute the best way of systematizing and keeping up with today's explosion of knowledge. They argue that mere "basic" skills provide insufficient preparation for life. Students need an academic knowledge base—what they call "cultural literacy" or "essential knowledge"—to deal with new ideas and challenges.[6]

Standards & Assessment ☑
■ Rigorous intellectual training and grading

Essentialism shares with perennialism the notion that the curriculum should focus on rigorous intellectual training, a training possible only through the study of certain subjects. Both perennialists and essentialists advocate educational meritocracy.

---

[2]Allan C. Ornstein, *Middle and Secondary School Methods* (New York: Harper and Row, 1992); and Ed Brazee, "Exploratory Curriculum in the Middle School" (December 2000), ERIC Clearinghouse on Elementary and Early Childhood Education at **http://ericeece.org/pubs/ digests/2000/brazee00.html**.

[3]Theodore Brameld coined these two terms in *Patterns of Educational Philosophy* (New York: Holt, 1950).

[4]Robert M. Hutchins, *The Higher Learning in America* (New Haven, Conn.: Yale University Press, 1936). See also Allan Bloom, *The Closing of the American Mind* (New York: Simon and Schuster, 1987); and E. D. Hirsch, *Cultural Literacy: Rediscovering Knowledge in American Education* (Boston: Houghton Mifflin, 1987); Ediger Marlow, *Philosophy of Testing and Measurement* (Lawrence: University of Kansas Press, 2002).

[5]For classic statements of this approach, see Arthur Bestor, *The Restoration of Learning* (New York: Knopf, 1956); and James B. Conant, *The American High School Today* (New York: McGraw-Hill, 1959).

[6]See, for example, E. D. Hirsch, "The Core Knowledge Curriculum—What's Behind Its Success?" *Educational Leadership* (May 1993), pp. 23–25, 27–30; Norman Bauer, *Essential Schools and the Basics; Resisting Technocratic Rationality, 1993* (ERIC Document No. 356560); Michael E. Wonacett, "Postmodernism: Yes, No or Maybe? Myths and Realities" (Washington, D.C.: U.S. Office of Educational Research and Improvement, 2001).

They favor high academic standards and a rigorous system of grading and testing to help schools sort students by ability. Today, many parochial schools and academically oriented public schools stress various aspects of the perennialist and essentialist curricula.

■ Public opinion favoring "basics"

■ Stress on solid subjects

Back-to-Basics Approach to Curriculum. In recent years many educators and laypeople have called for a **back-to-basics curriculum.**[7] Like the essentialist curriculum approach, "back-to-basics" connotes a heavy emphasis on reading, writing, and mathematics. So-called solid subjects—English, history, science, and mathematics—are required in all grades, and the back-to-basics proponents are even more suspicious than the essentialists of attempts to expand the curriculum beyond this solid foundation. Critics of this approach worry that a focus on basics will suppress students' creativity and shortchange other domains of learning, encouraging conformity and dependence on authority.[8]

Standards & Assessment ✔

■ Standards and testing

Back-to-basics proponents insist on the need to maintain minimum standards, and much of the state school reform legislation passed in recent years reflects this popular position. The push for national tests in major subject areas and annual assessment of student progress in reading and math required by federal No Child Left Behind legislation further emphasize the importance of mastery of basic subjects. In most states, standardized tests serve a "gatekeeping" function at selected points on the educational ladder. Forty-nine states also require students to pass a statewide exit test before receiving a high-school diploma.[9] For more on state competency tests, see the Taking Issue box.

Core Approach to Curriculum. The importance of basic subjects in the curriculum is also expressed by the term *core curriculum.* Unfortunately, in the post–World War II era, this term has been used to describe two different approaches to organizing curricula.

■ The first core curriculum

The first approach, which we will call *core curriculum,* originated in the 1940s and 1950s and is popular again today, especially in middle schools. In this approach, students study two closely related subjects taught by the same instructor (for example, math and science, or English and social studies). The teacher organizes instructional units in an interdisciplinary manner, showing how diverse subjects relate to one another.[10] This approach, sometimes called block scheduling (a block of time for math and a block for science), is tied to a progressive theory of education.

■ The new core curriculum

The second approach, in contrast, was born out of the 1980s educational reform movement and reflects the more conservative theory of essentialism. In this version, which we will call the **new core curriculum (core subjects approach),** students experience a common body of required subjects—subjects that advocates con-

[7]See the annual Gallup Polls published in the September or October issues of *Phi Delta Kappan,* 1976 to 2003.
[8]David W. Jardina, "Back to Basics: Rethinking What Is Basic to Education," *Alberta Journal of Educational Research* (Summer 2001), pp. 187–190; Elliot W. Eisner, "What Really Counts in School," *Educational Leadership* (February 1991), pp. 10–17; and Mary Anna Dunn, "Staying the Course of Open Education," *Educational Leadership* (April 2000), pp. 20–24.
[9]Allan C. Ornstein, "National Reform and Instructional Accountability," *High School Journal* (October–November 1990), pp. 51–56; Jo Anne Natale, "Write This Down," *American School Board Journal* (December 1995), pp. 16–20; and Brenda Welburn, "Executive Summary," *State Education Standard* (Spring 2000), p. 5.
[10]Allan C. Ornstein and Francis Hunkins, *Curriculum: Foundations, Principles and Theory,* 2nd ed. (Boston: Allyn and Bacon, 1998), pp. 160–161; Thomas Fowler-Finn, "I Think, I Can," *American School Board Journal* (October 2000), pp. 36–39; E. D. Hirsch, "Not So Grand a Strategy," *Education Next* (Spring 2003), pp. 68–72.

taking issue

Question Should every state require students to pass a statewide competency test to receive a high-school diploma?

State Competency Tests for Students

One feature of the back-to-basics movement has been a rise in statewide testing of students. The failure of many students to master even the most basic skills, especially in reading, writing, mathematics, and history, has prompted state, and even federal, lawmakers to demand proof that schools are meeting minimum standards. As a teacher, you will almost certainly be involved in statewide testing of your students. All states now employ statewide testing at one or more stages in the educational process. Many states, in fact, have established minimum-competency tests that students must pass before graduating from high school.

Arguments PRO

1 Statewide testing for high-school graduation forces schools to improve their minimum standards. Students are no longer passed automatically through the system, and every student is taught the skills required for basic literacy.

2 The rise in minimum standards brought about by statewide testing is especially important for students from disadvantaged backgrounds. To break the cycle of poverty and joblessness, these students must be given the skills needed for productive employment.

3 Besides improving minimum standards, statewide testing helps to shift curriculum emphasis back to the basics. All of our students need a firmer grounding in such essential subjects as reading, writing, and mathematics.

4 Testing for graduation shows the public that schools are being held accountable for their performance. The test results help to identify schools that are not doing their jobs properly.

5 Using the data provided by statewide testing, educators can discover where the overall problems lie. Policies can be modified accordingly, and curricula can be designed to address the problem areas.

Arguments CON

1 Statewide testing is cumbersome, costly, and may not lead to much improvement in minimum standards. The effort must come from the local level, where educators know the strengths and weaknesses of their own schools.

2 Statewide tests discriminate against minorities and the urban and rural poor, who fail the tests in disproportionate numbers. This failure stigmatizes them unjustly and further damages their prospects for employment.

3 When schools try to focus on "basics," they often neglect other important elements of education, such as problem solving and creative thinking. These higher-order abilities are increasingly important in a technological society.

4 Test scores by themselves cannot identify ineffective schools, and it is dangerous to use them for that purpose. There are too many complicating factors, such as the students' home environment and socioeconomic background.

5 Most teachers already know where the problems lie. Moreover, soon after a statewide test is established, many teachers begin to "teach the test." Thus, the data obtained from such examinations become meaningless or misleading.

sider central to the education of all students.[11] Mortimer Adler is best known for popularizing this new core curriculum idea at the elementary-school level. Ernest

---

[11]Richard W. Riley, "World Class Standards: The Key to Educational Reform" (Washington, D.C.: Department of Education, 1993); and John I. Goodlad, "A New Look at an Old Idea: Core Curriculum," *Educational Leadership* (December 1986–January 1987), pp. 8–16.

Boyer, John Goodlad, and Theodore Sizer are best known for their similar influence on high schools.[12]

■ Expanding the core units

Both Boyer and Sizer emphasize the humanities, communication and language skills, science, math, and technology. Boyer believes that the core units required for graduation should be expanded from one-half of the total curriculum (now the norm) to about two-thirds. Goodlad would like to see about 80 percent of the curriculum devoted to core courses, with only 20 percent reserved for the development of individual talents and interests.[13]

■ Stiffer requirements

The proponents of a new core curriculum have helped make subject-matter requirement changes in districts nationwide that you may have noticed as a student.[14] Those changes are summarized in Figure 14.1. In the decades after 1982, the percentage of high-school graduates who completed a basic curriculum in core subjects increased from 14 percent to more than 44 percent.[15]

■ Critiques of new core curriculum

The new core curriculum approach has drawn criticisms similar to those aimed at the back-to-basics curriculum. It may be argued that the new core curriculum turns the clock back to 1900, when subject-matter emphasis and academic rigor were the order of the day. These days, more students are college bound, and for them the academic core courses may be appropriate; yet increasing numbers of students are graduating from our schools as functional illiterates. To have value for all students, a core curriculum should take into account diverse populations of students, their individual differences and their career preferences.

Student-Centered Curricula

■ Emphasizing student needs

In direct contrast to subject-centered curricula, **student-centered curricula** of various types emphasize student interests and needs, including the affective aspects of learning. At its extreme, the student-centered approach is rooted in the philosophy of Jean Jacques Rousseau, who encouraged childhood self-expression. Implicit in Rousseau's philosophy is the necessity of leaving the children to their own devices, allowing them the creativity and freedom essential for growth.

■ Influence of progressivism

Progressive education gave impetus to student-centered curricula. Progressive educators believed that when the interests and needs of learners were incorporated into the curriculum, students would be intrinsically motivated and learning would be more successful. This does not mean that students' whims or passing fads should dictate the curriculum. However, one criticism of student-centered curricula is that they sometimes overlook important cognitive content.

■ Dewey's call for balance

John Dewey, a chief advocate of student-centered curricula, attempted to establish a curriculum that balanced subject matter with student interests and needs. As early as 1902, he pointed out the fallacies of either extreme. The learner was neither

---

[12]Ernest L. Boyer, *High School* (New York: Harper and Row, 1983); Theodore R. Sizer, *Horace's Compromise: The Dilemma of the American High School,* rev. ed. (Boston: Houghton Mifflin, 1985); and Joseph Creech, *High School Graduation Standards: What We Expect and What We Get* (Atlanta: Southern Regional Educational Board, 1996).

[13]Boyer, *High School;* Sizer, *Horace's Compromise;* John I. Goodlad, *A Place Called School* (New York: McGraw-Hill, 1984); and Ernest L. Boyer, *The Basic School: A Community of Learning* (Princeton: Carnegie Foundation, 1995).

[14]*Digest of Education Statistics, 2002* (Washington, D.C.: U.S. Government Printing Office, 2002), Table 142.

[15]"By the Numbers—Key Subjects," *Education Week,* June 14, 1995, p. 4; and *Digest of Education Statistics, 2000,* Table 141.

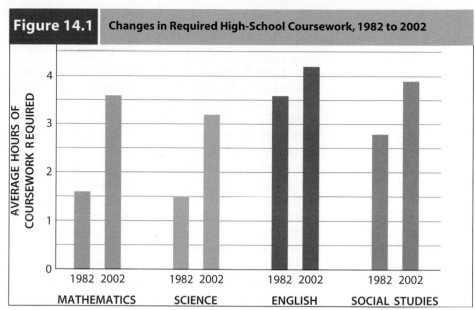

Figure 14.1 | **Changes in Required High-School Coursework, 1982 to 2002**

Source: The Condition of Education 1987 (Washington, D.C.: U.S. Government Printing Office, 1987), Table 1.37B, p. 84; and *Digest of Education Statistics, 2002* (Washington, D.C.: U.S. Government Printing Office, 2000), Table 139.

"a docile recipient of facts" nor "the starting point, the center, and the end" of school activity.[16] Dewey tried to emphasize the need for balance.

There are at least five major approaches to organizing student-centered curricula: activity-centered approaches, relevant curriculum, the humanistic approach, alternative or free schools, and values-centered curricula.

■ Lifelike, purposeful activities

Activity-Centered Approaches. The movement for an **activity-centered curriculum** has strongly affected the public elementary schools. William Kilpatrick, one of Dewey's colleagues, was an early leader. In contrast to Dewey, Kilpatrick believed that teachers could not anticipate the interests and needs of children, which made any preplanned curriculum impossible. Thus he attacked the typical school curriculum as unrelated to the problems of real life. Instead, he advocated purposeful activities as relevant and lifelike as possible and tied to a student's needs and interests,[17] such as group games, dramatizations, story projects, field trips, social enterprises, and interest centers. All of these facets of the activity-centered curriculum involved problem solving and active student participation. They also emphasized socialization and the formation of stronger school–community ties. Thus, they have relevance even today.

■ Constructivism

The recent development of *constructivist learning theory,* described in the chapter on Philosophical Roots of Education, draws on these and similar concepts.

---

[16]John Dewey, *The Child and the Curriculum* (Chicago: University of Chicago Press, 1902), pp. 8–9; George Debore, "Student-Centered Teaching in a Standards-Based World: Finding a Sensible Balance," *Science and Education* (July 2002), pp. 405–417; Violet R. Harade, "Building a Learning Community: Students and Adults as Inquirers," *Childhood Education* (Winter 2002–2003), pp. 66–71; William J. Reese, "The Origins of Progressive Education," *History of Education Quarterly* (Spring 2001), pp. 1–24.

[17]William H. Kilpatrick, "The Project Method," *Teachers College Record* (September 1918), pp. 319–335.

Constructivists favor an activity-centered curriculum in which students actively (mentally and physically) interact with knowledge and each other to construct meaning and new knowledge for themselves.[18]

Relevant Curriculum. By the 1930s, some reformers complained that the traditional school curriculum had become irrelevant: it had failed to adjust to social change and therefore emphasized skills and knowledge not pertinent to modern society. The 1960s and 1970s saw a renewed concern for a **relevant curriculum**, but with a somewhat different emphasis. Critics expressed less concern that the curriculum reflect changing social conditions and more concern that the curriculum be relevant to the students' personal needs and interests.

■ Requirements for a relevant curriculum

Proponents of this approach today suggest that educators (1) individualize instruction through such teaching methods as independent inquiry and special projects; (2) revise existing courses and develop new courses on such topics of student concern as environmental protection, drug addiction, urban problems, and cultural pluralism; (3) provide educational alternatives (such as electives, minicourses, and open classrooms) that allow more freedom of choice; and (4) extend the curriculum beyond the school's walls, through such means as distance learning (described in more detail later in this chapter).[19]

■ Psychological foundation

Humanistic Approach to Curriculum. A **humanistic approach to curriculum** emphasizes affective, attitudinal or emotional, in addition to cognitive outcomes. Such a curriculum draws heavily on the work of psychologists Abraham Maslow and Carl Rogers.[20] Advocates of humanistic education contend that the present school curriculum has failed miserably, that teachers and schools are determined to stress cognitive behaviors and to control students *not* for students' good but for the good of adults. Humanists emphasize more than affective processes; they seek higher

■ Higher domains of consciousness

domains of spirit, consciousness, aesthetics, and morality.[21] They stress more meaningful relationships between students and teachers; student independence and self-direction; and greater acceptance of self and others. Your role in teaching from a humanist approach would be to help learners cope with their psychological needs and problems and to facilitate self-understanding among students.

■ Freedom for students

Alternative or Free Schools Programs. Today, you are likely to find student-centered curriculum programs in **alternative** or **free schools**, often private or experimental institutions, some organized by parents and teachers dissatisfied with the public schools. These schools typically feature much student freedom, noisy

---

[18]Lois T. Stover, Gloria A. Neubert, and James C. Lawlor, *Creating Interactive Environments in the Secondary School* (Washington, D.C.: National Education Association, 1993), pp. 20–23; and Ina Claire Gabler, *Constructivist Methods for the Secondary Classroom: Engaged Minds* (ED 471198).

[19]Velma Menchase "Providing a Culturally Relevant Curriculum for Hispanic Children," *Multicultural Education* (Spring 2001), pp. 18–20. Michael W. Apple and Linda Christian-Smith, *The Politics of the Textbook* (New York: Routledge, 1991); and Arthur Powell, Eleanor Farrar, and David Cohen, *The Shopping Mall High School* (Boston: Houghton Mifflin, 1985).

[20]Abraham H. Maslow, *Toward a Psychology of Being* (New York: Van Nostrand Reinhold, 1962); Abraham H. Maslow, *Motivation and Personality,* 2nd ed. (New York: Harper and Row, 1970); and Carl Rogers, *Freedom to Learn,* 2nd ed. (Columbus, Ohio: Merrill, 1983).

[21]Elliot Eisner, *The Educational Imagination,* 3rd ed. (New York: Macmillan, 1993); John Miller, *The Holistic Curriculum: Revised and Expanded Edition* (Ontario: OISE Press, 1996); and Carol Witherell and Nel Noddings, *The Challenge to Care in Schools* (New York: Teachers College Press, 1992). See Paul Freire, *Pedagogy of the Oppressed* (New York: Herder and Herder, 1970); Henry A. Giroux, *Teachers as Intellectuals* (Granby, Mass.: Bergin and Garvey, 1988); Ivan Illich, *Deschooling Society* (New York: Harper and Row, 1971); Jonathan Kozol, *Free Schools* (Boston: Houghton Mifflin, 1972); and Jonathan Kozol, *Savage Inequalities: Children in America's Schools* (New York: Crown, 1991).

classrooms, and a learning environment, often unstructured, where students are free to explore their interests. Most are considered radical and antiestablishment, even though many of their ideas are rooted in the well-known student-centered doctrines of progressivism.

▪ Controversy about free schools

Paul Freire, Henry Giroux, Ivan Illich, Herbert Kohl, and Jonathan Kozol have stressed the need for, and in many cases have established, student-centered alternative or free schools.[22] Critics, however, condemn these schools as places where little cognitive learning takes place and that provide little discipline and order. Proponents counter that children do learn in student-centered alternative schools, which—instead of stressing conformity—are made to fit the students.

▪ Public alternative schools

A second type of alternative school is that which public-school systems run for students who experience persistent discipline problems (and who often also have learning problems). These schools start from the premise that schools must change to provide a more flexible approach to learning. They generally stress greater collaboration among staff members and between staff and students in terms of both curriculum and instructional methods. Many schools that have developed highly creative approaches are among the best examples of *restructured schools* in the country—that is, schools reorganized around improved student achievement, effective teaching, and improved school organization.[23] (See the chapter on School Effectiveness and Reform in the United States for further discussion of restructuring.)

▪ Restructuring

▪ Value confusion

Values-Centered Curriculum. A **values-centered curriculum**—more popularly known as *character education*—places special emphasis on moral and ethical issues. For example, advocates of multicultural education stress not only knowledge of American society's diverse cultures and ethnic experiences, but also appreciation and respect for cultures other than one's own. Thus, multicultural education fits into a values-centered curriculum. Even more fundamentally, some educators, parents, and community members have concluded that too many students lack a strong sense of right and wrong. It is up to the schools, these people argue, to teach such basic values as honesty, responsibility, courtesy, self-discipline, compassion, tolerance, and respect for the rights of others.[24]

▪ Multiculturalism and values

▪ Sense of right and wrong

▪ No quick fix

Kevin Ryan, director of the Center for the Advancement of Ethics and Character, says that the school curriculum, now increasingly devoid of moral authority and ethical language, has become sterile and meaningless. Ryan warns, however, that character education requires more than a quick-fix approach. Educators and their communities must define character education clearly and make it a focal point of the school's mission, finding a common ground of civic values that do not transgress upon religious and family values.[25]

---

[22]See, for instance, Diane Ravitch, *The Troubled Crusade* (New York: Basic Books, 1983); and Frank Smith, *To Think* (New York: Teachers College Press, 1990); Camilla A. Lehr, "Alternative Schools Serving Teachers With and Without Disabilities: What Are the Current Issues and Challenges?" *Preventing School Failure* (Winter 2003), pp. 59–65; Ron Miller, "John Holt: His Prophetic Voice," *Education Revolution* (Autumn 2002), pp. 28–33.

[23]Robin Ann Martin, *Alternatives in Education: An Exploration of Learner-Centered Progressive and Holistic Education*, 2002 (ED 466453).

[24]See, for example, Task Force on Values Education and Ethical Behavior, *How to Establish a Values Education Program in Your School* (Towson, Md.: Baltimore County Public Schools, 1991); and Linda Inlay, "Values: The Implicit Curriculum," *Educational Leadership* (March 2003), pp. 69–71.

[25]Tom Erb, "Nurturing Good People: The Editor Reflects," *Middle School Journal* (September 2002), pp. 1–4; Linda Darling, "The Essential Moral Dimensions of Citizenship Education: What Should We Teach?" *Journal of Educational Thought* (December 2002), pp. 229–247. Kevin Ryan, "Character and Coffee Mugs," *Education Week*, May 17, 1995, pp. 37, 48.

■ What values should we teach?

One potential drawback to values-centered curricula, like humanistic curricula, is a lack of attention to cognitive learning. Even more important, educators and community members rarely concur about which values to teach or how to teach them. In such controversial areas as sex, religion, and social justice, values education may become a minefield. The In This Case feature shows educators' concerns about including values in the curriculum.

■ Finding a consensus

Despite these problems, many educators contend that it is possible—even with our multicultural, multireligious population—to establish a set of values that represent an American consensus.[26] Table 14.2, for example, lists a "common core of values" developed by the school system in Baltimore County, Maryland. These values are emphasized throughout the curriculum, especially in social studies and English. Although the exact definitions of concepts such as "freedoms," "patriotism," and "tolerance" may be hard to determine, many educators believe that finding such a common core is an urgent responsibility of American schools.

Curriculum Contrasts: An Overview

■ Influence of school philosophy

As we noted earlier, subject-centered and student-centered curricula represent extremes on a continuum. You will find that most schooling in the United States falls somewhere between the two—keeping a tenuous balance between subject matter and student needs, between the cognitive and affective dimensions of students' development.

Decisions about what you should teach and how your teaching curriculum is organized will be influenced by the philosophical orientation of your school system or school. More traditional schools that subscribe to a perennialist or essentialist philosophy generally lean toward a subject-centered curriculum. Schools oriented more toward progressive or reconstructionist education tend to use a student-centered approach. Overview 14.1 summarizes the various subject-centered and student-

Table 14.2	A "Common Core of Values," as Defined by the Baltimore County (Md.) Public Schools	
Compassion	Reasoned argument	Justice
Due process procedures	Responsibility	Loyalty
Freedoms	Tolerance	Rational consent
Human worth and dignity	Courtesy	Respect for rights of others
Knowledge	Critical inquiry	Responsible citizenship
Patriotism	Honesty	Peaceful resolution of conflict

Questions
1. Which of the core values in Table 14.2 do you consider most important and why?
2. What core values would you add to Table 14.2?

Source: Task Force on Values Education and Ethical Behavior, *1984 and Beyond: A Reaffirmation of Values* (Towson, Md.: Baltimore County Public Schools, 1994).

[26]Ibid., pp. 37, 48; Kenneth Godwin, Carrie Ausbrooks, and Valerie Martinez, "Teaching Tolerance in Public and Private Schools," *Phi Delta Kappan* (March 2001), pp. 542–546; and Thomas Lasley, "The Missing Ingredient in Character Education," *Phi Delta Kappan* (April 1997), pp. 654–655.

IN THIS CASE

Curriculum Choices

Sandra Helenski is just one of several beginning teachers at Winkler Junior High. Bobby Owens and Laura Rittilini are also new to Winker Junior High and the profession. All are assigned to teach seventh-grade students. Sandra teaches English, Bobby teaches life science, and Laura teaches band. All would say they teach students first and the subject second.

Discussion in the teachers' lounge is warming up today as they debate a few of their concerns with the most experienced teachers at Winkler—also known as the "old-timers."

Mrs. Whipper, one of the old-timers, says, "I don't see how you can teach values if you want them to pass the state exam next March. You have to stay focused on the basics—the test content. If you want to last a few years here, I think you should stick to making sure your students can write correctly and read well. Also, you have to be very careful: Are you sure you know the values of the community or of the parents? If you teach tolerance of diversity that includes gays and lesbians, many conservative religious parents won't be happy. It's all too easy to be misunderstood and to step on someone's toes."

"But, when I have a perfectly good opportunity to use student needs and interests in teaching concepts in the state curricula that relate to values, perhaps through special projects or book assignments, why shouldn't I do that?" responds Sandra. "For example, why can't students learn to search for and evaluate authors' statements about honesty just as easily as they can learn to search for and evaluate metaphors?"

"I'm including some activities that emphasize respect for the environment," said Bobby. "Students will test water and take air samples near the county landfill. They'll analyze their lab results in teams and send reports to the county commissioners. Certainly we can include values with this approach." He turned to the old-timers. "What do you think?"

A more experienced teacher responded, "Well, I would be sure that my time was wisely used. That sort of activity can get away from you, and before you know it, March is here and your students aren't ready for the state exam. So, just be careful in how you plan and implement your ideas."

Laura chimed in with her observation that the skills, knowledge, and dispositions of each band member were important to her. She wanted to be sure that each student valued being part of a team and also valued the discipline and hard work it took from all members to form a championship band. "Certainly," she said, "each of us in our own way is teaching values anyway. Perhaps we need to reflect on what values we teach just doing everyday things."

Questions

1. What do all three new teachers hold in common? What kinds of curriculum organization are really under discussion here?

2. How do you react to the experienced teachers' comments to Sandra? How would you reply?

3. What curriculum approach do you favor? Why?

4. Do you agree with Laura's comment that all teachers teach values? How do you expect the experienced teachers to react to Laura's comment?

centered approaches to curricula and their corresponding philosophies, content emphases, and instructional emphases. As you begin to think seriously about in which district and school you want to teach, consider asking interviewers questions about curricular organization to ensure a "fit" between your philosophy and that of the district or school. In the next section, we move on to the curriculum development process and the main issues it raises.

OVERVIEW 14.1   *Curriculum Organization Approaches*

Curriculum Approach	Corresponding Philosophy or Theory	Content Emphasis	Instructional Emphasis
Subject-Centered			
Subject-area	Perennialism, essentialism	Three Rs; academic, vocational, and elective subjects	Knowledge, concepts, and principles; specialized knowledge
Perennialist	Perennialism	Three Rs; liberal arts; classics; timeless values; academic rigor	Rote memorization; specialized knowledge; mental discipline
Essentialist	Essentialism	Three Rs; liberal arts and science; academic disciplines; academic excellence	Concepts and principles; problem solving; essential skills
Back-to-basics	Essentialism	Three Rs; academic subjects	Specific knowledge and skills; drill; attainment of measurable ends or competencies
New core curriculum (core subjects)	Perennialism, essentialism	Common curriculum for all students; focus on academics	Common knowledge; intellectual skills and concepts; values and moral issues
Student-Centered			
Activity-centered	Progressivism	Student needs and interests; student activities; school–community activities	Active, experimental environment; project methods; effective living
Relevant	Progressivism, social reconstructionism	Student experiences and activities; felt needs	Social and personal problems; reflective thinking
Humanistic	Progressivism, social reconstructionism, existentialism	Introspection; choice; affective processes	Individual and group learning; flexible, artistic, psychological methods; self-realization
Alternative or free schools	Progressivism	Student needs and interests; student experiences	Play oriented; creative expression; free learning environment
Values-centered (character education)	Social reconstructionism, existentialism	Democratic values; ethical and moral values; cross-cultural and universal values; choice and freedom	Feelings, attitudes, and emotions; existentialist thinking; decision making

REFOCUS   One of the questions at the beginning of the chapter asked you to focus on how curriculum content reflects changes in society. Which societal changes do you believe have been most important in driving curriculum emphases? In your opinion, which social changes *should* be most important? Why?

▶ Issues in Curriculum Development

■ Curriculum at national and state levels

■ Curriculum at the local level

.

Standards & Assessment ☑

■ Influence of textbooks

■ Limitations of textbooks

Whether the curriculum is subject centered or student centered, the process of developing it involves (1) assessing learners' needs and capabilities (including those of culturally diverse populations, learners with disabilities, gifted and talented students, college-bound students, and those who wish to enter the work force) and (2) selecting or creating the instructional materials and activities.

At the national level, curriculum making is minimal and indirect, despite recent work on national goals, standards, and assessment. Curriculum development at the state level varies from state to state. Some state departments of education limit their involvement to publishing curriculum guides and booklets. These are prepared by a professional staff in the state department of education, assisted by curriculum consultants and college professors. State publications tend to focus on large-scale concerns such as the need for stronger math and science curricula. In many states, however, the guidelines are more specific, including lists of "core learning goals" and instructional materials either mandated or recommended or in some cases forbidden.

The greatest responsibility for curriculum development generally falls on the local school district—or, as school-based management becomes more widespread, on the schools themselves. Large school districts often employ personnel who specialize in curriculum development, including subject-matter specialists and test consultants. Smaller school districts generally assign curriculum development to a group of teachers organized by subject or grade level; sometimes parents, administrators, and even students participate.

College admission standards exert a strong influence on curriculum choices. Increasingly, too, local curriculum developers must pay close attention to state standards and academic requirements (including voluntary national standards).

Another major influence on curriculum—one whose importance is often underrated—is the textbook. Textbooks have long been the most frequently used instructional medium at all levels beyond the primary grades. As such, they can dominate the nature and sequence of a course and profoundly affect students' learning experiences. Because courses often reflect the textbook author's knowledge and biases, curriculum developers may shape the entire course just by choosing the textbook. For this reason, it is important for you to understand factors that govern textbook writing and publication.

In order to have wide application and a large potential market, textbooks tend to be general, noncontroversial, and bland. Because they are usually written for a national audience, they disregard local issues or community problems. Aiming for the greatest number of "average" students, they may fail to meet the needs and interests of any particular group or individual.[27] In summarizing large quantities of data, they may become superficial and discourage conceptual thinking, critical analysis, and evaluation. Furthermore, with the possible exception of mathematics textbooks, most quickly become outdated. Because they are expensive, however, they often are used long after they should have been replaced.

---

[27]Allan C. Ornstein, "Textbook Instruction: Processes and Strategies," *NASSP Bulletin* (December 1989), pp. 105–111; Jess E. House "Leverage on Learning: Test Scores, Textbooks and Publishers," *Phi Delta Kappan* (March 2003), pp. 537–541; and William Evers, "The Least Common Denominator," *Education Next* (Spring 2003), pp. 73–75.

Standards & Assessment ✓

■ Advantages of textbooks

Considering these criticisms, why do teachers rely so heavily on textbooks? The answer is that textbooks also have many advantages. A textbook provides teachers with an outline for planning lessons; summarizes a great deal of pertinent information; enables the student to take home most of the course material in a convenient package; provides a common resource for all students to follow; includes pictures, graphs, maps, and other illustrative material that facilitate understanding; and frequently includes other teaching aids, such as summaries and review questions.[28] Furthermore, textbook authors and publishers are increasing efforts to create materials that help teachers reach state standards. In short, the textbook is an acceptable tool if selected and used properly. However, it should not be the only source of knowledge for students, and it should not define the entire curriculum.

■ Censorship trends

Another issue in curriculum development is the question of censorship. In states that prepare lists of instructional materials for their schools, the trend is growing to "limit what students shall read." As the chapter on Governing and Administering Public Education indicated, the list of objectionable works has sometimes included such classics as *Little Red Riding Hood* and *Huckleberry Finn*. Today, almost any instructional material that contains political or economic messages, obscenity, sex, nudity, profanity, slang or questionable English, ethnic or racially sensitive material, or any material that could be interpreted as antifamily, antireligious, or anti-American is subject to possible censorship. Additionally, the use of commercial videos and unsupervised Internet access, as discussed in the Technology @ School box, is of much concern to teachers and parents.[29]

■ Subtle censorship

Although censorship is often overt, it can operate in subtle ways as well. Curriculum developers may quietly steer away from issues and materials that would cause controversy in the community. Moreover, textbooks often omit topics that might upset potential audiences or interest groups. Even pictures are important; some organizations count the number of pictures of one ethnic group versus another group, of boys versus girls, of business versus labor. Professional associations can also exert a type of censorship when they recommend certain changes in subject content and implicitly discourage other approaches. Educators must be sensitive to censorship because it is always present in one form or another. In dealing with such issues, we often find that Herbert Spencer's fundamental question "What knowledge is of most worth?" becomes "Whose knowledge is of most worth?"[30]

As teaching becomes more professionalized, teachers are increasingly expected to deal with curriculum choices and the complex issues they present. To avoid letting curriculum become "a political football," as Michael Apple terms it,[31] you will need a full understanding of community concerns, statewide standards and goals, and student needs.

---

[28]Allan C. Ornstein, "The Textbook-Driven Curriculum," *Peabody Journal of Education* (Spring 1994), pp. 70–85; search at **www.rethinkingschools.org/** for "Reading, Writing and Censorship" by Barbara Miner; Mitzi Lewison et al., "Dangerous Discourses: Using Controversial Books to Support Engagement, Diversity and Democracy," *New Advocate* (Summer 2002), pp. 215–226.

[29]Steven C. Schlozman, "To View or Not to View," *Educational Leadership* (December 2002), pp. 87–88; Jerry M. Weiss, "Rumbles, Bangs, Crashes! The Roar of Censorship," *ALAN Review* (Spring–Summer 2002), pp. 54–57. See also "Censorship and Challenges," American Library Association, January 29, 2001, at **www.ala.org/alaorg/oif/censors.html**.

[30]Joan Del Fattore, *What Johnny Shouldn't Read: Textbook Censorship in America* (New Haven: Yale University Press, 1992).

[31]Michael Apple, "Is There a Curriculum Voice to Reclaim?" *Phi Delta Kappan* (March 1990), pp. 526–530; Robert Seney, "The Challenge of 'Challenged' Books," *Gifted Child Today* (Spring 2002), pp. 28–32.

Protecting Students from Undesirable Material on the Web

Educators and parents alike agree that adult supervision of students' Web site selections, both at home and at school (a form of censorship), is critical. As a teacher, you need to educate your students about responsible online behavior and safety issues. An excellent Web site for this is Media Awareness Network at **www.media-awareness.ca/english/teachers/ wa_teachers/index.cfm**; scroll down to "Safe Passage." This site alerts teachers and students to safety issues associated with Web sites, chat rooms, newsgroups, instant messaging, and e-mail. It includes information on the benefits and risks of these activities and offers practical advice on how you can ensure that your students have safe and rewarding experiences. The site includes a button for parents with much the same information.

In addition to informing students about Internet safety, media awareness groups suggest other measures to ensure that students avoid exposure to inappropriate material online. To begin with, ask your students to sign contracts regarding appropriate Internet behavior. You should also occasionally monitor the sites they visit. The Media Awareness Network suggests easy ways to find out what Web sites your students have visited in an article called "Tracking Where Kids Have Been Online." (See **www.media-awareness.ca/ english/resources/special_initiatives/wa_resources/wa_shared/backgrounders/ tracking_kids_online.cfm**.)

If you find that students are distracted by visiting irrelevant or inappropriate Web sites at school, you can use technology to limit their choices. WebWhacker, a commercial program, lets you download Web sites to your class computers and use the sites without an Internet connection (see **www.bluesquirrel.com/products/whee/**). Because the computers are not actually connected to the Internet, this program permits 100 percent control over Web content viewed by children.

Another excellent tool for teachers is the EduHound HotList, which permits teachers (and parents) to create their own Web page of educational resources composed of educational links, questions, directions, explanations, and assignments. HotLists are passwords protected to ensure privacy and security, and a teacher can develop, free of charge, as many HotLists as he or she wishes (see **www.eduhound.com/hotlist/default.cfm**).

The approaches suggested above help teachers and parents ensure that their children spend productive learning time on the Internet, avoid inappropriate and undesirable material, and remain safe from those who would prey on children.

 How will you, as a teacher, respond if you feel pressured to censor materials or to follow a textbook-defined curriculum?

▶ Instructional Approaches

■ Interrelationship of curriculum and instruction

Although educators differ in the definition of curriculum, most recognize that curriculum and instruction are interrelated. To carry out the curriculum, one must rely on instruction—programs, materials, and methods. Even more than with curriculum approaches, most teachers incorporate a variety of instructional strategies in their classes. The search for new programs and methods of instruction is continual. The past four decades, in particular, have witnessed a major effort to improve learning outcomes, integrate technology into the lesson, and have students participate firsthand with the new tools of instruction.

Although we cannot survey all the major instructional innovations, the following sections describe several that have drawn considerable attention from educators. The chapter on School Effectiveness and Reform in the United States treats the subject of instructional approaches in the context of school reform and school effectiveness.

Individualized Instruction

In recent decades, several models have been advanced for **individualized instruction**. Although these approaches vary, they all try to provide a one-to-one student–teacher or student–computer relationship. Students proceed at their own rate with carefully sequenced and structured instructional materials, and usually with an emphasis on practice and drill.

▪ IPI

One of the early examples, the Individually Prescribed Instruction (IPI) project, was developed at the University of Pittsburgh in the late 1950s and early 1960s.[32] Teachers prepared an individual plan for every student, based on a diagnosis of the student's needs in each skill or subject. Students worked toward specific proficiency levels. Objectives were stated in behavioral terms. Teachers gave students individualized learning tasks and continually evaluated their progress.

▪ Significant gains reported

Field testing of individualized instruction programs has generally been positive. Reports on IPI and other approaches have shown significant gains in student achievement. Adaptive instruction, adjusted to students' individual strengths and weaknesses, seems to benefit all kinds of students, especially low-achieving ones or students with mild disabilities.[33] Nevertheless, most schools today continue to employ group methods of instruction and group expectations. Schools often consider individualized plans too expensive to implement because of the costs of materials and one-to-one teacher–student relationships.

Cooperative Learning

▪ Competition versus cooperation

Cooperative rather than competitive learning is also gaining acceptance as an important way to instruct students. In the traditional classroom structure, students compete for teacher recognition and grades. The same students tend to be "winners" and "losers" over the years because of differences in ability and achievement. High-achieving students continually receive rewards and are motivated to learn, whereas low-achieving students continually experience failure (or near failure) and frustration. The idea of **cooperative learning** is to change the traditional structure by reducing competition and increasing cooperation among students, thus diminishing possible hostility and tension among students and raising the academic achievement of all.

▪ Benefits of competition

This does not mean that competition has no place in the classroom or school. Under the right conditions, competition can be a source of fun, excitement, and motivation. The chief advocates of cooperation tell us that competition can be used

---

[32]Robert Glaser and Lauren B. Resnick, "Instructional Psychology," *Annual Review of Psychology* (no. 23, 1972), pp. 207–276.
[33]Mary Anna Dunn, "Staying the Course of Open Education," *Educational Leadership* (April 2000), pp. 20–24; William Malloy, *Inclusion: An Educational Reform Strategy for All Children* (ERIC Document 379856, 1994); and Laura M. Stough, "Special Thinking in Special Settings: A Qualitative Study of Expert Educators," *Journal of Special Education* (Winter 2003), pp. 206–222; Jillian Leaderhouse, "The Power of One-on-One," *Educational Leadership* (April 2003), pp. 69–71.

Cooperative learning offers students new chances to experience success in school and helps them develop a range of interpersonal and individual skills. *(Bob Daemmrich/The Image Works)*

successfully to improve performance on simple drill activities and speed-related tasks (such as spelling, vocabulary, and simple math computations), in low-anxiety games and on the athletic field.[34]

■ Benefits of cooperation

In cooperative learning, however, competition takes second place. According to a review of the research, cooperation among participants helps build (1) positive and coherent personal identity, (2) self-actualization and mental health, (3) knowledge and trust of one another, (4) communication with one another, (5) acceptance and support of one another, and (6) wholesome relationships with a reduced amount of conflict. The data also suggest that cooperation and group learning are

[34]David W. Johnson and Roger T. Johnson, *Learning Together and Alone: Cooperative, Competitive, and Individualistic Learning,* 4th ed. (Needham Heights, Mass.: Allyn and Bacon, 1999); see the University of Minnesota Cooperative Learning Center at **www.clcrc.com/**: click on "Cooperative Learning"; and Robert E. Slavin, *School and Classroom Organization* (Hillsdale, N.J.: Erlbaum, 1988); Richard H. Priest and Donna R. Sterling, "Team Science" (April 2003), pp. 38–40.

■ STAD

considerably more effective in fostering these social and interpersonal skills than are competitive or individualistic efforts.[35]

Of all the cooperative instructional arrangements, the two developed by Robert Slavin are most popular: Student-Teams Achievement Divisions (STAD) and Team-Assisted Individualization (TAI). Both methods have increased student achievement when the proper procedures have been followed.[36] In STAD, teams are composed of four or five members, preferably four (an arrangement that contradicts other research indicating that groups of four tend to pair off). Teams are balanced by ability, gender, and ethnicity. Team members provide assistance and feedback to each other and receive a group performance score on quizzes. They also receive recognition via bulletin boards, certificates, special activities and privileges, and letters to parents. The teams are changed every five or six weeks to give students an opportunity to work with others and to give members of low-scoring teams a new chance.[37]

Standards & Assessment ☑
■ TAI

The TAI approach puts more emphasis on mastery of particular skill sheets and on individual diagnosis through pre- and post-testing. Students first work on their own skill sheets and then have their partners or team members check their answers and provide assistance. Not until the student scores 80 percent or higher on a practice quiz is the student certified by the team to take the final test. Teams are scored and recognized in the same way as with STAD, but criteria are established for "superteams" (high performance), "great teams" (moderate performance), and "good teams" (minimum passing grade). Every day the teacher spends five to fifteen minutes of the forty-five-minute lesson period with two or three groups at about the same point in the curriculum. The other teams work on their own during this time.[38]

Mastery Instruction

Mastery instruction is an instructional plan for all grade levels and subjects. The approach most widely used in public schools is the Learning for Mastery (LFM) model, often referred to as mastery learning. Mastery learning has gained supporters, particularly in urban school districts that have an obvious and urgent need to improve academic performance.[39]

[35]Robert E. Slavin, *Cooperative Learning: Theory, Research, and Practice* (Boston: Allyn and Bacon, 1995); Robert J. Stevens and Robert E. Slavin, "Effects of a Cooperative Learning Approach in Reading and Writing on Academically Handicapped and Nonhandicapped Students," *Elementary School Journal* (January 1995), pp. 241–262; Robert Slavin, "Cooperative Learning and Intergroup Relations" (ERIC Document Number 382730, 1995) and David W. Johnson and Roger T. Johnson, "Making Cooperative Learning Work," *Theory into Practice* (Spring 1999), pp. 67–73; Sandra Pratt, "Cooperative Learning Strategies," *Science Teacher* (April 2003), pp. 25–29.
[36]Robert E. Slavin, "When Does Cooperative Learning Increase Student Achievement?" *Psychological Bulletin* (November 1983), pp. 429–445; Robert E. Slavin, "Synthesis of Research on Cooperative Learning," *Educational Leadership* (February 1991), pp. 71–82; Robyn Gilles, "The Behaviors, Interactions and Perceptions of Junior High School Students during Small Group Learning," *Journal of Educational Psychology* (March 2003), pp. 137–147.
[37]Robert E. Slavin, *Using Student Team Learning,* 3rd ed. (Baltimore: Johns Hopkins University Press, 1986).
[38]Thomas R. Guskey, "Benjamin Bloom's Contributions to Curriculum, Instruction and School Learning," 2001 (ED 457185); Thomas L. Good and Jere E. Brophy, *Looking in Classrooms,* 5th ed. (New York: HarperCollins, 1997); and Robert E. Slavin, "Team-Assisted Individualization: Combining Cooperative Learning and Individualized Instruction in Mathematics," in R. E. Slavin, ed., *Learning to Cooperate, Cooperating to Learn* (New York: Plenum, 1985), pp. 177–209.
[39]John B. Carroll, "The Carroll Model: A 25-Year Retrospective and Prospective View," *Educational Researcher* (January–February 1989), pp. 26–31.

Mastery approaches are based on the central argument that nearly all public-school students can learn much of the curriculum at practically the same level of mastery. Although slower students require a longer time to learn the same materials, they can succeed if their initial level of knowledge is correctly diagnosed and if they are taught with appropriate methods and materials in a sequential manner, beginning with their initial competency level.[40]

To accomplish this goal, you would focus attention on small units of instruction, and use criterion-referenced tests to determine whether a student has the skills required for success at each step in the learning sequence. An entire course such as third-grade mathematics is too complex to be studied in large units. Instead, you would break it down into smaller modules and see that your students master each of them thoroughly (scoring 80 to 90 percent correct on tests) before moving to the next module.

Hundreds of studies have examined mastery learning. After reviewing this broad span of literature, several observers have concluded that mastery strategies do have moderate to strong effects on student learning when compared to conventional methods.[41] Studies of entire school districts show that mastery approaches also succeed in teaching basic skills such as reading and mathematics on which later learning depends. Moreover, inner-city students profit more from this approach than from traditional groupings of instruction,[42] and even students at risk and those with learning disabilities achieve at mastery levels.[43]

Questions and criticisms remain unanswered, however. Many educators, for example, are unconvinced that mastery approaches can accomplish "higher-order" learning, even though Bloom has reported positive gains in higher-order thinking skills correlated with the mastery learning approach.[44] Educators are also uncertain how well the various mastery approaches work for affective learning or for different types of students. Moreover, it is unknown to what extent teachers are "teaching to the test" to avoid blame for students' failure to master the material.[45] Other critics claim that even though reading, writing, and mathematics are being broken down into discrete skills and mastered, the students still cannot read, write, or compute any better. Although students show gains on small skill-acquisition items, this does

---

[40]James H. Block, *Mastery Learning: Theory and Practice* (New York: Holt, Rinehart and Winston, 1971); Ronald Gentile and James P. Lalley, *Standards and Mastery Learning: Aligning Teaching and Assessment So All Children Can Learn,* 2003 (ED 473455); and Vahid Motamedi and William J. Sumrall, "Mastery Learning and Contemporary Issues in Education," *Action in Teacher Education* (Spring 2000), pp. 32–42.

[41]See, for instance, Lorin W. Anderson, "Values, Evidence, and Mastery Learning," *Review of Educational Research* (Summer 1987), pp. 215–223; Benjamin S. Bloom, "The Search for Methods of Instruction," in Allan C. Ornstein and Linda S. Behar, eds., *Contemporary Issues in Curriculum* (Boston: Allyn and Bacon, 1995), pp. 208–225; and Stephen Anderson, "Synthesis of Research on Mastery Learning" (ERIC Document 382567, 1994).

[42]Daniel U. Levine, "Achievement Gains in Self-Contained Chapter I Classes in Kansas City," *Educational Leadership* (March 1987), pp. 22–23; and Daniel U. Levine and Allan C. Ornstein, "Research on Classroom and School Effectiveness," *Urban Review* (June 1989), pp. 81–94.

[43]Perry D. Passaro et al., "Instructional Strategies for Reclaiming Schools," *Journal of Emotional and Behavioral Problems* (Spring 1994), pp. 31–34.

[44]Bloom, "The Search for Methods," pp. 220–222; and Robert Slavin, "Mastery Learning Re-Reconsidered," *Review of Educational Research* (Summer 1990), pp. 300–302; Karen Morse, "Is Homeschooling Right for You and Your Highly Gifted Child?" *Understanding Our Gifted* (Fall 2001), pp. 25–26.

[45]Herbert J. Walberg, "Productive Teaching," in Allan C. Ornstein, ed., *Teaching: Theory into Practice* (Boston: Allyn and Bacon, 1995), pp. 43–44, 49; Allan C. Ornstein, "Emphasis on Student Outcomes Focuses Attention on Quality of Instruction," *NASSP Bulletin* (January 1987), pp. 88–95; and Robert E. Slavin, "Mastery Learning Re-Reconsidered."

not necessarily prove learning.[46] Finally, mastery learning and other individualized instructional systems are difficult to implement. Responsibility falls on the teacher, who must adapt the instruction to each student. To implement such a plan, you must continually monitor each student's work, determine what skills and tasks each student has mastered, and provide immediate feedback—a challenge in a class of twenty-five or more students.

Critical Thinking

■ Intelligence that can be taught

Today, we speak of *critical thinking* and *thinking skills* to denote problem-solving ability. Interest in this concept has produced an outpouring of articles in the professional literature, a host of conferences and reports on the subject, and a majority of states' efforts to bolster critical thinking for all students.

■ Metacognition

Most of the commentators argue that **critical thinking** is a teachable form of intelligence. The leading proponents of this school are Matthew Lipman and Robert Sternberg.[47] Lipman seeks to foster thirty critical thinking skills, generally designed for elementary school grades. These skills include understanding concepts, generalizations, cause–effect relationships, analogies, part–whole and whole–part connections, and applications of principles to real-life situations.[48] Lipman's strategy for teaching critical thinking has children spend a considerable portion of their time thinking about thinking (a process known as *metacognition*)[49] and about ways in which effective thinking is distinguished from ineffective thinking.

■ Criticisms of critical thinking

Some critics of critical thinking approaches contend that teaching a person to think is like teaching someone to swing a golf club or tennis racket; it involves a holistic approach, not the piecemeal effort implied by proponents such as Lipman. Critical thinking, the critics say, is too complex a mental operation to divide into small processes; the result depends on "a student's total intellectual functioning, not on a set of narrowly defined skills."[50] Moreover, as Sternberg has cautioned, critical thinking programs that stress "right" answers and objectively scored test items may be far removed from the problems students face in everyday life.[51] Thus many educators believe that attempts to teach critical thinking as a separate program or as a particular group of defined skills are self-defeating. Ideally, one might argue, critical thinking should be integrated into all courses throughout the curriculum so that students are continually challenged to develop an inquiring attitude and a critical frame of mind.

---

[46]Linda Darling-Hammond, "Mad-Hatter Tests of Good Teaching," *New York Times,* January 8, 1984, sect. 12, p. 57; and Marilyn Cochran-Smith, "Word Processing and Writing in Elementary Classrooms," *Review of Educational Research* (Spring 1991), pp. 107–155.

[47]See, for example, Matthew Lipman et al., *Philosophy for Children,* 2nd ed. (Philadelphia: Temple University Press, 1980); and Robert J. Sternberg, "How Can We Teach Intelligence?" *Educational Leadership* (September 1984), pp. 38–48; Joanne Harris, "The Skeptical Surfer: Web Research and Critical Thinking on Controversial Issues," *Green Teacher* (Spring 2003), pp. 21–24.

[48]Matthew Lipman, "The Cultivation of Reasoning Through Philosophy," *Educational Leadership* (September 1984), pp. 51–56; Matthew Lipman, "Critical Thinking—What Can It Be?" *Educational Leadership* (September 1988), pp. 38–43; and Missy Garrett, "A Community of Learners: Empowering the Teaching/Learning Process," *Research and Training in Developmental Education* (Spring 1993), pp. 45–54.

[49]Matthew Lipman, "Critical Thinking," in Ornstein and Behar, *Contemporary Issues,* p. 149.

[50]William A. Sadler and Arthur Whimbey, "A Holistic Approach to Improving Thinking Skills," *Phi Delta Kappan* (November 1985), p. 200.

[51]Robert J. Sternberg, "Thinking Styles: Key to Understanding Student Performance," *Phi Delta Kappan* (January 1990), pp. 366–371; National Center for Education Statistics, *The Condition of Education, 2000* (Washington D.C.: U.S. Government Printing Office, 2001), Table 418.

Computerized Instruction

■ CAI

The role of computers in our schools continues to increase. In 1980, the nation's schools used about 50,000 microcomputers. Twenty years later, by the end of the twentieth century, this number had soared to more than eight million, and it continues to grow.[52]

Patrick Suppes, an early innovator of computer use in schools, coined the term *computer-assisted instruction (CAI)*. Suppes defined three levels of CAI: practice and drill, tutoring, and dialogue.[53] At the simplest level, students work through computer drills in spelling, reading, foreign languages, simple computations, and so forth. At the second level, the computer acts as a tutor, taking over the function of presenting new concepts. As soon as the student shows a clear understanding, he or she moves to the next exercise. The third and highest level, dialogue, involves an interaction between the student and the computer. The student can communicate with the machine—not only give responses but ask new questions—and the computer will understand and react appropriately.

■ Hypermedia browsing

More recent applications often involve a **hypermedia** approach, which represents a significant shift in how information is presented and accessed by students. Hypermedia structures information nonsequentially. "Nodes" or information chunks are connected through associative, or topically related, links and presented in the program through text, illustrations, or sound. Thus the hypermedia approach allows learners to browse through an information base to construct their own relationships. This process makes learning more meaningful because it relates to the student's knowledge structure rather than that of the teacher or a textbook.[54] Many educational CD-ROMs use a hypermedia approach. So, of course, does the World Wide Web, with its rapid links to diverse and far-ranging sites. Increasingly, the Web presents a variety of curriculum options for teachers who want to supplement their curriculum program.

■ Problem of equal access

Many teachers, once skeptical of computers, are abandoning the chalkboard in favor of the computer terminal because they believe computers add a challenging and stimulating dimension to classroom learning. Now, the problem that concerns many educators is computer access: as former NEA president Keith Geiger put it, the challenge is "how to ensure every student—rural or urban, rich or poor—access to the most important learning tool of our time."[55] A majority of students now have at least some computer access. In 2002, the National Center for Educational Statistics reported that 99 percent of the nation's schools were connected to the Internet (up from 35 percent in 1994). Although only about 14 percent of the nation's classrooms had Internet access in 1996, the number had reached 87 percent by 2002. The percentage of students with computer access at home (36 percent in 1993) reached 90 percent in 2002.[56] The next challenge is to make good educational use of the computers available.

---

[52]*Digest of Education Statistics, 2002*, Figure 31.

[53]Patrick Suppes, "Computer Technology and the Future of Education," *Phi Delta Kappan* (April 1968), pp. 420–423.

[54]Simon Hooper and Lloyd P. Rieber, "Teaching Instruction and Technology," in Ornstein and Behar, *Contemporary Issues*, pp. 258–259; Anthony K. Betrus, "Historical Evolution of Instructional Technology in Teacher Education," *TechTrends* (September–October 2002), pp. 18–21, 33.

[55]Keith Geiger, "Computer Learning Achieves Lift Off," *Education Week,* May 24, 1995, p. 11; Jennifer Jenson et al., "No One Way: Working Models for Teachers' Professional Development," *Journal of Technology and Teacher Education* 10, no. 4 (2002), pp. 481–496.

[56]Deb Reichmann, "Nerd Discipline Needed in Schools," *The Sun*, September 7, 1998, p. C4; and *The Condition of Education, 2000*, Table 418; *Digest of Education Statistics, 2002*, Figure 31.

Modern technology, including computers and video and satellite systems, has allowed many curriculum innovations, including an explosion in distance-learning programs. (© *Michael Newman/ PhotoEdit*)

■ Impersonal machine or increased human contact?

Early in the computer revolution, some educators worried that computerized instruction involved students with machines and materials that, in themselves, had minimal emotional and affective components. Such critics justifiably contended that substituting a machine for a human teacher left the student with no true guidance and with too little personal interaction. The expansion of the Internet and the increasing access to it in schools across the country should help combat this impersonal aspect of computers. With e-mail and other electronic means of contact, students can reach other people, not merely other collections of information.[57] Moreover, the computer can be used to build a sense of inquiry, to "mess about," to explore, and to improve thinking skills. When students learn how to think and explore with the computer, their potential for innovation and creativity is unlimited.[58]

Video and Satellite Systems

Along with the computer, advances in video technology have brought many other valuable tools for instruction. In foreign language, English, science, history, geography, government, and even the arts (music, drama, dance, creative writing, visual arts), teachers have discovered considerable value in the use of videotapes, videodisks, CD-ROMs, DVDs, satellite links, telecommunication networks (such as Channel 1 for news and current events), and even cable television, and believe this technology makes instruction more accessible and productive.[59]

[57]Odvard E. Dyrli, "Surfing the World Wide Web to Education Hot Spots," *Technology and Learning* (October 1995), pp. 44–51.
[58]Robert C. Johnston, "Connecting with Technology," *Education Week,* May 10, 1995, pp. 27–28; Daniel Kelley et al., "Equal Access: Integrating Technology into the Elementary and Secondary Classroom," *REview* (Summer 2001), pp. 63–69.
[59]Dennis Knapczyk, "Staff Development in Rural Schools Through Distance Education," *Educational Media International* (June 1993), pp. 72–82; Joseph Francis, "Use of Internet Resources in the Biology Lecture Classroom," *American Biology Teacher* (February 2000), pp. 90–93.

■ Widespread video use

A study by the Corporation for Public Broadcasting showed that television, video, and the Internet are becoming widely used and more fully integrated into the curriculum.[60] Other studies have shown increased student achievement in courses with integrated video segments.[61] Videotapes, DVDs, and disks serve in classroom instruction, libraries, resource centers, and students' homes. They can be played at any convenient time, so students need never miss a lesson. Hundreds of catalogs and Web sites offer videos, CD-ROMs, and DVDs on a wide range of subjects. Many school systems and teachers have also begun to produce their own videos for specific instructional purposes. A videoprinter can reproduce individual images from the screen—photographs, tables, graphs, or any other useful picture—on paper for further study. Educators are also investigating ways to use the popularity of videogames for teaching purposes. Math, reading, and writing lessons can be written in a videogame format, giving students more lively practices and drills in a game atmosphere.

■ Interactive videos

More and more, videos are designed to be interactive—that is, to respond to the student's input. The term *interactive video instruction (IVI)* applies to realistic simulations and action–reaction situations presented as part of an instructional program. The program can tell the viewer if a response is right or wrong or offer a choice of options and then display the outcome of the option chosen. Interactive videos supply either individual lessons or instruction in small groups.

■ Virtual reality

As one educator says, video technology "is the next best thing to being there." In fact, some applications invite students to enter a *virtual reality* far from their classroom. They might interact with zookeepers at the San Diego Zoo, plan their upcoming field trip with local museum staff, or interact directly with White House staffers on a "hot" issue before the Congress. Video use in schools has increased at such a staggering rate that teachers must plan ways to integrate it into the curriculum.[62] In an era when the number of videos rented from video stores surpasses the total number of books checked out of libraries, you should help your students become critical video consumers, aware of how visual images affect us as individuals and as a society.[63]

Distance Education. Many of the electronic systems discussed in the past two sections have the potential for transporting educational materials and instruction across long distances. "**Distance education**" refers to the many ways in which schools make use of this technology.

■ Educational television via satellite or cable

For example, schools may select television programs specifically developed for educational purposes and have them beamed into the classroom by satellite. This is particularly useful for small, rural schools with limited local resources, as well as for

---

[60]Corporation for Public Broadcasting, *Study of School Uses of Television and Video: 1996–1997 School Year Summary Report* (Washington, D.C.: Corporation for Public Broadcasting, 1997).
[61]William Harwood and Maureen McMahon, "Effects of Integrated Video Media on Student Achievement and Attitude in High School Chemistry," *Journal of Research in Science Teaching* (August 1997), pp. 617–631.
[62]George Peterson, "Geography and Technology in the Classroom," *NASSP Bulletin* (October 1994), pp. 25–29; see "Technology Focus" (2003) at **www.electronic-school.com**; and see "Windows on the World," *Education Week,* February 8, 1995, pp. 36–37.
[63]Allan C. Ornstein, "Video Technology and the Urban Curriculum," *Education and Urban Society* (May 1991), pp. 335–341; G. Eugene Martin, *Technology Education for the 21st Century: A Collection of Essays* (Reston, Va.: Council on Technology and Teacher Education, 2000); Wen-Tsai Sung, "Web Based Learning in the Computer Aided Design Curriculum," *Journal of Computer Assisted Learning* (June 2000), pp. 175–187.

■ Teleconferences

colleges and universities as they reach beyond their traditional service areas.[64] Schools can also make use of home cable systems that carry educational programming, such as the Discovery, Learning, and History channels, each of which offers special programs on a wide range of subjects.

Widely used in business and industry, teleconferences have also begun to appear in school systems. In a typical conference, viewers watch a resource person, teacher, or group of students on the television screen talking to or instructing other students or participants. Viewers can watch as if they were across the table, even though they may be thousands of miles away. The viewing audience can ask questions and make decisions about what further information should be presented.[65]

■ Rapid spread of distance education

With the expansion of videophone links and the Internet, distance education is becoming a resource not just for isolated or small schools but for any school that wants to extend its students' horizons. Widespread workplace computer use—more than 50 percent of all workers use computers on the job—motivates educators to integrate computer knowledge and skills into classroom instruction. Colleges and universities are outpacing public schools with Web-enhanced courses, distance learning, Web-based courses, and even complete Web-based academic programs. It will be a challenge for public-school teachers to match these creative efforts.[66] In addition, Web-based instruction in lifelong learning (see following text) and corporate training programs is growing dramatically. It will be interesting to see if elementary and secondary schools follow this lead.[67] But teachers also are using electronic technology to put their students in touch with experts, teachers, and other students around the globe. The point of contact can be as close as an adjacent school or as far away as the frigid Antarctic.

■ Teachers need technological competence

To some educators, our rapid technological advances spell the eventual demise of "pencil technology." In the twenty-first century, the textbook may not be the norm that it once was; it may be incidental, or it may take on different forms, such as wireless technology, hand-held devices and e-mail dialogue; it may monitor student progress and present information in a highly visual and stimulating way. Experts do agree, however, that technological knowledge and skills will be essential components in the preparation and repertoire of all teachers.

[64]Jerry D. Pepple, Dale A. Law, and Sheri Kallembach, "A Vision of Rural Education for 2001," *Educational Horizons* (Fall 1990), pp. 50–58; *Master Plan for Distance Learning: An Evolving Technological Process* (Austin, Tex.: Texas Higher Education Coordinating Board, 1996); Gary Marchionini, "Video and Learning Redux: New Capabilities for Practical Use," *Educational Technology* (March–April 2003), pp. 36–41; and Steve Bosak, "Bits in the Ether: Wireless LANS Leave Cables Behind," *American School Board Journal* (March 2000), pp. 38–39, 41.

[65]Allan C. Ornstein, "Curriculum Trends Revisited," *Peabody Journal of Education* (Summer 1994), pp. 4–20; and Allan C. Ornstein, "Bringing Telecommunications and Videos into the Classroom," *High School Journal* (April–May 1990), pp. 252–257.

[66]Peter West, "Satellite Space Crunch Seen Impeding Distance Learning," *Education Week,* March 22, 1995, p. 3; and *The Condition of Education, 2000,* Table 423; Gene I. Maeroff, "Classroom of One: The Promise of On-Line Learning," *American School Board Journal* (February 2003), pp. 26–28.

[67]"Distance Learning," *The Electronic School,* a supplement to *American School Board Journal* (January 1998), pp. A1–40; She-sheng Liaw and Hsiu-mei Huang, "Enhancing Interactivity in Web-based Instruction: A Review of the Literature," *Educational Technology* (May–June 2000), pp. 41–45; and Richard H. Hall and Steve E. Watkins, "The Horse and the Cart in Web-based Instruction: Prevalence and Efficacy" (2000), paper presented at the annual meeting of the American Educational Research Association, April 24–28, 2000 (ERIC Document No. 443425); Sharon Levitch et al., "Transmitting Instructor Skills to the Virtual Classroom," *Educational Technology* (March–April 2003), pp. 42–46.

R E F O C U S **Which of the instructional methods listed in this section (individualized instruction, cooperative learning, mastery instruction, critical thinking, and various methods of electronic instruction) do you feel most comfortable with as a teacher? Why? How can you prepare to make effective use of methods with which you are not yet comfortable?**

▶ Emerging Curriculum Trends: An Agenda for the Future

In discussing computer links and communications technology, we have already begun to step from the present into the future. Student learning will increase through interaction with computers. Not all learning will be centered in the school classroom, and use of computers and the Internet, both in school and at home, will greatly expand how you and your students access information and, just as importantly, what information you access. What other trends will the future bring to American classrooms? We describe several of the most important likely trends in the following list.

■ Education at many stages of life

1. *Lifelong learning.* Rapid social, technological, and economic changes have forced people to prepare for second or third careers and to keep themselves updated on new developments that affect their personal and social goals. Lifelong learning will be an especially important element in your professional life as a teacher.[68]

   Some observers believe that much of the learning provided by elementary, secondary, and postsecondary schools may in the future come from business and industry, especially to meet the needs of a skilled work force in high-tech and information-based industries.[69] Still other scenarios envision educating adolescents and adults through a network of community resources and small learning centers and libraries.

■ Nationwide efforts

2. *The restoration of geography.* In 1984 the National Geographic Association, in concert with the Association of American Geographers and the Association for Geographic Education, began a national program to improve understanding of the basic principles of geography and special methods for teaching the discipline. As a result of these efforts, geography has been undergoing a renaissance in the school curriculum and is being linked to various curriculum foci, such as back-to-basics, multicultural education, environmental education, and global education.[70]

---

[68]*National Goals for Education: Goals 2000* (Washington, D.C.: Department of Education, 1994); and *The National Educational Goals Report: Building a Nation of Learners* (Washington, D.C.: National Educational Goals Panel, 1998); Nola Purdie et al., "The Learning Needs of Older Adults," *Educational Gerontology* (February 2003), pp. 29–49.

[69]Allan C. Ornstein, "Curriculum Trends Revisited," in Allan C. Ornstein and Linda S. Behar-Horenstein, *Contemporary Issues in Curriculum,* 2nd ed. (Boston: Allyn and Bacon, 1999), pp. 265–276; Barbara L. McCombs, "Motivation and Lifelong Learning," *Educational Psychologist* (Spring 1991), pp. 117–128; and Lisa Holm and Carol Horn, "Bridging the Gap Between Schools of Education and the Needs of 21st Century Teachers," *Phi Delta Kappan* (January 2003), pp. 376–380.

[70]Donald Rallis and Helen Rallis, "Changing the Image of Geography," *Social Studies* (July–August 1995), pp. 167–168; and Christopher Shearer, "Geography Education: Learning the Why of Where," *Principal* (January–February 2003), pp. 32–35.

Standards & Assessment ☑
■ Ongoing discussion of national standards

3. *National curriculum standards.* The U.S. Department of Education has funded the development of national curriculum standards in seven subject fields: history, geography, economics, English, foreign languages, mathematics, and science. Many of these efforts have been spearheaded by professional organizations in the respective disciplines, such as the American Historical Association, the National Academy of Science, and the National Council of Teachers of Mathematics. Back-to-basics proponents are promoting national curriculum standards as a way to restore the primacy of basic content to the curriculum, and the federal government has offered financial incentives for states to adopt the national curriculum standards. The concept of national curriculum standards has not, however, been sufficiently accepted for states to buy into national standards; thus it remains a subject of considerable discussion among curriculum developers at the national, state, and local levels.[71]

■ Status of foreign language study

4. *International education.* As many educators and laypeople have pointed out, increasing interdependence among nations demands that Americans become more knowledgeable about distant lands. One area of international education that U.S. schools may particularly need to address is foreign language instruction. Although forty states require schools to offer two years of foreign language study, only twenty-seven states offer it as part of the core curriculum, on an equal footing with other major disciplines. In 2001, 46 percent of U.S. secondary students were enrolled in foreign language classes. An elementary-level study found the percentage of foreign language instruction at 30 percent, up dramatically from 20 percent in 1987.[72]

■ Most common languages

When students do study foreign languages, they do not necessarily concentrate on those most important in the current world economy. The most common spoken language in the world is Mandarin, for example, and the third most common is Hindi. However, few U.S. public schools teach Mandarin, and practically none offers Hindi. Failure to train students in the world's most common languages may severely limit the future growth of U.S. trade.

U.S. education probably must become more international in other ways as well. Educators may expand travel exchange programs and perhaps make study in another culture a graduation requirement. Emphasis on international geography, history, political science, and economics may increase. As the world becomes more interconnected and interdependent, such needs will become more evident and more funds may be devoted to the area of global curriculum.

■ AIDS epidemic

5. *Health education and physical fitness.* Health trends in the U.S. population are producing new pressures to expand or change the curriculum. For example, the epidemic of AIDS (acquired immunodeficiency syndrome), with its dire risk to sexually active adolescents, has forced educators to confront the issue of student health in a new way. However, only twenty-seven states require any

---

[71]Meg Sommerfield, "Sciences Group Quietly Unveils Final Standards," *Education Week,* December 13, 1995, pp. 1, 9; and Marion Brady, "The Standards Juggernaut," *Phi Delta Kappan* (February 2001), pp. 460–461; see also "About National Curriculum Standards" at **www .ash.udel.edu/ash/teacher/standards.html**; and Nell Noddings, "Thinking About Standards," *Phi Delta Kappan* (November 1997), pp. 184–189; Julie Bianchini and Greg Kelly, "Challenges of Standards Based Reform," *Science Education* (May 2003), pp. 378–389.
[72]Renate A. Schulz, "Foreign Language Education in the United States: Trends and Challenges." See Eric Review at **http://nces.ed.gov/programs/coe/2003/section4/indicator24 .asp;** Stephanie A. Neugent, "Foreign Language Instruction in a Global Community," *NASSP Bulletin* (January 2000), pp. 35–40.

form of health or sex education, and when health education is offered, it is more likely to be taught by science, physical education, or other subject-area teachers than by certified health teachers. Elementary teachers are generally poorly trained in this field.[73] Many educators believe that this problem must and will be addressed in the future.

■ Drug use

Drugs are another critical matter. As detailed in the chapter on Culture, Socialization and Education, after a decade of decline in illicit drug use among teenagers, we are seeing a disturbing trend toward increased use of marijuana, alcohol, and other drugs and finding more drugs on school campuses.[74]

Standards & Assessment ☑
■ Diet and exercise

Obesity, dietary habits, and exercise are yet another health concern. As one report summed up the situation, "We presently have a generation of adolescents that is heavier, less physically active and that is smoking more than its parents were at the same age." Increasingly, weight problems are a concern for elementary-age children, too. For that reason, the American Cancer Society and American Public Health Association have developed a draft set of national standards for health education and have called for its inclusion in the high-school curriculum as a core subject.[75]

■ Keep up with rapid change

6. *Technology Education.* Teachers, students and parents find themselves functioning, at work and at home, in an increasingly technological environment. In less than fifteen years, we have gone from audiotapes to videotapes, from CD-ROMs to CD burners and DVDs, and from transparencies to PowerPoint slides. Who knows what technology we will be talking about in the next decade, but you can be sure it will be challenging and exciting and have a significant impact on our lives. Our current generation of students—even elementary-grade students—are often more technologically proficient than their teachers and parents. School systems will need to commit both financial and human resources to help already overloaded faculty stay up-to-date technologically. Teacher-education programs must prepare new teachers for this technological world. And, as a teacher, you must continue to stay abreast of the latest technology before your students outpace you.

■ High immigration rate

7. *Immigrant education.* The education of immigrant children in America has growing implications for curriculum. The United States is currently in the midst of its second largest immigration wave since the beginning of the twentieth century. Legal immigration now accounts for up to one-half of the annual growth in the U.S. population. In fact, nearly one in ten U.S. residents in 1999 was foreign born—double the 1970 figure.[76]

■ Difficulties faced by immigrant families

Cultural differences in learning styles or thinking patterns may lead immigrant children to be mistakenly labeled "learning disabled" or "slow." Value

[73]Clark Robenstine, "The School and HIV Education After the First Decade of AIDS" (ERIC Document 379250, 1994), p. 8; Wanda Blanchett, "Sexual Risk Behaviors of Young Adults with LD and the Need for HIV/AIDS Education," *Remedial and Special Education* (November–December 2000), pp. 336–345.

[74]National Education Goals Panel, *National Education Goals Panel Report (1998)*, at **www.ed.gov/Mailinglists/EDInfo/Archive/msg00410.html**; and Lauran Neergaard, "Survey: Teens' Marijuana Use Nearly Doubled over Two Years," *Philadelphia Inquirer,* September 13, 1995, p. A9.

[75]"Core Subjects Status for Health Education Sought," *Education Week,* May 10, 1995, p. 5; Kathy Christie, "Even Students Are What They Eat," *Phi Delta Kappan* (January 2003), pp. 341–342.

[76]Center for Immigration Studies, "Immigration Related Statistics," *Backgrounder* (July 1995), pp. 6, 11; Randy Capps, "Hardship Among Children of Immigrants: Findings from the 1999 Survey of America's Families," at **http:www.urban.org/Content/Research/NewFederalism**.

hierarchies vary widely across cultures, so that immigrant children have diverse attitudes about school, teacher authority, gender differences, social class, and behavior, all of which have implications for their success in school.[77]

■ Debate about special programs

Many educators believe that immigrant children need special programs, such as expanded bilingual and multicultural education, to help them acclimate. Multicultural programs also help longer established groups understand how much the new immigrants can contribute to American society. However, as we saw in the chapter on Providing Equal Educational Opportunity, multicultural education remains a controversial subject, and schools are still working out their responses to the new rise of immigration. Some educators believe English-language immersion should take place as soon as possible. For example, California's Proposition 227, enacted in 1998, required the state's one thousand school districts to place limited-English-proficient students in English immersion classes rather than in bilingual classes.[78]

Words of Caution

Although curriculum should evolve to serve a changing society, we caution you on several fronts. Change for the sake of change is not good. Schools throughout the ages have thought their programs were on the cutting edge of progress, and they have often been wrong.

■ Balancing old and new

New knowledge, indeed, is not necessarily better than old knowledge. Are we to throw away most of Aristotle, Galileo, Kepler, Darwin, and Newton merely because they are not part of this century? If we stress only scientific and technological knowledge, we could languish physically, aesthetically, morally, and spiritually. We must learn to prune away old and irrelevant parts of the curriculum and integrate and balance new knowledge. As we modify and update content, we need to protect schools and students against fads and frills, and especially against extremist points of view. We must keep in perspective the type of society we have, the values we cherish, and the educational goals we wish to achieve.

REFOCUS **Which of the trends listed here do you believe will have the strongest influence on your career as a teacher? Why? In what ways will you be affected?**

▶ Summing Up

1 In organizing the curriculum, most educators hold to the traditional concept of curriculum as the body of subjects, or subject matter. Nevertheless, contemporary educators more concerned with the learner's experiences regard the student as the focus of curriculum.

2 Examples of a subject-centered approach include the following types of curriculum: (1) subject area, (2) perennialist and essentialist, (3) back-to-basics, and (4) new core.

3 Examples of a student-centered approach include the following types of curriculum: (1) activity-centered approaches, (2) relevant curriculum, (3) the humanistic approach, (4) alternative or free schools programs, and (5) values-centered curriculum.

[77]Xue Lan Rong and Judith Preissle, *Educating Impaired Students* (Thousand Oaks, Calif.: Corwin Press, 1998).
[78]Lynn Schnalberg, "Schools Gear Up as Bilingual Education Law Takes Effect," *Education Week*, August 5, 1998, p. 29; Jorge Ruiz-de-Velasco, *Overlooked and Underserved: Immigrant Students in U.S. Secondary Schools* (Washington, D.C.: Urban Institute, 2000).

④ Recent decades have produced significant instructional innovations, including (1) individualized instruction, (2) cooperative learning, (3) mastery instruction, (4) critical thinking, (5) computerized instruction, and (6) the use of video and satellite systems. The last two areas of innovation have made distance learning an increasingly important resource.

⑤ Future curricular trends will probably include the following: (1) lifelong learning, (2) return of geography, (3) national curriculum standards, (4) international education, (5) health education and physical fitness, (6) technology education, and (7) immigrant education.

▶ Key Terms

curriculum (414)
subject-centered curricula (415)
subject-area curriculum (417)
perennialist approach to curriculum (417)
essentialist approach to curriculum (417)
back-to-basics curriculum (418)
new core curriculum (core subjects approach) (418)
student-centered curricula (420)
activity-centered curriculum (421)

relevant curriculum (422)
humanistic approach to curriculum (422)
alternative (free) school (422)
values-centered curriculum (423)
individualized instruction (430)
cooperative learning (430)
mastery instruction (432)
critical thinking (434)
hypermedia (435)
distance education (437)

▶ Discussion Questions

① Discuss the benefits and limitations of using a single textbook as the basis for a course curriculum.

② Does your teacher-education program seem to favor one curriculum approach over another? Why might this be so? What kind of curriculum approach would you recommend for a teacher-education program? Relate your approach to your philosophy of education.

③ Which of the instructional approaches discussed in this chapter best fits your teaching style? Why? Share your thinking with a classmate.

④ List curriculum changes you expect to see in the future. How will these affect your work as a teacher?

▶ Suggested Projects for Professional Development

① How is curriculum organized in the schools you visit? Ask to see a curriculum guide for your subject field. Is it a general outline of content and activities, or is it a detailed list of objectives, activities, and materials and resources? Which approach do you believe is better for students? More helpful to teachers?

② In your visits to schools this semester, talk with teachers about the curriculum they teach. Do they use a subject-centered approach, and, if so, which of the four subject-centered approaches described in this chapter best describes their procedure? If they use a student-centered approach, which of the five student-centered approaches best describes what they do? Of the several schools you have visited, explain which school's approach best fits your ideas for a curriculum.

3 Talk with members of the educational faculty at your college. What do they see as the pros and cons of subject-centered versus student-centered curricula?

4 Draw up your own version of Table 14.1, reflecting what you see as the proper division of time for today's elementary schools. (Or do a similar chart for high schools or middle schools.) Show your chart to one or more classmates and defend your decisions.

5 Explore the Internet and other electronic resources for learning. Identify a series of topics about which you would like to know more to further your professional knowledge and development.

6 Using the following Internet resources section, select a topic or unit of instruction and develop a portfolio of resources and sample lesson plans to use as a teacher.

▶ Suggested Resources

Internet Resources

The development of national curriculum standards can be followed by checking the latest documents on the subject at the U.S. Department of Education's Internet site (**www.ed.gov**) or the ERIC database (**www.eric.ed.gov/**) and search for curriculum and instructional resources. There are hundreds of other interesting offerings on the World Wide Web, with new ones appearing every month. For a sample you might look at the Teachers College Record—at **www.tcrecord.org/**: click on "Technology," "Teaching," or "Curriculum," or go to **www.tcrecord .org/indexing.asp?** for recent articles on curriculum and instruction published by the Teachers' College Record in 2003.

Information on curriculum and instruction can also be found by exploring state-level sites and other links accessible at **www.nasbe.org** or by using Google, Infoseek, Yahoo, Alta Vista, or other search engines for "education journals," "curriculum," and "educational issues."

Publications

Altbach, Philip G., ed. *Textbooks in American Society.* Albany: State University of New York Press, 1991. *Focusing on how textbooks are produced and selected, this book explains the pressures placed on textbook authors and publishers.*

Beyer, Barry K. *Critical Thinking.* Fastback #385. Bloomington, Ind.: Phi Delta Kappa Educational Foundation, 1995. *A cogent monograph on the essential features of critical thinking and ways to use it in classrooms.*

Boyer, Ernest L. *High School: A Report on Secondary Education in America.* New York: Harper and Row, 1983. *An analysis of high-school curricula in the United States and proposals for a new core curriculum.*

Boyer, Ernest L. *The Basic School: A Community of Learning.* Princeton, N.J.: Carnegie Foundation, 1995. *A description of Boyer's proposed eight core commonalities in curriculum.*

Bruning, Roger, Christy Horn, and Lisa Putlik-Zillig. *Web-Based Learning: What Do We Know? Where Do We Go?* Greenwich, Conn.: Information Age, 2003. *A thorough discussion of Web-based learning and instruction, including critical thinking.*

Connelly, Michael F., and D. Jean Claudinin. *Teachers as Curriculum Planners.* New York: Teachers College Press, 1988. *Offers case studies on the role of teachers in planning and developing the curriculum.*

Doll, Ronald C. *Curriculum Improvement: Decision Making and Process.* 9th ed. Boston: Allyn and Bacon, 1996. *Provides an excellent overview of curriculum improvement, with emphasis on practical principles, problems, and solutions.*

The Electronic School, 2003. *Supplement to the monthly* American School Board Journal. *This quarterly supplement offers excellent suggestions on electronic education and electronic educational resources for schools.*

Johnson, David W. *Reaching Out: Interpersonal Effectiveness and Self-Actualization,* 5th ed. Needham Heights, Mass.: Allyn and Bacon, 1993. *Describes the theory and practice of cooperative learning and how to enhance student self-actualization.*

Marzano, Robert J. *A Different Kind of Classroom: Teaching with Dimensions of Learning.* Alexandria, Va.: Association for Supervision and Curriculum Development, 1992. *Describes teaching, the psychology of learning, curriculum planning, and assessment.*

Ornstein, Allan C., and Francis Hunkins. *Curriculum: Foundations, Principles and Issues,* 4th ed. Boston: Allyn and Bacon, 2004. An excellent book for researchers, theoreticians, and practitioners of curriculum involved in the development, design, and implementation of elementary- and secondary-school curriculum.

Sizer, Theodore R. *Horace's Compromise: The Dilemma of the American School.* Rev. ed. Boston: Houghton Mifflin, 1985. *This book on school reform remains quite relevant.*

Sizer, Theodore R. *Horace's School: Redesigning the American High School.* Boston: Houghton Mifflin, 1992. *Looks at the goals of U.S. secondary education and at high schools in particular, with a special focus on mastery learning.*

Slavin, Robert J. *Cooperative Learning: Theory Research and Practice.* Boston: Allyn and Bacon, 1995. *An excellent book on cooperative learning theory and practice.*

PART SIX

Effective Education International and American Perspectives

CHAPTER 15

International Education

M any educational reformers have suggested that the United States could improve its educational system by emulating other countries. Japanese education has received particular attention because it appears to have contributed in large measure to Japan's economic success during the past fifty years. But imitating educational practices from other countries raises questions. Would they work in an American context? Do they mesh with American beliefs and values?

Before beginning to answer such questions, we need to understand the varieties of educational systems other countries employ: how they resemble one another, how they differ, and which particular features are most effective in which contexts. In this chapter we offer an introduction to that kind of analysis. We then consider education in developing countries and international studies of school improvement. Finally, we offer a brief comment on the accomplishments of U.S. schools in an international context. As you read the chapter, see what answers you formulate to the following basic questions:

FOCUS QUESTIONS

- What do educational systems in various countries have in common? In what respects do they differ?
- How do educational systems differ with respect to the resources they devote to education and the percentage of students they enroll?
- How does the achievement of U.S. students compare with that of students in other countries?
- Which countries provide examples of outstanding educational activities that may be worth emulating elsewhere?
- What should be done to improve education in developing countries?
- How do the purposes and attainments of U.S. schools compare with those of other countries?

▶ Commonalities in Educational Systems

At first glance, classrooms around the world may seem to have little in common. Consider a classroom in a rural Sudanese village and one in contemporary Japan, for example. In Sudan, the building has no electricity and the earthen floor is uncovered. The students are all boys. None of the teachers has a high-school diploma; the curriculum and teaching, which rely heavily on memorization and recitation, are determined by the country's ministry of education. In highly developed Japan, by way of contrast, modern school buildings house classes of boys and girls, almost all of whom will complete high school. Teachers are highly respected professionals with college degrees. They are given considerable latitude in devising activities and adapting materials that satisfy the national guidelines, which emphasize development of children's thinking and problem-solving skills, as well as social, moral, and physical instruction that benefits the "whole person."

Despite the great variety in educational systems worldwide, however, certain commonalities exist. The following sections describe widespread characteristics and problems: the strong relationships between students' social-class origins and their success in school, the educational challenges posed by multicultural populations, typical teaching approaches, and professional conditions teachers face. Overview 15.1 also summarizes commonalities and differences among educational systems.

Social-Class Origins and School Outcomes

■ Privileged versus less privileged students

As we noted in the chapter on Social Class, Race, and School Achievement, various national and international studies have illustrated the strong relationships between students' socioeconomic background and their success in school and in the economic system. For example, World Bank studies have reported that family socioeconomic background is a salient predictor of students' achievement in both industrialized and developing countries. Similarly, Donald Treiman and others have found that individuals' social-class origins and background relate to their educational and occupational attainment regardless of whether their society is rich or poor, politically liberal or conservative.[1] A multitude of studies such as these also demonstrate that the family and home environments of low-income students generate the same kinds of educational disadvantages in other countries as in the United States.[2]

Multicultural Populations and Problems

■ Rising diversity

Except in a few homogeneous countries, nationwide systems of education enroll diverse groups of students who differ significantly with respect to race, ethnicity, religion, native language, and cultural practices. (Its geographic isolation and cultural insularity make Japan one of the exceptions to this generalization.) Most large

---

[1]Donald J. Treiman, *Occupational Prestige in Comparative Perspective* (New York: Academic Press, 1977); and Marlaine E. Lockheed, Bruce Fuller, and Ronald Nyirongo, *Family Background and School Achievement* (New York: World Bank, 1988). See also Daniele Checchi, "Education and Intergenerational Mobility in Occupations," *American Journal of Economics and Sociology* (July 1997), pp. 331–350; and Emma Smith and Stephen Gorard, "What Does PISA Tell Us About Equity in Education Systems?" (2003), paper prepared at the Cardiff University School of Social Sciences, available at **www.cf.ac.uk/socsi/whoswho/gorard.html**.

[2]Alan C. Purves and Daniel U. Levine, eds., *Educational Policy and International Assessment* (Berkeley, Calif.: McCutchan, 1975); and "A League Table of Educational Disadvantage in Rich Nations," *Innocenti Report Card* (November 2002), available at **www.unicef-icdc.org**.

OVERVIEW 15.1 *Areas of Similarities and Differences Among Educational Systems of the World*

Commonalities—Many educational systems in the world face the same challenges.

Social Class Origins and School Outcomes	Throughout most of the world, lower-income students are at an educational disadvantage.
Multicultural Populations	Nearly every nation must find ways to effectively educate diverse student populations.
Teaching Approaches and Conditions	Teachers in many countries share similar sources of frustration and reward, and research finds remarkable similarity in the teaching and learning processes of different school systems.

Differences—Many areas of distinction define individual countries' educational systems.

Resources Devoted to Education	The percentage of gross domestic income spent on education varies because of countries' incomes and the priority they give to education. Larger expenditures allow for more student enrollment and a higher level of educational services.
Extent of Centralization	Nations vary widely in how much educational decision making occurs at local and national government levels.
Curriculum Content and Instructional Emphases	The subjects and methods that receive most attention reflect the culture and priorities of each country.
Vocational Versus Academic Education	After the first few years of common schooling, some nations more commonly separate students into academic or vocational educational tracks for further education.
Enrollment in Higher Education	Emphasis on academics in earlier schools, resources devoted to education, and occupational requirements in different countries contribute to wide variations in enrollment and completion of college and university studies.
Nonpublic Schools	Differences in culture and governmental structure contribute to variations in the size and functioning of nonpublic education.
Achievement Levels	U.S. students rank toward the middle on most international achievement tests, which leads many to conclude that U.S. schools need improvement.

---

nations historically have included numerous racial/ethnic and cultural subgroups, but the twentieth century seems to have greatly accelerated the mixture of diverse groups across and within national boundaries. World and regional wars, global depressions and recessions, migration and immigration to large urban centers that offer expanded economic opportunity—these and other destabilizing forces have led some historians to see recent decades as the era of the migrant and the refugee.[3] These forces more or less ensure that you, as a teacher, will have students from other

---

[3]Roger Cohen, "Europe's Love–Hate Affair with Foreigners," *New York Times* (December 24, 2000); and Lauren M. McLauren, "Anti-Immigrant Prejudice in Europe," *Social Forces* (March 2003).

nations in your classes. As the In This Case feature describes, you might consider using the ease of global travel to your advantage now, to help you prepare for the opportunities and challenges of teaching international students.

■ Multicultural challenges

Not surprisingly, then, other countries encounter challenges in multicultural education similar to those of the United States: ineffective traditional instruction, providing bilingual education, and desegregating minority students. (See also the chapters on Providing Equal Educational Opportunity and The Purposes of Education.) This is partly because minority racial, ethnic, and religious groups in many nations, as in the United States, frequently are low in socioeconomic status. England, France, the Netherlands, and other European countries, for example, have many lower-income students from Africa, Asia, the Caribbean, and other distant locations. Germany is struggling to provide effective education for the children of Romany (Gypsy), Slavic, and Turkish migrants, and most West African nations include students from numerous disadvantaged tribal and minority-language groups.[4]

Teaching Approaches and Conditions

■ Similar teaching practices

Although instructional approaches vary considerably from one teacher to another and the conditions for teaching and learning change accordingly in different classrooms and schools, practices emphasized around the world typically show much similarity. Two researchers who analyzed data on fifth- through ninth-grade classes in mathematics, social studies, and science in ten countries found "remarkable similarity with respect to the teaching and learning process." In general, in all ten participating countries, the primary classroom activities included teacher-presented lectures or demonstrations plus seatwork activity.[5]

■ Similar pros and cons for teachers

Scholars in many countries report that teachers also share similar sources of frustration or reward. Around the world, teachers typically cite the following sources of "professional discouragement": lack of time to accomplish priority goals, a multiplicity of sometimes conflicting role demands, and lack of full support from administrators. Sources of "professional enthusiasm" generally center on relationships with students and satisfaction with students' accomplishments. Just as in the United States, these sources of teacher enthusiasm and discouragement reflect "the reality of schools."[6]

REFOCUS What other characteristics do you believe may be common to schools in many countries? In what other ways, besides those described, might you encounter situations similar to teachers in other countries?

---

[4]Nigel Grant, "Some Problems of Identity and Education," *Comparative Education* (March 1997), pp. 9–28; K. Lindholm-Leary, *Biliteracy for a Global Society* (Washington, D.C.: National Clearinghouse for Bilingual Education, 2000); and Chris Gaine et al., "Eurokid," *Intercultural Education* (September 2003), pp. 317–329. Reports on minority issues in Europe are available at **www.ecmi.de**.

[5]Angela Hilgard and Sid Bourke, "Teaching for Learning: Similarities and Differences Across Countries." Paper presented at the annual meeting of the American Educational Research Association, Chicago, April 1985, p. 17. See also J. Hiebert et al., *Highlights from the TIMSS Video Study of Eighth-Grade Mathematics Teaching* (Washington D.C.: National Center for Education Statistics, 2003).

[6]Herbert Fibler et al., "A Cross-Cultural Comparison of the Sources of Professional Enthusiasm and Discouragement." Paper presented at the annual meeting of the American Educational Research Association, San Francisco, April 1986, p. 21. See also Max Angus, *The Rules of School Reform* (London: Falmer, 1998); and Kathleen K. Manzo, "NEA, Overseas Unions Share Similar Concerns," *Education Week*, June 4, 2003.

IN THIS CASE

New Perspectives

Dr. Harris addressed the classroom of education majors: "I'm wondering if any of you know how many languages are spoken in Minneapolis schools, in New York City schools, Houston schools, or Los Angeles schools." He answered his own rhetorical question as he introduced his main topic for the day's discussion. "Right here in Minneapolis, we have students speaking more than ninety different languages.

"How many of you speak more than one language? How many of you have traveled to other countries to see how children are educated in various parts of the world? Whether or not you have traveled, whether or not you are bilingual, you will be working with students from different cultures and with parents who have differing expectations from educators.

"We have a responsibility to serve all our children well," he continued. "What do you think we can do to assist you preservice teachers in becoming prepared to deal effectively with students from other countries?"

"One obvious way is to have us read about the different types of schooling and the different approaches to teaching used around the world," suggested Michael Ervin.

"We could research ountries on the Internet to get a sense of how their schools are organized and run," commented Sally Newman.

"Why don't we use on-campus resources?" Bob Barrett said. "We could interview international students that we know about their country's educational process."

Tanghe Yu added, "I think the best way to gain an appreciation of the different perspectives would be to actually visit the site. That way, whether we're students or student teachers, we could immerse ourselves in the educational experiences of the students. I moved here from Taiwan when I was eight years old. I can tell you that my schooling there and here, even in the early years, differed substantially."

Dr. Harris responded. "Yes, those are all great suggestions. Tanghe, I think your idea has special merit. Since the 9/11 incidents, I have been thinking that we really need to help build more understanding between and among different groups. Who would like to travel and learn about schools in other countries?" About half of the class raised a hand. "Right now, we don't have the funds," he commented, "but perhaps we can start by looking at grant opportunities that may help us."

Questions

1. How are you, as a preservice teacher, preparing yourself to deal with the students and families who come to public schools with languages and cultural backgrounds different from your own?

2. How have the schools you observed in your own community worked with students and families with varying cultural backgrounds? What strategies do you consider most effective?

3. Would you want to participate in a program such as the one suggested by Dr. Harris? If so, to which country would you travel, and why? If not, why not?

▶ Differences in Educational Systems and Outcomes

Each nation's educational system also differs in important ways from other systems. We'll discuss some of the most significant differences in the following sections.

Resources Devoted to Education

■ Expenditures for education

One fundamental way in which nations differ is in the percentage of their resources they devote to education rather than to priorities such as highways, health care, and military forces. As a percentage of gross domestic product (wealth produced an-

Classrooms, schools, and school systems around the world differ in many ways, some obvious as in this picture, others less obvious. School also share commonalities such as the joys most teachers find in working with their students. *(Steven Starr/Stock Boston)*

nually), public expenditures on K–12 and higher education range from 3 to 4.5 percent in nations low in average income and/or that place relatively little priority on education, to more than 7 percent in nations with high average income and/or that emphasize education. In the world's poorest countries, average per capita expenditures on military forces are nearly one-third greater than per capita spending for education.[7]

■ Better student–teacher ratios in wealthy regions

Student–Teacher Ratios at the Primary Level. Relatively wealthy nations, as well as nations that allocate many of their resources to education, can provide a higher level of services than poor nations that mobilize relatively few resources for their schools. For example, average primary-level student–teacher ratios tend to be much higher in poorer regions than in wealthier regions. More than half of African nations report an average student–teacher ratio of more than thirty to one, whereas most European and North American nations average twenty to one or fewer. Large differences also emerge, however, when we compare wealthy countries with each other, and when we compare poor countries with other poor countries.[8]

■ Higher enrollment in wealthy regions

Enrollment Ratios. The resources devoted to education also help determine whether most children and youth attend school and whether they obtain diplomas

[7]George Psacharopoulos, *Planning of Education: Where Do We Stand?* (Washington, D.C.: World Bank, 1985); and Thomas D. Snyder and Charlene M. Hoffman, eds., *Digest of Education Statistics, 2002* (Washington, D.C.: U.S. Government Printing Office, 2003).
[8]*Education at a Glance* (Paris: Organisation for Economic Co-operation and Development, 2003).

or degrees. Data collected by UNESCO indicate that in "more developed regions" (Australia, Japan, New Zealand, North America, and most of Western Europe) nearly all children attend elementary schools. In what UNESCO designates as "less developed regions" (including most of Africa, the Arab states, much of Asia, and Latin America), nearly 20 percent of elementary-age children do not attend school. (In underdeveloped nations such as Liberia and Sudan, more than 60 percent of children are not in school.) Discrepancies in enrollment ratios between developed and less developed nations become even greater at the secondary and higher-education levels.[9]

■ Increasing female enrollment

Male and Female Enrollments.   We noted in the chapter on Culture, Socialization and Education that U.S. girls have higher reading scores than boys, and that females have become a majority in higher-education institutions. The same pattern has appeared in other developed nations. With a few exceptions, such as Japan and Turkey, female enrollment in colleges and universities in wealthy nations has been growing to the extent that more women than men obtain first degrees. However, the pattern is different in developing nations, where males frequently vastly outnumber females in higher education, secondary schools, and, sometimes, even elementary schools. Many analysts believe that the low enrollment ratio for girls compared to boys in many low-income countries in Africa and Asia is both a cause and an effect of economic development problems.[10]

The United States Among Industrial Nations.   For certain purposes it is instructive to compare wealthy or highly industrialized nations with each other rather than with poor or economically underdeveloped nations. Other factors remaining equal, nations with less wealth and fewer resources have a much harder time supporting education or other government services than do those with a strong economic base. Thus, to analyze how well the United States mobilizes resources for education, we should compare it with other developed countries.[11]

■ U.S. rank in expenditures

Several recent controversies have erupted about this subject. Although public-school critics have claimed that American education expenditures are "unsurpassed," many researchers disagree. When we subtract funding for higher education, the United States ranks near the middle on education expenditures. Figure 15.1 shows such a comparison in graphic form. In terms of public education expenditures for grades 1 through 12, as a percentage of gross domestic product, the United States ranks only fifth among twelve industrial countries.[12]

---

[9]*Education for All* (Paris: UNESCO, 2000); and Ken Parks, *The World Almanac and Book of Facts* (New York: World Almanac Books, 2003).

[10]Partha S. Dasgupta, "Population, Poverty, and the Local Environment," *Scientific American* (February 1995), pp. 40–45; and Christopher Colclough et al., "Gender and Education for All: The Leap to Equality" (2003), paper prepared for the UNESCO Education for All Global Monitoring Report 2003/4, available at **www.unesco.org/education/efa_report/2003_pdf/ summary_en.pdf**. The latter is a summary of the full report available at **www.efareport .unesco.org**.

[11]"Developed" nations as classified by the United Nations Educational, Scientific, and Cultural Organization (UNESCO) include Australia, Canada, most of Europe, Israel, Japan, South Africa, the former USSR, the United States, and New Zealand. All others are classified as "developing" nations.

[12]Joel Sherman and Marianne Perie, *International Resources and Expenditures for Elementary and Secondary Education* (Washington, D.C.: Pelavin Research Center, 1998); Ludger Woessman, "Why Students in Some Countries Do Better," *Education Next* (Summer 2001), pp. 67–74; available at **www.educationnext.org**; and Randall Parker, "An International Spending Study Is Misleading," September 16, 2003, posted at Parapundit, **www.parapundit.com**.

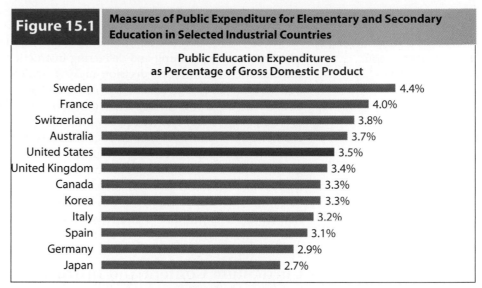

Figure 15.1 Measures of Public Expenditure for Elementary and Secondary Education in Selected Industrial Countries

Public Education Expenditures as Percentage of Gross Domestic Product

Sweden	4.4%
France	4.0%
Switzerland	3.8%
Australia	3.7%
United States	3.5%
United Kingdom	3.4%
Canada	3.3%
Korea	3.3%
Italy	3.2%
Spain	3.1%
Germany	2.9%
Japan	2.7%

Note: Expenditure data are for first grade through high school but exclude capital outlay and debt service. Various adjustments have been made to enhance comparability of the original data.
Source: Adapted from *Education at a Glance* (Paris: Organisation for Economic Co-operation and Development, 2003), Table B2.1b.

■ Comparing teacher salaries

Analysts also debate whether U.S. teacher salaries are high or low in comparison with those of other industrial countries. Data on teacher salary averages indicate that for both beginning and experienced teachers, average salaries in countries such as Ireland and Norway are a good deal lower than in the United States, but in some other countries they are generally higher.[13]

■ Comparing social-welfare expenditures

Sometimes the comparisons expand to other types of resources that support children's well-being and development. For example, Timothy Smeeding, comparing the United States with Australia, Canada, Germany, Sweden, and the United Kingdom, found that these five countries average about the same for government expenditures on children's education and health services as a percentage of gross domestic product. However, he also found that U.S. government expenditures to help provide income security for children's families are less than half the average for these countries. Smeeding concluded that high rates of divorce, out-of-wedlock births, and other social forces are creating a larger "urban and rural underclass," making it "increasingly hard to argue that all U.S. children have equal life chances."[14]

REFOCUS How do you think U.S. schools would be affected if the country devoted a greater percentage of its resources to education and children's well-being? What if the United States began to devote fewer resources to these?

---

[13]Daniel U. Levine, "Educational Spending: International Comparisons," *Theory into Practice* (Spring 1994), pp. 126–131; F. Howard Nelson, *How and How Much the U.S. Spends on K–12 Education* (Washington, D.C.: American Federation of Teachers, 1996); and "Facing Facts," *The Education Gadfly*, October 2, 2003, available at **www.edexcellence.net/foundation/gadfly**.
[14]Timothy M. Smeeding, "Social Thought and Poor Children," *Focus* (Spring 1990), p. 14. See also Lee Rainwater and Timothy M. Smeeding, *Rich Kids in a Poor Country* (New York: Russell Sage, 2003).

Extent of Centralization

Standards & Assessment ☑
▪ Decentralized versus centralized systems

All governments must decide whether to emphasize decentralized decision making, which allows for planning and delivering instruction in accordance with local circumstances, or centralized decision making, which builds accountability up and down a national or regional chain of command. Examples go far in either direction. In the United States, most important decisions are decentralized across thousands of diverse public school districts. At the other extreme, France, Greece, and Japan, for example, have highly centralized educational systems and decisions, following nationwide standards concerning acceptable class size and what will be taught in a given subject at a particular grade and time. In some countries, centralization has led to long lines of citizens from all parts of the nation waiting outside the ministry of education for appointments with central school officials who determine what schools children will attend and how students will be treated.[15] We consider centralized versus decentralized systems in the Taking Issue box.

Curriculum Content and Instructional Emphasis

Although, as we have seen, much instruction worldwide consists of teacher lectures and student seatwork, nations do differ with regard to curriculum content and instructional emphasis. The following well-known practices make certain countries distinctive:[16]

▪ Distinctive types of curriculum and instruction

- New Zealand primary schools are known for their systematic emphasis on learning to read through "natural language learning." Using this approach, children learn to figure out words in context as they read, rather than through phonics and decoding instruction.

- The education system in Finland has become known for high achievement and attainment at all levels from preschool through higher education (see Tables 15.1 and 15.2). Various observers have cited features they believe help account for this success: a national core curriculum that emphasizes thinking and students' active role in learning, an almost complete absence of streaming and tracking, provision and updating of science laboratory equipment and materials and computer hardware and software, and early intervention to help struggling students in elementary and secondary schools.

- Schools in certain Islamic countries build much of the curriculum around religious content and emphasize didactic memorization of religious precepts.

Vocational Versus Academic Education

▪ Divergence after primary years

School systems around the world also differ greatly in how they are organized to provide education through the postsecondary level. Although most nations now provide at least four years of first-level education during which all students attend

---

[15]Ami Voollansky and Daniel Bar-Elli, "Moving Toward Equitable School-Based Management," *Educational Leadership* (December 1995–January 1996), pp. 60–62; and Jackyung Lee, "School Reform Initiatives as Balancing Acts," *Education Policy Analysis Archives*, April 24, 2001, available at **http://epaa.asu.edu**.

[16]Elaine Jarchow, "Ten Ideas Worth Stealing from New Zealand," *Phi Delta Kappan* (January 1992), pp. 394–395; Heather Bell, "Learning to Read in New Zealand," *Reading Today* (April/May 2000), p. 32; John Crace, "Heaven and Helsinki," *Guardian*, September 16, 2003, available at **www.education.guardian.co.uk/schools**: search for "heaven"; and Jouni Välijärvi et al., "The Finnish Success in PISA—And Some Reasons Behind It" (2003), paper posted at the University of Jyväskylä Internet site, available at **www.jyu.fi/ktl/pisa/publication1.pdf**.

taking issue

Question Would a United States national curriculum be preferable to decentralized policies that allow individual school districts, schools, or teachers to select instructional objectives and materials?

Establishment of a National Curriculum

Countries with highly centralized public education generally expect teachers to follow a national curriculum that specifies the topics to be taught and the objectives and materials to be emphasized in each subject and grade level. Countries that follow a decentralized pattern primarily relegate decisions about subject matter and materials to a regional group of schools (such as a school district) or individual faculties or teachers. Government officials in some highly decentralized nations such as the United States are considering whether a national curriculum should be established to provide for a more standardized approach in planning and delivering instruction.

Arguments PRO

1 Availability of a national curriculum is partly responsible for the high achievement levels in Japan, Korea, and other countries.

2 A national curriculum based on the careful deliberation of subject-area specialists and experienced teachers makes it easier to achieve in-depth teaching of well-sequenced objectives and materials.

3 Uniformity in objectives and materials reduces the inefficiencies and learning problems that occur when students move from one classroom, school, or district to another.

4 A national curriculum will improve teacher education because preparation programs can concentrate on objectives and materials that trainees will teach when they obtain jobs.

5 Because it draws on a large base of resources, national curriculum planning can incorporate the best current thinking in each subject area and help prepare technically excellent tests.

Arguments CON

1 Establishment of a national curriculum runs counter to promising trends toward school-based management and professional autonomy for teachers.

2 A national curriculum is undesirable because its objectives and materials will be too difficult for many students and too easy for others.

3 Particularly in large and diverse countries such as the United States, the standardized materials that form the basis for a national curriculum will be uninteresting and demotivating for many students.

4 Even if the national curriculum allows flexibility in objectives and materials, teachers will be pressured to follow the same path as everyone else, and most likely funds will be unavailable for alternative materials. Therefore students and classes that might benefit from alternatives will suffer.

5 The extreme difficulty in preparing challenging national curriculum materials appropriate for use across a wide range of classrooms will reinforce tendencies to emphasize low-level skills and uncreative materials.

"primary" or "elementary" schools, above that level systems diverge widely. Most students continue in "common" first-level schools for several more years, but in many countries students are divided between academic-track schools and vocational schools after four to eight years of first-level education. This arrangement, which corresponds to the traditional European dual-track pattern described in the chapter on World Roots of American Education, is often known as a **bipartite system**.

◼ Wide variations in tracking

The proportion of secondary students enrolled in primarily vocational programs varies from less than one-tenth in industrial countries such as Denmark and the United States to more than one-fifth in others such as Germany. Similar variation appears in academic tracks. Some countries, beginning at the secondary level and extending into postsecondary education, enroll large proportions of students in academic schools designed to produce an "elite" corps of high-school or college graduates. In others, including Canada and the United States, most secondary students continue to attend "common" or "comprehensive" schools, and many enroll in colleges that are relatively nonselective.[17]

Enrollment in Higher Education

◼ Factors affecting enrollment in higher education

Countries that channel students into vocational programs tend to have low percentages of youth attending institutions of higher education. By contrast, more youth go on to higher education in countries that provide general academic studies for most high-school students. Other factors that help determine enrollment in higher education include a nation's investment of resources in higher education, emphasis on postsecondary learning rather than job market entry, traditions regarding the use of higher education to equalize educational opportunities, and the extent to which colleges and universities admit only high-achieving students.

◼ Developing versus industrial nations

Developing countries with relatively little funding available for higher education and struggling to increase elementary and secondary enrollments levels predictably have low proportions of youth participating in higher education. Thus Afghanistan, China, Ethiopia, Ghana, and many other developing nations enroll less than 20 percent of their young people in higher education. Most industrial countries provide postsecondary education for more than a third of their young adults (see Table 15.1).

◼ Differences among industrial nations

Once high-school graduates are enrolled in postsecondary institutions, numerous considerations determine whether they will stay enrolled and eventually gain their degrees: curriculum difficulty, financial aid opportunities, motivation levels, and access to preferred institutions and courses. Industrial nations differ greatly in the proportion of young people who obtain postsecondary degrees. As shown in Table 15.1, for example, the percentages of young adults who complete postsecondary education in industrial nations varies from 12 percent in Italy to more than half in Canada.

◼ Decline in U.S. ranking

Decline in U.S. Ranking for College Participation.   Until the 1990s, the United States generally had higher percentages of young people attending and completing higher education institutions than any other nation. Only Canada came close. The data in Table 15.1 indicate that this pattern no longer holds. Several nations now surpass the U.S. in postsecondary participation, and others are gaining rapidly. This change led the author of a study conducted for the Educational Commission of the States to conclude that "if current trends persist and students in the United States continue to enroll in college at the rate they do now, America is likely to slip further behind the growing number of developed nations that have stepped up their efforts over the last decade to increase educational attainment." She further warned of a se-

[17]Elliott A. Medrich and Susan A. Kagehiro, *Vocational Education in G-7 Countries: Profiles and Data* (Washington, D.C.: U.S. Department of Education, 1994); Klaus Breuer and Klaus Beck, eds., *Are European Vocational Systems Up to the Job?* (Frankfurt: Peter Lang, 2002); and Gerald W. Bracey, "Tracking, By Accident and By Design," *Phi Delta Kappan* (December 2003), pp. 332–333.

Table 15.1	Percentage of Twenty-five- to Thirty-four-Year-Olds Who Have Attained Postsecondary (Tertiary) Education, Selected Countries, 2001			
Australia	34	Italy	12
Belgium	38	Japan	48
Canada	51	Korea (South)	40
Denmark	29	Netherlands	27
Finland	38	Norway	38
France	34	Spain	36
Germany	22	Sweden	37
Iceland	26	United Kingdom	29
Ireland	48	United States	39

Source: Adapted from *Education at a Glance* (Paris: Organisation for Economic Co-operation and Development, 2003), Table A2.4.

rious risk "that competing public priorities and shrinking resources will put access to an affordable and high-quality college education further out of reach for more and more Americans."[18]

Nonpublic Schools

■ Proportion of students in private schools

Depending on their histories, political structures, religious composition, legal frameworks, and other factors, nations differ greatly in the size and functions of their nonpublic education sectors. In a few countries, such as the Netherlands, more than half of elementary and secondary students attend private schools. At the other extreme, governments in Cuba, North Korea, and other nations have prohibited nonpublic schools in order to suppress ideologies different from those supported by the state. In most countries, private-school students constitute less than 10 percent of total enrollment.[19]

■ Problems in defining a "private school"

Nations also vary widely in the extent to which they provide public support for nonpublic schools or students. They differ as to government regulation of nonpublic systems, people's perceptions of public and nonpublic schools, and the role that private schools are expected to play in national development. In some countries, nonpublic schools enroll a relatively small, elite group of students who later enter the most prestigious colleges; in others they serve a more representative sample of the nation's children and youth. Given this variety, it is not possible to cross-nationally define a "private school" or generalize about policies that encourage or discourage nonpublic schools. Clearly, productive national policies on nonpublic schools must reflect each country's unique mix of circumstances and challenges.[20]

---

[18]Sandra S. Ruppert, "Closing the College Participation Gap" (2003), paper prepared for the Education Commission of the States, pp. 6–7, available at **www.ecs.org**.
[19]Brian J. Caldwell, "Scenarios for Leadership and Abandonment in the Transformation of Schools," *School Effectiveness and School Improvement* (December 2000), pp. 475–499.
[20]Pauline Nesdale, "International Perspectives on Government Funding of Non-Government Schools," *Education Forum Briefing Papers* (March 2003), available at **www.educationforum.org.nz**.

Standards & Assessment

■ IEA, PISA, PIRLS, and TIMSS
studies

Achievement Levels

Differences in school achievement among nations have received considerable attention since the **International Association for the Evaluation of Educational Achievement (IEA)** began conducting cross-national studies in the 1960s. One of the first major IEA projects collected and analyzed data on the achievement of 258,000 students from nineteen countries in civic education, foreign languages, literature, reading comprehension, and science. This study showed a wide range in average achievement levels across nations. In general, the United States ranked close to the middle among the nations included in the study. Later studies, such as the Program for International Student Assessment (PISA), the Progress in International Reading Literacy Study (PIRLS), and the **Third International Mathematics and Science Study (TIMSS)**, also have found that our students above the fourth grade generally rank near the average for industrial countries (see Table 15.2).[21]

Table 15.2	Reading Literacy Scores of Fifteen-Year-Olds in Thirty-One Nations		
Finland	546	Switzerland	494
Canada	534	Spain	493
New Zealand	529	Czech Republic	492
Australia	528	Italy	487
Ireland	527	Germany	484
S. Korea	525	Lichtenstein*	483
United Kingdom	523	Hungary	480
Japan	522	Poland	479
Sweden	516	Greece	474
Austria	507	Portugal	470
Belgium	507	Russia*	462
Iceland	507	Latvia*	458
Norway	505	Luxembourg	441
France	505	Mexico	422
United States	504	Brazil*	396
Denmark	497		
		Average	**500**

*=non-OECD nations. The average score is for the twenty-seven nations belonging to the Organisation for Economic Co-operation and Development.

Source: Adapted from Marianne Lemke et al., *Outcomes of Learning: Results From the 2000 Program for International Student Assessment of 15-Year-Olds in Reading, Mathematics, and Science Literacy.* (Washington, D.C.: U.S. Department of Education, 2002), Table A3.1, available at **http://search.nces.ed.gov**.

---

[21]Purves and Levine, *Educational Policy and International Assessment;* Lawrence C. Stedman, "The Achievement Crisis Is Real," *Educational Policy Analysis Archives,* January 23, 1996, pp. 1–11, available at **http://epaa.asu.edu**; "What Can We Learn from TIMSS-Repeat?" *NCTM News and Hot Topics* (January 2001), available at **www.nctm.org/news/articles/2001-01cover.htm**; Lawrence T. Ogle et al., *International Comparisons in Fourth-Grade Literacy* (Washington D.C.: National Center for Education Statistics, 2003); and TIMSS Video Mathematics Research Group, "Understanding and Improving Mathematics Teaching," *Phi Delta Kappan* (June 2003), pp. 768–775.

■ Researchers' conclusions

Analyzing data from these international studies, scholars have reached conclusions that include the following:[22]

- National scores in subjects such as reading, math, and science tend to be highly correlated. For example, seven of the eight nations with the highest reading scores in data collected by PISA also were in the highest eight nations with respect to math and science scores.

■ More spread in U.S.

- As shown in Table 15.2, U.S. students scored well below students in the highest-scoring nations. Some nations, including the United States, have a much greater spread between the performance of low- and high-achieving students than do others such as Finland, Japan, and Korea. The performance of high-achieving American students, however, is comparable to that of the highest performers in other nations.

- Social class correlates strongly with achievement test scores in nearly all nations. However, the spread between working-class and middle-class students is much greater in nations such as the United States than in others such as Finland and Japan that have high average scores and relatively low spread between high and low achievers.

■ Emphasis on passive learning

- Instructional characteristics (including class size, amount of time allocated to instruction, teachers' experience, and amount of homework) generally do not correlate with achievement test scores. For example, most countries studied, including the United States, commonly use mathematics instruction based on "tell and show" approaches that emphasize passive, rote learning. Because some of these countries had scores considerably higher than U.S. scores, however, such approaches could not account for mediocre U.S. performance levels except in interaction with other variables.

■ U.S. math curricula repetitive, incoherent, and undemanding

- Some analysts have concluded that U.S. curricula and instruction, particularly in mathematics, generally are a "mile wide and an inch deep" and that the mediocre performance resulting from this superficial teaching poses a serious threat to our international competitiveness. Several scholars studying the U.S. math curriculum in an international context concluded that it is *unfocused,* with too many topics in too little depth; *highly repetitive; incoherent,* with little logical order to topics; and *undemanding,* particularly at the middle school level. In addition, U.S. mathematics curricula, in contrast to many other nations, are highly differentiated. That is, our middle-level students tend to be sorted into mathematics tracks that stress algebra and other advanced topics for high-achieving students and simple arithmetic for low achievers. Thus many students with low or medium achievement levels have little opportunity to proceed beyond basic skills. This is in marked contrast to Finland, Hungary, Japan, and some other locations where most students are challenged to perform at a higher level. Most analysts who have reviewed these patterns believe that action must be taken to reduce this kind of curriculum differentiation.[23]

---

[22]Pascal D. Forgione Jr., "Responses to Frequently Asked Questions About 12th-Grade TIMSS," *Phi Delta Kappan* (June 1998), pp. 769–772; Kathryn S. Schiller, "Beyond the 'One Best System,'" *International Journal of Educational Policy, Research and Practice* (Summer 2000); Stephen P. Heyneman, "Study Abroad," *Education Next* (Summer 2003), available at **www.educationnext.org**; and Deborah I. Nelson, "What Explains Differences in International Performance," *CPRE Policy Briefs* (September 2003), available at **www.cpre.org**.
[23]Tom Loveless and Paul Diperna, "How Well Are American Students Learning?" *Brown Center Report on American Education* (September 2000); and William Hook, "A World Class K–7 Math Curriculum Verified by Outstanding Experimental Research" (2004), paper prepared for the California State Department of Education, available at **www.educationnews.org/a-world-class-k-7.htm**.

Standards & Assessment

- Improvement in U.S. student performance will require systemic change involving setting of standards, assessment of students, teacher preparation, instructional methods, and other aspects of our educational system.

Publication of the PIRLS, PISA, and TIMSS studies has helped ignite emotional controversies. On one side, observers claim that our educational system is more satisfactory than it is often portrayed. While admitting that it needs major improvements, these observers point to factors like the following.[24]

■ Defense of U.S. schools

- Our students generally perform at a relatively high reading level through the fourth grade.

- Cultural factors, not deficiencies in the schools, may be causing much of the relatively low student performance. For example, the high levels of mathematics achievement reported for Hungary, Japan, and Korea may be attributable primarily to the great value their cultures attach to mathematics performance and to strong family support for achievement.

- Contrary to critics' statements, achievement in U.S. schools has improved during the past few decades, particularly considering the increased enrollment of minority students from low-income families. These improvements may be attributable in part to the positive effects of compensatory education and school desegregation (see the chapter on Social Class, Race, and School Achievement) and to efforts at educational reform.

■ Critique of U.S. schools

Critics of U.S. performance have been unappeased by such arguments. Frequently pointing to the particularly low scores that our students register on tests assessing higher-order skills such as math problem solving, they reiterate the importance of improving students' skills in comprehension, geography, math, science, and other subjects. They conclude that the rankings of U.S. students in numerous international achievement studies represent a deplorable performance level that cannot be corrected without radical efforts to reform or even replace our current system of education.[25]

 How might your work as a teacher be affected by international comparisons of achievement? How should it be affected?

▶ Problems and Prospects in Developing Countries

■ Education and economic development

Earlier in this chapter we saw that educational inadequacies in developing countries are both a cause and a result of poverty. For this reason, national governments and international organizations have strongly supported bolstering the economies of developing countries by expanding and improving their educational systems. Education usually is considered critical for economic development because it can give people the skills and knowledge to compete in international markets and because it

---

[24]Purves and Levine, *Educational Policy and International Assessment;* Gerald W. Bracey, "'Diverging' Japanese and American Scores," *Phi Delta Kappan* (June 2000), pp. 790–791; and David J. Hoff, "U.S. Students Rank Among World's Best and Worst Readers," *Education Week*, December 1, 2002.
[25]Chester E. Finn Jr., *We Must Take Charge* (New York: Free Press, 1991); William Schmidt, Richard Houang, and Leonard Cogan, "A Coherent Curriculum," *American Educator* (Summer 2002), available at **www.aft.org/american_educator**; and Harold W. Stevenson, "A TIMSS Primer" (undated), paper posted at **www.edexcellence.net/foundation/global/index.cfm**.

■ Problems in upgrading education

can help bring about a more equitable distribution of wealth and power, which in turn contributes to political stability and long-term economic growth.

However, it has proved exceedingly difficult to achieve widespread, lasting, and balanced improvement of educational systems in many developing countries. For example, extreme poverty in countries such as Rwanda has been partly responsible for restricting the availability of funds to less than one hundred dollars per primary student per year. Developing countries such as India and Nigeria also struggle to overcome educational problems associated with the use of dozens or even hundreds of different languages among their multiethnic populations. Numerous developing countries also confront a problem known as **brain drain**: the number of high-school and university graduates increases, but with no well-paid jobs suitable to their level of education, these well-trained people emigrate to wealthier countries with better employment opportunities.

To improve education in developing countries, researchers have suggested the following steps:[26]

■ Recommendations for developing countries

1. Invest more in primary schools to broaden the base of students who can participate in higher levels of education.

2. Avoid emphasizing higher-education subjects that students will tend to study abroad and perhaps not return.

3. Make private schools an integral part of educational expansion plans.

4. Expand efforts to improve students' cognitive functioning.

5. Work on overcoming obstacles that limit the education of girls and women.

6. Substantially improve teacher preparation.

7. Use modern technologies to expand educational opportunities at all levels.

 Which of these suggestions do you believe would be of most use to developing nations?

▶ Exemplary Reforms: A Selection

As in the United States, educators in other parts of the world are introducing reforms to make schools more effective. Some of these reforms are based on studies of unusually successful schools and how they function. Most research on these **effective schools** occurred in the United States, but important studies have also taken place in Australia, Canada, the Netherlands, the United Kingdom, and other countries. In this chapter we're considering substantial reforms many nations have introduced in their educational systems.[27] Some countries have been respected for many decades for the quality and effectiveness with which they provide early childhood opportunities, mathematics instruction, vocational schooling, or other important educational experiences. In the next chapter we'll explore in detail characteristics

---

[26]Gary Stix and Paul Wallich, "A Digital Fix for the Third World?" *Scientific American* (October 1993), p. 89; Andrew Curry, "Cap, Gown, Mouse," *Foreign Policy* (January–February 2003), pp. 102–103; and Judith L. Johnson, *Distance Education* (New York: Teachers College Press, 2003).
[27]L. Kyria Rides, R. J. Campbell, and A. Gagatsis, "The Significance of the Classroom Effect in Primary Schools," *School Effectiveness and School Improvement* (December 2000), pp. 501–529; and Helen S. Timperly and Viviane M. Robinson, "Partnership as an Intervention Strategy in Self-Managing Schools," *School Effectiveness and School Improvement* (September 2003), pp. 249–274.

of effective schools, as well as research indicating that systematic change and long-term commitment are the keys to successful schools.

Early Childhood Education in France

■ Varying child-care arrangements

Recognizing the critical importance of the preschool years in a child's social, physical, and educational development, many countries have taken steps to provide stimulating learning opportunities and positive day-care arrangements for most or all young children. For example, more than 90 percent of three- to five-year-olds in Belgium, Hong Kong, and Italy are enrolled in early childhood education programs, compared with little more than half in the United States. Outstanding child-care arrangements for infants are easily accessible to families throughout Scandinavia. The mix of preschool and day-care programs varies considerably from one country to another, as does the extent to which early childhood educators work with parents and families. Overall, however, early childhood education has become a topic of urgent interest throughout much of the world.

■ French preschool programs

France has what many observers consider a "vintage" approach to preschool services. Nearly all three- to five-year-olds are enrolled in preschool programs, and average salaries of preschool teachers are considerably higher than in the United States or most other countries. Participating children pursue stimulating activities before and after school, during vacation, and at other times when school is out. Equally important, parents have financial incentives to enroll their children in high-quality programs that provide pediatric and other preventive health services. Child-care specialists and civic leaders who examined the French system have reported the following aspects of French programs as worth considering in the United States:[28]

■ Positive features of French programs

- Virtually all children have access to a coordinated system linking early education, day care, and health services.

- Paid parental leave from jobs after childbirth or adoption helps to nurture positive parent–child relationships.

- Good salaries and training for early childhood teachers help to keep turnover low and program quality high.

- Nearly all young children are enrolled in preschool programs.

- The government provides additional resources to ensure high quality at locations enrolling low-income children.

Vocational and Technical Education in Germany

■ Advantages and disadvantages

Most European countries and many developing countries channel a high percentage of high-school and postsecondary students into vocational or technical schools. Students receive high-quality training for specific occupations, which they enter immediately upon receiving their diplomas or certificates. The "up" side of this bipartite system—early separation into vocational and technical versus academic tracks—is that many students unlikely to complete college can successfully prepare for employment. Thus the transition from adolescence or young adulthood to work is

---

[28]Karen Whiten, *Promoting the Development of Young Children in Denmark, France, and Italy* (Washington, D.C.: U.S. Government Accounting Office, 1995); Janet C. Gornick and Marcia K. Meyers, "Support for Working Families," *American Prospect,* January 1–15, 2001), pp. 3–7; and Michelle J. Neuman and Shanny Peer, *Equal From the Start* (New York: French-American Foundation, 2002), available at **www.frenchamerican.org/pubs/ Equalfromthestart.pdf**.

Many believe that certain elements of the German apprenticeship system—such as close supervision of apprentices by veterans and certification of employability—can be adapted and emulated successfully elsewhere. *(© Michael A. Dwyer/Stock Boston)*

smooth and easy. The "down" side is that these young people have fewer opportunities to pursue academic studies and obtain a college degree than students in Canada, the United States, and a few other countries.

Responding to this dilemma, government officials in many countries with severe tracking arrangements are introducing general studies programs into vocational education, expanding opportunities to attend academic high schools and postsecondary institutions, and establishing "informal" mechanisms such as correspondence courses for obtaining college degrees. Conversely, officials in the United States are beginning to establish apprenticeship programs and other vocational or technical courses that may help prepare high-school students for employment without placing them in separate tracks that exclude them from higher education.[29]

■ German apprenticeship program

Many authorities on vocational education see Germany's traditional apprenticeship program as one of the most effective in the world. Only about a third of high-school-age German students attend college-preparatory institutions; the remainder enroll in vocational and technical schools that combine academics with job training as an apprentice. Their work is supervised by experienced personnel and monitored by appropriate organizations, such as state agencies for health workers or industrial associations for students with jobs in commerce. The responsible organizations also administer exams that lead to completion certificates and often directly to employment. Although analysts recognize that the German apprenticeship system evolved gradually over centuries and cannot be simply re-created in other countries, many believe that certain elements, such as close supervision of

[29]John R. McKernan Jr., *Making the Grade* (Boston: Little, Brown, 1994); *Pathways and Participation in Vocational and Technical Education and Training* (Washington, D.C.: OECD, 1998); and Elisabeth Oehler, "Vocational Education in Germany" (2002), posting at the Goethe-Institute Zintrale Internet site, available at **www.goethe.de/kug/buw/sub/ein/en21491.htm**.

apprentices by skilled veterans and certification of a young person's employability, can be adapted successfully elsewhere.[30]

Standards & Assessment ✓

Elementary-School Reading and Mathematics in England

One of the most impressive school reform efforts has been in England's reading and mathematics instruction. Following recommendations of literacy and numeracy task forces, the national government initiated actions and activities, including the following, that affected about three million students in approximately twenty thousand elementary-level schools:[31]

■ British literacy and numeracy initiatives

- ■ A requirement that every school have at least a daily literacy hour and a daily mathematics hour, together with guidance and standards on what content should be emphasized at each grade level for students five to eleven years old.

- ■ A reduction in prescribed curriculum content outside these core subjects; the director of the government Standards and Effectiveness Unit described this reduction as "huge."

- ■ Additional funds and other resources for low-performing schools.

- ■ Providing the services of hundreds of expert literacy and numeracy consultants at the local level.

- ■ An emphasis on early intervention and catch-up for students who fall behind, including after-school, weekend, and holiday classes for students who need extra help.

- ■ The appointment of more than two thousand math teachers and several hundred literacy teachers as lead teachers to model best practice for their colleagues.

- ■ Major investments in books for schools.

- ■ Regular monitoring and extensive evaluation by a national inspection agency.

As a result of these actions and activities, the percentage of students scoring at least 4 (on a scale of 1 to 5) in reading increased from 48 percent in 1996 to 75 percent in 2000, and the corresponding percentages in mathematics were 44 percent in 1996 and 73 percent in 2000. Education officials in England are now working to increase student performance to still higher levels and to extend these gains to higher grades. For more on school reform in England, see the Technology @ School box.

Mathematics and Science Education in Japan

■ High performance

International achievement studies indicate that Japanese students consistently attain high scores in mathematics, science, and other subject areas. For example, the second International Study of Achievement in Mathematics reported that eighth

---

[30]Harvey Kantor, "Managing the Transition from School to Work," *Teachers College Record* (Summer 1994), pp. 442–461; Tim Hatcher, "From Apprentice to Instructor," *Journal of Industrial Teacher Education* (Fall 1995), p. 44; Susan B. Silverberg et al., "Adolescent Apprentices in Germany," *Journal of Adolescent Research* (July 1998), pp. 254–271; and Felix Buchel, "Successful Apprenticeship-to-Work Transitions" (2002), paper prepared for the Max Planck Institute for Human Development, Berlin.

[31]Michael Barber, "Large-Scale Reform Is Possible," *Education Week*, November 15, 2000; Arthur Seldon, ed., *The Blair Effect* (Boston: Little, Brown, 2001); Rebecca Smithers, "How Labour's Big Moves Measure Up," *Guardian,* March 2, 2001; Lynn Olson, "England Refines Accountability Reforms," *Education Week*, May 5, 2004; and various publications at **www .standards.dfes.gov.uk/literacy/publications**.

TECHNOLOGY @ School

An Internet Location Dealing with School Reform in England

In this chapter, we've mentioned that the effective reforms implemented at schools around the world might serve as useful examples for other schools with similar needs. As a teacher, you can use the Internet to learn the details of how exemplary school reforms have been implemented in other nations. Gathering this specific information can help you and your colleagues decide whether elements of international reform could be readily transferred to help meet the needs of students at your own school.

As an example, you could try learning more about the elementary-school reforms described in this chapter. Go to the United Kingdom's Department for Education and Skills "Standards Site" at **www.standards.dfes.gov.uk**. The literacy and numeracy reforms were combined in 2004 into a single Primary National Strategy. Go to that heading to read about the intent of the reforms, examine the curriculum frameworks teachers are to use in their classrooms, and download lesson plans suggested for teaching particular objectives and materials.

You also can find descriptions of practices at exemplary schools by clicking on "Beacon Schools" at the bottom of the first screen. The next screen lets you click on "Case Studies Index" to pursue topics of particular interest.

You may have a special interest in policy initiatives of the standards and effectiveness unit, listed at **www.standards.dfes.gov.uk/seu**, such as "Boys and Girls Achievement" or "Excellence in Cities."

Questions you might consider as you explore this site include the following:

1. Do the curriculum frameworks used for literacy and numeracy resemble those used in school districts where you live?

2. Do the practices described at Beacon schools apply to reforming schools in general? Would they make sense at schools in the United States?

3. Would you like to teach at English schools emphasizing policies and practices described at this Internet site?

4. Do you believe this site provides concrete help for teachers and administrators in England?

You can keep up with school reform developments in England and the controversies surrounding it by going to the Electronic Telegraph at **www.telegraph.co.uk**. Search for terms such as "school reform."

graders in Japan on average answered 62 percent of the test items correctly, compared with 45 percent in the United States and 47 percent across the eighteen countries included in the study. With respect to science achievement among eighth graders, Japanese students attained an average score of 571, compared with an average of 541 for other industrial nations included in the third assessment.[32]

■ Possible reasons for Japanese success

Certain aspects of Japanese education and society may help account for high achievement levels among Japanese youth. Most of the following characteristics apply to Japanese education in general, not merely to math and science programs. The

[32]Barbara J. Reyes and Robert E. Reyes, "Japanese Mathematics Education," *Teaching Children Mathematics* (April 1995), pp. 474–475; *The Condition of Education 1997* (Washington, D.C.: U.S. Government Printing Office, 1997); and *Before It's Too Late* (Washington, D.C.: America Counts, 2000), available at **www.ed.gov/inits/Math/glenn**.

list of pertinent factors is long, and researchers remain unsure which are important. Perhaps they all are.[33]

- ■ Outstanding day care helps prepare children for school success. In addition, socialization practices in the family and in early childhood education help students learn to adapt to classroom situations and demands. U.S. schools, in contrast, tend to attain good discipline by making instruction attractive and by "bargaining" with students to obtain compliance (see the chapter on Culture, Socialization, and Education), at great cost to academic standards and rigor.

■ Parental involvement

- ■ Intense parental involvement is expected. In particular, mothers feel great responsibility for children's success in school. Families provide much continuing support and motivation, ranging from elaborate celebration of entry into first grade to widespread enrollment of children in supplementary private cram schools *(juku)*, which students attend after school and on weekends. Compared with U.S. parents, Japanese parents emphasize effort over ability when asked to identify causes of success or failure in school.

■ Long school year

- ■ Students attend school 240 days a year (compared with less than 200 in the United States).

■ National curriculum

- ■ Large amounts of homework correlated with classroom lessons contribute to high student performance.

Standards & Assessment ✓

- ■ Careful planning and delivery of a national curriculum help students acquire important concepts within a sequential and comprehensive framework.

- ■ Compared with elementary-school practices in the United States and in many other countries, lessons de-emphasize rote learning.

- ■ Language patterns in Japan and other Asian countries facilitate academic learning. For example, math may be easier to learn in Japanese than in English because numbers are designated in a "ten plus one, two, etc." system.

■ Stress on character

- ■ The schools emphasize the development of students' character and sense of responsibility through such practices as assigning students chores and having them help each other in learning.

- ■ Educators tend to take responsibility for students' learning. For example, many teachers contact parents to recommend homework schedules and curfews.

■ Status of teachers

- ■ Prospective teachers must pass rigorous examinations and are intensely supervised when they enter the profession.

- ■ Japanese educators have relatively high social status, which enhances their authority in working with students and parents. Partly for this reason there are numerous applicants for teaching positions thus allowing administrators to select highly qualified candidates.

- ■ School schedules provide considerable time for counseling students, planning instruction, and engaging in other activities that make teachers more effective.

---

[33]Robert D. Hess and Hiroshi Azuma, "Cultural Support for Schooling," *Educational Researcher* (December 1991), pp. 2–12; Thomas P. Rohlen, "Differences That Make a Difference: Explaining Japan's Success," *Educational Policy* (June 1995), pp. 129–151; Andy Hargreves, ed., *Learning to Change* (San Francisco: Jossey-Bass, 2000); Wellford W. Wilms, "Altering the Structure and Culture of American Public Schools," *Phi Delta Kappan* (April 2003); and Harold W. Stevenson and Roberta Nerison-Low, "To Sum It Up" (undated), paper prepared for the U.S. Department of Education, available at **www.ed.gov/pubs/SumItUp**.

- Generous time and support available to help slower students helps produce less variability in achievement than in the United States and most other countries. Japanese schools have relatively few extremely low achievers.

■ **Criticisms of Japanese system**

People familiar with the Japanese educational system also point out some apparently negative characteristics:[34]

■ **Too little divergent thinking**

- Emphasis appears relatively slight on divergent thinking. Some observers believe that insufficient emphasis on creativity may severely hamper future social and economic development in Japan.

■ **Class and gender limitations**

- Opportunities for working-class students and women to attend postsecondary institutions and gain high occupational status appear severely limited. For example, one study found that only 11 percent of students in college-prep high schools had fathers who had not completed high school, compared with 32 percent of students in less academic high schools.

Standards & Assessment ☑

- Partly because of restricted higher-education opportunities, secondary education is exam driven—instruction covers immense quantities of factual information likely to be tested on entrance examinations. In turn, examination pressures further stifle divergent thinking and frequently lead to mental distress and even suicide.

- Students face relatively few demands once they are admitted to colleges and universities.

■ **Behavioral conformity**

- Behavioral standards and expectations in many Japanese schools are so narrow and rigid that some educators believe they generate too much conformity. In accordance with the old Japanese proverb "The nail that sticks out gets hammered down," students are told what school uniform to wear at each grade. In some cases, they have been required to dye their hair to conform to school regulations. However, rules governing student appearance and behavior have been significantly loosened in recent years.

- More than ever before, young people in Japan seem to be rejecting the traditional customs and values on which the educational system is founded.

- Many students with disabilities receive little help.

- Japanese schools have done relatively little to introduce computers and other aspects of modern technology.

■ **Neither ignore nor imitate**

In reviewing its various strengths and weaknesses, several thoughtful observers have concluded that we have much to learn from the Japanese educational system, but they add that we should make sure that promising practices from elsewhere are workable and appropriately adapted to our own situation. Likewise, government commissions in Japan have been considering reform proposals that incorporate the more positive aspects of education in the United States (for example, to reduce the emphasis on conformity). A professor of Japanese studies at Harvard University has summarized the situation in this way: "As a mirror showing us our weakness and as a yardstick against which to measure our efforts," Japanese education has great value for us. We should not, however, "allow ourselves either to ignore or to imitate" its approach. Instead, we should "look periodically into the 'Japanese mirror'

---

[34]Ken Schoolland, *Shogun's Ghost: The Dark Side of Japanese Education* (New York: Bergin and Garvey, 1990); Maso Miyamoto, *Straitjacket Society* (Tokyo: Kodansha, 1994); Kathleen K. Manzo, "Japanese Schoolchildren 'Cram' to Boost Achievement," *Education Week*, August 7, 2002; and John Nathan, *Japan Unbound* (Boston: Houghton Mifflin, 2004).

while we quite independently set out to straighten our schools and our system within our own cultural and social context."[35]

Multicultural Education in Europe and North America

Probably no country has responded adequately to the challenges posed by multicultural populations. However, many nations have made important efforts to deliver educational services suitable for diverse groups of students, particularly minority students who experience racial, ethnic, or religious discrimination or who do not learn the national language at home. Approaches like the following may become future models:[36]

■ Model multicultural programs

- As we discussed at length in the chapter on Providing Equal Educational Opportunity, the United States is trying to provide bilingual education for millions of English language–learner students.

- Canada has implemented sizable bilingual education programs, as well as numerous approaches for promoting multiethnic curriculum and instruction.

- France has provided in-service training nationwide to help teachers learn to teach French as a second language.

- Belgium provides *reception classes* in which immigrant children receive up to two years of instruction from both a Belgian teacher and a native-language teacher.

R E F O C U S   **What are the potential benefits of using other nations' educational reforms as models for improving our own schools? What are the drawbacks? What cautions should educators observe in adopting school reforms from other countries?**

▶ Conclusion: U.S. Schools in an International Context

■ Growing similarities among nations

Some observers believe that international study of education is becoming increasingly useful because developed societies are growing more alike. Throughout the world, more citizens are becoming middle class, and school systems and other institutions are emphasizing preparation for dealing with advanced technology and rapid social change. Mass media and other technologies exert a common influence across national borders. Even so, no two societies ever will be exactly alike, nor will cultural and social differences disappear entirely. Still, characteristics of social institutions (including the family and the school) will likely converge. For example, Kenichi Ohmae has remarked that Japan's "Nintendo Kids"—youngsters who have grown up with computers, video games, and global media—"have more in common with similar youngsters outside Japan than with other generations within Japan."[37]

[35]Thomas P. Rohlen, "Japanese Education: If They Can Do It, Should We?" *American Scholar* (Winter 1985–1986), p. 43. See also Catherine C. Lewis, *Educating Hearts and Minds* (Cambridge: Cambridge University Press, 1995); and Jackyung Lee, "School Reform Initiatives," *Education Policy Analysis Archives,* April 24, 2001, available at **http:epaa.asu.edu**.
[36]Bruce Carrington and Alastair Bonnett, "The Other Canadian 'Mosaic,'" *Comparative Education* (November 1997), pp. 411–432. See also Olusegen A. Sogunro, "Toward Multiculturalism," *Multicultural Perspectives* 3 (2001), pp. 19–34.
[37]Kenichi Ohnae, "China's 600,000 Avon Ladies," *New Perspectives Quarterly* (Winter 1995), p. 15. See also Pico Iyer, "The Diversity Debate: Point," *Utne Reader* (January–February 1996), pp. 35–36.

■ Much to learn, much to offer

If that is true, we have much to learn from studying effective education in other nations. Likewise, other nations can learn from the United States. Despite its many shortcomings described in this book, the United States has been an international leader in striving to educate all students regardless of their social background or previous achievement. Richard Kahlenberg and Bernard Wasow examined educational systems and achievement patterns internationally and reached the following conclusions with respect to implications for the United States: ". . . American public schools have helped make Americans out of wave after wave of immigrants. . . . That said, the public school system fails a substantial segment of the population, and this failure aligns sharply with class and race. Reform must preserve the achievements of the system while correcting the failures." [38]

 **Do you believe that increasing similarities between developed nations will eventually lead to increasingly similar educational systems?**

▶ Summing Up

① Although educational systems differ considerably between nations, they tend to confront the similar problem of providing effective instruction for large numbers of students whose opportunities and performance relate to their social and cultural background.

② Teaching conditions throughout the world appear fundamentally similar. In most countries, teachers and curricula emphasize presentation of information, and teachers struggle to find time to accomplish difficult and sometimes conflicting goals.

③ School systems around the world differ greatly in the resources they devote to education, enrollments, student and teacher ratios, male and female student ratios, the extent of centralization or decentralization, curriculum content and instructional emphasis, higher education and vocational education opportunities, nonpublic school availability and roles, and student achievement.

④ Scholars studying education in developing countries advocate an emphasis on improving teacher preparation and primary education, developing student cognitive functioning, and expanding education for girls and women.

⑤ Educational services or practices appear exemplary in several countries: early childhood education in France, vocational and technical education in Germany, elementary-school reading and mathematics in England, and mathematics and science education in Japan. Europe and North America in general have excelled in multicultural education. Researchers can learn much from studying educational systems in other countries, but it is not always easy to identify the reasons for a system's success or failure or its implications for different societies.

⑥ The United States has been an international leader in the effort to provide equal and effective educational opportunities for all groups of students, but it has been slipping in this regard in comparison with other nations.

[38]Richard D. Kahlenberg and Bernard Wasow, "What Makes Schools Work?" *Boston Review* (October–November 2003), available at **www.bostonreview.net**.

▶ Key Terms

bipartite system (457)
International Association for the Evaluation of Educational Achievement (IEA) (460)
Third International Mathematics and Science Study (TIMSS) (460)
brain drain (463)
effective schools (463)

▶ Discussion Questions

1 Why are teaching methods and teachers' joys and frustrations so similar from one country to another?

2 What are the most important educational problems in developing countries? What policies might be most appropriate in addressing these problems?

3 To what extent should U.S. education policies and practices emulate those in Japan? Which practices might be most "transportable," and which may be undesirable?

4 What are the advantages and disadvantages of offering higher education opportunities for a large proportion of young people? What might or should be done to counteract the disadvantages?

▶ Suggested Projects for Professional Development

1 Use Internet resources to find recent arguments for and against national tests and/or a national curriculum. Does the current seem to be moving toward or away from national standards and curricula? Searching ERIC for these terms at **www.ed.gov** can provide a useful start.

2 Examine one or more international studies of educational achievement (such as the ones cited in this chapter) to determine how far the United States ranks from the top or bottom. Has the U.S. position been improving or declining?

3 Research two or three educational policies or approaches used in other countries but not in the United States. Do they seem applicable to the United States? If so, what problems might occur in implementing them? How would you prepare a plan to convince school officials to let you try such a policy or approach in your subject or teaching field?

▶ Suggested Resources

◯ Internet Resources

Good sources of information regarding developments in educational systems elsewhere include publications such as *Education News,* at **www.educationnews.org**, and organizations such as the International Association for the Evaluation of Educational Achievement (**www.iea.nl**). Another useful Internet location is the World Bank's site dealing with school and teacher effectiveness internationally (**www1.worldbank.org/education/est**). Much information about education in Europe is available at **www.eurydice.org**.

Jackyung Lee's "School Reform Initiatives" (*Education Policy Analysis Archives,* April 24, 2001) examines developments in England, Japan, Korea, and the United States, and is available at **http:epaa.asu.edu**.

Publications

Caldwell, Brian J., and David Hayward. *The Future of Schools.* London: Routledge, 1998. *Gives particular attention to recent school reform efforts in Australia and the United Kingdom.*

Chris Colclough et al. *EFA Global Monitoring Report 2003/4.* Paris: United Nations Educational, Social and Cultural Organization, 2003. *This in-depth examination of educational opportunities for women focuses on the need for improvement in developing countries. It is available at **www.efareport.unesco.org**.*

Comparative Education Review. This journal emphasizes such topics as the development of national school systems, education and economic development, comparisons across nations, and international aspects of multicultural education.

Husen, Torsten, Albert Tuijnman, and William Halls. *Schooling in Modern European Society.* Oxford: Pergamon, 1992. *Discusses trends in curriculum and testing, economics and education, schooling for minorities, and other contemporary issues.*

International Journal of Educational Research. Recent theme issues have dealt with equal opportunity, giftedness, private education, science education, and other topics of worldwide concern.

Lane, John J., ed. *Ferment in Education: A Look Abroad.* Chicago: University of Chicago Press, 1995. *In addition to several general essays, this book includes chapters dealing with Africa, China, Israel, Japan, and Russia and Eastern Europe.*

CHAPTER 16

School Effectiveness and Reform in the United States

Much of this book is concerned with problems and trends in the reform of elementary and secondary schools. The material in this chapter deals even more explicitly with selected issues in school effectiveness and reform. After highlighting several major challenges that confront the U.S. educational system, we will examine research into the characteristics of effective instruction and effective schools. We will also look at the process of school improvement and reform and other important areas often discussed under the heading of school effectiveness.

Debates about school reform can be resolved only by analyzing actual research evidence. This chapter cannot discuss every suggested change, but it will examine the proposals that seem to have particular promise or that have received widespread attention. As you read, consider which ideas have solid evidence to support them. Think also about the prerequisites for success, the underlying conditions that may help make each suggested reform appropriate or inappropriate, and how each may affect your career as a teacher. Keep the following basic questions in mind:

FOCUS QUESTIONS

- What are the characteristics of effective teaching and effective schools?
- What are some keys to implementing effective school reform?
- How can we improve instruction at the classroom and school levels?
- How can schools help special populations of students such as low-income students, rural students, or gifted and talented students?
- What is the role of magnet and alternative schools?
- What reform efforts are being initiated in school districts and state school systems?
- Are nonpublic schools more effective than public schools?
- Will expansion of school choice plans improve education?

▶ **Imperatives to Improve the Schools**

■ Underprepared workers

Concern about American schools largely focuses on the need to bolster the nation's international economic competitiveness by teaching students work-related skills and on the related imperative to improve performance among disadvantaged students.

Several major national reports and studies have suggested that American students are leaving school unprepared to participate effectively in jobs that will, in an increasingly sophisticated and technology-based world economy, require them to "reason and perform complex, non-routine intellectual tasks." For example, surveys of employers have reported that nearly half of current workers are deficient in basic skills.[1]

■ Compelling need for equity

Nearly all the recent reports and studies dealing with educational reform call for improving the performance of economically disadvantaged students in order to make educational outcomes more equitable. In addition to the desire for fairness, educational equity has also been related to the need for economic competitiveness. For example, the Forum of Educational Organizational Leaders concluded that "if we wish to maintain or improve our standard of living, we must work smarter . . . [but] it is not possible to succeed if only middle class people from stable families work smarter. . . . [This capacity] must—for the first time in human history—be characteristic of the mass of our population."

Specific areas of concern for educators working to reform educational opportunities for disadvantaged students include the following:

■ CCSSO recommendations

■ *At-risk students and schools.* Social and economic opportunities have declined rapidly for low-achieving students and those without good postsecondary credentials. Perhaps the farthest reaching set of proposals for helping at-risk and disadvantaged students is in the policy statements of the Council of Chief State School Officers (CCSSO). CCSSO's statements argue that state laws should "guarantee" educational programs and other services "reasonably calculated to enable all persons to graduate from high school." Such a guarantee policy, the CCSSO has indicated, may require such strong measures as "state takeovers" of distressed school districts, support for students to transfer from low-achieving schools or districts to "successful" locations elsewhere, and reduction in the concentration of students at low-income schools. Similarly, Bob Chase, a former president of the National Education Association, has declared that

> there are public schools that middle-class parents, including me, would not want their children to attend. These schools . . . are struggling. Teachers often lack certification. School buildings are run down and overcrowded. This status quo is disastrous for children. It is morally wrong. . . . We are dealing here with the toughest—and most compelling—challenge in U.S. education . . . [that requires] heroic work—done school by school, and student by student.[2]

---

[1]Paul E. Barton, *Raising Achievement and Reducing Gaps* (Washington, D.C.: National Education Goals Panel, 2001); Paul E. Barton, "The Closing of the Education Frontier" (2002), report prepared for the Education Testing Service, available at **www.ets.org/research/pic**; and Lynn A. Karoly and Constantijn W. A. Panis, "The 21st Century at Work" (2004), paper prepared for the Rand Corporation, available at **www.rand.org**.
[2]*State Responsibility for Student Opportunity* (Washington D.C.: Council of Chief State School Officers, 1995); Bob Chase, "Answering the Alarm," available at **www.nea.org**: search for "Answering the Alarm"; Paul T. Hill, Kacey Guin, and Mary B. Cielo, "The Chasm Remains," *Education Next* (Spring 2003), available at **www.educationnext.org/20032**; and "State Support to Low-Performing Schools" (2003), report released by the Council of Chief State School Officers," available at **www.ccsso.org**.

■ Coordinated reform needed to combat declining opportunities

■ *Inner-city poverty.* As we pointed out in the chapter on Social Class, Race, and School Achievement and elsewhere, educational problems are particularly severe in inner-city minority neighborhoods of concentrated poverty. A workable response to the problems in these neighborhoods will involve employment, transportation, housing, affirmative action, and social welfare supports; desegregation and deconcentration of poverty populations; decreasing crime and delinquency; and other efforts—and elementary and secondary education must play a pivotal part.[3]

■ Pockets of rural poverty

■ *Concentrated rural poverty.* Some rural areas have communities of concentrated poverty similar in many respects to those in big cities. Among these are the Appalachian region in the eastern United States and the Ozarks region in the South. Although many poor rural communities have mostly nonminority populations, indicators of social disorganization—high teenage pregnancy rates, widespread juvenile delinquency, extremely low school achievement, and pervasive feelings of hopelessness—run as high or nearly as high as those in poor minority urban neighborhoods. For the U.S. economy as a whole to "work smarter," these rural students, like their inner-city counterparts, need effective education.[4]

Many observers believe that our response to these challenges will be of historic importance in determining whether the United States prospers or declines in the twenty-first century.

REFOCUS **What do you believe is the most urgent reason for educational reform?**

▶ Characteristics of Effective Classrooms and Schools

The push for greater educational effectiveness became a national growth industry in 1983, and since then has generated hundreds of research studies as well as thousands of discussion papers and improvement plans. Many studies have been designed to identify the characteristics of effective classroom teaching and **effective schools**.

Effective Teaching and Instruction

■ Much has been learned about effective instruction

We have learned a great deal about effective delivery of instruction in the classroom. This section summarizes what this research into effective teaching and instruction can tell you about classroom management, pedagogical methods, grouping of students, and related issues.

---

[3]*The State of the Cities—2000* (Washington, D.C.: U.S. Department of Housing and Urban Development, 2000); and James E. Rosenbaum, "Organizational Effects on Learning," Institute for Policy Research Working Paper WP-02020, May 14, 2002, available at **www.northwestern.edu/ipr/publications**.
[4]Maureen Sullivan and Danny Miller, "Cincinnati's Urban Appalachian Council and Appalachian Identity," *Harvard Educational Review* (February 1990), pp. 106–124; "Study Finds Child Poverty Worst in Rural Areas," *Rural Policy Matters* (July 2002), available at **http://ruraledu.org/rpm**; and Doris T. Williams, "Closing the Achievement Gap," *CSR Connections* (Spring 2003), pp. 1–10, available at **www.goodschools.gwu.edu/pubs**.

■ Effective classroom practices

Classroom Management.   Research on classroom management indicates that effective teachers use a variety of techniques to develop productive climates and to motivate students. Effective teachers emphasize practices like the following:[5]

1. Making sure that students know what the teacher expects
2. Letting students know how to obtain help
3. Following through with reminders and rewards to enforce the rules
4. Providing a smooth transition between activities
5. Giving students assignments of sufficient variety to maintain interest
6. Monitoring the class for signs of confusion or inattention
7. Being careful to avoid embarrassing students in front of their classmates
8. Responding flexibly to unexpected developments
9. Designing tasks that draw on students' prior knowledge and experience
10. Helping students develop self-management skills
11. Attending to students' cultural backgrounds
12. Ensuring that all students are part of a classroom learning community.

■ Time of active engagement

Time-on-Task.   Effective teaching as portrayed in various studies brings about relatively high student **time-on-task**—that is, time engaged in learning activities. As you might expect, students actively engaged in relevant activities tend to learn more than do students not so engaged. Time-on-task studies have pointed out that classrooms can be managed to increase the time students spend on actual learning activities. However, student learning involves more than time spent on academic work. Other variables, such as the suitability of the activities, the students' success or failure in the tasks attempted, and the motivating characteristics of methods and materials, are also important.[6]

■ Skillful questioning and wait time

Questioning.   One way to stimulate student engagement in learning is to ask appropriate questions in a manner that ensures participation and facilitates mastery of academic content. Several studies have identified questioning skills as an important aspect of effective teaching. In particular, research indicates that longer "wait time" (the interval between the posing of a question and selecting or encouraging a student to answer it) significantly improves student participation and learning. Research also indicates that "higher-order" questioning that requires students to mentally

---

[5]Anne Reynolds, "What Is Competent Beginning Teaching? A Review of the Literature," *Review of Educational Research* (Spring 1992), pp. 1–36; Jere Brophy and Janet Alleman, "Classroom Management," *Social Education* (January 1998), pp. 56–58; Susan M. Glazer, "Quiet Signals," *Teaching PreK–8* (October 2003) pp. 86–87; and Carol Weinstein, Mary Curran, and Saundra Tomlinson-Clarke, "Culturally Responsive Classroom Management," *Theory Into Practice* (Fall 2003), pp. 269–277.

[6]Mary Rohrkemper and Lyn Corno, "Success and Failure in Classroom Tasks," *Elementary School Journal* (January 1988), pp. 297–311; Michael Sadowski, "Time and Learning," *Harvard Education Letter* (March–April 1998); Cori Brewster and Jennifer Fager, "Increasing Student Engagement and Motivation" (2000), paper prepared for NWREL, available at **www .nwrel.org/request**; James H. Stronge, *Qualities of Effective Teachers* (Alexandria, Va.: Association for Supervision and Curriculum Development, 2002); and Mary Beth Coleman, "Helping Classroom Teachers Focus," *FPG Snapshot*, March 13, 2004, available at **www.fpg .unc.edu**.

Questioning skills—such as ensuring long "wait times" and asking "higher-order" questions—are an important aspect of effective teaching. *(Ellen Senisi/The Image Works)*

manipulate ideas and information is more effective than "lower cognitive" questioning that focuses on verbatim recall of facts.[7]

Direct Instruction and Explicit Teaching.   The terms **direct instruction** and **explicit teaching** (frequently used as synonyms) usually refer to teacher-directed instruction that proceeds in small steps. (Direct instruction also is sometimes referred to as "active teaching.") Research has shown a link between this method, properly implemented, and high levels of student achievement. Barak Rosenshine identified the following six teaching "steps" or "functions" as central to direct instruction:[8]

◼ Six teaching steps

1. Begin lessons with a review of relevant previous learning and a preview and goal statement.

2. Present new material in small steps, with clear and detailed explanations and active student practice after each step.

3. Guide students in initial practice; ask questions and check for understanding.

4. Provide systematic feedback and corrections.

5. Supervise independent practice; monitor and assist seatwork.

6. Provide weekly and monthly review and testing.

---

[7]Kenneth R. Chuska, *Improving Classroom Questions* (Bloomington, Ind.: Phi Delta Kappa, 1995); Kathleen Cotton, *The Schooling Practices That Matter Most* (Alexandria, Va.: Association for Supervision and Curriculum Development, 2000); and David Perkins, "Making Thinking Visible," *New Horizons for Learning* (Winter 2004), available at **www.newhorizons.org**: click on "Quarterly Journal."
[8]Barak Rosenshine, "Explicit Teaching and Teacher Training," *Journal of Teacher Education* (May–June 1987), pp. 34–36. See also Barak Rosenshine, "Advances in Research on Instruction" (1996), posting at the Arizona State University Internet site, available at **http:// epaa.asu.edu/barak**; and "What Characterizes an Effective Teacher?" (2002), interview with Barak Rosenshine published by the Heartland Institute, available at **www .heartland.org**.

Several other prominent advocates of explicit teaching, including Jere Brophy, Thomas Good, Madeline Hunter, and Jane Stallings, have outlined similar components of direct instruction.[9]

■ Critique of explicit teaching

Explicit Comprehension Instruction and Strategic Teaching. Direct instruction has often been criticized for its tendency to neglect important higher-order learning (reasoning, critical thinking, comprehension of concepts) in favor of small-step learning of factual material. In many schools where teachers have been told to follow a prescribed sequence of this kind, the practice emphasizes low-level learning and mindless regurgitation of facts and leaves little room for creativity and analytical thinking.[10]

■ Higher-order focus

However, direct instruction need not concentrate on low-level learning. Educators have been refining classroom techniques for explicitly teaching comprehension in all subject areas. David Pearson and his colleagues refer to many such approaches as **explicit comprehension instruction**. Barak Rosenshine has characterized the development of this approach since 1970 as an "enormous accomplishment" in which educators should take great pride.[11]

Like explicit teaching, explicit comprehension instruction emphasizes review and preview, feedback and correctives, and guided as well as independent practice, but experts suggest that teachers also systematically model conceptual learning, help students link new knowledge to their prior learning, monitor students' comprehension, and train students in summarizing, drawing inferences, and other learning strategies. Techniques and strategies associated with explicit comprehension instruction include the following:[12]

■ Techniques for explicit comprehension instruction

- "Prediction" activities in which students predict what will be found in the text based on their prior knowledge

- "Reciprocal teaching," student team learning, and other approaches to cooperative learning, through which students learn to take more responsibility for helping each other comprehend material

- "Semantic maps" and "semantic networks" that organize information

- Computer simulations designed to develop concepts and thinking skills

- "Metacognitive" learning strategies through which students monitor and assess their own learning processes

---

[9]Steven A. Stahl and David A. Hayes, eds., *Instructional Models in Reading* (Mahwah, N.J.: Erlbaum, 1996); Robert J. Marzano, Barbara B. Gaddy, and Ceri Dean, *What Works in Classroom Instruction* (Aurora, Colo.: Midcontinent Regional Educational Laboratory, 2000); and Susan J. Paik, "Ten Strategies That Improve Learning," *Educational Horizons* (Winter 2003), pp. 83–85, available at **www.pilambda.org/horizons/archive.html**.

[10]Arthur E. Wise, "Legislated Learning Revisited," *Phi Delta Kappan* (January 1988), pp. 328–329; Linda M. McNeil, *Contradictions of School Reform* (New York: Routledge, 2000); and Sandra Mathison & Melissa Freeman "Constraining Elementary Teachers' Work," *Education Policy Analysis Archives*, September 24, 2003, available at **http://epaa.asu.edu/epaa**.

[11]P. David Pearson and Janice A. Dole, "Explicit Comprehension Instruction," *Elementary School Journal* (November 1987), pp. 151–165; Ann L. Brown, "The Advancement of Learning," *Educational Researcher* (November 1994), pp. 4–12; "Effective Practices for Developing Reading Comprehension," *Educational Research Reports 2003*, March 15, 2003, available at **http://ed-web3.educ.msu.edu/reports**; and Barak Rosenshine, "The Case for Explicit, Teacher-Led Cognitive Strategy Instruction" (undated), paper at the Arizona State University Internet site, available at **http://epaa.asu.edu/barak**.

[12]Barak Rosenshine and Carla Meister, "Reciprocal Teaching: A Review of the Research," *Review of Educational Research* (Winter 1994), pp. 479–530; Miriam Alfassi, "Reading for Meaning," *American Educational Research Journal* (Summer 1998), pp. 309–332; and Donna Peterson and Carol VanDerWege, "Guiding Children to Be Strategic Readers," *Phi Delta Kappan* (February 2002), available at **www.pdkintl.org/kappan/karticle.htm**.

- ■ "Learning to learn" strategies
- ■ Problem-solving models that help students analyze learning situations
- ■ Collaborative study of increasingly complex questions and problems

■ Teachers as strategists

Beau Jones and her colleagues have described the effective use of such techniques as **strategic teaching**, a "concept which calls attention to the role of the teacher as strategist." Emphasis in strategic teaching is on the student's construction of meaning and growth in independent learning, with the teacher serving as a model and mediator of learning. As noted in the chapter on Motivation, Preparation, and Conditions of the Entering Teacher, many analysts use the term *reflective teaching* in describing this kind of instructional approach.[13]

Cognitive Instruction for Low-Achieving Students.   Emphasis on passive learning of low-level skills seems particularly pervasive in schools with concentrations of working-class students and low achievers. A change in this pattern will require new approaches for delivering cognitive instruction, as well as fundamental improvements in programming throughout the educational system.[14]

Specific programs aimed at improving the thinking skills of low achievers include the Higher Order Thinking Skills Program (discussed later in this chapter), the Productive Thinking Program, and the Chicago Mastery Learning Reading (Insights) Program. Research suggests that such approaches have indeed improved performance. However, specific obstacles must be addressed, including the preference many students have developed for low-level learning, teachers' low expectations for low achievers, and the high financial cost of effective instruction that emphasizes cognitive development.[15]

In summary, research on effective teaching and instruction suggests that successful reform projects might include several changes, including improving teachers' classroom management and questioning skills, increasing time-on-task, expanding the use of direct instruction and explicit comprehension instruction, and introducing cognitive instruction for low-achieving students.

 **Which of the characteristics of effective teaching are you most confident about demonstrating? Which will you need to work hard to develop?**

---

[13]Michael Pressley, Rachel Brown, Peggy Van Meter, and Ted Schuder, "Transactional Strategies," *Educational Leadership* (May 1995), p. 81; Michael Pressley, *Reading Instruction That Works* (Washington, D.C.: International Reading Association, 1998); and Bob Kizlik, "Information About Strategic Teaching, Strategic Learning, and Thinking Skills" (2003), posting at the Adprima Internet site, available at **www.adprima.com/strategi.htm**.

[14]Daniel U. Levine, "Teaching Thinking to At-Risk Students: Generalizations and Speculation," in Barbara Z. Presseisen, ed., *At-Risk Students and Thinking: Perspectives from Research* (Washington, D.C.: National Education Association and Research for Better Schools, 1988); Eric J. Cooper and Daniel U. Levine, "Teaching for Intelligence," in Barbara Presseisen, ed., *Teaching for Intelligence: A Collection of Articles* (Arlington Heights, Ill.: Skylight, 1999); and Cathy C. Block and Michael Pressley, eds., *Comprehension Instruction* (New York: Guilford, 2002).

[15]Stanley Pogrow, "Challenging At-Risk Students," *Phi Delta Kappan* (January 1990), pp. 389–397; Stanley Pogrow, "Making Reform Work for the Educationally Disadvantaged," *Educational Leadership* (February 1995), pp. 20–24; Stanley Pogrow, "What Is an Exemplary Program?" *Educational Researcher* (October 1998), pp. 22–29; and "Making Schools Better for 'At Risk' Students," *AISQ Briefings* (March 2003), available at **www.aisq.qld.edu.au/publications.html**.

▶ **Effective Schools Research**

■ Focusing on larger contexts

The preceding sections addressed effective teaching and instruction at the classroom level. However, reformers must also pay attention to the school as an institution and, in the final analysis, to the larger context of the school district and the environment in which schools operate. How effective schools and whole districts are helps determine what happens in each classroom.

■ Edmonds's research

Elementary Schools.   Most of the recent research on effective schools focuses on elementary education. Researchers usually define effectiveness at least partly in terms of outstanding student achievement. For example, Ronald Edmonds and others described an effective school as having characteristics such as the following:[16]

■ Characteristics of effective schools

1. A *safe and orderly environment* conducive to teaching and learning and not oppressive

2. A *clear school mission* through which the staff shares a commitment to instructional priorities, assessment procedures, and accountability

3. *Instructional leadership* by a principal who understands the characteristics of instructional effectiveness

4. A climate of *high expectations* in which the staff demonstrates that all students can master challenging skills

5. High *time-on-task* brought about when students spend a large percentage of time "engaged" in planned activities to master basic skills

6. Frequent *monitoring of student progress,* using the results to improve both individual performance and the instructional program

7. Positive *home–school relations* in which parents support the school's basic mission and play an important part in helping to achieve it

8. A *unified effort* in which all staff take responsibility for improving achievement

■ Coordinating methods and materials

Another characteristic that contributes to school effectiveness is **curriculum alignment**—the coordination of instructional planning, methods, materials, and testing. When staff development focuses on such coordination, teachers are less likely to rely solely on textbooks and more likely to select or create materials that are most appropriate for teaching a specific skill to a particular group of students.[17]

---

[16]Joan Shoemaker, "Effective Schools: Putting the Research to the Ultimate Test," *Pre-Post Press* (1982), p. 241. See also Ronald Edmonds, "Effective Schools for the Urban Poor," *Educational Leadership* (October 1979), pp. 15–24; Ali C. Picucci et al., "Driven to Succeed" (2002), report prepared for the Charles A. Dana Center, available at **www.utdanacenter.org**: click on "reports"; Robert J. Marzano, *What Works in Schools* (Alexandria, Va.: Association for Supervision and Curriculum Development, 2003); and Daniel U. Levine, *Unusually Effective Schools: An Update* (Bloomington, Ind.: Phi Delta Kappa, 2004).

[17]Daniel U. Levine and Joyce Stark, "Instructional and Organizational Arrangements That Improve Achievement in Inner-City Schools," *Educational Leadership* (December 1982), pp. 41–48. See also Daniel U. Levine and Lawrence W. Lezotte, *Unusually Effective Schools* (Madison, Wisc.: National Center for Effective Schools Research and Development, 1990); Craig Spilman, "Transforming an Urban School," *Educational Leadership* (December 1995–January 1996), pp. 34–39; Mike Schmoker, "The Real Causes of Higher Achievement," *SEDL Newsletter* (May 2002), available at **www.sedl.org**; George D. Holmgren, "School Improvement Process Works at Hood Canal School," *New Horizons for Learning* (Winter 2004), available at **www.newhorizons.org**: click on "Quarterly Journal"; and Lawrence W. Lezotte, "Correlates of Effective Schools" (undated), posting at the Effective Schools, Inc., Internet site, available at **www.effectiveschools.com/freestuff.asp**.

■ Other key factors

According to several recent research reviews, other key features of unusually effective schools are (1) attention to goals involving cultural pluralism and multicultural education; (2) emphasis on responding to students' personal problems and developing their social skills; (3) faculty who strive to improve students' sense of efficacy; (4) continuous concern for making teaching tasks realistic and manageable; and (5) targeting interventions on low-performing students. Researchers at the Northwest Regional Educational Laboratory have identified more than one hundred specific practices, grouped in eighteen categories, that contribute to school effectiveness.[18]

High Schools.   Relatively few studies have concentrated solely on the characteristics of unusually effective senior high schools. Because high school goals and programs are so diverse and complex, it is difficult to conclude that one is more effective than another, particularly when the social class of the student body is taken into account. In addition, hardly any high schools enrolling mostly working-class students stand out as being relatively high in achievement.[19]

■ Helping low achievers

However, in recent years, researchers have identified and described some high schools that appear unusually effective in educating a broad range of students. In general, these schools heavily emphasize helping low achievers in the entry grade (that is, ninth or tenth grade) and on providing additional support in later grades. They also strive to personalize instruction and avoid rigid grouping into permanent, separate tracks for low, medium, and high achievers.[20] In addition, the following approaches have frequently been successful:[21]

1. *Schools-within-a-school for low achievers.* Students who read more than two or three years below grade level are assigned to a special unit of eighty to one hundred students at the entry grade. If their teachers are selected for ability

---

[18]Daniel U. Levine, "Update on Effective Schools: Findings and Implications from Research and Practice," *Journal of Negro Education* (Fall 1990), pp. 577–584; Kathleen Cotton, *Effective Schooling Practices: A Research Synthesis 1995 Update* (Portland, Oreg.: Northwest Regional Educational Laboratory, 1995); Diane Massell, "The District Role in Building Capacity," *CPRE Policy Briefs* (September 2000), pp. 1–7; and Daniel U. Levine, "Effective Schools Highlights" (2004), paper prepared for the National Center for Effective Schools Research and Development Foundation, available at **www.effective-schools.org/effective-schools-resources/effective-schools-resource.asp**.

[19]Daniel U. Levine and Eugene E. Eubanks, "Organizational Arrangements in Effective Secondary Schools," in John J. Lane and Herbert J. Walberg, eds., *Organizing for Learning* (Reston, Va.: National Association of Secondary School Principals, 1988); Edys Quellmalz and Patrick M. Shields, *School-Based Reform* (Washington, D.C.: U.S. Government Printing Office, 1995), available at **www.ed.gov/pubs/Reform**; Charles Teddlie and David Reynolds, eds., *Research on School Effectiveness* (Levittown, Pa.: Falmer, 1998); and Gene Bottoms, Lingling Han, and Alice Presson, "Doing What Works" (2003), report prepared for the Southern Regional Education Board, available at **www.sreb.org**.

[20]James Traub, "Subject Matters," *Blueprint* (Fall 1999); Judy B. Codding and Marc S. Tucker, "A New High School Design Focused on Student Performance: Part I," *NASSP Bulletin* 84, no. 615 (2000), pp. 79–92; and Maxine Minkoff, "Head of the Class" (2003), report prepared for MassINC, available at **www.massinc.org**.

[21]Gary Wehlage, Gregory Smith, and Pauline Lipman, "Restructuring Urban Schools," *American Educational Research Journal* (Spring 1992), pp. 51–96; Kathleen Cotton, "Back to the Future," *NW Education* (Winter 2000), available at **www.nwrel.org/nwedu**; James J. Kemple and Jason C. Snipes, *Career Academies* (Washington, DC: Manpower Demonstration Research Corporation, 2000), available at **www.mdrc.org**; Adria Steinberg and Lili Allen, "From Large to Small" (2003), report prepared for Jobs for the Future, available at **www.jff.org**; Robert Rothman, "Transforming High Schools into Small Learning Communities," *Challenge Journal* (Winter 2002/2003), available at **http://annenbergchallenge.org**; Thomas Toch, *High Schools on a Human Scale* (Boston: Houghton Mifflin Beacon, 2003); Thomas Toch, "Small Schools, Big Ideas," *Education Week*, December 3, 2003; and Susan Black, "The Pivotal Year," *American School Board Journal* (February 2004), available at **www.asbj.com**.

and willingness to work with low achievers, participating students can make large gains in basic skills and transfer to regular courses.

2. *Career academies.* Functioning as schools-within-a-school that enroll students of various abilities across several grades, career academies focus on such fields as computers, biology or other science, humanities or the arts, or occupational studies such as law enforcement or journalism. Positive data have been reported regarding student engagement and achievement at career academies.

3. *Smaller high school units in general.* High schools that have low enrollment or have been divided into smaller units such as schools-within-a-school have more student engagement and higher achievement than traditional large high schools with similar students. Assigning students to these smaller schools or units can create a more personalized environment in which staff provide individual help to students.

■ Definitions differ

Evaluation of Effective Schools Research. Keep in mind the following points as we evaluate research on effective schools. First, we should recognize the widespread confusion about definitions. There are nearly as many definitions of effective schools as there are people discussing them. While some people have in mind a school with high academic achievement (taking account of social class), others are thinking about a "self-renewing" school that can identify and solve internal problems, a school that promotes students' personal growth, a school that has shown improvement in achievement, or a school that concentrates on developing independent study skills and love for learning.

■ Research focused on poverty schools

Second, many rigorous studies have focused on high-poverty elementary schools in which academic achievement is higher than at most other schools with similarly disadvantaged students. It is more difficult to identify unusually effective high schools and schools outside the inner city, where high achievement is more common. In addition, the key components of effectiveness outside the inner city may differ somewhat from those at poverty schools.[22]

■ Problems in research methods

Third, other methodological problems have left much of the research vulnerable to criticism. For example, schools identified as effective in a given subject (say, reading) during a given year may not be effective on other measures or in the next year. In addition, controls for students' social class and family environment are frequently inadequate. For instance, magnet schools enrolling inner-city students may be judged as unusually effective; but if later research shows that those schools draw their students from highly motivated poverty families dissatisfied with neighborhood schools, the high achievement might be attributable more to the students' background than to school characteristics.[23]

■ Begging the question

Fourth, the literature often tends to beg the question of what teachers and principals should do in the schools. For example, the claim that a school requires good leadership and a productive climate fails to specify these or ways to accomplish them.[24]

---

[22]Daniel U. Levine and Robert S. Stephenson, "Are Effective or Meritorious Schools Meretricious?" *Urban Review* no. 1 (1987), pp. 25–34; Thomas Corcoran and Margaret Goetz, "Instructional Capacity and High Performance Schools," *Educational Researcher* (December 1995), pp. 27–31; and Naomi G. Housman and Monica R. Martinez, "A Brief for Practitioners on Turning Round Low-Performing Schools," *NCCSP Issue Briefs* (April 2001).

[23]M. Donald Thomas and William L. Bainbridge, "All Children Can Learn: Facts and Fallacies," *Phi Delta Kappan* (May 2001), pp. 660–663; and William L. Bainbridge, "Leaving Children Behind," *Technos Quarterly* (Summer 2002), available at **www.findarticles.com**.

[24]Judith Chapman, "Leadership, Management, and the Effectiveness of Schooling," *Journal of Educational Administration* 31, no. 4 (1993), pp. 4–18; and Kathleen Cotton, *Principals and Student Achievement* (Alexandria, Va.: Association for Supervision and Curriculum Development, 2003).

Despite these qualifications, the research on effective schools has identified characteristics to consider in school reform and improvement projects. Research also has provided educators with advice on the best ways to proceed as they implement these projects.

 **What steps can you take during your teacher-preparation program to help you develop the skills of effective teachers described above?**

▶ Characteristics of Successful School Reforms

■ Solving day-to-day problems

From analysis of past school improvement efforts, we have a much better understanding of the steps that will ensure reform efforts of significant and lasting impact. We describe lessons learned from past efforts below.

1. *Adaptive problem solving.* An innovation frequently has little or no effect on students' performance because a host of problems arise to stifle practical application. For example, experts may devise a wonderful new science curriculum for fourth graders and school districts may purchase large quantities of the new curriculum materials, but teachers may either choose not to use them or not know how to use them. Innovations usually fail unless the organization introducing them is adaptive in the sense that it can identify and solve day-to-day problems.[25]

■ Focus on individual schools

2. *School-level focus.* Because the innovating organization must solve day-to-day problems, it must focus at the individual school level, where many problems occur.[26]

■ Compatibility and accessibility

3. *Potential for implementation.* Successful school reform also depends on whether changes can be feasibly implemented in typical schools. Three characteristics that make successful implementation more likely are an innovation's *compatibility* with the context of potential users, its *accessibility* to those who do not already understand the underlying ideas, and its *doability* in terms of demands on teachers' time and energy. Levine and Levine have pointed out that many approaches have high "potential for mischief" because they are so difficult to implement.[27]

[25]Linda Lambert, *Building Leadership Capacity in Schools* (Alexandria, Va.: Association for Supervision and Curriculum Development, 1998); Michael Fullan and Nancy Watson, "School-Based Management," *School Effectiveness and School Improvement* (December 2000), pp. 453–474; and Jeanne R. Century and Abigail J. Levy, "Sustaining Your Reform," *NCCSR Bookmarks* (Summer 2002), available at **www.goodschools.gwu.edu/pubs**.

[26]Daniel U. Levine, "Creating Effective Schools Through Site-Level Staff Development, Planning and Improvement of Organizational Cultures," in David H. Hargreaves and David Hopkins, eds., *Development Planning for School Improvement* (London: Cassell, 1994), pp. 37–48; and Kathleen Porter and Stephanie Soper, "Closing the Achievement Gap," *CSR Connections* (Summer 2003), pp. 1–10, available at **www.goodschools.gwu.edu/pubs**.

[27]David P. Crandall, Jeffrey W. Eiseman, and Karen E. Louis, "Strategic Planning Issues That Bear on the Success of School Improvement Efforts," *Educational Administration Quarterly* (Summer 1986), pp. 21–53; Jane Foley, "A Recipe for Restructuring," *School Administrator* (January 1996), p. 30; Daniel U. Levine and Rayna F. Levine, "Considerations in Introducing Instructional Interventions," in Barbara Presseisen, ed., *Teaching for Intelligence* (Arlington Heights, Ill.: Skylight, 1999), pp. 269–280; David Potter, David Reynolds, and Christopher Chapman, "School Improvement for Schools Facing Challenging Circumstances," *School Leadership and Management* (August 2002), pp. 243–256; and Darlene Y. Bruner and Bobbie J. Greenlee, "Analysis of School Work Culture in Schools That Implement Comprehensive School Reform Models," *Journal of Research for Educational Leaders* (Spring 2004), available at **www.uiowa.edu/~jrel**.

■ Sharing a vision

4. *Leadership and shared agreements.* Meaningful innovation requires change in many institutional arrangements, including scheduling of staff and student time, selection and use of instructional methods and materials, and mechanisms for making decisions. The building principal usually is the key person in making these arrangements, but the faculty also must have a shared vision of possible and necessary changes. Otherwise, staff members will likely discount proposals that ask them to make significant changes.[28]

■ Giving teachers a voice

5. *Teacher involvement.* People expected to alter their working patterns will not cooperate fully unless they have a voice in designing and implementing change. Teachers, therefore, must have an opportunity to help select and evaluate innovations.[29]

■ Staff development essential

6. *Staff training.* Staff development is a core activity in the school improvement process. In an elementary school, the entire staff should participate; in secondary schools, departments may be the appropriate unit for certain activities. Staff development should be an interactive process in which teachers and administrators work together at every stage.[30]

Standards & Assessment ✔

7. *Coherence.* Coherence in school reform efforts has at least two major dimensions. The first refers to coherence across grade levels: teachers in each grade must be willing to help students master the curriculum and standards established for their grade, or students will lack the skills required for success in the next grade. *Coherence* also refers to consistency and compatibility across the instructional programs and approaches used in the school. For example, some students probably will struggle to master reading if their teachers use differing materials that introduce key skills at different times and thus conflict with rather than reinforce each other. Some students will not master social skills if their teachers establish greatly different rules of behavior from one class to another.[31]

8. *Professional community.* Schools can ensure that all students learn only if teachers work together, trust their colleagues, and challenge each other to take responsibility for the difficult task of helping low achievers master increasingly

[28]Kenneth A. Leithwood, "The Move Toward Transformational Leadership," *Educational Leadership* (February 1992), pp. 8–12; Penny B. Sebring and Anthony S. Bryk, "School Leadership and the Bottom Line in Chicago," *Phi Delta Kappan* (February 2000), pp. 440–443; Barbara O. Taylor, "The Effective Schools Process," *Phi Delta Kappan* (January 2002), pp. 375–378; and Hajara Rahim, "Student Academic Progress," *New Horizons for Learning* (Winter 2004), available at **www.newhorizons.org**: click on "Quarterly Journal."

[29]Susan Moore Johnson, *Teachers at Work* (New York: Basic Books, 1990); Judith K. March and Karen H. Peters, "Curriculum Development and Instructional Design in the Effective Schools Process," *Phi Delta Kappan* (January 2002); pp. 379–382, available at **www.pdkintl.org/kappan/karticle.htm**; and David Foster and Pendred Noyce, "The Mathematics Assessment Collaborative," *Phi Delta Kappan* (January 2004), pp. 367–374.

[30]Bruce B. Joyce and Marcia Weil, *Models of Teaching,* 2nd ed. (Englewood Cliffs, N.J.: Prentice-Hall, 1991); Elizabeth G. Sturtevant, "The Literacy Coach" (2003), paper prepared for the Alliance for Excellent Education, available at **www.all4ed.org/publications**; and Dale Mann, "Technology Training for Teachers," *eSCHOOLNEWS* (February 2004), p. 28, available at **www.eschoolnews.com**.

[31]Fred M. Newman, BettsAnn Smith, Elain Allensworth, and Anthony S. Bryk, *School Instructional Program Coherence* (Chicago: Consortium on Chicago School Research, 2001), available at **www.consortium-chicago.org**: search for "School Instructional Program Coherence"; and "Instructional Program Coherence," *Educational Research Reports 2003,* July 24, 2003, available at **http://ed-web3.educ.msu.edu/reports**.

challenging material. Analysts refer to this aspect of reform as development of a "professional community."[32]

The In This Case feature describes a school improvement plan that features many hallmarks of effectiveness. As you read through it and the rest of this chapter, note which reform programs described seem to exemplify each of these best practices.

R E F O C U S How might you, as a teacher, participate in implementing reforms at your school? What do you believe teachers can do to best help with successful reform implementations?

▶ Improvement Approaches Across Grade Levels

The effective teaching practices cited earlier in this chapter work in individual classrooms, but numerous instructional approaches are designed for use at several or all grade levels in a school. For example, reading improvement programs often target students in kindergarten and the primary grades. We'll discuss several such improvement efforts in this section.

Higher-Order Thinking Skills (HOTS) Program

■ HOTS components

Developed by Stanley Pogrow and his colleagues, the HOTS program is specifically designed to replace remedial-reading activities in grades 4 through 6. The HOTS approach has four major components: (1) use of computers for problem solving; (2) emphasis on dramatization techniques that require students to verbalize, thereby stimulating language development; (3) Socratic questioning; and (4) a thinking-skills curriculum that stresses metacognitive learning, learning-to-learn, and other comprehension-enhancement techniques of the kinds described earlier. Now used in nearly two thousand schools, HOTS frequently has brought about extensive improvements in student performance in both reading and math.[33]

■ A faster pace

The developers of HOTS also have devised a thinking-based math curriculum and identified materials and methods for improving low-achievers' comprehension in science, social studies, and other subjects. According to Pogrow, results of the HOTS program show that at-risk students have "tremendous levels of intellectual and academic potential" but that many do not "understand 'understanding.'" This "fundamental learning problem can be eliminated if enough time and enough resources are made available."[34]

---

[32]Michael Fullan, "The Three Stories of Education Reform," *Phi Delta Kappan* (April 2000), pp. 581–584, available at **www.pdkintl.org/kappan/karticle.htm**; Cori Brewster and Jennifer Railsback, "Building Trusting Relationships for School Improvement" (2003), paper prepared for the Northwest Regional Educational Laboratory, available at **www.nwrel.org/request**; Robert J. Garmston and Bruce M. Wellman, "The Importance of Professional Community," *ENC Focus* (November 2003), pp. 7–9; and Mike Schmoker, "Tipping Point," *Phi Delta Kappan* (February 2004), pp. 422–432.

[33]Stanley Pogrow, "Teacher Feature . . . ," *Teachers.Net Gazette* (January 2002), available at **http://teachers.net/gazette/JAN02**. Information about the HOTS Program is available at **www.hots.org**.

[34]Stanley Pogrow, "What to Do About Chapter 1," *Phi Delta Kappan* (April 1992), pp. 624–630; Stanley Pogrow, "Helping Students Who 'Just Don't Understand,'" *Educational Leadership* (November 1994), pp. 62–68; and Stanley Pogrow, "Beyond the 'Good Start' Mentality," *Education Week*, April 19, 2000.

IN THIS CASE

School Reform

Paul and Henry are study partners in the college of education at their university. Paul waves a letter from across the library table. "Henry, you have to hear about this! My sister Melanie started teaching in this small rural school system last year. You ought to hear some of her stories about how the teachers come together to make things happen for those kids. They don't have much, compared to some of the suburban schools around here, but they do have fine student achievement. I'm thinking that when I graduate, I might want to go that route too—if they have a teaching position open."

Henry looks up from his notes. "How do you know that the student achievement is so good, Paul?"

"My sister sent me the results of the statewide exams," says Paul. "Not only is the district rated exemplary, but each of the three schools is rated exemplary, as well. That means that all schools showed 90 percent or more mastery in all the subjects tested. Larger schools have a hard time getting ratings like those. Melanie keeps saying smaller is better."

"You said that they don't have much. What do you mean by that?" Henry asks.

"Basically, they don't have all the equipment that most schools have," Paul replies. "They don't have extra staff to help with daily routines. The superintendent drives a bus, and each principal drives a bus, too.

"The school libraries have limited books and magazines. The high school has only fifteen computers, all located in the library for instructional purposes. Administrators have computers on their desks, but teachers have to go to the library to use a computer. The other schools have even fewer computers, all in the libraries, too."

"Amazing!" says Henry. "I don't know what I would do without a computer! How do they account for the top ratings? Are they still working on the achievement levels?"

"I visited Melanie over the holidays, and actually ended up interviewing her and a friend who teaches with her," Paul answers. "They say the community is close-knit, that faculty members feel like family. It's like moving back in time because everyone knows everyone else. All the students understand that the teachers know their parents, and even grandparents. Melanie says the superintendent and the principals really care. They see each student as a responsible individual. They expect the teachers to pitch in and help each other, to help the students, and yes, to help administrators when they need it. On the other hand, the administrators stand by the teachers, too. It's a team process on each campus. Every teacher who needs training gets it. When they work, they all work hard. When they play, they have fun and enjoy each other's company.

"And, yes," Paul continued. "They are still working to increase achievement levels. Melanie writes that their vision is 100 percent mastery of the statewide tests. They're continually problem solving looking for ways to help students."

"Is there any downside to all this?" laughs Henry.

"Well," Paul admits, "the pay *is* pretty low. But," he brightens. "There's not much to spend it on around there, either."

Questions

1. What characteristics of effective schools does this school district exemplify?
2. How does this district seem to support the process of school improvement and reform?
3. In addition to lower pay, what else might a new teacher consider deterrents to signing on as a team member in this small district?
4. Would you be willing to work in a school such as this? Why or why not?

Success for All

■ Comprehensive changes

Possibly the most comprehensive intervention for improving the achievement of disadvantaged students, Success for All provides intensive instructional support for students in elementary schools. It also emphasizes cooperative learning and mastery instruction (described in the chapter on Curriculum and Instruction), with technical support and staff development provided by full-time coordinators and resource persons assigned to participating schools. Measurable improvements in student achievement have been documented at numerous low-income schools in both urban and rural districts. According to its developers, Success for All demonstrates that schools neither exceptional nor extraordinary can routinely ensure success for disadvantaged students. However, the program does require a serious commitment to restructure elementary schools and to reconfigure the use of available funds.[35]

Degrees of Reading Power Comprehension Development Approach

Standards & Assessment ✓
■ Stressing real-life comprehension

Based in part on the Degrees of Reading Power (DRP) test originally developed by the College Board, the DRP approach is being implemented successfully at many urban schools. The test is unlike other standardized reading measures in that it assesses how well a student actually can comprehend written prose he or she encounters in or out of school, not just whether the student is above or below an abstract grade level. After using the DRP to determine their students' comprehension levels, teachers in all subject areas align their instruction accordingly. For homework and other independent assignments, they select materials that challenge but do not frustrate students; they use class work materials slightly beyond students' comprehension in order to help them improve.[36]

Comer School Development Program

■ Comer's approach

Developed by James Comer and his colleagues at Yale University, the School Development Program aims to improve achievement at inner-city elementary schools through enhanced social and psychological services for students, emphasis on parent involvement, and encouragement and support for active learning. Participating faculties involve parents in all aspects of school operation (including governance), and teachers, parents, psychologists, social workers, and other specialists form "Mental Health Teams" that design and supervise individualized learning arrangements for students with particular problems. Curriculum and instruction are coordinated across subject areas to emphasize language learning and social skills. Schools in various school districts have produced improvements in student achievement and

---

[35]Robert E. Slavin, "Can Education Reduce Social Inequity?" *Educational Leadership* (December 1997–January 1998); and Bruce Latta, "The Long-Term Effects and Cost-Effectiveness of Success for All," *NCCSR Research Briefs* (October 2003), available at **www.goodschools .gwu.edu/pubs**.
[36]Daniel U. Levine and John K. Sherk, "Implementation of Reforms to Improve Comprehension Skills at an Unusually Effective Inner City Intermediate School," *Peabody Journal of Education* (Summer 1989), pp. 87–106; Daniel U. Levine, "Instructional Approaches and Interventions That Can Improve the Academic Performance of African American Students," *Journal of Negro Education* (Winter 1994), pp. 46–63; and Daniel U. Levine, Eric J. Cooper, and Asa Hilliard III, "National Urban Alliance for Professional Development," *Journal of Negro Education* (Fall 2000), pp. 305–322, see later version available at **http://nuatc.org/articles/ pdf/achievement.pdf**.

behavior after implementing the School Development Program along with other innovations.[37]

Algebridge and Equity 2000

■ Transition to algebra

Jointly developed by the Educational Testing Service and the College Board, Algebridge helps students succeed in the transition from arithmetic to algebra. It since has evolved into the Equity 2000 project, which addresses additional aspects of mathematics education in secondary schools. Students receive assistance in prealgebra, algebra, geometry, and other courses. Recent data suggest that students frequently register large gains in mathematics performance, and that many are succeeding in algebra and other advanced math courses they otherwise would not be taking.[38]

Combinations of Approaches

■ Frequent combinations of approaches

Exemplary interventions such as those described above are not mutually exclusive. Educators frequently combine promising approaches to school-based management, comprehensive staff development, changes in testing, and mastery instruction with other innovations and interventions described elsewhere in this book. For example, faculties using the School Development Program can use the HOTS approach, cooperative learning, mastery learning, and other innovations in curriculum and instruction. School faculties throughout the United States are combining these kinds of exemplary interventions as part of districtwide or multischool projects.[39]

 **REFOCUS** Have you visited any schools that use programs described in this section? Which programs appeal most to you, as a teacher? Why?

▶ Reform Programs to Improve Whole Schools

■ Comprehensive reform

As described earlier, many reforms involve instructional interventions designed for single class use or across several grades. More ambitious programs, however, seek to improve most or all subject areas throughout all grades in an entire school. These efforts are variously referred to as "whole-school reform," "comprehensive building reform," and "school-level restructuring." Such initiatives generally reflect

---

[37]James P. Comer, "Educating Poor Minority Children," *Scientific American* (November 1988), pp. 42–48; Catherine Sullivan-DeCarlo, Karol DeFalco, and Verdell Roberts, "Helping Students Avoid Risky Behavior," *Educational Leadership* (September 1998), pp. 80–82; Thomas D. Cook, Robert F. Murphy, and H. David Hunt, "Comer's School Development Program in Chicago," *American Educational Research Journal* (Summer 2000), pp. 535–597; and Michael A. Rebell and Joseph J. Wardenski, "Of Course Money Matters" (2004), paper prepared for the Campaign for Fiscal Equity, available at **www.cfequity.org**. See also information at **www.info.med.yale.edu/comer**.

[38]Sandra Ham and Erica Walker, "Getting to the Right Algebra," *Manpower Demonstration Research Corporation Working Papers* (April 1999), available at **www.mdrc.org**; Stephen R. Green, "Closing the Achievement Gap," *Teaching and Change* (Winter 2001), pp. 215–224; and Berkeley Miller and James Stapleton, "Closing the Gap," *AIR News* (Fall 2002), available at **www.air.org/pdf/Newsletters/Fall2002.pdf**.

[39]Thomas R. Guskey, Perry D. Passaro, and Wayne Wheeler, "The Thorpe Gordon School," *Principal* (September 1991), pp. 36–38; Robert E. Slavin and Olatokunbo S. Fashola, *Show Me the Evidence* (Thousand Oaks, Calif.: Corwin, 1998); and Rebecca Sadinsky and Greg Tuke, "Powerful Schools," *New Horizons for Learning* (Winter 2004), available at **www .newhorizons.org**: click on "Quarterly Journal."

research-based recognition (described earlier in this chapter) that faculty at the building level ultimately determine whether change efforts are successful. They also allow for the intensive, ongoing staff development and technical assistance required to help teachers master new or different instructional approaches. Two of the most prominent of these initiatives involve the New American Schools project and the Comprehensive School Reform Demonstration Program.

New American Schools

■ Whole-school designs

New American Schools (NAS) is a nonprofit organization established in 1991 to support educational reform through widespread implementation of specific approaches (called "designs" by the NAS) that address all aspects of participating schools. With funds from the federal government and several foundations, the NAS sponsors "whole-school designs" that it helps schools implement during an initial three-or-more-year period. Designs include the Success for All approach described earlier in this chapter, the ATLAS approach, which coordinates high schools and their feeder schools, the Accelerated Schools teacher-empowerment approach, and the Turning Points approach for middle schools.[40]

■ Core features of successful reform

Having learned something about considerations that are central for successful implementation, NAS began taking designs that had succeeded in a few schools and introducing them at many schools. During this phase, analysts identified the following core set of features that must be present for schools to succeed in introducing a given design: an effective process for matching schools and designs, an ability to obtain sufficient focused resources, adequate school-based authority, an accountability system based on assessment of student and school performance, and coordination of professional development activities and external assistance.[41] You may recognize some of these core features as the best practices in school reform that we discussed earlier in the chapter.

■ NAS in Memphis

The NAS designs were an important part of the Memphis Public Schools Restructuring Initiative established in 1995. As part of this effort, thirty-four schools introduced one or another of the NAS designs. Data collected after the first year indicated that many teachers felt revitalized and were trying new or different instructional strategies, but need arose for more focused training, more time for collaboration, and better alignment of curriculum, instruction, and testing. Analysts also concluded that "restructuring a school requires tremendous energy, time, and commitment from the teachers, administrators, and school communities." In 2001, researchers reported that NAS schools in Memphis and elsewhere produced larger achievement gains than similar schools in their districts, but results were not consistently positive for all designs or from one district to another. Much depended, the authors concluded, on the quality of implementation and the suitability of a design for a particular school.[42]

---

[40]Thomas J. Glennan Jr., *New American Schools After Six Years* (Santa Monica, Calif.: Rand, 1998), available at **www.rand.org**; and Susan J. Bodilly, *New American Schools' Concept of Break the Mold Designs* (Santa Monica, Calif.: Rand, 2001), available at **www.rand.org**. See also information at **www.newamericanschools.org**.

[41]Mark Berends, Susan J. Bodilly, and Sheila N. Kirby, *Facing the Challenges of Whole-School Reform* (Santa Monica, Calif.: Rand, 2002); and Susan H. Fuhrman, "Redesigning Accountability Systems for Education," *CPRE Policy Briefs* (September 2003), available at **www.cpre.org/Publications/rb38.pdf**.

[42]Mark Berends, Sheila N. Kirby, Scott Naftel, and Christopher McKelvey, *Implementation and Performance in New American Schools* (Santa Monica, Calif.: Rand, 2001), available at **www.rand.org**; Mark Berends, Susan Bodilly, and Sheila N. Kirby, "Looking Back over a Decade of Whole-School Reform," *Phi Delta Kappan* (October 2002), pp. 168–175; and Marilyn S. Muirhead and Eric Collum, "Brokering External Policies to Raise Student Achievement," *CSR Connection* (Spring 2004), available at **www.goodschools.gwu.edu**.

Comprehensive School Reform Demonstration Program

■ Whole-school reform models

The federal **Comprehensive School Reform Demonstration (CSRD) Program** was initiated in 1998. The program provides up to seventy-five thousand dollars per year for three years to help participating Title 1 schools introduce "whole-school reform" models that affect all aspects of the school's operation and that have had documented success in improving student performance at other locations. Applicants were encouraged to select among twenty-seven models for which data were available to support their potential effectiveness.[43] Models include, among others, NAS designs (see above), the Direct Instruction approach for elementary schools, the HOSTS tutoring approach, Edison schools (described later in this chapter), the Comer School Development Program, the Effective Schools approach, and the Paideia "Great Books" approach (described in the chapter on Philosophical Roots of Education). As an alternative to a predeveloped program, schools can receive funding for locally developed approaches that meet government criteria for comprehensiveness. Congress has appropriated hundreds of millions of dollars for the CSRD program since 1999.[44]

► Related Efforts and Aspects Involving Educational Effectiveness

We lack space to describe all of the many activities and proposals related to the innovations discussed so far, but we'll mention several of the more important efforts in the following pages and summarize them in Overview 16.1.

Cooperation and Participation with Business, Community, and Other Institutions

Many schools and school districts are attempting to improve the quality of education by cooperating with other institutions, particularly those in business and industry. Promising efforts include the following:[45]

■ Types of cooperation

■ "Partnership" or "adopt-a-school" programs in which a business, church, university, or other community institution works closely with an individual school, providing assistance such as tutors or lecturers, funds or equipment for vocational studies, computer education, or help in curriculum development

■ Operation of professional development schools at which teachers and teacher educators work together to improve training and instruction

■ Funding of student awards for reading books or other positive behaviors

■ Donations of equipment and supplies

---

[43]Laura Desmione, "The Role of Teachers in Urban School Reform," *Clearinghouse on Urban Education Digest* (July 2000), available at **http://eric-web.tc.columbia.edu/digest/dig154.asp**; and James H. Lytle, "Whole-School Reform from the Inside," *Phi Delta Kappan* (October 2002), pp. 164–167.

[44]Joseph Murphy and Amanda Datnow, *Leadership Lessons from Comprehensive School Reforms* (Thousand Oaks, Calif.: Corwin, 2003); and documents available from the National Clearinghouse for Comprehensive School Reform at **www.goodschools.gwu.edu**.

[45]Celia B. Richardson, "Gift-in-Kind Clearing House," *Phi Delta Kappan* (June 1995), pp. 792–793; Karen Smith, "Tech Corps," *T.H.E. Journal* (October 1998), available at **www.thejournal.com**; "New Breed of Business Partners," *American School Board Journal* (January 1998); and "What Educators Need to Know About Work Keys" (2003), posting at the Work Keys for Education Internet site, available at **www.act.org/workkeys/education**.

OVERVIEW 16.1 *Examples and Trends Involving Efforts at School Reform or Improvement*

Area of Reform or Improvement	Examples and Trends
Business and Community Participation	• Community and business volunteers, donations, awards for schools
	• Boston Compact
	• School privatization
	• Guaranteed postsecondary access for high-school graduates
Technology	• Extensive introduction of computers, increases in Internet access in recent years
	• Research that guides effective technology use
	• Schools' efforts to improve equity in technology use
	• Researchers and educators offer cautions and concerns about ineffective use of technology.
Rural Education	• Research to determine effective improvement programs for rural areas emphasizes that unique approaches are needed, because rural areas are diverse.
	• Distance learning may help rural students.
Gifted and Talented Students	• Many possible approaches make it hard to determine ways to meet potential of gifted and talented students.
	• Most programs emphasize acceleration through curriculum, enriching curriculum, or a blend of both.
	• Schools must expand efforts to identify disadvantaged and minority gifted and talented students.
Increasing Time for Teaching and Learning	• Longer school years and year-round schools
	• Longer school days
	• After-school and summer learning programs
	• 21st Century Community Learning Centers

■ Development of approaches that enable employers to check students' school performance records before making hiring decisions

■ Boston Compact

An even farther-reaching example of cooperation with public schools is the Boston Compact. In forming the Compact in 1982, business leaders agreed to recruit at least two hundred companies that would hire graduates of the Boston public schools, as well as providing employment opportunities for students. In return, school officials agreed to establish competency requirements for graduation, increase placement rates of graduates into higher education as well as into full-time employment, and reduce dropout and absenteeism rates. City students got the message: "If you stay in school, work hard, and master the basics, you will be helped to find a job."

■ Expansion of the compact

By the early 2000s, more than four hundred companies were participating in the compact. Activities had expanded to include more than twenty local colleges and universities, and tens of thousands of Boston students had been placed in sum-

Many school districts are cooperating with business and industry to improve education quality in their schools. Business partners supply schools with mentors, supplies, funds, and apprenticeship opportunities or guaranteed postsecondary school funding for students. *(Michael Newman/PhotoEdit)*

mer jobs programs or had received help in obtaining full-time jobs after graduation. Data collected by Compact officials indicate that high proportions of high-school graduates in Boston either enter college or are employed full time, and most college entrants are persisting to graduation.[46]

■ Corporate projects

■ Support from foundations

The apparent success of the Boston Compact has helped stimulate major corporate and foundation efforts to help improve education. For example, the MacArthur Foundation provided forty million dollars to support reform efforts in the Chicago public schools, and the Bill and Melinda Gates Foundation and the Annenberg Foundation each have provided hundreds of millions of dollars to improve schools in Chicago, Los Angeles, New York, and many other school districts.[47]

■ Edison Schools

Privatization. **Privatization** occurs when public-school operation is contracted out to business corporations. The best-known privatization initiative has been the Edison Schools Corporation, conducted in a growing number of school districts. Edison won contracts to operate four schools in 1995 after three years of research and development to identify workable reform components such as longer school days and the introduction of technology. The company has since contracted with school districts to operate more than one hundred schools, including charter schools and schools using comprehensive reform funds (discussed earlier in this chapter). Few studies have been carried out regarding the success of Edison schools, and researchers disagree on whether or not Edison is having a substantial impact on student achievement.[48]

---

[46]Randy L. Dewar and Barbara Sprong, "No Diploma, No Job," *American School Board Journal* (October 1991), pp. 38–39; Robert C. Johnson, "Leaders Revisit Boston Compact," *Education Week*, May 17, 2000; and material available at **www.bostonpic.org**.
[47]See information at **www.gatesfoundation.org** and **www.whannenberg.org**.
[48]F. Howard Nelson and Nancy V. Meter, "Update on Student Achievement for Edison Schools Inc." (2003), paper prepared for the American Federation of Teachers, available at **www.aft.org/research/edisonschools**; and "Privatization" (undated), postings at the Education Commission of the States Internet site, available at **www.ecs.org**: click on "Education Issues." See also information at **www.edisonproject.com**.

Guaranteed Postsecondary Access for High-School Graduates.   As noted above, a key component in the Boston Compact (and similar projects elsewhere) is guaranteed support from businesses to help students attend postsecondary schools. Increasing numbers of communities are receiving similar support from wealthy individuals, foundations, community agencies, colleges and universities, and state or local governments.

■ Proliferation of programs

Programs that guarantee postsecondary access proliferated after 1981, when Eugene Lang established the "I Have a Dream" Project to pay college expenses for sixty-one sixth graders in New York. Of the fifty-four original Dreamers who remained in contact with the project, more than 90 percent earned high-school diplomas or certificates, and 60 percent went on to higher education. By 2003, philanthropists were supporting similar programs assisting more than thirteen thousand low-income students in more than sixty cities.[49]

Technology in School Reform

Educators confront many questions and challenges with respect to the introduction of new and emerging technologies as part of school reform efforts. We will consider several major topics, including the effective introduction of new technologies in schools and classrooms, equity and technology use in education, and cautions regarding developments that have occurred during the past decade.

■ Policies for technology

Effective Introduction of Computers and Other Technologies.   Analysts have identified many considerations that determine whether the introduction of computer-based technologies will produce or help produce substantial improvements in the performance of elementary and secondary students. It is useful to view such considerations as having implications for policy and practice at each level of the educational system: federal, state, district, school, and classroom. Federal officials and legislators have been grappling with broad issues, such as how to make Internet connections affordable for schools, how to obtain and disseminate research dealing with the effective use of computers, and how to help colleges and universities improve teacher education with respect to instructional technologies. State and district decision makers have been considering and often acting on recommendations such as the following:[50]

- State and district leaders must have a clear plan for supporting district efforts in introducing new technologies.

- Teachers must receive ongoing training and technical support in how to use technologies effectively. Technical support staff should be available at both the district and school levels.

- There should be a balance among investing in hardware, software, and training.

---

[49]Eleanore Chelimsky, *Private Programs Guaranteeing Student Aid for Higher Education* (Washington, D.C.: General Accounting Office, 1990), p. 2; and Michael Winerip, "When Data Don't Mean That One Way Is Best," *New York Times,* July 16, 2003. See also information at the "'I Have a Dream' Foundation" Internet site, at **www.ihad.org**.

[50]Sylvia Charp, "Classrooms of Tomorrow," *T.H.E. Journal* (January 1999), available at **www.thejournal.com**; Keith Oelrich, "Virtual Schools," *T.H.E. Journal* (June 2001), available at **www.thejournal.com**; Fred Carrigg and Margaret Honey, "No Miracles Here!" (2003), paper prepared for the Center for Children and Technology, available at **www2.edc.org/CCT**; Steve Rappaport, "Why We've Failed to Integrate Technology Effectively in Our Schools," *eSCHOOLNEWS* (August 2003), available at **www.eschoolnews.com**; and Corey Murray, "In Ed Tech, Leaders Matter Most," *eSCHOOLNEWS* (July 2004), available at **www.eschoolnews.com**.

Standards & Assessment ☑

- Teacher licensing standards should include assessment of knowledge and skills involving incorporation of technology in classroom lessons.
- Schools should have community partners who provide expertise and support.
- Research should be conducted on the use of computers in schools.

At the classroom level, researchers have found that variables associated with the successful implementation of computer-based technologies include the following:[51]

■ Concentration needed

- Computers must be sufficiently concentrated to make a difference. For example, one study found that placing one computer in a classroom did not change student achievement but that providing classrooms with three or more computers did produce better outcomes.
- Training must be sufficiently intensive to make a difference. For example, several studies found that providing teachers with more than ten hours of training results in much more change in instruction than shorter training periods.
- How teachers use computers helps determine student outcomes. For example, one major study using data from hundreds of schools supported the conclusion that eighth graders whose teachers emphasized problem solving and learning of concepts using computers learned significantly more than did those whose teachers emphasized low-level "drill and kill" exercises.

■ Coordination needed

- Plans for computer use must coordinate with arrangements for scheduling, testing, class size, and other aspects of instruction. If class periods are too short or classes are too large to allow the teacher to deliver a lesson effectively, or if teachers are preoccupied with preparing students for tests or with other urgent tasks, computer availability may make little or no difference.
- Teachers who use technology heavily should not neglect motivational and affective aspects of their instruction.

■ Training needed

The predominant theme throughout our preceding review of computer-based technologies and successful school reform is that substantial, appropriate teacher training is definitely a prerequisite. The federal government has recognized this imperative in provisions of the No Child Left Behind Act that require states to develop plans to ensure that teachers can use new technologies effectively. Many of these plans focus on training teachers to implement improved technologies in the classroom.[52]

■ Poverty schools bypassed

Equity and the Use of Technology.   Another key issue, particularly at national and state levels, is ensuring equal opportunity for all students to access the benefits of technology improvements. Whether in their schools or homes, low-income students

[51]Dale Mann and Edward A. Shafer, "Technology and Achievement," *American School Board Journal* (July 1997), available at **www.asbj.com**; Gary Lilly, "Tech Coaches," *Electronic School* (January 1999), available at **www.electronic-school.com**; Allan Perry, "Tech Versus the Human Touch," *Educational Horizons* (Summer 2003), available at **www.pilambda.org**; and Cathleen Norris and Eliot Soloway, "The Impact of Technology on K–12 Education," *eSCHOOLNEWS* (June 2004), available at **www.eschoolnews.com**.
[52]Fred Reiss, "Project T.E.A.C.H.—Technology Enrichment and Curriculum Help," *T.H.E. Journal* (October 1998), pp. 70–71, available at **www.thejournal.com**; James P. Tenbusch, "Teaching the Teachers," *Electronic School* (March 1998), available at **www.electronic-school.com**; Mary Burns, "From Compliance to Commitment," *Phi Delta Kappan* (December 2002), pp. 295–302; Kristen Loschert, "Are You Ready?" *NEA Today* (April 2003), available at **www.nea.org/neatoday**; and Mark A. Edwards, "Fulfilling the Promise of Ed Tech," *eSCHOOLNEWS* (February 2004), p. 6, 29, available at **www.eschoolnews.com**.

generally have less access to certain computer-based learning opportunities than do middle-income students. Until recently, many low-income families have been unable to afford computers. Schools enrolling high percentages of low-income students usually have computers available, but in recent years increasing reliance on Internet and multimedia usage in U.S. schools has bypassed numerous high-poverty schools in big cities. In addition, as we noted in the chapter on Culture, Socialization, and Education, girls also lag behind boys in certain indicators involving computer access and use. Educators at the National Educational Technology Consortium have been studying disparities among groups of students in opportunities to learn with and from computer-related technologies. They have offered many recommendations, including the following, for addressing the situation in a school or district:[53]

■ Addressing inequities

- Gather usage and course enrollment data and examine the data on the basis of race, gender, language status, disability status, and income.
- Collect and disseminate information on promising intervention strategies and discuss these possibilities with the staff.
- Assist faculty in developing plans for advancing equity.
- Evaluate staff on how well they incorporate activities ensuring equitable computer use.

■ Community technology centers

Many efforts to enhance equity in technology access involve making computers available not in schools but in community locations. Neighborhood computer centers in low-income urban and rural communities are allowing residents—both adults and children—to learn about and benefit from advanced technologies. One researcher commented that "community technology centers ensure that we don't leave part of our population behind with nineteenth-century skills as we move into a twenty-first-century economy." This approach may become widespread in the future and may tie in with school-based efforts to reduce technology-related inequities.[54]

■ Silicon snake oil?

Cautions Regarding Computer-Based Technologies in Education. Not everyone is optimistic about the likelihood that technology will produce productive reforms in the educational system. Skeptics abound, and their ranks include some of the most knowledgeable analysts of recent developments in the schools and of the evolution of computers in general. For example, Clifford Stoll, widely known for his contributions to Internet development, has written a book titled *Silicon Snake Oil* in which he points out that although computers may be fun to use in the classroom, entertainment is not synonymous with learning. Stoll sees computers as potentially

---

[53]Michael Dertouzos, "The Rich People's Computer?" *Technology Review* (January–February 1999), available at **www.techreview.com**; and "Closing the Equity Gap in Technology Access and Use" (undated), posting at the National Educational Technology Consortium Internet site, available at **www.netc.org/equity**. See also John H. Holloway, "The Digital Divide," *Educational Leadership* (October 2000); and James T. Gordon, "Curriculum Access in the Digital Age," *Harvard Education Letter* (January–February 2002), available at **http:// edletter.org/past**.
[54]Mitchell Resnick and Natalie Rusk, "Computer Clubhouses in the Inner City," *American Prospect* (July–August 1998); Helen Silvis, "Forget Isolation, We're Online Now," *NW Education* (Winter 2000), available at **www.nwrel.org**; and Rebecca P. Pierik, "Beyond the Digital Divide," *Ed. Magazine*, July 1, 2003, available at **www.gse.harvard.edu/~news**: click on "Technology & Learning."

equivalent to the grainy films and the disjointed filmstrips that teachers used years ago mainly to keep their students occupied.[55]

■ Idle clicking?

Similarly, Jane Healy had become well known as an enthusiast about the computer's potential for opening new worlds to students and then shocked many of her readers with a 1998 book in which she questioned the effects of new technologies on children both inside and outside the schools. After two years spent visiting classrooms, she concluded that computers in many classrooms are supervised by "ill-prepared teachers" whose students engage mostly in mindless drills, games unrelated to coherent learning objectives, "silly surfing," and/or "idle clicking." Other analysts, also on the basis of visits to numerous schools and classrooms, have reached the conclusion that expensive multimedia setups frequently serve more as a medium for classroom control than as a learning tool. In reaching such conclusions about computer-based technologies in the schools, Healy and other skeptics typically offer the following cautions and criticisms:[56]

- Research indicating that computers are producing widespread gains in student performance generally is badly flawed and mostly invalid.

■ Creativity reduced?

- Computers too often detract from students' creativity by constraining them within prescribed boundaries of thought and action.

- Schools respond to perceived or real public demands and expectations that classrooms should be loaded with advanced technologies by buying expensive equipment that soon becomes obsolete.

- The high costs of these soon-outdated technologies force schools to severely cut back on industrial arts, art and music, and other "frills."

- Particularly for young children, time on the computer too often replaces time needed to develop motor skills and logical thinking.

- Much of students' time online involves commercial sources mainly seeking loyal customers.

■ Reduced attention span of screenagers?

- Even more than television, digital technology is reducing the attention span of children and "screenagers" (adolescents growing up in the Internet era).

- Fantasy worlds and other imaginary digitized environments are distorting children's sense of reality.

- According to Paul Saffo, digitized technologies are an "even more potent time-sink" than television, "serving up parent-fretting violence and vapid, content-less drivel" that constitutes a vast, "cyberspace wasteland."

■ Scaling up a problem

- Isolated examples of a few classrooms, schools, and even districts that effectively use computer-based technologies do not tell us anything about what is

---

[55]Clifford Stoll, *Silicon Snake Oil: Second Thoughts on the Information Superhighway* (New York: Doubleday, 1995). See also Todd Oppenheimer, "The Computer Delusion," *Atlantic* (July 1997), available at **www.theatlantic.com**; Kirk A. Johnson, "Do Computers in the Classroom Boost Academic Achievement?" (2000), paper prepared for the Heritage Foundation, available at **www.heritage.org**; Todd Oppenheimer, *The Flickering Mind* (New York: Random House, 2003); and "Experts Speak Out Against Computers for Youngsters," *Education Reporter* (January 2004), available at **www.eagleforum.org**.

[56]Stoll, *Silicon Snake Oil*; David Tyack and Larry Cuban, *Tinkering Toward Utopia* (Cambridge, Mass.: Harvard University Press, 1995); Jane M. Healy, *Failure to Connect* (New York: Simon and Schuster, 1998); Paul Saffo, "Neo-Toys," *Civilization* (November 1998); Joan Almon, ed., *Fool's Gold* (College Park, Md.: Alliance for Childhood, 2000), available at **www .allianceforchildhood.net**: click on "Projects," then "Reports"; Carol Tell, "The I-Generation—From Toddlers to Teenagers," *Educational Leadership* (October 2000); and Jamie McKenzie, "The Technology Presumption," *From Now On* (May 2003), available at **www.fno.org**.

happening or likely to happen in most situations. Indeed, the educational system has a long and inglorious history of failure in half-hearted attempts to "scale up" from a few promising implementations to widespread use throughout the system.

In reviewing these cautions, we should keep in mind preceding parts of this section as well as earlier parts of this chapter that identified actions associated with the successful implementation of computer-based technologies and other substantial efforts to reform the schools. Will schools and districts provide large-scale and ongoing training and the meaningful technical support required for teachers to use technology effectively? Will educators carefully align the introduction of such technologies and coordinate them with curriculum objectives, testing, and school climate improvements? Fortunately, many educators are working to make this happen.

Rural Education

■ Rural diversity

More than one-third of public-school students attend rural schools, and about one-half of school districts are rural. In trying to improve rural education, educators must confront the extreme diversity of rural locations, which makes it difficult to generalize across communities. One group of observers defined rural school districts as those that have fewer than 150 residents per square mile and are located in counties in which at least 60 percent of the population resides in communities with populations under 5,000. Even within this fairly restricted definition, rural communities exemplify hundreds of "subcultures" that differ in racial and ethnic composition, extent of remoteness, economic structure, and other characteristics.[57]

This diversity is partly why the particular problems of rural schools have received relatively little attention during the past fifty years. Recently, however, a small group of scholars has been trying to determine how to provide high-quality education in a rural setting. They have reached several major conclusions:[58]

■ Conclusions about rural schools

1. The critical elements for rural school improvement are community dependent. For this reason, innovations that succeed in urban areas tend to fail in rural areas.

2. The tremendous diversity in rural America requires similarly diverse school improvement efforts that also address multicultural education goals.

3. The small scale of rural schools offers advantages. Teachers can know students and parents personally, and schools can work closely with community agencies.

4. Cyclical economic recessions have made public education an increasingly important force in providing skilled personnel and jobs in rural communities.

---

[57]Robert C. Johnston, "Rural Education," *Education Week,* December 16, 1998; Michael L. Arnold, "Rural Schools: Diverse Needs Call for Flexible Policies," *McREL Policy Brief* (May 2000), available at **www.mcrel.org/topics/policybrief.asp**; and Kathleen K. Miller and Bruce A. Weber, "Persistent Poverty and Place" (2003), paper prepared for the Economic Research Service, available at **http:srdc.msstate.edu/measuring/series/miller_ weber.pdf**.

[58]Craig R. Howley, "Studying the Rural in Education," *Education Policy Analysis Archives* (April 30, 1997), available at **http://epaa.asu.edu**; Dennis Sparks, "Low Income, High Hurdles," *Journal of Staff Development* (Summer 2000); "Rural Alaska Schools Look to Online Courses for NCLB Success," *eSCHOOLNEWS,* July 2, 2003, available at **www.eschoolnews.com**; and Judith K. March and Karen H. Peters, "A Collaborative Approach for Small Districts to Use the Effective Schools Process for Comprehensive School Reform" (2004), paper prepared for the Ohio Center for Effective Schools, available at **www.effective-schools.org/ effective-schools-resources/effective-schools-resource.asp**.

5. Educators should make sure that children and youth in rural communities feel appreciated. They should understand that they have a part to play in the future of their communities.

6. Teachers in rural schools frequently require substantial technical support.

7. Many rural schools can benefit from distance learning and other forms of advanced technology.

Other authors have concluded that teacher-training programs for rural areas should prepare teachers in more content areas and for a broader age range of students than do conventional programs. As the chapter on Governing and Administering Public Education points out, educators also are reassessing the desirability of school consolidation in light of the possible advantages small schools offer.

■ **Teacher shortages and distance education**

Many rural schools face serious problems in attracting qualified teachers. States have increased certification requirements and reduced the flexibility to employ teachers without proper certification, which has left many rural districts unable either to find or to afford sufficient teaching personnel, particularly in science, math, and foreign languages. But school systems can overcome this problem, in part, by using television, interactive computers, and other forms of **distance education** that deliver cost-effective instruction.[59]

■ **Adapting curriculum and instruction**

Educators working with low-income students in Appalachia and other areas of rural poverty are looking for ways to adapt curriculum and instruction to their students' social and cultural backgrounds. The Foxfire approach provides examples of such adaptation in its use of oral history and local cultural materials to help improve students' understanding and motivation inside and outside the school.[60]

Gifted and Talented Students

■ **Trends in gifted education**

Research on the education of gifted and talented students has increased. Widespread program trends include "radical acceleration" of learning opportunities for gifted and talented students; special "mentoring" assistance; increased emphasis on independent study and investigative learning; use of individualized education programs (IEPs), as with students with disabilities; opportunities to engage in advanced-level projects; instruction delivery in accordance with students' learning styles; special schools, Saturday programs, and summer schools; increased community resource use; varied instructional approaches to match student interests and abilities; and "compacting" curriculum to streamline content that students already know and replace it with more challenging material.[61]

---

[59]Troy K. Corley, "Tapping into Technology in Rural Communities," *Educational Leadership* (May 1998), pp. 71–73; Kathy Christie, "The Rural Bellwether," *Phi Delta Kappan* (February 2001), pp. 425–427; and Cynthia Reeves, "Implementing the No Child Left Behind Act" (2003), paper prepared for the North Central Regional Educational Laboratory, available at **www.ncrcl.org/policy/pubs/html/implicate**.

[60]Eliot Wigginton, "Foxfire Grows Up," *Reform Report* (January 1993), pp. 1, 4–7; Bobby A. Starnes, "On Dark Times, Parallel Universes, and Deja Vu," *Phi Delta Kappan* (October 2000), pp. 108–114; and information available at **www.foxfire.org**.

[61]John F. Feldhusen, "How to Identify and Develop Special Talents," *Educational Leadership* (February 1996), pp. 66–69; Karen L. Westberg and Francis X. Archambault Jr., "A Multi-Site Case Study of Successful Classroom Practices for High Ability Students," *Gifted Child Quarterly* (Winter 1997), pp. 42–51; Dana T. Johnson, "Teaching Mathematics to Gifted Students in a Mixed-Ability Classroom," *ERIC Clearinghouse on Disabilities and Gifted Education Digest* (April 2000); and Joan F. Smutny, *Gifted Education* (Bloomington, Ind.: Phi Delta Kappa, 2003).

■ Differing approaches

A major issue involving gifted and talented students is the selection of effective approaches to curriculum and instruction. In general, educators have tended to emphasize either acceleration through the regular curriculum or enrichment that provides for greater depth of learning, but some have argued for a "confluent" approach that combines both. Developing this idea, analysts have advocated combining elements: (1) a "content" model, which emphasizes accelerated study; (2) a "process-product" model, which emphasizes enrichment through independent study and investigation; and (3) an "epistemological" model, which emphasizes understanding and appreciation of systems of knowledge.[62]

■ Including more minority students

Much concern has been expressed about the low participation of minority students and economically disadvantaged students in gifted education. Evidence indicates that selection criteria frequently fail to identify disadvantaged students who might benefit from participation. For this reason, many efforts are under way to broaden definitions of giftedness to include indicators such as very strong problem-solving skills, high creativity, high verbal or nonverbal fluency, and unusual artistic accomplishments and abilities.[63]

Increasing Teaching and Learning Time

Several national reports, including *A Nation at Risk* and *Prisoners of Time,* have recommended providing more time for teaching and learning. Possible approaches include extending the school year, lengthening the school day, or offering after-school and summer learning programs.

■ Extending time controversial

Longer School Years or School Days. Numerous school districts have lengthened the school day or the school year. Some offer **year-round schools** that run on rotating schedules so that three-quarters of students attend for nine weeks while the remaining quarter are on vacation for three weeks. Year-round schools have usually been established where schools are seriously overcrowded. More than two million students now attend year-round schools.

Such moves usually provoke controversy because they require a significant increase in staff costs and may disrupt parents' child-care arrangements. Action to extend time for learning also will require substantial changes in curriculum and instruction if it is to improve student achievement.[64] For a debate on this topic, see the Taking Issue box.

---

[62]Joyce Van Tassel-Baska, "Effective Curriculum and Instructional Models for Talented Students," *Gifted Child Quarterly* (Fall 1980), pp. 162–168; and Ann Robinson and Pamela R. Clinkenbeard, "Giftedness," *Annual Review of Psychology* no. 49 (1998), pp. 117–139. See also E. Jean Gubbins, "NRC/GT Looks at Self-Reflection of Classroom Practices," *National Research Center on the Gifted and Talented Newsletter* (Spring 2003), available at **www.gifted.uconn.edu/newslttr.html**.
[63]James J. Gallagher, "Education of Gifted Students: A Civil Rights Issue?" *Phi Delta Kappan* (January 1995), pp. 408–410; Wendy Schwartz, "Strategies for Identifying the Talents of Diverse Students," *ERIC Clearinghouse on Urban Education* (May 1997), available at **www.ericfacility.net/databases/ERIC_Digests/ed410323.html**; and Mary R. Coleman, "The Identification of Students Who Are Gifted," *ERIC Digest* (June 2003), available at **http://ericec.org/digests/e644.html**.
[64]National Education Commission on Time and Learning, *Prisoners of Time* (Washington, D.C.: U.S. Department of Education, 1994); Carolyn M. Shields and Steven L. Oberg, *Year-Round Schooling: Reviewing What We Know* (Bloomington, Ind.: Phi Delta Kappa, 2000); John G. Morgan, "School Calendar Choices in Tennessee" (2003), paper prepared for the Tennessee Office of Educational Accountability, available at **www.comptroller.state.tn.us/orea/reports**; and "Don't Change School Calendars Because . . . Summer Matters!!" (undated), postings at the Summer Matters Internet site, available at **www.summermatters.com**.

taking issue

Question Should the United States extend the amount of time students spend in school?

More Time in School

One suggestion for improving student achievement has been to increase the amount of time students spend in school by lengthening the school day or school year or both. This idea is based in part on observations of countries such as Japan, where students spend considerably more time in school than do American students. It also reflects research indicating that time-on-task is an important determinant of students' performance.

Arguments PRO

1 Extending the school year or school day will give teachers more contact time and an opportunity to teach students in depth. This is particularly vital for at-risk students, who need special services and remedial work.

2 Experience in countries such as Japan indicates that increased time spent in school can assist in raising achievement scores. Many national task-force reports have also recommended extending time in school.

3 Extending school time can help to solve the problems of latchkey children, who must look after themselves while their parents work. In this way, schools can benefit the family as well as improve education.

4 Lengthening students' time in school will indicate to taxpayers that schools are serious about raising educational standards. Taxpayers will therefore be more willing to support the schools.

5 The present system of school attendance originated in an agrarian period when families needed children's help with farm tasks. In an industrial society, the best use of students' time is to give them additional schooling that prepares them for the world of the twenty-first century.

Arguments CON

1 Extending time in school will not compensate for the poor teaching that takes place in too many schools. The problem is not quantity but quality of schooling, and longer hours could well *reduce* quality.

2 So many social and cultural differences exist between Japan and the United States that simple comparisons are not valid. Little hard evidence indicates that increasing students' time in school will raise achievement levels in the United States.

3 Extending the time children spend in school will add to the growing institutional interference with basic family life. Such interference, however well intentioned, contributes to the fragmentation of the modern family.

4 Extending school time will require major new expenditures to increase salaries and refurbish buildings. Taxpayers will not willingly pay for these expenses.

5 We know too little about the effects of lengthening the school day or year. Do children in our culture *need* ample breaks from school? Do their originality and creativity suffer when they are kept too long in classes? Until we have answers, we should not make students spend more time in school.

■ 21st Century Learning Centers

After-School and Summer Programs. Rather than increase the school year or school day for all students, many districts have been initiating or expanding after-school and summer learning programs. After-school and summer programs can provide struggling students with more time for learning or offer safe and educational opportunities for latchkey and other children (see the chapter on Culture, Socialization, and Education). These programs have grown rapidly in recent years as the

No Child Left Behind Act resulted in the identification of thousands of schools not making adequate yearly progress. The federal government now provides millions of dollars annually to support them under the **21st Century Community Learning Centers** legislation, and state and local sources provide still more support. The 21st Century Community Learning Centers, supported through the No Child Left Behind Act, provide tutoring, after-school classes, summer school, and other academic enrichment activities for students attending low-performing schools. Analysts and evaluators who have studied the centers and similar efforts have reached several conclusions:[65]

■ Successful if implemented well

1. After-school and summer programs can improve academic performance if they are implemented well.

2. Implementation considerations include selecting and training staff, providing appropriate materials, and making sufficient resources available.

3. Progress is difficult to measure because students typically make relatively small gains on tests that assess regular schooling, let alone after-school and summer programs. Therefore officials should assess attendance, parent support, student effort, and other possible correlates of improved achievement.

4. Nonacademic goals such as providing a safe environment, expanding students' interests, and developing social skills are worthwhile and should be addressed in implementing after-school and summer programs.

5. Particularly successful programs should be analyzed and emulated.

REFOCUS Would you enjoy teaching in a school or school district that has implemented the reforms described in this section? For example, would you like to teach in a year-round school? How will you prepare to effectively teach gifted and talented students?

▶ School Choice

In recent years, **school choice** plans have been advocated as a way to introduce greater flexibility and accountability into education. The basic idea is to enhance students' opportunities to choose where they will enroll and what they will study. School choice is a broad goal and many different programs offer students and their families varying levels of choices. Advocates of school choice point out that parents typically find only one model of education in any given public-school neighborhood. Some advocates argue for creating choices within the public-school system; others contend that the only true alternatives are outside the system. Recent efforts

---

[65]Linda Lumsden, "After-School Programs," *Research Roundup* (Fall 2003), available at **http://eric.uoregon.edu/publications/roundup**; "Reflections on System Building," *Out-of-School Time Policy Commentary* (May 2003), available at **www.forumforyouthinvestment.org/comment/ostpc3.pdf**; Robert C. Wagner and Thomas Kane, "Improving the Quality of After-School Programs," *Education Week*, February 18, 2004; and information available at **www.ncrel.org/21stcclc/index.html**.

to increase school choice represent a spectrum of plans representing these two views and ideas between the two extremes. They include the following: [66]

Today's magnet schools

- *Magnet and Alternative Schools.* Many school districts offer their students the opportunity to choose magnet schools or alternative schools within the district. **Magnet schools**, as described in the chapter on Providing Equal Educational Opportunity, are designed to attract voluntary enrollment by offering special programs or curricula that appeal to students from more than one neighborhood. They are often part of a reform effort aimed at decreasing segregation and providing students with opportunities to participate in instructional programs not available in their local schools. More than one thousand magnet schools are now functioning in public school districts.

Types of alternative schools

Alternative schools provide learning opportunities unavailable in the average public school. From this point of view, magnet schools are a type of alternative school. So, too, are many parochial and other nonpublic schools and institutions such as street academies, storefront schools, and high-school "outposts" designed to make education more relevant for inner-city students. Studies of alternative schools have indicated that they usually enroll students who have not succeeded in traditional schools or who want a different kind of education.

Advantages of alternative schools

Compared to traditional schools, alternative schools allow for greater individualization, more independent study, and more openness to the outside community. They tend to offer small size, high staff morale, high attendance, satisfied students, freedom from external control, and strong concern for noncognitive goals of education.[67]

Voluntary-enrollment charter schools

- *Charter schools.* As discussed in the chapter on Financing Public Education, charter schools funded by public-school districts also frequently provide opportunities for parents and students to choose among schools. More than forty states now allow for establishment of charter schools, and nearly three thousand charter schools are operating nationally.[68]

NCLB choice

- *Open public-school enrollment.* As noted in the chapter on Providing Equal Educational Opportunity, provisions of the No Child Left Behind Act require that school districts provide opportunities for students at schools designated as not making adequate yearly progress to transfer to other schools in the district.

[66]Adam Meyerson, "A Model of Cultural Leadership," *Policy Review* (January–February, 1999), available at **www.policyreview.com**; David Myers et al., *School Choice in New York City After Two Years* (Washington, D.C.: Mathematica Policy Research, 2000); Stacey Bielick and Christopher Chapman, "Trends in the Use of School Choice" (2003), report #2003031, prepared for the National Center for Education Statistics, available at **http://nces.ed.gov/pubsearch**; and Dan Murphy, "Overview of the Milwaukee Voucher Program" (undated), paper prepared for the American Federation of Teachers, available at **www.aft.org/research/vouchers**.

[67]Daniel U. Levine, "Educating Alienated Inner City Youth: Lessons from the Street Academies," *Journal of Negro Education* (Spring 1975), pp. 139–148; "Support for Smaller Learning Communities," *NW Education* (Winter 2000), pp. 5–9, available at **www.nwrel.org**; Mary Ann Raywid, "What to Do with Students Who Are Not Succeeding," *Phi Delta Kappan* (April 2001), pp. 582–584; and C. A. Lehr and C. M. Lange, "Alternative Schools and the Students They Serve," *Policy Research Brief* (January 2003), available at **http://rtc.umn.edu/pdf/141.pdf**.

[68]Thomas L. Good and Jennifer S. Braden, "Charter Schools," *Phi Delta Kappan* (June 2000), pp. 745–750; and Katrina Bulkley and Jennifer Fisler, "A Decade of Charter Schools," *CPRE Policy Briefs* (April 2002), available at **www.cpre.org**.

■ Open enrollment attendance options

Several states have also created plans that allow all students the option to transfer to their choice of public schools within, or sometimes outside, their local school district. Colorado laws, for example, require that all districts allow students to transfer freely within their boundaries. Minnesota's comprehensive choice plan not only supports both intradistrict and interdistrict transfers but also expands alternative schools and programs. Washington's legislation provides students who experience a "special hardship or detrimental condition" with an absolute right to enroll in another school district that has available space; it also requires districts to accept students who transfer to locations close to their parents' place of work or child-care site.

■ Privately funded vouchers

■ *Privately funded school choice vouchers.* Philanthropists in numerous locations have provided vouchers to enable students to attend nonpublic schools. After a group of business executives funded scholarships that helped 2,200 New York City students (out of more than 40,000 applicants) to attend nonpublic schools in 1998 and 1999, a larger group raised millions of dollars for a national program to provide inner-city students with similar scholarships. Thousands of students have received such scholarships. Income tax deductions for contributions to private voucher programs also are allowed in Florida and Pennsylvania.

■ Arizona tax credits

■ *Tuition tax credits.* Initiated in 1997, Arizona's universal tax credit approach allows any taxpayer who pays tuition for a child attending a public or nonpublic school to take a dollar-for-dollar deduction (up to half what the local public schools would have spent) in state tax liability. In addition, taxpayers can receive a credit of up to five hundred dollars for donations to "private tuition" charities that spend at least 90 percent of this income for tuition assistance to low-income students.

■ Government-funded vouchers

■ *Publicly funded school choice vouchers.* Although small government-funded voucher programs have been in place in Cleveland and in Colorado, Florida, Maine, Ohio, and Vermont, the best-known voucher project is the sizable program funded by the Wisconsin legislature for low-income students in Milwaukee. Originally initiated to help students attend nonreligious private schools, the Milwaukee program expanded in 1998 to include attendance at religious schools. A major government-funded voucher program also was approved for the District of Columbia beginning in 2004.[69]

Controversy About School Choice

As programs have been implemented to expand school choice, numerous recommendations for and against additional action are being put forward. Those who support complete choice recommend policies such as enrollment across school district boundaries, vouchers to attend both public and nonpublic schools, magnetization and/or charterization of entire school districts and regions, and creation of alternative-school networks. Supporters of choice emphasize the following arguments:[70]

[69]"Case Studies: The Milwaukee and Cleveland Voucher Programs" (undated), papers at the "Voucher Home Page of the American Federation of Teachers," available at **www.aft.org/ vouchers/report/casstudy.htm**.

[70]Matthew J. Brouillette, "The Case for Choice in Schooling" (2001), paper posted at the Mackinac Center for Public Policy Internet site, available at **www.mackinac.org/ s2001-01**; John E. Chubb, "Ignoring the Market," *Education Next* (Spring 2003), available at **www.educationnext.org;** and John Danner and J. C. Bowman, "The Promise and Peril of Charter Schools," *Texas Education Review* (Winter 2003–2004), available at **www.educationreview.homestead.com**. See also studies listed at **www.free-market .net/directorybytopic**: click on "School Choice."

- Providing choice for disadvantaged students will enable them to escape from poorly functioning schools.

- Achievement, aspirations, and other outcomes will improve for many students because they will be more motivated to succeed at schools they select.

■ Arguments favoring choice

- Both existing public schools and alternative learning institutions (whether public or nonpublic) will provide improved education because their staffs will be competing to attract students.

- Increased opportunities will be available to match school programs and services with students' needs.

- Parents will be empowered and encouraged to play a larger role in their children's education.

Critics of school choice plans question these arguments, particularly in cases that involve public financing of nonpublic schools. The critics maintain the following:[71]

■ Arguments against choice

- Choice plans will reinforce stratification and segregation because highly motivated or high-achieving white and minority students will be disproportionately likely to transfer out of schools that have a substantial percentage of students with low achievement or low social status.

- Much of the student movement will consist of middle-class students transferring to nonpublic schools. That will reduce the middle class's willingness to support the public schools.

- Public financial support for nonpublic schools is unconstitutional.

- Competition among schools to attract transfer students will not by itself result in improved achievement; other emerging reforms described in this chapter are more important.

- The opening and closing of numerous schools based on their competitive attractiveness will disrupt the operation of the entire educational system.

- There is little or no reason to believe that most schools that presently enroll relatively few disadvantaged students will be more successful with such students than are their present schools.

- Even if one assumes that schools capable of substantially improving the performance of low achievers are widely available in a choice plan, many students and parents lack the knowledge necessary to select them, and these outstanding schools may not accept many low achievers.

- Although accountability may increase in the sense that unattractive schools will lose students and may even be closed, overall accountability will be reduced because nonpublic schools receiving public funds will not be subject to government standards. Alternatively, nonpublic schools' participation would result in more government regulation for those schools.

- Public financing of nonpublic institutions will result in the establishment of "cult" schools based on divisive racist or religious ideologies.

---

[71]Herbert J. Grover, "Private School Choice Is Wrong," *Educational Leadership* (January 1991), p. 51; Martin Carnoy, "School Choice? Or Is It Privatization?" *Educational Researcher* (October 2000), pp. 15–20, available at **www.aera.net/pubs/er**; Luis Benveniste, Martin Carnoy, and Richard Rothstein, *All Else Equal* (New York: Routledge Falmer 2002); and Emily Van Dunk and Anneliese M. Dickman, *School Choice and the Question of Accountability* (New Haven, Conn.: Yale University Press, 2003).

■ Fear of increased separatism

These worries about school choice are shared even by people who have supported proposals to expand student options. For example, John Leo thinks that school choice is "reform's best choice" but also is education's "600-pound gorilla." He believes it may harm education by funding schools that encourage social, racial, and economic separatism. In this context, many analysts have been trying to identify policies that could make choice plans as constructive as possible. They have suggested policies including the following:[72]

■ Policies for constructive school choice

- Ensure that students and parents receive adequate counseling and information.
- Provide free transportation, scholarships, and other support to make sure that choices are fully available and do not depend on social status.
- Include guidelines to avoid segregation and resegregation.
- Ensure that enrollment and admissions procedures are equitable and do not exclude large proportions of students from the most desirable schools.
- Include provisions to release government-operated schools from regulations not imposed on nonpublic schools.
- Create an environment in which both "regular" public schools and alternatives provide effective instruction. Many observers believe that both regular and alternate schools enrolling low-income students would benefit particularly from loosening or eliminating seniority rules currently a major aspect of collective bargaining agreements with teachers. Such changes would allow schools to replace unqualified or ineffective teachers with others better able to address their students' needs.
- Do not ignore other reform necessities and possibilities; instead, treat choice as part of a comprehensive reform agenda that involves systemic reform of the kind described elsewhere in this chapter.

■ Research on choice alternatives

Research to date has not conclusively established that students with school choice achieve at a higher level than comparable students in regular public schools. Evaluations of Edison and other privatized schools, voucher programs, and charter schools have tended to conclude that achievement gains generally were small and inconsistent.[73]

■ Effectiveness of nonpublic schools

Research comparing the effectiveness of public and nonpublic schools has spurred debate among researchers and others interested in school-choice plans that include funding for students to attend private schools. For example, James Coleman and his colleagues compared nonpublic and public schools and concluded that (1) after accounting for family background variables, students in nonpublic schools have higher achievement than students in public schools; (2) nonpublic schools provide a safer and more orderly environment; (3) except for Catholic schools, nonpublic schools are smaller, have smaller classes, and encourage more student partic-

---

[72]John Leo, "School Reform's Best Choice," *U.S. News and World Report,* January 14, 1991, p. 17; Stacy Smith, "The Democratizing Potential of Charter Schools," *Educational Leadership* (October 1998), pp. 55–58; John H. Holloway, "School Choice and Lessons Learned," *Educational Leadership* (December 2000–January 2001); Paul T. Hill, "Doing Choice Right," *Education Week,* November 19, 2003; and Diane Ravitch, ed., *Brookings Papers on Education Policy* (Washington, D.C.: Brookings Institution, 2004).
[73]"Comparison of Achievement Results for Students Attending Privately Managed and Traditional Schools in Six Cities" (2003), report published by the U.S. Government Printing Office, available at **www.gao.gov/atext/d0462.txt**; Jeanne Allen, Meghan E. Cotter, and Anna V. Marcucio, "Charter Schools" (2003), report prepared for the Center for Education Reform, available at **www.edreform.com**; and Frances C. Fowler, "School Choice," *Educational Researcher* (March 2003), available at **www.aera.net/pubs/er**.

ipation than do public schools; (4) nonpublic schools require more homework and have better attendance; and (5) superiority in school climate and discipline accounts for the higher achievement of students in nonpublic schools.[74]

■ Conclusions by Chubb and Moe

John Chubb and Terry Moe of the Brookings Institution also have studied achievement differentials between public and nonpublic schools. They, too, concluded that nonpublic schools produce higher achievement. A major reason for this difference, they said, is that nonpublic schools tend to function more autonomously and with less bureaucracy. For example, principals of public schools are much more constrained than their counterparts in nonpublic schools with respect to hiring and firing teachers. In addition, public schools tend to be more complex and more susceptible to pressures from a variety of external constituencies (such as central offices, state government officials, or groups representing taxpayers). As a result, teachers and students in public schools are more likely to receive mixed messages about the priority goals in their schools, and they are less inclined to work together to achieve these goals.[75]

■ Debate about research findings

However, many educators disagree with the conclusion that nonpublic schools produce higher achievement than public schools. Critics give the following reasons for their disagreement: (1) obtaining better measures or otherwise taking better account of family background variables virtually eliminates the achievement superiority of nonpublic students; (2) taking account of achievement level upon entry to high school also eliminates or greatly reduces the achievement difference between public and nonpublic students; (3) the statistical methods the researchers employed were inappropriate and led to misleading and unjustified conclusions; and (4) whatever differences may exist between Catholic or other nonpublic schools on the one hand and public schools on the other are trivial and have few long-term effects.[76]

Coleman and his colleagues, as well as Chubb and Moe, have responded with more data and further arguments supporting their original conclusions. In particular, they have argued that nonpublic schools enhance achievement by placing a relatively high percentage of students in college-bound programs. Because it is difficult to isolate differences in student motivation even after accounting for family background and social class, researchers probably will continue to argue over the relative effectiveness of public and nonpublic schools.[77]

---

[74]James Coleman, Thomas Hoffer, and Sally Kilgore, *Public and Private Schools* (Washington, D.C.: National Center for Education Statistics, 1981); Barbara Schneider, Kathryn S. Schiller, and James S. Coleman, "Public School Choice," *Educational Evaluation and Policy Analysis* (Spring 1996), pp. 19–29; and Richard D. Kahlenberg, "Learning From James Coleman," *Public Interest* (Summer 2001), pp. 54–73.

[75]John E. Chubb and Terry M. Moe, *Politics, Markets, and America's Schools* (Washington, D.C.: Brookings Institution, 1990). See also Edith Pasell and Richard Rothstein, eds., *School Choice* (Washington, D.C.: Economic Policy Institute, 1994); Paul E. Peterson, "Vouchers and Test Scores," *Policy Review* (January–February 1999), available at **www.policyreview.com**; and Paul T. Hill, "Eye of the Beholder," *Education Next* (Winter 2004), available at **www.educationnext.org**.

[76]Ellis B. Page and Timothy Z. Keith, "Effects of U.S. Private Schools," *Educational Researcher* (August–September 1981), pp. 7–22; Timothy Z. Keith and Ellis B. Page, "Do Catholic High Schools Improve Minority Student Achievement?" *American Educational Research Journal* (Fall 1985), pp. 337–349; David Baker and Cornelius Riordan, "The 'Eliting' of the Common American Catholic School and the National Education Crisis," *Phi Delta Kappan* (September 1998), pp. 16–23; "School Vouchers" (2001), report #GAO=01-914, prepared for the General Accounting Office, available at **www.gao.gov**; and "Voucher Effects Revisited," *ASCD Research Brief*, March 18, 2003.

[77]James S. Coleman and Thomas Hoffer, "Response to Taeuber-James-Cain-Goldberger and Morgan," *Sociology of Education* (October 1983), pp. 218–234; Lee Shumow, Deborah L. Vandell, and Kyungseok Kang, "School Choice, Family Characteristics and Home-School Relations," *Journal of Educational Psychology* no. 18 (1996), pp. 451–460.

■ Overall choice conclusions

The most notable and detailed document attempting to identify productive general policies regarding choice is a 2003 report from the National Working Commission on Choice in K–12 Education. *School Choice: Doing It the Right Way Makes a Difference* generally endorsed policies such as those summarized above. It pointed out both potential benefits and dangers in pursuing alternatives that expand choice, and that productive outcomes depend on adequate funding, careful design, ongoing evaluation, and workable accountability procedures. The report summarized much of the situation as follows:[78]

> Because so much depends on . . . [policies and practices involving design and implementation] choice is unlikely to be the panacea for American schools trumpeted by its advocates. It is equally unlikely to be the death of public support for American education, the fear of its detractors. . . . Choice's outcomes, for good or ill, depend heavily on how communities structure and implement it. . . . Communities can decide whether to make expansion of choice a conscious strategy, or they can let choice happen to them. Expanding choice implies that communities will provide some schools in new ways and also eliminate inequitable policies that plague district-run schools serving the poor.

REFOCUS Are you planning to teach in a public or nonpublic school? In either case, how do you believe expanded school choice programs would affect your teaching career?

▶ Systemic Restructuring and Standards-Based Reform

■ Improving the entire system

In recent years many reform efforts have been discussed in terms of **restructuring** all or part of the educational system. Although this term has been interpreted in many different ways, it increasingly is used to indicate the need for **systemic improvement**—that is, reform that simultaneously addresses all or most major components in the overall system. For example, officials of the Education Commission of the States have stated that all parts of the educational system from "schoolhouse to statehouse" must be restructured to bring about systematic improvement in teaching and learning. Systemic restructuring deals with instructional methods; professional development; assessment of student, teacher, and/or school performance; curriculum and materials; school finance; governance; course requirements; and other aspects of education.[79]

Standards & Assessment ✓

■ Making reforms coherent

When many changes are introduced simultaneously, restructuring and reform activities must be coherent; they must be compatible with and reinforce each other,

---

[77]James S. Coleman and Thomas Hoffer, "Response to Taeuber-James-Cain-Goldberger and Morgan," *Sociology of Education* (October 1983), pp. 218–234; Lee Shumow, Deborah L. Vandell, and Kyungseok Kang, "School Choice, Family Characteristics and Home-School Relations," *Journal of Educational Psychology* no. 18 (1996), pp. 451–460.
[78]National Working Commission on Choice in K–12 Education, "School Choice" (2003), report prepared for the Brookings Institution, pp. 4, 36, available at **www.brookings.edu**.
[79]Ronald A. Wolk, "Empower Schools," *Teacher Magazine* (January 1999); "What Is Systemic Reform?" (2001), posting at the National Academies Internet site, available at **www.nas .edu/rise/backg3.htm**; "Systemic Reform in Practice" (2003), paper prepared for the Merck Institute for Science Education, available at **www.cpre.org/Publications/mise .pdf**; and Susan H. Fuhrman and Richard F. Elmore, eds., *Redesigning Accountability Systems for Education* (New York: Teachers College Press, 2004).

rather than becoming isolated fragments that divert time and energy from priority goals. Because systemic reforms work for coherence by identifying student performance standards and then aligning testing, instructional methods and materials, professional development, and other aspects of education, they frequently are referred to as "standards-based" reforms.

State-Level Systemic Reform

One of the best examples of state-level systemic reform is in Kentucky, where in 1989 the state supreme court declared the state's "system of common schools" unconstitutional on the grounds that it was ineffective and inequitable. The court then instructed the legislative and executive branches to improve the "entire sweep of the system—all its parts and parcels." As a result, the following changes, among others, have been phased in as part of the Kentucky Education Reform Act (KERA):[80]

■ Provisions of Kentucky plan

- Curriculum, instruction, and student assessment are performance-based, emphasizing mastery-oriented learning and criterion-referenced testing.
- Schools have established governance councils with authority to make decisions on curriculum and instruction and on budget allocations.
- Parents can transfer their children out of schools they consider unsatisfactory.
- Faculty at unsuccessful schools receive help from state-appointed specialists.
- Youth and family service centers have been established in communities where 20 percent or more of students are from low-income families.
- All districts offer preschool programs for disadvantaged four-year-olds.
- Taxes have been increased by billions of dollars to pay for the changes.

Standards & Assessment ☑
■ Gains in Texas

Texas educators and legislators also have been introducing many components of systemic reform. The Texas Assessment of Academic Skills (TAAS) has been used to identify and provide support for modifying instruction in low-performing schools and districts. Particularly large gains have been reported for low-income students and for minority students. Among schools in Brazosport, for example, intensive staff development, tutoring for low achievers, and other reform efforts helped increase the percentage of low-income students passing the mathematics test from 55 percent in 1992 to 96 percent in 2001. For the state as a whole, the percentage of low-income students passing the reading, writing, and math sections of the TAAS increased from 39 percent in 1994 to 70 percent in 2000. Although some observers complain that too much time is spent preparing students for tests and that too many low achievers are excluded from testing, many analysts have applauded Texas teachers' efforts to improve the performance of all students.[81] For Internet sources of information on state reforms, see the Technology @ School box.

---

[80]Thomas R. Guskey and Kent Peterson, "The Road to Classroom Change," *Educational Leadership* (December 1995–January 1996), pp. 10–15; Marc S. Tucker and Charles S. Clark, "The New Accountability," *American School Board Journal* (January 1999); "Tough Love," *Insights* (August 2000), available at **www.sedl.org/policy/insights**; and Hilda Borko, Rebekah Elliott, and Kay Uchiyama, "Professional Development," *Teaching and Teacher Education* (November 2002), pp. 969–987.

[81]Tyce Palmaffy, "The Gold Star State," *Policy Review* (March–April 1998), available at **www.policyreview.org/mar98/goldstar.html**; Craig D. Jerald, "Real Results, Remaining Challenges" (2001), paper prepared for the Business Roundtable, available at **www.brt.org/pdf/532.pdf**; Linda Skrla, "Accountability, Equity, and Complexity," *Educational Researcher* (May 2001), available at **www.aera.net/pubs/er**; and Patricia Davenport and Gerald Anderson, *Closing the Achievement Gap* (Houston: American Productivity and Quality Center, 2002).

TECHNOLOGY @School

Accessing Information on State Assessment and Accountability Practices

State standards for your students' achievement will undoubtedly affect you as a teacher. You'll also encounter the growing movement to hold students, teachers, and schools accountable for their levels of achievement.

Margaret Goertz and Mark Duffy of the Consortium for Policy Research (CPRE) helped conduct a survey of state practices and prepared a 2001 report titled "Assessment and Accountability Across the 50 States." The report is available at **www.cpre.org/Publications/ Publications_Policy_Briefs.htm** and also free from the CPRE at the University of Pennsylvania Graduate School of Education, 3440 Market Street, Suite 560, Philadelphia 19104-3325.

The authors found that all states have "embarked on educational initiatives related to high standards and challenging content" that involve a "common set of academic standards for all students, the assessments that measure student performance, and accountability systems that are at least partially focused on student outcomes." They also reported that all the states publish, or require districts to publish, school or district report cards. But they acknowledge wide variability in how challenging the assessments are, the levels of performance considered proficient, the rewards and punishments in place based on a school's or district's performance, and the amount and types of assistance made available to low-performing schools. As you saw in the chapter on Providing Equal Educational Opportunity, these challenges continue to affect standards-based efforts including the No Child Left Behind laws.

You can obtain information about states' specific standards in various grades and subjects by searching at the Web site of Achieve, Inc., a bipartisan, nonprofit organization established in 1996 by governors and corporate leaders. Search from the home page at **www.achieve.org** to learn, for example, that the first English standard expected of sixth graders in Alaska involves the capacity to "Apply knowledge of word origins, structure, and context clues, and root words, and use dictionaries and glossaries, to determine the meaning of new words and to comprehend text." Another way to learn about state standards is to visit any state's education agency Web site. Find all such sites at **www.nasbe.org**. What are the English standards for sixth graders in your state?

District-Level Systemic Reform

Standards & Assessment ✓

■ High-performing districts

In the chapter on Motivation, Preparation, and Conditions for the Entering Teacher, we described systemic reform efforts in the Rochester, New York, public schools, and in the preceding section we cited systemic reforms in Brazosport and other districts in Texas. Many other districts throughout the nation have initiated outstanding reform approaches that are producing large gains on their states' standards-based assessments of student performance. In addition, we are learning much about what districts should do to make their reform plans successful. For example, a study conducted for the Educational Research Service reported that the following practices were characteristic of six districts rated high in performance, based on having brought about substantial achievement improvements while enrolling significant proportions of low-income students:[82]

---

[82]Gordon Cawelti and Nancy Protheroe, *How Six School Districts Changed into High-Performance Systems* (Arlington, Va.: Educational Research Service, 2001); and Jason C. Snipes, Fred Doolittle, and Corinne Herlihy, *Case Studies of How Urban School Systems Improve Student Achievement* (New York: MDRC, 2002), available at **www.mdrc.org/Reports2002/achievementgap/ achievement_exsummary.htm**.

- The superintendent and other leaders developed widely shared beliefs about the necessity for high expectations.

- Budgeting was decentralized to the building level to increase possibilities for accountability.

- Extensive work was done to align curriculum with state tests.

- Regular assessments of student performance helped ensure tutoring for students falling behind.

Districts registering clear gains in student performance on state standards-based assessments include some of the nation's largest districts that enroll disproportionately large percentages of low-income students, minority students, and limited-English learners. The Council of Great City Schools has surveyed its big-city member districts and reported the following:[83]

- The "Great City Schools have made meaningful gains in math scores on state assessments" and also on other independent tests such as the National Assessment of Educational Progress.

■ Gains in big cities

- Gains also were found on state assessments of reading, but these gains were not as well confirmed independently using other tests.

- "Preliminary evidence" indicates that gaps in math achievement between minority and nonminority students "may be narrowing" as districts report progress in reducing the gaps at certain schools.

■ Baltimore and Charlotte-Mecklenburg

Impressive examples of gains in student performance on state assessments and other tests have been particularly evident in Baltimore, Charlotte-Mecklenburg (North Carolina), and several other cities. In Baltimore, students have improved both their reading and math scores at every grade tested by the state. Baltimore elementary students also made major progress on nationally normed tests. The percentages of fifth graders reading at or above the national average increased from 18 percent in 1998 to 41 percent in 2001, and comparable scores for first graders improved from 29 percent to 56 percent. In Charlotte-Mecklenburg the percent of third graders at or above grade level in reading increased from 63 percent in 1997 to 78 percent in 2002, and the comparable percentages for fifth graders increased from 66 to 81 percent. Observers have attributed these gains to such coordinated reform initiatives as professional development dealing with balanced literacy; standards-based teaching in reading, writing, and math; increased early childhood, after-school, and summer learning opportunities; and requirements for student promotion from one grade to the next. Gains of this magnitude have contributed to overall improvements in the performance of students statewide in Connecticut, Maryland, North Carolina, Virginia, and other states.[84]

---

[83]*Beating the Odds* (Washington, D.C.: Council of Great City Schools, 2001); and Anthony D. Lutkus and Arlene W. Weiner, "Results of the NAEP 2003 Trial Urban District Assessment" (Washington, D.C.: National Center for Education Statistics, 2003), available at **http:// nces.ed.gov/nationsreportcard/pdf/dst2003/2004459.pdf**.
[84]Liz Bowie and Erika Niedowsi, "Improving Test Scores Hailed as Turnaround," *Baltimore Sun*, May 18, 2001; Michael Casserly, "Beating the Odds III" (2003), report prepared for the Council of Great City Schools, available at **http://cgcs.org/pdfs/bto3.pdf**; and "Baltimore Builds for Success," *American Teacher* (December 2003–January 2004), available at **www.aft.org/publications**.

▶ Conclusion: The Challenge for Education

■ Key role for new teachers

To help meet national challenges to compete internationally and to address the problems of disadvantaged citizens, education in the United States must become more effective than it is today. This is particularly true with respect to the development of higher-order skills in all segments of the student population and specifically among disadvantaged students.

Recent national proposals for educational reform have reflected these emerging concerns. During the same time, we have learned much about improving educational effectiveness at district, school, and classroom levels. However, using this knowledge to fundamentally improve the schools is a difficult and complex task. As a teacher, you will face this task because you will play an important part in determining whether the reform effort is successful.

▶ Summing Up

1. The educational system is being challenged to improve achievement in order to keep the United States internationally competitive and to provide equity for disadvantaged and other at-risk students.

2. Research on effective teaching and instruction provides support for appropriate emphasis on efficient classroom management, direct instruction, high time-on-task, skillful questioning of students, explicit comprehension instruction, and other methods that promote achievement.

3. Research indicates that schools unusually effective in improving student achievement have a clear mission, outstanding leadership, high expectations for students, positive home–school relations, high time-on-task, frequent monitoring of students' achievement, and an orderly, humane climate. Research also has identified somewhat more specific characteristics such as curriculum alignment and schoolwide emphasis on higher-order skills. In high schools, researchers found that schools-within-a-school, career academies, and smaller units were effective.

4. It now seems possible to create more effective schools, provided educators use what we have learned about the school improvement process.

5. Many efforts, such as the Higher-Order Thinking Skills Program, seek to improve instruction across grade levels.

6. Research efforts designed to improve whole schools stem from research indicating that the individual school level is crucial in bringing about reform.

7. Many school districts and states have undertaken improvement efforts involving cooperation with business and other institutions, year-round schooling, and improving rural education and education for gifted and talented students.

8. Emerging technologies offer great potential for improving elementary and secondary education, but effective use of technologies will require considerable effort and resources.

9. Many possibilities exist for improving education through expanding school choice, but many potential dangers also exist.

10. Highly promising efforts are now under way to bring about systemic, coherent restructuring and reform.

► Key Terms

effective schools (476)
time-on-task (477)
direct instruction (478)
explicit teaching (478)
explicit comprehension instruction (479)
strategic teaching (480)
curriculum alignment (481)
Comprehensive School Reform Demonstration Program (491)

privatization (493)
distance education (499)
year-round school (500)
21st Century Community Learning Centers (502)
school choice (502)
magnet schools (503)
alternative schools (503)
restructuring (508)
systemic improvement (508)

► Discussion Questions

1. What are some major obstacles in working to improve students' higher-order skills? What can be done to attain this goal?

2. Why is school effectiveness so dependent on what happens in the school as a whole, not just in individual classrooms? What are the most important actions a teacher can take to help improve school effectiveness?

3. What does research say about the effectiveness of nonpublic schools? Do they produce higher achievement than public schools? If yes, what considerations account for the difference?

4. Why should educators be somewhat cautious in interpreting research on effective schools? What mistakes in interpretation are most likely?

5. Would you be willing to work in a high-poverty school even though teaching there might be more difficult than in a middle-class school? What philosophical commitments might be important in undertaking this assignment?

► Suggested Projects for Professional Development

1. Collect and analyze information about cooperation between schools and other institutions (such as businesses and colleges) in your community. To what extent has such cooperation helped the schools?

2. Visit a nearby school with a high proportion of low-income students. Talk with both teachers and students. Write a description of the school comparing its programs and practices with the characteristics of unusually effective schools discussed in this chapter. Organize your material for inclusion in your personal portfolio.

3. List the first actions you would take to improve the effectiveness of a typical high school. Defend your list. How do your proposals reflect research on school effectiveness? How do they reflect your personal philosophy?

4. In a recent book , journal, or article available on the Internet, find a proposal for a basic reform or restructuring in the public schools. What does the author propose to reform? How? Is the proposal realistic? What philosophic perspectives does it represent? What conditions or resources would be required to implement it successfully? What is the likelihood of success?

▶ Suggested Resources

 Internet Resources

The Internet is a treasure trove of places where you can read descriptions and analyses of successful schools. The following are a brief sampling:

- the state of Maryland's "Benchmarking Successful Schools" site at **www.mdk12.org/ process/benchmark/benchmark.html**
- "Schools to Watch" from the National Forum to Accelerate Middle Grades Reform, **www.mgforum.org/Improvingschools/STW/STWbackground.htm**
- No Excuses (**www.noexcuses.org**), an organization dedicated to publicizing "lessons from high-performing, high-poverty schools"
- The World Bank's "Effective Schools and Teachers" site, **www1.worldbank.org/ education/est.**

Lawrence W. Lezotte's *Correlates of Effective Schools* is available at **www.effectiveschools .com/freestuff.asp**.

The Fall–Winter 2000 issue of the *Future of Children,* available at **www.futureofchildren.org/ homepage2824/archive.htm**, is devoted to the theme "Children and Computer Technology."

Studies opposing school choice approaches are emphasized in analyses at the American Federation of Teachers "Vouchers Home Page," **www.aft.org/research/vouchers**. Studies supporting school choice approaches are emphasized in a list of school choice magazines and periodic columns collected by the International Society for Individual Liberty at **www.free-market .net/directorybycategory/magazines/T17.3**. David J. Ferrero's essay on "Why Choice Is Good for Teachers" in the Winter 2004 issue of *Education Next* at **www.educationnext.org** discusses the teaching career impact of school choice.

Many of the topics discussed in this chapter are discussed and updated frequently in the bimonthly newsletter of the 21st Century Schools Project available at **www.ppionline.org**: click on "Education," and the weekly bulletin *Education Gadfly* available at **www.edexcellence .net/institute**. Both offer free subscriptions.

Thoughtful articles dealing with school reform are presented in the online journals *Education Next,* available at **www.educationnext.org**, and *Education Policy Analysis Archives,* available at **http://epaa.asu.edu**.

Publications

Fuhrman, Susan H., and Richard F. Elmore, eds., *Redesigning Accountability Systems for Education.* New York: Teachers College Press, 2004. *Full description and discussion of issues involving school reform, assessment, and accountability.*

Fullan, Michael. *The New Meaning of Educational Change.* New York: Teachers College Press, 1991. *Excellent analysis of both the theoretical basis and the practical implications of research on the school change process.*

Healy, Jane M. *Failure to Connect.* New York: Simon and Schuster, 1998. *Many of Healy's classroom observations raise important questions about the appropriate use of computers and other digital media.*

Jones, Beau Fly, and Lorna Idol, eds. *Dimensions of Thinking and Cognitive Instruction.* Hillsdale, N.J.: Erlbaum, 1990. *Here is much of what you always wanted to know about instruction to develop higher-order skills.*

Witte, John F. *The Market Approach to Education.* Princeton, N.J.: Princeton University Press, 2000. *Concentrating on but not limiting his attention to the Milwaukee voucher program, Witte assesses both the promise and dangers of vouchers, open enrollment, and other choice mechanisms.*

▶ Glossary

A Nation at Risk A landmark national report critical of public education in the United States that resulted in raising high school graduation requirements in most states.

a priori ideas Ideas derived from self-evident first principles; they are deductions or conclusions based on reason alone. The theory of *a priori* ideas is associated with realism, Thomism, and perennialism.

academic freedom A protection permitting teachers to teach subject matter and choose instructional materials relevant to the course without restriction from administrators or other persons outside the classroom.

academy A type of private or semipublic secondary school dominant in the United States from 1830 through 1870.

accountability Holding teachers, administrators, and/or school board members responsible for student performance or for wise use of educational funds.

acculturation The process beginning at infancy by which a human being acquires the culture of his or her society.

activity-centered curriculum A type of student-centered curriculum that emphasizes purposeful and real-life experiences and, more recently, student participation in school and community activities.

adequate yearly progress The regular increments of achievement gain that schools and districts must register to have all students attain academic proficiency in 2013–2014.

aesthetics The branch of axiology that examines questions of beauty and art.

alternative certification Teacher certification obtained without completing a traditional teacher-education program at a school or college of education.

alternative school A school, public or private, that provides learning opportunities different from those in local public schools. Some such schools follow a student-centered curriculum characterized by a great deal of freedom for students and a relative lack of structure.

American Federation of Teachers (AFT) The second largest organization that represents teachers in America. Affiliated with the AFL-CIO, it often is associated with union representation.

Americanization The dominant ideology in public schools with regard to immigrant and minority group children in the nineteenth and early twentieth centuries. The emphasis was on teaching in English rather than the language the children spoke at home and rejecting the values of the minority child in favor of what was termed American values.

axiology The area of philosophy that examines value issues, especially in ethics and aesthetics.

back-to-basics curriculum A type of subject-centered curriculum that emphasizes the three Rs at the elementary level and academic subjects at the secondary level; also includes a defined minimum level of academic standards.

basic skills testing Testing that examines preservice teachers' basic skills with respect to subjects such as reading, mathematics, and communications.

bilingual education Instruction in their native language provided for students whose first language is not English.

bipartite system A dual-track system consisting of academic schools and vocational schools.

block grants General-purpose funding from the federal government, allowing each state considerable freedom to choose specific programs on which to spend the funds.

boarding schools Residential institutions where students live and attend school. Boarding schools were used to assimilate Native American children into white culture by insisting they speak only English and study a required industrial training curriculum. In these schools, Native American pupils were not permitted to use their own vernacular languages and engage in tribal customs.

Brahmins Members of the highest caste and primary recipients of education in ancient India.

brain drain The emigration of educated people to wealthier nations.

breach of contract What occurs when one side fails to perform as agreed in a contract.

caste system A system of social stratification traditionally used in India.

categorical grants Funds designated for specific groups and purposes; the standard method of federal education funding before the 1980s and again more recently.

central office staff A cadre of supervisors and specialists who work closely with the superintendent to carry out school board policy.

certification State government review and approval that permits a teaching candidate to teach.

character education See *values-centered curriculum.*

charter school A public school governed by a community group granted a special contract (charter) by the state or the local school board. Charter schools often form to offer educational alternatives unavailable in regular public schools.

chief state school officer The chief executive of the state board of education; sometimes called the state superintendent or commissioner of education.

child benefit theory A theory that government aid directly benefits the child rather than a nonpublic institution he or she attends.

child depravity theory A theory that children, because of their sinful nature, need strict discipline to create a personal sense of order and civility.

classical humanism The leading educational theory and general method during the Renaissance. Refers to the study of the classical Greek and Roman texts with an emphasis on their humanistic (human-centered) meaning.

collective bargaining A procedure for resolving disagreements between employers and employees through negotiation. For teachers, such negotiation pertains to many aspects of their work and salary as well as their relationship with students, supervisors, and the community.

Commission on the Reorganization of Secondary Education A commission appointed by the National Education Association to study and make recommendations for reforming American secondary education. Its 1918 report, *The Cardinal Principles of Secondary Education,* recommended a curriculum based on fundamental personal, social, cultural, and economic needs within a comprehensive institutional setting.

Committee of Ten A committee, chaired by Charles Eliot, appointed by the National Education Association in 1892 to bring greater coherence to secondary education in the United States. It recommended a four-year program and a curriculum that emphasized academic subjects for all students.

common school A publicly supported and locally controlled elementary school.

community control An elected community council or board that shares decision-making power with the local school board.

community education The school serves as a partner or coordinating agency in providing educational, health, social, legal, recreational, and/or cultural activities in the community.

community participation Citizen advisory committees at either the local school or school board level.

compensatory education An attempt to remedy the effects of environmental disadvantages through educational enrichment programs.

Comprehensive School Reform Demonstration Program A federal program that provides three years of funding to help participating Title 1 schools introduce whole-school reform models.

concrete-operational period A stage of human development identified by Jean Piaget that occurs from ages seven to eleven years, when children organize their concepts in performing increasing complex mental operations.

Confucius (551–478 B.C.) Chinese philosopher and government official who devised an ethical system still in use in China today and in other parts of the world.

consolidation The combining of small or rural school districts into larger ones.

constructivism A learning theory that emphasizes the ways in which learners actively create meaning by constructing and reconstructing ideas about reality.

continuing contract An employment contract that is automatically renewed from year to year without need for the teacher's signature.

controlled choice A system in which students can select their school as long as their choices do not result in segregation.

cooperative learning A form of instruction in which teams of students work cooperatively on specific tasks or projects.

critical theory (critical pedagogy) An interpretation of schooling that views public school systems as functioning to limit educational opportunities for students marginalized because of race, class, and gender biases. Proponents argue that teachers should be "transformative intellectuals" who work to change the system. Also known as "critical discourse."

critical thinking Solving problems by means of general concepts or higher-order relationships. Instruction in critical thinking generally emphasizes basic analytical skills applicable to a wide variety of intellectual experiences.

cultural pluralism Acceptance and encouragement of cultural, ethnic, and religious diversity within a larger society.

cultural relativism This theory asserts that ideas and values are products of specific cultural groups formulated during a particular historical period. Ideas and values depend on the place, time, circumstances, and situations in which they arise. Cultural relativism denies the existence of universal and eternal truths and values. It is associated with pragmatism, progressivism, social reconstructionism, and critical theory.

culture Patterns of acquired behavior and attitudes transmitted among the members of society.

curriculum Planned experiences provided through instruction through which the school meets its goals and objectives.

curriculum alignment Coordination of instructional planning, methods, materials, and testing in order to accomplish important learning objectives.

de facto segregation Segregation associated with and resulting from housing patterns.

de jure segregation Segregation resulting from laws or government action.

deconstruction Critical examination of texts or canons to determine the power relationships embedded in their creation and use. Often used by educators who follow a postmodernist philosophy.

deductive logic The process of thinking by which consequences or applications are drawn out of general principles or assumptions; the process of thought in which conclusions follow from premises.

deprofessionalization The process of removing from professional status.

desegregation Attendance by students of different racial backgrounds in the same school and classroom.

direct instruction A systematic method of teaching that emphasizes teacher-directed instruction proceeding in small steps, usually in accordance with a six- to eight-part lesson sequence.

distance education Instruction by people or materials distant from the learner in space or time; many distance education projects use interactive television, the Internet, and other modern communication technologies.

dual-track system The traditional European pattern of separate primary schools for the masses and preparatory and secondary schools for upper socioeconomic classes.

due process A formalized legal procedure with specific and detailed rules and principles designed to protect the rights of individuals.

due process clause A Fourteenth Amendment statement that government shall not deprive any person of life, liberty, or property without due process of law.

Ebonics Frequently used as a synonym for Black English, Ebonics also refers to analysis of a dialect used by many African Americans and of how it might play a part in teaching Standard English.

ecological intervention Comprehensive efforts to improve the environments of young children.

Education for All Handicapped Children Act (Public Law 94–142) A law passed in 1975 that mandated that children with handicaps must have access to a full public education in the least restrictive educational environment.

educational ladder The system of public schooling developed in the United States that begins with kindergarten, proceeds through elementary education, and leads to secondary education.

educational voucher A flat grant or payment representing a child's estimated school cost or portion of the cost. Under a typical voucher plan, the parent or child may choose any school, public or private, and the school is paid for accepting the child.

effective schools Schools that are unusually successful in producing high student performance, compared with other schools that enroll students of similar background; sometimes defined as schools in which working-class students achieve as well as middle-class students.

empiricism An epistemology that relies on human experience, especially sensation and observation, as the source of knowledge about reality. It emphasizes experimentation and the scientific method.

enculturation The process beginning at infancy by which a human being acquires the culture of his or her society.

environmentalist view of intelligence The belief that intelligence is mostly determined by environment.

epistemology The area of philosophy that examines knowing and theories of knowledge.

equal protection clause A Fourteenth Amendment statement that government shall not deny any person the equal protection of the law.

essentialism An educational theory that emphasizes basic skills and subject-matter disciplines. Proponents generally favor a curriculum consisting of the three Rs at the elementary level and five major disciplines (English, math, science, history, and foreign language) at the secondary level. Emphasis is on academic competition and excellence.

essentialist approach to curriculum A subject-centered educational theory based on six major disciplines: English, mathematics, the sciences, history, foreign languages, and geography.

establishment clause A constitutional provision that prohibits the establishment of a government-sanctioned religion.

ethics The branch of axiology that examines questions of right and wrong and good and bad.

ethnic group A group of people with a distinctive history, culture, and language.

ethnicity A shared cultural background based on identification and membership with an ethnic group.

exclusive product rights Special privileges whereby commercial enterprises pay a fee for the exclusive right to market their product (for example, Pepsi Cola) in the school district.

existentialism A philosophy that examines the way in which humans define themselves by making personal choices.

experience As defined by John Dewey, the interaction of a person with his or her environment.

explicit comprehension instruction Classroom techniques specifically for teaching comprehension.

explicit teaching See *direct instruction.*

fair use A principle allowing use of copyrighted material without permission of the author, under specific, limited conditions.

Family Educational Rights and Privacy Act (Buckley Amendment) A law passed in 1974 to curb possible abuses at institutions receiving federal funds.

first-language maintenance Continued teaching in a language while introducing instruction in another language.

Follow Through A program that concentrated on improving achievement of low-income children in the primary grades.

formal-operational period A stage of child development identified by Jean Piaget that occurs from ages eleven to fifteen years, when individuals formulate abstract generalizations and learn how to perform complex problem-solving processes.

free exercise clause A constitutional provision that protects rights of free speech and expression.

gender roles Socially expected behavior patterns for girls and boys, men and women.

goals Broad statements of educational purpose.

Goals 2000 The 1994 revision of the *National Educational Goals* that added two additional goals and updated states' progress on the *National Educational Goals* while providing additional services, programs, and classes as needed.

Head Start A federal government program that provides preschool education for economically disadvantaged four- and five-year-old students.

hereditarian view of intelligence The belief that intelligence is mostly determined by heredity.

hidden curriculum What students learn, other than academic content, from the school milieu or environment.

high school A school for students in the upper secondary grades, commonly serving grades 9 or 10 through 12.

highly qualified teachers An aspect of the No Child Left Behind Act, which specifies that teachers should have (1) a bachelor's degree; (2) full state certification and licensure as defined by the state; and (3) demonstrated competency as defined by the state in each core academic subject he or she teaches.

homogeneous grouping The practice of placing together students with similar achievement levels or ability.

hornbook A single sheet of parchment, containing the Lord's Prayer, letters of the alphabet, and vowels, covered by the translucent, flattened horn of a cow and fastened to a flat wooden board. It was used during the colonial era in primary schools.

humanistic approach to curriculum A student-centered curriculum approach that stresses the personal and social aspects of the student's growth and development. Emphasizes self-actualizing processes and moral, aesthetic, and higher domains of thinking.

hurried children Children highly pressured to excel at an early age.

hypermedia A computer approach that allows learners to browse through an information base to construct their own knowledge relationships and connections.

idealism A philosophy that construes reality to be spiritual or nonmaterial in essence.

in loco parentis The idea that schools should act "in place of the parent."

inclusion Educating students with disabilities in regular classrooms in their neighborhood schools, with collaborative support services as needed.

individualized education program (IEP) Plans including both long- and short-range goals for educating students with disabilities.

individualized instruction Curriculum content, instructional materials, and activities designed for individual learning. Considers the learner's pace, interests, and abilities.

Individuals with Disabilities Education Act (IDEA) Legislation enacted in 1990.

inductive logic The process of reasoning from particulars to generalities, from the parts to the whole, and from the individual to the general. It is the basis of the scientific method, emphasized by Dewey and the pragmatists.

integration The step beyond simple desegregation that includes effective action to develop positive interracial contacts and to improve the performance of low-achieving minority students.

intermediate unit An educational unit or agency in the middle position between the state department of education and the local school district; usually created by the state to provide supplementary services and support staff to local school districts. Also known as a regional educational service agency (RESA).

International Association for the Evaluation of Educational Achievement (IEA) A research group that began conducting cross-national studies in the 1960s.

Islam Religion founded by Mohammed (569–632); currently practiced in many Middle Eastern and other countries.

junior high school A two- or three-year school between elementary and high school, commonly for grades 7–9.

Koran The most sacred book of the Islamic religion and culture.

land grant An arrangement used to found many of today's state universities. The Morrill Act of 1862 granted thirty thousand acres of public land for each senator and representative in Congress, the income from which was to support at least one state college for agricultural and mechanical instruction.

land-grant college A state college or university offering agricultural and mechanical curricula, funded originally by the Morrill Act of 1862.

latchkey children Children unsupervised after school.

Latin grammar school A college preparatory school of the colonial era that emphasized Latin and Greek studies.

learning styles Distinctively different ways students learn, such as emphasis on oral or visual activities.

least restrictive environment A term used in educating students with disabilities to designate a setting that is as normal or regular as possible. Federal law requires that children with disabilities be placed in special or separate classes only for the amount of time necessary to provide appropriate services.

liberation pedagogy An educational theory advanced by Paulo Freire that encourages students to develop a critical consciousness into the conditions that oppress them and to free themselves from this oppression.

litigants Parties in a lawsuit.

local school board A body of citizens, either appointed or elected, who set policy regarding schools in a local school district.

macrocosm The universal whole or entirety. In idealism, it is the most universal, complete, and abstract idea from which all subordinate ideas are derived.

magnet school A type of alternative school that attracts voluntary enrollment from more than one neighborhood by offering special instructional programs or curricula; often established in part for purposes of desegregation.

mainstreaming Placing students with disabilities in regular classes for much or all of the school day, while also providing additional services, programs, and classes as needed.

mastery instruction An approach in which students are tested after initial instruction, and those who fail to master the objectives receive corrective instruction and retesting. Emphasizes short units of instruction and learning defined skills.

mediated entry The practice of inducting persons into a profession through carefully supervised stages.

mental discipline approach Strengthening the mind through mental activities, just as the body is strengthened through exercise.

merit pay A plan that rewards teachers partially or primarily on the basis of performance or objective standards.

metaphysics The area of philosophy that examines issues of a speculative nature dealing with ultimate reality.

microcosm A miniature version of the larger part, the macrocosm, from which it is derived.

middle class Professionals and small-business owners, as well as technicians and sales and clerical workers.

middle school A two- to four-year school between elementary and high school, commonly for grades 6–8.

mill A unit of the local tax rate representing one thousandth of a dollar.

monitorial method A method of instruction also known as mutual instruction and designed by Andrew Bell and Joseph Lancaster, working independently of each other in the early nineteenth century. It sought to provide an inexpensive form of mass basic schooling by using more advanced students—monitors—to teach less advanced students.

Montessori schools Early childhood institutions that follow Maria Montessori's philosophy and method of instruction. They emphasize that children learn by developing sensory, motor, and intellectual skills by using didactic materials in a structured environment.

multicultural education Education that focuses on providing equal opportunity for students whose cultural and/or language patterns make it difficult for them to succeed in traditional school programs. Many multicultural programs also emphasize positive intergroup and interracial attitudes and contacts.

municipal overburden Severe financial crunch caused by population density and a high proportion of disadvantaged and low-income groups.

National Assessment of Educational Progress (NAEP) A periodic assessment of educational achievement under the jurisdiction of the Educational Testing Service, using nationally representative samples of elementary and secondary students.

National Board for Professional Teaching Standards (NBPTS) A national nonprofit organization that issues certificates to teachers who meet its standards for professional ability and knowledge.

National Council for Accreditation of Teacher Education (NCATE) Prestigious national organization that works closely with state departments of education to review and evaluate teacher-education programs at colleges and universities.

National Education Association (NEA) The largest organization that represents teachers in the United States.

The National Education Goals A 1990 National Governors' Conference report on education in America that delineated six educational guidelines for state and local education agencies.

National Education Goals Panel Report A 1998 report that reviewed the progress on the eight goals and twenty-six indicators in *Goals 2000*.

national reports Major reports in the 1980s and 1990s that spurred reform by designating student low performance and other problems as deficiencies in the educational system.

naturalistic theory An educational theory that argues that the natural stages of human development should be the basis of instruction and education.

new core curriculum (core subjects approach) A curriculum of common courses that all students are required to take. Emphasis is usually on academic achievement and traditional subject matter.

No Child Left Behind Act (NCLB) The federal Elementary and Secondary Education Act passed in 2001, which requires states and school districts that receive federal funding to show adequate yearly progress, as measured by standardized tests of students in grades 3–8, and to provide all students with "highly qualified" teachers.

normal school A two-year teacher-education institution popular in the nineteenth century.

norms A social entity's rules of behavior.

nuclear family Mother and father living with their children.

object lesson A method developed by Johann Heinrich Pestalozzi, who used concrete objects as the basis of form, number, and name lessons.

objectives Specific statements of educational purpose, usually written for a particular subject, grade, unit, or lesson; commonly defined in behavioral terms so that student experiences and performance can be observed and measured.

occupational prestige The special status accorded to certain occupations and not to others.

outcomes-based education (OBE) Education guided by the principle that success should be judged by student "outcomes" (generally seen in terms of abilities to function in real-life contexts) rather than by "inputs" such as programs, courses, or funding. Many proponents would revise traditional curricula that fail to produce desired outcomes.

overloaded schools Schools with a high incidence of serious problems that make it difficult for educators to function effectively.

The Paideia Proposal *The Paideia Proposal*, developed by Mortimer J. Adler, uses the Greek term *paideia*, the total educational formation, or upbringing of a child in the cultural heritage, to assert that all students should pursue the same curriculum consisting of intellectual skills and organized knowledge in language, literature, the arts, sciences, and social studies. It is a modern form of perennialism.

Parent Teacher Association (PTA) A national organization of parents, teachers, and students to promote the welfare of children and youth that has affiliated local groups in school communities.

parent-teacher group An organization of parents and teachers in a local school community.

peer culture Behaviors and attitudes of similar-age children or youth in an institution or society.

perennialism An educational theory that emphasizes rationality as the major purpose of education, asserting that the essential truths are recurring and universally true. Proponents generally favor a curriculum consisting of the three Rs at the elementary level and the classics at the secondary level.

perennialist approach to curriculum A fundamentally subject-centered educational theory that the main purpose of education is the cultivation of the best of the past, the classics.

personal income tax A tax based on a percentage of personal income.

philosophies Fully developed bodies of thought each representing a generalized worldview.

plaintiffs Persons who sue.

Plato's *Republic* Plato's most systematic philosophical statement on politics and education. Using the format of dialogues, it portrays a perfect city ruled by philosopher-kings according to the principle of justice.

postmodernism A philosophy that is highly skeptical of the truth of metanarratives, the canons, that purport to be authoritative statements of universal or objective truth. Rather, postmodernists regard these canons as historical statements that rationalize one group's domination of another.

pragmatism A philosophy that judges the validity of ideas by their consequences in action.

preoperational stage A stage of human development identified by Jean Piaget that occurs from ages two to seven years, when children create categories, classify, add to, and reconstruct their conceptions of reality through systematic environmental explorations.

principal The chief administrative officer of the school, responsible for school operation.

privatization The operation of public schools is contracted to private businesses.

profession An occupation that rates high in prestige and requires extensive formal education and mastery of a defined body of knowledge beyond the grasp of laypersons. Members of many professions control licensing standards and have autonomy in their work environment.

professional development school (PDS) An elementary or secondary school operated jointly by a school district and a teacher-training institution that emphasizes thoughtful analysis of teaching and learning. The participants usually include future teachers as well as practicing teachers, administrators, and teacher educators.

professional practice board A state or national commission that permits educators to set professional standards and minimal requirements of competency.

progressive taxes Taxes based on the taxpayer's ability to pay, for example, income taxes or property taxes.

progressivism An antitraditional theory in American education associated with child-centered learning through activities, problem solving, and projects. The Progressive Education Association promoted progressivism as an educational movement.

property tax The main source of revenues for local school districts, based on the value of real property (land and improvements on land).

pullout approach Taking low achievers out of regular classes for supplementary instruction in reading and math.

race Groups of people with common ancestry and physical characteristics.

realism A philosophy that considers reality to be objective and dualistic in nature. That is, reality has both a material and a formal or structural component.

reflective teaching A style of teaching that emphasizes reflective inquiry and self-awareness. Reflective teachers analyze their own teaching behavior and consider the factors that make their teaching effective or ineffective.

regional educational service agency (RESA) See *intermediate unit.*

regressive taxes Taxes that require lower-income groups to pay relatively more of their income than higher-income groups.

relevant curriculum Curricula that addresses social change, emphasizing knowledge, skills, and attitudes pertinent to modern society.

reminiscence The recalling or remembering of ideas that Plato asserted were latently present in the mind. Through skilled questioning, the teacher stimulates students to bring these ideas to consciousness.

resistance theory The view that working-class students resist the school in part because a hegemonic traditional curriculum marginalizes their everyday knowledge.

restructuring Multiple changes to bring about systemic improvement in a school or group of schools.

revisionist view of schools The belief that elite groups have channeled disadvantaged students into second-rate schools and inferior jobs.

rhetoric The theory and practice of public speaking, declamation, and oratory in ancient Greece. During the Middle Ages it tended to emphasize written discourse as well as speaking. Along with grammar and logic, rhetoric was part of the *trivium* of the liberal arts.

sales tax A tax based on purchase of taxable goods (generally not food or services).

Scholasticism The intellectual and educational approach used by educators in medieval universities, involving the study of theological and philosophical authorities.

school-based management A system of school governance in which individual schools make many important decisions, rather than the superintendent or board of education. This system usually gives teachers substantial decision-making responsibility.

school choice A system that allows students or their parents to choose the schools they attend.

school infrastructure The basic physical facilities of the school plant (plumbing, sewer, heat, electric, roof, windows, and so on).

scientific method A systematic approach to inquiry in which hypotheses are tested by replicable empirical verification. Although usually identified with the laboratory method in the natural sciences, the scientific method is also used in philosophy, where it is associated with pragmatism.

sensorimotor stage A stage of child development identified by Jean Piaget that occurs from age eighteenth months to two years, when children develop their earliest concepts by environmental exploration.

Social Darwinism An ideology that applies Darwin's biological principles of the "survival of the fittest" and competition to individuals in society. During the late nineteenth century, it was a highly influential rationale for unregulated capitalism as the economic system best designed to promote progress.

social reconstructionists A group of progressive educators who believe schools should deliberately work for social reform and change.

socialization The process of preparing persons for a social environment.

socialized education The educational philosophy developed by Jane Addams, who advocated that schools emphasize teaching about urbanization, industrialization, technology, and cultural diversity.

socioeconomic status (SES) Relative ranking of individuals according to economic, social, and occupational prestige and power; usually measured in terms of occupation, education, and income and generally viewed in terms of social-class categories ranging from working class to upper class.

Socratic method An educational method attributed to the Greek philosopher Socrates by which the teacher encourages the student's discovery of truth by asking leading and stimulating questions.

Sophists Members of a group of itinerant educators in ancient Greece during the period from 470 to 370 B.C. who emphasized rhetoric, public speaking, and other practical skills. Their approach contrasts with that of the speculative philosophers Plato and Aristotle.

staff development Continued education or training of a school district's teaching staff. Such programs often emphasize teacher input as well as collaboration between the school district and a college or university.

state board of education An influential state education agency that advises the state legislature and establishes policies for implementing legislative acts related to education.

state department of education An agency that operates under the direction of the state board of education. Its functions include accrediting schools, certifying teachers, apportioning state school funds, conducting research, issuing reports, and coordinating state education policies with local school districts.

state school code A collection of state laws that establish ways and means of operating schools and conducting education.

state standards Performance indicators showing students have achieved academic mastery at levels set by state boards of education.

strategic teaching An approach that emphasizes students' construction of meaning and growth in independent learning, with the teacher serving as a model and mediator of learning.

student-centered curricula Curricula that focus on the needs and attitudes of the individual student. Emphasizes self-expression and the student's intrinsic motivation.

subject-area curriculum A type of subject-centered curriculum in which each subject is treated as a largely autonomous body of knowledge. Emphasizes traditional subjects that have dominated U.S. education since the late nineteenth century, including English, history, science, and mathematics.

subject-centered curricula Curricula defined in terms of bodies of content or subject matter. Achievement is judged according to defined outcomes such as test scores, correct answers, or responses deemed appropriate.

superintendent of schools The executive officer of the local school district, implements policies adopted by the school board.

supply and demand Market conditions that affect salaries such that pay decreases during a large supply of teachers and rises when supply is low and teachers are in high demand.

synthesizers' view of intelligence The belief that intelligence is determined by interaction of environment and heredity.

systemic improvement Reform efforts that simultaneously address all or most major components in the overall educational system.

tax base Basis upon which taxes to support public schools are assessed at state and local levels—for example, property tax, sales tax, transportation taxes, and special fees.

taxpayer resistance When taxpayers show reluctance to continue paying increased taxes to support public schools.

teacher empowerment The process of increasing the power of teachers and their role in determining school policies and practices.

tenure Permanence of position granted to educators after a probationary period, which prevents their dismissal except for legally specified causes and through formalized due-process procedures.

theories Sets of ideas or beliefs, often based on research findings or generalizations from practice, that guide educational policies or procedures.

Third International Mathematics and Science Study (TIMSS) A research group that has conducted cross-national research since 1996.

time-on-task Classroom time engaged in learning activities.

Title 1 A portion of the federal Elementary and Secondary Education Act that provides funds to improve the education of economically disadvantaged students.

torts Civil wrongs involving individuals who sue because of improper conduct of others.

town school The eighteenth- and early-nineteenth-century elementary school of New England that educated children living in a designated area.

traditional view of schools The belief that the educational system provides economically disadvantaged students with meaningful opportunities.

transitional bilingual education (TBE) A form of bilingual education in which students are taught in their own language only until they can learn in English.

tuition tax credits Tax reductions offered to parents or guardians of children to offset part of their school tuition payments.

21st Century Learning Centers These centers, supported through the No Child Left Behind Act, provide tutoring, after-school classes, summer school, and other academic enrichment activities for students attending low performing schools.

underclass Section of the lower working class subject to intergenerational transmission of poverty.

upper class Wealthy persons with substantial property and investments.

U.S. Department of Education A cabinet-level department in the executive branch of the federal government, in charge of federal educational policy and the promotion of educational programs.

user fees Special fees charged specifically to those who use a facility or service (for example, recreational facilities, bus service, or after-school centers).

utilitarian education The teaching of skills and subjects applicable to daily life, work, and society. Herbert Spencer argued that the subject of most use, or utility, was science. Utilitarian education is often contrasted with the Greek and Latin classical curriculum.

values-centered curriculum Places special emphasis on moral and ethical issues. More popularly known as *character education.*

Vedas One of the key religious texts used in Hinduism; the focus of ancient Indian education.

vernacular schools Primary institutions provided instruction in students' common language, in contrast to schools that instructed in classical languages such as Greek or Latin.

whole-child concept The view that schools must concern themselves with all aspects of students' growth and development, not merely with cognitive skills or academic learning.

working class Skilled crafts workers and unskilled manual workers.

year-round schools Rotating schedules that allow students to attend school for three out of four quarters during a chronological year.

Name Index

Subject Index

New!

In This Case feature helps students apply and think critically about concepts discussed in each chapter. This boxed feature contains brief, fictional case scenarios that describe situations in which new teachers might find themselves, and ask readers to answer questions that encourage critical and applied thinking.

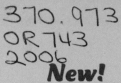

IN THIS CASE

Students' Perceptions and Feelings and the Official Curriculum

The following case study is excerpted from Peter McLaren, *Life in Schools: An Introduction to Critical Pedagogy in the Foundations of Education.* The case study is based on the experiences of McLaren, a critical theorist philosopher, while teaching in a school in the Toronto suburb of North York, Canada. The school's neighborhood includes many low-income residents, giving the school characteristics of an inner-city school. The case study discussion appears as a diary entry in which Fred, the school principal, and McLaren discuss students' feelings or perceptions of their own reality.

Tuesday, April 25 For the first time since I came to this school, most of the parents showed up for interviews. Although I had scheduled parents for only fifteen minutes each, sometimes the interviews lasted over an hour.

When they had all left, I saw Fred in the hallway and we walked down to his office for a quiet talk. I told him how depressed I was to find that over half my class came from

"As teachers, we can't ignore that, but we can't let it get in our way, either. We have to try to make these kids feel like people who feel like they're worth something.". . .

"You have to ask yourself if there is any way you can get children to feel good about themselves. . . .

"Listen. Teachers have to understand about the prejudices they bring to their job. Somehow, they have to respect the kids' own values, and where the kid is at. We can impose our values on them, but that implies their values aren't any good. That would be destructive. We've got to develop relationships with these kids, and relationships involve feelings, not simply content or information. With poor kids, it's even harder, because you almost have to say to them that they are worthwhile human beings, that you don't care how they dress or where they come from." Fred was getting very emotional. His jaw tensed, his arms waved as he spoke, his eyes burning right through me.

"The way you reach a poor kid who's doing badly at school is not by concentrating on arithmetic, but by getting something going with him or her that tells them that you care about them as people. Forget about the curriculum, at least for the time being. Reach your kids through feelings."

n in the students' education?

ir autobiographies, as a basis for teaching and learning?

ognitive dimension) and feeling (the affective dimen-

between Fred and McLaren?

IN THIS CASE

Meeting All Needs

Bob and Don are graduating this year and heading for their first year of classroom teaching. Bob looks over at Don. "I don't know about you, Don, but I'm pretty overwhelmed by what we're expected to do with and for special-needs students in an inclusion program. I know it's important for special-needs students to spend as much time as possible in the least restrictive environment, but just dealing with the requirements for normal students will be plenty of responsibility for me in my first year of teaching."

Don nods. "I agree. I suspect that inclusion helps the school district's financial situation. Look at the state formula for funding special education. More money comes to the districts that practice inclusion. But I'm not at all sure that inclusion is the best practice for most students with disabilities. *I* certainly don't have the training to deal with emotionally disabled students. If a disabled student becomes disruptive, how does a teacher proceed normally?" Don taps his finger on the table. "I am also really wondering how all of this affects learning for regular students. We'll have to follow Individual Education Plans for all disabled students. Couldn't following the IEP sometimes lead regular students to suspect unfairness? Before I took Overview of Special Education this year, even I kind of thought special education students could get away with doing almost nothing and call it 'adapting the curriculum.' How can I explain the differences to my class?"

Bob sighs. "I was only worried about meeting the spe-

cial ed needs. But I can see potential problems in developing or maintaining effective education for regular students, too. In the effort to serve disabled students, I might be tempted to ease up on my preparation for regular students, and vice-versa. And behavior problems of just one student can easily distract a whole class, causing all of us to waste valuable time. I wonder how new teachers feel about this after their first year."

Don makes a note on a notepad. "Let's ask Professor Goodwin if we could have a panel discussion. She would know which of last year's graduates are teaching in a school using full inclusion. Then we could ask all our questions about this issue."

Bob looks over at the notepad. "I think we should include teachers who have lots of experience and who have seen how other arrangements work, as well. I remember the old resource rooms where they used to send most of the disabled students. That set-up may have worked better for some kids, but I also remember the disruption in class when they gathered up their stuff to go for their special sessions.

"Maybe the working teachers can talk about team teaching," Bob adds. "We don't necessarily have to work alone, you know. I've heard of shared teaching responsibilities, where a special education teacher teams with the regular teacher. I would definitely like to learn more about that. And there are always aides. Some of them serve as teachers even though they're not certified. Let's ask about these—and more."

Questions

1. What arrangements do local schools use to provide services to special education students?
2. What do you see as the most effective way to serve disabled students?
3. Do you have concerns about working with certain classes of disabled students?
4. Arrange to talk to regular and special education teachers. What arrangements do special ed teachers believe serve special education students best? How do regular classroom teachers answer the same question?